CONTENTS

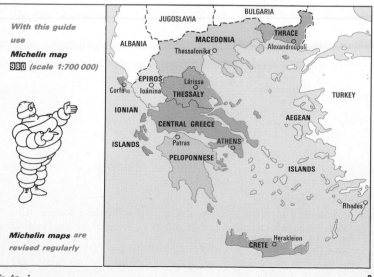

With this guide
use
Michelin map
980 (scale 1:700 000)

Michelin maps are
revised regularly

PRINCIPAL SIGHTS

Worth a journey	★★★
Worth a detour	★★
Interesting	★

The names of towns or sights described in the guide appear in black on the maps
See the index for the page number.

0 _____ 100 km

Three major organisations:

Greek National Tourist Organisation (GNTO), Elinikós Organismós Tourismoú (EOT):

Athens, 2 Odós Karagiórgi Servías, ☎ 322 2545 (information); 2 Odós Amerikis, 322 3111 (administration).

London, 195-197 Regent Street, W1R 8DR, ☎ 734 5997.

New York, 645 Fifth Avenue, Olympic Tower, NY 10022, ☎ (212) 421 5777.

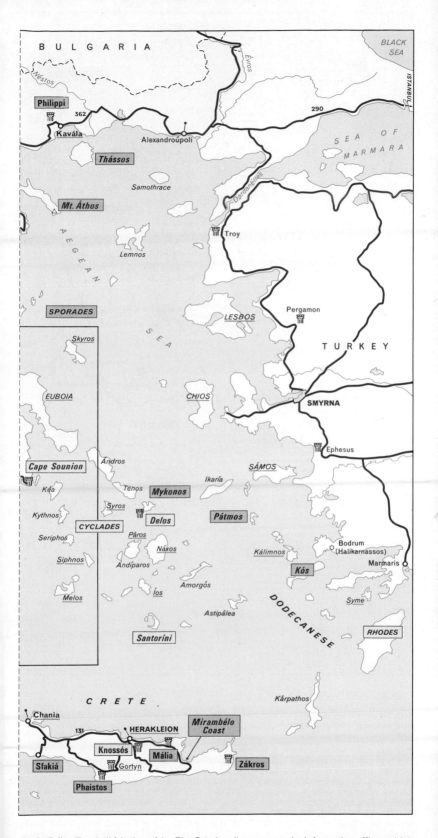

Tourist Police (Touristikí Astinomía). – The Greek police runs tourist information offices which supply all sorts of information, particularly on where to stay (rooms in private houses for example) and on transport (destinations and timetables).

ELPA: 2-4 Odós Messogíon, Athens, ☏ 779 1615

ELPA (Greek Automobile Touring Club) has representatives in all the major towns and runs a roadside breakdown service (☏ 104) which is free to members of other national Automobile or Touring Clubs.

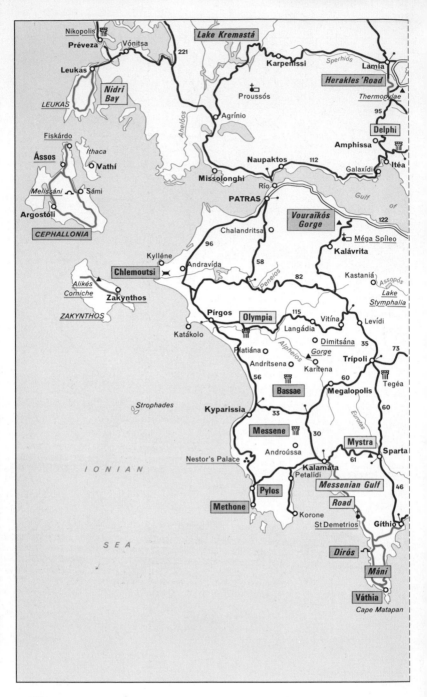

REGULATIONS

Entry documents. – Passport or valid identity card (for a stay not exceeding three months); international driving licence for the driver, international green insurance card for the vehicle (or temporary insurance taken out at the border).

Exchange. – The currency is the drachma which is worth about 1/2 p (200 Dr = £1). There is a limit (3 000 Dr) on the amount of Greek currency which can be imported into Greece.

The banks in Greece are usually open from 8am to 2pm during the week (closed Saturdays, Sundays and holidays). In country districts the hours may be restricted to certain times and days. In popular tourist areas extended hours are in operation: National Bank of Greece, Síndagma Square, Athens (daily); Athens International Airport (24 hour).

Foreign currency, travellers' cheques and Eurocheques can be changed in banks or exchange offices at the legal rate and in hotels at a much lower rate. Credit cards (particularly Visa) can be used to obtain Greek currency and in many hotels and shops.

Customs. – The duty and tax free allowances available on certain categories of goods – tobacco, alcohol: spirits and table wine, perfume and toilet water, and other goods – vary depending on whether the goods were obtained duty free or outside the EEC as opposed to duty paid within the EEC.

A pamphlet explaining the allowances and categories is available from HM Customs and Excise at any airport or from Dorset House, Stamford Street, London SE1 9PS or any local office.

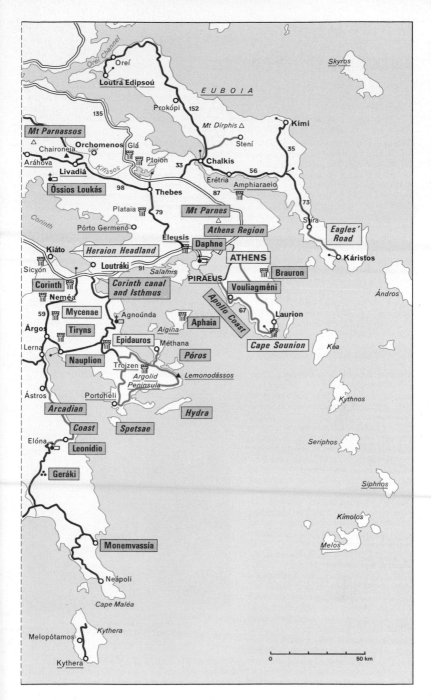

THE CLIMATE

The climate is more varied than one might imagine; it is continental in the north of the country and Mediterranean in the south and the islands. The mountains are snow-capped until the late spring... even in Crete. Moreover, the rainfall on the west coast is considerably higher than on the east: 1 300mm – 507ins in Corfu as opposed to 350mm – 136ins in Athens.

Winter. – The weather is severe in central and northern Greece when the north wind *(voriás)* blows. On the coast and in the islands, however, it is milder and the average temperature in January in Herakleion (Crete) or Rhodes is 12°-13 °C – 55 °F; these are the main centres for winter tourism. The rain falls in brief but violent storms.

Spring. – Despite the snow on the mountains and the occasional showers of rain, the spring flowers provide a mass of colour. May is most pleasant when the heat and the numbers of visitors are not excessive although the sea may be chill.

Summer. – From June to September the unchanging blue sky and the bright sunlight attract the sun and sand worshippers. In July and August the weather is very hot but tempered in southern Greece and in the Aegean Islands by the north wind *(meltémi) (p 10)*. In Thessaly and Macedonia it is sultry.

Autumn. – For some the autumn, until the end of November, is the most agreeable season. The evenings are drawing in and there are occasional rain storms but the vegetation revives, the temperatures are mild and the sea is warm.

7

APPEARANCE OF THE COUNTRY

Greece lies at the southern end of the Balkan peninsula. Its 131 944km² – 50 944sq. miles is divided up into regions by mountains and fragmented by the sea. The broken coastline extends for 15 020km – 9 332 miles. The country's most distinctive characteristic is its many islands; between Thássos and Crete, a distance of 600km – 373 miles, there are 427 islands, of which 134 are inhabited.

Topography. – The country, which rises to its highest point in Mount Olympos at 2 917m – 6 289ft, presents a rugged but fragmented and complex topography, which can however be divided into two distinct zones.

In the east, an ancient primary substratum, consisting of crystalline metamorphic (granite, gneiss, marble...) rocks alternating with sedimentary limestone, has been raised by movements of the earth's crust: the mountain ranges of Thrace and Macedonia, the foothills of the Rhodope massif in Bulgaria; Mount Olympos, its high peaks shaped by ice-age erosion, Mounts Óssa and Pelion extending into Euboia; the Aegean Islands, traces of a continent submerged at the end of the tertiary era by earthquakes which created troughs in the seabed up to 4 850m – 15 912ft deep (Santoríni volcano – *p 176*).

In the west, a tertiary chain, the Jugoslavian Dinaric Alps, continues south to form the spine of Greece, composed mainly of **karst,** a limestone rock eroded by running water to form caves, chasms and swallow holes **(katavóthres)** into which lakes and ponds drain away underground. This mountain range, which contains many small rounded depressions **(doline)** and runs mainly north-south despite many divergent minor chains, includes the peaks of the Pindos range (2 637m – 8 652ft) and the Ionian Islands, Mounts Óthris and Parnassos (2 457m – 8 061ft), the mountains of the Peloponnese including Erímanthos (2 224m – 7 297ft), Parnon and Taÿgetos (2 407m – 7 897ft), ending in the mountain spine of Crete which rises to 2 456m – 8 058ft in Mount Ida.

CONTINENTAL GREECE

Central Greece and Euboia. – Pop 1 099 841, excluding the Athens conurbation.

Attica, the heart of Greece, occupies a promontory consisting of low hills and plains covered in vineyards and olive groves. The city of Athens, which is bounded by Mounts Parnes, Pentelikon and **Hymettos**, extends its suburbs to the northeast and the Bay of Eleusis (W), to the port of Piraeus (S) and along the Apollo coast (SE), enveloping the plain where olive trees used to flourish. Between Mount Hymettos and the famous Laurion silver mines lies the Messógia *(map p 69),* once a marshy swamp but now parcelled out into orchards, fields and vineyards.

North of Mounts Parnes and Kithairon lies **Boeotia**; its main towns, Thebes and Livadiá, are agricultural markets. Wheat, corn and barley are grown in the Boeotian plain while the Tanágra basin is devoted to potatoes and tomatoes; the reclaimed land which once flooded to form Lake Copaïs is now a huge cotton plantation. The island of **Euboia** *(p 110)* lies

Hymettos. – Kessarianí Monastery

parallel to the east coast of the Attic peninsula to which it is linked by a bridge.

The western boundary is marked by Mount Parnassos with its bauxite mines which have promoted the development of the important industrial complex of Andikíra for the production of aluminium; beyond lies Phocis (Fokída), famous for the sanctuary at Delphi and the "sea of olive trees" which fills the Amphissa basin.

Etolía on the west coast comprises a cool mountainous district clothed with holm-oaks round the huge reservoir, Lake Trihonída, and the River Aheloós expanding into the Agrínio basin where olives, tobacco and early vegetables are raised; the gleaming lagoon at Missolonghi (salt marshes) lies on the north coast of the Gulf of Patras.

Peloponnese. – Pop 1 012 528. The Peloponnese, which is linked to Attica by the Isthmus of Corinth, now breached by the Corinth Canal, is a vast and mountainous peninsula also known in the Middle Ages as **Morea**. The landmass is made up of high peaks, inland basins caused by subsidence and irrigated coastal plains; many of the people have emigrated providing Athens with a large proportion of her civil servants and politicians.

The eastern coastal plain, the Argolid, which is dominated by the citadels of Argos and Mycenae, is devoted to cereals, as well as orchards, market gardens and cattle.

In the north lies a fertile coastal strip divided into **Corinth** *(east)* and **Achaia** *(west)*. The vines which are cultivated to produce wine and raisins often alternate with rows of vegetables or fruit trees (oranges). Patras, which is the third largest town in Greece and an important centre for wine merchants, is also a port where many tourists disembark.

Down the west coast extends the monotonous plain of **Elis** (Ilía), partially composed of the alluvium deposited by the River Alpheios, which has been successively reclaimed since the Middle Ages. Small-scale enterprises are engaged in cereal cropping, market-gardens, orchards and vineyards; their products are processed in local factories: canning plants, fruit juice extractors etc.

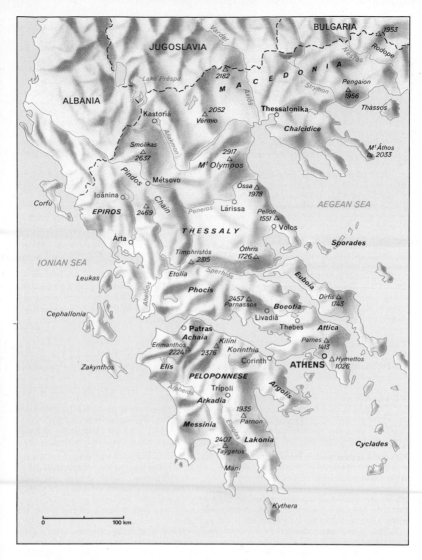

The southern coast is split into three promontories; the longest an extension of the Taÿgetos massif, is **Máni** *(p 130),* a wild limestone region inhabited by people of spirit. Taÿgetos is flanked by alluvial plains, free from winter frost: **Lakonía** *(east)* round Sparta and **Messinía** *(west)* round Kalamáta. The smiling fields produce grain and early vegetables while the figs and olives of Kalamáta are well known for their quality.

At the centre of the Peloponnese, round Trípoli, between 600m and 800m – 1 968ft and 2 625ft above sea level, lie the pasturelands of **Arkadía.**

Epiros. – Pop 324 541. Between the Ionian Sea and the western border of Thessaly rise the mountains of Epiros; the landscape is majestic and harsh, deeply furrowed by valleys and gorges. Its severe climate and isolation allowed the people a certain autonomy under the Turks. Even today the Epirots retain many of their traditional customs in dress, dancing, crafts etc.

The mountain pastures round Métsovo are devoted to flocks of sheep tended by their shepherds while the thick forests still shelter a few bears and wolves.

The capital, Ioánina, is situated on a beautiful site by a lake; round the shores are meadows where cattle and sheep are raised. Northeast rise the limestone heights of Zagória with their handsome stone houses.

To the south extends the plain of Árta with its orange plantations while the plain of Préveza produces early vegetables (tomatoes and melons).

Thessaly. – Pop 695 654. Thessaly, which has two main centres at Lárissa and the port of Vólos, is composed of a rich agricultural basin, watered by the River Peneios and surrounded by high peaks: Pindos to the west, Olympos to the north, Pelion and Óssa to the east and Timphristós in the south. Cold and damp in winter and very hot in summer, the country, which was formerly a marshy plain where buffalo roamed, now produces an abundance of wheat, barley, corn, sugarbeet and animal fodder. Almond trees crowd the slopes of Óssa while the famous "Volos olives" are grown on Pelion; a few picturesque towns boast traditional houses with balconies and flat stone roof tiles.

At the foot of Pelion lies the port of Vólos providing maritime communications. Road and rail links with Macedonia to the northeast pass through the famous Vale of Tempe at the foot of Mount Óssa while the road to Ioánina and Epiros in the northwest climbs over the Métsovo Pass (alt 1 705m – 5 594ft), the highest road pass in Greece. As it rises into the Píndos range the road passes the curious pillars of rock created by erosion which are known as the Metéora *(p 135).*

9

Macedonia. – Pop 2 121 953. The huge northern province of Greece with its continental climate stretches from west to east along the border with Albania and Bulgaria.

At the centre of the province lies the vast alluvial plain of the River Axiós (or Vardar) with its characteristic rows of poplars, its canals, its ancient salt marshes converted into rice fields or cotton plantations and its simple houses. Further west the crescent formed by Édessa, Náoussa and Véria on the lower slopes of Mount Vérmio has for centuries been a very fertile area which enabled Philip and Alexander of Macedon to develop and extend their power: apples, cherries, apricots and particularly peaches, food crops, grain, barley for brewing, root crops and fodder for cattle. East of the mouth of the Axiós, at the head of a small gulf (Kólpos Thessaloníkes), lies the port of Thessalonika, the second largest town in Greece.

Chalcidice *(p 77),* the region southeast of Thessalonika consists of bare hills, where cereals are grown, ending in three wooded peninsulas; the most easterly shelters the famous monasteries of Mount Áthos.

The country further east round Kavála is composed of broad valleys and inland depressions where tobacco with some cereals and sugarbeet is grown overlooked by high plateaux and Mount Pangaion with its famous gold mines.

In the mountains of western Macedonia, round Kastoriá, there are some fine examples of typical Macedonian houses with balconies and shingle roofs. This region abounds in beautiful lakes particularly Préspa, a nature reserve on the Jugoslavian border.

Thrace. – Pop 345 220. Thrace is the most easterly province of mainland Greece, flanked by Bulgaria and Turkey; it became part of Greece after the Second World War. Its dependent island, Samothrace, joined the Greek state in 1912.

The country consists of hills and plains devoted to growing tobacco, cereals, cotton and also mulberry trees for feeding silk worms. There is still a Turkish minority, particularly round Komotiní, and a few reminders of the Ottoman presence: the country women wear shawls on their heads, the four-wheeled farm carts are drawn by oxen... even camels are occasionally seen.

THE SEA AND THE ISLANDS

Thálassa, thálassa ! – The sea, the sea ! According to Xenophon this was the cry raised by the Greek mercenaries of Cyrus, the heroes of the Retreat of the Ten Thousand in 401 BC when they finally caught sight of the Black Sea after an exhausting march fighting a rearguard action over the mountains of Asia Minor.

The sea is never far distant in Greece; the long coastline is extended by countless bays and gulfs which are excellent for underwater fishing. There is no tide and the salinity reaches 3.8%. The water is usually transparent and blue but it can get choppy; the absence of currents and the excellent visibility are favourable to navigation and fishing.

Fish and fishermen. – Small-scale fishing still thrives in many of the little ports on the coast and in the islands. The major item of equipment is the boat, the wooden **caique** *(kaíki)* which has almost no keel but sits well in the water, bobbing like a cork on the short, sharp, foam flecked waves of the Mediterranean. The caiques, which are still built locally, no longer hoist their traditional double sails which have been replaced by a stout motor but they are often decorated in vivid colours, sometimes with a figure on the prow; the stern and the deck are finished with a balustrade.

The open boats propelled by a motor *(venzínes)* are crewed by only one or two men; they usually carry lights, which are strung out at dusk to dazzle the fish which are caught in a net: red mullet, mackerel, sardines and whitebait *(marída).* A typical catch includes squid *(kalamári)* and octopus *(oktapódi);* the latter are beaten on a stone to make them tender and then hung on a line to dry.

One sometimes sees flying fish and dolphins, which make a graceful escort for a boat but cause great damage to fishing nets.

Sponge diving, once common on many of the Aegean Islands, now survives only on Hydra, Syme (Sími) and Kálimnos; the caiques set out in the spring round the coasts.

Aegean Islands. – Pop 428 533. Exposed to the wind, the sea and the sun, the Aegean Islands are scattered between the Greek mainland and Turkey. The larger islands near the coast of Asia Minor – Lemnos, Lesbos, Chios and Sámos – are green and fertile and have not suffered much loss of population. In the Cyclades *(p 92)* and the Dodecanese *(p 219)* the cuboid houses under their dazzling whitewash contrast starkly with the barren rock-strewn land.

Under the brilliant light the islands are exposed to the prevailing wind which blows from the north. In winter it is known as the **"voriás"** but in spring and summer it becomes the **"meltémi"** which can blow for two or three days at a time, attaining a force of 6 to 8 (39 to 73km/h – 24 to 45mph); it makes the sea rough but refreshes the air.

Most of the Aegean Islands have a port or a landing place called **"skála"** (steps) in a sheltered bay, a town called **"hóra"** (place) on a hill out of reach of pirates and a **"kástro"**, which may have begun as an ancient Greek acropolis, become a *"froúrio"* under the Byzantines and then a castle or citadel under the Venetians and the Turks.

Ionian Islands. – Pop 182 651. They are strung out in the Ionian Sea off the west coast of Greece; there are seven main islands running from north to south: Corfu, Paxí, Leukas, Cephallonia, Ithaca, Zakynthos (or Zante) and Kythera which is separate from the other six and lies off the southern tip of the Peloponnese. They are pleasant and agreeable islands, slightly lacking in character compared with the Aegean Islands but better suited to holidays owing to their mild climate and tourist facilities.

Their propinquity to Italy and their long occupation by the Venetians (15C-18C) has made them as much Latin as Greek. The architecture shows strong Venetian influence, particularly in Corfu which has not suffered from earthquakes.

The rainfall in the autumn and winter means that the islands are fertile, producing abundant supplies of cereals, olives, fruit and grapes and supporting a reasonably large population (nearly 100 people to the km² – 250 to the sq. mile).

Crete, Rhodes and the Dodecanese. – *Description pp 199 to 229.*

FLORA AND FAUNA

The flora, which consists of over 6 000 species, will provide ample interest for the amateur botanist; it is at its best in the spring.

Trees. – In antiquity the Greek countryside was well forested but the trees were gradually decimated by goats and by over exploitation for ship building.

Cultivated trees are commonly to be found on farmland or in the plains and on the lower slopes of the hills, grown in plantations: olives more or less everywhere up to 600m – 1 969ft, citrus fruits (oranges, lemons, citrons) on irrigated land, almonds in sheltered spots and mulberries, figs, pomegranates and jujubes on the outskirts of villages. Protective shade along the roads and in the towns and villages is provided by the stately plane tree, the aromatic eucalyptus and the pepper tree which resembles a weeping willow. In open country and in scrubland the holm oak predominates, growing singly or in clumps and providing shade for the shepherds and their flocks. The cypress, tamarisk and Aleppo pine trees are to be found along the coasts while in the mountains over 1 000m – 3 281ft oaks, chestnuts, beeches, Corsican pines and fir trees thrive.

| Olive tree | Almond tree | Holm Oak | Aleppo Pine |

Olive tree: calcareous or siliceous soil: lives for 300 years or more; twisted trunk, silvery leaves.
Almond tree: plains and valleys; early pink flower; seed known as the almond.
Holm oak or holly oak: calcareous soil, below 800m – 2 625ft; evergreen leaves.
Aleppo pine: calcareous coastal slope; light foliage; twisted trunk and grey bark.

Shrubs. – They are usually evergreen and grow on grazing land or scrubland together with thyme, lavander, rosemary, basil and above all **majoram** (pink flowers); the roads and paths are more likely to be lined with bushes of scented broom, jasmin, mimosa, rhododendron and **oleander;** the latter are particularly common along water courses.

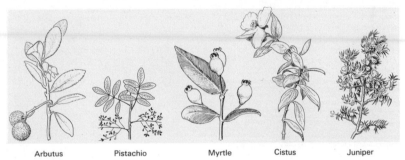

| Arbutus | Pistachio | Myrtle | Cistus | Juniper |

Arbutus: shiny leaves; whitish flowers and red fruit.
Pistachio: sparse foliage growing in groups of five to eleven leaflets; very small red fruit which darkens as it ripens *(p 74)*; also terebinth and mastic *(p 81)* pistachio.
Myrtle: white scented flowers, blue-black berries; symbol of amorous passion.
Cistus: dark green leaves; pink or white flowers with separate petals.
Juniper: prickly leaves; purple berries attractive to birds (quails, blackbirds).

Plants. – The common species, bulbs or succulents, grow in the open air.
Asphodel: long stems ending in white or yellow star shaped flowers.
Bougainvillea: climbing plant with clusters of purplish leaves.
Hibiscus: Shrub with large vivid red flowers.
Acanthus: long, curved, denticulate leaves.
Cactus: strangely shaped succulent plant with spikes and cylindrical, annulate stems.
Agave: succulent plant with thick leaves ending in a black spike; yellow flowers.

Fauna. – There may have been lions in Greece in antiquity since they appear frequently in Hellenistic art. During the Turkish occupation, there were jackals in the Peloponnese and caravans of camels plodding the paths of Macedonia, Thrace and Central Greece.

Nowadays a few species which are relatively rare in the rest of Europe are still to be found in Greece. The huge **tortoises,** which appear on the coins of certain ancient currencies, are sometimes seen in Attica and Boeotia. The forests on Mount Pindos still harbour brown bears and a few wolves. Wild boars are more numerous, so too are the birds of prey (eagles, falcons, vultures) which swoop over the mountain peaks and passes. In Epiros they breed "arrow" pigeons, which climb very high in the sky and then, in response to a whistle, plummet vertically towards the earth.

A familiar bird in central and northern Greece is the stork searching for its food in the river deltas, the lakes and lagoons and marshy coastal plains: Missolonghi lagoon, the plains of Árta and Lárissa, the lakes at Ioánina and Kastoriá and in Macedonia and Thrace.

ECONOMIC ACTIVITY

In 1981 Greece joined the European Economic Community (Common Market).

Agriculture. – 27.60 % of the active population is engaged in agriculture.

Sufficient **wheat** (2 308 471 tonnes) is grown to meet domestic needs. High yields are obtained on the red soil of Boeotia and Thessaly.

Vines are tended to produce wine (6 910 000 hl) to which resin *(retsína)* is often added as a preservative. The major wine merchants congregate round Patras.

The **olive** reigns throughout central and southern Greece: the owners beat the trees to bring down the fruit which they press to extract as much oil as they need for their own use before sending the surplus to the refineries.

Improved methods of cultivating **citrus fruits** (993 595 tonnes in 1984) in the coastal basins of the Peloponnese and Epiros mean that a quarter of the harvest can be used for juice extraction. The peach orchards in the Náoussa region in Macedonia provide largescale exports to the U.S.S.R. (1/3 of production) and to the Common Market.

The hot and humid plains of Boeotia, Thessaly, Macedonia and Thrace produce sugarbeet, corn, barley, rice and **cotton**, of which Greece is the major European producer. Tobacco is grown by small holders in Macedonia and Thrace and Epiros.

Industry and commerce. – Greece lacks natural resources in minerals and energy.

The total power of the hydroelectric installations is only 2 852 000 kW while the other power stations produce 13 876 000 kW. The only solid fuel is **lignite;** the oil discovered near the island of Thassos meets only 20% of the nation's needs.

The main product of the mining industry is **bauxite** (2 700 000 tonnes per annum) which is extracted from Mount Parnassos and converted into aluminium in Andikíra near Delphi. Production of cement, fertilisers, textiles and electric appliances is growing.

Half of Greece's external trade is with the Common Market, 20% with Arab countries; this produces a trade deficit of 98 000m: 172 000m of imports (oil, meat, manufactured goods) against 74 000m of exports (aluminium, textiles, tobacco, fruit and vegetables). The deficit is made up by "invisible earnings" from **merchant shipping** (Greek crews only) which carried 50 600 818 tonnes in 1981 (3rd in the world and 1st in Europe), tourism (5 000 000 visitors annually) and money repatriated by Greeks abroad.

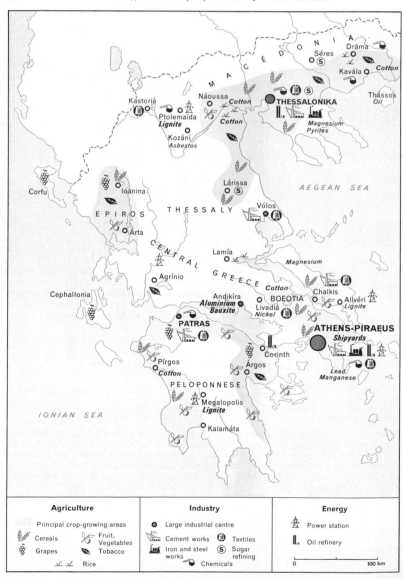

Agriculture	Industry	Energy
Principal crop-growing areas	Large industrial centre	Power station
Cereals — Fruit, Vegetables	Cement works — Textiles	Oil refinery
Grapes — Tobacco	Iron and steel works — Sugar refining	
Rice	Chemicals	0 100 km

POPULATION

The population of Greece (9 740 417) is fairly homogenous, only 5 % being aliens. In Epiros there are a few **Vlachs,** nomadic shepherds from the north, speaking a language derived from Latin, while the Peloponnese, Attica and the Saronic Islands contain small Albanian communities. There are Greeks of Turkish origin (100 000) in Thrace and in the Dodecanese; the gypsy people have no fixed abode. The Greeks who fled from Asia Minor in 1922 have settled on the outskirts of large towns in the **"new"** (néa) communities named after their lost homes, such as New Smyrna (Néa Smírni) in Athens.

There is also a large and powerful Greek expatriate community.

The greater number is made up of Greeks who emigrated in 19C, establishing themselves in Egypt, the home of an influential group of businessmen (Benáki), in Central Europe (Sína the banker in Vienna), on the Black Sea (Odessa), in the Middle East and particularly in the U.S.A. where their political weight is not to be ignored.

More recent emigrants were attracted by the high salaries of the industrial countries, such as Canada, Australia, South Africa and Federal Republic of Germany; they return to Greece after a few years or on retirement.

The number of expatriate Greeks is about 4 000 000; 250 000 in Germany and 30 000 in France, mainly in Paris, Marseille and Lyon.

GREEK WAY OF LIFE

Daily Life. – Although egocentric and individualistic in character, the Greeks are also hospitable and exuberant; they have a powerful need to talk and use their hands a great deal. To pass the time they often resort to worry beads (**komboloi**), which resemble a rosary, endlessly clicking the beads of amber, box wood or plastic between their fingers. Their gaiety, however, hides a deep pessimism which is expressed in the melancholy strains of their popular songs and music. Time is of little importance to them and punctuality is not their forte. Although they enjoy drinking, there is little drunkenness. The Greeks combine a talent for business with a reputation for deep personal honesty.

In physique the Greeks rarely resemble the image received from ancient documents. Although they may be called Odysseus or Aristotle, Iphigenia or Antigone, they seldom have the traditional traits of the Greek hero – curly hair, fine features and straight noses – but seamed faces with aquiline noses. The women, who are dignified and highly respected in their old age, play an important role.

On rising the Greeks take a single cup of coffee before starting work but at mid-morning they pause for a snack of bread and cheese or a *koulouri,* a bread ring sprinkled with sesame seeds. Lunch, which is eaten between 1 and 2pm, consists of a main dish with a salad and bread accompanied by wine or beer.

Then comes the delicious siesta until 4 or 5pm when work resumes until 7 or 8pm.

The early evening is the best part of the Greek day when the men meet in the café (**kafenío**), the centre of social life, and talk interminably over an *oúzo (p 31),* or a tiny cup of Greek coffee *(kafedáki)* with a simple glass of water; the main topics are football, politics and their fellow countrymen; some play cards or backgammon (**távli**). In the provinces this is the time for the **"perípato"** or *"vólta"* when people stroll in the main square.

Dinner, at home, is served about 10 o'clock or even later and is the heaviest meal of the day with a dish of meat or fish, vegetables, various salads, wine or beer. The evening ends at the café or out in the open air or watching television. Sometimes there is a performance at the shadow theatre **"Karagiósis"** (Evil Eye) which is named after the main character in the show, a resourceful person, previously very popular, whose adventures often evoke the Turkish occupation.

Orthodox Christianity. – This is the established church to which 97% of the population belong; the remaining 3% is divided among Muslims (100 000 in Thrace and the Dodecanese), Roman Catholics (35 000 in the Cyclades and the Ionian Islands) and Jews (65 000).

During the Turkish occupation the Greek church conducted secret schools and helped to keep Greek culture alive and during the struggle for Independence *(p 24)* in 19C it sided with the people. Under the nominal tutelage of the Patriarch of Constantinople, the church is administered by a Synod presided over by the Archbishop of Athens; the Metropolitans (bishops) are responsible for their dioceses; each parish is in the charge of a pope *(papás)* who is free to marry a wife *(pappadiá)* while still a deacon but cannot then aspire to being a bishop.

There are over two hundred monasteries *(moní)* inhabited by monks *(kalógeri)* or nuns; the most famous are at Metéora or on Mount Áthos. Under the authority of a superior *(igoúmenos)* they follow a fairly relaxed rule apart from the obligation to attend services and provide hospitality.

Priests and monks can be recognised by their black robes (blue for informal occasions); their round high hats *(skoúfia),* their beards and long hair tied up in a bun in the Byzantine manner; bishops and abbots wear a pectoral cross.

The Byzantine rite has an ancient liturgy rich in symbolism. The faithful receive communion in both kinds, make the sign of the cross from right to left and revere icons of Jesus, the Virgin and the saints. Their services are punctuated by magnificent unaccompanied chanting, in which the base voices predominate. Baptism is by immersion and at weddings the bride and bridegroom are crowned with white wreaths joined by a ribbon. In church the congregation usually stands, women on the left, men on the right.

Local arts and traditions. – Traditional dress is worn for patronal festivals or feasts of the Virgin (processions), at weddings, during the carnival or, in a simpler form, on market day. The women are resplendent in embroidery and chased ornaments chiefly displayed on their bodices and skirts. A few men still wear the heavy pleated kilt (**fustanélla**), which is the uniform of the soldiers *(évzoni)* of the Guard *(p 57),* as well as the pompom shoes (**tsaroúhia**). Local costumes are most common at Métsovo in Epiros, on Leukas, in the Northern Sporades, in the Peloponnese, on Kárpathos and Astipálea in the Dodecanese and also in Crete; women spinning are often to be seen in the country districts.

Popular music is played at festivals and other ceremonies (weddings and funerals), in the cafés and squares where the men meet in the evenings. On these occasions the traditional local instruments are used: a sort of lute (bouzoúki), (various rustic flutes, the Epirot clarinet, the lyre, a three-stringed viol played with a bow, the *sandoúri* which is played by striking its steel strings with small hammers.

Three or four of these instruments accompany the singers whose plaintive style owes much to oriental music: the *"kléftikos"* attributed to the klephts *(p 24)* in the War of Independence and the famous rebétika, nostalgic songs from the urban slums.

Some dances are of oriental origin such as the *zembétiko,* performed by a man on his own, or the *hassápiko,* the butchers' dance, for a couple of men; others such as the Cretan *pendozáli* imitate war; a clarinet accompanies the *mirológia,* funeral dances and dirges. The national dance, the *kalamantianós,* is danced in a ring and recalls the sacrifice of the Souliot women *(p 120).* The lively sirtáki is a recent development of the *hassápiko.*

MAJOR FESTIVALS *(1)*

DATE *(2)* and PLACE	TYPE OF EVENT
6 January (Epiphany) ......Piraeus and other ports	Blessing of the sea and immersion of a cross, retrieved by swimmers.
February-March: 8 days before the 1st Monday in Lent .... Patras	Carnival, the most important in Greece: procession of floats.
Athens	Carnival with masks and disguises.
Skyros	Carnival; costume procession; traditional dances.
Náoussa (Páros)	Carnival of the "Boúles", masked dancers.
Monday before Lent .... Athens	Popular songs and dances near the temple of Zeus and the Pnyx Hill; kite-flying competition.
Palm Sunday and Holy Saturday .... Corfu	St Spiridon's procession.
Good Friday ..... Throughout Greece	Procession of the Epitáfios (image of Christ).
Easter Sunday	Midnight mass out of doors; pascal lamb feast.
Easter Tuesday .....Mégara (Attica)	Local festival: traditional dances in costume.
Easter Week ......Káristos (Euboia)	The Voriatikí (North Wind), a men's dance.
Kálimnos	Blessing of the boats for sponge fishing.
23 April (St George's Day) Aráhova	Religious festival: singing, dancing and games.
Assí-Goniá (Crete; SW of Rethymnon)	Mass and popular festival; blessing of the cattle.
5-6 May .Skinés (Crete: S of Chania)	Orange festival; Cretan dancing and singing.
21-23 May .... Langadás (NE of Thessalonika) and Agiá Eléni (Séres)	Ritual ceremonies (Anastenária): the "Anastena-rídes", in a trance, dance barefoot on hot coals holding icons of Constantine and Helena.
May .... Lesbos	Animal sacrifices, horse racing, dancing, religious festival *(see p 126).*
May – September .... Athens	Dancing by the Dora Stratou company. Athens Festival: ancient Greek drama; concerts and ballet.
Saturdays and Sundays, end June – early September .... Epidauros	Festival of ancient drama.
End June – July ..... Coastal towns	Nautical Week.
Early July .... Rethymnon (Crete)	Representation of a Cretan wedding; wine festival.
10 July – September ......Daphne	Greek wine festival: free tasting; dancing.
17-18 July ...... Vóni (Crete: SE of Knossós)	Festival of Cretan dancing and singing.
25 July .... Throughout Greece	Pilgrimages to peaks dedicated to Elijah (Ilías).
July – August ....Delphi	Festival of ancient drama.
July – August ....Philippi – Thassos	Ancient Drama Festival
July – early September ....Rhodes	Wine festival: free tasting of Greek wine.
August .... Leukas	Arts and folk festival.
6 August .... Corfu	Procession of boats to the isle of Pondikonísi.
11 August .... Corfu	St Spiridon's procession.
13-15 August ...... Neápoli (Crete)	Festival of popular art; wine tasting.
15 August ....Tenos	Pilgrimage to the miraculous image of the Virgin.
Markópoulo (Cephallonia)	Procession of serpents.
27-28 August ....Dodona	Performances of ancient Greek drama.
Last Sunday in August Kritsá (Crete)	Representation of a traditional country wedding.
End August – early September ....Zakynthos	International Medieval and Popular Drama Festival.
9-23 September ...... Thessalonika	International Fair.
October .... Thessalonika	Film Festival.
26 October .... Thessalonika	St Demetrios' procession; cultural events.
8 November ....Arkádi (Crete)	Parade and traditional dances in memory of the sacrifice of the defenders of the monastery.
30 November (St Andrew's Day) .... Patras	Procession in honour of the patron saint of Patras.
24 December .... Thessalonika	Children sing "Kálanda" in the streets.

(1) For the exact dates apply to the Tourist office.
(2) In the Orthodox Church, the feasts from Lent to Whitsun are not celebrated on the same dates as in the western church; they may fall from one to four weeks later.

ART AND CIVILISATION

ANTIQUITY

Below is a comparative table of the great periods of civilisation in the eastern Mediterranean.

BC	GREECE		ORIENT
	Historic facts	**Artistic eras**	
3000		**Cycladic (3000-2000):** ceramics, idols, small useful objects	Sumer
			Egypt: Ancient Empire (2800-2100)
2500			
2000	Achaian and Ionian invasions	**Minoan (2000-1500):** frescoes, low relief sculptures, ceramics, statuettes.	*Pyramid of Cheops*
			Egypt: Middle Empire (2100-1600)
			Abraham (2000)
1500		**Mycenaean (1500-1100):** masks, golden vessels and funerary objects, ivory and rock crystal trinkets, arms, helmets	Babylon: First Empire (2000-1400)
1200	Capture of Troy by the Achaians		Anatolia: Hittites (2000-1300)
1150	Dorian invasions		Egypt: New Empire (1600-1200)
1100	Colonisation of Asia Minor by the Greeks (Ionians)	**Geometric (1100-700)** ceramics with linear decoration, small bronzes, implements, funerary objects.	*Tutankhamen (1450)* *Ramses II (1250)* *Moses (1250)*
1000			Lebanon: the Phoenicians (1500-1000)
900	Homer		
700	Lycurgus (Sparta) Greek colonies in Syria, Italy, Sicily, Egypt, Euxine (Black Sea), Liguria (Marseille)	**Archaic (700-500):** temples of tufa and sculptures in oriental style, *kouros* and *korai*, Corinthian vases, black figure ceramics.	Assyrian Empire (1400-600)
			Kings of Judah: Saul, David and Solomon (1000)
			Italy: Etruscans (750-500)
600	Solon (Athens) Peisistratos (Athens)		*Foundation of Rome*
500	1st Persian War: Persians defeated at Marathon (490)		Egypt: Saitic Renaissance (650-500)
			Assurbanipal (650)
480	2nd Persian War: Persians defeated at Salamis (480)	**Classical (500-300):** marble temples, marble, gold and ivory sculptures, great bronzes, red figure ceramics.	Babylon: Second Empire
			Capture of Jerusalem by Nebuchanezzar (587)
450	Age of Pericles (5C): Socrates and Plato in Athens		
400	Peloponnesian War won by Sparta		Persian Empire (500-300)
350	Philip of Macedon: Greeks defeated at Chaironeia (338)		*Cyrus, Darius, Xerxes (Ahasuerus)*
330	Alexander the Great (330-280)	**Hellenistic (300-100):** Macedonian tombs and treasuries, stoas, great statues in marble and bronze, Tanágra figurines.	Rome: the Republic (500-100)
200	First Roman incursions		
100	Greece a Roman province: capture of Athens by Sulla (86) battle of Actium (31)		Empire of Alexander the Great (300-200)
			Egypt: The Ptolemies (Ptolemy, Cleopatra)
			Rome: the Empire
AD			*Capture of Jerusalem by Titus*
50	Paul the Apostle in Greece	**Roman:** urban complexes, administrative buildings, baths, arches, busts, portraits, mosaics.	
130	The Emperor Hadrian and his favourite Antinoüs in Greece		
200	Barbarian invasions.		

GODS AND MYTHS

The ancient religion was devoid of dogma or a sense of sin; the legendary adventures of its many divinities constituted Greek mythology which was based on the forces of nature and the fear which they inspired.

The divinities and their cults. – The three oldest divinities (Rheia, Gaia and Kronos) were followed by a group of about twenty major gods and goddesses among which twelve were pre-eminent and lived in majesty on Mount Olympos hidden in the clouds with Zeus the thunderer at their head. There was also a crowd of lesser divinities: local gods, Egyptian and Syrian gods, demi-gods born of the love affairs between the greater gods and mere mortals, and heroes who were deified mortals.

The gods were consulted through oracles whose priestly attendants interpreted the messages. The temple (**hieron**), dedicated to the god or goddess, stood within a sacred precinct (**témenos**) which was entered by a grand gateway (**propylaia**). Purified with lustral water, the worshippers entered the precinct and processed along the sacred way past the **treasuries**, small buildings for the reception of offerings, the semi-circular bench seats (**exedra**) and the **votive offerings** (inscriptions, statues) which also surrounded the temple. The altar, where the libations were poured and the animals were sacrificed, stood in the open in front of the temple. After the sacrifice the people entered the temple to see the statue of the divinity in the inner chamber (**naós**) (p 18).

Names	Identity and Symbol	Attributes	Principal place of worship
Zeus (Jupiter)	Lord of the gods and the world.	Eagle, sceptre, thunder.	Olympia, Dodona, Neméa.
Hera (Juno)	Zeus' wife. Marriage	Peacock, diadem.	Árgos, Sámos, Perachora, Olympia.
Athena (Minerva)	Wisdom. Arts and crafts. Victory in war.	Shield (aegis), helmet, owl, olive branch.	Athens (Parthenon).
Apollo (Apollo)	Physical beauty. Fine Arts.	Lyre, arrows, laurel, sun.	Delos, Delphi, Corinth, Bassae, Líndos.
Artemis (Diana)	Chastity, hunting. Twin of Apollo.	Bow, quiver, crescent moon.	Delos, Brauron, Corcyra, Delphi, Artemision.
Hermes (Mercury)	Messenger of the gods and souls. Commerce, eloquence.	Winged sandals and cap. Caduceus, ram.	
Hephaistos (Vulcan)	Aphrodite's husband. Fire, metal.	Anvil, hammer.	Athens "Theseion", Lemnos.
Hestia (Vesta)	Family hearth.	Fire.	
Ares (Mars)	Aphrodite's lover. War.	Helmet, arms and armour.	
Aphrodite (Venus)	Born from the sea. Mother of Eros. Love and beauty.	Doves, shell.	Kythera, Corinth, Rhodes.
Demeter (Ceres)	Agriculture, maternal love.	Ear of corn, sceptre, scythe.	Eleusis.
Poseidon (Neptune)	Amphitrite's husband. Sea and storms.	Trident.	Athens, Cape Sounion, Isthmía.

Other important gods

Asklepios (Aesculapius)	Apollo's son. Healing.	Serpent, rod.	Epidauros, Kos.
Dionysos (Bacchus)	Born from Zeus' thigh. Wine, joy.	Vine, thyrsus, panther.	Athens, Delos, Parnassos and Pangaion.
Hades (Pluto)	Kingdom of the dead.	Throne, beard.	Ephyra Nekromanteion.
Persephone or Kore (Proserpina)	Demeter's daughter Death. Renewal.	Cock, plants.	Ephyra Nekromanteion.
Helios (Phœbus)	A Titan. Sun.	Sun's rays, chariot.	Rhodes.

Demi-gods and heroes

Achilles. – Son of Thetis and Peleus, pupil of the centaur Cheiron. Impetuous and brave. Invulnerable except on his heel at which Paris aimed his fatal arrow.

Adonis. – A handsome youth; Aphrodite was inconsolable when he died.

Centaurs. – They had horses' bodies with human busts and fought the Lapiths.

Dioscuri (Castor and Pollux). – Twin sons of Zeus and Leda. Adventurous warriors.

Aiolos. – He kept the Winds tied up in a skin and released them on the orders of Zeus.

Giants. – They attacked the Olympian gods: **Gigantomachia** (battle of the Giants).

Herakles (Hercules). – The most famous hero, son of Zeus and Alkmene. He performed the legendary Twelve Labours (p 194) and is shown with a mace, a bow and a lion skin.

Jason. – Thessalian hero, leader of the Argonauts who went in search of the Golden Fleece.

Muses. – Daughters of Zeus and associates of Apollo, patrons of writers and artists, the nine Muses (p 36) dwelt on Mount Parnassos.

Orpheus. – Son of one of the muses, musician and poet, husband of Eurydice whom he tried in vain to rescue from the underworld. Attribute: a lyre.

Pan. – Rustic and lecherous demi-god with horns on his head and cloven hoofs for feet. Attribute: pan pipes (7 tubes). Shrines: the Corycian Cave (Delphi), the caves at Marathon.

Perseus. – Son of Zeus and Argive hero; he beheaded Medusa, one of the three Gorgons, and married Andromeda whom he rescued from a dragon with the aid of Pegasos.

Theseus. – Assisted by Ariadne he killed the Cretan minotaur in the Labyrinth.

Odysseus (Ulysses). – King of Ithaca, courageous and cunning, he fought in the Trojan War. His adventures on the journey home are told in Homer's "Odyssey".

ARCHITECTURE

Quarries. – The chief building material was stone: limestone tufa (often shell limestone), and marble from the quarries on Pentelikon, Thássos and Náxos.

The stone blocks were quarried with a pickaxe and extracted with the aid of metal or wooden wedges – the latter were soaked to make them expand. Often the blocks were then shaped on the spot into architectural elements: columns, capitals etc.

Transport. – The blocks were removed from the quarry down a slipway constructed so as to have a regular gradient. Weighing on average 5 tonnes, they were loaded on to wooden sledges which were lowered on ropes hitched round fixed bollards. The blocks were then transferred to carts or drays drawn by bullocks for transport to the building site.

Building sites. – On the site the rough or prepared blocks were unloaded with the aid of levers and rollers and sent to the workshop to be dressed or decorated (fluting, moulding) or carved (capitals, pediments and metopes).

The blocks were raised into position with a block and tackle and hoist or derrick. The dressed stones which were placed one upon another without mortar were held in place by H or N cramps. Wooden or metal pins were used to secure the piles of drums which made up a column: the holes which held them can still be seen. Stone columns received a coat of stucco.

| Cyclopean Bonding | Polygonal Bonding | Trapezoidal Bonding | Rectangular Bonding |

Bonding. – In large-scale constructions the blocks of stone were cut and placed in various ways according to the purpose and period of the building and the means and time available. No bonding material was used. This gives Greek stonework an almost unrivalled aesthetic and functional value.

The **Cyclopean** style of construction, rough but sturdy, is to be found in some Mycenaean structures, especially at Tiryns. **Polygonal** bonding was used in all periods, often for foundations; at first the blocks were rough hewn, then came curved surfaces and finally flat ones. **Trapezoidal** bonding, with varying degrees of regularity, was widespread in 4C BC. **Rectangular** bonding, which occurred in all periods, was used most frequently in the Classical period.

PALACES AND FORTRESSES
(2000-1000 BC)

Minoan Period. – 2000-1500 BC. The Minoan dynasties which ruled the cities of Crete built complex fortified palaces which inspired the myth of the labyrinth *(p 210)*: blind external walls, symmetrical entrances, a cordon of storerooms and workrooms within the outer walls, at the centre a vast courtyard surrounded by the religious and royal apartments grouped round light wells on several floors which were linked by a maze of stairs and corridors. Villas, such as Tylissos, show the same plan on a smaller scale.

The best examples of Cretan palaces are Knossós, Mália, Phaistos and Zákros on Crete itself; other examples on Melos and particularly Santoríni.

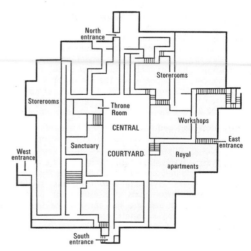

Cretan Palace

Mycenaean Period. – 1500-1100. The Mycenaean palace was less sophisticated than the Cretan and stood within a fortified city *(acropolis)* composed of Cyclopean walls, so called because legend said they had been built by giant masons, the Cyclops. The palace itself had a simple and logical plan: one entrance, a courtyard with the throne room on one side preceded by a vestibule and the main reception rooms on the other. The largest room was the **megaron** with four columns supporting the roof and surrounding the central hearth which served both domestic and religious purposes. Beyond lay the private apartments of the king and queen, usually furnished with baths.

The best examples of Mycenaean palaces are Mycenae, Tiryns, Pylos and Gla.

The dead were buried on the edge of the city in three different sorts of graves: a pit grave, a rock sepulchre or a circular domed chamber *(thólos)* with an entrance passage *(drómos)*. The skilled craftsmanship of the objects found in these tombs indicates that the princes who were buried in them were astonishingly rich; for many years the graves were known as "Treasuries".

The best examples of Mycenaean graves are at Mycenae, Pylos and Vapheio.

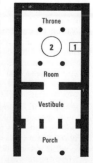

Mycenaean megaron
1 Throne 2 Hearth

TEMPLES (from 700 BC)

The temple was the dwelling place of the god or goddess to whom it was dedicated and housed his or her statue; some temples were dedicated to more than one divinity.

Proportions. – The temples, which were thought to represent the architectural ideal, are essentially a blend of structural simplicity and harmonious proportions. The proportions were governed by the **module,** the average radius of the column, which determined the height since the column was the basic element in the elevation of a building.

In some buildings the architects departed from rigid verticals and horizontals to create a different effect.

The horizontal entablatures were slightly

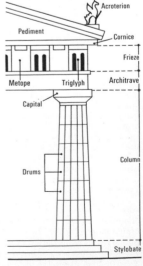

Off-set columns.

bowed making the centre imperceptibly higher than the ends; each column was inclined towards its inner neighbour as it rose, the angle of incline increasing from the centre of the colonnade towards the outer corner.

Decoration. – The sculpted figures, which were often didactic, were placed where they would be most visible: the tympanum (pediment) and the metopes (architrave).

The temples were painted; the background was generally red with the prominent features in blue to form a contrast. These brilliant colours made the stone or white marble sculptures stand out. A gilded bronze colour was used to pick out certain decorative motifs such as shields or acroteria.

Plan. – There were three main types:
– the large peripteral temple, consisting of a central oblong chamber (**naós**) containing the statue of the divinity and entered by a door, with a porch at either end screened by two columns; one porch *(prónaos)* led into the *naós,* the other *(opisthódomos)* contained the temple's most precious offerings. The roof of the *naós* might be supported on two rows of columns. Behind the *naós* there was occasionally an inner chamber *(adyton)* which only the priest might enter. This central section was surrounded by a colonnade (peristyle) and

THÓLOS

IN ANTIS

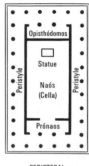

PERIPTERAL

the temple was described in terms of the number of columns in the front and rear colonnades: hexastyle – six. The length of a temple was usually twice its width.
– the "in antis" temple consisting of a *naós* and *prónaos* screened by two columns placed between two pilasters (*antae* in Latin) at the ends of the extended walls of the *naós.*
– the **"thólos"**, a votive or commemorative circular building with a peristyle.

Elevation and orders. – The main elements of a temple were the base (**stylobate**), the columns, the entablature supporting a wooden roof frame covered with tiles and a pediment at either end. The articulation of these elements gave rise to the different orders.

Doric Order. – It developed on the mainland among the Dorian people and was the most common style in Greece from 7C onwards. The columns, which had twenty flutes, rested directly on the stylobate without bases; the capitals were plain. The entablature consisted of three parts one above the other: the architrave, the frieze and the cornice; the frieze was composed of **metopes,** panels often carved in high relief, alternating with **triglyphs,** stone slabs with two vertical grooves. The triangular pediments were sculpted with scenes in high relief and also adorned with decorative motifs (**acroteria**) at the angles. Along the sides above the cornice were sculpted ornaments (**antefixa**) which served as gargoyles.

Ionic Order. – This style developed among the Ionians who had settled in Asia Minor in 5C BC and was considered a feminine style; its delicate grace and rich ornament contrasted with the austere strength of the Doric order. Its main characteristics are tall slim columns with 24 flutes resting on moulded bases and crowned by **capitals** in the form of a **double scroll** *(photo p 33);* an entablature consisting of an architrave, a continuous sculpted frieze and a cornice decorated with egg and dart and leaf and dart moulding; a pediment with acroteria shaped like palm leaves at the angles.

Corinthian Order. – It was invented in Corinth in 5C BC but did not spread until 4C BC; it was very popular in the Roman period. It is a derivative of the Ionic order and its chief distinction is the scroll capital almost entirely covered in curled acanthus leaves.

The capital was invented by Kallimachos, a sculptor and contemporary of Pheidias; he is thought to have been inspired by a basket filled with flowers.

Doric elevation

THEATRES

Nearly all religious sites in ancient Greece included a theatre which was originally designed for the Dionysiac festivals which included hymns or dithyrambs which developed into tragedy.

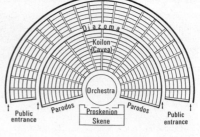

Theatre.

The original wooden structures were later built of stone and from 4C BC comprised:
– a central circular area (**orchestra**) where the chorus performed round the altar of the god and the actors wearing the appropriate mask acted their parts;
– tiers of seats (**koilon** or **theatron**) extending round more than half the orchestra to form the segment of a circle; the first row of seats was reserved for the priests and officials; a promenade (**diázoma**) ran round between the upper and lower tiers of seats. The audience reached their seats from above, from the *diázoma* or through passages (**parodos**) leading into the orchestra;
– a proscenium (**proskenion**), a sort of portico forming a backdrop, and a stage (**skene**) which was originally a store room where the actors waited their turn; in the Hellenistic period it was incorporated into the performing area so that the actors could develop their roles.

Odeons were covered theatres which became very numerous in the Roman period.

The major theatres are in Athens (Theatre of Dionysos), Delphi, Árgos and Epidauros (4C BC) and Dodona (3C BC).

SCULPTURE

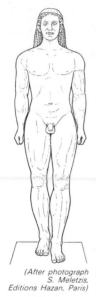

(After photograph
S. Meletzis,
Editions Hazan, Paris)

Kouros

Archaic Period. – 700-500 BC. In 7C BC the Greek world began to produce its first full size statues, strange rigid figures with ecstatic expressions made of wood *(xoanon)* inspired by Asiatic, particularly Egyptian, models.

In 6C two well known and distinctive types of statue were produced: the **kouros**, a naked young man, and the **kore**, a young woman dressed in a tunic, Doric peplos or Ionian chiton. The figures, which were life size or larger, were sometimes made of bronze, like the Piraeus Apollo which was discovered in 1959, but more often of limestone *(poros)* or marble and then painted with vivid colours.

The high reliefs, carved in stone and also painted, mostly come from pediments and are impressive for their realistic and expressive appearance; the bronze sculptures are more stylised.

The Acropolis Museum in Athens has an important series of Archaic figures *(kouroi* and *korai,* high relief pedimental sculptures, *moscophoroi)* while the National Museum displays the Warrior of Marathon and several *kouroi* including the *kouros* of Sounion, the oldest known (600 BC), and the *kouros* of Anávissos; the Piraeus Apollo (late 6C BC) is to be found in the Piraeus Museum.

(After photograph
S. Meletzis,
Editions Hazan, Paris)

Kore

Other examples typical of Archaic art are the stone Gorgon from the temple of Artemis in Corcyra (Corfu Museum), the marble frieze from the Siphnian Treasury and two *kouroi* representing Cleobis and Biton (Delphi Museum).

Classical Period. – 500-300 BC. There was a transition period, marked by the **Charioteer from Delphi** (475 BC: Delphi Museum), where the figure turns slightly to the right and takes his weight on one hip; Classical statuary then freed itself from the rigid frontal stance passing through two distinct phases.

In the idealistic phase (5C BC) Greek sculpture reached its height in the work of Polykleitos and Pheidias. The former established a standard model, the **canon**. The latter created an ideal standard of beauty composed of strength, majesty and serenity in the delicately carved lines of his marble figures: his genius is expressed in the Parthenon sculptures (British Museum, Louvre); unfortunately the famous chryselephantine (gold and ivory) statue of Zeus at Olympia has been destroyed.

During the "naturalist" phase (4C) majesty gave way to grace and the female nude made its appearance. Artists began to compose from nature *(illustration p 104)* giving their figures expressive faces; the best known are Skopas, Lysippos the sculptor of Alexander the Great, and Praxiteles who produced tall figures such as the famous **Hermes of Olympia**. The Apollo Belvedere (Vatican) also dates from this time as do the great bronzes in the Athens Museum: the Ephebe from Antikythera and the Poseidon from Artemision.

Tanágra in Boeotia produced the famous funerary figurines in terracotta.

Hellenistic Period. – 300-100 BC. Sculpture began to be influenced by expressionism and orientalism. A realism, sometimes excessive, was used to express not only pain but also movement as in the Laocoon (Vatican) and the Victory of Samothrace (Louvre); at the same time it could produce the beautiful serenity of the Melos Aphrodite (Venus de Milo). Artists took delight in representing children, such as the bronze jockey from Artemision in the Athens Museum.

PAINTING AND CERAMICS

Except for the Minoan frescoes in Crete or Santoríni and the Hellenistic funerary paintings in Macedonia *(pp 124 and 196)* few examples of ancient Greek painting have survived. In fact, although painting played a major role in the decoration of sculptures and monuments, it was less important as an art form in its own right and the works of the great painters of 4C BC – Zeuxis and above all **Apelles**, Alexander the Great's favourite artist – have not survived the passage of time. For a knowledge of Greek painting one must study the decoration of pottery on the many vases which have come down to us.

Vases. – The ornamentation painted on vases is one of the major sources of information about Greek religion and civilisation.

| Pithos | Krater | Hydria | Amphora | Pelike |

| Oinochoë | Krater | Kantharos | Kylix | Lekythos | Rhyton |

The *pithos* was used for storing grain, the *amphora* for the storing and transport of oil or wine. The *pelike, krater* and *hydria* were used as jars for oil, wine and water respectively.

The *oinochoë* was used as a jug for pouring water or wine into a *kantharos;* the *kylix* was a drinking cup and the *rhyton* was a vessel shaped like a horn or an animal's head. The *lekythos* was a funerary vase.

Styles. – The styles developed in step with the great artistic periods *(see table on p 15);* there were several types.

Creto-Mycenaean vases (1700-1400 BC): scenes of flora and fauna treated with great freedom and decorative sense. Typical examples: octopus amphora; Phaistos krater (Herakleion Museum).

Archaic vases (1000-600 BC): geometric style in the Cyclades and Attica with large kraters or amphorae decorated with dotted lines, the key pattern, checks, lozenges and sometimes animals; orientalising style in Rhodes and Corinth where small vessels were decorated with oriental motifs: roses, lotus sprays, sphinxes and deer.

Typical examples: amphorae from the Kerameikos and the Dipylon (National Museum in Athens); perfume flasks (Corinth Museum).

Black figure vases (600-480 BC): subjects for decoration drawn from mythology or history: silhouettes in black painted on a red ochre ground.

Typical examples: krater showing Herakles and Nereus (National Museum in Athens).

Red figure vases (480-320 BC): subject for decoration not only mythological (so called "severe" style – 5C BC) but also familiar and more lighthearted: scenes and figures drawn in detail and accentuated by a black or white ground *(lekythoi).*

Typical examples: krater from Kalyx and lekythoi from Eretria (National Museum in Athens).

GLOSSARY

Abaton: inviolate holy place

Adyton: Holy of Holies in a temple

Agora: chief public place in a town

Archon: town magistrate

Bema: rostrum for orators

Bouleuterion: Senate House

Boule: Senate

Chiton: a woollen shirt worn next to the body

Chryselephantine: made of gold and ivory

Chrysobull: golden bull, document sealed with a gold seal

Exedra: semi circular bench

Hoplite: heavy-armed foot soldier carrying a pike and a large shield

Nymphaeum: monumental fountain

Oikos: house, place of religious worship

Palestra: wrestling ring, sports ground

Peplos: ample outer garment for women

Propylaia: monumental entrance gate

Prytaneion: townhall where the local governors met

Quadriga: four horse chariot

Stoa: portico

Term: a pedestal tapering towards the base, supporting a bust or merging at the top into a sculptured human, animal or mythical figure

Thyrsos: a staff wreathed in ivy or vine tendrils topped with a pine cone borne by Dionysos

Trireme: a war ship with three banks of oars and a ram

Anastylosis is the total or more often partial reconstruction of a monument using the original fragments found on the site and making up the missing parts with an easily distinguishable modern material (e.g. cement).

HISTORICAL TABLE

BC	**ANCIENT GREECE** *See also pp 15 and 41-43 (Athens)*
c **1250**	Troy captured by the Achaians.
Early 5C	Persian Wars in which the Greeks were victorious.
Mid 5C	Apogee of Athens: 'Age of Pericles'.
431-404	Peloponnesian War: Athens defeated by Sparta.
Early 4C	Thebes predominates over Athens and Sparta.
359-323	Domination by Philip II of Macedon and his son Alexander the Great.
214 BC	Beginning of Roman penetration into Macedonia.

AD	**BYZANTINES AND FRANKS**
313	Edict of Milan permitting freedom of worship to Christians.
330	Founding of Constantinople by the Emperor Constantine.
379-395	Reign of Theodosius I the Great; banning of pagan cults and suppression of the Olympic Games (in 393).
395	On Theodosius' death, division of the Roman Empire: Greece is included in the Eastern empire of which the capital is Byzantium (Constantinople).
527-565	Reign of **Justinian I** and his wife Theodora; reconquest of Italy. Justinian publishes a Legal Code in Greek. Golden age of Byzantine art.
Early 7C	Invasions of waves of Slavs who were gradually assimilated.
726-843	Under iconoclasm *(p 22)* many 'images' are destroyed; theological disputes.
867-1056	Macedonian dynasty (Basil I, Constantine VII, Nikephoros Phokas, Basil II). Prosperity and second golden age of Byzantine art.
963	Foundation of the monastery of the Great Lavra on Mount Athos.
1054	Schism between the Greek and Roman churches at Constantinople.
1081-1203	Comnenos and Angelos dynasties.
11C-12C	Normans from Sicily raid and occupy the Ionian Islands and Epiros.
1204	Fourth Crusade: the Crusaders capture Constantinople.
1204-1261	Latin Empire of Constantinople *(see p 23)*.
1261	Constantinople retaken by the Byzantines.
1267	Baldwin II of Flanders cedes Morea to Charles of Anjou and to the Angevins of Naples (dynasty of Anjou-Sicily).
1261-1282	Michael VIII Palaiologos, Emperor of Byzantium. The Greeks recapture the southeast of Morea.
1311	Battle of Kephisos near Lake Copaïs *(p 162)*.
Mid 14C	Organisation of the 'Despotate of Morea' by the Greeks *(p 147)*.

TURKISH OCCUPATION

1453	Constantinople captured by the Turks.
1444-1481	Reign of Mehmet II who completes the conquest of eastern Greece.
1480	Siege of Rhodes by the Turks who force the Knights of St John of Jerusalem to withdraw; Rhodes eventually falls to **Suleiman the Magnificent** in 1522.
1536	Signature of the **'Capitulations'**, an agreement between François I of France and Suleiman the Magnificent, by which France protected the Roman Catholics in the Levant and received certain commercial privileges.
1571	The Christians curtail Turkish expansion at the Battle of Lepanto *(p 152)*.
1669	Herakleion (Crete) falls to the Turks: end of Venetian control of Crete.
1687-1715	The Venetians re-occupy the Peloponnese and Aigina; they retain control of Corfu and the other Ionian Islands until the French Revolution.
Early 18C	Depopulation of Greece; Albanian settlers introduced by the Turks.
18C	Rebirth of national feeling: resistance fighters **(klephts)** in the mountains, pirates in the islands, secret schools organised by the Orthodox Church.
1797	French troops temporarily occupy Corfu from 1807 to 1814.
1814	The Ionian Islands become a British Protectorate until 1863.
1821	The Bishop of Patras, Germanós, gives the signal for revolt at the monastery of Agía Lávra. Ali Pasha of Ioánina joins the movement.
1822	Kolokotrónis and his soldiers **(palikares)** defeat the Turks in the Dervenáki Gorge: the Peloponnese is freed; independence proclaimed in Epidauros.
1824	The Turks react. **Ibrahim Pasha** reconquers and ravages the Peloponnese.
1824-1826	Death of Byron and capture of Missolonghi by the Turks: the remaining defenders blow themselves up. Birth of the **Philhellene Movement** *(p 24)*.
1827	Intervention of the Great Powers (UK, France and Russia): the allied naval forces destroy the Turkish fleet at Navarino (Pylos).
1829	French expedition to Morea: the Turks are driven out of the Peloponnese.

INDEPENDENCE

1830	Greece is recognized as an independent state; internal dissension.
1831	Kapodistrias, the Prime Minister, is assassinated in Nauplion.
1833-1862	Reign of Otho I of Bavaria, a Roman Catholic and centralist. Greece remains under the influence of the UK, France and Russia.
1863-1913	Reign of George I of Denmark, constitutional monarch.
1863	The Ionian Islands, British possessions since 1814, become part of Greece.
1881	Greece recovers Thessaly from the Turks.
1882-1893	Building of the Corinth Canal.
1912-1913	Balkan War. Under **Venizélos** the Greek army liberates Macedonia and Epiros from the Turks. Crete becomes part of Greece.
1914-1919	First World War. Venizélos brings Greece into the war on the side of the allies. In 1919 Greece receives Thrace and Smyrna.
1919-1922	New conflict with the Turks who are victorious; 15 000 Greeks flee from Asia Minor to Europe (the **Catastrophe**).
1940	The Greeks say 'No' **(Ohi)** and repulse the Italian invasion of Epiros.
1941-1944	German occupation.
1941-1949	Civil War.
1967-1974	Military dictatorship.
1974	Greece becomes a republic.
1981	Greece joins the E.E.C. (Common Market).

GREECE UNDER THE BYZANTINES

In 330 AD Constantine transferred the capital of the Roman Empire to **Byzantium,** soon to be known as Constantinople. He called his city "New Rome" and practised religious toleration. In 380 however Theodosius the Great established Christianity as the official religion and Greek, the language of the Church and the Near East, soon replaced Latin as the official language. Although the inhabitants saw themselves as Romans (Romaioi) with an obligation to maintain the Roman Empire, the Byzantine Empire developed into a Greek Christian theocratic state, in which the Emperor and the Patriarch were interdependent; the former ensured the défence of the state and the latter preserved the orthodox faith. The state was seen as the final order on earth and the people were acutely concerned with matters of doctrine since error could endanger not only their own souls but the security of the state.

As Christianity had developed through a number of autonomous churches each interpreting the new religion in the light of their own previous beliefs, heresies arose which weakened the state both internally and in its external relations. The **Monophysite** heresy (5-6C) which denied the dual nature of Christ, was widespread in the eastern territories which later fell easy prey to Islam. **Iconoclasm,** introduced by Leo III to attract the eastern people back into the Christian fold, required the destruction of all images but it only caused internal strife and aggravated the division between the eastern and western churches. Iconoclasm was abandoned in 843 and icons remain a prominent feature of Orthodox worship to this day. The other subjects of dispute were the nature of the Eucharist and the Procession of the Holy Ghost. Despite many attempts to achieve unity a gulf arose which remains to this day between Orthodoxy and Catholicism.

Throughout its thousand years of existence the Byzantine Empire was under constant threat of invasion. Despite the great achievements of **Justinian** (527-565), **Heraclius** (610-641) and **Basil II** (976-1025) in winning back lost territory, the general pattern is of retrenchment until only Constantinople and its hinterland remained. In the west the threat came from the barbarians, the Normans, Franks and Venetians; in the north from the Slavs, who occupied the Greek mainland and the Peloponnese from 6C to 8C; in the east from the Persians, Arabs and finally the Turks. As the Empire diminished so did food supplies, recruits for the army and taxes to sustain the vast centralised bureaucracy which had grown up in Constantinople.

The Byzantines resisted their enemies not only by warfare – they invented the famous **Greek fire** (c 674) which gave them a great advantage particularly at sea – but also by intrigue and diplomacy; they bought off some enemies, received tribute from others and even converted their northern Slav neighbours to Christianity, hence the presence of the Orthodox faith in Bulgaria and Russia.

The **Crusades** were launched in the west in 11C and 12C by the Pope to help the Byzantines repulse the Moslems from the Holy Land but the Franks were more interested in the acquisition of land and the Venetians in commercial gain. In 1204 the Fourth Crusade was re-directed against Constantinople itself, ostensibly to settle the disputed succession to the throne, and the city was captured and sacked. The Empire was reduced to three successor states in Epiros, Trebizond and Nicaea. The latter proved the most enduring; it re-captured Constantinople in 1261 and established the **Despotate of Morea** (p 147) in the Peloponnese. Constantinople finally fell to the Turks in 1453.

The most visible expressions of Byzantine culture are the churches (see below) which were decorated with icons and mosaics. The Byzantines also took great interest in engineering, medicine and mathematics. There had always been scholarly exchange between east and west, which was stimulated by an influx of eastern scholars to the west after the fall of Constantinople; the Renaissance owes much to Byzantine study over the centuries in the fields of Classical literature, history, law, scientific knowledge, the organisation of universities and monasticism.

Art and Architecture. – Byzantine art, which came to be identified with oriental Christian art, was mystical and hieratical, a blend of the influences coming from Rome and Asia Minor.

The main characteristics of Byzantine architecture are demonstrated in the religious buildings: symmetrical plan, dome symbolising the heavenly vault, use of brick either alternating with stone or on its own but arranged in a decorative pattern.

First Golden Age: "Age of Justinian" 5C-6C. – The church opened off a court (atrium); it was built on the basilical plan (nave and two aisles) or the Greek cross plan, with a massive dome on pendentives and interior galleries for the women (gynaecea). Typical examples: Agia Sophia in Constantinople; in Thessalonika and Philippi in Greece.

Second Golden Age 9C-12C. – The buildings were often small scale but perfectly proportioned; they were built on the cross-in-square plan with the arms of the cross more evident on the exterior; a narthex preceded the main entrance and the dome was raised higher by the introduction of a "drum"; the walls were adorned with marble low relief sculptures decorated with coloured enamels. Typical examples in Greece: Old Metropolitan and St Theodore in Athens, Daphne, Óssios Loukás in Boeotia, Panagía Halkeón in Thessalonika, Néa Moní in Chios and Agía Sophía in Monemvassía.

Third Golden Age: "Palaiologos Renaissance" 13C-16C. – The buildings combine the basilical plan (ground floor) and the Greek cross plan: multiplicity of domes, widespread use of frescoes for decoration. Many examples in Thessalonika (Holy Apostles, St Catherine's), Árta, Kastoriá, Mystra etc.

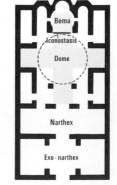

Byzantine church

The churches were richly decorated with multicoloured marble floors, frescoes (from 13C) and mosaics in warm colours embellished with gold that fired the imagination. The decorative scheme followed a well defined liturgical and doctrinal arrangement: **Christ Pantocrator** (Ruler of All) in the dome, surrounded by archangels, apostles or evangelists; the Virgin Theotókos (Virgin Mother) flanked by the Archangels Michael and Gabriel in the apse; scenes from the Life of Christ or the Virgin, not always in chronological order but according to the calendar of feasts, in the nave and narthex.

The icons, which were painted on wood, were hung on the **iconostasis,** a screen separating the nave from the sanctuary *(bema)* where the priest officiates.

The subjects of Orthodox iconography include: the Preparation **(Hetoimasia)** shown by an empty throne awaiting the return of the Lord to judge the world; the Descent of Christ into Hell; the Dormition of the Virgin and the Three Angels at Abraham's table. The most venerated saints are the Three Hierarchs or Doctors of the Church (John Chrysostom, Basil and Gregory of Nazianzus), John the Baptist (Pródromos = Forerunner) represented with wings, St George on horseback piercing the dragon with his spear, St Andrew of Patras, St Demetrios of Thessalonika, Sts Michael, Nicholas, Athanasios, Cyril and Pantaleon and the two Theodores.

The best collections of Byzantine mosaics are preserved in the monasteries at Daphne, Néa Moní in Chios and Óssios Loukás in Boeotia while the great series of frescoes can be seen in Mystra, in Kritsá in Crete and in the monasteries of Mount Áthos.

GREECE UNDER THE FRANKS (13C-15C)

The Fourth Crusade brought together the knights of Burgundy, Champagne, the Ile-de-France, Picardy and particularly Flanders as well as Lombards and Venetians from Italy. The religious arm was subordinated to commercial interests by the Venetians and Lombards who turned the army against Constantinople; the city was taken by assault on 13 April 1204 and sacked.

Latin Empire of Constantinople. – A college of six Venetians and six French elected **Baldwin of Flanders** emperor. Greece, except for Epiros, was divided up between the Crusaders, according to the feudal system; the Venetians took the islands and the coastal sites to further their trading activities and the French and Lombards colonized the land.

As his personal fief the Emperor Baldwin held Constantinople, which he shared with the Venetians, Thrace and the adjacent parts of Asia Minor but he was killed by the Bulgars at the battle of Adrianople in 1206. He was succeeded by his brother Henry of Flanders, then by Peter and Robert de Courtenay and finally by **Baldwin II de Courtenay** in 1261.

Two small states, the kingdom of Thessalonika and the principality of Morea (the Peloponnese) were nominally dependent on the Emperor. When the kingdom of Thessalonika was attached to the Despotate of Epiros in 1224, the principality of Morea, "where people spoke French like the Parisians", became the main area of Frank domination.

Principality of Morea. – The princes, who took the tittle of Duke of Achaia, ruled through 12 vassal barons who bore the main responsibilities. The first princes were from Champagne, William de Champlitte and then the de Villehardouin *(p 118)* who were succeeded by the Anjou-Sicily dynasty in the person of Charles I of Anjou, brother of Louis IX of France. In 1261, however, the Byzantines recaptured Constantinople and then proceeded to re-conquer the Peloponnese ending with the capture of Clarence *(p 122)* in 1428.

The princes of Morea, whose history is told in the Chronicle of Morea, also held sway over the Duchy of Thebes and Athens which had devolved to the La Roche *(p 43)* who were succeeded by the Brienne: when Gautier de Brienne and his knights died in the battle of Kephisos *(p 162)* in 1311, the duchy fell into the hands of the Catalans whence it passed in 1388 to the Acciaiuoli, Florentine allies of the Anjou-Sicily dynasty.

Other territories dependent on the principality of Morea were: the county of La Sole, the marquisate of la Bondonice, the duchy of Náxos including the Cyclades with the Venetian nobles, the the county of Cephallonia including Zakynthos and Leukas which were controlled by the Venetians.

Oecumenism. – The Cistercian Order played a major role in the organisation of the Fourth Crusade and also in the establishment of the French in Greece in 13C and 14C.

Once the land had been apportioned, the white monks began to establish themselves preferably in the Flemish, Burgundian or Champagne fiefs, occupying the Byzantine monasteries or founding new houses. It is difficult to plot their movements owing to a lack of documents and the alterations subsequently made to religious buildings. Various architectural features, however, make it possible to trace their presence: the Duchy of Thebes and Athens where they settled at Daphne and at Óssios Loukás and Orchomenos (Boeotia); in the Peloponnese where they occupied the abbey at Zaraká by Lake Stymphalia and the monastery of Vlacherna near Clarence on the Kyllene peninsula.

The Cistercians were helped in their efforts in Morea by the **Templars,** who were replaced in 14C by the Knights of St John of Jerusalem who had commanderies at Malvoisie, on Mount Ithómi, on Náxos (still extant) and others in Andréville, Clarence and Corinth which have now disappeared. They were joined by the Dominicans and the Franciscans, who had a few convents both on the mainland and in the islands particularly in Crete.

At Pope Innocent III's behest the main task of all these monks was to work for oecumenism (union between the eastern and western churches) which was to be sealed at the **Council of Lyon** (1274) held by Pope Gregory X in the presence of the Latin Emperor Baldwin II de Courtenay and the Byzantine Emperor Michael VIII Palaiologos but it failed owing to the opposition of the populations involved.

Their efforts have, however, left their mark in curious double churches with two naves, one for the Roman Catholics and one for the Orthodox: Pórta Panagía in Thessaly, Óssios Loukás in Boeotia, Holy Apostles in Kalamáta in the Peloponnese; in Parikía on Paros and in Belonia on Náxos, St Catherine's in Herakleion, at Toploú, Vrondissí and Valsamónero in Crete, at Filérimo in Rhodes also.

A second attempt at oecumenism in Greece was made in 1438 at the Council of Florence which brought together Pope Eugenius IV, the Emperor John VIII Palaiologos, Cardinal Bessarion and the philosopher Gemistos Plethon *(p 147)* but the invasion of Greece by the Turks in 1461 brought these projects to nought.

GREECE UNDER THE TURKS

The Turks imposed their own system of government, which was administered in the regions (pashaliks) by a **pasha**; the Greek communities were represented by their **primates**. Religious toleration allowed the Orthodox monasteries to keep their vast domains and permitted Roman Catholic communities to settle in the country. On the other hand the Turks imposed heavy taxes, favoured extorsion and abducted young boys to serve as mercenary soldiers, **Janissaries**, and in the fleet.

Their long occupation left few architectural traces: some fountains and bazaars, a few houses with screened balconies and mosques with the **mihrab**, the recess which indicated the direction of Mecca; most minarets have been demolished.

INDEPENDENCE

The Struggle for freedom. – There had been revolts in 17C but it was in 18C that a feeling of nationalism began to develop under the influence of the Orthodox church which was teaching young Greeks in its "secret schools". In addition there were secret societies (**eteríes**); largest was the Filikí Etería, founded in Odessa in 1814; these societies consisted of merchants and civil servants, ship owners from the islands and merchants, bankers and writers living abroad. In the mountains bands of **klephts** (the word literally means robber in Greek) began to harass the Turks.

The Patriarch Germanós raised the flag of revolt, a white cross on a sky blue ground, on 25 March 1821 at the Agía Lávra Monastery near Kalávrita. The revolt spread throughout the Peloponnese, into Epiros ruled by Ali Pasha *(p 115)* and to the islands of the Saronic Gulf. By 1822 Kolokotrónis and his troops, **palikares**, were in control of the Peloponnese and Greek independence was proclaimed at Epidauros.

The next two years were marked by violent and sometimes bloody dissension among the Greeks. The Turks launched a counter attack led by Mehmet Ali *(p 121)*, viceroy of Egypt, against the Peloponnese and in 1825 he captured Missolonghi.

These tragic events and the subsequent repression gave rise in Western Europe to the **Philhellene Movement** which consisted of altruistic liberals who campaigned for the Greek cause mainly through the work of writers, poets and artists. Committees were set up in various countries to raise money. Eight shiploads of volunteers arrived in Greece from Europe and were formed into the Philhellene Battalion; there was a large contingent of Germans, many of whom died at Peta; the English and Americans numbered nearly 100. The Americans were particularly sympathetic towards a country struggling for independence and the war brought many travellers as well as volunteers: Mark Twain, Herman Melville and Julia Ward Howe, the author of the "Battle Hymn of the Republic".

(From doc. Bibliothèque Nationale, Paris)

Ali Pasha

Chief among these "friends of Greece" was Lord Byron who was persuaded by the London Greek Committee to carry arms and funds, raised in London in 1823, to the Greeks under Mavrokordatos. Two more substantial loans were raised in the City in 1824 and 1825. In 1827 General Sir Richard Church and Admiral Lord Cochrane were appointed to command the Greek forces by land and sea.

In the same year the United Kingdom, Russia and France decided to intervene to enforce an armistice "without however taking any part in the hostilities". The allied fleet went to parley with the Turkish fleet anchored in Navarino Bay (Pylos) and ended up destroying it *(p 174)*.

The French dispatched a military mission under General Maison in October 1828, which drove out the Turks while the Russians threatened Constantinople.

The Treaty of Adrianople in 1829 recognized Greece's autonomy; its independent status was recognized by the Great Powers in 1830 and by the Porte in 1832; Otho of Bavaria became king in 1834 *(p 46)*.

Heroes of the Greek struggle for independence.

Lascarína Bouboulína (1771-1825).
She fought the Turks at sea and in the Peloponnese *(p 181)*.

Markos Bótsaris (1790-1823).
Originally from Souli, he fought at Missolonghi *(p 139)* and was killed near Karpeníssi.

John Kapodístrias (originally Capo d'Istria) (1776-1831).
Born in Corfu; a diplomat in the Russian service. Head of the government in 1827, he organised the administration and founded the Bank of Greece. Assassinated in Nauplion.

Constantine Kanáris (1790-1877).
Sailor from Psará, specialist in fire ships *(p 113)*, then a politician.

Theodore Kolokotrónis (1770-1843).
A native of the Peloponnese. Military leader who first defeated the Turks in the Dervenáki Gorge. Equestrian statues in Nauplion, Tripoli and Athens.

Germanós (1771-1826).
Bishop of Patras. At Agía Lávra *(p 119)* he blessed the flag of Greek independence and preached the cause at Patras on 25 March 1821 (Greek national holiday).

Andréas Miaoúlis (1769-1835).
Sailor from Hydra *(p 113)* who fought the Turkish fleet between 1822 and 1825.

CONTEMPORARY ASPECTS

In 1981 Greece had 9 740 417 inhabitants, i.e. an average density of 69 inhabitants per square kilometre as opposed to 15 only in 1830. The figure for Greeks living abroad was 4 million.

The dominant features in social activity are the absence of rigid social classes and the passion for discussion; Athens retains her ancient reputation as the "town of gossips". The Greeks are fiercely individualistic and have inherited from their forebears, who invented democracy, a taste for argument and a propensity to dissension which has caused the country many political crises.

Political and administrative organisation. – Since 1974, when the monarchy was abolished in a referendum, Greece has been a republic. Legislative power lies with the National Assembly which is composed of 300 members, elected by universal suffrage, who choose the President of the Republic by a two-thirds majority. The President is the guardian of the Constitution, which was approved in 1975, together with the Constitutional Council, and presides over the Council of Ministers; he also has a representative role.

Executive power is in the hands of the Prime Minister and his Ministers but is also widely decentralised since many administrative responsabilities are exercised by the 9 regions *(p 3)* and 52 departments *(nomí)* which are themselves divided into eparchies, demes and kinotites.

Greek women have been able to vote since 1952 and about 35% of them work; the army numbers 300 000 men.

Education. – The Greeks have a high regard for education since it is their chief means of promotion and 45% of students come from average backgrounds.

Primary and secondary education, public or private, is obligatory for 9 years. The pupils wear a uniform in the national colours of blue and white; in May they can be seen on educational outings to the historic sites.

Higher education which involves 4.8% of the active population is provided by the Universities of Thessalonika, Komotiní, Ioánina, Patras, Heracleion and Rethymnon (Crete) and Athens which is also the home of the Polytechnic; many students go abroad to study in Italy, Germany, France and the United Kingdom.

Graduates tend to enter the liberal professions (lawyers, doctors).

Press and information. – The press, which is widely read, deals essentially with politics; about 150 daily papers are published in Greece: 17 in Athens and 3 in Thessalonika which are distributed throughout the country. Television has made rapid strides since 1975: in 1983 there were 1 800 000 sets.

SPOKEN GREEK

Modern Greek is a simplified version of ancient Greek from which it has evolved. It is difficult to pronounce and, owing to being an inflected language, it is complicated.

Demotic Greek is used in conversation, literature and education. A more formal and archaic version of the language *(katharévousa)* which was officially abandoned in 1976, is still seen in certain official publications. In this guide we have used demotic Greek transcribed according to the system used on the road signs in Greece; the accent marks the stressed syllable.

Pronunciation. – The equivalents given below are the nearest available in the English language.

vowels: **e** pronounced as in "wet" and never silent
      o pronounced as in "hot"
      a pronounced as in "hat"
      i pronounced as in "meet"

consonants: **d** when it is transcribed from the Greek delta, is pronounced like th in "then"
      g before a, o and ou is pronounced as in "gone"
        before e and i is pronounced as in "yet"
      h (transcription of the Greek X)
        before a, o and ou is pronounced like the final ch in "Scottish loch"
        before e and i is pronounced as in "hue"
      th is pronounced as in "thing"
      x is pronounced ks as in "exam"
      z is pronounced as in "zone"
      s is always soft as in "set"

GREEK ALPHABET – transcription into Latin alphabet

álpha	A	α	a	ní	N	ν	n
víta	B	β,δ	v	ksí	Ξ	ξ	x
gámma	Γ	γ	g	ómicron	O	o	o
délta	Δ	δ	d	pí	Π	π	p
épsilon	E	ϵ	e	ró	P	ρ	r
zíta	Z	ζ	z	sígma	Σ	σ,ς	s ou ss
íta	H	η	i	táf	T	τ	t
thíta	Θ	θ	th	ípsilon	Y	υ	i
ióta	I	ι	i	phí	Φ	ϕ	f
káppa	K	κ	k	hí	X	χ	h
lámda	Λ	λ	l	psí	Ψ	ψ	ps
mí	M	μ	m	oméga	Ω,O̲	ω	o

AI	$\alpha\iota$	e	ΓX	$\gamma\chi$	nh	NT	$\nu\tau$	nd, d
AY	$\alpha\upsilon$	av, af	EI	$\epsilon\iota$	i	OI	$o\iota$	i
ΓΓ	$\gamma\gamma$	ng	EY	$\epsilon\upsilon$	ev, ef	OY, O	$o\upsilon$	ou
ΓK	$\gamma\kappa$	ng, g	MΠ	$\mu\pi$	mb, b	TZ	$\tau\zeta$	dz

NUMBERS

1	éna, mía	30	triánda
2	dío	40	saránda
3	tría, tris	50	penínda
4	téssera, tésseris	60	exínda
5	pénde	70	evdomínda
6	éxi	80	ogdónda
7	eptá	90	enenínda
8	októ	100	ekató
9	enéa	101	ekato éna (etc)
10	déka	200	diakóssia
11	éndeka	300	triakóssia
12	dódeka	400	tetrakóssia
13	dekatría	500	pendakóssia
14	dekatéssera	600	exakóssia
15	dekapénde	700	eptakóssia
16	dekaéxi	800	oktakóssia
17	dekaeptá	900	eneakóssia
18	dekaoktó	1 000	hília
19	dekaenéa	2 000	dío hiliádes
20	íkossi	3 000	trís hiliádes
21	íkossi éna	5 000	pénde hiliádes
22	íkossi dío (etc)	10 000	déka hiliádes

VOCABULARY (the accent indicates the syllable which is stressed)

General expressions

Yes, no	né, óhi	Ok, all right	endáxi
Good morning	kaliméra	How much does this	
Good evening	kalispéra	cost?	pósso káni aftó?
Goodbye	adío, giá sas,	I do not understand	dén katalavéno
Good night	kaliníhta	good, bad	kaló, kakó
Sir, Madam	kírie, kiría	well, beautiful	kalá, oréo
And, not	ké, dén	half	missó
Please	parakaló	hôtel	xenodohío
Thank you	efkaristó	restaurant, taverna	estiatório, tavérna
Very	polí	breakfast	proïnó, prógevma
Excuse me	mé sinhoríte	lunch, dinner	gévma, dípno
I would like	thá íthela	post	tahidromío
What?	ti?	stamps	gramatóssima
What do you have?	tí éhete?	bank	trápeza
Do you have a room?	éhete domátio?	Great Britain	Megáli Bretanía
for one person	monó	England	Anglía
for two people	dipló	Wales	Oualía
Where? How much?	poú? pósso?	Scotland	Skotía
with, without	mé, horís	Ireland	Irlandía
Where is the lavatory?	poú íne i toilétes?	America	Amerikí
I am listening	oríste	Canada	Kanadás
of course, indeed	málista	Australia	Afstralía
towards	prós	New Zealand	Néa Zilandía

Tourism and travelling

ruins	arhéa	saint	ágios, agía
cathedral	mitrópoli	temple, shrine	naós, ieró
castle, citadel	kástro, froúrio	tower	pírgos
church	eklissía, naós	view	théama
river	potamós	entrance, exit	íssodos, éxodos
cave	spíleo	closed, open	klistó, anihtó
island	nissí	street, road	odós, drómos
lake	límni	square	platía
monastery	moní, monastíri	the road to	o drómos prós
mountain	vounó, óros	on the right, on the left	dexiá, aristerá
mosque	dzamí	straight on	efthía
beach	aktí, paralía	up, down	páno, káto
port, harbour	limáni	fill up	na to gemíssete
boat, ship	vapóri, várka	petrol, oil	venzíni
bus	leoforío	Michelin tyre	lástiko Messelínne
ticket	issitírio	film	film

In a restaurant *(see also p 31)*

Do you have?	éhete	butter, honey	voútiro, méli
plate	piáto	sandwiches	sandouíts
spoon	koutáli	bread	psomí
fork	piroúni	red wine	mávro krassí
knife	mahéri	red wine	kókino krassí
bottle, glass	boukáli, potíri	rosé wine	rosé krassí
bill	logariasmó	white wine	áspro krassí
menu	katálogo	resinated wine	retsína
salt and pepper	aláti ke pipéri	water, beer	neró, bíra
sugar	záhari	milk coffee	kafé me gála
oil, vinegar	ládi, xídi	fruit juice	himó froútou
Greek coffee	kafé elinikó	tea	tsáï
milk	gála	yoghurt	giaoúrti

The Greeks often express "No" by closing their eyes and nodding their head upwards.

LITERATURE

Poets and poetry. – Two Nobel prizes awarded to Greek poets in sixteen years shows that Greece is still a land of poets.

Even under the Turkish occupation a tradition of popular and patriotic verse survived but it was the Ionian Islands that nourished the first neo-Hellenic poets: the leader of this "Ionian School" was **Dionysos Solomós** (Zakynthos 1798-1857) who in 1824 wrote the Hymn to Liberty, of which part is now the Greek national anthem.

The end of 19C and the early years of this century have been dominated by Kóstas Palamás (1859-1943), founder of the "New School of Athens", and Constantine Cavafy (1863-1933), a cultured intimist poet, who lived in Egypt for many years.

The 1930s generation is illustrated by three names:

– **George Seféris** (1900-1971), who was influenced by symbolism, expressed his anguish at life in astonishingly powerful evocative verses; Nobel prize in 1963.

– **Odysséas Elytis** (born in 1911), Nobel prize in 1979, whose poetry is shot through with surrealism, reveals the sacred feeling Greeks have for their natural environment: the land, the sea and above all the light.

– **Yánnis Rítsos** (born in 1909) writes grand dramatic poems, reflecting the trials he has undergone.

Essayists and Novelists. – **John Psichári** (1854-1929), who lived in Paris for many years, contributed to the pre-eminence achieved by demotic Greek in neo-Hellenic literature.

The short stories and novels of Aléxandros Papadiamántis (1851-1911), a native of Skíathos, had already described the world of the fishermen and farmers struggling against adversity in a still untamed country but, as for poetry, it was the 1930s generation which produced the greatest writers including two Cretans: Kazantzákis and Prevelákis.

Nikos Kazantzákis, who was born in Herakleion in 1885 and died in 1957, wrote about the wild and heroic character of Crete in his famous novels, *Zorba the Greek* and *Christ Re-crucified* which have been turned into very successful films.

Pandelís Prevelákis (1909-1986) described his native Rethymnon in *Tale of a City.*

BIBLIOGRAPHY

Art and Archaeology

The Glory that was Greece, J. C. Stobart, revised R. J. Hopper, Sidgwick & Jackson
The Architecture of Ancient Greece, William Bell Dinsmoor, Batsford 1975, 1985
The Sea Peoples, N. K. Sandars, Thames & Hudson 1978
The Mycenaean World, John Chadwick, Cambridge University Press 1976
Writing in Gold – Byzantine Society and its Icons, Robin Cormack, George Philip 1985
The Rediscovery of Greece, Fani-Maria Tsigakou, Thames & Hudson 1981
The Victorians and Ancient Greece, Richard Jenkyns, Blackwells 1980

Geography and History

Greece – an introduction, E. M. Pantelouris, Blueacre Books Glasgow 1980
Atlas of the Greek World, Peter Levi, Phaidon Press Oxford
A Concise History of Ancient Greece, Peter Green, Thames & Hudson 1973
The Ancient Greeks, M. I. Finley, Penguin 1963
The Spartans, L. F. Fitzhardinge, Thames & Hudson 1985
The Ancient Olympic Games, Judith Swaddling, British Museum Publications Ltd. 1980
Crete: Its Past, Present and People, Adam Hopkins, Faber & Faber 1977
Byzantium – An Introduction, Philip Whitting, Blackwells 1971, 1981
The Byzantine Empire, Robert Browning, Book Club Associates 1980
Mediaeval Greece, Nicolas Cheetham, Yale University Press 1981
Mistra, Steven Runciman, Thames & Hudson 1980
Britain's Greek Empire, Michael Pratt, Rex Collings 1978
Lord Elgin and the Marbles, William St. Clair, OUP 1967, 1983
That Greece might still be free, William St. Clair, OUP 1972
Modern Greece – A short history, C. M. Woodhouse, Faber & Faber 1968, 1977
The Philhellenes, C. M. Woodhouse, Faber & Faber 1969
Ill Met by Moonlight, W. Stanley Moss, George G. Harrap 1950
The Mountain War, Kenneth Matthews, Longman 1972
The Greek War of Independence, C. M. Woodhouse, Russell & Russell 1952, 1975

Travel books; literature

The Greek Islands, Lawrence Durrell, Faber & Faber 1978
Prospero's Cell (Corfu), Lawrence Durrell, Faber & Faber 1960
Reflections of a Marine Venus (Rhodes), Lawrence Durrell
Roumeli, Patrick Leigh Fermor, John Murray 1966, Penguin 1983
Mani, Patrick Leigh Fermor, John Murray 1958, Penguin 1984
Deep into Mani, Journey to the Southern Tip of Greece, Peter Greenhalgh & Edward Eliopoulos, Faber & Faber 1985
The Cretan Runner, George Psychoundakis, tr. by P. Leigh Fermor, John Murray 1955
Greek Myths, Robert Graves, Cassel 1955
The Dark Crystal: Cavafy, Sikelianos, Seferis, Elytis, Gatsos, translated by Edmund Keeley and Philip Sherrard, Denis Harvey 1981
Eleni, Nicholas Gage, Fontana-Collins 1983

General

Greek Food, Rena Salaman, Fontana Paperbacks 1983
Cooking the Greek Way, Anne Theoharous, Methuen Paperbacks 1979
The Companion Guides to Mainland Greece; Southern Greece; the Greek Islands, Collins 1983
Greece on Foot, Marc Dubin, Cordee, Leicester 1986
The Customs and Lore of Modern Greece, Rennell Rodd, Argonaut Press, Chicago.

PRACTICAL INFORMATION

See also pp 4 to 5 and consult the brochure "General Information about Greece" published by the Greek National Tourist Organization (GNTO).

TRAVELLING TO GREECE

By air. – There are daily flights by British Airways to Athens and by Olympic Airways to Athens (3 1/2 hours), Corfu and Thessalonika (3 hours).

In summer there are charter flights from London and most UK provincial airports to all or some of the following destinations: Alexandroúpolis, Andravída, Athens, Cephallonia, Chania, Corfu, Herakleion, Kalamáta, Kos, Lesbos, Lemnos, Mykonos, Mytilene, Préveza (Aktio), Rhodes, Sámos, Santoríni, Skíathos, Thessalonika and Zakynthos.

Olympic Airways flights to Athens land at Eliniko-West (the national terminal for domestic flights to the islands and elsewhere in Greece – *see p 29*); bus shuttle to the international terminal; Olympic Airways bus to central Athens, 96 Avenue Singrou (45 Dr); KTEL bus 133 to Sindagma Square (40 Dr); KTEL buses 107 and 109 to Piraeus (40 Dr). Foreign airline flights land at Eliniko-East (the international terminal); bus shuttle to national terminal; ELPAP express bus to Sindagma Square (60 Dr); KTEL bus 18 to Sindagma Square (40 Dr); KTEL buses 101 and 19 to Piraeus (40 Dr). Taxis are also available (10km – 6 miles to central Athens).

British Airways, 65-75 Regent Street, London W1, ☏ 897 4000.
Olympic Airways, 164-165 Piccadilly, London W1, ☏ 846 9966

By car. – There are two main options:
– overland all the way from the French coast (3-4 days); the quickest route is via Strasbourg, Munich, Salzburg, Zagreb, Belgrade and Thessalonika.
– by land and sea; by motorway through France to Italy and then by an Italian or Greek shipping line: from Venice to Piraeus or Corfu or Herakleion; from Ancona to Piraeus or Corfu or Igoumenítsa or Patras or Herakleion or Rhodes; from Bari to Corfu or Igoumenítsa or Patras; from Brindisi to Corfu or Igoumenítsa or Cephallonia or Ithaca or Patras or Herakleion; from Otranto to Corfu or Igoumenítsa.
Daily bus service every 45 minutes from Patras to Athens (3 1/2 hours). Train service is slower, less frequent but cheaper.

Hellenic Mediterranean Lines, 9 Hanover Street, London W1R 9HG, ☏ 499 0076.
Minoan Lines, c/o Townsend Thoresen Car Ferries, 127 Regent Street, London W1R 8LB, ☏ 437 5644

PLACES TO STAY

The Michelin map 980 marks the major resorts, the places with hotels, the official camping sites, the ports with moorings and the beaches with facilities.

The GNTO publishes a list of hotels classified according to towns and categories (except for D and E) and pamphlets on the various regions of Greece with information about the resorts and accommodation.

Hotels. – Although many hotels have been built since the 1960s there is still not enough accommodation in the high season; it is wise to reserve in advance. Prices, service charges and taxes vary according to the categories: from the luxury class downwards from A to E. The average tourist is advised to choose B and C class hotels which are usually clean and reasonably comfortable; hotels in category C rarely have restaurants. Reception will ask for passports *(diavatírio)* and hold them overnight.

On the coasts modern holiday complexes, known as **"beaches"** have been developed; they are equipped with air conditioning, swimming pools, tennis courts, night clubs, water skiing and sail boarding; they are often isolated and best suited to groups.

Xenia Hotels and Tourist Pavilions. – These are state-run chains of hotels and restaurants.
The Xenia hotels are comfortable and well decorated and built on pleasant sites.
The Tourist Pavilions are to be found near the main archaeological or tourist sites; they have few bedrooms but serve drinks and meals.

Traditional lodgings. – The GNTO (EOT) lets accommodation in traditional buildings in typical settings: on Cephallonia (Fiskárdo), on Chios (Mestá), on Psará, on Santoríni (Ía – cave dwellings), in Epiros (Zagória) and in Thessaly (Vizítsa on Mount Pelion).

Rooms in private houses. – Outside the large towns and resorts it is common to take a room in a private house, particularly in the Aegean Islands where the boats are met by householders offering rooms. It is prudent to seek accommodation through the local GNTO (EOT) office or the Tourist Police *(p 5)* who check the rooms and make the introduction. Standards of comfort vary but the rooms are almost always clean.

Camping. – There are some hundred official camping sites near the major towns and resorts run by the GNTO (EOT), the Greek Touring Club and private owners. Consult the Michelin map 980 and apply to the GNTO (EOT) or the Tourist Police. There is a Greek Camping Guide. Although camping outside the official sites is forbidden, it is sometimes possible with the permission of the owner of the site or of the Tourist Police.

CLOCK AND CALENDAR

Time. – The time in Greece is GMT + 2 hours in winter and GMT + 3 hours in summer.

Public holidays: 1 January, 6 January (Epiphany), 1st Monday in Lent, 25 March (Independence Day), Good Friday, Easter Sunday and Monday (Orthodox calendar), 1 May, Whit Sunday and Monday (Orthodox calendar), 15 August (Assumption), 28 October (Ohi Day: *p 21*), 25 and 26 December (Christmas).

The Orthodox religious festivals from Lent to Whitsuntide are fixed according to the Julian calendar and are not on the same dates as in the west.

TRANSPORT

Road system. – Consult Michelin Map 980. The Greek road network, which now consists of over 40 000km – 24 850 miles of roads, has improved considerably during the last twenty years. There are two motorways (tolls payable) linking Athens to Patras and Thessalonika with a speed limit of 100km/h – 62mph. The other roads, surfaced or not, are slow and winding owing to the terrain. The roads are poorly signposted although many of the signs are written in Roman as well as Greek lettering. Petrol stations *(venzíni)* are frequent enough except on some mountain roads.

Buses. – The buses (some have air-conditioning) are a cheap and picturesque, if not particularly comfortable, means of travel; there is a service to even the most remote places. Information from the Central Bus Station (KSAYLE), 4 Odós Pireos, Omonia, Athens ℡ 523 1876) or the KTEL offices in Athens (℡ 512 4910 and 831 7171-9).

Car and cycle hire. – Car hire is fairly expensive but practical in the more distant islands (Crete and Rhodes). The international car hire companies (Hertz, Avis etc.) have offices in most of the tourist towns but it is advisable to reserve in the high season; in the smaller agencies make sure that proper insurance cover is provided. In the islands bicycles and motor scooters can be hired.

Boat services. – Consult Michelin Map 980. Most services are operated by modern ships: some of the ferries can carry 100 cars and their passengers at speeds of 20 knots. In the high season it is necessary to book in advance for cars.

The ships on the major routes have two or three classes. Normally it is all right to travel Tourist (C) class where the accommodation consists of a lounge fitted with armchairs and a bar-restaurant, with easy access to the upper deck for a good view. Tickets are issued at mobile counters on the dockside or in the shipping line offices.

The less busy routes, known as "barren lines" since they are not profitable, are served by smaller craft with basic facilities, more to the taste of solitary travellers.

Information: lists published by the GNTO (EOT), "Greek Travel Pages", 12 Dimotikoú Stadíou, Kallithéa-Athens, ℡ 958 9859, and "Key Travel Guide", 6 Odós Kriezotou, Athens, ℡ 363 2572.

Pleasure cruising. – For the hire of caiques, yachts and motor cruisers, with or without crew, apply to the GNTO (EOT). Michelin Map 980 marks the main moorings for pleasure craft.

Air lines. – *See plan below.* Olympic Airways, the national Greek airline, provides services from Athens to a large number of other towns on the mainland and in the islands; most destinations are not more than 1 hour's flying time from Athens Airport (Elenikó-West terminal).

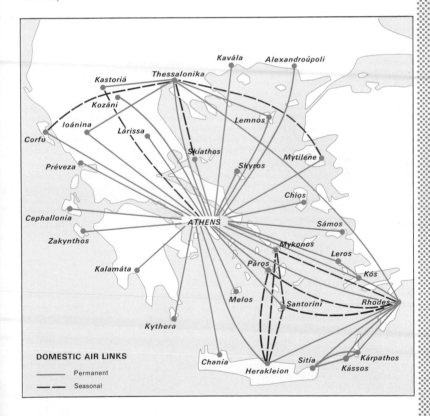

DOMESTIC AIR LINKS
—— Permanent
– – – Seasonal

Post. – Letter boxes are yellow, the official colour of the postal service. Letters between Athens and London take about 3 or 4 days; postcards from more remote places are unpredictable.

Poste restante in Athens, 100 Odós Eólou, near Omonia Square.

Telephone (OTE). – The telephone service is not housed in the same building as the post office. It works very well and is not expensive. To ring a foreign number direct dial 00 followed by the country code (44 for the United Kingdom), the city or district code and the subscriber's number.

SHOPPING

Shops are usually open from 8am to 1.30pm and 5 to 8pm on Tuesdays, Thursdays and Fridays and from 8am to 2.30pm on Mondays, Wednesdays and Saturdays.

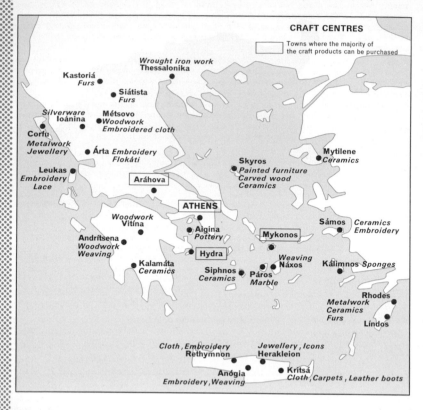

CRAFT CENTRES

Towns where the majority of the craft products can be purchased

Wrought iron work
Thessalonika

Kastoriá
Furs

Siátista
Furs

Silverware
Ioánina

Métsovo
Woodwork
Embroidered cloth

Corfu
Metalwork
Jewellery

Árta Embroidery
Flokáti

Mytilene
Ceramics

Skyros
Painted furniture
Carved wood
Ceramics

Leukas
Embroidery
Lace

Aráhova

ATHENS

Woodwork
Vitína

Sámos Ceramics
Embroidery

Aigina
Pottery

Mykonos

Andrítsena
Woodwork
Weaving

Hydra

Weaving
Náxos

Kálimnos Sponges

Kalamáta
Ceramics

Siphnos
Ceramics

Páros
Marble

Rhodes
Metalwork
Ceramics
Furs

Líndos

Cloth, Embroidery
Rethymnon

Jewellery, Icons
Herakleion

Anógia
Embroidery, Weaving

Krítsá
Cloth, Carpets, Leather boots

Specialities. – Honey *(méli),* Turkish delight *(loukoúmi),* macaroons *(amigdalotá),* olives *(eliés),* pistachio nuts *(phistíkia),* fortified wine (Samian muscat, Mavrodaphne etc.) liqueurs *(oúzo, rakí),* cigarettes *(tsigára).*

Souvenirs. – Pottery and ceramics, hand-woven carpets and cloth, long-haired rugs **(flokáti)**, embroidered clothes, furs, lace, carved or turned wood, "Greek shoulder bags", sponges, worry beads **(komboloï)**, dolls dressed in regional costumes, jewellery and gold and silver work, reproduction icons, marble or onyx carvings.

Antiquities or works of art must be declared for export: 13 Odós Polignótou, Athens.
National Craft Council, 9 Odós Mitropóleos, Athens, ☎ 322 1017.

Electric current. – Usually 220 Volts.

Newspaper stalls (períptera). – As well as newspapers, they sell cigarettes, postage stamps, sweets, razor blades, sun glasses, suntan lotion etc. Often they have a telephone too.

Tipping. – In theory prices are net but it is usual to round up (restaurants, tavernas, taxis) and to give a few drachmas (30-40) to the boy *(mikró)* in a restaurant and to porters.

Dress. – Women in mini skirts or trousers and men or women in shorts or with bare shoulders are not admitted to monasteries.

Current prices (1986). – Given as a rough guide; £1 = 200 Drachmas.

Ordinary petrol, per litre	75 Dr
Super petrol, per litre	80 Dr
Taxi ride, hire charge and per mile	25 Dr
Bus ride (Athens and inner suburbs)	40 Dr
Letter to UK or elsewhere within the EEC	27 Dr
Postcard to UK or elsewhere within the EEC	20 or 27 Dr
Local telephone call	5 Dr
Telephone call to UK, per minute	92,40 Dr
Greek coffee, Nescafé	25 to 100 Dr
Cup of tea	25 to 100 Dr
Bottle of beer (50cl)	80 to 200 Dr
Oúzo	40 to 190 Dr
Icecream (in a glass)	120 to 400 Dr
Cakes	100 to 250 Dr
Greek cigarettes (packet of 20)	50 Dr
Gauloises cigarettes (packet of 20)	95 Dr
Other cigarettes (packet of 20)	90 to 150 Dr
English or American newspaper	75 to 110 Dr
One night in a C hotel, double room (with breakfast)	1330 to 2000 Dr
One night camping (per person)	150 to 200 Dr
One restaurant meal (per person)	600 to 3000 Dr
One taverna meal (per person)	300 to 1000 Dr

FOOD AND WINE

Greek dishes are simple but tasty; even in 4C BC they were being praised by a Sicilian Greek called Archestratos. Their main elements are Mediterranean: olive oil, tomatoes, lemons, herbs and aromatic spices (origano, mint, sesame). The pastries and cakes, which are very sweet and flavoured with honey and cinnamon, evoke the orient.

Authentic but inexpensive Greek dishes are to be found in the tavernas and some more modest restaurants *(estiatório)* in the towns and the country.

Eating in the Greek way. – A Greek meal consists of a starter or a main dish or both accompanied by a vegetable or cheese or, most likely, a salad. A starter can be a small portion of a main dish. It is usual to choose from a display counter or in the kitchen but rarely from a menu. Sometimes fruit is also available but usually dessert is eaten in a pastrycooks *(zaharoplastío)* and coffee drunk in a café *(kafenío)*.

A *psistariá* specializes in roast meat and a *psarótaverna* in fish.

Lunch is eaten about 1 pm and dinner between 8 and 9pm according to location.

Soup. – Psarósoupa (fish soup); soúpa avgolémono (broth with rice and eggs beaten with lemon juice).

Starters. – Dolmádes (vine leaves stuffed with meat and rice), kokorétsi (offal sausages spit-roasted), melidzanosaláta (aubergine puree with black olives), tzatzíki (yoghurt with chopped cucumber and garlic), **taramosaláta** (purée of fish roe and bread crumbs or potatoes), piláfi (rice with tomatoes), gemistá (stuffed tomatoes, peppers, aubergines).

Main dish. – **moussaká** (aubergines and minced meat baked beneath bechamel sauce) and pastítsio (macaroni and minced meat baked in bechamel sauce).

Fish (psári). – Astakós (lobster); **barboúni** (red mullet); **garídes** (prawns); glóssa (sole); koliós (mackerel); ksifías (swordfish); marídes (white bait); kalamári (squid); **okotapódi** (octopus); tsipoúra (John Dory); sardéles (sardines); **sfirída** (whiting).

Fish is boiled (vrastó), fried (tiganitó) or grilled (psitó); price according to weight.

Meat (kréas). – Arní and arnáki (mutton and lamb); moshári (veal); hirinó (pork); kotópoulo (chicken); **souvláki** or kebabs (gobbets of beef, lamb or goat with tomatoes and onions on a spit); soutzoukákia, **keftédes** and biftéki (minced meat balls, grilled or fried).

Meat is also served in cutlets (brizóla), roasted, boiled or braised (stifádo) with a tomato and oil sauce seasoned with onions and herbs.

Vegetables. – Melidzánes (aubergines); **patátes** (potatoes); rísi (rice); domátes gemistés (tomatoes stuffed with rice); fassolákia (string beans); domatosaláta (tomato salad); saláta horiatikí (country salad of tomato, cucumber, onion, green pepper and féta cheese).

Cheese (tirí). – **Féta** (goat or sheep's milk cheese); **graviéra** (sort of Gruyère); kasséri (mild, similar to Cheddar).

Fruit (froúta). – **Eliés** (olives: those from Vólos, Kalamáta and Ámfissa are famous); fráoules (strawberries); karpoúzi (water melon); kerássia (cherries); lemóni (lemon); pepóni (melon); portokáli (orange); síka (figs); stafília (grapes); veríkoko (apricot); rodákino (peach).

Cakes and pastries (gliká). – **Baklavá** (millefeuilles with walnuts or almonds and cinnamon); **kadaïfi** (rolls of thread-like pastry with honey and walnuts or almonds); galaktoboúreko (cold custard pie); rizógalo (cold rice pudding); **loukoumádes** (mini doughnuts with honey and sesame or cinnamon); bougátsa (flaky pastry turnover with cream and cinnamon).

Snacks. – **Mezédes** or **pikilía** (olives, almonds, shrimps, hard boiled eggs, cheese, saganáki (fried cheese), pieces of octopus or squid, served with drinks); omelétta (omelette); spanakópita (spinach puffs); **tirópita** (cheese puffs); souvlakópita (pieces of grilled meat wrapped in a pancake); **yaoúrti me méli** (yoghurt with honey); amigdalotá (macaroons); loukoúmi (Turkish delight). Snacks are served in cafés, bars, dairies (galaktopolío) and at street stalls.

Refreshments. – Lemonáda (soda or fruit juice with lemon); **portokaláda** (orangeade); graníta (sorbet); **pagotó, pagotá** (ice, ices); frapé (iced coffee).

Wine. – With its dry warm climate and limestone or volcanic soil Greece is an excellent country for producing wine; the main wine regions are the northern Peloponnese, Attica, Crete, Rhodes and Sámos. Except in Sámos the business is not strictly controlled and the wine is sold under the name of the grower or a cooperative. It is worth while trying wine from the vat (**krassí** híma) served in carafes or copper pitchers. Greeks seldom get drunk and in antiquity they always diluted their wine with water.

The most well-known Greek wine is probably **retsína**, a white wine to which pine resin has been added as a preservative; this gives it an unusual taste, which is too suggestive of paraffin for some palates, but much appreciated by others. Retsína is not expensive and, served chilled as it usually is, it is very refreshing without being heavy.

Among the unresinated wines (aretsínoto) some have earned a particular reputation: the well-rounded dry white wines of Hymettos and Palíni in Attica, the scented rosé from Aráhova near Delphi, the sparkling dry white wine of Zítsa in Epiros, the full-bodied reds from Náoussa in Macedonia, the white wines of Chalcidice that preserve their quality well, the fruity reds from Neméa in the Argolid and the popular white wines of Achaia (Demestica, Santa Laura, Santa Helena). In the islands there are the generous reds and rosés from Crete, dry whites from Lindos in Rhodes, the heady and scented wines from the Cyclades, particularly Náxos and Santoríni, and from the Ionian Islands: Zakynthos (Verdéa), Cephallonia (the famous Róbola, fruity and musky) and Leukas (Santa Maura).

Mavrodaphne from Patras and Samian muscat are dessert wines.

Coffee and liqueurs. – Coffee is served in tiny cups together with a glass of cold water; the coffee grounds sink to the bottom of the cup. Coffee is ordered more or less sweet according to taste: glikó – very sweet, métrio – medium sweet and skéto – without sugar.

First among the liqueurs is **oúzo**, a colourless aniseed spirit, served in tiny glasses accompanied by a glass of water or diluted in a glass of water which turns cloudy. There is also Cretan **rakí**, a strong fruit brandy, and mastíka, a sweet liqueur flavoured with mastic gum.

KEY

Sights

★★★ **Worth a journey**
★★ **Worth a detour**
★ **Interesting**

Sightseeing route with departure point and direction of tour
on the road   in town   on an archaeological site

Panorama – View	Building
Monastery	Church
Ancient site	Mosque
Ruins	Ancient theatre
Castle	Ramparts – Tower
Cave	Windmill
Miscellaneous sights	Statue, small building
	Gateway
	Letter locating a sight

Other Symbols

Dual carriageway, interchange	Hospital – Stadium
Major through road	Covered market
Stepped street	Telephone – Poste restante
Footpath	Tourist information centre
Lighthouse – Factory or power station	Greek Automobile Club
Quarry – Tower	Station
Dam – Mine	Coach station
Cable car	Underground station
Swimming pool – Fountain	Airport
Cemetery	Airline (domestic flights)
Garden, park, wood	Car park
Distance (in kilometres)	Ferry services:
Pass – Altitude	Passengers and cars
Reference grid on town plans	Passengers only

Abbreviations

H Town Hall   M Museum   T Theatre

TOWNS, SIGHTS
AND
TOURIST
REGIONS

The opening times and admission charges given in this guide are usually those in force during the tourist season. Alterations and price increases are inevitable between the compilation of the guide and its publication; we hope our readers will make allowances.

The prices are given in drachmas.

The monuments, museums and archaeological sights often close on one day a week (usually Tuesday) as well as on the following public holidays: Christmas, 1 January, 25 March, Good Friday and Easter (Orthodox calendar).

(Photograph J. Bottin)

Delphi

AGNOÚNDA Monastery

Peloponnese – Argolis – Michelin map 980 fold 30

This charming little fortified monastery *(open 8.30am to 1pm and 5.30pm until sunset)* is just off *(signpost)* the fast new road linking Corinth and Epidauros.

At the centre stands the domed church; the exterior is decorated with Byzantine reliefs and the interior is adorned with icons and fine wall paintings (especially the Last Judgment).

The surrounding buildings house the communal rooms and the monks' cells.

The chapel of St John the Evangelist in the shade of a tall pine tree is decorated with 18C wall paintings.

AMBELÁKIA

Thessaly – Lárissa – Pop 487 – Michelin map 980 fold 17

Ambelákia is splendidly situated on the northwest slope of Mount Óssa in the Vale of Tempe *(p 185)* with an extensive view of the River Peneios Basin and of the heights of Mount Olympos. Although it is now only a small town with a few tavernas, Ambelákia was once a prosperous place with a population of 4 000.

In 17 and 18C there were thriving workshops producing silk and cotton fabrics, dyed scarlet with madder from the neighbouring plain. In 1780 these workshops combined in a cooperative for production and sales, the oldest of its type, which had commercial agents throughout Europe, particularly in France in Lyon and Rouen. Its members numbered 6 000. Unfortunately it was disbanded in 1811 owing to competition from British industrial manufactures, the disruption caused by the Napoleonic wars and the heavy taxes imposed by Ali Pasha *(p 114)*, the tyrant of Ioánina.

George Schwarz' House★ (Arhontikón). – *Guided tour*. This was the residence of the head of the cooperative and his brother, Demetrios. It is a superb example of a typical 18C Thessalian house with projecting upper storeys, balconies and carved and turned wooden partitions. The interior has typical rounded fireplaces and is richly decorated with painted ornaments and landscapes; the offices were on the ground floor and the living rooms upstairs.

AMPHIARAEIO   *Amfiaraío*

Central Greece – Attica – Michelin map 980 east of fold 30

In a narrow peaceful valley, watered by a stream and shaded by pine trees, lie the ruins of a sanctuary dedicated to **Amphiaraos,** king of Argos and warrior who took part in the expedition of the Seven against Thebes *(p 187);* he was also a seer and healer whose cult developed in these remote parts as did the cult of Asklepios in Epidauros.

Access and tour. – *Approach via Kálamos*. The road down affords fine views over the strait (Evrípos) to Euboea. *Open 8.45am to 3pm (Sundays 9.30am to 2.30pm); 100 Dr. Entrance on the right of the road from Kálamos.*

Ruins. – The ruins were excavated by the Greek Archaeological Society; the major part dates from 4C BC.

To the right of the path was the temple of Amphiaraos with the base of the cult statue and the offering table in the centre; in front of the temple was a huge altar where a ram was sacrificed and the oracle was consulted; lower down under the trees is a fountain into which pieces of money were thrown by the pilgrims who had been cured.

On the other side of the path is the "Statue Terrace"; the pedestals date from the Roman period.

Beyond was the portico *(abaton)* where the sick lay down to sleep; Amphiaraos was thought to send his instructions for their treatment through the medium of their dreams which were interpreted by the priests. Note the feet of the supports for the marble bench which ran the whole length of the portico.

Further on was the theatre (3 000 seats) where the votive festival (Amphiaréa) took place every four years; the marble seats of the priests and dignitaries are well preserved.

AMPHIPOLIS   *Amfípoli*

Macedonia – Séres – Michelin map 980 east of fold 6

The ancient city of Amphipolis lay in a favourable position not far from the mouth of the River Strymon and **Mount Pangaion** (Pangéo: alt 1 956m – 6 417ft), known as the "holy mountain" to the ancients as much for the cult of Dionysos and his followers the Maenads as for its gold mines and thick forests.

Amphipolis was founded in 5C BC and prospered under Philip and Alexander of Macedon (353-323 BC). It was a staging post on the Via Egnatia *(p 189)* under the Romans and was still an important centre during the Byzantine period.

The Lion. – On the left of the road from Thessalonika, just before the bridge over the Strymon, stands a huge marble lion which was reconstructed in 1937 from Hellenistic fragments: it resembles the lion of Chaironeia *(p 77)* although it is later, dating from the end of 4C BC.

Ruins. – *After crossing the bridge over the Strymon, take the road to Séres (left); after 1.5km – 1 mile turn left to the modern village of Amfípoli and then left again towards the church; after 0.5km – 547yds a path to the right leads to the ruins.*

On the plateau, not far from what was probably the agora, are traces of paleo-Christian basilicas: mosaics of birds *(partially covered)*.

Work is in progress to expose the Hellenistic precinct of Amphipolis.

The rival of Delphi in antiquity, Amphissa is now the capital of Phocis (Fokída) and an important olive market; it is built against the curved slope at the head of the valley of olive groves which runs down to Itéa.

Known as **Salona** in the Middle Ages, Amphissa was a medieval stronghold and in 13C was the seat of a Frankish domain held by the Autremencourt family from Picardy. In the following century Louis de Salona laid claim to the Duchy of Athens when it and Salona too were occupied by the Spanish. Salona was taken by the Turks in 1394.

In the First World War Amphissa regained its strategic importance as it lay on the new road built by the Allies over Mount Parnassos to Brálos and Lamía to supply their forces in Thessalonika and avoid the sea route through the Aegean which was longer and threatened by submarines.

Castle (Froúrio). – *Access by Odós Froúriou (signpost "Pros Froúrion").*
Called Château de la Sole by the Franks, the fortress with its three defensive walls was built early in 13C on the site of the old acropolis which can still be traced in the occasional massive blocks of stone.

Within stood the city; traces of two churches and some cisterns still survive. The castle proper occupied the top of the site: remains of the keep, the living quarters and a 13C round tower.

There are fine views of Amphissa and of the olive groves in the valley.

ANDRÍTSENA

Peloponnese – Pop 863 – Alt 765m – 2 510ft – Michelin map 𝟵𝟴𝟬 fold 28

The red roofs of this typical mountain town stand out against the slopes of the peaks bordering Elis to the east. Among these mountains is the famous Mount Lykaion (Líkeo) (alt 1 421m – 4 662ft); it was a primitive sanctuary for the worship of Zeus, involving human sacrifice and ritual cannibalism.

Andrítsena is a market town and an excursion centre *(hotels)*. It has many old wooden houses with projecting upper storeys and craft workshops (blacksmiths, wood turners, weavers...) lining the streets where goats, donkeys and pigs roam at will. A fountain in the shade of a plane tree lends charm to the main square.

Andrítsena possesses a library of some 25 000 volumes which was started with a nucleus of 6 250 works presented in 1840 by **Agathophros Nikolopoulos** (1786-1841), a scholar and philologist, who died in Paris after twenty years at the Bibliothèque de l'Institut: many incunabula; plays by Alembert with comments by J.-J. Rousseau.

EXCURSION

Temple of Apollo at Bassae ★ ★ (Vassés). – *14km – 8 miles south.* Access by a fine modern road up the side of the Andrítsena Basin.

The temple at Bassae *(open 8.45am to 3pm; 9.30am to 2.30pm Sundays; restoration in progress)* stands alone on a lofty cheerless **site ★ ★** (alt 1 130m – 3 707ft) on the southern face of Mount Kotylion (Paliovlátiza) surrounded by ravines *(bassai);* on the distant horizon rise the mountains of Lakonía (SE) and Messinía (SW).

It was built from 450 to 420 BC by the inhabitants of Phigaleia (SW) in honour of Apollo who had preserved them from the plague. According to Pausanias (2C AD) the architect was Iktínos, one of the designers of the Parthenon in Athens. Forgotten for many centuries it was discovered in 1765 by a French architect, Joachim Bocher, who was working for the Venetians. In 1811 C.R. Cockerell *(pp 62 and 74)* and Haller von Hallerstein visited the temple and the latter together with Baron Stackelberg made a record of the architecture in 1812. The internal frieze and other fragments were auctioned in Zakynthos and acquired by the British Museum where they are now displayed. It is one of the

(From photograph Tzaferis S.A., Athens)

Bassae. – Temple of Apollo

best preserved of Greek temples but was in imminent danger of collapse when restoration work began in 1975.

It is built of greyish limestone in the Doric style and is completely surrounded by a colonnade. It is not outstanding but its merit lies in its pleasant proportions and its harmony with the landscape. The building has several unusual characteristics:
– exceptional length in relation to its width (15 columns by 6);
– north-south orientation as opposed to east-west, with the entrance facing north *(uphill);*
– opening in the long east side to shed light on the statue of Apollo in the *naós (p 18);*
– Ionic half-columns in the *naós* linked to the walls by buttresses.

At the southern end of the *naós* stands a Corinthian column, the first known in this style; the base is extant but the capital which was decorated with acanthus leaves is missing; the two flanking columns may also have been Corinthian.

The architrave was surmounted by a frieze of sculpted metopes while the walls of the *naós* were decorated on the inside with another frieze of low-reliefs representing the battles between the Greeks and Amazons on the one hand and the Centaurs and Lapiths on the other; this is the earliest example of a sculptured frieze decorating the interior of a Greek building.

There is an overall view of the site from above the keeper's house.

ARÁHOVA★

Central Greece – Fokída – Pop 2 793 – Michelin map 980 north of fold 29

Once over the **Aráhova Pass** (alt 940m – 3 084ft) on the traditional road from Livadiá to Delphi, the traveller is greeted by a very fine **view★★** down on to the site of Aráhova, a small mountain town (alt 905m – 2 696ft) on the southern face of Mount Parnassos above the Pleistos ravine.

The climate is fairly harsh with snow in winter and rain in spring and autumn which feeds the many fountains in the town; in summer the temperature stays quite cool.

In spring on St George's Day (23 April) the town attracts the people from the country round who come dressed in their traditional costume to take part in the folk dancing while the old men compete in a race in which the winner receives a lamb presented by the shepherds of Parnassos.

Main Street. – The narrow street winds its way between tavernas and workshops. In the tavernas one can savour a dish of soft fried cheese – *formaéla* – and the mountain cheeses together with a delicious red wine which tastes of redcurrants. The workshops sell shoulder bags, carpets and long haired rugs *(flokáti)* in bright colours.

St George's Church. – Picturesque streets lead up to the terrace which offers a **view★** of the Pleistos ravine and Mount Kírphis.

EXCURSIONS

Corycian Cave★★ and Mount Parnassos★★. – *45km – 27 miles by car, about 2 1/2 hours, by the road from Aráhova. Leave Aráhova towards Delphi; turn right towards Lílea. After 11km – 7 miles, just beyond Kalívia, turn left (signpost "Chat Tours") into a narrow stony track which winds uphill for 5km – 3 miles to a car park. From there it is 5 minutes on foot to the cave.*

Corycian Cave★★ (Koríkio Ándro). – In antiquity the cave was devoted to "the god **Pan** and the Nymphs"; on the neighbouring slopes orgies in honour of Dionysos were organised by his attendant Thyiads.

The cave is 1 300m – 4 265ft above sea level and very extensive. It was already in use in the neolithic and Mycenian periods as excavations made in 1970 by the French School of Archaeology have shown. Subsequently it was used as a refuge. One can penetrate right into the cave which is naturally well lit; there are a few stalactites. From the threshold there are views towards Parnassos, the Pleistos Valley and the Bay of Itéa.

Return to the road to Lílea.

Mount Parnassos★★. – The road follows the hanging valley of **Kalívia** where sheep are pastured. After about 15km – 9 miles turn right into a good road which climbs through a mountain landscape of pine trees to a chalet belonging to the Athens Ski Club (alt 1 900m – 6 234ft). From here one can make the ascent of **Mount Liákoura** (2 457m – 8 061ft), the highest peak of Parnassos *(6 hours on foot Rtn; July to August only; guide essential);* on a clear day, which is rare, there is a superb panorama of a large part of Greece from the Peloponnese to Mount Athos (E).

Parnassos, which is often under snow or enveloped in clouds, was thought to be the home of Apollo, whose main sanctuary was nearby, and of the nine **Muses:** Clio (History), Euterpe (Music), Melpomene (Tragedy), Thalia (Comedy), Terpsichore (Dancing), Urania (Astronomy), Erato (Elegy), Polyhymnia (Lyric poetry) and Calliope (Epic poetry).

The Parnassos range, which is not easy of access and still harbours a few wolves, was the base of the local klephts *(p 24)* during the Greek War of Independence and served again after the Second World War as the stronghold of the E.L.A.S. resistance movement which survived there until 1949. There are many bauxite mines.

ARCADIAN Coast★★

Peloponnese – Arkadía – Michelin map 980 south of fold 29

The east coast of the Peloponnese from Ástros to Leonídio, which forms part of Arkadía, has long been overlooked by tourists as it was accessible only by sea. Since 1976 however a new sometimes corniche road has been built which follows the course of the lonely winding coastline overlooking the Argolic Gulf. It is still not much used and offers a succession of views across the gulf to the Argolid peninsula and Spetsae Island.

The Arcadian coast is formed by the foothills of the **Mount Parnon** range which rises to 1 935m – 6 348ft; its limestone slopes are mostly barren except at altitude where a few wolves inhabit the forests. Life is still traditional: many peasants go to work in their fields riding on a donkey or a mule, the women spin by hand and the fishermen pull their boats up on the shore... Extended villages of white houses topped by pantile roofs appear in the distance clustered in coastal depressions amid orchards fed by irrigation channels.

FROM ÁSTROS TO LEONÍDIO★★

50km – 31 miles by car, about 2 hours; petrol stations are rare

Ástros. – Pop 2 459. Ástros is an agricultural centre specialising in the cultivation of fruit trees (olives, citrus fruits and particularly peaches); there is a small seaside resort (Paralía Ástros) down on the coast at the foot of a promontory below the remains of an ancient citadel refurbished by the Franks. In 1823 Ástros was host to the Second National Assembly of Greece which met to revise the 1821 Constitution.

Beyond Ágios Andréas the road passes above several inlets which are suitable for bathing.

Tirós★. – Pop 304. An old town which spreads out like a fan among terraced olive groves. On the coast there is a resort (Paralía Tiroú – pop 552) with a beach and several hotels.

Beyond Tirós a corniche road offers beautiful views across the sea to Spetsae.

Sambatikí★. – Pop 57. Attractive site in a curving bay protected by a watch tower; beach and fishing boats.

The road runs high up above Leonídio Bay and the fertile coastal strip which produces olives, citrus fruit and vegetables. The river mouth is flanked by two small beaches – Lékos and Pláka *(tavernas; ships to Piraeus).*

Leonídio★★. – Pop 3 557. Timeless and peaceful *(at least out of season)* the little town of Leonídio extends from the bank of its river to a high red cliff. It has a certain old-world charm: a 12C fortified house *(recently restored),* old rough-cast houses with balconies and Saracen chimneys, the workshops of craftsmen and tradesmen (baker's oven), old woodpanelled cafés with marble topped tables.

Walk to the far end of the town for a view (near the ruined tower) over the site and the coastal basin down to the sea.

Further inland *(32km – 20 miles Rtn)* along the road lies the **Elóna Monastery** huddled against the rocks on a wild **site★** overlooking a narrow valley.

The continuation of the road beyond Elóna is magnificent but the further section from Kosmás to Geráki is very rough.

ARGOLID Peninsula★ _____ *Argolída*

Peloponnese – Argolis – Michelin map 980 folds 29 and 30

This peninsula, which separates the Saronic and Argolic Gulfs, is composed of limestone hills, often covered with pine woods and olive groves, while the coastal plains are planted with citrus orchards.

The little ports and sheltered creeks for bathing which are dotted along the shore were formerly accessible only by sea but now there is a coast road serving the modern hotels and resorts and offering attractive views of the islands of Póros, Hydra and Dokós.

ROUND TOUR FROM PORTOHÉLI★

About 186km – 116 miles – 1 day

Portohéli★. – Pop 756. Well sheltered in its attractive bay, Portohéli (Eel Port) is a fishing village and port for Spetsae and an excellent mooring for caïques and yachts. In recent years a seaside resort with modern hotels has developed which is linked to Zéa (Piraeus) by hydrofoil.

Take the road up to Kranídi and then continue towards Ligourió. Just before Trahiá turn right to Fanári. Beyond **Fanári,** clinging to the steep hillside, a corniche road descends the cliff face providing spectacular **views★★** of the Saronic shoreline and the **Méthana** peninsula which ends in Mount Helóni (743m – 2 438ft), an extinct volcano. *7km – 4 1/2 miles beyond Kaloní turn left towards Méthana.* The road crosses the neck of land leading to the former volcanic island of Méthana, jagged and mountainous. In 1820 Colonel Fabvier *(p 46)* pitched camp on the island before going to relieve the Acropolis in Athens and the place is still known as Faviópoli. Just before Méthana there is an attractive view of the town and the harbour.

Méthana. – Pop 988. There is a boat service from Piraeus to Méthana which has a small harbour protected by a wooded promontory where traces of a 4C BC fortress have been found. It is a seaside resort and also a spa; its warm sulfurous waters are used in the treatment of rheumatism and skin diseases.

Return to the crossroads on the mainland and turn left towards Galatás; after 2km – 1 1/4 miles turn right (signpost) into a minor road leading to Trizína (formerly Damalas) (pop 645) where the third Greek National Assembly at which Kapodistria was elected head of the new state took place in 1827. *Go through Trizína to reach the site of ancient Troizen level with the "Hellenistic tower".*

Troizen★ (Trizína). – A few traces of the ancient city have been excavated by the French School of Archaeology. It was the birthplace of Theseus *(pp 41 and 210)* and the scene of dramatic events which form the theme of famous tragedies by Euripides and Racine. **Phaedra,** Theseus' wife, fell in love with her step-son, Hippolytus who rejected her; she denounced him falsely as her seducer to Theseus who delivered his son to the fury of Poseidon; in despair Phaedra took her own life.

The tower is part of an ancient 3C BC fortress; the upper section dates from the Middle Ages. It stands at the lower end of the **Devil's Gorge★** which is worth exploring *(1 hour on foot Rtn)* by a difficult but picturesque path (views of the coast and then the mountain) which climbs up beside a mountain torrent between steeply sloping cliffs. The Devil's Bridge is a natural rock formation linking both sides of the gorge; it is overshadowed by thick plane trees in a wild and impressive site.

Another 1/2 hour's walk will bring you past a terrace, where there used to be a sanctuary to Pan, up to the ancient **fort of Damalet,** the seat of a 13C Frankish barony (fine view).

ARGOLID Peninsula ★

Return to the road to Galatás. The fertile coastal plain is a sea of orchards growing oranges, lemons, citrons, figs and carob-beans, dotted with the occasional dark plume of a cypress tree.

Galatás. – *Ferries and hire boats to Póros.* Magnificent views ★★ of the straits and Póros Island.

Continue along the coast south to Ermióni.

Lemonodássos ★. – On the coast opposite Póros Island there is a huge lemon grove of about 30 000 trees covering a gentle slope above Alíki beach. These delicate trees die if the temperature drops below –3 °C (26.6°F) but bear flowers and fruit throughout the year.
Park the car beside the road near the signpost by a chapel. From there one walks up the hill *(1/2 hour on foot Rtn)* through the scented lemon grove which is irrigated by narrow channels of running water. The path *(signpost: Pros Kéntron Cardassi or Restaurant Cardassi)* soon reaches the Cardassi taverna surrounded by oleanders, bougainvilleas and banana palms near a cool spring; attractive view of Póros Island *(p 173)*.

The coast road to Ermióni is a recent construction opening up views of Hydra and Dokós through the ubiquitous olive groves.

Hydra Beach ★ (Plepí). – Pop 299. New resort with a pleasant aspect: villas and flats attractively sited, harbour for leisure craft. *Motor launches from Plepí.*

Ermióni. – Pop 2 104. Former Byzantine see; now a resort and sheltered fishing port. *Regular services to Hydra.*

Continue along the coast road bearing left at the fork to Kósta.

Kósta. – Pop 61. Modern resort. *Ferry to Spétses (p 181).*

Return to Portohéli.

When visiting London use the **Green Guide** *"London"*

– *Detailed descriptions of places of interest*
– *Useful local information*
– *A section on the historic square mile of the City of London with a detailed fold out plan*
– *The lesser known London boroughs - their people, places and sights*
– *Plans of selected areas and important buildings.*

ÁRGOS

Peloponnese – Argolis – Pop 20 702 – Michelin map 980 fold 29

From afar a spit of rock crowned by a citadel indicates Árgos, capital of ancient Argolis (Argolída), whose population equalled that of Athens.

The town was burned by Ibrahim Pasha during the War of Independence and rebuilt on a grid plan so that it is now a featureless overgrown village, which acts as a communications centre and a market for the agricultural produce of the coastal plain: cattle, tobacco, cereals, fruit and vegetables (particularly tomatoes, artichokes and melons).

The oldest town in Greece. – The Ancients believed that Árgos was the oldest town in Greece, having been founded by an Egyptian, Danaos, father of the famous **Danaids** who killed their husbands and threw their heads into the Lerna marshes *(p 125);* they were condemned by the god of the underworld to fill a leaking vessel with water. Later the city of the Argives, like Mycenae, came under the control of Perseus and his descendants among whom was Diomedes, the faithful companion of Odysseus in the Trojan war.

Árgos grew to prominence in 8C. Throughout the Archaic period the city with its twin citadels, Lárissa and Aspís, dominated the northeast of the Peloponnese in rivalry with Sparta. Although it began to decline at the end of 6C, during the Classical period it supported a brilliant civilisation which produced a school of sculptors in bronze including **Polykleitos,** second only to Pheidias.

In 272 BC during the Hellenistic period, **Pyrrhus,** king of Epiros, was killed in Argos in street fighting by a tile which an old woman threw down from the roof of a house; it was this Pyrrhus who, thanks to his elephants, had won a victory against the Romans but at great cost, hence the expression "a Pyrrhic victory".

Under the Roman occupation Argos again enjoyed a period of prosperity but, despite having the strength to hold out for seven years against the Franks, the city was subsequently supplanted by Nauplion in importance not only under the Franks but also during the later occupations by the Venetians and Turks.

The city did however feature in the Greek War of Independence: in 1822 Kolokotrónis and D. Ypsilántis (1793-1832) held out against the Turks from the citadel *(kástro)* and the Greek National Assembly held sittings in the ancient theatre in 1822 and 1829.

SIGHTS *2 hours*

Ancient ruins ★ (Arheótites). – *Open 8.45am to 3pm (9.30am to 2.30pm Sundays).*

Excavations being carried out by the French School of Archaeology on a site at the foot of the hill below the citadel *(kástro)* have uncovered Greek and Roman remains.

By the western entrance to the site is an ancient road leading to a theatre to the left of which are the remains of a large building comprising a vaulted chamber with a crypt and an apse and three rooms opening into a courtyard surrounded with porticoes. Roman **baths (B)** were built here in 2C, surrounded by their hypocausts for the heating; the porticoes in the western section have been converted into a room; next comes the frigidarium with its three pools and the three caldaria which were decorated with numerous statues now in the museum.

38

The **theatre (T)**, which dates from 4C BC, was altered by the Romans who converted the orchestra into a *naumachia* for staging mock sea-fights.

Together with the one at Dodona, this theatre was one of the largest in Greece: the terraces, which were either hewn out of the rock or supported by an embankment, could accommodate 20 000 spectators. The central terraces (81 rows), the orchestra and the entrances and exits are well preserved.

On the wall in the south corridor there is a low relief sculpture of the Dioscuri on horseback.

South of the theatre are the remains of an **odeon (T1)** (2C-3C AD), a small indoor theatre, of which the curved terraces, the entrances and the stage remain.

On the opposite side of the road are the remains of the agora **(A)**, which dates from 4C BC: traces of a meeting room followed by a double doorway and two nymphaea (2C BC) – the second is linked to the city sewer.

Museum (M). – *Open 8.45am to 3pm (9.30am to 2.30pm Sundays); closed Tuesdays; 100 Dr.*

Built and organised by the French School of Archaeology, the museum displays the finds excavated at Árgos and Lerna *(p 125)*.

They are attractively presented in chronological order: in the righthand room a superb suit of armour (8C BC) including a crested helmet such as Homer's heroes wore and a fragment of painted pottery (7C BC) showing Odysseus and his companions putting out the eye of the cyclops, Polyphemus.

Under a portico in the garden there is a Roman mosaic evoking Bacchus, the Seasons and hunting scenes.

Lárissa Citadel★. – The Deirás Gap separates Aspís Hill (traces of a sanctuary to Apollo and a fortress) from Lárissa Hill. *Bear left at the crossroads into the road which winds round the back of the hill to the top* (alt 290m – 951ft).

The citadel on this wild and isolated but very beautiful site was built by Byzantines and completed by the Franks of the house of Enghien in 13C-14C on the foundations of an ancient acropolis from which a few huge blocks of masonry remain; Gautier de Foucherolles from Burgundy was the governor early in 14C.

The building was altered by the Venetians and the Turks and now consists of an outer wall with towers and the castle itself. The water cisterns are impressive.

There is a fine **view★★** of the fertile plain of Argolis stretching from the barren mountains to the gulf of Nauplion.

ÁRGOS

Bouboulinas	ΜΠΟΥΜΠΟΥΛΙΝΑΣ	2
Danaou	ΔΑΝΑΟΥ	3
Fidonos	ΦΕΙΔΩΝΟΣ	5
Makariou	ΜΑΚΑΡΙΟΥ	6
Metaxa	ΜΕΤΑΞΑ	7
Nikitara	ΝΙΚΗΤΑΡΑ	9
Vas. Sofias	ΒΑΣ. ΣΟΦΙΑΣ	12

EXCURSIONS

Argive Heraion★ (Iréo). – *9km – 5 1/2 miles northeast. Leave the centre of Árgos by the road towards Náfplio and then bear left towards Corinth; after 200m – 220yds take the road (Odós Papaikonómou) to Hónikas. Beyond Hónikas, level with an oratory, turn right into a stony track which leads to the Heraion.*

Open 8.45am to 3pm.

The sanctuary, which was consecrated to **Hera,** the tutelary goddess of fertile Argolis, was already in existence in the Mycenaean period and the Greek chiefs may have sworn their oath of loyalty to Agamemnon here before setting out for the Trojan War. The ruins which were discovered in 1831 occupy three terraces cut into the mountain side, a magnificent solitary **site★★** above the plain of Árgos.

On the first terrace stand the bases of the columns which formed a 5C BC portico or stoa; at the back, built of limestone blocks, is the retaining wall of the second terrace, which is reached by steps at the righthand end of the portico.

On the second terrace stood a Classical temple (late 5C BC) containing a huge statue, overlaid with gold and ivory, of Hera. The extant foundations reveal the design of the building which measured about 40m – 131ft by 20m – 66ft; the sculptures are on display in the Athens museum.

On the upper terrace are the massive lower courses of an Archaic Doric temple (early 7C BC) which burned down in 423 BC owing to the negligence of the priestess Chryseis, who fell asleep while her lamp was still burning.

The cult of Hera was still celebrated on this spot in Roman times; Roman baths have been found on the west slope; Nero is known to have presented the goddess with a purple robe and Hadrian made a gift of a peacock (Hera's symbol), gilded and set with precious stones.

39

Kefalári. – Pop 533. *9km – 5 1/2 miles southwest. Take the road to Trípoli. After 5km – 3 miles turn right into a track which leads to the Erássinos spring.*

The river gushes from a cave consecrated in antiquity to Pan and Dionysos; a sanctuary stands on the terrace above. The ancients thought that the water flowed beneath the mountain from Lake Stymphalia (Stimfalía) (NW).

In summer the cool shade of the huge plane trees and the tall poplars is particularly welcome *(open air cafés)*.

Mérbaka (Agía Triáda). – Pop 1 167. *10km – 6 miles east. Take the road to Náfplio and then turn left.*

Mérbaka is named after Wilhelm van Mœrbeke, a Fleming who was archbishop of Corinth in 1280 during the Frankish occupation and was the first to translate Aristotle. The apse of the beautiful 12C church is decorated with its original carving, quite unlike the traditional Byzantine style.

ÁRTA★

Epiros – Pop 18 283 – Michelin map 980 fold 15

Árta, which was known in antiquity as Ambracia, is situated in a bend in the River Árahthos and dominated by a 13C citadel built on ancient foundations.

It was a thriving city which Pyrrhus, king of Epiros in 3C BC who died in 272 BC in Argos *(p 37)*, and the despots of the Comnenus dynasty in 13C-14C chose as their capital; in 1259 Anna Comnena was married here to William de Villehardouin *(qv)*. Nowadays the town is above all a market for the citrus fruits which are grown in the neighbourhood and also a craft centre: embroidery, long-haired rugs *(flokáti)*.

SIGHTS *1 hour*

Bridge★. – The 17C hump-backed bridge over the Árahthos on the edge of Árta (Ioánina road) is celebrated for its elegant curve and its wide arches alternating with smaller ones which ease the flow of water when the river is in spate. The bridge has inspired several legends; one recounts that the architect used his wife's body to reinforce the foundations.

Panagía Parigorítissa★. – *Open 8.45am to 3pm (9.30am to 2.30pm Sundays; closed Tuesdays; 100 Dr.*

The great church of the Virgin Comforter near Skoufá Square was built at the end of 13C by Anna Palaiologos wife of the Despot Nikephoros I. With its six domes it was inspired by the churches in Constantinople and was restored after the Second World War.

From the outside it looks like a huge square palace and is constructed of bricks and stones forming a decorative pattern.

The interior is surrounded by galleries for women *(gynaecea)*. The central dome is raised on three stages of projecting columns (some of them ancient). The base of the dome is supported on squinches of such an unusual type that the only other example is St Theodore's Church in Mystra *(p 149)*.

The mosaics (Christ Pantocrator; the Prophets) are of the same date as the church itself; so too are the original Italian sculptures which decorate the vaulting and the bases and capitals of the columns of the third stage.

There is an **archaeological museum** (icons, sculptures etc.) in a neighbouring building.

St Theodora's Church (Agía Theodóra). – *Northwest of the main street going towards the citadel.* The church was originally attached to a convent, which has since disappeared, to which Theodora, wife of Michael II, Despot of Epiros, withdrew in 13C. On the left of the entrance is Theodora's tomb, set up by her son Nikephoros I and reconstructed from 13C pieces found in the last century. The massive capitals in the sanctuary probably came from one of the first Christian churches in Nikopolis *(p 174)*.

St Basil's Church (Ágios Vassílios). – *Further on towards the citadel.* This charming little 14C church is decorated with bricks and glazed tiles *(keys at the house opposite)*.

Vlacherna Monastery. – *2km – 1 1/4 miles NE of Árta. Open all day until sunset except between 1 and 5pm.*

The convent stands on the top of a hill in the country. The church, which was built in 13C on the basilical plan, has retained some of its original decoration (mosaic floor, frescoes) and contains two marble tombs which are thought to belong to Despot Michael II and his sons.

EXCURSION

Rogóus Fortress. – *15km – 9 1/2 miles west, near the village of Néa Kerassoús on the Préveza road.* Above a bend in the River Loúros stand the ruins of this ancient fortress; it is impressive for its size and state of preservation. It was built late in 5C BC on older foundations, partially destroyed by the Romans and then restored by the Byzantines. Fine polygonal stonework. The frescoes in the little church are somewhat spoiled.

Michelin main road maps

980 *Greece*
986 *Great Britain, Ireland*
987 *Germany, Austria, Benelux*
988 *Italy*
989 *France*
990 *Spain, Portugal*
991 *Yugoslavia*

ATHENS★★★ _____ _Athína_

Central Greece – Attica – Pop 885 737 (Greater Athens: 3 027 331) Michelin map 980 fold 30

The attractive site, the brilliant light (sometimes hazy with pollution), the beauty of the ancient monuments and the quality of the museums all contribute to the pleasure of visiting Athens, the city of Athena, the cradle of European civilisation.

Athens also has many Roman and Byzantine souvenirs and certain districts, such as the old Bazaar, have a strong and enticing oriental flavour. It is remarkable that, although Athens numbered less than 10 000 inhabitants in 19C, as the capital of modern Greece it has now become a huge conurbation, lively and cosmopolitan, extending for 15km – over 9 miles from Piraeus to Kifissiá.

PRACTICAL INFORMATION _(see also pp 5, 6 and 29)_

Traffic. – Driving in Athens is difficult: crowded narrow streets, mostly one-way; lack of discipline among drivers who rely on their horns. Pedestrians should pay great attention when crossing the road. It is almost impossible to park in the town centre although an underground car park has recently been constructed in Klafthmónos Square. Sometimes there are spaces near Zápio Park or the Pedío Áreos.

Transport. – The best method of transport for the tourist is a taxi which can be hailed anywhere in the street; the fares are relatively inexpensive; taxis tend to be scarce in the rush hour. Buses and trolleybuses are cheap (single fare: 40Dr) but often crowded. There is only one underground line running north-south from Kifissiá to Piraeus.

Hotels and restaurants. – The hotels are often full and it is wise to reserve a room a week or two in advance in the high season; failing that, apply to the Greek Tourist Office (EOT), Eleniko airport or 2 Karagiórgi Servías Street. The most luxurious hotels are to be found in the districts round Síndagma Square, Kolonáki and Vassilíssis Sofías Avenue; more modest establishments are situated near Omónia Square and Karaiskáki Square. The same is true for restaurants. Tavernas are most numerous in Pláka, in the Omónia-Patissíon district and in the other central districts.

Shopping. – Except for Minion in Patissíon Street there are few large shops or supermarkets. The small shops are open in summer from 8am to 2.30pm and again from 5.30 to 8.30pm; they are closed on Sundays and Mondays all day and after 2.30pm on Wednesdays and Saturdays.

Useful addresses:

Greek National Tourist Office (EOT): information office and foreign currency exchange, 2 Odós Karagiórgi Servías (Síndagma), Tel: 322 2545
British Airways, 10 Odós Óthonos (Síndagma), Tel: 322 2521
Olympic Airways, 6 Odós Óthonos (Síndagma), Tel: 923 2323
Central Post Office: 100 Odós Eólou (Omónia): poste restante.
British Embassy: 1 Odós Ploutárhou, Tel: 723 6211
British Council: 17 Kolonáki Square, Tel: 363 3211
Anglican church: 29 Odós Philellinon.
Roman Catholic church: St. Dionysius' Church, 24 Leofóros Venizélou (Latin mass at 11am).

Other practical information to be found in the Greece-Athens brochure available in the Tourist Office (EOT), in hotels and at airports, the "Week in Athens" magazine, the monthly magazine "The Athenian" and "Athens News", a daily information sheet.

Athens in a day. – In the morning take the funicular to the top of Lycabettos, then visit the Acropolis by way of the Temple of Zeus (Olympieion). After the Acropolis (excluding the museum) walk down to Monastiráki (former bazaar) and then to Omónia Square passing through the Central Market. Lunch.

In the afternoon visit the National Museum (Greek antiquities) before walking along Leofóros Venizélou (Panepistimíou) to Síndagma Square for a pre-dinner stroll. In the evening take a walk in Pláka, a pedestrian precinct devoted to restaurants and shops selling jewellery and souvenirs.

HISTORICAL AND GEOGRAPHICAL NOTES

Ancient Athens

Birth of Athens. – The Acropolis was built on a natural defensive site consisting of a hill about 156m – 512ft high with steep sides, not far from the sea, the approaches protected by two rivers (Kifíssos – west and Ilissos – east) and a circle of hills forming outposts. Athens is thought to have been founded by Creops, the king of a prehistoric race; he was deified in the form of a serpent with a human torso and believed to have introduced the cult of the owl.

In all the mythical accounts Poseidon, the bellicose god of the Sea, and Athena, the goddess of Wisdom, are said to have rivalled one another in the performance of miracles for the good of the first inhabitants; one produced a spring and a horse, the other the olive tree, symbol of peace and harmony.

Erechtheos, a descendant of Creops, established the cult of Athena, the goddess who was associated with the olive and the owl : the cult was practised in the king's palace itself, on the site where the Erechtheion now stands. There are fragments of a wall dating from this period near the Propylaia.

Aigeus' son, **Theseus** (12 or 11C BC) made Athens the capital of a coherent state covering present-day Attica and afforded great importance to the processions in honour of Athena, called the Panathenaia. He was the Athenian national hero throughout antiquity. In his reign the area covered by the city was scarcely larger than the Acropolis which contained the royal palace and the houses of the patricians (Eupatrides). A few shrines were built however on the banks of the Illissos, near the Kallirhoë fountain; an agora was created and the first graves were dug at the roadsides.

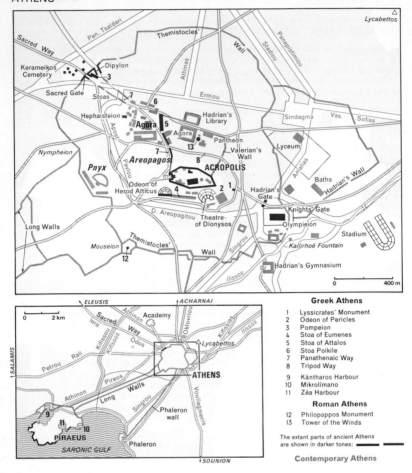

Greek Athens

1	Lyssicrates' Monument
2	Odeon of Pericles
3	Pompeion
4	Stoa of Eumenes
5	Stoa of Attalos
6	Stoa Poikile
7	Panathenaic Way
8	Tripod Way

9	Kántharos Harbour
10	Mikrolímano
11	Zéa Harbour

Roman Athens

12	Philopappos Monument
13	Tower of the Winds

The extant parts of ancient Athens are shown in darker tones: ▬▬ ▬ ▬

Contemporary Athens

Athens in her glory. – **6-5C BC.** After the great urban reforms introduced by Solon and the enlightened dictators, Peisistratos and his sons (561-510), the city developed extensively. A new circuit wall was built enclosing the Areopagos hill northwest of the Acropolis, where certain assemblies were held, as well as the two agoras of Theseus and Solon, which became the political centre of the city. At the same time various municipal undertakings were being carried out in the lower town: public buildings constructed of tufa, provision of water, sewers and roads. The first coins were struck bearing the effigy of Athena and the owl; the Lyceum and the Academy, famous gymnasia surrounded by gardens, were established.

When Kleisthenes rose to power in 508 BC he organised Athens into a direct democracy and introduced ostracism so that any individual who was a danger to the state could be excluded from public affairs.

Legislative power was exercised by an assembly of the people *(Ecclesia)* which met three or four times a month on the Pnyx *(p 61)*, a Senate *(Boule)* of 500 members which was subordinated to the Assembly and a tribunal *(Heliaia)* comprising elected magistrates and juries chosen by lot.

Executive power was exercised by the *archons* and the *strategi;* the latter were in command of the army.

Following the damage caused by the enemy in 479 BC at the end of the Persian Wars, Themistocles, the victor of the battle of Salamis, gave orders for the construction of the wall which bears his name and of which a few traces remain; he also built the "Long Walls", a sort of fortified corridor linking Athens and Piraeus.

In the Age of **Pericles,** that great Athenian statesman, who gave his name to the period, devoted himself to the reconstruction of Athens with the advice of the sculptor Pheidias. An overall plan was drawn up for the Acropolis; various buildings in white Pentelic marble rose against the blue sky: the Propylaia, the Parthenon, the Erechtheion and the temple of Athena Nike surrounded by votive monuments and statues. In the lower town the agora was restored and enlarged. Almost the whole area within the walls was covered by brick houses, usually built round a central courtyard; they were particularly dense on two hills near the beginning of the Long Walls west and southwest of the Acropolis, the Mouseion and the Nympheion. The Kerameikos cemetery, beside the road leading to Plato's Academy, was the largest in the city where the most important citizens were buried.

Athens in decline. – **4-2C BC.** The Peloponnesian War (431-404), in which Athens was defeated by Sparta, marked the beginning of a decline in the moral sphere which is illustrated by the death of the philosopher **Socrates** who was unjustly condemned to drink hemlock (399 BC) in the presence of his pupil Plato.

Despite the exhortations of the great orator **Demosthenes,** the Greeks failed to agree on a concerted policy and after the Battle of Chaironeia (338 BC) Athens became subject to Philip of Macedon who was succeeded by Alexander the Great.

Secure under the Macedonian "protection" which lasted until the end of 3C BC, the Athenian municipal authorities embarked on public works of embellishment particularly under the orator Lycurgus (338-326 BC): the theatre of Dionysos and the choregic monument of Lysicrates.

The Hellenistic period which began with the death of Alexander (323 BC) was marked by the division of the Macedonian empire into several kingdoms. Athens vegetated; only the building of a few porticoes and gymnasia, in the reigns of the kings of Antioch and Pergamon, reveal the city's continuing intellectual power.

Conquered by Rome, Athens conquers Rome. – 1C BC – 4C AD. The political independence of Athens came to an end in 86 BC when the city was captured by Sulla and the walls were rased.

Nonetheless the "Roman peace" enabled Athens to retain its leadership in cultural affairs in the Mediterranean world; the Romans carried away or copied her works of art, imitated her citizens' way of life and sent their sons to Athens to complete their education. In 1C BC a temple to Rome and Augustus was built on the Acropolis hill and a Roman forum and a hydraulic clock, known later as the "Tower of the Winds", were built at the foot; a covered theatre (Odeon) was built on the old agora.

In 53 AD Christianity was brought to Athens by **St Paul** who preached the gospel, without much success it is true, and exalted the "unknown god" on the Areopagos; Paul did however convert one member of the famous tribunal, Dionysius the Areopagite, who was the first bishop and martyr of the new community...

Later, in 2C AD, the **Emperor Hadrian** who cherished all things Greek was very generous in his embellishment of Athens: he completed the temple of Zeus (Olympieion) begun by Peisistratos, built a library and aqueducts and a new district east of the Acropolis protected by a wall. Herod Atticus, a wealthy Athenian, contributed to these public works by constructing a theatre (Odeon), which still bears his name, on the southern slope of the Acropolis and a splendid white marble stadium, which has been restored in recent years, on the east bank of the Ilissos.

Byzantine and Medieval Athens

Byzantium and the rise of Christianity. – 5C-13C. Following the Germanic invasions in the middle of 3C the division of the Roman empire in 395 attributed Athens to the emperor residing in Byzantium (Constantinople).

The Edict of Milan in 313 allowed Christians to practise their religion legally and their proliferation in Athens from 5C to 7C led to the suppression of the schools of philosophy and the establishment of Christian basilicas in the Parthenon, the Erechtheion, the Hephaisteion (Theseion), the theatre of Dionysos, Hadrian's library etc.

The majority of the Byzantine churches however date from 9C and often incorporated fragments of ancient buildings. They were small but well proportioned and carefully decorated and quite a few have survived: the Holy Apostles (late 10C) in the Greek agora, St Theodore (11C), the Kapnikarea (11C) and the Old Metropolitan (12C).

Until the late 12C when Athens was sacked by the Saracens, it was a flourishing city with a stable population protected by the castle on the Acropolis.

The Dukes of Athens. – 13C-15C. The Fourth Crusade which captured Constantinople in 1204 caused Athens to fall into the hands of the Frankish knights who also held Thebes.

Athens passed to a family of Burgundian origin, La Roche, who had a castle in Thebes: during their tenure Athens was raised to a Duchy by Louis IX of France (1260).

They were succeeded by Gautier de Brienne but he was killed by the Catalans at the Battle of Kephisos (1311) near Lake Copais in Boeotia *(p 162)* and the Frankish domination of Athens came to an end. The Franks fortified the Acropolis and altered the Propylaia to form a palace guarded by a keep, known as the Frankish Tower, which was 28m-92ft high and stood until it was demolished in 1875.

The Catalans then occupied the region but established their stronghold in Thebes rather than Athens so that in 1387 Nerio Acciaiuoli, a member of a Florentine family involved in banking and arms manufacture, broke out of Corinth where his family was detained and captured Athens after a long siege.

After a brief Venetian interlude from 1394 to 1403 the Acciaiuoli reigned over Athens until 1456 when they were obliged to submit to the Turks who had captured Constantinople three years earlier.

Athens under the Turks

Athens asleep. – 1456-1687. Sultan Mahomet II, who captured Constantinople, granted a certain degree of autonomy to Athens and the Turks allowed several churches to be built; in 17C they even permitted the Jesuits and Capucines to found monasteries.

The Acropolis was fortified to form the kernel of the Turkish fortress; in 1466 the Parthenon was converted into a mosque with an adjoining minaret; the Propylaia was used as a powder magazine and the Erechtheion housed a harem.

Athens was simply a small provincial town which was thought in the west to have degenerated into the fishing village of Porto Leone (in fact Piraeus, *p 64*) since in 16C most knowledge of Greece was acquired from merchants and chaplains in the British Levant Company and as there was no trade with Athens few people went there. A few intrepid travellers however did visit the ancient city. In 1675 Sir George Wheler described the Parthenon as "absolutely both for matter and art the most beautiful piece of antiquity remaining in the world".

Athens at its lowest ebb. – 1687-1821. After reconquering the Peloponnese, the Venetian troops led by the Doge Morosini and by Koenigsmark laid siege to Athens in 1687; during the bombardment a powder magazine on the Acropolis exploded causing grave damage to the Parthenon and the Turks surrendered. They recaptured the town a year later but the Venetians had meanwhile removed the great white marble lions which now guard the entrance to the Venice Arsenal and drawn up a plan of the town.

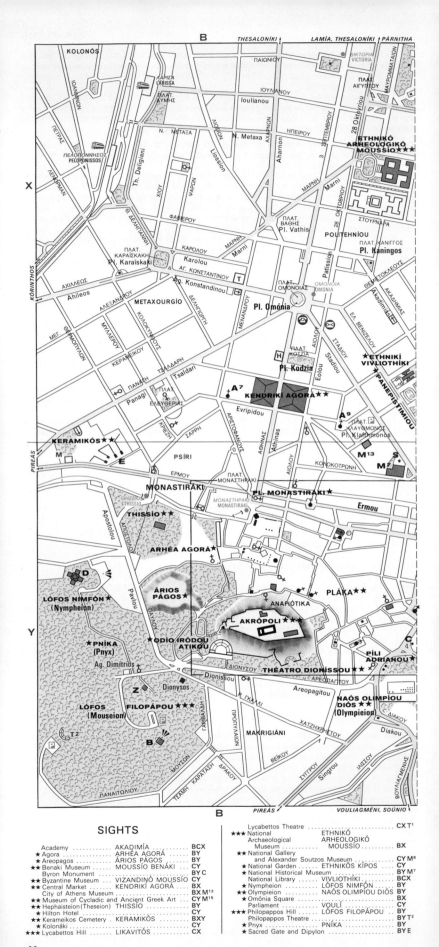

SIGHTS

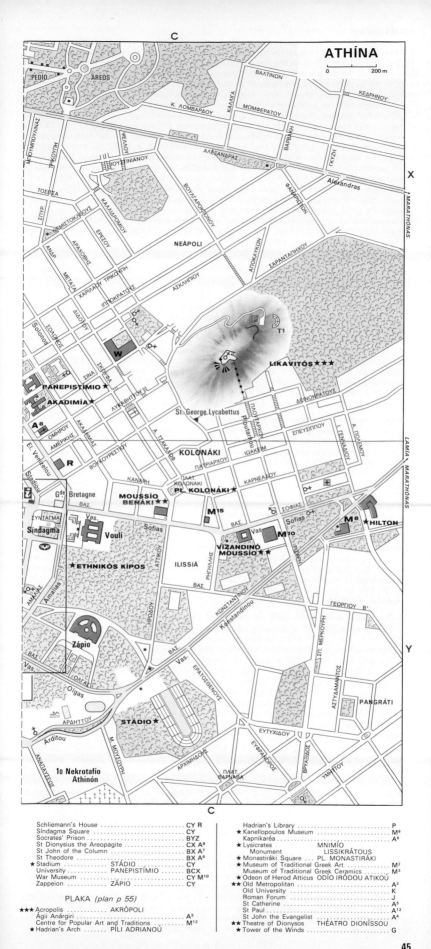

ATHÍNA

0   200 m

PEDÍO ÁREOS

ΒΑΛΤΙΝΟΝ
ΚΕΔΡΗΝΟΥ
Κ. ΛΟΜΒΑΡΔΟΥ
ΚΑΛΛΙΓΑ
ΜΟΜΦΕΡΑΤΟΥ
ΑΛΕΞΑΝΔΡΑΣ
ΒΑΡΒΑΚΗ
ΓΚΥΖΗ
Alexandras

X

ΜΠΟΥΜΠΟΥΛΙΝΑΣ
ΤΡΙΚΟΥΠΗ
ΙΟΥΣΤΙΝΙΑΝΟΥ
ΒΟΥΛΓΑΡΟΚΤΟΝΟΥ
ΦΑΝΑΡΙΩΤΩΝ
ΓΕΝΝΑΔΙΟΥ

ΤΟΣΙΤΣΑ
ΣΠΥΡ
ΘΕΜΙΣΤΟΚΛΕΟΥΣ
ΚΑΛΛΙΔΡΟΜΙΟΥ
ΕΡΕΣΟΥ
ΝΕΑΠΟΛΙ
ΑΠΟΚΑΥΚΩΝ
ΣΑΡΑΝΤΑΠΗΧΟΥ

AMP
ΑΡΑΧΩΒΗΣ
ΜΕΤΑΞΑ
ΧΑΡΙΛΑΟΥ ΤΡΙΚΟΥΠΗ
ΙΠΠΟΚΡΑΤΟΥΣ
ΑΣΚΛΗΠΙΟΥ

ΔΙΔΟΤΟΥ
ΣΟΛΩΝΟΣ
W
ΣΙΝΑ
ΣΚΟΥΦΑ
ΛΥΚΑΒΗΤΤΟΥ

T1

LIKAVITÓS ★★★

PANEPISTÍMIO ★

AKADIMÍA ★

St. George Lycabettus

A 8
ΟΜΗΡΟΥ
ΑΜΕΡΙΚΗΣ
ΑΚΑΔΗΜΙΑΣ
Α. ΤΣΑΚΑΛΩΦ
Πλουτάρχου
Plutarhu
ΔΕΙΝΟΚΡΑΤΟΥΣ
ΣΠΕΥΣΙΠΠΟΥ
Ι. ΓΕΝΝΑΔΙΟΥ
Α. ΠΟΛΕΜΩΝ

El. Venizélou
R
ΒΟΥΚΟΥΡΕΣΤΙΟΥ
ΚΟΛΩΝΑΚΙ
ΚΟΛΩΝΑΚΙ
ΠΑΤΡΙΑΡΧΟΥ ΙΩΑΚΕΙΜ

Stadíou
Gde Bretagne
ΒΑΣ
ΚΑΝΑΡΗ
ΠΛΑΤ. ΚΟΛΩΝΑΚΙ
PL. KOLONÁKI ★
ΚΑΡΝΕΑΔΟΥ

MOUSSÍO BENÁKI ★★

ΣΥΝΤΑΓΜΑ
Síndagma
Vas.
Vouli
Sofias
ΒΑΣ
Μ 15
Vas.
ΒΑΣ
Vas.
Sofias
Σοφίας
Μ 10
Μ 8
HILTON

★ ETHNIKÓS KÍPOS
ΑΤΤΙΚΟΥ
ILISSIÁ
ΡΗΓΙΛΛΗΣ
VIZANDINÓ MOUSSÍO ★★

Amalías
ΗΡΩΔΟΥ
ΒΑΣ
ΚΟΝΣΤΑΝΤΙΝΟΥ
Konstandínou
ΓΕΩΡΓΙΟΥ Β΄

Zápio
ΒΑΣ
Vas.
ΕΡΑΤΟΣΘΕΝΟΥΣ
ΣΠ. ΜΕΡΚΟΥΡΗ
ΑΣΤΥΔΑΜΑΝΤΟΣ
PANGRÁTI

ΟλΓας
Olgas
ΑΡΔΗΤΤΟΥ
STÁDIO ★
ΕΥΤΥΧΙΔΟΥ
ΕΦΟΡΙΩΝΟΣ
ΒΡΥΑΞΙΔΟΣ
ΥΜΗΤΤΟΥ

Ardítou
Ardítou
Μ. ΜΟΥΣΟΥΡΗ
ΑΡΧΙΜΗΔΟΥΣ
ΑΝΑΠΑΥΣΕΩΣ
ΠΛΑΤ. ΒΑΡΝΑΒΑ
1o Nekrotafío Athinón

From then until independence Athens was just a small town of about 10 to 15 000 inhabitants living in the narrow streets crowded on the northern slopes of the Acropolis hill. There were about 1 500 Greek families as opposed to 400 Turkish ones who, together with the garrison, lived in the citadel on the Acropolis and in the Bazaar district near the old Roman forum; their cemetery lay west of the Acropolis.

Although only an unimportant backwater in the Ottoman Empire, Athens began to attract many visitors from western Europe who, having been introduced to Greek architecture in southern Italy, desired to visit the source of such excellence. From 1751-53 "Athenian" Stuart and Revett were at work in Athens preparing "an accurate description of the antiquities of Athens"; the first volume was published in 1762. Richard Chandler, who visited Athens some ten years later, remarked that it was "to be regretted that so much admirable sculpture as is still extant... should be all likely to perish... Numerous carved stones have disappeared; and many, lying in the ruinous heaps, moved our indignation at the barbarism daily exercised in defacing them". Lord Elgin, British Ambassador in Constantinople at this period, is famous for his acquisitive activities which incidentally protected the marble sculptures from further deterioration. His chief rival in the collection of antiquities was Fauvel, who had acted as agent for the French Ambassador, Choiseul Gouffier, and remained in Athens, adding to his collection and acting as cicerone to all important visitors.

Athens the capital of Greece

Athens resurrected. Independence. – 1821-1834. On 25 April 1821 the Athenians rose in rebellion and occupied the town except for the Acropolis which held out until 10 June. Unfortunately a counter-attack launched by Ibrahim Pasha in 1826 enabled the Turks to capture Missolonghi *(p 139)* and to lay siege to Athens. Although 500 volunteers under Colonel **Fabvier,** a Frenchman, managed to breach the blockade and enter the Acropolis, the Greek troops were forced to surrender on 24 May 1827. Eleven months of fighting and bombardment had devastated the town from which the inhabitants had fled and the great olive grove of 150 000 trees to the west of the town had been almost totally destroyed by fire. Worse still, despite the War of Independence ending in 1829, the Acropolis remained in Turkish hands until 1834 when Otho of Bavaria made his triumphal entry into Athens which succeeded Nauplion as the capital of the new state of Greece; the population numbered barely 4 000.

Athens transformed: first neo-Classical era. – 1834-1900. In 1832 the Great Powers imposed on Greece a German king, the young **Otho of Bavaria,** son of Ludwig I of Bavaria, who had a passion for both Greece and Lola Montes.

In the reign of Otho and Queen Amalia, a policy of great works was inaugurated under the aegis of the Bavarian architect, Leo von Klenze. A new town with straight streets was traced out in a triangular area based on Odós Ermoú with Odós Pireós (Panagí Tsaldári) and Odós Stadíou forming the two sides and meeting in Omónia Square. After 1860 new districts were developed: to the east of Síndagma Square (the foreign embassy district and to the north round the axes formed by Odós Patissíon and Odós Sólonos. In 1861 the population of Athens reached 41 298.

Many of the buildings from this period were in the neo-Classical style: imposing and severe public monuments, modest houses with cornices and acroteria; the latter have unfortunately almost all been pulled down. The main German contributions were the Royal Palace, the University, the Academy and the Observatory. The parliament building, however, was designed by a French architect, Boulanger, and another Frenchman, Daniel, was responsible for public works (roads, sewers etc.). Kleanthes, a Greek architect, worked more on houses for private clients: the Duchess of Plaisance' residence in Ilissia and his own house in Pláka.

Athens' expansion. – After 1900. When the Greeks from the district of Smyrna in Asia Minor were expelled by the Turks in 1922, a wave of refugees settled in Athens, mainly in the district north of Piraeus, as can be seen from the popular suburb of New Smyrna **(Néa Smírni)** where the population rose from 292 991 in 1920 to 452 919 in 1928.

The city has continued to expand: the old-fashioned cornice houses have been replaced with concrete blocks of flats often mounted on arcades. The lower slopes of Lycabettos have been covered by the elegant Kolonáki district; the Ilissos now runs underground beneath a broad highway; the outer districts of detached houses now extend from Kifissiá in the north to Phaleron (Fáliro) in the south. After the Second World War new buildings were concentrated along Leofóros Vassilíssis Sofías: Hilton Hotel and the American Embassy by Gropius and the Athens Tower at Ambelókipi are the most striking constructions.

THE ATHENIAN WAY OF LIFE

For tourists the centre of Athens is Síndagma Square with its large hotels, its travel agencies and airline companies, its banks and famous open-air cafés. Bars and night clubs crowd the side streets. Women's dress shops line Odós Ermoú which extends the axial perspective from the main square towards Piraeus.

Southwest of Síndagma Square lies Pláka, an old district of narrow streets and little squares with terraces perched on the lower slopes of the Acropolis hill; it is very lively in the evenings when tourists throng the souvenir shops and the tavernas resound with bouzoúki music interspersed with the exploits of sirtáki dancers. Lysikrates Square (Platía Lysikrátous) is the home of the shadow theatre "Karagiósis" *(p 13).*

Pláka merges into Monastiráki *(northwest),* an old Turkish bazaar which has become a sort of flea market *(particulary on Sunday mornings).*

Northeast of Síndagma Square lies Kolonáki, an elegant district where the wealthy Athenians live. Beyond Kolonáki Square the streets run straight up the slopes of Lycabettos; some are so steep they end in flights of steps and cars are excluded. Here are the luxury shops: antiques, high class groceries and pastrycooks.

Síndagma Square is joined to Omónia Square *(northwest)* by two busy shopping streets, Odós Stadíou and Odós Venizélou, which is better known to Athenians as Odós Panepistimíou, lined by smart hotels and restaurants and shops overflowing on to the pavement.

Omónia Square is a very lively and crowded place in the less expensive part of town which has retained some of its oriental atmosphere. The streets are full of small shops and businesses belonging to tradesmen and artisans. Running south from Omónia Square Odós Athinas passes through the Central Market (Kendrikí Agorá), a huge covered market which sells a fascinating and astonishing variety of foodstuffs.

On fine evenings the Athenians stroll in Síndagma or Omónia Square or in the Zapio Garden where they dine at the restaurants or attend the popular musical entertainment. Lycabettos *(café-restaurant)* has a magnificent view south over Athens while Pedío Áreos is known for its open-air cinemas. Well worth while are the open-air productions at the Herod Atticus Odeon (Athens Festival of music and theatre), at the Philopappos Theatre (**T2** – traditional national dancing) and at the new Lycabettos Theatre (**T1**). The Son et Lumière spectacle on the Acropolis *(see below)* is also to be recommended.

THE SITE OF ATHENS

The hills surrounding the centre of the city give a good view of the natural location in which the conurbation has developed and of the different districts and main features.

Lycabettos★★★ (Likavitós) (CX). – Lycabettos (Wolves' Hill) rises to 277m – 909ft and is crowned by a chapel dedicated to St George. Its characteristic silhouette is marked by the steep sides and the pink-grey limestone peak (old quarries). Formerly it was isolated in the barren countryside but now it has been planted with pine trees and cactus bushes and the lower slopes have been invaded by housing.

Access. – *By funicular from the top of Odós Ploutárhou to the summit (large café-restaurant).* The descent can be made on foot by a winding path which ends at the Hotel St George-Lycabettos (**CX**).

Other paths wind through the pine trees to the Kolonáki district (attractive views down over Athens and the Acropolis). It is also possible to drive up by car to the terrace between the main peak and the new tubular theatre (**CX T1**).

The two terraces next to St George's Chapel offer an admirable **panorama★★★** embracing the city of Athens, the Acropolis, the sea coast at Piraeus and the Saronic Gulf as well as the major mountain peaks: the long ridge of Hymettos (SE) silhouetted against the sky, the Pentelikon (E) riddled with quarries and Parnes (N) with its massive bulk.

Philopappos Hill★★★ (Lófos Filopápou) (BY). – *Access: by car taking the road which ends in a car park below the Philopappos Monument; on foot taking the winding path which starts near the Dionysos Restaurant.*

In antiquity Philopappos Hill (alt 147m – 482ft) was dedicated to the Muses and bore the name **Mouseion.**

The path climbs up through groves of pine trees and oleander bushes past ancient troglodyte cave-dwellings; one was long thought to be **Socrates' prison (Z)** where he was detained before drinking the fatal hemlock and from which he refused to escape despite the exhortations of Krito.

The hill is dominated by the **Philopappos Monument** (116 AD) **(B)**, which was raised by the Athenians in memory of a prince of Syrian origin, who became a Roman consul and a citizen and benefactor of Athens. The major part of the façade has survived; it is decorated with low reliefs *(lower level)* of the prince upright in his chariot and *(above in a recess)* with an effigy of the prince seated. On the base are scratched the names of three 18C French travellers: Choiseul-Gouffier, French Ambassador to the Porte in 1783, who toured in Greece in 1776 and 1780; Foucherot, a draughtsman, who accompanied him in 1176 and Fauvel, a painter, who accompanied him in 1780 and later acted as his agent in Athens with instructions to "pillage" all he could.

From the monument there are spectacular **views★★★**, particularly at sunset, of the Acropolis, Athens, Hymettos and the plain of Attica extending south to the Saronic Gulf.

The road down passes St Demetrios' Chapel (Ágios Dimítrios) (Byzantine paintings) near a Tourist Pavilion *(refreshments)*. The road circles round to the south to the **Philopappos Theatre (T2)** (remarkable performances of traditional dances produced by the Dóra Strátou company every evening in summer) which is set about with pine and cypress trees.

PRINCIPAL SIGHTS

Ancient Athens

Acropolis★★★ (Akrópoli) (BY). – *Open 7.30am to 7.30pm (8am to 6pm Sundays); 8am to 5.30pm in winter; 400 Dr.*

Main entrance in Leofóros Dioníssou Areopagítou which passes the Theatre of Dionysos *(p 53)* and the Odeon of Herod Atticus *(p 54)*. The no. 16 bus from Síndagma Square stops near the entrance. There is another path on the north side of the hill which can be reached via Pláka or the old Agora and the Panathenaic Way. In summer avoid the midday heat. An extensive programme of restoration and conservation work is in progress on the Acropolis; it is scheduled to last until 1993 so some areas may be closed temporarily.

The artistic climax of Greek architecture, the Acropolis, meaning the upper town, which attracts about 4 500 000 visitors per year, stands on the summit of a steep rock platform. It measures 270m – 885ft long by 156m – 512ft wide and covers an area of 4 ha – just under 10 acres. It reaches a height of 156m – 512ft and dominates the lower town by 100m – 329ft.

The Acropolis comprises traces of construction from various periods dating back to the second millenium BC (Mycenaean period) but the principal buildings – the Propylaia, the Temple of Athena Nike, the Erechtheion and the Parthenon – are all in white Pentelic

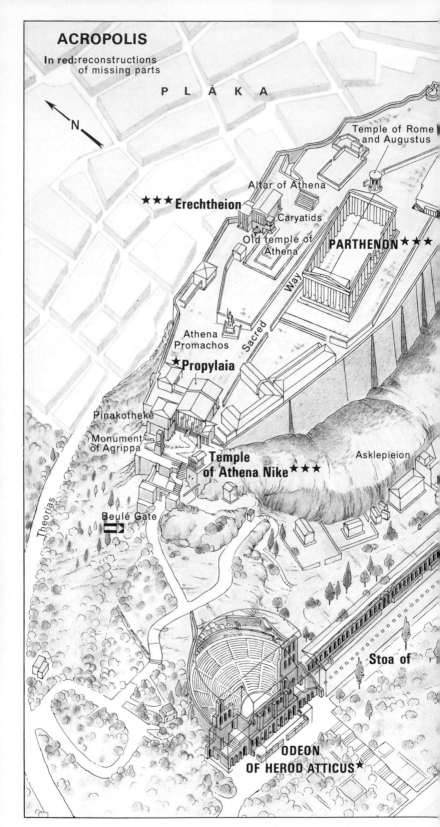

ACROPOLIS

In red: reconstructions of missing parts

PLÁKA

N

Temple of Rome and Augustus

Altar of Athena

★★★ Erechtheion

Caryatids

Old temple of Athena

PARTHENON ★★★

Sacred Way

Athena Promachos

★ Propylaia

Pinakotheke

Monument of Agrippa

Asklepieion

Temple of Athena Nike ★★★

Theorias

Beulé Gate

Stoa of

ODEON
OF HEROD ATTICUS ★

marble and belong to the Age of Pericles (5C BC). The air pollution in recent years has
made it necessary to take steps to protect the stone and to replace the remaining
sculptures with copies.

The entrance to the Acropolis is known as the **Beulé Gate** since it was discovered in
1853 beneath the Turkish bastion by a French archaeologist Ernest Beulé. The gate, which
was flanked by two towers, is late Roman. Beyond is a flight of steps, also Roman, which
is flanked by the Temple of Athena Nike *(south) (p 51)* and a pedestal of grey Hymettos marble
(north) (12m-39ft) which in about 15 BC supported the quadriga of Agrippa, Augustus'
son-in-law. Before the Roman period the entrance to the Acropolis was below the Temple

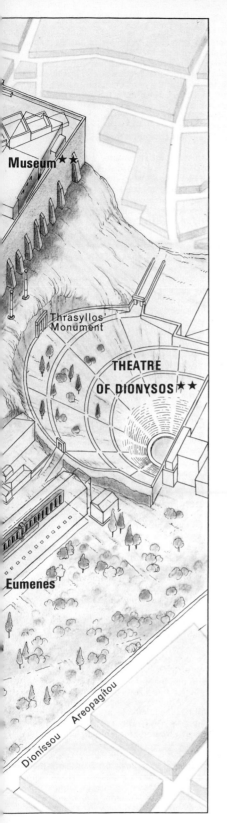

Museum ★★

Thrasyllos' Monument

THEATRE OF DIONYSOS ★★

Eumenes

Dionissou

Areopagitou

of Athena Nike; it consisted of a steep ramp continuing the Sacred Way along which the Panathenaic processions made their way up to the temple.

A projecting terrace north of the Agrippa Monument gives a good view of the three hills to the west: Philopappos, the Pnyx and the Areopagos; in the Middle Ages steps led down from the terrace to the Klepsydra Spring which was discovered in 1873.

Propylaia ★. – The monumental gates to the Acropolis, the Propylaia, were built by the architect Mnesikles using a combination of blue Eleusinian marble and Pentelic marble. They consist of a central section flanked by two asymetrical returning wings.

From 12C to 15C they were adapted to create a palace for the bishops and dukes of Athens; a square defensive tower, the "Frankish Tower", was erected on the south wing. The Turks reinforced the fortifications by the addition of bastions and it was not until 1836 that the Propylaia were stripped of their military accretions; the Frankish Tower was demolished by Schliemann in 1875.

The central section was preceded by a portico with a triangular pediment; it was supported on fluted Doric columns without capitals of which six remain. The vestibule in the central section consisted of three parallel passages divided by two rows of three Ionic columns; part of the coffered ceiling has been reconstructed. Part of the east wall of the vestibule still exists; it contained five wooden doors of which the one in the centre opened into a Doric portico similar to the western porch and giving access to the Sacred Way within the Acropolis.

The north wing was divided into a portico and a gallery for exhibiting paintings, the Pinakotheke; the south wing consisted simply of a portico.

On passing through the Propylaia, one comes face to face with the graceful silhouette of the Erechtheion *(left)* and the majestic golden pile of the Parthenon *(right);* the intervening space is scattered with blocks of marble, fragments of monuments or votive offerings long gone. Opposite the Propylaia stood the **statue of Athena Promachos** (9m – 30ft high), an impressive warrior figure, designed in bronze by **Pheidias** to commemorate the Athenian victory over the Persians.

The Sacred Way skirts the north side of the Parthenon to reach the entrance.

Parthenon ★★★. – The Doric temple known as the Parthenon was built under Pericles and dedicated to Athena whose statue in gold and ivory, designed by Pheidias, adorned the sanctuary. Pheidias was also responsible for the sculptures decorating the pediments, friezes and metopes, all of which were painted in vivid colours.

The statue of Athena was removed to Constantinople in the Byzantine period and destroyed by the inhabitants in 1203 when the city was besieged by the Crusaders. The Parthenon was then converted into a church dedicated to the Holy Wisdom and richly decorated with frescoes and mosaics; the entrance was moved to the west end. After eight centuries of Orthodox worship the church was plundered by the Franks who converted it to the Roman rite under the title of St Mary of Athens.

The Turks converted the Parthenon into a mosque and built a minaret at the southwest corner. The building however still retained the majority of its sculptures which were recorded by Jacques Carrey, a painter employed by the Marquis de Nointel, before the explosion of the powder magazine in 1687 destroyed many of them and brought down the Parian marble roof slabs, the walls of the *naós* and 28 columns.

ATHENS ★★★

When **Lord Elgin** arrived in Constantinople as British Ambassador to the Porte he obtained a firman from the Sultan granting him permission to make copies and models of ancient buildings, to erect scaffolding, to dig down to the foundations and to remove any interesting pieces. His agents in Athens induced the local Turkish authorities to allow pieces of sculpture to be removed from the temple itself. About eighteen months later he obtained further written documents saying that the Turkish government approved all that the local authorities in Athens had done to assist him in his acquisitions. Elgin's purpose in acquiring his collection of antiquities had been to improve artistic taste and design in Britain. His expenses, which he had hoped to recover from the government, made him bankrupt and he was finally forced to sell his collection to the British Museum at half the cost of obtaining it.

Since 1834 efforts have been made to restore the structure, particularly the re-erection of the colonnades, a difficult operation known as anastylosis *(p 18)*, which was carried out by Greek archaeologists after the First World War. The iron clamps used in this early work have since rusted causing the marble to crack and are now being replaced by titanium clamps. The current programme, which is scheduled to last for ten years, also involves protecting the stone from atmospheric pollution and the rock floor from the erosion caused by the feet of thousands of tourists.

Exterior. – The Parthenon rests on a marble stylobate and is surrounded by a peristyle of 46 fluted columns (8 at the ends and 17 down each side) which measures 10.43m – 34 1/4ft high, 1.90m – 6 1/4ft across at the base and 1.45m – 4 3/4ft across at the height of the capitals.

The pediments were decorated with painted sculptures against a blue background. The east pediment showed the Birth of Athena, rising fully armed from the head of Zeus in the presence of the Sun (Helios) and the Moon (Selene) who are driving their chariots; this description of the scene is taken from the mouldings of the originals now kept in the British Museum. The west pediment represented the Quarrel between Athena and Poseidon for possession of Attica; two very damaged pieces have survived.

The Doric frieze consisted of the usual triglyphs alternating with 92 metopes showing sculpted battle scenes against a red ground: the Battle between the Giants and the Olympian Gods *(east),* the Battle between the Lapiths and the Centaurs *(south),* the Battle between the Greeks and the Amazons *(west)* and the Siege of Troy *(north).* Only a few of the original metopes still exist; there are 15 in the British Museum, one in the Louvre in Paris and several others in the Acropolis Museum *(p 51).*

The shields presented by Alexander the Great were attached to the architrave.

Interior. – *Closed to the public.* The east portico *(prónaos – p 18)* where the offerings were placed led into the sanctuary through a door 10m – 33ft high.

The inner chamber *(naós)* contained a gigantic statue of Athena (12m – 39ft high); it was made of a wooden frame covered with ivory and gold (more than a tonne of gold was used); a few base blocks show where it stood.

Behind the *naós* there was another chamber, the Parthenon itself, which housed the treasure of the Delian League; four Ionic colums supported the ceiling.

The wall enclosing the *naós* and the Parthenon was decorated on the outside with the **frieze of the Panathenaia;** it was 160m – 525ft long and started at the southwest corner extending round both sides towards the entrance. This famous band of sculpture, which contained 400 human figures and 200 animals, showed the procession which took place every four years at the end of the festival in honour of Athena; it consisted of the young girls bearing gifts and baskets *(kanephoroi)* and the magistrates, musicians and men on horseback coming to offer the goddess the tunic which had been woven and embroidered by the young Athenian women. About 50 pieces, the best preserved, are displayed in the British Museum; a few others can be seen in the Acropolis Museum.

The west portico *(opisthódomos)* was a symmetrical counterpart of the *prónaos;* there are traces of a Turkish minaret near the southwest corner.

Cross the area between the Parthenon and the Erechtheion: foundations of the earlier temple of Athena built in the early 6C BC and destroyed a hundred years later to make room for the Erechtheion.

Erechtheion ★★★. – *Restoration in progress: interior closed.*

The design of this little Doric and Ionic temple, which was completed in 407 BC, is unexpectedly complicated because of the sloping ground and because several existing shrines had to be incorporated in it; the most important of these were the shrines of Athena, Poseidon and of Erechtheos and Creops, kings of Athens, to which the Panathenaic procession made its way. During the following centuries the building was used as a church, a palace, a harem and a military powder magazine. After Greece had gained her independence it was restored under the auspices of Piscatory, the French Ambassador in Athens.

The famous southern portico faces the Parthenon. It is known as the **Porch of the Caryatids** because it is supported by six statues of young women, over 2m – 6ft 6ins high; their expressions are calm and noble and their garments fall in vertical parallel folds resembling the fluting on the columns which they replace. In fact the present figures are copies; one of the originals was removed by Elgin and is in the British Museum; the others were removed in 1977 to protect them from further decay and are on display in the Acropolis Museum.

The eastern portico, supported on six Ionic columns, opens into the sanctuary which contained the oldest statue of Athena which was made of olive wood.

The western façade was altered in the Roman period. The olive tree in the adjoining courtyard was planted as a reminder that the sacred olive tree of Athena was venerated in this temple.

From the belvedere in the northeast corner of the site there are dramatic views★★ over the Roman town (E) (Hadrian's Arch, temple of Zeus), down into the old district of Plaka (N) and over the northern suburbs of Athens.

Make for the Acropolis Museum skillfully recessed in a hollow in the rock.

Acropolis Museum ★ ★ ★. – *Open 7.30am to 7.30pm (8am to 6pm Sundays); closed Tuesdays.*
It contains the sculptures and other objects found during the excavation of the Acropolis, in particular a remarkable series of Archaic works. The entrance hall contains a bust of Alexander the Great (end of 4C BC). Rooms 1 *(entrance)* and 2 *(left)* display the pediments or fragments of pediments, carved and painted, which date from 7C and 6C BC; these pieces are often in tufa rather than the marble of the Classical period. The subject of the sculptures is often the legend of Hercules (Herakles in Greek): Hercules and the many headed Hydra of Lerna *(Room 1)*, the Apotheosis of Hercules from the old temple of Athena *(Room 2)*, Hercules' struggle with Triton and a three headed monster *(Room 2)*. Also in Room 2: a beautiful fragment (the forequarters) of a marble quadriga, the Pediment of the Olive Tree showing the olive tree against the house wall *(left)*, and above all the **Moscophoros**, a young man carrying a sacrificial calf, a painted marble statue with eyes originally of glass paste.
Room 3 presents a Bull being attacked by a lion in front of a sphinx-like acroterion. In Room 4 a seated figure of Athena is surrounded by a collection of statues of young women called **korai**, in coloured marble (6C BC) with slight malicious smiles: early *korai* standing erect like columns, Ionian *korai* richly ornamented, Attic *korai* more austere. One of the latter is by Phaidimos, the oldest Attic sculptor to have been identified; also by him are an extraordinarily life-like Dog, a Horseman and a Lion's Head.
Room 5 contains four statues from the pediment (*c*525 BC) from the old temple of Athena, which were part of a scene illustrating the Battle between the Gods and the Giants: Athena brandishing a lance.
Near the entrance *(left)* to Room 6 is the famous "**mourning Athena**", a 5C votive relief; nearby is the "Fair Head" of a young man in marble which was formerly coloured yellow (early 5C BC). Also in this room: young man's head in marble from Pheidias' studio and the forequarters of a horse (5C BC).
Room 7 is devoted to reconstructions of the Parthenon pediments: Birth of Athena, Quarrel between Athena and Poseidon. There is one original metope from the Doric frieze showing a Centaur abducting a Lapith woman.
Room 8 contains sculptures removed from the temples: the Panathenaic procession from the Parthenon and from the temple of Athena Nike the figure of **Nike** (Victory) undoing her sandal before offering a sacrifice, a marvellously balanced and fluid figure.
In the last room the famous **caryatids** from the Erechtheion are displayed behind a protective glass screen.
On leaving the museum walk along the southern edge of the Acropolis hill: interesting views down over the theatres of Dionysos and Herod Atticus.

Temple of Athena Nike ★ ★ ★. – *Closed to the public.* The temple, which was formerly but incorrectly known as the **temple of Nike Apteros** (Wingless Victory), stands on a projecting bastion west of the Propylaia overlooking the Sacred Way. According to legend, Theseus' father, old Aigeus, threw himself down from here believing his son to be dead, when he saw the black sail hoisted instead of the white on the vessel in which his son was returning from Crete after defeating the Minotaur *(p 210)*.
It was a small (8.27m by 5.44m – 27ft by 18ft) but graceful Ionic temple (late 5C BC) which was reconstructed by the Bavarian archaeologists of King Otho. It consisted of a chamber *(naós)* between two porticoes supported on monolithic columns. The *naós* contained a statue of Athena Nike (bringer of victory) which was later confused with the figure of Victory which was usually represented without wings *(apteros)*. The exterior frieze, which is badly damaged, comprises a few original pieces (east and south sides); the rest is made up of copies.
From the temple there are extensive views south over the Attic plain, the coast at Piraeus and the Saronic Gulf.
Leave the Acropolis by the Beulé Gate and bear north to the Areopagos.

Areopagos ★ (Áríos Págos) (BY). – Theseus' enemies, the Amazons, camped on this limestone hill (115m – 377ft high) and consecrated it to Ares, god of War. Another legend says that **Orestes**, who was being pursued by the Furies *(p 123)*, the avenging divinities, for murdering his mother Clytemnestra, was judged here by the forerunner of the Council of the Areopagos which originally was a judicial tribunal and political assembly but later reduced to safeguarding laws and customs. In 375 BC the courtesan Phryne, friend and model of the sculptor Praxiteles, appeared before this open-air court on a charge of impiety and was acquitted; appealing to the jury in her defence Hyperides bared her bosom saying "Can such beauty be guilty?".
It was here too that **St Paul** is thought to have preached when he converted the senator who was to become St Dionysius the Areopagite, the first bishop of Athens; he was later confused with Dionysius, the Pseudo-Areopagite who invented the celestial hierarchy with nine choirs of angels.
Fine view of the Acropolis and of the Greek agora and Roman forum below.

Hephaisteion (Theseion) ★ ★ and Agora ★ (BY). – *Archaeological site open 9am to 6pm (10am to 4pm Sundays); 150 Dr. Entrances in Leofóros Apostólou Pávlou (W), Odós Adrianóu (N) and the Panathenaic Way (SE). From the Acropolis one can walk down the Sacred Way. Visitors are advised to begin with the Hephaisteion (Theseion).*

Hephaisteion ★ ★ (Thissío). – This 5C BC Doric temple, one of the best preserved in the Greek world, stands on a mound (66m – 217ft) dominating the agora, the centre of Athenian public life in antiquity.
Known since the Middle Ages as the Theseion (temple of Theseus), it is in fact the **Hephaisteion** mentioned by Pausanias, the temple of Hephaistos, god of smiths and metal workers who were as numerous then as they are today in the neighbouring district (Odós Iféstou – *p 53*).
In the Byzantine period the temple was converted into a church dedicated to St George and the entrance was moved to the west end. Under the Turks it became the burial place of Englishmen and other protestants; some of the memorial plaques have been transferred to St Paul's Church *(p 62)*. Even in the last century it was still out in the country and on

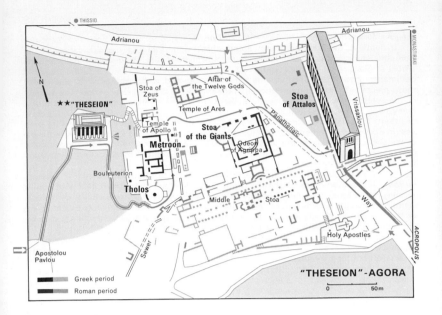

N

★★"THESEION"

Stoa of
Zeus

Altar of
the Twelve Gods

Temple of Ares

Temple
of Apollo

Metroon

Stoa
of the Giants

Stoa
of Attalos

Vissakiou

Panathenaic

Odeon
of Agrippa

Bouleuterion

Tholos

Middle   Stoa

Way

Holy Apostles

ACROPOLIS

Apostolou
Pavlou

Sewer

Greek period

Roman period

"THESEION"-AGORA

0   50m

Easter Sunday people would come from Athens dressed in their best to dance nearby. The last service was held in 1834 when the building was used to house the first collections of the National Museum. Pomegranates and myrtle trees have been planted round the temple to recall the trees which covered the slopes in antiquity.

The Hephaisteion, which is older and smaller than the Parthenon, is built of stone rather than marble but it is well proportioned and was originally painted. It measures 31.77m by 13.72m – 104ft by 45ft and has 26 columns down each side and 12 at each end which narrow towards the top and incline slightly inwards. The sculptures of the external frieze, which are badly damaged and difficult to discern, recall the exploits of Herakles (Hercules) and Theseus.

The east portico (*prónaos* – *p 18*) with its marble coffered ceiling still in place leads into the *naós*, which resembles the nave of a church with its doorways and barrel vaulting (5C AD); one of the funerary plaques on the north wall in memory of George Watson, who died in Athens in 1810, bears a Latin inscription by Byron.

The temple terrace offers fine views of the Agora, the Monastiraki district and the Acropolis.

Agora ★ (Arhéa Agorá). – The Agora which is now a confused jumble of ruins was originally a rectangular open space covering about 2.5 ha – 6 acres and divided diagonally by the Panathenaic Way which ran past the Altar of the Twelve Olympian Gods from which the distances to other Greek cities were measured. Large trees, fountains, statues and votive offerings dotted the ground which was enclosed within administrative buildings, temples and long porticoes of shops (stoas) where the idlers gathered to hear the news and listen to the orators.

The Romans encroached on the open space with buildings such as the Odeon of Agrippa and the temple of Ares. In 267 AD the Agora was destroyed by barbarians. Under the Byzantines a district grew up round the Church of the Holy Apostles (Ágii Apóstoli). Here lived Fauvel, French Consul during the Napoleonic Wars, who produced a plan of Athens and acted as guide to the more important travellers. His house (model in Benaki Museum) was more like a museum owing to the huge collection of antiquities he was amassing on behalf of Choiseul-Gouffier the French Ambassador in Constantinople. In 1931 the buildings were expropriated and demolished to clear the site for excavations which were conducted by the American School of Archaeology.

Leave the temple terrace and descend the slope into the agora where the first ruins are those of the thólos.

The **thólos,** which dates from about 470 BC, was a round building where the 50 senators *(prytaneis)*, responsible by turn for the government of the state, met to take their meals; the standard weights and measures were also kept here.

To the north of the *thólos* stood the **Metroon,** the temple of the Mother of the gods, behind which stood the Bouleuterion, the Senate house; beyond the Metroon stood the temple of Apollo Patroos and the Stoa of Zeus. Only the foundations of these buildings remain but there are also traces of a great drain which passed to the east of them and of pedestals for statues: one of them bears the likeness of the emperor Hadrian (1).

Turning east one sees the **Stoa of the Giants,** named in modern times after the Giant and two Tritons which originally decorated the Odeon of Agrippa, a covered chamber for 1 000 people which was built by the son-in-law of the Emperor Augustus, destroyed by the barbarians and converted into a gymnasium in about 400 BC; there is little left.

Follow the Panathenaic Way south to enter the Stoa of Attalos.

The **stoa,** which was built in 2C BC by **Attalos,** king of Pergamon, has been reconstructed. It is a long (116m by 19.5m – 380ft by 64ft), two-storeyed building which displays the articles found during the excavations in the Agora *(open 7.30am to 7.30pm; 8am to 6pm Sundays)*. The external gallery displays the Apollo Patroos (4C BC), which is headless, and the interior gallery contains objects from everyday life in antiquity, an amphora with a seated sphinx (7C BC) and a Spartan shield in bronze (5C BC) *(centre)*.

Near the entrance in Odós Adrianóu there is a mosaic reconstruction (2) showing the Agora as it was in antiquity.

Olympieion★★ and Hadrian's Arch★ (BY). – *Access: no. 16 bus from the Acropolis; no 16 bus or no 2 or no 12 trolleybus from Síndagma Square.*

Olympieion★★ (Naós Olimpíou Diós). – *Open 8.45am to 3pm (9.30am to 2.30pm Sundays); 100 Dr.*

A Corinthian colonnade is all that is left of the majestic temple of Olympian Zeus which stood on a platform of rock overlooking the Ilissos Valley and the Kallirhoë Fountain which are now covered by a modern boulevard.

As early as 6C BC the Peisistratids had chosen this site for a colossal temple in the Ionic order; a few drums measuring 2.38m – 7 3/4ft across have been found but the work was interrupted when they fell from power and not resumed until 2C BC on the initiative of Antiochos Epiphanes, king of Syria. This time the Corinthian order was adopted and marble was used instead of tufa but the death of the king halted construction and the temple was not completed until 132 AD under the Emperor Hadrian who also built the precinct and erected a colossal chryselephantine statue to Zeus. The barbarians wrecked the temple which was used as a stone quarry during the Middle Ages. In 17C it was called Hadrian's Palace; on the top of the ruins a stylite hermit established a shack which survived into the reign of Otho. Of the 84 original columns only 17 then remained. This number fell to 15 when one was pulled down in 1759 to be turned into chalk and another was brought down in a storm in 1852.

A grand gateway *(propylaia)* led into the temple which was one of the largest in the Greek world: it had two rows of 20 columns down each side and three rows of 8 columns at each end; the podium measures 107.75m by 41.10m – over 350ft by 134ft. Even today, the 15 fluted Corinthian columns with their remarkable sculpted capitals are impressive owing to their width and height: Chateaubriand compared them to Egyptian palm trees. It is worth studying the fallen column to appreciate the size of the marble drums.

From the temple precinct there are fine views of Pláka and the Acropolis silhouetted against the sky.

Hadrian's Arch★ (Píli Adrianóu). – This grand Corinthian gate in Pentelic marble looks more like a commemorative arch. The openings in the upper level were originally filled with marble plaques forming recesses for statues. In 17C it was thought to have been the entrance to Hadrian's Palace which in fact never existed.

Hadrian's Arch was built in 131-132 AD and separated the Greek city from the new Roman city as was stated in two inscriptions in Greek engraved on the frieze: "This is Athens, the ancient city of Theseus" *(west side)* and "This is the city of Hadrian and not of Theseus" *(east side)*.

Hadrian's new Roman city (Hadrianopolis) extended from the present-day Leofóros Amalias as far as the Ilissos, which is now covered: temples, villas and baths, of which several traces have been found, were surrounded by gardens and shrubberies.

Northeast of Hadrian's Arch against the southwest corner of the National Garden stands the **Byron Monument (C)** by Chapu and Falguière, French sculptors.

Theatre of Dionysos★★ (Théatro Dioníssou) (BY). – *Open 8.45am to 3pm (9.30am to 2.30pm Sundays); 100 Dr.*

The first stage to be built on this spot was set up in 6C BC within the sacred precinct dedicated to Dionysos Eleutherios where the Dionysiac Festivals consisting of mime, the chorus and the dancing of satyrs and maenads took place.

Early in the following century these rather basic facilities were improved by the addition of a real theatre equipped with wooden terraces where the great classical dramas were played: the Persians by Aeschylus, Oedipus Rex by Sophocles, Medea by Euripides and the Wasps by Aristophanes.

The present stone structure which dates from the time of Lycurgus (4C BC) provided 12 000 seats and was also used for the popular assemblies which had formerly been held on the Hill of the Pnyx.

Extensive alterations were carried out by the Romans. Following the barbarian invasions the theatre was abandoned and used for raising crops. It was restored by the German Archaelogical Society early in 19C.

Beyond the remains of a temple to Dionysos and a portico lies the stage of the theatre; its foundations date from 4C BC but it was rebuilt under Nero (1C AD): the front of the stage facing the orchestra is decorated with sculptures dating from this period which evoke the legend of Dionysos including a crouching Silenus. The marble paving of the orchestra describes a lozenge shape; at the centre stood the altar to Dionysos round which the chorus was grouped during the ancient performances.

The terraces (4C BC) are partially preserved; they rose as high as the monument to Thrasyllos, 30m – 98ft *(below)*. In the first row were the seats reserved for individuals bearing the names of the officials, priests and dignitaries who occupied them in 2C AD; the one in the centre belonged to the priest of Dionysos and is decorated with lions, griffons, satyrs and grapes.

From the top there is a good view of the site; on the left are traces of the **Odeon of Pericles,** a covered theatre which was mostly used for rehearsals.

Choregic monument of Thrasyllos. – There is nothing left but the pedestal of this votive monument which was set up by Thrasyllos, a chorus-leader *(choregós)* in 4C BC in honour of Dionysos, who was worshipped in the cave *(below)* which was later converted into a chapel (Panagía Spiliotissa) for Christian worship. The two Corinthian columns above, which date from the Roman period, bore two choregic tripods *(p 55)*.

Sanctuary of Asklepios (Asklepieion). – A long terrace west of the upper part of the theatre of Dionysos bears the remains of two sanctuaries to Asklepios (Aesculapius); one dates from 4C BC *(east)* and the other *(west)* from 5C BC. Each consisted of a small temple, a sacred spring where the sick were purified and a portico where they slept.

Stoa of Eumenes. – Below the Asklepieion, facing south, is the stoa of Eumenes II, king of Pergamon, who had it built in 2C BC. It was 163m – 535ft long and comprised two storeys of colonnades; the column bases are clearly visible. The stoa was used as a shelter and promenade for the theatre of Dionysos and later for the Odeon of Herod Atticus.

Odeon of Herod Atticus ★ (Odío Iródou Atikoú) (BY). – It is not open except for performances but there is a good view from the south path up to the Acropolis.

The Odeon was built in memory of his wife, Annia Regilla by Herod Atticus, a Greek patron of Roman origin, who became an archon, consul and senator; it was completed in 161 BC the year after her death and would then have had a cedar wood roof.

The **façade ★** is fairly well preserved; it is typically Roman with its round-headed doors and arches; there were three entrances. Inside it has been completely restored to provide a setting for the dramatic and lyric performances of the Athens Summer Festival: it can accommodate from 5 000 to 6 000 spectators.

It was through the ruins of the Odeon that help arrived for the besieged Greeks on the Acropolis on 17 December 1826 when Colonel Fabvier, a famous French Philhellene, accompanied by 500 volunteers broke through the Turkish blockade.

Byzantine and Turkish Athens *2 hours, plan p 55*

On the northern slopes of the Acropolis old Athens still survives in the Pláka and Monastiráki districts, the only ones in the capital which can evoke the atmosphere of Athens in the Middle Ages or during the Turkish occupation. The conservation of the old buildings and the exclusion of traffic have greatly enhanced the charm of the area.

Pláka ★★. – Particularly in the steeper part Pláka consists of a network of picturesque and peaceful narrow streets and alleys opening out into tiny squares and terraces linked by steps. There are a few Byzantine churches tucked in between the old houses with their pantile roofs and wooden balconies; sometimes the plume of a cypress or pine tree or the straggling branches of a fig betray the existence of a hidden garden. Here and there one catches a glimpse of the city or the Acropolis. The broader streets below the slope are thronged with shops and inexpensive guest houses.

After dark Pláka comes alive. The tavernas with their cavernous rooms decorated with barrels and their trellis covered terraces are illuminated with multicoloured lights: crowds of Athenians and tourists tarry late into the night, savouring the Greek cuisine with glasses of *retsína*, listening to the *bouzoúki* (or electric guitar) music and the latest singers and dancing the modern *sirtáki*. As well as the tavernas there are night clubs where food and drink are offered together with a show which is well done when it is based on traditional music.

From the southwest corner of Síndagma Square take Odós Mitropóleos: on the left under the arcade of a modern building is the tiny chapel of Agía Dínami (17C) which belongs to the Pendéli Monastery *(p 72)*. The street opens into a square, Platía Mitropóleos: the Orthodox cathedral, which is known as the **New Metropolitan (A1)** and dates from 19C, dwarfs its neighbour the Old Metropolitan.

Old Metropolitan ★★ (A2). – The Old Metropolitan, which is dedicated to the Virgin who answers prayers swiftly (Panagía Gorgoepíkoos), is a charming 12C Byzantine church built on the Greek cross plan with a dome; its modest proportions reflect the general height of houses in Athens at that period.

Incorporated in the external walls are many decorative pieces from an earlier age: between the two Corinthian capitals flanking the façade stretches an unusual ancient frieze (4C BC) showing the months and the signs of the Zodiac together with their corresponding festivals or activities. There are also several 9C-10C AD low reliefs of symbolic Christian motifs: lions flanking a cross *(door lintel)*; griffins feeding on the eucharistic grape and peacocks drinking at the source of eternal life. On the other hand the cross with a double bar and the arms of the La Roche and de Villehardouin families *(pediment)* were added in the Frankish period (13C).

Other sculpted marbles, both ancient and Byzantine, decorate the side walls and the chevet where there is a low relief from the Archaic period showing some dancing girls.

Take the streets going south and west, Odós Paleologou Venizélou, Odós Erehthéos and Odós Kirístou, to reach the Tower of the Winds.

Tower of the Winds ★ (G). – This is an octagonal building in white marble rising to 12.80m – about 42ft which dates from the reign of Julius Caesar (1C BC) and was then part of the Roman forum. It takes its name from the eight winged figures carved on the eight faces of the tower and identified by inscriptions; the figures represent the winds which blow in Athens.

On the north side, facing Odós Eólou, is Boreas, the cold north wind, shown as a bearded man blowing into a conch shell; on the west the gentle Zephyr strews flowers from her lap.

In fact the tower was built to house a hydraulic clock invented by Andronikos of Kyrrhos in Syria or Macedonia. The water supply came from the Klepsydra spring on the north slope of the Acropolis hill whence came the word clepsydra meaning a water clock. The semi-circular tower attached to the south face was the reservoir from which the water flowed in a steady stream into a cylinder in the main tower; the time was indicated by the level of the water in the cylinder; the northwest door of the tower stood open so that people could consult the clock.

Athens. – Tower of the Winds

In 6C the Tower of the Winds was converted into a chapel; under the Turkish occupation it became a *tekke,* a Muslim convent, and in 18C it was occupied by whirling dervishes. At that period it was thought to have been the tomb of Socrates.

North of the Tower on the corner of Odós Eólou are the remains of an 18C Muslim seminary *(medresse).*

Roman Forum (Romaikí Agorá) **(J)**. – Walk round in an anti-clockwise direction *(Odós Diogénous)* passing an old 16C mosque with domes and an attractive columned porch.

On the west side stands the monumental Forum gateway completed by the Romans in 2 AD with funds provided first by Julius Caesar and then by Augustus. The gateway consists of four columns supporting a pediment and gave access to the forum proper; the interior court, which was paved with marble and surrounded by a peristyle, has been excavated.

Walk south down Odós Dioskoúron as far as the Kanellopoulos Museum (p 63); turn left.

A little way along on the right stands the small church of the Transfiguration (Metamórfossis) which dates from 12C-14C; its dome of semicircular tiles rises above the houses of the semi-rural district of Anafiótika which was founded by refugees from Anaphe in the Cyclades.

Below and to the north of the church lies the "**Old University**" (19C) **(K)** which was originally the house of the architect Kleanthes. It housed the first university founded by the new Greek state in 1837 which later moved to its present site *(p 57).* The building is now used for exhibitions.

Continue east along Odós Stratónos to the **Church of Ágii Anárgiri (A3)** *(left),* a 17C building near two tall cypress trees in the courtyard of the convent of the Holy Sepulchre. Further on stands the 12C **Chapel of St John the Evangelist (A4)**.

Bear round to the south along the **Street of the Tripods** (Odós Tripódon), a very ancient street linking the theatre of Dionysos to the Agora, where the winners in the Dionysiac Games used to erect choregic monuments supporting the bronze tripods which they received as prizes *(see also p 53).*

Lysicrates' Monument ★ (Mnimío Lissikrátous). – The only survivor of the votive monuments in Odós Tripódon was erected in 334 BC. Subsequently in 1669 it was incorporated in the French Capucine convent where many Christian travellers, such as Sir George Wheler, Richard Chandler and Lord Byron, used to stay during the Turkish occupation. The monument was used by the holy fathers as a library and was known as the **lantern of Demosthenes** since tradition wrongly asserted that the great orator had worked there on his speeches.

The monument of Lysicrates escaped the turmoil of the War of Independence, which destroyed the convent, and was restored in 1845 by the French School of Archaeology in Athens; it is still French property.

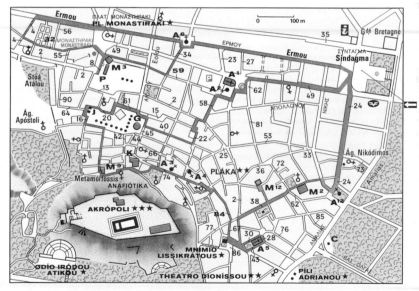

PLAKA

The monument is in the form of a rotunda, 10.20m – about 33.1/2ft high; its six columns with their remarkable Corinthian capitals are linked by white marble plaques. Above runs the dedicatory inscription together with a carved frieze showing Dionysos changing pirates into dolphins, which is presumed to be the subject of the drama competition which Lysicrates won. The roof consists of a single marble plaque topped by several acanthus leaves which supported the tripod, now disappeared. Recent excavations *(in progress)* have uncovered the bases of other similar monuments.

One of the rare "Karagiosis" shadow puppet theatres *(see p 13)* is be found on the south side of the square.

Further east on the far side of a shady square stands **St Catherine's Church** (Agía Ekateríni) **(A5)**; it was built in 13C but has been altered several times since. *(Excavations in progress)*.

Turn right into Odós Kidathinéon and then left to reach Odós A. Hatzimiháli and the Centre for Popular Art and Traditions (M12 p 63); return to Odós Kidathinéon which contains the Museum of Traditional Greek Art (M2 p 63); at the next corner turn right into Odos Nikis to visit St Paul's Anglican Church (p 62).

Turn north into Odós Filelínon to visit the Russian church of St Nicodemus (Ágios Nikódimos), an 11C building with a dome, which was extensively altered in the last century.

The north end of the street opens into Síndagma Square.

Monastiráki ★. – This was the centre of the Turkish town with the bazaar and the souks as well as the main mosques and administrative buildings sheltering under the citadel on the Acropolis hill. Now it is a popular commercial district incorporating the Athens flea market.

Start from Síndagma Square. Go west down **Odós Ermoú**, a busy shopping street lined with boutiques selling feminine apparel, dress materials and ready-to-wear clothes, furs and shoes, leather goods and jewellery.

Kapnikaréa (A6). – The church, which stands in the middle of the street at road level, is attached to the University of Athens and probably takes its name from one of its founders. In fact it is a double church consisting of two adjoining chapels, one *(right)* dates from 11C and is built on the Greek cross plan, the other dates from 13C and is roofed with a dome. The narthex joining the two was also built in 13C. Although in the Byzantine style, the paintings are in fact modern.

From the church walk south down Odós Kapnikaréas and turn right into Odós Pandróssou.

Odós Pandróssou ★. – This is a narrow street, thronged with busy crowds, tightly packed; it resembles a market with awnings and pavement stalls where the proprietors stand touting for custom. There is an amazing range of articles for sale: Turkish slippers, shoes with pompoms *(tsaroúhias)*, carpets and embroidery, *palikares'* belts, gold and copper work, incised or embossed, icons and ceramics, etc.

On the left was the entrance to the bazaar, a market set up in the ruins of Hadrian's Library which burned down in 1885.

Odós Pandróssou ends in Monastiráki Square.

Monastiráki Square ★. – This square, with its frippery goods displayed on open air stalls, is one of the attractions of Athens; it is always very lively, particularly in the morning. The church, Pandánassa, is a 17C building heavily restored, which originally belonged to the convent from which the square takes its name.

At the junction of Odós Pandróssou with Odós Áreos stands the former **Djisdaráki Mosque (M3)** (1759); it has lost its minaret but it was skillfully restored in 1975 to house the **Museum of Traditional Greek Ceramics** *(temporarily closed)*; pottery and porcelain from the different regions is pleasantly displayed in the setting of a Muslim place of worship with its mihrab (recess facing Mecca) and its galleries.

Hadrian's Library (P). – The destruction by fire of the bazaar in 1885 made it possible to investigate the remains of the Library built by the Emperor Hadrian in 132 BC and described by Pausanias.

It was an impressive rectangular building, 122m by 82m – 400ft by 269ft, with a peristyle of 100 columns, which was devastated by the barbarians and restored in 5C BC when a quatrefoil building was constructed in the library courtyard; this building was subsequently replaced by two churches, one in 7C, the other in 11-12 C; the remaining columns belonged to the 7C church.

The façade containing the entrance (Odós Áreos) is quite well preserved, particularly the Corinthian colonnade which is made of Euboian marble. It is about half the length of the original façade which preceded the courtyard where the foundation of the Byzantine church are visible. The Library proper, where the books were housed, stood on the far side of the courtyard.

Return to Monastiráki Square and continue westwards along **Odós Iféstou**, the street which is named after Hephaistos, the god to whom the nearby temple, the Hephaisteion (Theseion) *(p 51)* is dedicated. Nowadays as in antiquity it is devoted to metal workers, particularly coppersmiths.

Modern Athens *2 hours*

Central Market ★★ (Kendrikí Agorá) **(BX)**. – When the Bazaar was burnt down in 1885, the Athens market was moved to the new part of town which developed in the reign of King Otho where it still functions in a quasi-oriental atmosphere presenting an extraordinary variety of goods for sale to both city dwellers and country folk against an aroma of exotic spices.

The meat market with its stalls lining the long alleys is a spectacular sight; so too are the egg vendors whose merchandise is hung on the walls and the goldsmiths and money changers with their scales on the north side (Odós Sofokléous).

There is a project to transfer the market to another site, "Varvakiós agorá", and to retain the present buildings as a historic monument.

From the south side of the market go west along Odós Evripídou to no. 72 where at the back of a small square stands the **Chapel of St John of the Column (A7)**, which was built round a Corinthian column; the chapel is much sought after for curing fevers.

Kodziá Square, to the north of the Central Market, was formerly named after Otho's father, Ludwig of Bavaria, and was the centre of Athens in the second half of 19C; the square was planted with palm trees and lined with private mansions such as the residence of the Duchess of Plaisance *(pp 60 and 72);* at the centre stood the Municipal Theatre. The National Bank of Greece (Ethnikí Trápeza tis Eládos) on the east side was founded in 1842 by a Philhellene J.-G. Eynard (Lyon 1775-Athens 1863). Opposite stands the original Town Hall; the offices are to be transferred to Vathis Square – 22 Odós Liossíon while the building will be used to house a public library, meeting rooms and an exhibition hall for modern sculpture.

Síndagma Square – Omónia Square★. – **Síndagma** (Constitution) **Square** (Platía tou Sindágmatos) **(CY)** is a spacious piece of town planning in the elegant part of Athens which attracts the tourists. The east side is filled by the former royal palace, built by the Bavarian architect, Gartner for Otho I of Bavaria, which became the Parliament *(Vouli)* House in 1935. It is a solemn and austere building, covered with a coat of rose-tinted ochre plaster which catches the light particularly at sunset. The Constitution of 1843 was proclaimed by King Otho from the balcony. To the south lies an extensive garden.

In front of the palace, before the Monument to the Unknown Soldier, two soldiers **(évzoni)** stand guard; they are dressed in the distinctive kilt *(fustanélla)* and pompom shoes *(tsaroúhias).* From time to time they emerge from their boxes to perform a sort of military ballet, very graceful but precise, before retreating like two automata into their boxes. The spectacle is particularly grand on Sundays *(11am)* when the ceremony is conducted with additional military personnel, dressed in smarter uniforms and accompanied by a band.

On the north side of the square stands the famous Hotel Grande Bretagne, which began life in 1843 as a private house, was occupied from 1856 to 1874 by the French School of Archaeology and was then rebuilt from the first floor up as a hotel. It was occupied successively by Greek, German and British forces during the Second World War; an attempt to blow it up on Christmas Eve 1944 when Churchill was visiting Athens was fortunately foiled.

Panepistimíou★ (BCXY). – Venizelos Avenue (Leofóros Venizélou), which starts from the northwest corner of the square, is better known to the Athenians by its former name, University Avenue (Leofóros Panepistimíou). At first it is lined by luxury hotels, large terraced cafés, restaurants, cake shops and smart boutiques. **Schliemann's House** (Iliou Melathron) **(R)** *(right)* is a large private house which the brilliant German archaeologist had built in 1879 in the style of a Venetian Renaissance palace; it is now used for exhibitions but is scheduled to house the Numismatic Museum *(p 60).* Further on stands the Roman Catholic cathedral, consecrated in 1865 to **St Dionysius the Areopagite (A8)** *(right).*

Academy, University, Library★ (BCX). – These three 19C buildings in white Pentelic marble compose an architectural group in the elegant but slightly arid neo-Classical style.

The University (Panepistímio) in the centre is the oldest of the three buildings; it was designed by Christian von Hansen, the Danish architect, and built between 1837 and 1864; the pure design of the façade is outstanding. Near the pavement stands a statue of Gladstone *(p 83)* who is also remembered in the name of a nearby street.

The Academy (Akadimía) *(right)* was paid for by Baron Sina, a Greek banker in Vienna, and designed by Theophilos von Hansen (1813-91), Christian's brother, in the style of an Ionic temple; it is flanked by two tall columns surmounted by statues of Apollo and Athena.

The National Library (Ethnikí Vivliothíki) *(left),* which is reminiscent of a Doric temple, countains 500 000 volumes and 3 000 manuscripts.

The entrance hall displays a collection of books, newspapers and other documents connected with the Greek struggle for independence including a History of the Greek Revolution by George Finlay *(p 63)* and a Prospectus (1824) for a news sheet to be called the "Greek Telegraph" and to be compiled in Missolonghi.

Omónia Square (BX). – A complete contrast with Síndagma Square is provided by Omónia (Concord) Square with its noise and crowds, its marked oriental atmosphere which is more obvious to a Western European in the evening.

In Platía Kanningos, northeast of Omónia Square, stands a statue of **George Canning** who as Foreign Secretary in 1823 reversed the previous British indifference to the Greeks' struggle for independence and subsequently supported their aim through a policy of "peaceful interference". The other name is that of a relative who was killed in Greece in the Second World War.

Return to Síndagma Square by Odós Stadíou (southeast corner), parallel to Odós Panepistimíou.

At the start Odós Stadíou is a shopping street; half way along on the south side is Klafthmónos (Wailing) Square, named after the civil servants of the neighbouring ministries who came there to bewail their lot when they were dismissed. In the west corner stands **St Theodore's Church (A9)** (11C), the oldest in Athens; the dome rests on the walls instead of columns.

Beyond Klafthmónos Square *(east)* stands an equestrian statue of **Kolokotrónis (S),** a hero of the War of Independence, in Kolokotrónis Square in front of the old Parliament which was built by Florimond Boulanger from 1858 to 1871 and vacated in 1935; the chamber has been preserved and the attendant rooms now house the National Historical Museum *(p 63).*

Return to Síndagma Square.

National Garden★ (Ethnikós Kípos) and **Zappeion** (Zápio) **(CY).** – The former royal garden, which was designed by Friedrich Schmidt (1811-1889) for Queen Amalia, covers only 14ha – under 35 acres and is not laid out to a regular plan but it is pleasant to stroll in the shade of its abundant vegetation, past its pools and flower beds, its fine palm trees, orange trees, cypresses and Aleppo pines, particularly in the heat of high summer. There are some 500 species of trees and plants, a botanical museum (charming neo-Classical building) and a small zoo. The statues of several famous men – Kapodístria, J.-G. Eynard and John Moréas – have been set up here and there.

Adjoining the National Garden to the south is the Zappeion Park overlooking the Ilissos Valley. It is named after the Záppas brothers, who gave the land, and is very popular, particularly in the evenings, with the Athenians who come to listen to the singing.

The **Zappeion Hall** (Zápio) is a pleasant neo-Classical building which is now used for exhibitions; it was designed by Florimond Boulanger and T. von Hansen and built between 1874 and 1888. The internal peristyle is a successful combination of an Ionic colonnade at ground level and an upper gallery of short columns shaped like herms. The instrument admitting Greece to the Common Market (EEC) was signed here in 1979.

Museums

National Archaeological Museum ★★★ (Ethnikó Arheologikó Moussío) (BX). – *Open 8am to 7pm (8am to 6pm Sundays); 8am to 5.30pm in winter; closed Mondays; 300 Dr. Snack bar (and WC) in the basement. Light refreshments in the shade in the forecourt.*

The Archaeological Museum, which is devoted to ancient art from the neolithic period to the Roman era, is one of the richest in the world and displays the major works of art from the Greek archaeological sites, except for Macedonia, Delphi, Olympia and Crete. It was founded in 1834 in the Hephaisteion (Theseion) and transferred in 1874 to the present neo-Classical buildings which were later enlarged. Sculpture is displayed on the ground floor, ceramics on the first floor.

It is easier to envisage the exhibits in their original setting and period and therefore more worthwhile to visit the Museum after seeing the main archaeological sites on the mainland and the islands.

Neolithic antiquities (8000-3000 BC) and **Cycladic** (3000-2000 BC):

Room 5. Idols and ceramics originating in Thessaly in particular.

Room 6. Stylised marble idols with rounded contours originating in the Cyclades: near the entrance a female figure of the earth-mother goddess from Amorgós and some musicians *(see also Museum of Cycladic and Ancient Greek Art, p 61).*

Mycenaean antiquities (16C-11C BC):

Room 4. This room, the most famous in the museum, is mainly devoted to the finds from the excavations conducted at Mycenae since 1876 by Schliemann and his successors. There are also objects from the same period found on other sites in the Peloponnese such as Tiryns, Argos and Pylos:

1 – in a case left of the entrance, the "**mask of Agamemnon**", the famous funerary mask of an Achaian king discovered by Schliemann in the Mycenae acropolis (5th tomb in the 1st circle) and believed by him to be the mask of Agamemnon; in the same case, bronze daggers with blades encrusted with gold, silver and enamel (Mycenae, same tomb); in a neighbouring case, hexagonal wooden box covered with embossed gold plate showing lions pursuing deer (same tomb)

2 – a flask (rhyton) used for libations in the shape of a **bull's head** in silver with gold horns and muzzle and a gold rosette (Mycenae, 4th tomb in 1st circle)

3 – a shallow vessel, like a sauceboat, in the shape of a duck made of rock crystal (tomb in 2nd circle)

4 – a woman's or sphinx's head in limestone painted so as to pick out the features in vivid colours (Mycenae: house on the acropolis)

5 – two admirable **Vapheio Cups** wrought in embossed gold, discovered at Vafió near Sparta and decorated with scenes showing (on one) the capture of a bull and (on the other) the animal's domestication by man; in a further case, a seal ring in gold: spirits with lions' heads offer libations to a goddess holding a cup (Tiryns Treasury)

Return to the entrance hall and turn right into Room 7.

Geometric and Archaic art (10C, 6C BC)

Room 7. The main attraction is the huge geometric amphora (6) dating from mid-8C which had been placed on a tomb in the Kerameikos cemetery: the key pattern decoration frames a funeral cortege. The wooden statue of Artemis was found on Delos.

Room 8. The "Dipylon Head" which was found near the gate of the same name *(p 61)* is beautifully sculpted, particularly the hair; it belonged to a funerary *kouros (p 19)* standing on a tomb. The huge votive *kouros* from Sounion (7) once stood in front of the first temple to Poseidon erected on Cape Sounion *(p 67).*

Room 9. Several *kouroi* or *korai* from Attica and the Cyclades.

Room 11. The most remarkable exhibit here is the funerary stele of Aristion, "**the warrior of Marathon**" (8), sculpted by Aristokles who signed his name at the bottom. There is also a small funerary stele in the name of Antiphanes found in the Kerameikos.

Room 12. Here is an unusual tombstone showing a "running hoplite" or a Pyrrhic dancer.

Room 13. It contains a superb funerary *kouros* (9) from Anávissos in Attica: an inscription states that the statue used to decorate the tomb of Kroisos. The statue of Aristodikos, one of the later *kouroi*, shows the transition from Archaic to Classical art. The bases of statues discovered in Themistocles' wall are decorated with low reliefs showing ephebes practising physical exercises: wrestling, throwing, hockey and chariot racing.

Room 14. Among the tombstones and votive tablets there is a votive relief in honour of a goddess with a pure Greek profile holding an apple (Aphrodite?).

Classical art (5C-4C-3C BC):

Room 15. Two of the museum's masterpieces are exhibited here:

(10) the extraordinary **Artemision Poseidon**, a bronze statue which was salvaged from the sea off Cape Artemision at the northern end of Euboia. The Sea god holds the symbolic trident in his right hand; the figure is superbly posed with a delicate and noble head, although the ivory eyeballs are missing from the sockets.

(11) the **Eleusinian Relief** is admirable for its solemnity and the composition of the figures; Demeter *(left)*, the goddess of fertility and protector of agriculture, accompanied by her daughter Persephone, is presenting an ear of corn to Triptolemos, son of the king of Eleusis, who has been entrusted with teaching agriculture to the human race.

Room 20. Here stand Roman copies of the Parthenon Athena, a lost work by Pheidias.

Room 18. Hegeso's tombstone (12), formerly in the Kerameikos, shows a young girl sitting on an unusually elegant seat: she is studying a piece of jewellery taken from a coffer presented by her servant.

Room 21. The astonishing Horse and **Jockey of Artemision** (13) is a 2C BC Hellenistic bronze which, like the Poseidon, was salvaged from the sea off Cape Artemision; the galloping horse and the spirited rider are vigorously sculpted.

Turn left at the end of the hall *(Room 35)* to reach the huge Room 40 where the large bronzes are exhibited. The Ephebe of Marathon was retrieved from the Bay of Marathon; it is a 4C Classical work of such plasticity and elegance that it may have come from the school of Praxiteles.

Return to the hall (Room 34) and Room 21.

Room 22. Interesting series of 4C BC sculptures from the temple of Asklepios (Aesculapius) at Epidauros; attractive acroteria.

Room 28. Three remarkable works attract attention. The Ephebe of Antikythera (14) (4C), which was found in the sea off the isle of Antikythera, shows Paris offering the apple *(missing)* to Aphrodite. A stone head of Hygeia (15) with soft lines and an introspective expression is by Skopas or Praxiteles. A high relief (16) of a spirited horse held by a black slave comes from a 2C funerary monument found in Athens in 1948 near Lárissa station; this lively and realistic work shows the transition from Classical to Hellenistic art.

Hellenistic art (3C-2C BC):

Room 30. This room is dominated by the colossal and dramatic statue of Poseidon of Melos (17) (2C BC) and by three bronze portraits which are decidedly individualistic and astonishingly expressive: a philosopher's head (3C BC) salvaged at the same time as the Ephebe of Antikythera, a pugilist's head from the shrine at Olympia and a pensive poet's head (2C BC) excavated on Delos.

Helene Stathátos Collection

Room 32. An impressive collection of ancient and Byzantine gold jewellery mostly from Macedonia and particularly Thessaly: bracelets representing serpents or finished with bulls' heads, pendant earrings, brooches, necklaces, pendants, diadems etc.

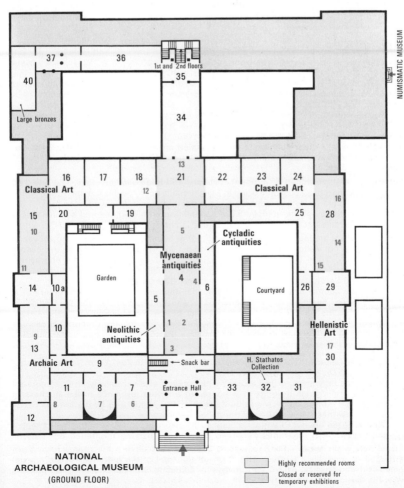

NATIONAL
ARCHAEOLOGICAL MUSEUM
(GROUND FLOOR)

Highly recommended rooms

Closed or reserved for temporary exhibitions

ATHENS★★★

Ceramics

First floor: access by the stairs in Room 35. The collections are exhibited in chronological order; turn right at the top of the stairs into Room 49.

Although the exhibits in the ceramics department are less arresting than those in the sculpture galleries, a careful study of the scenes depicted on the pieces will yield many curious details about the adventures of the gods and mythological heroes as well as about daily life in ancient Greece.

A distinction is to be made between early ceramics with Geometric decoration and Archaic ceramics (7C-6C BC) decorated with plants or fantastic animals. Ceramics from the Classical period are decorated with black figures on a light ground in 6C BC and with red figures on a black ground in 5C-4C BC *(on ceramics see also p 20)*.

Among the most precious pieces are the Nessos Amphora and the four kraters from Melos *(Room 51)*, a krater showing Herakles (Hercules) struggling with Nereus *(Room 52)* and white-ground funerary lekithoi *(Room 55)*.

Santoríni Frescoes *(temporary display on 2nd floor)*

The magnificent frescoes discovered in the 1970s by Professor Marinatos on Santoríni together with ceramics from the same site are a most valuable source of information about life on the island in 16C BC. They are very lively descriptive murals reflecting the influence of Minoan Crete but executed with great elegance and grace. They have survived without much damage although some areas have been reconstructed. They depict various aspects of Cycladic civilisation: two boys engaged in fisticuffs, a fisherman with his catch, springtime, antelopes, young women and a long panel showing a "naval expedition". The ceramics found on Santoríni include some highly original pots of local manufacture: graceful pitchers, sometimes nippled, with spouts in the shape of a bird's beak.

South Wing: Epigraphic and Numismatic Collections

The numismatic museum *(1st floor, open 8.30am to 1.30pm; 2pm Sundays; closed Tuesdays; proposed transfer to Schliemann's House – p 57)* is the more interesting with 215 000 coins of which 2 000 are gold and 4 000 silver. Greek coins are among some of the oldest in the world: they were first minted in 7C BC.

Benaki Museum★★ (Moussío Benáki) (CY). – *Open 8.30am to 2pm; closed Tuesdays; 150 Dr. Snack bar on top floor; attractive view of National Garden and the acropolis.*
This museum, which is devoted mainly to Greek and oriental art, houses the collection of Antonis Benaki (1873-1954), a patron of the arts who founded a family in Egypt and made a fortune in cotton. The exhibits which have been augmented by later bequests are appropriately displayed in the setting of an early 19C patrician mansion in Benaki's own house. *Reorganisation in progress.*

Ground Floor. – The rooms on the left of the entrance hall, where the collection of Greek art is displayed, contain an exceptional series of golden artefacts and jewellery, ancient workmanship such as some cups from Euboia (3000-2800 BC), a 7C BC funerary frieze from Kos, 3C and 1C BC earrings and necklaces, a 3C BC broach representing Aphrodite.

The rooms of Byzantine and post-Byzantine art display in particular a remarkable series of icons on subjects such as the Hospitality of Abraham which is very well drawn (late 14C), St Demetrios (15C), a fine Transfiguration (16C) and an extraordinary composition by Th. Poulakis (Crete, 17C), a pictorial synthesis of the Hymn to the Virgin and the Last Judgment. There also a superb representation of St James and two youthful works by El Greco: the Adoration of the Magi (1560-65) and St Luke (1560).

The room at the rear contains a rare collection of porcelain, said to be from Rhodes but in fact made in Isnik (Nicaea) in Asia Minor from 16C to 18C, and some 11C-12C Fatimid ceramics.

Basement. – Large collection of regional costumes and traditional jewellery. The late 18C reception room from a house in Kozáni in Macedonia is not to be missed; the room, which was reconstructed by Helene Stathátos and is decorated with fine wood carvings, is the setting for a display of the goldsmith's art containing both religious and secular pieces (jewellery): famous pectoral cross from Patmos in the shape of a caravel (17C).

First Floor. – There are four rooms devoted to the War of Independence including souvenirs of Lord Byron but visitors may be more interested in the gallery devoted to the history of Athens from 17C to 19C as depicted in paintings, water colours, drawings, engravings and models made by English (Sir Charles Eastlake, J. Stuart, W. Gell and Edward Lear), French (David Leroy, J.-B. Hilaire, Cassas etc) and German artists.

There are additional collections of traditional embroidery and Islamic art: ceramics, textiles, glasses... beautiful 18C bed hangings for a tester bed from Rhodes; the traditional costumes from the Dodecanese are some of the best in the museum.

A rich collection of works of art from the Far East – particulary Chinese porcelain – is on display in the Museum annex at Old Phaleron (Paleó Fáliro) in a neo-Gothic building (**AV M14**) on the coast road.

Byzantine Museum★★ (Vizandinó Moussío) (CY). – *Open 8am to 7pm (6pm Sundays); closed Mondays; 100 Dr.*
This is the only museum in Europe which concentrates exclusively on Byzantine art and it is particularly rich in icons. It is housed in a former residence of the Duchess of Plaisance *(pp 57 and 72)* which was built between 1840 and 1848 by the famous Greek architect, Kleanthes (1802-1861) in the Italian Renaissance style.

First visit the courtyard which is flanked by two wings of low outbuildings which housed the Duchess' enormous Pyrenean dogs whose barking frightened her visitors.

Ground Floor of the house. – For the display of religious sculpture the rooms have been arranged to resemble churches. The room on the right of the entrance recalls a small paleo-Christian basilica: 4C-5C AD gravestone depicting Orpheus charming the animals with his music.

The second room contains the Byzantine sculptures properly speaking (low reliefs from 9C to 13C). The third room represents a small Greek cross church with a dome such as is frequently seen in Athens. The fourth room represents a church at the time of the Turkish occupation (15C-19C): richly sculpted iconostasis (17C-18C).

First Floor. – The collection of icons covers 9C to 15C (in particular note a Virgin and Child and a Crucifixion both from 14C); there are also fragments of frescoes, liturgical objects and embroideries including the famous Epitaphios of Salonika (14C), originally used as a corporal-cloth (to cover the blessed Sacrament) and therefore ornamented with Eucharistic scenes surrounding the Dead Christ.

Outbuildings. – Rich collection of icons, grouped chronologically and according to subject. There is also an astonishing version of the Evangelistary (1765) composed of small plaques of silver incised and inset with precious stones: scenes from the Old and New Testaments, figures of saints.

In an adjoining building is the Loverdos collection of 8C to 17C frescoes arranged in chronological order.

Museum of Cycladic and Ancient Greek Art ★★ (CY M15). – *Open 10am to 4pm (1pm Saturdays); closed Thursdays and Sundays; 150 Dr (no charge on Saturdays). Snack bar (and WC) in basement. Commentary in English and Greek.*

The private collection of N.P. Goulandris illustrates the developement of Greek art over a period of 5 000 years. The quality of the exhibits is matched by their superb presentation.

First floor. – 230 objects produced by the Cycladic island civilisation (3000-2000 BC) which traded with mainland communities: marble and pottery vessels, some with herring bone decoration; magnificent collection of Cycladic marble **idols** with folded arms and lyre or almond shaped heads where only the nose was in relief, the other features being painted; these figurines are remarkable for their austere style and clarity of line.

Second floor. – Minoan and Mycenaean artefacts; fine collection of vases with red and black figure decoration: in particular from the Attic workshop a bell krater (430 BC) showing a girl flautist and two male dancers and a lekythos showing horse racing (560-550 BC); the Lambros Evtaxias Collection of cult and household **bronze vessels** (8C BC – 1C AD) including a bronze kados from Thessaly with two handles and elaborate plant decoration: gold and bronze jewellery and clay vases from Skyros (1000-700 BC); South Italian fish plates; oil lamps; loom weights; glass perfume flasks; marble sculpture.

ADDITIONAL SIGHTS

Ancient Athens

Pnyx ★ and Nympheion ★ (BY). – *After descending from the Acropolis (SW) the road rises between the Philopappos and the Pnyx hills up to the Tourist pavilion (refreshments, meals) near to which is the entrance to the Pnyx.*

Pnyx ★ (Pníka). – *Son et Lumière about the Acropolis in English every night from 9 to 9.45pm 1 April to 31 October (except Good Friday).*

Facing the Parthenon *(east)* and overlooking the ancient Agora *(north)*, the Pnyx (literally a place where people are squashed together) forms a sort of amphitheatre, 119m by 70m – 390ft by 230ft, where the Assembly of the people (Ecclesía) met between 6C and 4C BC when it began to meet in the Theatre of Dionysos. The assembly was a democratic meeting of citizens to discuss proposed legislation. Each man was entitled to speak for a certain length of time and many famous orators, such as Themistocles, Pericles and Demosthenes, addressed the Assembly.

In the early days attendance at the Assembly was good but gradually, despite the indemnity paid to those who attended, apathy grew so that in 4C archers had to be sent out to compel the Athenians to perform their civic duties; the quorum was 5 000.

The orators' platform is thought to have stood at the foot of the escarpment below an altar to Zeus. From the terrace where the citizens gathered and where spectators now stand for the Son et Lumière there is a splendid **view ★★★** of the Acropolis.

Nympheion ★ (Lófos Nimfón). – The road which skirts the archaeological site of the Pnyx makes an agreeable walk to the Nympheion, the Hill of the Nymphs, which is scattered with traces of dwellings. To the west was the Barathron, a chasm now half filled in, where the bodies of those condemned to death were thrown. View of the Parthenon.

The Nympheion (alt 104m – 341ft) is crowned by an astronomical **Observatory (D)**, built in 1846 according to the design of the architect Theophilos von Hansen at the expense of a banker, Baron Sina. It is a neo-Classical cruciform building with a telescope mounted in the revolving dome. It was completed in 1957 with the addition of a seismology station.

Kerameikos Cemetery ★★ and Dipylon ★ (BXY). – *Open 8.45am to 3pm (9.30am to 2.30pm Sundays); museum closed Tuesdays; 100 Dr. Entrance in Odós Ermoú.*

Kerameikos Cemetery ★★ (Keramikós). – Like most ancient cemeteries the Kerameikos, the largest in Athens, was situated outside the city wall on either side of two public highways, one going to Eleusis and the other to the Academy *(p 73)*.

The cemetery, which was first used in 10C BC, takes its name from the clay *(kéramos)* used by the potters to make funerary vases. At first the graves were simply grave mounds, then from 6C BC terraces were built retained by masonry and marked with gravestones and statues which reached their most flamboyant in the age of Pericles. Some of them were destroyed during the construction of Themistocles' wall (479 BC) and the reinforcement of the fortifications after the victory of the Macedonians at Chaironeia (338 BC). The cemetery was then abandoned and used as a public rubbish tip. The site was first excavated in 1863 and has yielded some handsome finds which are now displayed in the National Museum; a few statues and stones have been left in place.

Leaving the museum on the left descend the path (South Way) which leads to the best preserved part of the cemetery: tombs dating from 4C BC to 1C AD.

Turn left into the West Way which is lined by tombs erected in 4C BC by rich Athenian families; on the corner there is a family tomb with a low relief *(moulding)* of a cavalry man fighting; this is Dexileos who was killed in 393 BC in the war against the Corinthians. Further on there is a group of three monuments belonging to a family from Herakleia in the Euxine near the Black Sea. The tomb of Dionysos, the treasurer, is recognizable from the bull standing on a pillar while the monument to Lysimachides, the archon, and his family is crowned by a dog. On the other side of the West Way stand the funerary column of Bion and the famous grave stone of Hegeso *(moulding)*; the original is in the National Museum.

Return to the crossroads on the Sacred Way and turn left.

On the south side is the gravestone of Antidosis which was painted as were probably most of the others, and the lekythos (vase – *p 20*) of Aristomachos.

Northeast of the Sacred Way on the far side of the Eridanos stream near the Dipylon were other tombs (6C-5C BC): some private such as Pericles' grave and some communal for soldiers.

Sacred Gate and Dipylon ★ (E). – The Sacred Gate was built at the same time as Themistocles' wall (5C BC), of which the footings are identifiable. The Sacred Gate, which was later altered, marks the beginning of the Sacred Way to Eleusis *(p 106)* where the famous "mysteries" were celebrated; only the foundations remain.

The Dipylon, which dates from the same period but is better preserved, was a double gate, as its name implies, and the main entrance to Athens. It was rectangular in plan with a pair of square towers at each corner. The road from the Agora to the Academy *(p 73)* passed through it.

Between the Dipylon and the Sacred Gate stood the Pompeion, a building surrounding a rectangular courtyard where the things required for the Panathenaic processions *(p 50)*, which started from here, were kept.

Modern Athens and Museums

Stadium ★ (Stádio) (CY). – A natural depression running down between two wooded hills to the River Ilissos, now covered by a broad highway, was the site of the ancient stadium laid out under Lycurgus in 4C BC and rebuilt by Herod Atticus in 144 AD. It fell into ruin and was turned into a wheat field. In 1896 it was rebuilt on its original plan for the modern Olympic Games. From the top of the white marble terraces which can accommodate 70 000 spectators, there is a view of the National Garden and the Acropolis.

Kolonáki Square ★ (CY). – This is a charming little square on a slope round a public garden, named after the column at its centre and ringed with luxury shops, pastry cooks, sweet shops, restaurants, cafés with terraces where the cream of Athenian youth meet for a chat; since the age of Pericles Athens has been known as the "Town of gossips".

Kolonáki Square is at the centre of the Kolonáki district, a modern and elegant part of town on the slopes of Lycabettos. The streets are lined with the smartest shops in Athens: fashion and haute couture, tailors, shoe makers, jewellers, book shops and art galleries, high class grocers etc.

Hilton Hotel ★ (CY). – This is the largest hotel in Athens (480 rooms); it enjoys the usual "Hilton style" facilities: luxury boutiques, swimming pool, bars, night clubs, conference and exhibition halls.

It was built in 1963 by the Greek architect Vassiliadis; it has an unusual façade facing Leofóros Vassilíssis Sofías: a white ground relieved by decorative "graffiti" symbolic of Greece, painted by Yannis Moralis.

Americain Embassy (AV Z). – The embassy building, which is contemporary with the Hilton, was designed by the famous architect Gropius. The two-storey glazed structure is surrounded by a peristyle of concrete columns recalling ancient Greece.

British School of Archaeology. – *Odós Souidías (Kolonáki).* The school, which was founded in 1886 for the study of Greek archaeology, also promotes research into other aspects of Greek culture and history in all periods. Its work is published in the "Annual of the British School at Athens". Its most famous excavations are those conducted at Knossós in Crete, in Perachora near Corinth and in Mycenae.

Sites for excavation are allocated by the Greek authorities and any one nation is not expected to work on more than three sites at once.

There are other national schools in Athens including the **American School** (1882) *(next door)* which has similar aims and includes the **Gennadion Library** *(opposite)* which was donated by a former Greek minister in London and housed by the Carnegie Foundation in a neo-Classical building with a central portico (1926) *(open 9am to 2pm and 5 to 8pm; Saturdays 9am to 2pm; closed Sundays and holidays).*

St Paul's Anglican Church (Ágios Pávlos) (A12 *on plan of Pláka p 55*). – *Open 9am to 1pm Tuesdays to Saturdays.*

The church, which was begun in 1838 and consecrated in 1843, is built in the simple Gothic style of three types of local limestone from Lycabettos, Hymettos and Aigina. The original plans were drawn by Sir W. Henry Acland, then travelling in Greece, and later amended by C. R. Cockerell, the English architect who had been excavating at Bassae *(p 35)* and on Aigina *(p 74)*, and by the Danish architect C. Hansen *(p 57)*, who acted as consultant during the construction.

The church contains some interesting memorials. The east window commemorates the Dílessi Murders *(p 70)*; the transept windows General Sir Richard Church (buried in the First Cemetery, *p 63*), who was appointed commander of the Greek forces in 1827 and remained in Greece until his death in 1873. There is a plaque *(left on entering)* to Sir Henry Acland who designed the church; another tablet to George Stoakes of Limehouse and two other Englishmen who died in 1685; a tablet to Captain Frank Abney Hastings of the Royal Navy who harrassed the Turks in the Gulf of Corinth with his steam-driven frigate "Kartería" (Perseverance) during the War of Independence, destroyed a Turkish fleet in the Bay of Itéa (then Salona) in 1827 and died on Zakynthos in May 1828 after being mortally wounded at the battle of Anatolikon; a plaque to an engineer employed by the Lake Copais Co. *(p 162)* which also contributed to the cost of relaying the chancel floor in 1954; a plaque to Clement Harris, another old Harrovian who died fighting for Greece in 1897.

Outside the church *(east of the door)* are monuments to Lusieri, an Italian landscape painter who acted as Lord Elgin's agent for 20 years helping to record and preserve the Parthenon sculptures and lived in Athens for 25 years until his death in 1821; fragments of a monument to John Tweddell, an exceptional scholar and Fellow of Trinity College Cambridge, who spent four years on a grand tour collecting a mass of material before dying of fever in the arms of Fauvel in Athens in 1799; he was buried in the "Theseion" and eventually two epitaphs were erected on pieces of marble from the Acropolis – one with a Latin inscription by Elgin set up by Lusieri and another in Greek by a party of Englishmen including Lord Byron; the latter has disappeared.

First Cemetery (Prótó (1o) Nekrotafión Athinón). – *Odós Anapafseos. Open 7.30am to 12.30pm and 2.30 to 5pm (8am to 1pm Sundays).*

In 1830s the Protestant graves in the "Theseion" cemetery were moved to a new burial ground by the Ilissos, purchased jointly by several Protestant governments – United Kingdom, the Netherlands, Denmark, Sweden, Prussia and Bavaria. When Queen Amalia required the land for her palace garden, the bodies were transferred to the Protestant corner of the Athens First Cemetery.

Here are memorials to Sir Richard Church *(obelisk);* George Finlay, the historian of mediaeval and modern Greece, whose library forms part of the British Archaeological School; Carl Blegen (1887-1971), an American from Minneapolis who came to Greece in 1910 and devoted his life to Mycenaean archaeology; he excavated at Pylos *(p 157)* and at Troy.

Kanellopoulos Museum★ (Pláka: M9). – *Open 8.45am to 3pm (9.30am to 2.30pm Sundays and holidays); closed Tuesdays; 100 Dr.*

The collections are well presented in an elegant 19C mansion: remarkable series of ancient ceramics, Tanagra figurines, busts of Sophocles and Alexander, jewellery, Byzantine icons, popular works of art etc.

Centre for Popular Arts and Traditions (Pláka M12). – *Open 9am to 1pm and 5 to 9pm (9am to 1pm Sundays); Tuesdays and Thursdays open all day; closed Mondays.*

This handsome mansion, once the house of Angelika Hatzimihali (1895-1965), who made a detailed study of traditional Greek culture, now houses a museum exhibiting collections of woven cloth and embroidery (coloured lace and embroidery), regional costumes, musical instruments, old agricultural implements etc. A reconstruction of the typical beehive hut of the nomadic Sarakatsani *(1)* has been erected on the first floor.

Museum of Traditional Greek Art★ (Pláka: M2). – *Open 10am to 2pm; closed Mondays; no charge.*

This is a most attractive museum where the exhibits, most dating from 18C and 19C, are skillfully displayed.

Copper pots and plates, rural and domestic articles and ceramics from Rhodes are accompanied by a large collection of embroidery (borders of table cloths, bed hangings), richly coloured or delicately decorated with motifs which are often of Byzantine origin.

On the second floor there is a reconstruction of a village interior with wooden panels decorated by the naive painter Theophilos (1873-1934; *pp 127 and 168):* scenes from history and daily life. The upper floors display the great variety of traditional costumes: the sober and hard wearing woollen dress of the Sarakatsani who are nomadic shepherds, the cheerful colours of the clothes worn by the Balkan Greeks, the sumptuous embroidery of ceremonial dress, heavy with silver ornaments, and the elegant costumes of Central Greece and the Peloponnese.

City of Athens Museum (BX M13). – *Open 9am to 1.30pm Mondays, Wednesdays, Fridays; closed in July; 100 Dr (no charge on Wednesdays).*

The museum traces the history of Athens since the days of the Frank invasion (13C); eventually it will consist of three sections. At present only one is in being and it is housed in a neo-Classical mansion (known as the "Old Palace"), designed by the German architects, G. Lueders and J. Hoffer, in 1833-4, which became the royal residence for five years from 1837 to 1842.

The exhibits illustrate daily life and social customs during the reign of King Otho (a meeting of local tradition and western European manners).

On the first floor the rooms have been arranged and furnished as they were during the king's residence: paintings by visiting European artists including Edward Lear, Dodwell and Gasparini.

National Historical Museum★ (BY M7). – *Open 9am to 2pm (1pm Saturdays and Sundays); closed Mondays; 100 Dr (no charge Thursdays).*

This museum is housed in the old Parliament building *(p 57)* and should be visited by those who are interested in modern Greece and more especially in the period from the fall of Byzantium to the end of the Second World War.

In the rooms left of the entrance is a series of water colours by a Scotsman, James Skene, showing views and monuments of Greece between 1838 and 1845.

There is a section on the Philhellene movement which assumed a special importance during the War of Independence: souvenirs of Byron (his helmet, sword, pistols and chest in Room E) and other foreign participants.

In the final rooms a rich collection of traditional Greek dress from the islands and regions (18C-19C-20C), some of which were worn by famous Greeks who took part in the struggle for independence.

---

(1) An fascinating account of these people is given by Patrick Leigh Fermor in "Roumeli".

National Gallery and Alexander Soutzos Museum★★ (CY M8). – *Open 9am to 3pm (10am to 4pm Sundays); closed Mondays; 30 Dr.*

Pride of place in the collection goes to four remarkable works by D. Theotocopoulos (El Greco, *p 209*) including his famous "Concert of the Angels", and to a selection of post-Byzantine icons.

The second floor, which is devoted to the different periods in Hellenic art since its inception, presents a number of 18C works from the Ionian Islands and a collection of 19C canvases illustrative of the Munich School (Gysis, Lytras, Iacovides, Volanakis etc); one room is devoted entirely to C. Parthenis (1878-1967) whose influence is decisive in the development of 20C Hellenic art.

Between the floors are displayed a dozen frescoes and canvases by the naive painter Theophilos (1873-1934, *pp 127 and 168*).

The first floor is devoted to contemporary Hellenic painting particularly from the 1930s.

The rich collection of sculpture is displayed in two rooms and the garden. The first room – 19C work influenced by Classicism – is dominated by the work of the great Greek sculptor Yiannoulis Halepas; the second room displays more modern trends up to 1940.

War Museum (CY M10). – *Open 9am to 2pm; closed Mondays; 100 Dr (no charge Tuesdays and Thursdays).*

Outside some early (Farman 1912) and some more recent (Spitfire, Tiger Moth, Helldiver) aircraft are on display.

Inside on the ground floor there is a gallery of ancient weapons: ostentatious oriental arms in white with incised or damascene decoration, pistols, powder horns etc. The first floor presents documents and souvenirs of battles in which the Greek army has taken part, particularly between 1941 and 1945.

THE SUBURBS

PIRAEUS★ (PIREÁS)

10km – 6 miles southwest of the centre of Athens. Access by underground, by bus (from Omonia or Síndagma Square), by car down Odós Piréos or Leofóros Singroú; the latter is less direct but quicker.

Piraeus (pop 476 304) is a typically Mediterranean port, lively and cosmopolitan. Together with the capital it forms one huge conurbation. It is the first port of Greece and the country's major industrial centre. Even in antiquity it was chosen as the port of Athens owing to its exceptional situation: it consists of a peninsula *(aktí)* which forms a deep inlet on the west side and is favoured with two well protected natural round harbours, Zéa and Mikrolímano, on the east coast. It is the point of embarkation for the islands and the roadstead has often been used as an anchorage by Mediterranean fleets.

Piraeus is a modern town with a noisy vibrant population, tavernas serving fish and seafood and popular cabarets which attract sailors from every corner of the world.

The port in antiquity. – It was **Themistocles** in *c*493 BC who decided to move Athens' harbour from Phaleron *(p 65)*, which was too exposed to the wind, to Piraeus. The new town was protected and linked to Athens by the Long Walls, nicknamed the Long Legs by the Athenians, which formed a fortified corridor.

In the age of Pericles the town was rebuilt according to a grid plan designed by **Hippodamos of Miletus,** a philosopher and geometer. For several hundred years the inhabitants enjoyed great commercial prosperity produced by the "display of samples" in the great porticoes (stoas).

In 85 BC however the Romans under Sulla sacked Piraeus and set it on fire; three bronze statues, then lying in the basement of a warehouse waiting to be shipped to Rome, were discovered by chance in 1959 in Leofóros Georgiou-A.

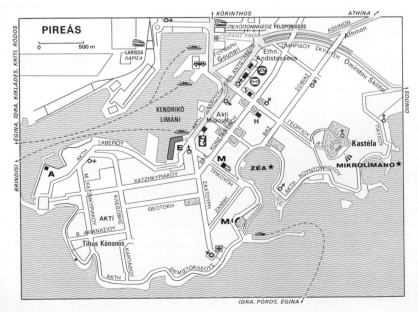

In the Middle Ages Piraeus came to be known as **Porto Leone** after the ancient lion at the harbour entrance which served as a leading mark and was carried away by the Venetians and set up in front of the Arsenal in Venice in 1687.

Later the island of Syros *(p 184)* in the Cyclades developed as the main port of Greece and when Otho of Bavaria arrived in Piraeus in 1834 the population had fallen to about 50 but the designation of Athens as the capital of Greece and the opening of the Corinth Canal in 1893 marked the beginning of a commercial revival.

The modern port. – The modern port complex consists of Piraeus harbour, Herakles harbour, the Eleusinian Gulf (Kólpos Elefsínas) and the two small harbours, Zéa and Mikrolímano, which accommodate pleasure craft and fishing boats.

The main Piraeus harbour comprises: the central harbour (Kendrikó Limáni) for goods but more particularly for domestic and international passenger liners; for the latter there is a large maritime station (**E**); Alón harbour (northern section of the central harbour) is used by coasting vessels; the outer port deals in wood and containers.

Herakles harbour *(west)* is reserved for freighters fitted with hatches in the bow or stern or sides of the ship opening directly from the hold on to the quay. The ship builders and ship repair yards are to be found in the Eleusinian Gulf.

Traffic in the port rose in 1984 to 12 451 114 tonnes of goods and 5 173 398 passengers. From Piraeus to Eleusis the coast is lined with petrol refineries, metal works, food processing plants, cement works and tobacco factories.

Tour *about 1/2 day*

Zéa★. – In antiquity this round bay which is almost completely enclosed was a large port for triremes: the ship-sheds which sheltered these war ships spread round the bay; traces of them are still visible.

Zéa harbour can now accommodate up to 400 pleasure craft. The waterfront is lined with fish restaurants and tavernas which are usually crowded.

Zéa harbour is the embarkation point for the hydrofoils serving the Saronic Gulf Islands and the Peloponnese.

The **Archaeological Museum★** (**M**) *(open 8.45am to 3pm; 9.30am to 2.30pm Sundays; closed Tuesdays; 100 Dr)*, which has been recently reorganised, contains (ground floor) an interesting collection of Greek and Roman sculptures some of which were rescued from an ancient shipwreck in Piraeus harbour or found in the local cement works. The most remarkable (found in 1959) are displayed on the first floor: the Piraeus Apollo (c525 BC), a splendid Archaic *kouros* which is probably the oldest known Greek statue in bronze and the Piraeus Athena (c340 BC) wearing a peplos and a crested helmet and holding a statuette or a cup in the right hand and a shield or lance in the left. Two other bronze statues represent Artemis.

The **Naval Museum** (**M1**) *(open 9am to 12.30pm; closed Sundays and Mondays in August; 50 Dr)* contains 12 rooms illustrating the history of navigation in Greece from antiquity to the Second World War: models of ships, paintings, reconstructions of sea battles.

The battleship **Avéroff** (which used to be at Póros) belongs to the museum and is now moored in Trocadero Harbour in Phaleron Bay (P. Fáliro, **AV**). Launched in 1910, it took part in all the Balkan wars; it was withdrawn from service in 1946.

Mikrolímano★. – Like Zéa, Mikrolímano was a harbour for triremes in antiquity and is now lined by fish tavernas. The semi-circular harbour lies at the foot of Mounychía Hill (Kastéla), 87m – 285ft high, which was crowned by an acropolis and a sanctuary to Artemis. From the neighbourhood of the open-air theatre *(traditional dances in summer)* there is a fine view of Piraeus, the coast and the Saronic Gulf.

Aktí. – The coast road round the peninsula gives attractive views of the port and the coast. There are traces of the sea wall (Tíhos Kónonos) built by Konon in 4C BC. Near the public garden at the western end of the peninsula stands the tomb of Miaoúlis (**A**), a famous Hydriot admiral *(p 113)*.

PHALERON (FÁLIRO)

10km – 6 miles south of the centre of Athens. Access by bus from Síntagma Square or by car down Leofóros Singroú.

In antiquity before the harbour was built in Piraeus the Athenians beached their triremes in **Phaleron Bay** (Fáliro). The long sandy beach was popular with the modern Athenians for bathing until industrialisation fouled the water; efforts are however now being made to remove the pollution. The shoreline which was open country only fifty years ago is now covered with housing.

In a **cemetery** on a gentle slope overlooking the marina et Álimos are buried 2 067 Commonwealth troops who fought against the German invading force in 1941 or in 1944 when the enemy retreated.

KIFISSIÁ★ *2 1/2 hours*

14km – 9 miles northeast of Athens. Access by underground (1/2 hour from Omónia Square; plan p 63) or by road (leave central Athens by Leofóros Vassilíssis Sofías).

Kifissiá is an elegant residential town (pop 31 876) which is pleasantly cool and fresh in summer owing to its altitude (276m – 906ft), its water and its trees: even in antiquity the Athenians came up to Kifissiá for refreshment.

Kifissiá comprises: the lower town near the underground station and the public park; its shops and tavernas give it a relaxed atmosphere; the upper town, an elegant district, with avenues of plane trees where luxury hotels and restaurants are interspersed among the handsome 19C villas built in the Italian style and surrounded by gardens luxuriant with pine trees, cypresses and eucalyptus trees.

Goulandris Museum of Natural History★. – *13 Odós Levidou* (**AU M**). *Open daily 9am to 2pm (10am to 4pm Sundays); closed Fridays; 100 Dr. Commentary in English and Greek.*

The subject of this museum, which is housed in an elegant 19C villa and modern wing, is natural history: stuffed animals including native species under threat of extinction, molluscs, insects, plants and fossil plants *(ground floor);* fossils, mineralogical and geological specimens *(basement);* sections devoted to the region of Lavrion and to seismology showing the evolution of the Mediterranean.

The herbarium contains 200 000 different varieties of plants from the Mediterranean basin. There is a section devoted to paleontology and paleobotany.

The Goulandris Research Institute, which is in the same building, publishes an annual scientific review "Annales Musei Goulandris".

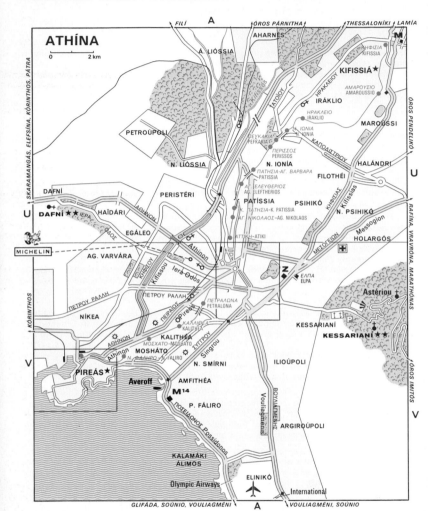

KESSARIANÍ MONASTERY★★
AND MOUNT HYMETTOS★★

9km – 5 1/2 miles east of Athens. Access by bus 234 (bus stop behind the Archaeological Museum, Odós Akademías and Leofóros Vas. Sofías) plus 1/2 hour on foot.

Beyond the suburb of Kessarianí *(bus terminus)* the road climbs in leisurely bends up the verdant slopes through fragrant groves of pine and eucalyptus trees. After 3 km – 2 miles the Kessarianí Monastery appears on the right.

Kessarianí Monastery★★ (Moní Kessarianí) (**AV**). – *Open 9am to 3pm (2pm Sundays).*
The fresh water of the springs, the shade of the plane trees, pines and solemn cypresses and the silence, which is barely broken by the murmuring of the bees on Mount Hymettos, all add to the charm of a visit to this monastery. It was founded in 11C and dedicated to the Presentation of the Virgin. Formerly it was famous for the wisdom of its superiors and for the richness of its library but it was destroyed during the War of Independence and is now deconsecrated *(illustration p 8).*

A recess in the outer wall of the monastery on the east side of the first courtyard contains the famous **Ram's Head Fountain,** a sacred spring in antiquity which was celebrated by the Latin poet Ovid in his Ars Amatoria.

The inner courtyard is cooled by running water and scattered with ancient fragments. In the Middle Ages the 11C building *(left)* was the monks' bath house: the main room is roofed with a dome. The building was later converted into cellars with a press. The adjoining wing has a gallery at first floor level serving the monks' cells.

The **church,** *katholikon (right),* on the Greek cross plan dates from 11C but the domed narthex and the side chapel with its belfry were added in 17C. The interior is decorated with murals: those in the narthex date from 1682; those in the church itself are probably 18C and show Christ Pantocrator in the dome, the Virgin in majesty between the Archangels Michael and Gabriel in the top of the apse and the Life of Jesus around the transept. Four ancient columns support the dome and the choir screen comes from a paleo-Christian basilica *(see below).*

Facing the church is the kitchen around a central hearth and chimney and the refectory which ends in a recess where the superior *(igoúmenos)* sat.

Leave the monastery on this side and take the path which climbs up through the olive trees and cypresses (1/4 hour on foot Rtn) to a sanctuary southeast of the monastery. Here there are traces of a 10C church with a nave and two aisles built on the foundations of a paleo-Christian basilica; adjoining the basilica was a 13C vaulted Frankish church dedicated to St Mark; there is also a later chapel dedicated to the Archangels.

All these buildings incorporate ancient fragments. Fine **views** of Athens, Attica and the Saronic Gulf.

Mount Hymettos★★ (Óros Imitós). – Continue up the road which climbs Mount Hymettos through the pine trees; soon the 11C **Asteri Monastery (AV)** appears on the left; then the road emerges from the woods into scrub. There are views of Athens and the Saronic Gulf as far as the Peloponnese to the west and of the Attic peninsula (Mesógia), its eastern shore and Euboia to the east. The summit is prohibited *(military zone)* but in antiquity it was crowned by a statue of Zeus.

The Hymettos range, which rises to 1026m – 3366ft, extends north south for about 20km – 12 1/2 miles and is well known for turning a delicate purple hue at dusk. Hymettos was already famous for its honey in antiquity. Il also boasts a vineyard on the lower slopes of the eastern face which produces a high quality white wine.

Another Hymettan speciality is the grey blue marble which is still quarried in St George's Valley not far from Kessarianí.

ATHENS Region★★

Michelin map 980 folds 30 and 31 – local map pp 68 and 69

CAPE SOUNION★★★ (ÁKRI SOÚNIO)
Itinerary 1 *– Round trip of 143km – 89 miles*

It is traditional to visit Cape Sounion at sunset and return to Athens in the evening twilight but for a better appreciation of the region it is advisable to make a whole day excursion: spending the morning exploring the Apollo Coast by the new coast road, lunching at Cape Sounion and returning to Athens by the old inland road.

Leave Athens Leofóros Singróu; in Fáliro (beach, roadstead, Karaiskákis stadium and bouzoúki tavernas) turn left into the new "expressway" which, after skirting the south side of the Elenikó Airport, follows the coast of the Saronic Gulf which is called the Apollo Coast.

Apollo Coast★★ **(Aktí Apólona).** – The road from Phaleron (Fáliro) to Sounion offers frequent views of the Saronic Gulf and the islands. Unfortunately it has been spoiled in places by unattractive modern developments.

Glifáda★. – Pop 44 018. This is a sizable resort just south of the Elinikó Airport which comprises a beach with facilities, a marina and an 18 hole golf course. *Numerous hotels, bungalows, fish restaurants, night clubs.*

The road passes through Voúla (beach with facilities) and Kavoúri skirting many small bays.

Vouliagméni★★. – Pop 2 743. An elegant resort, Vouliagméni is pleasantly situated at the head of a deep inlet flanked by two promontories indented by many small creeks. The fragant pine trees, one huge beach with facilities and several smaller beaches, a safe mooring and several hotels, including the luxurious Astir Palace with its bungalows, add to the attractiveness of the resort.

From the southern headland beyond the harbour there is a **view** of the bay and the coast extending south towards Cape Sounion.

The road continues to Várkiza, a new seaside resort on Várkiza Bay, and then to **Lagoníssi,** another summer resort *(bungalows)* which has a sandy beach in an attractive bay partially enclosed by a reef.

The broken rocky coastline becomes more dramatic with views of the Saronic Gulf and the isle of Patroclos which is named after one of Ptolemy II's admirals who fortified the island in 260 BC.

Anávissos. – Pop 1 837. Seaside resort; old salt pans. One of the most famous *kouroi* in the Athens Museum was found in Anávissos.

Sounion. – Pop 401. A small seaside resort has grown up on the site of the ancient town and port of Sounion. In an inlet near the headland dry dock facilities for two triremes have been found. View★ of Cape Sounion, crowned by the columns of an ancient temple.

Cape Sounion★★★ **(Aktí Soúnio).** – *Tourist Pavilion.* The "sacred headland" (Homer) is the outpost of Attica; it occupies a commanding position facing the Aegean Sea and the Cyclades at the entrance to the Saronic Gulf. The situation is enhanced by the ruins of a **temple to Poseidon,** the sea god invoked by sailors rounding the cape, which crowns the precipitous headland some 60m – 197ft above sea level.

Known formerly as Cape Colonna, the headland was celebrated by romantic writers such as Byron and the sailor-poet, William Falconer, whose once popular work "The Shipwreck" was inspired by his own experience in a storm in 1750. The site now attracts busloads of tourists.

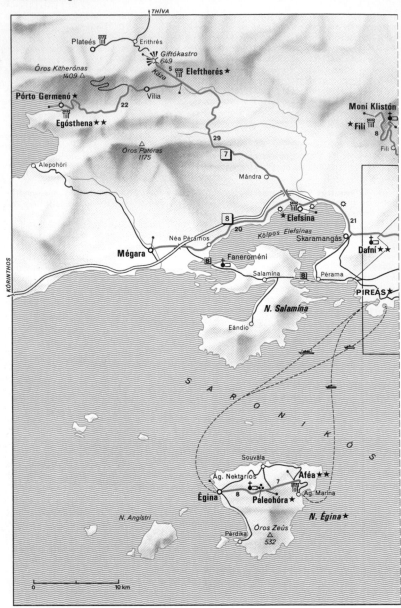

The sanctuary. – *Open 9am to sunset; 100 Dr.*

The path leading up to the temple crosses the wall, which enclosed the ancient acropolis and is fairly well preserved (traces of square towers), and then enters the sacred precinct *(peribolos)* at the point where the original gate *(propylaia)* stood, flanked *(right)* by a large portico where the pilgrims assembled.

The temple, which was built of marble between 444 and 440 BC on the orders of Pericles, was dedicated to Poseidon. It was a Doric building with a peristyle replacing an earlier 6C BC santuary of tufa which had been destroyed in the second Persian War. Abandoned for many years to the ravages of the weather and treasure seekers, it was restored in 19C: during the excavations two colossal Archaic *kouroi* were found which are now in the Athens Museum; several columns have been re-erected.

The entrance façade *(facing east)* consisted of a portico leading into the *naós (p 18)* of which the corner pillars have been preserved: the one on the right is covered with "graffiti" including the name of Byron, although not perhaps in his own hand, who visited the temple in 1810.

The 16 columns of the peristyle which remain of the 34 originals which supported the architrave seem very tall although they are only 6.10m – 20ft high; they have no entasis and the diameter is only 1m – 3 1/4ft at the base and 0.79m – just over 2 1/2ft at the top.

A tour of the ruin reveals the variation in thickness of the podium which was built for the original Archaic temple to provide a level base: it is several metres deep at the northwest corner.

The temple steps, where the votive stele were placed, give a beautiful **view** of the sea, which is often quite choppy, the islands (Makronísi to the east with Kéa beyond) and the Saronic Gulf.

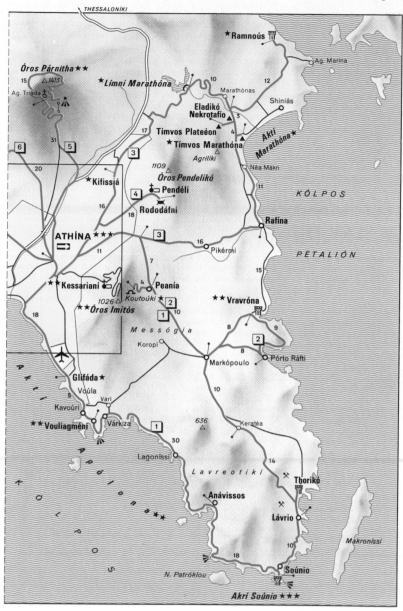

From Sounion to Laurion (Lávrio) the road winds its way along the east coast of Cape Sounion. The landscape is more verdant than on the western side; villas and hotels are dispersed among the pine and olive trees above little beaches nestling in the creeks.

Laurion (Lávrio). – Pop 8 921. Laurion, a small industrial town (foundries) and mineral port, is surrounded by a desolate landscape of spoil heaps at the foot of Mount Laurion (Lavreotíki); the mines were well known even in antiquity.

Recent excavations by Belgian archaeologists suggest that the mines were already being worked early in 3000 BC but it was early in 5C BC on the advice of Themistocles that the deposits of silver bearing sulphides began to be systematically exploited bringing wealth and power to Athens. Shafts were sunk up to 100m – 328ft deep leading to radial galleries, no more than 1m – 3 1/2ft high, where the mineral was extracted; it was then crushed and smelted. At its peak activity up to 20 000 slaves worked in the mine. In 2C BC the lodes became exhausted and extraction had to cease.

In 1864 a new process for treating the mineral made it possible for mining to be restarted and a French company founded in 1876 was responsible for almost the whole output not only of silver but also of zinc until 1981.

From Lávrio there is a narrow road along the coast to Thorikó: bear right following the sign "Théâtre antique".

Thorikó. – Thorikó was a large fortified city with two ports where wood was imported from Euboia for the metal foundries in Laurion. It was inhabited from 2 000 BC until the Roman period. The site is being excavated by the Belgian School in Athens; they have found a **theatre** *(free access)* capable of seating 5 000 spectators on its unusual elliptical terraces facing a rectangular orchestra, and a residential district below an acropolis.

Views of Mount Laurion and its mining installations.

Return towards Lávrio to rejoin the road to Athens. Beyond Keratéa the road enters the **Messógia** (inland), a sparsely inhabited plain caused by subsidence which was formerly marshy but has since been drained and now produces cereals, olives and vines.

Peanía. – Pop 7 278. The birthplace of Demosthenes. A good road leads to the **Koutoúki Cave★** *(open 9am to 7pm)* 500 m – 1 640ft up the slope of Mount Hymettos; it has recently been arranged to show off the beautiful stalactites, stalagmites and variously coloured curtains.

Vorrés Museum (modern and popular art). *Open 10am to 2pm Saturdays and Sundays.*
It presents over 300 paintings and 40 sculptures by Greek artists in the post-war years: paintings by Fassianos, Moralis, Gaitis, Tsarouchis, Vassiliou etc.

Return to Athens by the road which passes over the saddle between Hymettos and Pentelikon.

BRAURON★★ (VRAVRÓNA)
Itinerary ② *– Round trip of 81km – 50 miles*

Leave Athens by the road to Rafína bearing right to Markópoulo. The route crosses the Messógia Plain past wheat fields, olive groves, orchards and vineyards. *In Markópoulo (wine making centre) turn left (northeast) into the road which descends towards Vravróna and Pórto Raftí.* After 8km – 5miles one reaches the Brauron archaeological site which has been excavated since 1846 by the Greek Archaeological Society.

Brauron★★ (Vravróna). – Pop 51. The Brauron sanctuary was set among hills not far from the Aegean shore *(beach);* anciently it was a place of pilgrimage dedicated to Artemis Brauronia. According to a legend referred to by Euripides in his "Iphigenia in Tauris" Agamemnon's daughter, Iphigenia *(p 79),* who had escaped being sacrificed and fled to the land of the Tauris in the Crimea, returned with the sacred statue of Artemis, to live out her days in Brauron. To atone for the sacrifice of a bear protected by Artemis – the goddess had a special association with the bear – Iphigenia founded the santuary of Artemis Brauronia which was served by young priestesses, known as "bears", who were dressed in saffron robes and dedicated to the goddess at the age of seven.

Sanctuary. – *Open 8.45am to 3pm (9.30am to 2.30pm Sundays); 100 Dr.*
Beyond a 6C AD paleo-Christian basilica *(left)* is the sacred fountain which flowed into a stream spanned by a 5C BC bridge.
On the right, below St George's Chapel (15C) are the foundations of the temple of Artemis (5C BC); behind in a crack in the rock is the "Tomb of Iphigenia".
Opposite was the grand peristyle courtyard which was flanked on three sides by the "parthenon" where the "bears" lived; the rooms were furnished with wooden beds and stone tables. Part of the colonnade has been re-erected.

Museum. – *Closed Tuesdays.*
It displays geometric vases (9C-8C BC), a low relief votive sculpture showing the figures of Zeus (seated), Leto, Apollo and Artemis (5C BC) and particularly a series of ravishing statuettes or marble heads of little "bears" (4C BC) with unusually delicate expressions: the **"Bear with a bird"** is a masterpiece.
Return to Markópoulo via **Pórto Ráfti** (Pop 2 984). a seaside resort and the port of the Messógia (Limáni Messogéas), At the mouth of the bay there is an island crowned by a colossal Roman marble figure of a man sitting cross-legged; it is popularly called the tailor *(ráftis)* and was probably used as a leading mark.

(From photograph Tzaferis S.A., Athens)

Brauron.
Statue of a "Bear"

Return to Athens by the same road as for the outward journey.

MARATHON COAST★ (AKTÍ MARATHÓNA)
Itinerary ③ *– Round trip of 108km – 67 miles*

Leave Athens by the road to Rafína which passes between Hymettos and Pentelikon.

Pikérmi. – Pop 479. This village hit the headlines in 1870 owing to the Marathon Massacres, also called the **Dilessi Murders.**
On 11 April a party of eight consisting of Lord and Lady Muncaster, Edward Lloyd, an English barrister, and his wife and daughter (aged 6), Edward Herbert, third Secretary at the British Legation in Athens, Frederick Vyner, a young Englishman, and Count Alberto de Boÿl, a Piedmontese nobleman from the Italian Legation, made an excursion to the battlefield at Marathon. On the return journey their coach outstripped the escort of infantry and just before the bridge at Pikérmi (known subsequently as "the bridge of the Lords" but demolished in 1954 in a road improvement scheme) they were abducted by brigands. The women and child were released immediately and Lord Muncaster followed soon after to raise the ransom. The brigand leader, who was led to believe his prisoners were "kings", altered the terms for their release almost daily. The authorities mishandled the matter and sent troops to block the road. On 21 April the soldiers caught up with the brigands, who were moving from Skála Oroupoú on the north coast of Attica to Dílessi, and opened fire. The brigands, true to their code, promptly murdered their four captives.
The bodies of Herbert and Vyner were sent home after first being buried in the Protestant Cemetery in Athens *(p 63).* The victims are commemorated in the east window in St Paul's Anglican Church in Athens *(p 62).*
This incident inspired the film "Megalexandros" made by Angelopoulos in 1981.

Rafína. – Pop 4 984. The ferries for Euboia and the eastern Cyclades leave from Rafína which is a commercial and fishing port. Fish tavernas line the waterfront and the beach.

Take the road north along the coast past a series of beaches where the Athenians flock on Sundays and then rejoin the main road at Néa Mákri; after 5km – 3 miles there is a righthand turning leading to the Marathon battlefield.

Marathon Barrow ★ (Tímvos Marathóna). – The barrow standing isolated in the coastal plain was raised over the Athenian dead after the battle which took place in 490 BC and was described by Herodotos.

The Warriors of Marathon. – The Persian fleet set sail from Asia Minor to punish the Athenians and Eretrians (Euboia) for supporting the revolt of Miletus in 499. The archers and cavalry were landed in the Bay of Marathon to march on Athens. The Athenian hoplites had however taken up their position on the lower slopes of Mount Agrilíki at the southern end of the plain. They probably numbered about 7 000 assisted by 1 000 Plataians whereas the Persians numbered about 20 000.

For eight days the two armies faced each other. Then the Persians re-embarked some of their troops and the Athenians, commanded by **Miltiades**, attacked the remainder and overwhelmed them so that they fled to their ships across the marsh to the north. According to tradition there were 6 400 Persian dead while the Greeks lost only 192 men.

The victory won, Miltiades sent a messenger to Athens to announce the good news. The runner is supposed to have made the journey from Marathon to Athens without pausing for breath. On arrival he announced the victory and dropped dead of exhaustion.

This feat inspired the Marathon race which is part of the modern Olympic Games and has recently become a popular mass event among amateur runners in many major cities. The official distance is 42,195 km – 26 miles 385 yards, which was established in 1908 when the Games were held in England and the Marathon was run from Windsor Great Park to the White City Stadium. At the first modern Games in 1896 the distance was shorter, 40 km – 24.9 miles, which more nearly corresponds to the distance from Marathon to Athens.

Tour. – *Open 8.45am to 3pm (9.30am to 2.30pm Sundays); 100 Dr.* The barrow which was raised over the Athenian hoplites who died at Marathon is 9m – 30ft high. At the foot is a reproduction of the gravestone of Aristion, the so-called Soldier of Marathon; it is a low relief showing a hoplite like those who fought on the battlefield (original in the National Museum in Athens).

Originally gravestones bearing the names of those who died were set round the sides of the barrow *(disappeared)*. From the top *(closed temporarily)* there is a fine view of the plain, formerly uncultivated but now used for crops, and the surrounding mountains.

Return to the main road and 1km – 1/2 mile further north turn left to the Barrow of the Plataians. Immediately on the right stands a hangar covering a cemetery.

Helladic cemetery (Eladikó Nekrotafío). – This cemetery is proof of very ancient human occupation of the plain of Marathon where, according to mythology, Theseus killed the bull, brought by Herakles from Crete, which was devastating the countryside. The tombs which have been excavated date from 2000 BC and contain perfectly preserved skeletons.

Further on (left) is the Barrow of the Plataians.

Barrow of the Plataians (Tímvos Plateéon). – *To visit enquire at the museum.* It covers the graves in which were buried the remains of the soldiers of the Boeotian city of Plataia who died in the battle of Marathon.

Museum. – *Closed Tuesdays.* It contains an interesting collection of primitive objects from the Helladic and Mycenaean periods which were found during recent excavations: funerary urns, one of which, for a child, is most unusually shaped like a cocoon; statuettes; helmets and weapons; mirrors...

Near the museum is a Helladic and Mycenaean cemetery; one of the graves contains the skeleton of a horse.

Return to the main road continuing north; just before Marathon turn right to the pleasant beach at Shiniás (beautiful pine grove) and Ramnoús.

Ramnoús★. – *Open 8.45am to 3pm (9.30am to 2.30pm Sundays).*

The ruins of ancient Ramnoús lie in a remote valley running down to the sea opposite Euboia. Its name is thought to derive from a thorny shrub *(rámnos)* which still grows in the area and is classified by botanists in the same family as the buckthorn under the name rhamnaceae.

The first ruins to greet the visitor are a platform bearing the foundations of two Doric temples built side by side. The smaller (6C BC) was dedicated to Themis, goddess of Justice (statue in the National Museum in Athens); the larger (5C BC) contained a famous effigy of Nemesis, goddess of Punishment and divine Retribution, whose head is now displayed in the British Museum in London.

Continue down the path to the headland where the acropolis stood; the ruined fortress dates from 5C-4C BC. There are traces of the enclosing wall, which had one gate flanked by square towers, of a small theatre, of various buildings and of a citadel which stood on the top of the hill.

There are fine views of the wild and rocky coast; the position of the ancient lower town can be surmised as well as the harbour at the mouth of the stream.

Return to the Marathon road. On leaving Marathon turn left into the new road which passes Lake Marathon.

Lake Marathon ★ (Límni Marathóna). – *Private property but access allowed; Tourist Pavilion.*

This is an artificial lake which occupies a fresh and pleasant site in a valley surrounded by meadows and wooded slopes which have been partially made into a park.

The reservoir was created by a dam, 72m – 236ft high and 285m – 935ft long, which was built in 1926 to provide Athens with drinking water.

Return to Athens by the motorway.

MOUNT PENTELIKON
Itinerary ④ – 36km – 22 1/2 miles Rtn

Access from Athens by car or by no 105, 421 or 430 bus leaving from behind the Archaelogical Museum.

The road passes through an uninteresting suburb until it reaches Néa Pendéli and then climbs the slopes of Mount Pentelikon to a shady terrace *(cafés, tavernas)* in front of the entrance to Pendéli Monastery.

Pendéli Monastery. – *Free entrance.* A lively Orthodox community occupies the monastery which was founded by St Timothy in 1578 and quickly became one of the richest in Greece. Under the Franks (13C-14C) it was occupied for a period by the Franciscan Order. The present buildings are almost all modern or date from 19 C.

In antiquity Mount Pentelikon was crowned by a gigantic statue of Athena (alt 1 109m – 3 642ft) and was famous for its quarry *(spiliá)* where the white marble was extracted to create the great monuments of ancient Athens (the Parthenon, the Hephaisteion, the Olympieion etc).

Continue by car for 1km – 1/2 mile to the junction near the palace of the Duchess of Plaisance, signpost "Rhododaphni Palace".

Rhododaphne Palace. – *The interior is not open but one may view the exterior; concerts in summer.*

This charming white marble palace was built between 1839 and 1842 in neo-Gothic style for the Duchess of Plaisance who chose her favourite architect Kleanthes (1802-1862) to design it.

Sophie de Barbe-Marbois, **Duchesse de Plaisance** (1785-1854), wife of General Lebrun, was renowned for her intelligence and originality. She was a fervent supporter of the cause of Greek independence and subsidised Kapodistria's government which she had accompanied to Nauplion between 1829 and 1831.

Following the death of her daughter Elisa, whose embalmed body she kept in a crystal coffin, she took up residence in Athens in 1837. She dressed in a curious, vaguely Greek costume of her own desgin – white robe, white girdle, white flowing veil, gloves and upward curving red slippers – and astonished the court and the city with her eccentricities: she devoted herself to the education of young girls, whom she ruled with a rod of iron, took to fasting, which she imposed on her guests also, and kept a dozen Pyrenean dogs which inspired terror all around them.

She had a passion for building *(pp 57 and 60)* and was buried together with the ashes of her daughter and two of her favourite dogs in Néa Pendéli in the garden of a villa (La Maisonnette) which she had just completed when she died in 1854. There is a fine portrait of her by R. Lefevre in the National Gallery in Athens.

MOUNT PARNES★★ (ÓROS PÁRNITHA)
Itinerary ⑤ – 95km – 59 miles Rtn

Mount Parnes *(signposted on the outskirts of Athens)* stands on the border between Attica and Boeotia; it rises to 1 413m -4 636ft but there is no access to the summit *(military zone)*.

There are winter sports facilities on the southeast slopes; in summer many Athenians are attracted by the coolness of the high altitude.

Leave Athens by the Thessalonika road; at the edge of the conurbation turn left.

After passing the bottom station of the cable car which serves the hotel-casino on Mount Parnes, the road, which is broad and well engineered, winds its way up the rocky slopes of the mountain (extensive **views** of Athens and Attica) before entering the band of coniferous forest which gives the countryside an alpine look.

First the Hotel Xenia appears among the pine trees, then the Tourist Pavilion *(restaurant in the season)* and Holy Trinity Chapel (Agía Triáda) where the road divides; the lefthand turning makes a circular tour of the mountain *(about 1 1/2 hours)* just below the summit (glimpses of Kithairon to the west).

The main road continues up to the hotel-casino of Mount Parnes (alt 1 050m -3 445ft), a luxury establishment *(swimming pool, night club)*; the cafeteria terrace *(open in the season)* offers views of Athens and Attica.

PHYLE FORTRESS★ (FILÍ)
Itinerary ⑥ – 56km – 35 miles Rtn

Leave Athens by Odós Liossíon (BX) which follows the railway to Néa Lióssia and then Áno Lióssia. Beyond the village of Phyle the road starts to climb Mount Parnes. A righthand turning off one of the bends in the road leads to Moní Klistón (signpost).

Convent of the Gorge (Moní Klistón). – Alt 500m – 1 640ft. The convent of nuns known as The Virgin of the Gorge (Panagía ton Kleistón) takes its name from its spectacular **position★** above a deep gorge riddled with caves, some of which were occupied by hermits. Some of the buildings date from 14C.

The road continues upwards (beehives on the slopes) past the track (right) to the Plátani Kriopigí taverna; soon after turn left to reach Phyle Fortress.

Phyle Fortress★ (Filí). – Alt 683m – 2 241ft. Only flocks of goats disturb the empty landscape round the ruins of Phyle which merge with the rock escarpment on which they stand commanding one of the passes between Attica and Boeotia. Considerable sections of the enclosing wall are still standing; it was built in 4C BC of huge rectangular blocks up to 2.70m – over 8ft thick and reinforced with several square towers and one round one *(partially collapsed)*.

PÓRTO GERMENÓ★

Itinerary ⑦ *– 32km – 20 miles Rtn*

Leave Athens by Leofóros Athinón. On leaving Eleusis (Elefsína) bear right into the Thebes (Thíva) road which climbs gently towards the Kithairon range which forms the border between Attica and Boeotia. *Continue past the turning (left) to Vília;* the ruins of Eleutherai (Eleftherés) are soon visible on a rock spur (right).

Eleutherai Fortress★ (Eleftherés). *– Leave the car near the petrol station and return to the path (left) which leads up to the fortress (1/2 hour on foot Rtn).*

The fortress stands on a desolate site, exposed to the wind, commanding the way over the Kithairon range at the southern end of the Káza Pass. The walls were built by the Athenians in 4C BC with gates and posterns and reinforced with high towers and provided with a parapet walk which is quite well preserved particularly on the north side; views of Attica.

At first the city of Eleutherai was Boeotian but in 6C BC it was attached to Athens when the wooden statue of Dionysos Eleutheros was taken to Athens where it became a cult object.

Continue by car to the **Giftókastro Pass** (alt 649m – 2 129ft) where there is a magnificent view westwards over Mount Kithairon and northwards over the fertile Boeotian plain. *Return downhill to the turning (right) to Vília.* The road runs through the pleasant little town of **Vília** *(hotels, restaurants),* past the military road *(right)* which leads to the summit of **Mount Kithairon** (Óros Kitherónas) which reaches 1 409m – 4 623ft *(military zone)* and winds down through stands of Aleppo pines to the bay of Pórto Germenó.

Pórto Germenó★. – Pop 94. This quiet seaside resort is a modern development with a huge beach. It is pleasantly sited in a bay at the eastern end of the Gulf of Corinth. The white houses are scattered among the pines and olives which cover the lower slopes of Kithairon.

Aigosthena Fortress★★ (Egósthena). *– Access by the narrow coast road. Free access. (Restoration work in progress).* Above the olive groves stands a very well preserved acropolis which is a good example of Greek military architecture in the late 4C BC: the enclosing wall (180m – 590ft long) is built of rough blocks of stone, with posterns, huge lintels and high towers; the most handsome tower *(on the right going up)* rises 9m – 30ft above the curtain wall.

In 13C the fortress was restored by the Franks – there are traces of a monastery – and linked to the seashore by two fortified walls enclosing the lower town; part of the northern wall is still extant.

DAPHNE – ELEUSIS – MÉGARA★★

Itinerary ⑧ *– 82km – 51 miles Rtn*

Access by bus from Platía Eleftherías (Odos P. Tsaldari) along the ancient Sacred Way (Iera Odós) **(AUV)**; *by car leaving Athens by Leofóros Athinón (map p 66).*

On the right beyond the junction of Leofóros Athinón with the road to Thessalonika is the site of the garden of the **Academy,** the famous school of philosophy founded by Plato near the town of **Colona** (Kolonós) where Sophocles was born in 496 BC.

On the left just before the beginning of the motorway to Corinth at the foot of a wooded hill stands the Daphne Monastery. A famous **wine festival** *(mid July-early September)* takes place in the adjoining park; the price of entry includes free tasting of the major Greek wines.

Daphne Monastery★★ (AU). *– Description page 94.*

From Daphne to Eleusis the road skirts the Bay of Eleusis which is guarded by the island of Salamis *(below)* and cluttered with unchartered ships. **Skaramangás** is the home of the national shipyards, formerly the property of Niarchos. **Eleusis** (Elefsína) is now an industrial town (pop 20 320) on the edge of a fertile plain where Demeter is supposed to have taught Triptolemos how to cultivate wheat *(p 106).* Drive through the town to reach the sanctuary of Eleusis *(signpost).*

Sanctuary of Eleusis★ (Elefsína). *– Description p 106.*

On leaving Eleusis follow the corniche coast road southwest to Néa Péramos: attractive views of the Bay of Eleusis. *After passing under the Athens to Corinth motorway the road reaches Mégara.*

Mégara. – Pop 17 719. Modern Mégara is an agricultural centre; its population is of Albanian origin and its terraced houses have an oriental look; the town is known for its Easter Tuesday festival. From 8C BC the city was a rival of Athens and established colonies in Sicily (Megara Hyblaea and Selinous) and the Bosphorus (Chalcedon and Byzantium, the latter in 657 BC).

THE ISLANDS: SALAMIS AND AIGINA★

The islands of the Saronic Gulf described here are those closest to Athens. The others – Hydra, Póros and Spetsae – can be reached not only from Piraeus but also from the Peloponnese and are described separately.

Salamis (Salamína). – Pop 20 807. *Access by ferry and launch from Pérama (1/2 hour crossing) and from Piraeus.* The island, which almost blocks the entrance to the Bay of Eleusis, has few interesting sights except for the beautiful 18C frescoes (Last Judgement) in the church of the **Faneroméni Monastery** (17C) but many Athenians have a holiday house on the island.

The battle of Salamis (480 BC). – The name of Salamis survives in the annals of the second Persian War because of the famous naval engagement described by Aeschylus in his play "The Persians". The Persians had overrun Athens and Attica and assembled their fleet in the Bay of Phaleron while the Greek triremes had withdrawn into the Bay of Eleusis. By a ruse Themistocles induced the Persian fleet to launch an attack off Pérama to confine and destroy the Greek ships but it was unable to manoeuvre in the narrow channel and was dispersed and mostly destroyed under the eyes of Xerxes, the "king of kings", who was following the battle from his throne on the cliffs.

Aigina★ (Égina). Pop 11 893. *Map p 68. Numerous services by motor boat, hydrofoil and ferry (1 1/4 hour crossing from Piraeus to Aigina Town and, in summer, to Agía Marína Beach also.*

The isle of Aigina, which covers 85km² – 33 sq. miles, comprises a series of volcanic heights in the centre and the south which culminate in Mount Zeus (alt 532m – 1 745ft), now known as Mount Profítis Ilías; its pyramidal silhouette, formerly crowned by a temple to Zeus, acted as a landmark for sailors. To the north and west the island consists of a coastal plain and low hills covered by plantations of pistachio nuts, almonds and olives and a few vineyards.

In Greek mythology the island was known as the kingdom of **Aiakos,** Achilles' grand-father, who, together with Minos and Rhadamanthos, was made judge of the underworld.

In the Archaic era (7C-6C BC) Aigina was a powerful maritime state, minting its own coins, marked with a tortoise, exporting its ceramics and bronzes and establishing colonies round the Mediterranean. Its rivalry with Athens, however, proved fatal and in 455 BC the islanders were defeated and had to emigrate.

Aigina Town. – Pop 6 333. The low, pink and white houses of the town cluster round the little harbour of coastal and fishing vessels protected by a charming chapel dedicated to St Nicholas, the patron of sailors. The shops along the waterfront sell the local specialities: pottery, pistachio nuts *(fistíkia)* and marzipan *(amigdalotá);* some of the boats act as floating shops dealing in fish, fruit and vegetables.

Aigina enjoyed a brief moment of glory during the struggle for independence from 1827 to 1829 when it was the capital of the new Greek state and Kapodistrias *(p 153)* set up his government on the island. Printing presses produced the first books and newspapers of free Greece and the first national money was minted bearing a phoenix, symbol of rebirth.

On **Cape Colonna,** north of the town, stands a fluted column crowned with a capital (8m – 23ft high), once part of a temple to Apollo erected in 5C BC; excavations in the neighbourhood have uncovered the remains of a theatre and a stadium, as well as a prehistoric dwelling.

Paleohóra★; temple of Aphaia★★. – *16km – 10 miles east by the road to Agía Marína (bus and taxi).* The road climbs slowly through pistachio orchards dotted with country cottages before reaching the **sanctuary of St Nectarios** (Ágios Nektários), a popular place of pilgrimage, since 1953, dedicated to the most recently canonized Greek saint who restored the nunnery and died on the island in 1920. *A track leads to Paleohóra.*

Paleohóra★ was the capital of the island under the Venetians and the Turks when the coast was vulnerable to piracy. In 18C the town counted 400 houses and about 20 religious establishments; it was abandoned by its inhabitants early in 19C. The houses were demolished but the cathedral, a basilical building, and the churches and chapels, most of which are 13C, have been restored; some are adorned with interesting frescoes and iconostases *(apply to the keeper in Paleohóra or in Ágios Nektários).* The Venetian castle on the hilltop provides a good view of Mount Zeus and the northwest coastline.

The road to Agía Marína climbs through pine woods, which produce the resin used as a preservative in the local wine *(retsína),* before reaching the temple of Aphaia.

Temple of Aphaia★★ (Aféa). – *Open 8.45am to 3pm (9.30am to 2.30pm Sundays); 100 Dr.*

(Photograph J. Bottin)

Aigina. – Temple of Aphaia

The temple stands on a magnificent site on the summit (alt 199m – 653ft) of a wooded hill overlooking the bay of Agía Marína and the rocky coast where sponge divers used to operate *(east)* and Athens and Mount Hymettos, Salamis and the Peloponnese *(north and west).*

The temple, which is quite well perserved, was built in the Doric style; some of the 22 limestone columns (5.27m – 17 1/4ft high) are monolithic. The scale is modest but well proportioned. The temple dates from the beginning of 5C BC and was dedicated to Aphaia, a local divinity. The pediments of sculpted marble depicted Athena presiding over a battle between Greeks and Trojans. These carvings, known as the Aigina Marbles, were bought in 1812 by Prince Ludwig of Bavaria, later King Ludwig I, and displayed in Munich.

The temple is approached by a ramp from the east near the sacrificial altars. The position of the *naós (p 18),* containing the statue of Aphaia, is clearly visible in the interior. South of the temple are traces of an entrance gate *(propylaia)* and the priest's lodgings.

The site was first excavated in April 1811 by C.R. Cockerell and von Hallerstein and again in 1901-03 by Bavarian archaeologists under Furtwängler. Traces of an Archaic temple were discovered in 1969.

CEPHALLONIA★★ _____ *(Kefalonía)*

Cephallonia is formed of jagged hilly limestone. It is 50km – 31 miles long and the largest (735m² – 284sq miles) of the Ionian Islands. The landscape is varied; smiling terraces by the sea contrast with the more arid mountain slopes which nonetheless support clumps of cypresses among the olives.

Mount Ainos (Énos), the highest point (alt 1 628m – 5 941ft), is covered by a particular kind of spruce peculiar to the island.

The Cephallonians are reputed to be a spirited people whose patriotism was praised by Byron. The island has not only produced soldiers, sailors and enterprising emigrants, but has also fostered an aristocratic and cultivated society which produced scholars and politicians such as Metaxas (1871-1941) who rejected the Italian ultimatum on 28th October 1940.

Practical information. – *Daily ferry from Patras to Sámi, time 3 1/2 hours;* the boat passes through the waters where the naval battle of Lepanto took place (south of Oxiá Island). *Ferries from Kilíni to Póros and Sámi; from Leukas (Lefkáda) and Ithaca to Fiskárdo. In summer ship from Brindisi to Sámi. Daily aircraft from Athens to Argostóli.*

Argostóli, the chief town, provides hotel accommodation, in particular two large residential hotels at Lássi and Platís Gialós (fine sandy beaches). The villages offer a variety of hotels and lodgings supervised by the GNTO (EOT) in Fiskárdo. There are many small uncrowded beaches.

Local specialities include the delicious Robóla wine, dishes composed of meat and rice and thyme-flavoured honey.

Invasions and invaders. – Cephallonia did not play a major role in antiquity although several Mycenaean tombs have been discovered.

During the Middle Ages the island first belonged to the Norman kings of Sicily, one of whom, Robert Guiscard, died on Cephallonia in 1085. Then it became the County of Cephallonia, one of the great fiefs of the Frankish principality of the Morea, and included Ithaca and Zakynthos. For three hundred years it was ruled by Italian overlords: the Orsini from 1155 to 1356 and the Tocchi until 1478.

The Turks held the island for only twenty years; by 1500 the Venetians, assisted by the Spanish troops of **Gonzales of Cordoba,** the Great Captain, had recaptured the island and they held it until 1797. After 1808 Cephallonia was occupied by the British, who promoted many improvements under the Residency of **Sir Charles Napier.** In 1823 Byron spent four months in a rented house in Metaxáta near Argostóli before sailing to Missolonghi. The island was finally returned to Greek control in 1864.

When Marshall Badoglio signed an armistice with the Allies in 1943, 9 000 Italians belonging to the "Acqui" Alpine division held out for 9 days against the German air and land attack. When they finally surrendered, the survivors – 3 410 officers and 4 750 soldiers – were shot en masse on Hitler's orders; only 34 escaped.

In 1953 an earthquake caused severe damage throughout the island.

TOUR *1 day*

Sámi. – Pop 935. The port of Sámi nestles in a gently curving bay *(beaches)* where the fleet of the Holy League assembled on the eve of the battle of Lepanto *(p 152)*. There is a fine view of the narrow entry to the bay and of the stark coast of Ithaca.

Melissáni Cave★. – *3km – 2 miles northwest; take the road to Agía Ef mía, turn left into the track which leads to the cave. Open 8am to 6pm; best times to visit between 10am and 2pm because of the light; 100 Dr.*

The underground lake which receives its water via subterranean passages from the swallow holes *(katavóthres)* near Argostóli, is explored by boat. The roof has fallen in places but the intensity and variety of the colours of the water, the contrast of light and shadow and the resonance and echo produce a fantastic effect.

Drongaráti Cave. *2km – 1 1/4 miles southwest; take the road to Argostóli and after 2km – 1 1/4 miles turn right into a track. Open 8am to 7pm; 30 Dr.*

A flight of steps leads down into this cave, which is easy to explore. Among the beautiful concretions are some enormous stalagmites.

Argostóli. – Pop 6 788. The road from Sámi crosses the **Agrapídies Pass** which gives a magnificent view of the **site★★** of Argostóli, stretching away below along a promontory towards the Lixoúri peninsula.

The main approach to Argostóli is over a bridge, 650m – 711yds long, which crosses the Koútavos Lagon and was built between 1810 and 1814 by Bosset, a Swiss working for the British.

After the earthquake in 1953 the capital of the island had to be rebuilt and has unfortunately lost its Greco-Venetian atmosphere. It can however be recaptured by visiting the **Korgialénios Museum★** *(open 8.45am to 3pm; 9.30am to 2.30pm Sundays and holidays; 100 Dr):* remarkable collection of old costumes, documents relating to Argostóli in the past, reconstructions of the interiors of aristocrats' houses and craftsmen's workshops.

Swallow-holes *(katavóthres).* – Near the end of the promontory, level with a restaurant, the sea water flows into a fissure and disappears underground before reappearing on the other side of the island in the Melissáni cave on the principle of communicating vessels.

The hydraulic power thus created was used to turn the mills of which one example with its paddle wheel can be seen.

View of the sea and the Lixoúri peninsula.

Tour of the Island★★. – *Leaving from Argostóli (167km – 104 miles by car, plus 1 1/2 hours of walking and sightseeing).* Leave Argostóli by the English Bridge and turn left into the coast road which climbs up the mountain side with extended views of the Argostóli Gulf and the Lixoúri peninsula. After crossing the isthmus, the road runs high up in a corniche providing spectacular **views★★** of the Mírtos Gulf and the empty Ionian Sea and then winds downhill towards the Ássos peninsula.

75

Ássos ★. – Pop 72. This is a fishing village *(guest houses, tavernas)* on an enchanting **site ★ ★** on the neck of a hilly peninsula which is crowned with a Venetian fortress (16C); the road up offers attractive views of the harbour below. The combination of the sea and the mountain, the scent of the pine trees, the sense of peace emanating from the little port and its shady square surrounded by flower-bedecked houses, make Ássos one of the most charming places in Cephallonia. The reconstruction of "Paris Square" after the earthquake in 1953 was financed by the city of Paris in France.

(Photograph GNTO)

Ássos. – Entrance to the fortress

The corniche road, where eagles are often sighted, continues north overlooking the many creeks which punctuate the coastline. Just before Fiskárdo there is a remarkable **view point ★ ★** over the straits which separate Cephallonia and Ithaca from the cliffs of Leukas (Lefkáda) *(p 128)* and the coast of Akarnanía.

Fiskárdo ★. – This charming sheltered port was spared by the earthquake in 1953 and has therefore kept its character. Its name derives from **Robert Guiscard,** the Norman king of Sicily, who died of typhoid on Cephallonia in 1085; he may have been buried in the ruined church with its two Norman towers, which is visible on the other side of the bay.

Fiskárdo has become a very popular resort in recent years.

Return to Diveráta and bear left at the T junction. The road crosses the mountains and skirts Sámi Bay: fines views of the bare mountainous coast of Ithaca.

Sámi. – *Description p 71.*

The road from Sámi to Póros, which is picturesque but very circuitous and sometimes in a poor state of repair, passes through several inland valleys where olive and cypress trees grow.

Póros. – Pop. 479. A little seaside resort *(hotels and tavernas)* in a rocky inlet.

The road climbs back up the ravine from the sea and then continues to the south coast through gorges studded with slim cypresses.

Markópoulo. – On 15 August, the feast of the Assumption, so it is said, serpents with black crosses on their skins appear for the day only to be gone next morning.

Beyond Markópoulo there are attractive views across the sea to Zakynthos *(p 198)*. Below the road on the left lie the ruins of the Franciscan convent of Sissíon, named after St Francis of Assissi.

The olive groves in the fertile plain of Livathó are over a hundred years old.

St George's Castle ★ (Ágios Geórgios). – *Apply to the keeper.* The curtain wall, 600m – 656yds long and reinforced with three bastions, encloses a 13C keep. Until 1757 it was the capital of the island with 15 000 inhabitants, but was severely damaged by an earthquake in 1636. Among the ruins beneath the pine trees are traces of St George's collegiate church with the arms of the Orsini over the door.

The castle stands on a height (320m – 1 050ft) overlooking the Livathó Plain (SE), the Lixoúri Peninsula (NW) and Zakynthos (S). *The road returns to Argostóli.*

EXCURSION

Isle of Ithaca (Itháki). – *Access by ferry from Sámi and Fiskárdo.* The smallest (after Paxí) of the Ionian Islands (103km² – 123sq yds; pop 4 952) is composed of two mountains joined by an isthmus. The steep west coast contrasts with the eastern shoreline which is less stark and more welcoming.

Ithaca is famous as the island of **Odysseus** and corresponds closely to the descriptions in Homer's Odyssey. Schliemann *(p 143)* began his archaeological career on Ithaca in 1860 by digging on what he judged to be the sites described in the Odyssey. Subsequent research by scholars and excavations carried out in 1930 by the British School at Athens have confirmed the Homeric story and identified the places where Odysseus, his father Laertes, his wife Penelope and their son Telemachos lived.

When **Byron** visited the island in August 1823 *(commemorative plaque in Vathí)* he found it so beautiful that he considered buying it and living there permanently.

Itháki. – Pop 2 037. Itháki, which is also known as Vathí, is the capital of the island, a port and a resort. It occupies a charming **site ★** at the head of a deep and narrow inlet; the green slopes on either side are covered with smart white houses built after the earthquake in 1953.

It was here that the Phaeacians (Corfiots) set down the sleeping Odysseus. The road from Itháki to Stavrós and then a path to the left lead to the **Nymph's Cave,** 190m – 623ft up, with a clump of cypresses at the entrance *(1 1/2 hours on foot Rtn)*; here Odysseus is supposed to have hidden the treasure given him by the Phaeacians before making himself known to his swineherd Eumaeos.

Stavrós. – Pop 364. The village *(tavernas)* is reached from Itháki by a fine road built high on the cliff face; it is the starting point for two walks.

One walk climbs to the top of Pelikáta *(1/2 hour on foot Rtn)* where excavations have uncovered Mycenaean remains which may have been the palace where Odysseus presented himself to Penelope disguised as a beggar.

The other walk *(1 1/2 hours on foot Rtn)* goes down into Pólis Bay where the port is thought to have been in Odysseus' day; bronze tripods contemporary with the King of Ithaca have been found in a cave sanctuary to the north.

CHAIRONEIA — *Herónia*

Central Greece – Boeotia – Michelin map 980 northeast of fold 29

The Kifíssos Valley, traditionally the route for invasions from the north, is now the route south for the road and railway. Beside the road stands a monumental marble lion recalling the battle and the ancient town of Chaironeia.

North versus South. – At the battle of Chaironeia in 338 BC the phalanxes of **Philip of Macedon** (30 000 infantry armed with pikes, 2 000 cavalry) were ranged against the slightly less numerous forces of the Greek cities who had come to the aid of Thebes owing to the exhortations of Demosthenes who took part in the fighting. The southern Greeks were overwhelmed by the heavy infantry and the Macedonian cavalry in which Alexander, then 18 years of age, was making his debut in battle. The famous Theban Sacred Band *(p 188)* fought to the death and Greece fell into the control of Philip of Macedon.

The biographer **Plutarch** (*c*50-127 AD), who wrote the Lives of Eminent Men, was born and died in Chaironeia.

The Lion. – A clump of cypresses marks the position of the colossal lion (5.50m – 18ft high) which gazes down from its pedestal at the passing cars. It was set up after the Battle of Chaironeia on the ossuary containing the remains of the soldiers of the Sacred Band who were killed on that fatal day: when the mausoleum was excavated 254 skeletons were discovered.

The lion was discovered by a party of English travellers in 1818 half buried in the ground. It was smashed to pieces in the War of Independence because it sounded hollow and was supposed to contain treasure. Nothing was found and it was restored early this century.

The **museum** contains the bones, arms and vases excavated from the tumulus of the Macedonian dead *(4km – 2 1/2 miles northeast near the railway line)*.

Public holidays in Greece: 1 and 6 January (Epiphany), 1st Monday in Lent, 25 March (Independence Day), Good Friday, Easter Sunday and Monday, 1 May, Whitsunday and Monday, 15 August, 28 October (Ohi Day, p 21), 25 and 26 December.

In Greece the religious festivals from Lent to Whitsun are fixed according to the Gregorian calendar and may be from one to four weeks later than in western Europe.

CHALANDRITSA — *Halandrítsa*

Peloponnese – Achaia – Pop 963 – Michelin map 980 north of fold 28

Chalandritsa lies deep in the hills above the coastal plain. During the Frankish occupation it was an important town, the seat of a barony which was first held by Robert de la Trémouille *(p 119)*. Reminders of this period still exist in the centre of the town: a huge square tower and several Gothic churches with flat chevets and pointed vaults, of which the most typical is St Athanasius'.

CHALCIDICE★ — *Halkidikí*

Macedonia – Halkidikí – Michelin map 980 folds 6, 7, 18 and 19

The peninsula of Chalcidice extends like a three-fingered hand from the coast of north eastern Greece into the Aegean Sea. Its northern limit is marked by two lakes – Korónia and Vólvi – lying in a depression between the Strymon Gulf *(east)* and the Gulf of Theassalonika *(west)*. It is a region of gently rolling hills where grain is grown.

The fingers are three mountainous wooded promontories: Kassándra, Sithonía and Mount Áthos which is known for its unique monastic life.

MOUNT ATHOS★★

No female creature of any kind has been allowed on Mount Áthos since 1060; it is also closed to tourists. Only those with genuine religious or cultural reasons may enter. Apply to the Greek authorities through the British Consul in Thessalonika or the British Embassy in Athens. Access is usually by boat from Ouranópoli (hotels and restaurants) to Dáphni.

In the summer there are boat excursions from Órmos Panagías on Sithonía which skirt the coast of the Holy Mountain.

The most easterly of the three peninsulas, the **Holy Mountain** (Ágio Óros), is 45km – 27 miles long by 5km – 3 miles, covererd with forests (oaks, chestnuts and pines) culminating at the southern tip in Mount Áthos, 2 033m – 6 670ft high. The steep slopes drop sheer into the sea which is often turbulent. Since 10C the peninsula has been a sort of monastic Orthodox republic with **Kariés** as the capital; the Greek state is represented by a governor.

Unique theocratic state. – The first community *(lávra)* of monks dates from 963 when **St Athanasius of Trebizond** was encouraged by the Emperor Nikephoros Phokas to found the monastery of the Grand Lavra. Other communities were established from 13C onwards and by 16C there were 30 000 monks in about 30 monasteries. Before the First World War the monks numbered 9 000.

At the last census in 1981 there were 1 472 monks (309 more than in 1971), in about twenty monasteries; the majority are Greek but a few monasteries receive other nationalities, e.g. Russians (Ágiou Panteleímonos), Bulgarians (Zográfou) and Serbs (Hiliandaríou). Most of the monks are old and they all wear beards. There are several different life styles; the idiorrhythmic rule, which the larger monasteries follow, relies on individual discipline; the coenobitic communities live a communal life with a very strict diet; smaller groups of monks live in ascetics' dwellings *(skétes),* while there are anchorites living in remote huts or isolated caves and also a few peripatetic monks.

Mount Athos is administered by four supervisors *(epistátis)* based in Kariés. Each monastery is governed by a superior or abbot *(igoúmenos)* who is in charge of the novices *(rasophori),* the professed monks *(kalógeri)* and the lay brothers *(parámikri);* visitors are received by the head of the guest house *(arhondáris).* The church services are announced by beating on a piece of wood **(símandro)** with a mallet.

The major monasteries, which are immense and decorated in brilliant colours, were usually arranged round a courtyard and fortified with towers, the highest of which acted as the keep, to protect them from pirates in earlier centuries. The buildings round the courtyard accommodate the guest house, the monks' cells giving on to external balconies and the refectory *(trápeza)* in front of which stands the washing place *(fiáli).* In the centre of the court stands the church *(katholikon),* a cross-in-square building roofed with one or several domes. The walls of the churches and refectories are decorated with frescoes; the most beautiful were painted by artists such as M. Panselinos (14C), Theophanes the Cretan, Zorzio or Frango Kastellanos (16C). The libraries, which are often housed in the keep, contain upwards of 10 000 ancient manuscripts, some of which are unfortunately badly damaged.

The Monasteries. – Those mentioned here are the most famous or the most easily visited. *They all close at sunset.*

Grand Lavra (Megístis Lávras). – The oldest (963 AD) and the largest (104 monks) of the monasteries on the Holy Mountain is situated not far from the end of the peninsula at the foot of cloud-capped Mount Athos. Commanding the sea and its own natural harbour, the monastery looks like a fortified city and contains over 100 relics.

Athanasius, the founder, is buried in the 10C-11C church beneath the huge dome. Outside the immense 16C refectory stands a handsome *fiáli* (16C) with a porphyry basin; within the chairs and tables are of stone and the walls are covered with famous frescoes also 16C by **Theophanes the Cretan.** The library contains 5 000 volumes, about half of which are manuscripts.

Further south lies a stony waste known as the Hermits' Desert because a number of anchorites have established themselves in the cavities in the rugged cliff overlooking the sea.

Vatopedíou. – This huge monastery was established in 980 in an idyllic site overlooking a bay and a little port. It was fortified early in 15C. The maze of buildings includes some fifteen chapels as well as the church, a red building dating from the late 11C. The 15C bronze entrance doors came from Agía Sophía in Thessalonika; the mosaic is a remarkable piece of 11C work. Within are some interesting 13C to 16C icons.

The Treasury boasts some rare gold reliquaries and a 15C jasper cup on an enamelled silver base belonging to Manuel Palaiologos. The Library is well stocked with manuscripts (about 600) including a 12C copy of Ptolemy's Geography.

Ivíron. – This 10C monastery, which was originally dedicated to St John the Baptist, is hidden in a hanging valley overlooking the sea and surrounded by olive and pine trees. The church is 11C; a chapel contains the miraculous icon of the Mother of God of the Gate (Panagía Portaítissa) (10C). The library possesses many illuminated manuscripts (11 to 13C).

Símonos Pétras. – The lofty 14C coenobitic monastery with its row upon row of wooden balconies occupies a spectacular site atop a rock barely attached to the western face of the mountain.

Ágiou Dionissíou. – This monastery was founded in 16C on a rocky site overlooking an inlet on the west coast. The church and refectory are decorated with remarkable frescoes dating from 16C by Zorzio the Cretan and from 17C. The library contains a 7C evangelistary.

SITHONÍA Peninsula★★

Since the recent construction of roads and tourist facilities, the natural beauties of Sithonía have become more accessible: forests of sea and umbrella pines, fine sandy beaches in secluded bays and inlets, deep fjords with sheer rock walls penetrating the rugged coastline and providing under-water fishing.

To drive round the peninsula (109km – 68 miles, 3 1/2 hours) follow the coast road clockwise; it runs past many beauty spots, becomes a corniche road along the cliffs and opens up extensive views particularly east to Mount Áthos although the summit is often shrouded in clouds.

Órmos Panagías. – Pop 22. Picturesque hamlet in a rocky bay.

Sárti. – Pop 777. Small cultivated coastal plain running down to a sandy bay.

Cape Drépano★. – Rocky promontory deeply indented with many inlets extending into fjords particularly at Koufós and round Kalamítsi.

Toróni Bay★. – The long sandy beach of this idyllic bay curves gently south into a tiny peninsula which bears the remains of an ancient fortress mentioned by Thucydides *(excavations in progress).*

Pórto Carrás ★ ★. – Seaside resort masterminded by the oil tycoon, John C. Carras and completed in 1980. It is a spectacular undertaking with accommodation for 3 000 people centred on two hotels of imposing design, a charming seaside village with a harbour where three-masted sailing ships for local cruising are based, a golf course, tennis courts, a casino, a riding stable etc.

Nearby John Carras established a model farm with lemon and olive groves, almond orchards and vineyards producing an excellent wine.

KASSÁNDRA Peninsula

The Kassándra peninsula, which is served by a modern road running round the coast, is less wooded and less attractive than Sithonía but it is more fertile (wheat, olives) and more densely populated.

The isthmus has been breached by a canal at Néa Potídea, the site of ancient Poteidaia. The peninsula offers pleasant beaches and a number of hotels especially at Saní, Kalithéa, Agía Paraskeví and **Palioúri★** which lies at the southern end looking across a bay to the Sithonía peninsula.

CHALKIS *Halkída*

Euboia – Pop 44 867 – Michelin map 🗓🗓🗓 fold 30

Chalkis is the capital of Euboia (Euboea) which is separated from the mainland by the **Euripos,** a channel 39m – 128ft wide which is spanned by a bridge. The town is built on the edge of a fertile plain; it is a port, a market for agricultural produce and an industrial centre (cement works, textiles, food processing). The ramparts built by the Venetians to protect the town they knew as **Negroponte** have been demolished leaving a modern seafront composed of hotels, fish restaurants and cafés; the beaches lie along the coast north of the town.

Venetians and Turks. – From 13C to 15C the Venetians held a commanding position in Chalkis which they developed into an important commercial centre exporting the products of Euboia and controlling the maritime trade in the north of Greece. Italian and Greek merchants traded in competition with the Jews whose cemetery still exists.

The Venetians fortified both Chalkis and the bridge over the Euripos (Evrípos). Their name for the town (and also of the whole island) was derived from a corruption of Evripo (Egripo – Negripo) which the Venetians rationalised into Negroponte (black bridge – *p 110*). Despite its defences Negroponte was attacked several times in 14C both by the Catalans and by the Genoese who captured 23 Venetian ships in 1350.

In 1470 the town was captured by Sultan Mahomet II himself but nonetheless remained a lively trading centre with many commercial companies. In 1658 even the Jesuits succeeded in establishing themselves and one of them, Father Coronelli, who was a geographer, sketched a profile of the town.

In 1688 15 000 Venetian soldiers tried to recapture the town by laying siege to it but they were decimated by malaria which carried off their leader, Koenigsmark, and were forced to retire.

SIGHTS *1 1/2 hours*

Karababá Fort. – It was built on the mainland on the site of a Venetian fortress in 1686 by the Turks to serve as a bridgehead and was in use until 1856.

From the west bastion, there is a fine **view★** of Chalkis, the Euripos and the **Bay of Aulis** *(south)* where the Greek fleet mustered before setting out for Troy and where, so it is said, Agamemnon sacrificed his daughter **Iphigenia** to obtain a favourable wind.

Euripos Bridge. – A variety of bridges has served since the first in 411 BC. The present bridge (1962), consisting of two half spans decked with wood, which drop down and then roll back on rails beneath the approaches, replaces the famous fortified bridge with its central bastion which can be seen in many old prints and which was longer than the present structure since one of the arms of the Euripos has been filled in. The bridge is opened from time to time to allow the passage of leisure craft and coastal shipping moving with the flow of the current.

This **current** can attain 7 or 8 knots and it changes direction from north-south to south-north at least six and as many as fourteen times a day. This natural phenomenon can easily be observed but the cause of it has never been completely understood. **Aristotle** is supposed to have drowned himself in the Euripos because he could not explain the enigma; in fact he did die in Chalkis in 322 BC but of natural causes.

Archaeological Museum. – *Open 8.45am to 3pm (9.30am to 2.30 Sundays); 100 Dr.*

It contains some beautiful Archaic sculptures (early 5C BC) from the Temple of Apollo in Erétria *(p 111):* a group showing Theseus abducting Antiope (Hippolyta) and a bust of Athena holding a shield (aegis) bearing a Gorgon's head; also a 2C Roman work of Antinoüs disguised as Bacchus.

Beyond the museum there is a picturesque market with an oriental atmosphere.

St Mary's Basilica (Agía Paraskeví). – *Second street on the left coming from the bridge.* The church, which is situated in the old town, is Byzantine in origin and rests on ancient columns of cipolin marble; in 13C-14C it was converted into a Gothic cathedral probably by a Frenchman: Latin cross plan, rib vaulting in the chapels flanking the square chancel, rose window in the façade.

Not far away in the small square (Platía Kóskou) there is a disused mosque, now being restored to house a Byzantine museum, and a Turkish fountain; at the beginning of the 19C there were 1 600 Turkish families living in Chalkis.

Before the Second World War there was also a large Jewish community which had its own cemetery to the east of the town centre.

Pop 49 865 – Michelin map 980 fold 33

The island of Chios, which lies a mere 8km – 5 miles off the Turkish coast, is less verdant than its neighbours, Lesbos and Samos, but the countryside is varied with groves of olives, oranges, lemons and pomegranates to which the cypress trees add a sombre note; the painted houses are decorated with balconies and carved wooden screens in the Ottoman style.

The island is dominated to the north by mountains of volcanic origin – the highest point is Mount Pelinéo (alt 1 297m – 4 255ft); the hillsides and coastal plains, which are well watered by winter rainfall, are given over to the cultivation of citrus fruit, mulberries, vines, cotton, tobacco, fruit and vegetables.

In the south the Chiots traditionally grow the lentisk or mastic tree; its aromatic resin is used in the production of alcoholic drinks (mastíka, rakí), in chewing gum and in oriental cakes, syrups and preserves.

Access and accommodation. – *By boat or ferry from Piraeus daily (in season) at about 10am; by air from Athens every day at about 1pm.* Chios Town (Híos) is the main resort. Attractive beach at Mármaro on the north coast.

HISTORICAL NOTES

Mediterranean maritime trading centre. – Chios lies on the shipping routes to Thessalonika, and Constantinople, Smyrna, Crete, Rhodes and Cyprus, the ports of the Levant and Egypt. From antiquity to 19C the island has played a major role in the exchanges between east and west.

This pivotal role was made easier since the island was included in the Christian sphere of influence for over four centuries; it became Venetian in 1172, then Byzantine and from 1346-1566 was the centre of a Genoese "empire" which incorporated Samos, Lemnos, Lesbos, Samothrace and Thassos.

In fact in Chios the Genoese authority was delegated to a *"mahone"*, a financial and military body controlled by the Republic. The mahone of Chios, which was known as the Giustiniani mahone after the Genoese family which administered it, held a near monopoly of commercial traffic in the eastern Aegean. The port attracted commodities from the near East, cotton and spices, oil and soap, silk from the Caspian sea, Turkish wheat, Genoese cloth and slaves; but the two most important items of trade were the local mastic and alum from the Phokaian mines in Anatolia, which was essential to the dyeing process and exported mainly to Bruges.

Despite conflicts with the Venetians and the threat of the Turks, who captured Constantinople in 1453, Chios harbour was full of shipping: Genoese brigantines, Venetian galleys, Mediterranean tartanes and xebecs and Turkish feluccas. Bankers, lawyers and insurance agents set up offices in the town where the great merchants had their counters and their agents.

The Turkish occupation of Chios did not damage the island's trade although Barbery pirates used it as a base; in 1680 many of them were sunk just offshore from Chios Town by a French squadron under Duquesne.

The island even retained a measure of independence: the Turks, represented by a governor, who in the early 18C was a French renegade, Count Bonneval (Achmed Pasha), demanded only allegiance and tribute. In 19C the Chiot ship owners had a merchant fleet to rival those of Hydra, Spetsae or Psará.

"Chios Massacres". – At the beginning of the War of Independence, in 1821, the island rose against the Turks at the instigation of the inhabitants of Samos who had fled to Chios. The revolt failed and the Turks exacted a terrible vengeance which lasted five years: over 30 000 Christians were massacred or enslaved.

This cruel punishment aroused intense emotion in western Europe, particularly in France under the leadership of Chateaubriand: Delacroix's famous painting "the Massacres in Chios", Alfred de Vigny's poem Helena, and Victor Hugo's verses "The Greek Child" were inspired by it.

A few years later in 1827 Colonel Fabvier *(p 46)* and his Greek troops tried to take the town and besieged the castle but they had to retire finally in the face of numerous Turkish reinforcements. Chios finally became part of Greece in 1912.

The two humanists, Adamantios Koraïs and John Psichári, came of families of Chiot origin although they died in Paris in 1833 and 1929 respectively; Koraïs founded a library on the island which is now the fourth largest in Greece (95 000 volumes); John Psichári is buried there.

CHIOS TOWN (HÍOS) *1 hour*

The main town (pop 24 070), which was defended by a citadel, has been rebuilt several times, most recently after the earthquake in 1881. It has a pleasant position at the foot of Mount Épos, overlooking the harbour and the "Chios Strait".

Kastro. – The citadel was built by the Venetians and the Genoese from 13C to 15C and bears the coat of arms of the Giustiniani family; within its picturesque confines are St George's Church and several old houses dating from the Genoese period.

EXCURSIONS

Néa Moní★★. – *9km – 5 1/2 miles west. Open all day (except from 1 to 5 pm); informal dress inadmissible.* A superb panoramic road climbs the foothills of Mount Épos to the monastery which stands in a wooded valley guarded by cypress trees.

It is one of the most important buildings of the Byzantine era and was founded on the spot where a miraculous icon of the Virgin had been found. It was built in 11C by Constantine Monomachos in gratitude to the three hermits of Chios who had predicted that he would accede to the throne.

It is the work of architects and painters from Constantinople. The church, which is octagonal, is the best example of the architecture of this period in Greece. The walls of the interior are beautifully faced with plaques of coloured marble and mosaics; the latter are noteworthy for their originality and uniform style. The iconography conforms strictly to Christian doctrine. The figures are severe with vivid colours and expressions.

The church was damaged in the earthquake in 1881. The dome was replaced in 19C and is decorated with frescoes. There are more frescoes in the exo-narthex which are later than the mosaics.

In addition to the church it is worth visiting the cistern (11C), the refectory and a defensive tower. The cells are of more recent date.

Mastikohória★. – Armália *(26km – 16 1/4 miles southwest of Chíos Town)* is the beginning of "mastic country" which covers all the southern part of the island and comprises some twenty communities. This is where the lentisk grows; it is a bush about 2m – 6 1/2ft high which is cupped for its resin, mastic, which is collected in the summer. Average annual production is about 300 tonnes. The villages are very attractive; the old flower-bedecked houses are crowded together in the narrow lanes and vaulted passages, evoking the Middle Ages.

Pirgí★. – Pop 1 204. Picturesque medieval town with a Genoese fortress. Unusual houses with balconies and geometric sgraffito decoration. The church of the Holy Apostles (Ágii Apóstoli) and its frescoes both date from 12C.

Mestá. – Pop 400. A very typical village where the houses have been refurbished.

Emboriós. – This archaeological site near the sea has yielded traces of prehistoric, Greek, Roman and Christian settlement (paleo-Christian basilica built on the foundations of a 6C BC temple). It was excavated by the British School in 1954 when underwater reconnaissance by divers was employed for the first time in an archaeological survey.

Volissós. – Pop 479. *46km – 28 miles northwest.* Charming medieval fortress village with winding streets. According to tradition it was the birthplace of Homer.

CHLEMOUTSI Castle★★ _____ *Hlemoútsi*

Peloponnese – Elis – Michelin map 𝟿𝟾𝟶 fold 27

Chlemoutsi Castle, the watchtower of Frankish Morea and a masterpiece of medieval military art, reigns proudly over the Kyllene (Kilíni) peninsula from its position on top of Cape Chelonátas (alt 256m – 840ft) overlooking the Ionian Sea to Zakynthos.

From Geoffrey to Ibrahim. – This fortress, which was the most powerful in Morea, was built between 1220 and 1223 by **Geoffrey II de Villehardouin,** who called it Clermont, from which the Greek Chlemoutsi is derived. Late in 13C it passed to the Angevins of Naples *(p 122)* who held Marguerite de Villehardouin captive in the castle until she died in 1315; she was the daughter and only descendant of William de Villehardouin.

Subsequently it was dubbed **Castel Tornese** by the Italians probably because of the coins *(tournois)* produced by the local mint which bore the façade of St Martin's Church *(destroyed)* in Tours in France on one face. The castle passed into the possession of the Palaiologi, the despots of Mystra and other places in the Peloponnese, in 1427; in 1460 it was captured by the Turks who adapted it for the use of artillery, added a bastion and then abandoned it. It was damaged again in 1827 by the forces of Ibrahim Pasha.

Tour. – *Open 8.45am to 3pm. Access from the village. Restoration in progress.*

The fortress consists of an outer court and the castle proper, which is built on a polygonal plan according to a formula apparently inherited from the crusader castles.

Outer court. – The entrance, a mini fort in itself, leads into the outer court, which was the domain of the servants; it is enclosed by a curtain wall, which dates back to 13C but was extensively altered by the Turks. The buildings which backed up against the curtain wall have almost all been destroyed leaving only their fireplaces and foundations.

There is a fine view of the walls of the castle; originally the round towers were some 6m – 20ft higher than the walls.

Castle. – The impressively large vaulted entrance is flanked *(left)* by the chapel which is on two floors, the lower one for the servants and the upper one for the owner and his suite, and *(right)* by a vast structure, 70m – 230ft long, also with two floors, the lower one being a guard room and the upper being a hall where the assemblies of the Frankish barons of Morea were probably held.

At the centre of the castle is a hexagonal court, 53m by 30m – 174ft by 98ft, where jousts and other entertainments were held. Surrounding it are vast halls built against the outer curtain wall which is in places up to 8m – 26ft thick. These chambers, which originally had an intermediate floor, have vaulted ceilings supporting a terrace above.

From the terraces there is a splendid **panorama★★** of Zakynthos (W) and the other Ionian Islands (NW); the coast by Missolonghi (N); the plain of Elis (E), which is bordered to the north by Mount Skólis and Sandoméri, named after a castle built in 14C by Nicolas II de St Omer; and the valley of the River Peneios (E), the mountains of Arcadia (SE) and Cape Katákolo (S).

Michelin Guides

The Red Guides (hotels and restaurants)

Benelux – Deutschland – España Portugal – Main cities EUROPE – France – Great Britain and Ireland – Italia

The Green Guides (beautiful scenery, buildings and scenic routes)

Austria – Canada – England: The West Country – Germany – Italy – London – New England – New York City – Portugal – Rome – Scotland – Spain – Switzerland and 7 guides on France

CORFU★★★ _____ *Kérkira*

Ionian Islands – Pop 97 102 – Michelin map 980 fold 14

Corfu, which lies just off the coast of Albania (Shqipëria) and Epiros, is the most attractive of the Ionian Islands. Its charm derives from its very varied coastline washed by the violet-blue sea, its rolling hills and luxuriant gardens, its gentle climate and the smiling welcome of its inhabitants. Greek by language and tradition, the island spent many years under foreign domination – British and French but mainly Venetian – and is now a most attractive summer and winter resort with a cosmopolitan atmosphere.

Practical information. – *Access by ferry; frequent crossings from Igoumenítsa (Epiros) (1 3/4 hours); also from Patras (Peloponnese), Ancona, Bari and Brindisi (Italy); by air daily from Athens (1 hour). Traditional dancing in local costume on St Spyridon's Day and feast days (particularly 21 May – anniversary of union with Greece).*

Many hotels in all categories; two 18-hole golf courses; famous Club Mediterranée village in **Ipsos**; casino in the Achilleion.

Main beaches (sand): Ágios Spiridónas and Róda (north coast); Ágios Geórgios, Mirtiótissa, Glifáda and Ágio Górdis (west coast); Kávos (southern promontory).

Cars and motorbikes for hire in Corfu Town.

Specialities: fish including crayfish, *sofritó* (beef or veal cooked in a sauce of garlic, vinegar and black pepper), *graviéra* (type of gruyère cheese), honey, *dzinzerbíra* (ginger-beer), kumkwat (mini oranges in alcohol); white "Paloúmbi" wine.

GEOGRAPHICAL AND HISTORICAL NOTES

Corfu is 60km – 37 miles long and culminates in the north in Mount Pandokrátor (906m – 2 972ft). It is formed of limestone rock, very worn by erosion: fissures, caves, inland valleys lined with deposits of marl and clay.

The climate, which is warm and damp in winter and hot in summer, favours the growth of vegetation which is further encouraged by the depth of soil: a forest of age-old olive trees, sometimes quite large, citrus fruits, vineyards, maize, semi-tropical trees such as magnolias, palms, jujubes, succulents and myrtle clothe the island in a green mantle which contrasts sharply with the barrenness of the mainland.

Isle of the Phaeacians. – In the Odyssey Homer tells how Odysseus lingers on the Isle of Ogygia for love of the nymph Calypso, is set free by the intervention of Hermes and is on course for Ithaca when a storm throws him up on the coast of the isle of Scheria, identified as Corfu.

There he is discovered by the gracious **Nausicaa**, "of the white arms", who is playing ball with her companions, and she conducts him to her father, Alcinoüs, king of the Phaeacians. He receives Odysseus in his palace, which is surrounded by enchanting gardens, lays on a banquet in honour of Laertes' son who recounts his adventures, offers him rich presents and finally provides him with a ship to return to Ithaca *(p 76)*.

In 8C BC the Corinthians founded a colony on the island which became known as Corcyra until the Middle Ages.

The mark of the Lion (1386-1797). – From 1267 to 1386 the Angevin kings of Naples, following in the train of Charles I of Anjou, brother of St Louis, controlled Corfu but then the Venetians took command and made the island the main port of call for their "**galleys**" (merchant ships) on the route to the Levant.

During the Venetian occupation Corfu had to face attacks by the Turks on several occasions. They ravaged the island in 1537 under Suleiman the Magnificent (1494-1566) but failed to take the citadel. In 1571 a force of 1 500 Corfiot sailors took part in the naval battle of Lepanto *(p 152)*. Finally in 1716 an army of 30 000 Turks invaded the island but the fierce resistance of the garrison, a mixed force of Greeks, Slavs, Italians and Germans, under the command of a Saxon mercenary, Count von der Schulenberg, beat them back.

Through their representative, *provveditore,* the Venetians imposed their rule on Corfu, which became an arsenal and warehouse, with the assistance of the local nobility who were inscribed in a Golden Book as in Venice. Italian became the official language, Roman Catholicism held a privileged position and the Venetian government paid a sequin for every new olive tree planted, since Venice lacked oil.

This period of Venetian domination saw the building of rectangular churches with flat ceilings and detached bell towers, of tall narrow houses some with loggias, of wells with sculpted surrounds and arcaded Italian farmhouses *(fattorias);* many of the icons are the work of artists who were driven out of Crete by the Turks in 17C; the most famous is Emmanuel Tzanes (1610-1690).

Corfu under the French. – When French Republican troops occupied Venice in June 1797, several thousand men were sent to Corfu under General Gentili, a Corsican, who was welcomed with shouts of enthusiasm. Trees of Liberty were planted, the Golden Book was burned and Greek was reinstated as the official language. But the French incurred the anger of the Corfiots by their lack of respect for the relics of St Spyridon, patron saint of the island. Two years later they were driven out by the Russians and the Turks who set up the Septinsular Republic covering all the Ionian Islands including Kythera.

In 1807 under the Treaty of Tilsit France regained Corfu which Napoleon considered the key to the Adriatic. Seven years of enlightened government under General Donzelot mounted 500 canons on the fortifications, improved the appearance of Corfu Town (arcades on the Spianáda) and encouraged agriculture by extending the use of the plough. The press which had been created in 1797 was extended and in 1808 the first Ionian Academy was founded consisting of 26 members including Foscolo *(p 198)* Fauvel *(pp 46 and 52)*, and the famous Greek philosopher Koraïs who at that time lived in Paris.

British Protectorate (1814-1864). – Under the Treaty of Paris the Ionian Islands were granted independent status under the protection of the British government. In reality, although the constitution was drawn up in favour of the islanders, the British High Commissioner held the effective power.

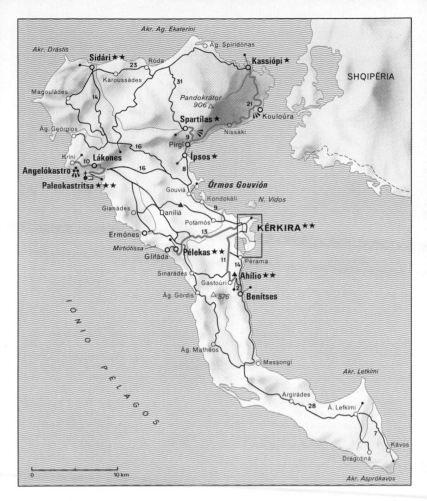

Nonetheless, Sir Thomas Maitland and Sir Frederick Adam, whose wife was a Corfiot, a member of the Palatianos family, provided the island with a solid infrastructure: public buildings, a road network, water supplies etc.

In 1824 Lord Guilford (1766-1827), a Philhellene who dreamed of reviving the spirit of ancient Greece and adopted the Orthodox religion, founded a second Ionian Academy with four faculties – theology, law, medicine and philosophy – and presented it with an extensive library. Originally he had intended to site his university on Ithaca.

In 1856 Edward Lear, who called Corfu a paradise and spent long periods on the island between 1848 and 1863 and painted many views of it, was offered the post of Director to the new Art Department in the University but he declined.

Corfu developed as an intellectual centre attracting the poets Kalvos, who lectured at the Academy, and **Solomós**, who composed the National Greek anthem.

Although the Corfiotes were prevented from playing an official part in the Greek War of Independence, they supplied money and volunteers and the first head of the new Greek state, **John Kapodistrias** (1776-1831), who came of an ancient line of Istrian origin and was buried in the Platitera Monastery on Corfu.

In 1861 Gladstone, who had served as Lord High Commissioner Extraordinary in the Islands in 1858-59 and was then Chancellor of the Exchequer, declared that "it would be nothing less than a crime against the safety of Europe" to cede the islands to Greece but a year later in December 1862 the decision to cede was made and the islands joined the new independent Greek state on the accession of George I to the throne (1863).

CORFU TOWN★★ (Kérkira – Pop 33 561).

The old town of Corfu between the old and new citadels has retained its Greco-Venetian atmosphere while the Spianáda, where Corfiot and tourist meet, supplies a touch of British dignity. Barouches drawn by horses sporting plumes and pompoms provide an agreeable means of transport.

Spianáda★ (B). – Once an open space for drilling soldiers and now a popular place for walking, the Spianáda (Platía) was planted with gardens, palm and eucalyptus trees during the Napoleonic occupation.

It is liberally adorned with commemorative monuments and statues: neo-Classical rotunda in memory of Maitland the High Commissioner, statues of Schulenburg (18C near the entrance to the citadel), of Lord Guilford and of Kapodistrias (near the former Academy to the south).

The west side of the Spianáda is lined by the "Liston", an arcaded terrace housing restaurants, tea rooms and bookshops; the building which was designed by Mathieu de Lesseps, father of the builder of the Suez Canal, dates from the French Empire Period (1804-14) and was inspired by the Rue de Rivoli in Paris.

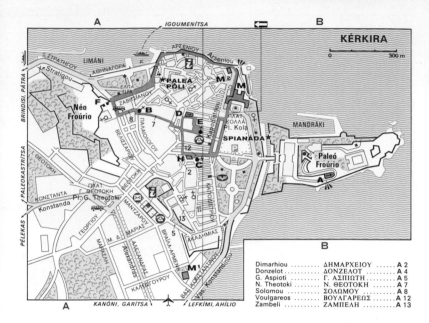

A | IGOUMENÍTSA | B

KÉRKIRA

0   300 m

B

The Spianáda also incorporates the famous Corfu **cricket pitch**. The Corfiots were introduced to the game under the British Protectorate and have played with enthusiasm ever since. There are four local teams which play on Wednesdays, Saturdays and Sundays. The tradition of touring teams, which dates back to the annual visits of the Mediterranean fleet before the Second World War, is now maintained through the Anglo-Corfiot Cricket Association (founded in 1970-71).

Ancient Citadel (Paleó Froúrio) (B). – *Open in the season 9am to 3pm; closed Tuesdays. Son et Lumière 15 May to end September. Traditional Greek dancing from 1 June.*

A promontory, consisting of two hills linked by a saddle and separated from the Spianáda by a canal, was the site of the early township of Corfu. By the Middle Ages fortifications already covered the twin peaks, the "sea fort" and the "land fort", protecting the houses which huddled round the Cathedral of St Peter and St Paul. The citadel is now occupied by a Military Academy.

In 16C the Venetians repaired the fortifications; they dug the canal and built the two powerful bastions which flank the bridge linking the promontory to the Spianáda.

The interior is much changed; **St George's Church** (Ágios Geórgios) (B A) was built in the form of a Doric temple for the British garrison in 1830 and the former Venetian barracks dominate the little port of Mandráki where the Venetian galleys rode at anchor. Fine views of the town and the roadstead.

Palace of St Michael and St George. (B M). – It was built from 1818 to 1823 as an official residence for the British High Commissioner and designed by Col George Whitmore. It is a neo-Classical building preceded by a Doric colonnade containing 32 columns. In 1864 it became a royal residence for the Greek monarch. The statue of Sir Frederick Adam in front of the façade is by the Corfiot sculptor Pavlos Prosalentis.

The palace now houses an interesting **Museum of Asiatic Art** ★ *(open 8.45am to 3pm; closed Tuesdays; 100 Dr)* (containing 10 000 items: funerary urns and Chinese bronzes, incense flasks, rare lacquers, ceramics and engravings, Japanese screens richly decorated; also a beautiful series of 17C and 18C icons by the Creto-Venetian school.

Old Town ★ (Paleá Póli) (A). – A walk *(about 1 1/2 hours)* takes in the narrow streets where the washing is hung out to dry, the little paved squares resembling theatre sets, the elegant church façades and the high arcaded houses which made old Corfu so picturesque during the Venetian period.

Leave the Spianáda by the northwest corner, pass the left side of the Palace to emerge on the corniche which is lined by old houses, some with Venetian loggias, overlooking the Corfiot roadstead and the Epirot coast. Here stands a small **Byzantine Museum (B M2)** displaying mainly icons *(open 8.45am to 3pm;*

(From photograph Editions Thira, K. Voutsas)

Corfu. – The old town

84

9.30am to 2.30pm Sundays; 100 Dr). Just offshore is the **Islet of Vídos** which was so densely covered with olive trees in 17C that it was described as "a forest swimming on the waves". It was denuded by 3 hours of heavy shelling in an allied attack on the French in 1798 when only 50 of the original 700 defenders survived.

Odós Donzelot, bordered by handsome houses belonging to shipping magnates, leads down to the quays of the Old Port *(fish tavernas)* where the ferries from Igoumenítsa and the mail boats from Paxí dock.

New Citadel (Néo Froúrio) **(A)**. – *Not open.* It was built in 16C and 17C but altered in 19C; a Venetian doorway bears the winged lion of St Mark **(A F)**.

Odós Solomoú leads into the upper town. At the beginning of Odós Nikifórou Theotokí stands St Antony's Church **(A B)**, a 14C building with an 18C Baroque iconostasis. Halfway up this street, which has many shops and was the main artery of Venetian Corfu, turn left to St Spyridon's Church.

St Spyridon's Church (Ágios Spiridónas) **(A D)**. – This 16C church with its tall detached bell tower was dedicated to a 4C Cypriot bishop whose relics were transferred from Constantinople in 1456 and who became the patron saint of Corfu. A chapel houses the silver coffin which contains the mummified body of the saint. From time to time it is solemnly paraded round the town particularly on the Orthodox feasts of Palm Sunday, Holy Saturday, 11 August and the first Sunday in November.

Southeast of St Spyridon's Church is a charming little square flanked by the church of Our Lady of Strangers (Panagía ton Xenón) **(A E)**. *Continue to the Town Hall.*

Town Hall Square (Platía Dimarhíou) **(A H)**. – Since 1903 the Town Hall has occupied the low building decorated with medallions; which was built as a loggia in 1693 and converted into a theatre in 1720; at one end is a monument to Morosini who expelled the Turks from the Peloponnese in 1691.

On the east side of the square stands the Roman Catholic cathedral **(A C)**, which dates from 17C and was restored after the last war; it contains a delicate 15C Venetian painting of the Madonna *(third chapel on the right)*.

Return by Odós Voulgáreos (attractive arcades) and Odós Kapodistríou (busy shops) to the starting point.

Archaeology Museum ★ **(A M1)**. – *Open 8.45am to 3pm (9.30am to 2.30pm Sundays); closed Tuesdays; 100 Dr.*

This modern style museum displays three Archaic works from ancient Corcyra (south of Garítsa Bay);
– the Gorgon pediment (6C BC) which belonged to the temple of Artemis and consists of a colossal figure of the Gorgon (Medusa) scowling with two serpents entwined about her waist; it is flanked by two feline creatures; anyone who gazed upon this Gorgon was supposed to turn to stone;
– a curious high relief sculpture of a Dionysiac banquet;
– the Archaic "lion of Menecrates" (7C BC) which covered a warrior's tomb.

There is also a collection of terracotta votive offerings and a head of the Athenian poet Menander (342-292 BC).

EXCURSIONS

Canon Walk (Kanóni) ★★. – *4km – 2 1/2 miles south.* Follow the attractive curve of Garítsa Bay as far as the suburb of Anemómilos where the villas are surrounded by gardens, and then bear right into Odós Iássonou Sossípatrou which leads to a 12C Byzantine church, Ágios Iássonas-Sossípatros. In the narthex are four fine 17C icons by Emmanuel Tzanes: St Jason and St Sossipater, disciples of St Paul who brought the Gospel to Corfu, and St John of Damascus and St Gregory Palamas.

The road which is narrow and congested skirts the villa known as **Mon Repos** *(not open)* which is surrounded by a beautiful park and stands on the site of the ancient acropolis of Corcyra. It was designed as a summer residence for Adam, the British Commissioner, in 1824 by Col George Whitmore, an engineer officer. Later it was given to the Greek royal family and Prince Philip, Duke of Edinburgh, was born there in 1921.

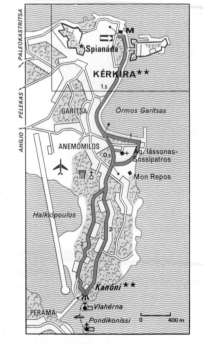

Kanóni ★★ *(hotels and restaurants).* – The platform at the end of the peninsula was built by Napoleon's soldiers as a battery for a single canon to command the entrance to the Halkiópoulos Lagoon which is now bisected by the airport runway.

From the gun emplacement there is a **view** ★★ down on to the monastery of Vlahérna (17C) *(accessible on foot)* and beyond it to round Mouse Island (Pondikoníssi) which also has a monastery *(accessible by boat from Vlahérna).*

Achilleion (Ahílio) ★★. – *11km – 7 miles south; leave Corfu Town by the road to the airport and continue through Gastoúri.*

On a wooded hillside (alt 145m – 476ft) stands the Achilleion *(open 9am to sunset).* It was designed in 1890 by an Italian architect for the Empress **Elisabeth of Austria** (1837-1898) who greatly admired the Greek hero Achilles and named her palace after

85

him. After her assassination by an anarchist in Geneva, the villa stood empty and was then bought in 1907 by Kaiser Wilhelm II who came for a month each spring until 1914, when it was confiscated by the Greek government. In 1916 the French turned it into a hospital and it served in this capacity during the Second World War. In between it became a museum and now it has been restored and converted into a casino *(open evenings only)*.

The villa is built in the neo-Classical style and divided into large rooms decorated with frescoes and ancient motifs; there are souvenirs of Elisabeth (portrait by Winterhalter) and Wilhelm (his desk).

The Italian terraced gardens are planted with flowers and Mediterranean trees and adorned with statues including The Dying Achilles (1884) by the German sculptor Herter opposite which Wilhelm II set up a huge bronze of Achilles the Victor.

From the end of the upper terrace there are extended views★★ of the northern end of the island and of the Albanian coast.

(Photograph J. Bottin)

Achilleion. – Statue of Achilles

Pélekas★★. – Pop 399. *13km – 8 miles west.* The "Kaiser's Throne" *(signpost; restaurant)* is an alternative name for this viewpoint where Kaiser Wilhelm II often used to stop to admire the superb panoramic view★★ of the countryside in the centre of the island; below on the coast is the huge and popular beach at Glifáda.

Gouviá Bay (Órmos Gouvión). – *9km – 5 1/2 miles north.* Sheltered and gently curving the bay is very popular. On the shore are the remains of an 18C Venetian arsenal. During the First World War the bay was used as a naval base by the French fleet.

2km – 1 1/4 miles southwest of Gouviá, lies **"the Village" (Daniliá)** which evokes the traditional Corfiot way of life; reconstructions of interiors and workshops, museum of arts and crafts and folklore. Traditional festivals are organised in the season.

Benítses. – Pop 611. *13km – 8 miles south.* Typical fishing village and seaside resort at the end of a valley thick with olive groves.

In an orange grove *(private property: apply for permission to enter)* a few traces (mosaics) survive of some Roman baths.

There is also the beginning of an aqueduct built by the British to supply water to Corfu Town.

DISTANT SIGHTS

Paleokastrítsa★★★. – Pop 159. Very popular seaside resort.

The Bay★★. – *Several hotels and restaurants, Tourist Centre, shellfish a speciality.* At the foot of a steep hillside cloaked in holm oaks, olive and cypress trees, the ochre rocks of the coastline are broken up into half a dozen sandy creeks, one of which provides a harbour.

The road runs to the end of the promontory where the monastery of Paleokastrítsa was founded in 13C; the present buildings date from 18C; the church contains some precious icons.

This may be the site of Scheria, the city of Alcinoüs, king of the Phaeacians, who gave hospitality to Odysseus. The Ermónes creek *(southeast)* may be the spot where Nausicaa was approached by Odysseus.

View of the site★★★. – Excellent bird's eye views of the site can be obtained from Lákones and Angelókastro *(20km – 12 1/2 miles Rtn by car plus 1 1/2 hours walking).*

Lákones. – Pop 574. A terrace about 800m – 875yds beyond the village of Lákones *(signpost, parking)* provides an extraordinary view★★★ of the many rocky inlets in Paleokastrítsa Bay.

Continue towards Kríni. Before entering the village bear left into a narrow road to Angelókastro *(signpost)* which leads to a hamlet and then to a restaurant. Park the car nearby and take the path to Angelókastro *(1 hour on foot Rtn).*

Angelókastro. – The ruins of Angelókastro on their hilltop recall an Angevin citadel mentioned in 13C in the Neapolitan archives and named Sant'Angelo in honour of the Archangel Michael.

From near St Michael's Chapel there are splendid views★★★ of the coast.

Sidári★★. – Pop 218. This little resort at the northern end of the island commands a view of a curious **rock formation★★** towards Cape Drástis where the sea has eaten away the parallel strata of tertiary sediment forming rocky inlets, some with little beaches, islets and promontories resembling piles of ruins, caves and caverns where the sea rushes in.

About 15km – 9 miles south lies **St George's Bay** (Ágios Geórgios: *tavernas*) with its magnificent beach.

Ípsos★. – Pop 426. This pleasant resort is situated on the edge of a huge sandy bay which is ideal for all water sports: bathing, sailing, water skiing etc. At the other end of the bay is **Pirgí**, also a popular resort.

Spartílas★ (alt 424m – 1 391ft). – Pop 644. *9km – 5 1/2 miles north*. The road loops its way up through the olive groves providing beautiful glimpses of the coast south to Corfu Town and of Albania on the mainland.

Kassiópi★. – Pop 594. *21km – 13 miles northeast*. This charming fishing port and resort is approached by a spectacular **corniche road★★** which goes to **Kouloúra** where the writer Lawrence Durrell lived with his wife before the Second World War. He had first come to live on Corfu in the 30s with his mother and sister and brothers; his younger brother Gerald has written several accounts of his idyllic boyhood. Remarkable views of the Albanian coast.

Kassiópi is dominated by the remains of a 13C feudal Angevin fortress. The 16C church contains 17C icons and frescoes.

CORINTH★★   *Kórinthos*

Peloponnese – Korinthía – Michelin map 980 fold 29

An impressive acropolis and the remains of many buildings recall "wealthy Corinth", one of the busiest trading cities in antiquity, a cosmopolitan and dissolute city which comprised an acropolis on its hill, the town proper on a lower plateau and Lechaion the port on the coast, all of which was protected by walls up to 20 km – 12 1/2miles in length.

The modern town (pop 22 658) was built in 1858 at the head of the gulf after the old town, which was further inland, was wrecked by an earthquake. It is both a port and an agricultural market dealing particularly in sultanas which have been exported since 14C. The local *souvláki (p 31)* are particularly good.

HISTORICAL NOTES

Corinth, the metropolis. – Corinth occupied an eminently favourable position at the crossroads of the land and sea routes linking Attica and the Peloponnese, the Ionian and the Aegean Seas; its almost impregnable acropolis, Acrocorinth, high on its hill controlled movement in all directions on the isthmus of Corinth. Moreover the hinterland was well watered with springs and fertile with olives and grapes.

According to legend, the city was founded by Korinthos, grandson of the sun god, Helios; one of the early kings was **Sisyphos,** grandfather of Bellerophon who, mounted on the winged horse Pegasus, killed the Chimaera. In the Mycenaean period Corinth was dependent on Argos.

In the Archaic era Corinth became very prosperous. The city was governed by a local oligarchy or by tyrants, such as the cruel Periander, who was yet considered one of the Seven Sages of Greece, and imposed considerable taxes on the passage of goods across the isthmus. The warehouses were filled with wheat from Sicily, papyrus from Egypt, ivory from Libya, leather from Cyrenaica, incense from Arabia, dates from Phoenicia, apples and pears from Euboia, carpets from Carthage and slaves from Phrygia.

The Corinthians also used the coastal clay to make the ceramic vases, often very tiny (perfume flasks), which they exported throughout the Mediterranean basin; in addition they developed the production of bronze (cuirasses, statues), glass and purple dyed cloth; their naval shipyards launched the first triremes. They facilitated their trade by establishing colonies, in particular in Leukas, Corcyra (Corfu) and above all in Syracuse (734 BC). After a partial eclipse by Athens in 5C BC Corinth regained its lustre in the following century when she took her place at the head of the Greek cities in the "League of Corinth" under Philip of Macedon and Alexander the Great.

The Corinthian capital *(p 18)* is thought to have been invented in 5C BC.

Their great wealth led the Corinthians astray into the paths of luxury and sensual pleasure. Corinth became known throughout the ancient world for her courtesans; at certain moments they numbered over 1 000: priestesses *(hierodules)* engaged in sacred prostitution in the precincts of the Temple of Aphrodite; dancers and flautists and oboists *(hetairai)* who attended the banquets. These servants of Aphrodite included the famous Lais whose tomb in the pine woods by the Kraneion on the outskirts of Corinth was described by Pausanias the historian as being "crowned with a ram in the clutches of a lionness".

In the following century, however, Corinth became famous for the presence of the austere philosopher **Diogenes** the Cynic who lived in a barrel, in fact a large earthenware jar. When Alexander asked him if he wanted anything he replied "Yes, don't keep the sun off me".

Corinth, a Roman colony. – In 146 BC the Consul Mummius captured the city which was then pillaged and burned by his legions: the bronze, an alloy of gold and silver, on the statues was removed to be used for the roof of the Pantheon in Rome whence it was later removed by Pope Alexander VII to make the baldaquin in St Peter's.

In 44 BC Julius Caesar founded a new town, Colonia Julia Corinthiensis, on the ruins of ancient Corinth. It became the capital of Roman Greece and was mainly populated by freedmen and Jews, who were Latin speakers. During the next two centuries Corinth developed into a rich city devoted to business and pleasure which attracted merchants, ship owners, and tourists in large numbers. Everyone dreamed of going to Corinth despite the high cost of the entertainment available.

Between 51 and 52 AD however **St Paul** spent eighteen months in the city; in his Epistle to the Corinthians he castigated the shameless behaviour of the citizens. He preached Christianity equally to the pagans and the Jews and the Jewish priests dragged him before the Proconsul Gallion in the agora but he was acquitted.

Nero visited Corinth 67 AD to announce the independence of the Greek cities and to take part in the Isthmian games. Hadrian in his turn erected many buildings, refurbished the baths and built an aqueduct to bring water from Lake Stymphalia *(west)*. Under the combined effect of barbarian invasions and earthquakes Corinth was brought low; only Acrocorinth retained a certain importance as a military stronghold.

ANCIENT CORINTH★★ (ARHÉA KÓRINTHOS)

7km – 4 1/2 miles southwest of the modern town. Leave the car in the car park near the Tourist Pavilion (restaurant); the entrance is on the west side of the archaeological site. Open 8.45am to 3pm (9.30pm to 2.30pm Sundays, holidays); 200 Dr.

During the Turkish occupation ancient Corinth disappeared under urban development except for the Temple of Apollo which was described by the majority of travellers. The earthquake which destroyed the town in 1858 did however assist the Americans in their excavations which began in 1896 and uncovered a jumble of ruins, mostly Roman; the large number of small shops bears witness to the commercial importance of ancient Corinth.

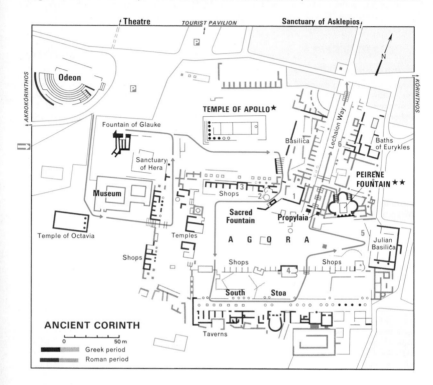

TOUR *about 2 hours; follow the route shown on the plan*

First move south to the **Temple of Octavian,** a Roman building from which three fine Corinthian capitals found in 18C by the French architect Foucherot have been re-erected.

Museum. – *Open 8am to 7pm (6pm Sundays); closed Tuesdays.*

The collections consist of most of the pieces produced by the excavations presented in a clear and informative manner. The gallery of Hellenistic antiquities (vestibule-*right*) houses several examples of the beautiful Archaic ceramics with an oriental decoration which Corinth exported in large quantities in 8C-7C BC. The gallery of Roman antiquities (vestibule – *left*) contains a statue of Augustus and a head of Nero; mosaics and, at the far end of the room, huge statues of captives from the agora.

Make for the upper level of the agora with its rows of shops and then bear left round an old sanctuary to Hera to reach the adjoining **Fountain of Glauke;** this fountain is named after Glauke (also known as Creusa), the second wife of Jason, who threw himself into the water to cool the burning caused by the poisoned robe which Medea the witch had given him.

Temple of Apollo★. – The highest point on the site of ancient Corinth is still marked by 7 of the 38 monolithic Doric columns, made of tufa and originally covered with white stucco, which belonged to the 6C BC temple. According to the description given by Dr Spon in 17C and the drawings made by the architects Leroy and Stuart in 18C, it was surrounded by a peristyle. The high ground affords spectacular views of the Gulf of Corinth and of Acrocorinth.

A grand flight of steps built in 5C BC leads down to the lower level of the agora. The façade (1) of a Roman "basilica", which stood in the centre of the north side, was adorned with four huge statues of captives, of which two are displayed in the museum.

Sacred Fountain. – A wall surmounted by tripods and statues marked the eastern side of the fountain; the base with its rhythmic frieze of triglyphs is still recognizable. Steps lead down to the underground spring which was linked by a secret passage, with the Sanctuary of the Oracle (2); its position nearby (NW) is marked by the foundations. A priest hidden beneath the altar answered the petitioners who were thus led to think they were in direct communication with the god.

Agora. – This huge open space, which provides remarkable views up to Acrocorinth, comprises a rectangle on two levels measuring 150m by 90m – 492ft by 295ft.

Along the north side, below the terrace supporting the great Temple of Apollo, are the remains of 15 Roman shops; the one in the centre (3) is still roofed.

The west side of the agora is marked by the foundations of six small Roman temples.

South Stoa. – The south side of the agora, on the upper level, is filled by the South Stoa, an immense building which was used by the Greeks as a guest house and converted by the Romans into an administrative centre. The bases of the colonnade are still extant and at the west end one can still trace the arrangement of each "compartment" with its courtyard and well; in the Greek period they were probably places of refreshment.

In front of the stoa, separating the upper and lower sections of the agora, are the remains of a row of Roman shops. In the centre stood the **Bema** (4), a sort of platform from which the governor Gallio passed judgment on St Paul (there was a church on the site in the Middle Ages).

To the east lie the remains of the **Julian Basilica**, a former law court and meeting room dating from the Roman era. Excavations in front of it have revealed earlier Greek paving with the starting line of a race track (5).

Propylaia. – Only the base of the monumental entrance to the agora remains. In the Roman era it was surmounted by two great gold chariots belonging to Helios and his son Phaeton.

Below the Propylaia on the right is the Peirene Fountain.

Peirene Fountain ★★ – It dates originally from 6C BC but has been remodelled many times. The original Greek part is at the back of the atrium *(south side)*: six stone arches preceding a row of underground reservoirs.

The colonnade in front of the arches, the rectangular basin and the three niches creating a nymphaeum were added under the Romans.

Leave the ancient city by the Lechaion Way, the beginning of a road running from the agora to the harbour at Lechaion. In the Roman period it became a ceremonial way leading to the Propylaia and bordered by porticoes housing the Baths of Eurykles with their public latrines (6) which are well preserved.

ADDITIONAL SIGHTS

Odeon. – Excavations have revealed a small Roman theatre dating from 1C AD; its semi-circular plan is clearly visible. The banks of seats, most of which are hewn out of the rock, could accommodate about 3 000 spectators.

In the reign of Herod Atticus the Odeon was linked to the theatre by a colonnaded court which can be traced in places.

Theatre. – Begun in 5C BC it was remodelled several times particularly in 3C AD when the stage was enlarged to accommodate gladiatorial combats and nautical spectacles. It held about 18 000 people.

A little further north are the remains of a brick-built Roman bath house.

Sanctuary of Asklepios. – The plan of the temple dedicated to the god of Medicine set in a colonnaded rectangular courtyard can be clearly traced on the ground. Near the entrance *(east)* is an unusual stone offertory.

West of the temple there is a huge cistern (Fountain of Lerna) which supplied the hydrotherapy facilities.

ACROCORINTH ★★★ (AKROKÓRINTHOS)

Same opening times as for Ancient Corinth (duration of visit: about 2 hours on foot; 100 Dr; take a torch. It is a steep climb from the entrance to the top of the site; the less agile are advised to go only as far as the entrance to admire the view.

Take the road *(7km – 4 1/2 miles by car Rtn)* which passes the Hotel Xenia and the old potters' district on the right, bears left in front of a Turkish fountain not far from the excavated remains of a temple to Demeter and then climbs in a succession of bends up to the citadel entrance *(taverna)*.

Poised between heaven and earth and almost indistinguishable from the rock, the ruins of Acrocorinth are some of the most impressive in the world owing to their extent, the desolate grandeur of their elevated site and the immense panorama which they command.

Acrocorinth was first a Greek acropolis, then a Roman citadel and then a Byzantine fortress. It was captured by the Franks in 1210 after a five year siege, became a fief of the de Villehardouin and then in *c*1325 came under Philip of Tarentum, of the Angevin dynasty, who ruled Naples. In 1358 it passed to the Florentines when Robert II of Tarentum gave the seigneury of Corinth to Nicolo Acciaiuoli *(p 122)*, an arms manufacturer and banker, who had been adviser to his mother Catherine of Valois, Princess of Morea. Subsequently Acrocorinth was held by the Palaiologi of Mystra (1394), by the Knights of Rhodes and from 15C by the Turks except for a Venetian interlude from 1687 to 1715.

The access ramp from the car park to the fortress offers spectacular views of the three lines of defence and the three gates which protect the citadel on the western approach.

First Gate. – It dates from 14C and is defended by a moat hewn out of the rock.

Second Gate. – It too dates from 14C but was almost entirely rebuilt by the Venetians; it is flanked by a tower.

Third Gate. – It is flanked by two powerful rectangular towers; the one on the right is mainly ancient (4C BC); the one on the left is Byzantine. The curtain walls on either side, which are reinforced with rectangular towers, date principally from the Byzantine era.

From the entrance a steep path leads up the slope among the ruins through the old Turkish district (remains of mosque – *left*) to the rampart and the northern postern. Return to the decapitated minaret and pass a fine brick-vaulted cistern to reach the medieval keep.

Keep. – It dominates the remains of the Frankish castle of the Villehardouin, princes of Morea in 13C and 14C; in 1305 Isabelle de Villehardouin and her husband Philip of Savoy commanded the Frankish barons of Morea and Attica to gather at the castle to take part in a tournament which assembled over 1 000 knights in passages of arms. Fine view of the Byzantine ramparts with their rectangular towers, the surrounding heights and the Gulf of Corinth.

From the keep return along the south ramparts and continue eastwards (view of the mountains of the Peloponnese) to the Peirene Spring which is to be found near a bend in the wall next to a ruined Turkish barracks.

Peirene Spring. – Modern steps lead down into a Hellenistic underground chamber (ancient graffiti) which was re-roofed by the Romans. More steps led down into another chamber which has since flooded with water. Some authors say that the spring was created by the winged horse Pegasus stamping its foot; Pegasus was then captured by Bellerophon while drinking at the spring.

Temple of Aphrodite. – The site of the famous temple of Aphrodite on the highest point of Acrocorinth (alt 574km – 1 883ft) is now marked by a column. There

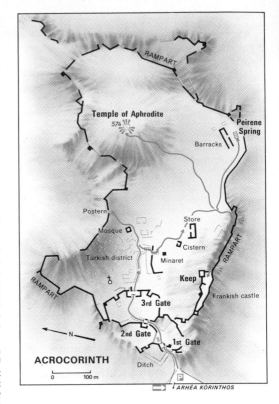

is a splendid **panorama**★★★ extending beyond the isthmus of Corinth to Mount Parnassos (N), across Attica (E) and to the mountains of the Peloponnese (S). To the southwest, perched on a rocky peak, are the medieval ruins of the Frankish castle of Montesquiou, built according to the Chronicle of the Morea under Geoffrey de Villehardouin and now known as Pendeskoúfi, possibly a corruption of the original French name.

Return to the entrance to Acrocorinth and so to the car.

CORINTH Canal and Isthmus★★

Peloponnese – Korinthía – Michelin map 980 folds 20 and 30

The Corinth Canal, which provides a maritime short cut between the Gulf of Corinth and the Saronic Gulf, traces a straight line across the isthmus, the narrow neck of land joining the Peloponnese to mainland Greece.

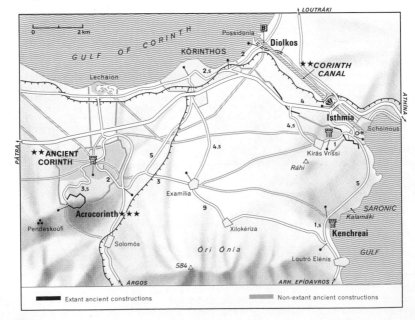

Extant ancient constructions   Non-extant ancient constructions

A superb strategic position. – Since the isthmus is only 6km – 4 miles wide and of easy passage, attempts to defend it have been made since the Mycenaean period. Recent excavations near Isthmía have uncovered several sections of a Cyclopean wall dating from 13C BC. Another wall, built in 480 BC to contain the Persian invasion, spanned the isthmus; it was reinforced with towers and kept in good repair until the Venetian period.

The ancient Greeks also sought to cut a channel through the isthmus to avoid ships having to circumnavigate the Peloponnese or be hauled over the *diolkós (see below)*. Both Periander and Alexander the Great had considered the question but it was Nero who inaugurated the digging in 67 AD with a golden shovel: 6 000 prisoners were employed on the work. Unfortunately the site was abandoned after about 3 or 4 months when Nero returned to Rome.

In those days the isthmus was more densely inhabited than it is now: there were two ports on the east coast at Schoinous and Kenchreai and one on the west at Lechaion. Every two years the Isthmian Games, second only to the Olympic Games in the whole of Greece, were held at the local religious sanctuary and the roads were thronged with chariots.

THE CANAL★★ (DIÓRIGA KORÍNTHOU)

The canal was begun in 1882 by a French company, the Société Internationale du Canal Maritime de Corinthe, inspired by a proposal made in 1829 by Virlet d'Aoust, a member of the Morean Commission *(p 24)*. Work stopped in 1889 when the company went bankrupt but the canal was completed by the Greeks in 1893. This spectacular undertaking permanently altered the shipping routes and Piraeus took the place of Syros *(p 184)* in the Cyclades as the major port of Greece.

The canal is 6.343km – nearly 4 miles long, 8m – 26ft deep and 24.60m – 27yds wide at water level. The walls rise to 79.50m – 260ft at the highest point. The channel is so narrow that it is not used regularly except by a few coastal traders and cruising ships drawn by tugs.

View★★. – The bridge which carries the Athens-Corinth road over the canal offers an impressive view of the almost vertical walls of the dead straight channel which broadens slightly at the centre to form a dock. People with a geological bent can analyse the different strata: alluvium and marine sand at the top, then clay and

(Photograph J. Bottin)

Corinth. – The canal

limestone. Photographers will obviously want to catch that rare moment when a train crossing the viaduct coincides with the passage of a ship beneath.

ADDITIONAL SIGHTS

"Diolkós". – On the road from the canal to the outskirts of Corinth there is a righthand turning which leads after 2km – 1 1/4 miles to the west end of the canal. The central section of the bridge sinks on to the canal bed to let the shipping pass.

Near the bridge on either side of the modern road one can see the *"diolkós"*, an ancient portage way paved with stone along which the ships were dragged on chariots or on wooden rollers across the lowest and narrowest part of the isthmus *(shown on the map on page 90)*. On the side near the Gulf of Corinth the paving stones are marked with letters of the Corinthian alphabet but their purpose is unknown; on the other side can be seen the ruts worn by the chariots.

This stone slipway was probably built in 6C BC and was still in use in 12C AD.

Isthmian Sanctuary (Isthmía). – By the road from the canal to Epidauros at the foot of Mount Ráhi a new museum marks the entrance to the excavations of the Isthmian sanctuary.

Museum and excavations. – *Open 8.45am to 3pm (9.30am to 2.30pm Sundays).*
The museum contains a clear presentation of the objects found during the excavations of the Isthmian sanctuary and the port of Kenchreai. Apart from the usual finds there are some unusual glass mosaics found in submerged packing cases at Kenchreai; they were probably imported from Egypt for the internal decoration of houses.

The excavations carried out from 1952 to 1960 by the Americans have revealed the foundations of a temple to Poseidon (5C BC) near which the Isthmian Games took place: note the 16 grooves made in the stone which diverge near the starting line.

Beyond are the ruins of a Roman theatre as well as the remains of the defensive wall and the Roman fortress: the latter was probably rebuilt c400 AD using Greek material.

Port of Kenchreai. – In antiquity, this was the port for Corinth on the Saronic Gulf. Traces, mainly Roman, of harbour installations extend beneath the water. To the south are the foundations of a Christian basilica (4C) which replaced a temple to Isis.

St Paul the Apostle disembarked at Kenchreai in 51 AD and founded a Christian community.

Central Aegean Islands – Pop 87 531 – Michelin map ⬚⬚⬚ folds 31, 32, 43, 44 and 45

The islands received their name in antiquity because they form a rough circle *(kíklos)* round the sacred island of Delos. Nowadays they attract tourists seeking the combined pleasures of transparent blue sea, constant sunshine and marvellously clear nights.

The brilliant light shows a landscape rich in contrasts, both harsh and colourful, oriental looking towns with windmills, chapels and immaculately white cubic houses, rocky inlets and deserted beaches, giving the visitor the feeling of being in a different world.

GEOGRAPHICAL AND HISTORICAL NOTES

Poverty offset by beauty. – The Cyclades form the largest group of islands in the Aegean Sea; there are 39 in all of which 24 are inhabited; the capital is Ermoúpoli on the island of Syros. They are divided into three groups: the western Cyclades (Kéa, Kythnos, Seriphos, Siphnos, Kímolos and Melos); the central Cyclades (Syros, Páros, Náxos, Amorgós, Íos, Síkinos, Folégandros and Santoríni (or Thera); the northern Cyclades (Ándros, Tenos, Mykonos and Delos).

The islands are the visible part of a sunken plateau, a shelf of ancient rocks forming an extension of the Attic peninsula beneath the sea, the average level of which is between 100 and 200m – 329 and 626ft below sea level. Some of them (Melos and Santoríni) have suffered volcanic eruptions. Their physical relief is clearly defined although only **Mount Náxos Días** (1 001m – 3 284ft) on the island of Náxos exceeds 1 000m in height.

The Cyclades are largely arid and the poverty of their soil coupled with the infrequency of communications has led, since the beginning of this century, to heavy emigration which is now abating in the islands where tourism is developing.

The more fertile islands produce wine, cereals, fruit and vegetables (Syros, Páros, Náxos, Santoríni); on some there is mining for iron-ore (Seriphos), manganese or sulphur (Melos); others have quarries for marble (Páros, Tenos, Náxos), emery-stone (Náxos), pumice stone or pozzolana (Santoríni). Some, like Santoríni, have so little water that extra supplies have to be imported by tanker; on such islands only a few olives, figs, carobs and oleanders are to be found in sheltered spots.

Cycladic art and civilisation. – A the end of the prehistoric era, between 3200 and 1750 BC, the islands which lay on the sea routes north from Crete were involved in considerable maritime trade which encouraged the development of a brilliant civilisation; it reached its apogee in about 2000 BC and was obliterated by the cataclysm which devastated the Aegean in about 1500 BC.

There are a number of traces of this Cycladic civilisation. For the period from 3000 to 2000 BC these are the famous "**idols**", female effigies, with minute heads, whose pure lines are scarcely outlined in the white marble: some are displayed in the Náxos museum, others in the Museum of Cycladic Art in Athens *(p 61)*; there are also black ceramics with spiral motifs. For the following period (2000 to 1500 BC) there are the delicately drawn and freshly coloured narrative **frescoes** which were discovered on Santoríni and are related to the Minoan art of Crete.

In 8C BC the islands began to enjoy a certain degree of prosperity in the orbit of Athens as is shown by a number of ruins, particularly those on Delos.

From the Serene Republic to the Sublime Porte. – Early in 13C, as a result of the Fourth Crusade, the Venetians established themselves in the Cyclades and the islands were handed out as fiefs to the great Venetian families. The group as a whole was placed under the sovereignty of the Dukes of Náxos *(p 155)* who themselves were under the Princes of Morea; Venice's interest was represented locally by a "bailiff".

The Cyclades served as ports of call on the sea route to Constantinople and flourished despite the inroads of Algerian pirates who forced the citizens to take refuge inland. It was at this time that Roman Catholic parishes were founded which are still thriving, particularly on the islands of Syros, Náxos, Tenos and Santoríni.

The Turks established themselves in the Archipelago by degrees, notably in 1537 and 1566 when Barbarossa captured Náxos; Tenos and Mykonos fell only in 1718. The Turks allowed the islands a certain autonomy and Italian remained the official language until 1830. Similarly, under the "**Capitulations**" between Francois I and Suleiman the Magnificent, the local Roman Catholics were placed under the protection of France; missions were launched by the Capucines in 1633 and then by the Jesuits, Lazarists, Ursulines etc. who played a prominent role in the educational and social fields (schools, hospitals). In 17C missions of a different type were launched by the English for the acquisition of antiquities which ended up in the collections of Charles I, the Duke of Buckingham and the second Earl of Arundel.

With the exception of Mykonos, the Cyclades took almost no part in the Greek War of Independence but were generous in receiving refugees from the mainland. During the First World War the islands played a strategic role on the route to the eastern front.

PRACTICAL INFORMATION

Access by sea. – *There are several shipping lines operating vehicle ferries and passenger steamers from Piraeus, with the possibility of changing from one route to another in certain ports:*
– the Cyclades line, daily departure in the morning for Syros, Páros, Náxos, Íos and Santoríni (Thera) arriving the same day; less frequent departures for the islands on the so called barren route: Amorgós, Kouphoníssi, Donoússa, Iráklia, Shinoússa, Anáfi, Folégandros, Síkinos and Kímolos.
– the western Cyclades line calls at Kythnos, Seriphos, Siphnos, Melos and Kímolos (in bad weather departure from Lávrio north of Cape Sounion).
– the boats sailing to Sámos and the Dodecanese Islands usually call at Syros or Páros.
– there is also a regular service to the Cyclades (Ándros, Mykonos, Syros, Páros, Náxos and Tenos) from Rafína east of Athens.

– similarly there are also boats from Lávrio to Kéa and Kythnos.
– there is a hydrofoil service linking the islands of Syros, Tenos, Mykonos, Íos, Náxos and Páros.

Caiques and motor launches provide supplementary and connecting services. Except in special cases, vehicles cannot be landed on Mykonos, Íos and the smaller islands. In bad weather delays can reach 5 or 6 hours for the more distant islands. Ships generally have first class, tourist class and third class accommodation as well as a cafeteria or snackbar.

In the season it is best to make reservations in advance for vehicles. Timetables are available from the offices of the GNTO (EOT).

Access by air. – In the season Olympic Airways provide daily flights from Athens-Elenikó-West to Mykonos (1/2 hour), Melos (3/4 hour) and Santoríni (1 hour).

Accommodation. – Andros and the islands served by the first two shipping lines are reasonably well supplied with hotels; the western Cyclades, except for Kéa and Siphnos, are less favoured. For accommodation in private houses, apply to the local Tourist Police or to the owners who offer rooms (domátio) on the dockside. There are buses on most islands and bicycle hire.

Beneath the trellises of the picturesque tavernas one can enjoy succulent prawns, squid, octopus, sword fish, red mullet, sardines and mackerel accompanied by white wines, the best of which come from Náxos, Santoríni and Melos.

Local crafts: ceramics, wickerwork, hand-woven cloth, carpets and mats.

Climate. – The best time of the year for visiting the Cyclades is without doubt May and June: the islands are not crowded, the plants are in flower, fresh water is plentiful and the cold north wind (meltémi) blows only occasionally. This wind, which can reach gusts of up to Force 6 or 8, is more frequent in July and August producing white horses on the crests of the waves; the Turks called this part of the Aegean the "white sea". The wind is refreshing and often dies away at nightfall.

Dolphins and flying fish sometimes accompany the ships' course.

NORTHERN CYCLADES★★

Ándros. – Pop 9 020. Access by ferry from Rafína in about 3 hours.
This large island is mountainous but fertile and more wooded than its neighbours; it is a pleasant summer resort, particularly popular with the Athenians, and has several beaches, the principal one being at Batsí. The **Messaría valley,** which is parcelled out into vineyards and orchards growing figs and citrus fruits, is studded with dovecotes, square towers like those on Tenos.

Ándros (pop 1 631), the capital with its typical white cubic houses, stands on a rocky promontory above the harbour. There are traces of a fortress built by the Venetians who occupied the island from 1207 to 1556. The chapel of Zoodóhos Pigí (Life-giving Spring) contains an iconostasis dating from 1717. There is also a well-presented archaeological museum.

Elsewhere on the island there is the beautiful site★ of the ancient port of Palaiopolis of which few traces remain and the medieval village of Kórthio dominated by the ruins of a Venetian castle.

Mykonos★★ and **Delos★★★.** – Description pages 145 and 95.

Tenos. – Description page 185.

CENTRAL CYCLADES★★★

Amorgós. – Pop 1 722. Access by ferry from Piraeus four days a week at 10am.
The island which is long and narrow has about 100km – 62 miles of coastline with endless beaches and deserted inlets. Amorgós will appeal to those who like nature and open spaces, to exploring on foot and by boat, particularly the southeast coast where the land rises in spectacular limestone cliffs.

The capital, also called Amorgós, is a typical Cycladic town. About 8 miles north the **Monastery of the Presentation of the Virgin** (Hozoviótissa) occupies an impressive **position★★** clinging to the precipitous cliff face; it was founded in 1088 by the Byzantine emperor Alexis Comnenos and owns some precious icons and manuscripts.

Excavations on the island carried out by the French School have yielded a number of Cycladic idols, some of which are now in the Louvre in Paris.

Íos★. – Pop 1 451. Access by boat daily from Piraeus. A few hotels, rooms in private houses, camping. Large beach in the main bay; several smaller beaches in the isolated inlets on the east coast.
Despite being very popular with the international young set, Íos has retained its pure Cycladic character; it is a rugged, mountainous island, rising to 713m – 2 340ft in Mount Pírgos, barren and without roads; the terraced hills support a little wheat, windmills, cubic houses and nearly 400 dazzling white chapels with domes.

The landing (Skála) with its attractive chapel dedicated to St Irene lies in a deep bay where the mail boat from Piraeus comes to anchor; from there the road climbs up to the main town (Hóra), hidden in a cleft from which a good beach is accessible. Further east (2 1/2 hours on foot Rtn for good walkers) are the ruins of the Venetian castle built by the Crispi in 15C where the islanders used to take refuge from pirates.

According to an apocryphal Life of Homer, the blind poet died on Íos during a sea voyage and was buried on the shore.

Náxos★. – Description page 155.

Páros★. – Description page 165.

Santoríni (Thera)★★★. – Description page 176.

Syros★. – Description page 184.

WESTERN CYCLADES ★

Kéa. – Pop 1 652. *Access by ferry from Lávrio (SE of Athens) four times a week in the season in about 1 1/2 hours.*

Despite reasonable hotels and good beaches on the west coast (Korissía, Koúndouros), this mountainous island is not popular with tourists. Apricots and vines grow in the fertile valleys.

The ferry puts in at Korrisía (Livádi) deep in a sheltered bay. To the north, not far from Vourkári, on the **St Irene peninsula** *(restaurant),* American archaeologists have excavated traces of a village dating from the Minoan period (2 000 BC).

A surfaced road *(bus)* runs up from Korissía to **Kéa** (Hóra) (pop 568), the main town on the island where a museum was opened in 1979. 1km – 1/2mile northeast a colossal antique lion, 9m – 30ft high, has been carved in the rock.

Kímolos. – *Description page 134.*

Kythnos (Kíthnos). – Pop 1 502. *Access by boat from Piraeus five times a week in the season. Frequent services from Lávrio (SE of Athens).*

Although the landscape is unexciting, there are hot springs at Loutrá (treatment for eczema and rheumatism), St Saba's (Ágios Sávas), a 17C church at Kythnos (pop 631), the capital of the island, and the ruins of a medieval fortress at Cape Kéfalos (N). Basketwork is a speciality.

Melos ★. – *Description page 133.*

Seriphos (Sérifos). – Pop 1 133. *Access by boat: in the season from Piraeus six times a week; out of season from Lávrio (SE of Athens).*

The island was famous in antiquity for its iron-ore mines which are now almost exhausted. Its name means denuded. Seriphos is well known for its traditional wedding dances.

It is not far from the port of Megá Livádi *(hotel, beach)* to Seriphos (pop 409), the main town on the island where the houses are painted white. From there a path leads north *(4 hours on foot Rtn)* to the 17C monastery of the Taxiarchs.

Siphnos ★ (Sífnos). – Pop 2 087. *Access by ferry: from Piraeus daily in the season in 6 to 8 hours; out of season from Lávrio (SE of Athens).*

This is the most popular of the Western Cyclades with tourists *(several hotels);* it has a very fine beach at Platís Gialós, varied landscape (olive groves) and the villages are built in the pure cubic style of architecture peculiar to the Cyclades.

Out of the proceeds of their gold and silver mines the ancient Siphniots were able to build the "Treasury of Siphnos" at Delphi *(p 102).* The island has remained prosperous owing to its abundant water supply and the fertility of the soil as much as to the skill of its potters and cooks who make good use of the local olive oil and the capers which are famous all over Greece.

The island is dotted with refuge towers and has good roads linking the main sites:
– **Kamáres,** the landing for boats (Skála) where many potters are at work.
– **Apolonía** (pop 841), the capital with its church, Ágios Sotírios, which is decorated with frescoes and a carved wood iconostasis.
– **Artemónas,** picturesque little Cycladic town *(restaurants, tavernas, "night clubs")* with many windmills.
– **Kástro ★**, the old capital, an abandoned Venetian fortress built on the site of an ancient city of which a few traces have been discovered (walls, dwellings, temple).

DAPHNE Monastery ★★   *Dafní*

Central Greece – Attica – Michelin map ▨▨▨ fold 30 – Local maps pp 66 and 68

Open 8.45am to 3pm (9.30am to 2.30pm Sundays); 100 Dr. Tourist Pavilion (restaurant-bar). Wine Festival mid-July to early September in the adjacent park: free tasting of Greek wines. Bus 864 or 873 from Platía Eleftherías (N of Monastiráki) in Athens.

The monastery, which is tucked between the Athens-Corinth road *(north)* and a sweet-scented pine-clad hill *(south),* is known to art enthusiasts for its church and its Byzantine mosaics.

The Duke of Athens' Burial Place. – The monastery stands on the site of a Temple to Apollo which was originally surrounded by laurel trees *(dáfni),* Apollo's favourite trees because they reminded him of the nymph Daphne whom he had loved. The monastery was founded in 5C AD and dedicated to the Dormition of the Virgin; it was reduced to ruins by the barbarian invasions and rebuilt in the late 11C.

When the crusaders arrived in 1205 Attica passed under the domination of the French. The new lords of Athens, who were natives of Burgundy or Champagne, took the monastery under their protection and the first of them, Otho de la Roche, gave it to the Cistercians. The monks of St Bernard restored it and under the name of Dalphinet it became the chosen burial place of the Dukes of Athens in imitation of Citeaux in France where the Capetian Dukes of Burgundy were buried; Guy I de la Roche was buried at Daphne in 1263 and Gautier de Brienne in 1311 but the Turkish invasion in 1458 forced the Cistercians to leave.

TOUR *about 1 hour*

There is a fine overall view of the site from the slope of the hill south of the precinct *(access via the car park):* original entrance to the west, **rectangular precinct** with a well preserved section of 5C to 6C wall complete with sentry walk and square towers on the north side parallel with the main road, the cloister and the church in the foreground.

Return to the present entrance.

Cloister. – The peaceful paved court with its solemn cypress trees is flanked on the east side by a typically Cistercian arcade with double arcatures; the cells were added in 16C. Under the western arcade are ducal sarcophagi; one is decorated with fleurs de lys and heraldic serpents (guivres). Fragments of stonework discovered in the crypt.

Church. – The domed Byzantine church was built over the crypt in 11C and enlarged and refurbished in 13C by the Cistercians who were responsible for a certain number of windows including the triple ones, the exonarthex and the creation within of a number of chapels for the monks whose rule required them to celebrate mass daily and simultaneously.

Exterior. – There is a fine view from the cloister of the south front of the church with its brick window frames. The entrance to the **exo-narthex** is composed of twin arches supported on a central antique column. This narthex, which is crenellated, must have been built on the model of Citeaux for the use of the lay brothers whose accommodation is likely to have been nearby; the tombs of the Dukes of Athens were placed here. The pointed arches of the west front and traces of a groined vault suggest the inspiration of Burgundian architecture.

On the north side of the church, beyond the square tower which protected the church on this side, are the remains of the 11C refectory. The elevation of the church and the dome can be admired; the small windows date from 11C; the others are probably 13C.

Interior. – The church is magnificently decorated with late 11C **mosaics**★★ against a gold background which are remarkable for their delicacy of line and colouring. The most beautiful scenes, which are arranged according to the theological concepts of those days, include:
– in the dome, Christ Pantocrator, surrounded by the 16 prophets; in the squinches, the Annunciation (**1**), the Nativity (**2**), the Baptism (**3**) and the Ascension (**4**) of Christ;
– in the apse, the Virgin Mary (**5**) flanked by the Archangels Michael (**6**) and Gabriel (**7**);
– in the transept arms, gospel scenes including the Birth of the Virgin, the Entry of Christ into Jerusalem (**8**) and the Crucifixion (**9**) *(north transept)*, the Adoration of the Magi, Christ rising from the dead (**10**), doubting Thomas (**11**) *(south transept)*;
– in the narthex, the Betrayal by Judas (**12**) and a scene from the legend of Joachim and Anne (**13**) are opposite the Last Supper (**14**) and the Presentation of the Virgin in the Temple (**15**).

DELOS★★★ — *Dílos*

Cyclades – Pop 16 – Michelin map 𝟿𝟾𝟶 fold 32

Delos lies at the heart of the Cyclades, an island of granite and gneiss culminating in Mount Kynthos. Despite its minute size (14sq miles), it played an important role in antiquity, both commercial and religious, when the sanctuary to Apollo attracted pilgrims and riches.

Nowadays Delos is a desolate wind-swept sea-girt place of pilgrimage for tourists only but the ruins are still imbued with a sense of mystic fervour and nostalgia.

PRACTICAL INFORMATION

Access by caique (3/4hr) from the port of Mykonos; departure every morning at 9am weather permitting; embarkation at West Mole, called the "caique mole". When the north wind (meltémi) is blowing the crossing can be cold and rough: take a woollen jacket.

After rounding the northern point of Delos the boat enters the straits separating Delos from Reneia (Rínia) past two islets and moors by the West Mole which separated the sanctuary harbour (sacred port) from the commercial harbour in antiquity; if the sea is too rough the boat puts in to Goúrna Bay in the northeast of the island. *The boat generally leaves for the return journey to Mykonos at 12.30pm.*

The day tripper therefore has about 2 1/2 hours for visiting the ruins and climbing Mount Kynthos. Beware of sunstroke and in the more remote places of vipers.

DELOS ★★★

MYTHOLOGICAL AND HISTORICAL NOTES

Apollo's Isle. – According to legend, **Leto** whom Zeus had seduced and then abandoned wandered about the world pursued by the anger of Hera who had forbidden anyone to receive the pregnant goddess. Leto eventually found a haven on the barren island of Ortygia (Quail Land) where after nine days and nights in labour she gave birth to twins, Apollo and Artemis, at the foot of a palm tree. In recognition of this event Ortygia became known as Delos (illustrious) and the Apollo sanctuary was to become, together with the shrine at Delphi, the most important in the Greek world.

Delos was already thriving in the Mycenaean era (1400-1200 BC); traces of a palace and precious objects have been found in the course of excavations.

Delos became the capital of an **"Amphictyony"**, a confederation of neighbouring islands and was evoked by Homer in the Odyssey and the Hymn to Apollo; it reached its religious apogee in 7C-6C BC, first under the Naxiots and then under the Athenians. In about 550 BC the Athenian tyrant, Peisistratos, ordered the first purification of the island so as to preserve its sacred character: no births or deaths were allowed on Delos and people near their time had to be removed to the neighbouring island of Reneia.

In 478 BC, after the Persian wars, Athens united the Amphictyony and Attica in the Delian Confederacy and the Treasure, which was contributed by the participating cities, was first kept in the Apollo sanctuary before being transferred in 454 to the Acropolis in Athens. In 426 the Athenians ordered a new purification of the island and the graves and their contents were removed to a great pit on Reneia.

At the same time the Athenians lent new lustre to the sanctuary, building a new temple to Apollo and organising the famous **Delian Festival** which took place every four years in May: processions of pilgrims crowned with flowers and chanting the "paean" sacrificed oxen, took part in sacred dances in front of the altar, attended banquets and watched competitions in sports, music and drama. A commercial market complemented the religious festival which flourished until 1C AD and was even enhanced by the assimilation of other cults from Egypt, Syria and Phoenicia.

Commercial and cosmopolitan centre. – Despite its only average harbour, from 4C BC onwards Delos gradually became the main port in the Aegean Sea. Its central maritime position and its sacred status, which preserved it from attack, favoured its economic development which resulted in the construction of quays, warehouses and ship yards. Delos was the principal market in the eastern Mediterranean for grain and slaves as well as the storage and redistribution centre for oil, wine and wood.

Its status as a free port which was granted by the Romans in 166 BC attracted merchants, bankers and shipping magnates from Italy, Greece, Syria and Egypt; residential districts were built to accommodate them. Early in 1C BC the prosperity of Delos reached its zenith and the town numbered 25 000 inhabitants.

The decline of Apollo's island began with the capture and sack of Delos in 88 BC by Mithridates, king of Pontus, who rose against the Romans. Pilgrimages became less popular, depradations by pirates grew and the main shipping routes moved elsewhere.

During the Venetian occupation of the Cyclades several works of art were removed to Venice and Rome. On 28 August 1628 **Sir Kenelm Digby**, who had set out from England in two ships in January of that year on a privateering expedition, "spent the day at Delos in search of antiquities"; he acquired fragments from Apollo's temple for Charles I's collection. Many other works of art ended up in the lime kilns.

Excavations. – The French School of Archaeology has been responsible for the exploration of the site; excavations, begun in 1872, have been carried out in parallel with those at Delphi. In 1904 with the aid of a patron, the Duc de Loubat, M. Holleaux began the "great excavation" which uncovered public buildings and private houses, some of which have been partially reconstructed by the Greek Anastylosis Service *(p 20)*. Work is still in progress particularly in a Hellenistic district to the north.

RUINS ★★★ *2 1/2 hours*

Open 8.45am to 3pm (9.30am to 2.30pm Sundays); 200 Dr.
The modern mole, made by the spoil from the excavations, leads directly to the entrance to the archaeological site.
Refreshments and simple lunches available at the Tourist Pavilion which has only three bedrooms.

Sanctuary (Hieron)

The paved open space is called the **Agora of the Competialists** because there freedmen and slaves honoured the Lares Compitales, roman gods of the crossroads: remains of a monumental altar (1).

Sacred Way ★. – This was a processional road, 13m – 43ft wide, used by the pilgrims to reach the sanctuary; it was lined by votive monuments, standing alone or in a semi-circular recess; some of the bases are still visible.

On either side stretched two porticoes; their positions are marked on the ground by the drums of columns and pieces of architrave; the portico on the left, the Stoa of Philip, was built by Philip of Macedon in 3C BC; the one on the right, the Pergamon Stoa, was built in the same period by the kings of Pergamon, a city in Asia Minor.

The Sacred Way ends in front of the Propylaia, the entrance to the sanctuary.

Propylaia. – Little is left of this monumental entrance but the numbers of pilgrims who crossed the threshold in antiquity can be judged by how much the three steps are worn away. On the right stands a marble statue of a bearded Hermes (4C BC) (2).

House of the Naxiots ★. – On the right beyond the Propylaia lie the foundations of a rectangular building from the Archaic period where the religious brotherhood of Náxos used to meet.

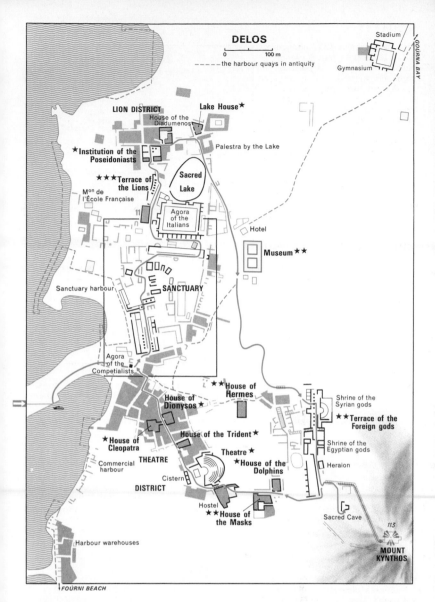

DELOS

0   100 m

- - - - - the harbour quays in antiquity

Stadium
Gymnasium
GOURNA BAY

LION DISTRICT
House of the Diadumenos
Lake House★

★Institution of the Poseidoniasts
Palestra by the Lake

★★★Terrace of the Lions
M^on de l'École Française
Sacred Lake

11
Agora of the Italians
Hotel

Museum★★

Sanctuary harbour
SANCTUARY

Agora of the Competialists

★★House of Hermes
House of Dionysos★
Shrine of the Syrian gods

★★Terrace of the Foreign gods
Shrine of the Egyptian gods

★House of Cleopatra
House of the Trident★
Theatre★
★House of the Dolphins
Heraion

Commercial harbour
THEATRE
Cistern
DISTRICT
Hostel
★★House of the Masks
Sacred Cave

113
MOUNT KYNTHOS

FOÙRNI BEACH

Against the north wall stands an enormous block of marble (3) which bears the following inscription in Archaic Greek letters: I am a single block, statue and pedestal. It was the base of a **statue of Apollo** (6C BC), a colossal votive offering erected by the Naxiots, which the Venetians tried to remove; some parts of it can be seen near the sanctuary of Artemis.

Stoa of the Naxiots. – On the left beyond the Propylaia are traces of this 6C BC portico; in the angle stands the circular base (4) granite on which stood the famous "**palm tree of Nikias**", a colossal bronze tree, which was erected in 417 BC by the Athenian Nikias to represent the palm tree beneath which Leto had given birth to Apollo and Artemis.

Continue along the Sacred Way between the precinct (témenos) of Apollo (right) and the precinct of Artemis (left).

Precinct of Apollo★★. – Lying south to north are traces of three successive temples of Apollo.

The temple of Delian Apollo (5), a Doric building, was the largest of the three; its construction was begun by the Deliots in 5C BC but was not completed until 3C BC because of Athenian hostility to it.

The Athenian temple (c420 BC) was also Doric (6) and the *naós (p 18)* contained seven statues set on a semicircular pedestal of black marble.

The smallest and oldest was the Porinos temple (7), built of hard limestone tufa, which contained an Archaic statue of Apollo and the treasure of the Delian League.

Near the Porinos temple stand two pedestals for statues; one (8) is decorated with a Doric frieze of alternating roses and bucranes (ox heads) and the other (9) in blue marble is inscribed in honour of Philetairos, first king of Pergamon.

Behind the three temples and beyond are the foundations of five small buildings (6C-5C BC) ranged in an arc which were probably the meeting places (**oikoi**) of the religious brotherhoods.

Precinct of Artemis★ (**Artemision**). – Set back from the Sacred Way, on the site of an ancient Mycenaean Palace, are the truncated columns of the façade of the temple of Artemis, a Hellenistic building (2C BC) in the Ionic style, which had succeeded two others;

digging nearby in 1946 uncovered a foundation trench, which
yielded numerous Mycenaean
objets *(in the museum)*.

Behind the temple of Artemis lie pieces of the colossal
Statue of Apollo ★★ (10) which was
hauled this far by the Venetians
in 1422; there are the torso,
partially covered with curly hair,
and the pelvis, which contains
holes to carry a belt; one of the
hands is in the local museum;
one of the feet is in the British
Museum.

*Cross the Sacred Way to reach
the Stoa of Antígonos Gonatás.*

Stoa of Antígonos Gonatás ★.
– The stoa which bordered the
sanctuary on the north side was
120m – 394ft long and consisted
of 48 Doric columns supporting
a frieze of bulls' heads. It was
built in 3C BC by a Macedonian
king. The ground plan shows two
galleries separated by a row of
columns ending in two short
wings. Two rows of statues lined
the façade; their bases still
exist.

Behind the eastern end of
the portico stands the **Minoë Fountain** which dates from 6C BC. Nearby are the remains
of the precinct wall and of a temple to Dionysos with two curious votive monuments
representing a phallus.

Return to the Sacred Way to leave the sanctuary and enter the ruined Lion District.

Lion District

This urban part was built in the Hellenistic period.

The path out of the sanctuary passes between the impressive remains of a granite
building **(11)** *(left)* and the walls of the **temple of Leto** *(right)* which dates from 6C BC and
has a bench outside. East of the temple extends the **Agora of the Italians** (2C BC) surrounded
by a portico into which opened the cells of the Italian merchants who settled on Delos
(several mosaics).

Terrace of the Lions ★★★. – Facing
the Sacred Lake *(see below)* is the row
of famous Archaic lions sculpted in
grainy Naxian marble. Originally there
were at least nine; only five remain;
a sixth was removed in 17C by the
Venetians and now stands guard,
with a different head, at the entrance
to the Arsenal in Venice.

These stone animals have long
bodies and scarcely perceptible
manes; they are sitting on their haun-
ches at different levels and give an
impression of restrained power. Their
hieratism and their stylised form suggest Asiatic influence.

Sacred Lake. – It was the habitat of
the swans sacred to Apollo but was
filled in 1924 because it caused
malaria.

Institution of the Poseidoniasts ★.
– It was an association of merchants
and ship owners from Beirut (Leba-
non) who worshipped under the aegis
of Poseidon. In the peristyled court
were discovered a group of Aphrodite

(Photograph D. Clement/Explorer)

Delos. – A lion

and Pan *(now in Athens Museum)* as well as a damaged statue of the goddess Rome.

Beyond are the remains of the **House of the Diadumenos** *(Athens
Museum)* of the famous Diadumenos by Polykleitos was discovered.

The path slopes down to the Lake House.

Lake House ★. – This is a Hellenistic house well-preserved (stucco and mosaics) with a
charming pillared court and a cistern.

*Turn south beside the Palestra by the Lake and along the eastern edge of the Sacred
Lake to the Museum (p 99) and then take the path and steps up the slopes of Mount
Kynthos.*

Mount Kynthos

Terrace of the Foreign Gods★★. – The terrace was built in 2C BC to take the shrines of the non-Greek divinities frequented by the many immigrants who lived on Delos.

Shrine of the Syrian gods. – On either side of the path which was once bordered by porticoes are traces of semicircular shrines and meeting rooms. One of the porticoes enclosed a small theatre where orgiastic mysteries were celebrated in honour of Atargatis, the Syrian Aphrodite.

Shrine of the Egyptian gods. – This is a continuation of the previous shrine; it contains the remains of a temple to Serapis and a temple to Isis of which the façade has been restored; in front of the latter temple stood an altar for offerings and its *naós* sheltered a statue of the goddess.

Heraion. – The foundations and two columns of the façade mark the site of a little Doric temple built of marble and dedicated to Hera (6C BC); numerous cult objects *(in the museum)* were found in the *naós*.

Ascent of Mount Kynthos★ *(3/4 hour on foot Rtn).* – *Visitors who do not want to climb Mount Kynthos should go straight to the Theatre District; the others should continue uphill to the sacred cave on the right.*

Sacred Cave. – This opening in the rock was covered in the Hellenistic era with enormous slabs of granite to form a shrine to Herakles.

Summit (alt 113m – 370ft). – There are traces of a sanctuary to Zeus and Athena (3C BC) and a magnificent **panorama★★★** over Delos and the Cyclades.

Return to the Heraion and descend towards the Theatre District.

Theatre District

The Theatre District was built from 2C BC onwards to house the many foreigners who came to live on Delos. It comprised many luxurious houses built round courtyards and decorated with superb mosaic floors in lively colours.

The path downhill passes the House of the Dolphins and the House of the Masks.

House of the Dolphins★. – The central courtyard is paved with a great mosaic signed by Asklepiades of Arados. In each corner is a dolphin in harness driven by a winged Cupid; one of the dolphins has a crown in its mouth.

House of the Masks★★. – This is a huge two-storeyed house, recently restored, with a central courtyard surrounded with a peristyle supported on stuccoed columns. The rooms giving on to the courtyard are decorated with magnificent mosaics showing figures wearing theatre masks: a dancing Silenus and an astonishing scene in the Asiatic style showing Dionysos with a thyrsos and a tambourine, dressed in a long robe and sitting on one of the panthers he subdued in India.

Continuing downhill the path passes the remains of a "hostel" with many rooms round a huge courtyard.

Theatre★. – This was a majestic construction, dating from the Hellenistic era, and is fairly well preserved, with marble walls and 43 rows of seats which could accommodate 5 000 spectators.

Opposite is a deep **cistern** with arches which once supported a roof.

House of the Trident★. – *Closed at present.* This house stands just below the theatre. Its mosaics are decorated with a trident, a dolphin entwined round an anchor and geometric motifs.

Further down the hill are the House of Cleopatra (left) and the House of the Dionysos (right).

House of Cleopatra★. – In 2C BC it was inhabited by a woman named Cleopatra and her husband Dioskourides whose damaged effigies can be seen on the north side of the peristyled courtyard.

The well still provides excellent drinking water.

House of the Dionysos★. – The central motif of the mosaic in the peristyled courtyard shows Dionysos again on a panther but this time with wings and seated astride. The panther's head is remarkable for its expression and colouring.

ADDITIONAL SIGHTS

House of Hermes★★. – The house is named after a fine head of Hermes *(in the museum)* which was found there. It is a two-storeyed building dating from 2C BC which was excavated and restored between 1948 and 1950 and is well preserved; the ground floor includes a vestibule, an inner courtyard bordered on three sides by a portico and a nymphaeum; stairs lead up to the first floor which includes a gallery and rooms leading off it.

Museum★★. – *Open 8.45am to 3pm (9.30am to 2.30pm Sundays); closed Tuesdays.*

The main room contains a remarkable series of Archaic sculptures including in particular votive statues of the *kouros* and *kore* type *(p 19)*; almost all the female figures were found in the sanctuary of Artemis.

Other rooms are devoted to Classical art from 5C BC (acroteria figures from the temple of the Athenians) to Romano-Hellenistic sculptures found in the private houses, little bronzes, ivories and Mycenaean jewellery.

Harbour warehouses. – Traces of quays, warehouses and stores along the shore towards Foúrni beach in the south.

Sports facilities. – Traces of the gymnasium (3C BC) and of the stadium are to be found northeast of the site.

In antiquity Delphi was one of the most important religious centres; the sanctuary of Apollo, which is situated above the River Pleistos gorge against the backdrop of Mount Parnassos, attracted a host of pilgrims who came to consult the oracle. Even now an aura of mystery invests the sparse ruins exposed on the rocky slope where the trees – olive, pine, cypress and lentisk – struggle for a toehold. A visit to Delphi tends to be a more impressive experience than any other in Greece. *Drama Festival in summer.*

The site★★★. – The road from Athens runs east to west through the archaeological site to the modern village (pop 2 426).

Beneath the silent watch of birds of prey the ancient ruins range down the mountain side below two roseate rock faces, the Phaidriades, 250m to 300m – 820 to 984ft high. Between them is a deep cleft from which emerges the Kastalian Spring. This awesome and majestic landscape is subject to occasional earthquakes and violent thunderstorms.

The view to the south, on the other hand, at the foot of the mountain presents a contrasting and smiling spectacle. The deep valley of the River Pleistos, silver-grey with olive groves, winds west and south round the foot of Mount Kírphis towards the coastal basin, forming the famous "sea of olive trees" which extends to the shore where the waters of the Bay of Itéa gleam in the pearly light.

The European Cultural Centre, founded in 1977, works in collaboration with the "Save Delphi" committee and other associations for the preservation of the site.

LEGEND AND HISTORY

The primitive earth goddess. – According to legend, Delphi was founded by Zeus. The historians of antiquity, who thought that the world was shaped like a flat disc, recounted how the leader of the gods wanted to know the position of the centre of the earth over which he reigned and sent two eagles out to reconnoitre. The two birds met above Mount Parnassos and identified the *omphalos* which was to make Delphi the hub of the universe.

In fact, the sanctuary's origins go far back into the past. In the 2nd millenium BC Delphi was already a place of worship dedicated to the earth goddess (Ge or Gaia) and her daughter Themis, one of the Titans, who expressed themselves in the booming of earth tremors, the rustle of vegetation and particularly the murmuring of water flowing from faults in the rock. The goddess hid at the bottom of one of these faults, guarded by her son, the snake Python; the divine pronouncements were already being interpreted by an oracle.

An archer takes the stage. – It was at the end of the Mycenaean period that **Apollo,** Olympian God and guarantor of universal harmony, is supposed to have overcome the old underworld deities. A hymn attributed to Homer tells how, after his birth on Delos *(p 95)* Zeus' son came to Delphi, killed the snake Python with his bow and arrow and took his place, becoming the god Python, who gave oracles through the intermediary of the Pythia.

The cult of Apollo, which was inaugurated by the Cretans, was joined by the cult of Dionysos *(p 36)* and Athena. Early in 6C BC, when the Athenians where the major power in central Greece, they instituted the Pythian Games at Delphi at which sports and poetic contests were held. This was the heyday of Delphi as a panhellenic sanctuary attracting pilgrims from all over the Greek world, from Spain to the Black Sea.

The sanctuary was maintained by the dues paid by those who consulted the oracle and enriched by offerings from both Greeks and barbarians. Despite the depredations of war and earthquakes and the pillaging of Sulla and Nero, Delphi was still thriving under the Emperor Hadrian in 2C AD.

When Julian the Apostate (361-363), the last pagan emperor of Rome, sent his quaestor, Oribasius, to consult the Pythian oracle, its utterance was worthy to be its own epitaph: "Go tell the king – the carven hall is felled;

       Apollo has no cell, prophetic bay

       Nor talking spring; his cadenced well is stilled."

It was finally closed in 381 by the Byzantine Emperor Theodosius the Great.

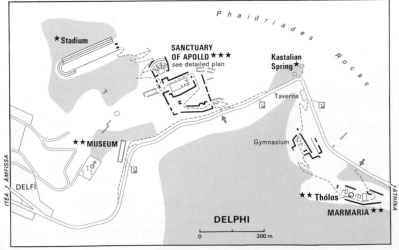

The oracle. – Originally the priestess of the sanctuary was chosen from among the local virgins but later she had to be a woman of over 50 whose life was beyond reproach. Known as the **Pythia** and later as the Delphic Sibyl, she delivered replies inspired by Apollo in answer to the questions put by the pilgrims. First she drank from the Cassotis fountain near the temple which was supposed to bestow the gift of prophecy; then she entered the temple crypt where she breathed the fumes of burning laurel leaves (Apollo's tree) and barley meal. Finally she took her seat on the famous tripod, a sort of three-footed cauldron, near to the *omphalos* and Dionysos' tomb.

The pilgrims (men only) were admitted to the neighbouring room where they gave their questions to the priests who passed them on to the Pythia. She went into a trance; the sounds that she uttered, her posture and her convulsive movements were interpreted by the priests who delivered the oracle couched in ambiguous phrases in hexameter verse. The replies took the form of advice rather than predictions.

The Pythia seems to have been well up in politics; in turn she favoured Xerxes during the Persian invasions, then Athens, Sparta and Thebes in 4C BC, then Philip of Macedon and finally Alexander the Great whom she proclaimed invincible.

The Pilgrim Way. – Having come overland or disembarked at Kirra near to Itéa, the pilgrims climbed the northern slope of the Pleistos valley and approached the temple past present-day Marmaria where they made their devotions to Athena. Then they proceeded to the Kastalian spring for ritual ablutions before crossing the agora and entering the sacred precinct. Once within they started up the Sacred Way, stopping at their national Treasury to deposit their offerings. Finally, after making the ritual propitiatory libations and sacrifices, they reached the temple.

As well as the sanctuary itself, the religious territory of Delphi included the Pleistos valley and the coastal plain. This sacred domain was administered by a sort of Greek Society of Nations, the **Amphictyony**, in which each of the twelve Greek "peoples" was represented by two deputies. Nonetheless there were rivalries and in 339 BC the Thessalians and Boeotians, who were members, invited the intervention of Philip of Macedon. The sanctuary itself was served by two high priests, a steward, a treasurer, five priests, of whom Plutarch was once one, and several acolytes, who attended the Pythia.

Excavations and restoration. – Although a village grew up over the sanctuary, the site of the Delphic oracle was never completely forgotten; it was visited by Cyriacus of Ancona in 15C, George Wheler and Dr Spon in 17C and by Byron and other 19C travellers. The credit for its excavation, however, goes to the French School at Athens.

1838: Laurent, an architect, studied the site and the visible traces;

1880: B. Haussoulier, an archaeologist, made confirmatory trials;

1892: the French Parliament voted a sum of 750 000FF to demolish the village and rebuild it away from the archaeological site;

1892-1902: excavations directed by **T. Homolle,** Director of the French School and E. Bourguet; 400 workmen uncovered the temple and the theatre from under a layer of earth up to 20m – 66ft thick in places; the spoil was evacuated by narrow gauge railway using 75 wagons over 3km – 2 miles; inauguration of the first museum.

1903-1950: further excavation and reconstructions by anastylosis *(p 20);* discovery in 1939 of a cache of precious objects beneath the Sacred Way.

since 1950: investigations in the direction of the Kastalian spring; display of the paleo-Christian mosaics in the modern town and excavation of the stadium; reorganisation of the museum.

Access by bus. – *From Athens, five services daily, bus station: 260 Odós Liossíon.*

Accommodation. – *Youth hostel; several hotels, restaurants, tavernas; camping site in Delphi (Itéa road) and by the sea near Itéa. For a longer stay, Galaxídi (p 105, 18km – 11 1/2 miles SW of Itéa; hotels, camping) would be more agreeable.*

Tour. – *The visitor who is pressed for time can visit the Apollo sanctuary and the museum in 1/2 day. Those interested in archaeology can take 1 1/2 days to visit the site following the path of the pilgrims of old (Marmaria, Kastalian spring, sanctuary of Apollo, stadium) with 1/2 day reserved for the museum and the views.*

SANCTUARY OF APOLLO★★★

Open 8am to 7pm (6pm Sundays); 200 Dr. Car park. It is a short walk uphill to the entrance.

Agora. – The Romans remodelled the agora and added some houses and baths built of brick; traces of these buildings are visible above the agora and road.

Down one side of the agora ran an Ionic portico with shops for the pilgrims; a few of the columns have been re-erected. There are fragments from a paleo-Christian church displayed (1) in the far corner.

Four steps lead up to the main entrance, one of nine, to the sacred precinct (**témenos**). The wall is 4C BC except in places (west side – polygonal construction) where it is 6C BC; it encloses a trapezoidal area 200m – 656ft by about 130m – 427ft, of which the lower part contains the votive offerings (statues, inscriptions etc) and the Treasuries, small temples erected by the Greek city states to receive the offerings made by their respective citizens; the whole area is thickly studded with monuments.

Walk up the Sacred Way.

Sacred Way. – No vehicles were allowed on the Sacred Way which leads up to the temple of Apollo; the paving dates from the Roman period.

Votive offerings. – On the right, as one enters, stands the base of the bull of Corcyra (2), a bronze animal offered in 5C BC by the city of Corcyra (now Corfu). Again on the right is the votive monument of the Arcadians (3) next to that of the Lakedaimonians *(p 180);* on the left the votive monument of Marathon, which the Athenians decorated with statues by Pheidias is followed by the monument of the Argives. These monuments, what little is left of them, testify to the rivalry between the Greek cities.

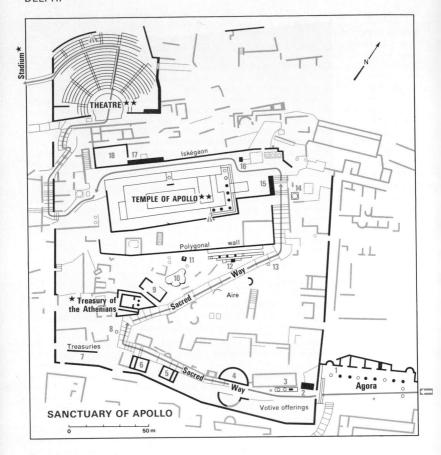

Stadium ★

THEATRE ★★

18   17   Iskégaon

16

TEMPLE OF APOLLO ★★

15

14

Polygonal   wall

11

12

13

10

Way

9

Aire

★ Treasury of
the Athenians

Sacred

8

Treasuries

7

6

5   Sacred   4

Way

3

1

2

Agora

SANCTUARY OF APOLLO

Votive offerings

0   50 m

The Sacred Way then passes between the foundations of two semi-circular structures erected by the Argives. The best preserved *(right)* was the monument of the king of Argos (4), built in 368 BC; it was decorated with 20 statues of the kings and queens of Argos; the dedicatory inscriptions were written from right to left.

Treasuries. – The first is the treasury of Sikyon (5), northwest of Corinth; the bases remain; it was built of tufa to a rectangular plan with two columns at the entrance (6C BC).

Beyond stands the wall of the Treasury of Siphnos (6), which was built in about 525 BC by the inhabitants of this Cycladic island out of the proceeds of its gold mines. It was an Ionic building in marble with a sculpted pediment supported by two caryatids and a beautiful sculpted frieze *(in the museum)*.

In the southwest corner of the precinct stood the Treasury of Thebes (7); the tufa foundations are visible; it contrasted with its neighbour by the austerity of its grey limestone architecture. Nearby on the outside of the bend in the Sacred Way stood a limestone version of the *omphalos* (8).

The **Treasury of the Athenians** ★, which has been reconstructed by anastylosis *(p 20)*, is a Doric building (490 – 480 BC) in white Parian marble, paid for with part of the booty captured from the Persians at Marathon. It was decorated with sculptures illustrating the Athenians' favourite themes: the battle between the Greeks and the Amazons, the legends about Theseus and Herakles *(in the museum)*.

The Treasury was built on a mound and preceded by a triangular terrace. The south wall of the terrace bears a dedication inscribed in huge letters: The Athenians to Apollo, after their victory over the Persians, as an offering to commemorate the battle of Marathon. The base and walls of the Treasury bear other inscriptions accompanied by crowns of laurel: for the most part the inscriptions are in honour of the Athenians.

After the Treasury come the sparse ruins of the Senate of Delphi (9) *(bouleuterion)*, followed by a pile of rocks (10) marking the site of the early Delphic oracle, which was guarded by the snake Python; behind the rocks stood the sanctuary of the Earth goddess, Ge or Gaia. Further on are the fallen drums of an Ionic marble column (11), 10m – 33ft high, a gift from the Naxiots to Apollo in about 570 BC; the column was surmounted by a sphinx *(in the museum)*.

Polygonal wall. – The famous polygonal wall retaining the terrace on which the temple of Apollo is built is 83m – 272ft long; it was built in 6C BC of huge blocks of random-shaped limestone. The wall is inscribed with more than 800 acts granting slaves their freedom during the Hellenistic and Roman periods.

Three columns of Pentelic marble mark the Stoa of the Athenians (12) which dates from about 480 BC; it contained the naval trophies captured from the Persians.

At this point the Sacred Way crosses a circular area *(halos)* where processions to the temple formed up before proceeding; note the handsome Ionic capital (13) and the curved seat *(exedra)* for the priests. On the edge of this area stood the Treasury of the Corinthians; nearby under the Sacred Way a cache of precious objects *(in the museum)* was discovered in 1939.

Temple approach. – The Sacred Way rises steeply to the level of the temple of Apollo. The circular pedestal *(right)* bore the Tripod of Plataia (14), erected in commemoration of the famous battle of Plataia *(p 172)*; it consisted of three bronze serpents intertwined forming a column and was transferred by Constantine the Great to Constantinople where it has remained. On the left are the foundations of the great altar to Apollo (15) which dates from 5C BC; it was also called the altar of the Chiots because they wrote the dedicatory inscriptions.

The huge stone pillar (16), to the right of the temple façade, bore an equestrian statue of Prusias (2C BC) king of Bithynia in Asia Minor.

Temple of Apollo ★★. – The existing ruins date from 4C BC; the previous building, the temple of the Alcmeonids (6C BC), which was partly financed by Croesus, was destroyed by an earthquake.

The outline of the 4C BC temple is clear; some half dozen columns have been re-erected. It was a Doric building with a peristyle, 60.30m – 198ft long by 23.80m – 781ft wide, with tufa columns faced with stucco 12m – 39ft high. The portico, in which stood a statue of Homer, was inscribed with the precepts of the Sages of Greece: "Know thyself", "Nothing in excess", etc. The *naós (p 18)* at the centre of the temple was furnished with altars and statues; beyond was the crypt *(adyton)* where the Pythia sat near the *omphalos* and the tomb of Dionysos.

The views from here are magnificent; to the south the temple columns stand out against the backdrop of the Pleistos Valley; to the northwest rise the perfect curves of the theatre.

Parallel with the uphill side of the temple runs a retaining wall "Iskégaon", built in 4C BC; at the western end, on the site of the votive offering of Polyzalos (17), was found the famous Charioteer of Delphi *(in the museum)*.

The rectangular base of a votive offering (18) has preserved the dedicatory stone on the back wall on the left. The monument was set up *c*315 BC by one Krateros *(p 170)* who had saved the life of Alexander the Great in a lion hunt; a bronze group by Lysippos recalls the scene.

Steps lead up to the theatre.

Theatre ★★. – The original theatre dates from 4C BC but it was remodelled two hundred years later by the Romans who refurbished the orchestra and the stage. The 35 terraces of seats could accommodate 5 000 spectators who came to watch the "mysteries" re-enacting the struggle between Apollo and the Python as well as to hear recitals in honour of the god; in the first row are the seats for the priest and other officials.

From the top row there is a marvellous **view ★★★** down over the sanctuary ruins, across the Pleistos Valley with its carpet of olives to the silent mass of Mount Kírphis.

The gangway *(diázoma)* running round the theatre half way up continues westwards as a path winding up the hillside to the Stadium; very fine views of the site of Delphi *(1/2 hour on foot Rtn)*.

Stadium ★. – It is surrounded by the silent conifers which clothe the hillside. Before the first stone seating was built in 3C BC the stadium was surrounded by earth terraces buttressed along the south side by a polygonal wall. In 2C AD it was altered by Herod Atticus who built the present terraces, which can hold 6 500 people, and erected a monumental **gateway** of which the columns have been partially rebuilt at the east end of the track.

The southern terraces were buttressed by a rampart which has half collapsed; those on the north side are built into the rock; at the centre is the presidential enclosure.

The starting and finishing lines are still in place, 178m – 584ft (600 Roman feet) apart.

In summer during the Festival of Delphi plays are performed in the stadium.

MUSEUM ★★

Open 8.45am (10am Sundays, holidays) to 3pm ; closed Tuesdays; 250 Dr.

The museum displays the works of art excavated at Delphi by the French School in a clear and pleasant presentation.

At the top of the steps stands a conical block of marble covered by a sculpted lattice effect, representing the *agrenon*; it is a Hellenistic copy of the famous **omphalos ★** (navel) which was kept in the crypt of the temple of Apollo and supposed to mark the centre of the world.

Enter the Hall of Shields and turn right into the Hall of the Siphnians.

Hall of the Siphnian Treasury ★. – Devoted to Archaic sculpture (6C BC).

In the middle stands the winged Sphinx of the Naxiots mounted on its column. It is flanked by two caryatids from the Treasuries of Knidos and Siphnos.

Around the walls are pieces of the frieze from the Siphnian Treasury, made of white Parian marble; the sculptured decoration was painted in bright colours, traces of which survive in places. The scenes depict: the Trojan War showing Aeneas and Hector in combat with Menelaos and Ajax (fine horses) under the interested gaze of the gods of Olympos; a beautifully composed Gigantomachy, the war between the Giants and the gods.

Return to the Hall of Shields and turn right into the Hall of the Kouroi.

Hall of the Kouroi ★. – The two *kouroi*, which were part of votive offerings, are huge Archaic statues from 6C BC, representing Cleobis and Biton, twins from Argos, who died of exhaustion after pulling their mother's chariot for 45 stadia (just under 5 miles); she was a priestess of Hera hurrying to the Argive Heraion to perform a sacrifice.

Continue into the small adjoining room, the Hall of the Bull.

Hall of the Bull ★. – Assembled here are the cult objects found in 1939 beneath the Sacred Way where they had been buried in two pits, probably because they were no longer in use, in accordance with an ancient custom which persisted in Christianity.

The principal item is an Archaic bull (6C BC) which was made of silver plates attached to copper strips fixed to a wooden framework. Dating from the same period are several gold panels, engraved or embossed, which probably adorned a statue and a statuette in ivory of a god taming a fawn. The bronzes include an incense burner held by a young girl dressed in a *peplos (p 20)* (5C BC).

Return through the Halls of the Kouroi and of the Shields and turn right into the Hall of the Athenian Treasury.

Hall of the Athenian Treasury. – The sculpted metopes *(damaged)* which date from the Archaic period, belonged to the Athenian Treasury. They illustrate the legends of Herakles and Theseus; some of the heads, particularly the head of Theseus *(left)*, are very fine.

Pass straight on through the Halls of the Temple of Apollo and of the Tholos into the Hall of the Monument of Daochos.

Hall of the Monument of Daochos★★. – A magnificent group of **three dancers** (4C BC) in Pentelic marble stands on an Acanthus Column; the dancers are bacchantes or Thyiads, priestesses of Dionysos. The column was a votive offering erected by the Athenians in front of the Monument of Daochos, which stood above the open space before the temple of Apollo.

Against the wall *(right)* are the statues from the monument (4C BC) of Daochos II, who represented Thessaly in the Amphictyonic league; note the figure of the athlete Agias *(second from the right)* who won the pancration in the Olympic and Delphic Games.

Hall of the Charioteer★★★. – The Charioteer of Delphi, which is wonderfully well preserved, is one of the most beautiful Greek statues from the late Archaic period (478 BC); it was discovered in 1896 not far from the theatre. The figure was part of a bronze votive offering representing the winning quadriga (four horse chariot) in the Olympic Games of 473 and 474; it was presented by Polyzalos, Tyrant of Gela in Sicily.

The noble, life-size figure (1.80m – 5ft 9ins) is facing slightly to the right (Polyzalos is thought to have been at his side) and holding the horses' reins in his hands. He is wearing the victor's headband. The great beauty of the modelling of the head is enhanced by the original eyes composed of enamel and coloured stones. The feet are so realistic that they seem to have been moulded from nature.

A showcase in the same room displays another work of art, a white libation cup (5C BC) showing Apollo seated, wearing a crown of laurel and holding a tortoise-shell lyre; he is pouring a libation in the presence of his sacred bird, the crow.

Delphi. – The Charioteer.

Return to the previous room and turn right into the Hall of the Antinoüs.

Hall of the Antinoüs★. – The marble statue (2C BC) of Antinoüs is one of the best representations of the favourite of the Emperor Hadrian, who deified him after his death.

There is a fine marble **head** thought to represent the Roman general T. Q. Flaminius. The showcases contain votive figurines offered to Pan in the Corycian cave *(p 36)*.

By the exit are displayed paleo-Christian mosaics, discovered recently near the modern town.

ADDITIONAL SIGHTS

Marmaria★★ (Sanctuary of Athena Pronaia). – *South of the road to Aráhova; main entrance to the east marked by a sign "Temple of Athena Pronaia".*

The sanctuary of Athena Pronaia which the pilgrims visited before going on to the sanctuary of Apollo, stood on a beautiful site looking across the Pleistos Valley to Mount Kírphis. Now in ruins, the sanctuary has been known as Marmaria since it was used as a quarry for marble.

Old Temple of Athena. – All that remains of this Archaic Doric temple, built of tufa in 6C BC, are the bases of some columns and some sections of wall. The building was damaged by rock falls and eventually abandoned in 4C BC. It incorporated elements of an earlier 7C BC temple, particularly some capitals which can be seen resting on the ground or on the remains of columns.

Between this temple and the rotunda *(thólos – p 18)* are the remains of two Treasuries; the second probably belonged to Massalia, present-day Marseille.

Thólos★★. – This elegant peristyle rotunda, built of marble in 4C BC, probably as a shrine of the earth goddess (Ge or Gaia), is picturesquely recalled by what remains: a stylobate *(p 18)*, drums of fluted columns, lower courses of a circular wall and three Doric columns (re-erected) supporting an entablature.

New Temple of Athena. – The old tufa building was replaced in 4C BC by a smaller temple built of limestone without a peristyle. The foundations are visible.

A steep path leads to the upper terraces where a gymnasium, built in 4C BC and remodelled by the Romans, extended over two levels; on the lower level, there are traces of a peristyle court which served as the palestra and of a circular pool; on the upper level traces of the covered track *(xystos)* are visible: part of the end wall and colonnade dating from the Roman era.

Return to the road by the path past the taverna.

Kastalian Spring ★. – The spring where the nymph Kastalia is said to have drowned herself to escape from the attentions of Apollo wells up at the end of the wild ravine which divides the Phaidriades Rocks. Here the pilgrims of old performed ritual ablutions to purify themselves before entering Apollo's sanctuary; the water is now chanelled to irrigate the olive groves.

Part of the ancient arrangements are still visible: a huge Archaic paved basin excavated in 1958, a longer basin hewn out of the rock at the base of the cliff with steps leading down into it and above it part of the side of the reservoir which supplied the basin below through openings which are still visible.

It is from the top of the Phaidriades Rocks that **Aesop** (6C BC), who composed the fables, is supposed to have been hurled for mocking the Delphians.

EXCURSIONS

Corycian Cave ★★ and Mount Parnassos ★★. – *Description page 36. 90km – 56 miles by car Rtn, about 2 1/2 hours by the Aráhova road.*

Itéa. – *17km – 11 miles to the southwest*. The road descends in long loops down the slopes of the Pleistos Valley into the olive groves in the coastal plain which belonged to the sanctuary of Apollo and was the setting of the ancient race course.

The famous olive groves, aptly referred to as a **sea of olives ★**, are tended and watered with care. Together with the more recent plantations on the slopes of the Pleistos Valley, they number some 400 000 olive trees; harvesting begins in September. The mills in which the olives are pressed are powered by the waters of the Pleistos.

Itéa (pop 3 414) is a bathing resort and port at the head of Itéa Bay; a new coast road links it to Naupaktos further west. It was chosen by the Allies in 1917 as the base town on the supply route which ran via Amphissa, Brálos and Lamía to the eastern front. To the east of Itéa lay the ancient port of Delphi, **Kirra**; there are traces of an ancient jetty.

Galaxídi ★. – Pop 1 264. *33km – 21 miles southwest via Itéa and the coast road:* fine view of the Bay of Itéa. Galaxídi is a charming old town *(hotels, guest houses, camping)* with a sheltered harbour, which until early this century was a rival to Syros *(p 184)*. The fine stone houses with their balconies suggest former days of wealth; in 19C Galaxídi traded throughout the Mediterranean; there were 50 shipping magnates out of a population of 6 000. A small **maritime museum** evokes the port's past glories. The cathedral at the top of the town contains a beautiful 19C carved wood iconostasis.

DIMITSÁNA ★

Peloponnese – Arkadía – Pop 612 – Michelin map 980 centre of fold 28

Buried at the heart of the Peloponnese is the old medieval city of Dimitsána which is built on a spectacular **site ★★** (alt 850m – 2 789ft) on a ridge overlooking the narrow and rugged Loússios Valley.

In 18C its remote position and inaccessibility made it a good centre for the national revival with its secret schools which were attended by several patriots who later became leaders in the independence movement, such as the Patriarch Germanós *(p 119);* owing to its arsenal and powder magazine, it took on a military role at the outbreak of war against the Turks.

Leave the car at the entrance to the town and stroll through the maze of narrow streets and steps lined by old houses, some of which are shaded by awnings: glimpses of the Loússios Valley and the surrounding peaks.

DION ★★   *Dío*

Macedonia – Pieriá – Michelin map 980 fold 17

At the foot of Mount Olympos *(16km – 10 miles south of Kateríni)* in the fertile Peiriá plain lies the sacred town of ancient Macedon; its name declares its link with Zeus (Días).

It was famous in the past for its athletic and dramatic festival which was known as the "**Olympic Games of Dion**" and instituted by Archelaos in 5C BC in honour of the Muses. At the height of its prosperity the town numbered 15 000 inhabitants. The site lies on the bank of a navigable river and was served by a river port. The fortifications were built in the reign of Alexander the Great who had a particular liking for the town.

Excavations. – *Open 8am to 7pm (6pm Sundays); 100 Dr (site and museum).*

Excavations to date have revealed three sections of interest: the town, the sanctuary and the cemetery.

The town, which was laid out according to the custom of that time, had a complete network of streets (22 have been excavated so far). Administrative buildings, warehouses, houses, baths and public latrines etc. have been uncovered. A Hellenistic theatre, two Roman odeons and a stadium bear witness to the cultural activities which took place in Dion and which put the town on a level with the thriving cities of southern Greece.

The largest sanctuary discovered was dedicated to the Egyptian divinities, Isis, Serapis and Anubis and consisted of several temples.

Museum. – *Open 8am to 7pm (6pm Sundays); 8.45am to 3pm Mondays and Wednesdays; closed Tuesdays.*

It contains the objects found during the excavations at Dion and neighbouring sites.

The ground floor is devoted to the sanctuaries and the upper floor to objects found in the town and on neighbouring sites.

Walkers, campers and smokers please take care.
Fire is the scourge of forests everywhere.

DIRÓS CAVES★★ *Spílea Diroú*

Peloponnese – Lakonía – Michelin map 980 fold 41 – Local map p 131

Part way down the west coast of Máni *(p 130)*, opening into Dirós Bay are two caves which were explored after the Second World War. The largest, Glifáda, is one of the most spectacular natural sights in Greece. *Bathing from the seashore.*

Glifáda Cave. – *Guided tours every day from 8am to sunset; 280 Dr; snack bar.*

The cave consists of chambers and a gallery created by an underground river forcing its way through the limestone of Máni to reach the sea below the actual entrance.

The cave is well organised for visitors with floating lights and coloured light projectors. The guided tour consists of a boat trip *(about 2km – 1 1/4 miles)* along both arms of the river which splits in two in the cave. All along the route are white or coloured concretions: pillars, curtains, stalactites and stalagmites which can appear like human silhouettes, fabulous beasts, fantastic flowers or surrealist buildings (the Dragon's Cave, the Cathedral, the Pavilion...).

The water is up to 15m – 50ft deep in places with a temperature of 12 °C – 54 °F. The air temperature varies from 16 to 20 °C – 62 °F to 70 °F.

Alepótripa Cave. – *Closed temporarily for excavations.* The entrance to this cave, which is called the fox hole, is about 200m – 656ft below the road; within are two lakes and traces of prehistoric occupation.

ÉDESSA

Macedonia – Péla – Pop 16 054 – Michelin map 980 folds 4 and 5

Édessa was built on the edge a plateau overlooking the Macedonian plain. In antiquity it was one of the main strongholds in Macedon, not far from the site of Philip II's assassination *(p 197)* in 336 BC. The town is known for its situation and the flowing waters of the River Vódas which make it a refreshing and agreeable summer resort.

Waterfalls★. – *East of the town, signpost "Waterfalls" and "Pros Kataráktes".* A public garden shaded by huge plane trees *(restaurant)* leads down to the point where the various streams which flow through the town meet in an impressive waterfall; the water tumbles 25m – 82ft down a rock face covered by luxuriant vegetation.

Old mosque. – This charming building houses an archaeological museum (stele, mosaics).

ELEUSIS, Sanctuary of★ *Elefsína*

Central Greece – Attica – Michelin map 980 fold 30 – Local map p 68

The sanctuary at Eleusis where the cult of the "great goddesses", Demeter and Persephone, was celebrated was one of the great shrines of antiquity. It was linked to Athens by the Sacred Way and was the setting for the initiation ceremonies which could not be divulged on pain of death; death was also the punishment for non-initiates who penetrated the sanctuary.

The sanctuary as built against a low hill topped by an acropolis overlooking Eleusis Bay and Salamis Island. The ruins were first discovered in 1815 by the Society of the Dilettanti and excavated in a series of digs, the first by French archaeologists in 19C. The topography is confused as the ruins are part Greek and part Roman.

Statue of Demeter. – The statue of a woman with a basket on her head at the entrance to the village was already well known to 18C travellers when **Edward Clarke**, an Englishman who acted as travelling tutor to young noblemen, visited Eleusis early in 19C and decided to acquire the statue. The goddess stood "in a dunghill buried to her ears"; the statue was worshipped by the villagers who placed lighted lamps before it in the belief that it protected the fertility of their corn fields. With the gift of a telescope Clarke obtained a firman from Athens for the purchase of the statue and after two days of delay and dispute with the villagers he succeeded in removing his treasure. The Eleusinians predicted disaster; the ship which carried the statue to England went down off Beachy Head. Demeter was however rescued and now stands in the Fitzwilliam Museum in Cambridge.

The Eleusinian mysteries. – In mythology it was at Eleusis that Demeter found her daughter, Persephone, who had been abducted by Hades, king of the underworld, near Lake Pergusa in Sicily. Keleos, king of Eleusis, gave the goddess hospitality and in return she gave **Triptolemos**, the king's son, the first grain of wheat and showed him how to make it bear fruit. At the same time she is supposed to have entrusted Eumolpos with the ritual of the fertility cult.

The secret rites, known as the "Eleusinian mysteries", were celebrated until 4C BC. Initiation, which was open to all, took place during the great Eleusinian festival in the autumn and consisted of two stages. In the second year the *"mystai"*, those partially initiated, met on the third day of the festival in the Stoa Poecile in Athens where they had to prove that they had not committed murder and were Greek-speaking. On the following day they were conducted to Phaleron Bay *(p 65)* where they plunged into the water (purification rite) together with a young pig destined to be sacrificed. The following days were devoted to retreat, fasting, sacrifices and a solemn procession which brought back to Eleusis along the Sacred Way the sacred objects *(ierá)* which had been taken to Athens at the beginning of the festival.

During the last three days the priests proceeded with the last part of the initiation in the heart of the sanctuary. This is thought to have consisted of revelations, a sort of sacred pageant on various themes: the union of Zeus and Demeter, a sign of fertility; the legend of Persephone detained in the world of the dead for six months, symbol of Nature being dormant during the winter and re-awakening in the spring; the journey to the underworld, evocation of man's final destiny. At the end of the ceremony the sacred objects were revealed to the initiates.

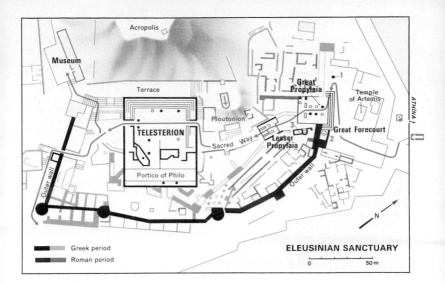

ELEUSINIAN SANCTUARY

Greek period
Roman period

0   50 m

TOUR *about 1 hour*

Open 8.45am to 3pm (9.30am to 2.30pm Sundays); 200 Dr.

Great Forecourt. – 2C AD. The square, which is paved with marble, was laid out in the Roman era. Near the site of a temple to Artemis is the colossal medallion bust of the Roman emperor Antoninus Pius (1) from the pediment of the Great Propylaia.

Great Propylaia. – 2C AD. This was the entrance to the sanctuary, which the Romans rebuilt on the model of the propylaia in Athens. Traces of steps and the bases of columns mark the two Doric outer doors and the three passages divided by Ionic columns.

To the left of the entrance *(outside)* is the **Kallichoron well** (2) (6C BC) round which the sacred dances were performed in honour of Demeter. Again on the left but inside are traces of the Roman sewer *(cloaca)* (3).

Lesser Propylaia. – 1C BC. To the right are parts of the architrave decorated with symbolic ears of corn.

The Sacred Way, which was paved by the Romans, leads *(right)* past caves hollowed out of the hillside to symbolize the entrance to the underworld; at the base on a triangular terrace stands a little temple dedicated to Hades, the Ploutonion.

Telesterion. –The Telesterion at the heart of the sanctuary was a majestic building in which the mysteries were revealed. It was almost square measuring 54m by 52m – 177ft by 170ft and the ground floor consisted of a huge room divided by six rows of columns and surrounded by raked seating which could accommodate about 3 000 people; another room *(megaron)* on the first floor under the wooden roof held the sacred objects. A paved portico, the **portico of Philo**, runs along the southeast front.

The building has been refashioned many times and retains traces of every period, from the Mycenaean to the Roman via Peisistratos (6C BC), Pericles (5C BC), Philo (4C BC) and Antoninus Pius (2C AD), which are very difficult to disentangle. The overall plan is, however, easily traced as well as the bases of votive statues.

Beyond the Telesterion it is possible to go outside the precinct and look at the Classical Greek walls surrounding the site.

Then climb the steps of a terrace which gave access to the upper floor of the Telesterion to reach the Museum which overlooks the Bay of Eleusis and Salamis Island (laid-up ships).

Museum. – *Open same times as the excavations; closed Tuesdays.*

The courtyard displays a horse's head dating from the Hellenistic period, which once decorated the base of a statue, and a sarcophagus from the Roman era with sculptures of Meleager hunting the boar which was ravaging the Calydon region (near Missolonghi).

The museum contains sculptures found during the excavations: low-reliefs of Demeter, Persephone, Triptolemos and a curious caryatid (2C AD) from the Lesser Propylaia. There is also a reconstruction of the sanctuary in its heyday.

EPHYRA NEKROMANTEION★ _____ *Efíra*

Epiros – Michelin map ❐❐❐ centre of fold 15 – southeast of Párga

Near the village of Messopótamo (pop 554) stood a sanctuary dedicated to the Oracle of the Dead (Nekromanteion) on the banks of the River Acheron (Ahérondas), the ancient "river of the Underworld". Gradually the estuary was filled and drained to form the present Fanári Plain which supports the cultivation of corn and rice and the raising of buffalo.

The entrance to the kingdom of the Dead. – In antiquity the **Acheron** (Ahérondas) emerged from a wild ravine and spread out to form an inaccessible and mysterious lagoon, Lake Acheroussia. The ancient people used to tell how the shades of the Dead had to cross this marshy lake to reach the infernal kingdom of **Hades** and his wife Persephone (Kore). The Dead who had not been buried according to the ritual were condemned to wander endlessly in the forests and reed beds which lined its banks. The others gave **Charon** the ritual coin and embarked in his boat; the fierce ferryman steered his craft into the sinister gorge which led to the bowels of the earth where **Cerberus**, a monstrous many-headed dog, kept guard.

Only two living souls managed to penetrate the kingdom of the Dead, Herakles (Hercules) and **Orpheus** whose lyre enabled him to snatch the nymph Eurydice from the infernal deities but he lost her again because he turned to look at her before they had emerged from Hades.

Charon often appears as a symbol of death in the popular songs of modern Greece.

Souliot Country. – The Acheron flows through a wild and desolate mountainous region, where in 15C Christians took refuge from the Turks. Albanian in origin, the people were named after their major settlement, Souli, which consisted of a few villages on a plateau 2000 ft up in the Acheron Gorge. They kept flocks if goats and sheep and survived on brigandage and tribute from their subject villages in the plains (Parasouli).

Although few in number (about 5 000), the **Souliots** were brave and indomitable. Divided into clans and protected by the inaccessibility of their mountain fortresses, they maintained their autonomy for a long time.

Eventually they were defeated in battle at Nikopolis and in 1803 at Zálongo *(p 120)* by the troops of Ali Pasha but he could not destroy them. They rose again in revolt against the Turks in 1820-23, taking part in the defence of Missolonghi under the orders of one of their own leaders, the famous Bótzaris.

Since then the Souliots have been dispersed; many of them live in Leukas, Cephallonia and Naupaktos.

THE SANCTUARY ★

Entrance signposted. Open 8.45am to 3pm (9.30am to 2.30pm Sundays); 100 Dr.

A chapel on a rocky hillock near the Acheron and the site of Lake Acheroussia marks the position of the Nekromanteion which was a sanctuary dedicated to Hades and Persephone at the entrance to the Underworld, where the people came to consult the spirits of the Dead through the oracle.

The Nekromanteion was already in existence in the Mycenaean period but the traces of the building which are now visible are Hellenistic (3C BC). It was constructed of fine polygonal stonework and comprised a series of corridors and rooms culminating in the sanctuary itself, a huge chamber where the priests wreathed in sulferous vapours pronounced the oracle to the pilgrims who had previously been through a propitiatory rite and taken hallucinogenic drugs. The oracle was located in a crypt, hollowed out of the rock beneath the central chamber, which was thought to communicate with the abode of Hades.

The items found during the excavations are on display in Ioánina Museum.

EPIDAUROS ★★★   *Arhéa Epídavros*

Peloponnese – Argolis – Michelin map 𝟿𝟾𝟶 folds 29 and 30

At the heart of the gentle Argolid hills, set about with pine trees and oleanders, lie the ruins of the famous sanctuary of the hero Asklepios, the god of medicine, where people from all over ancient Greece would come to consult the oracle. Modern crowds congregate here to admire the perfect proportions of the theatre, one of the marvels of Greece and very well preserved.

Access. – *Beside the road from Návplio is a huge car park. A path through the trees leads past the hotel-restaurant Xénia to the archaeological site.*

Tour. – *Open 8am to 5pm; 200 Dr.*

Epidauros Festival. – *Every weekend in the evening from 15 June to beginning of September. For times and programmes see the brochure issued by the EOT. Organised excursions from Athens, Návplio, Portohéli and the Saronic Gulf islands.*

LEGENDARY AND HISTORICAL NOTES

Beneath the Caduceus. – Asklepios (Aesculapius in Latin) was the son of Apollo and Koronis, a Boeotian princess; he was suckled by a nanny goat and educated by **Cheiron,** the wise centaur *(p 168),* who taught him surgery and the art of healing with plants. Owing to Cheiron's teaching and his own innate supernatural gifts, Asklepios became so knowledgeable that he was able to resuscitate the dead; this attracted the ill will of Hades and Zeus, jealous of a power reserved for the gods alone. So Zeus sent a thunderbolt to strike Asklepios dead and his body was buried at Epidauros.

However that may be, from 6C BC Asklepios became the object of a cult which reached its greatest intensity in 4C BC and even extended to the persons of his children including his two daughters, Hygieia and Panaceia. The great Greek doctors *(archontes),* even the famous Hippocrates of Kos, claimed authority from him.

Asklepios is generally represented as a bearded figure leaning on an augur's wand accompanied by the magic serpent; these elements later came to be included in the caduceus, the doctor's emblem.

The Epidauros treatment. – The sick, who came from Árgos, Troizen or from the town of Epidauros itself which was a few miles away on the east coast, would first make a sacrifice to the gods and accomplish a ritual purification and then spend the night in the sacred dormitory *(abaton)* where they lay on the skin of the animals which had been offered in propitiation. During their sleep they might be cured instantly or Asklepios might appear to them in dreams which the priests would translate into treatment accompanied, according to the different cases, by physical exercices or relaxation or baths or intellectual pursuits. This explains the importance given to the theatre and the sports facilities (stadium, gymnasium, palestra) and to the Asklepian Games which were held every four years and consisted of sporting contests and poetic or musical competitions. The people expressed their gratitude with the sacrifice of a cock and votive offerings in the shape of the part of the body which had been cured.

Under the Romans thaumaturgy gradually yielded its place to a more scientific form of medicine. Late in 5C AD a Christian basilica was built on the site of the ancient sanctuary.

Nothing more was heard of Epidauros until the beginning of 19C when an English traveller and topographer, Sir William Gell, made a plan of the ruins. In 1822 the independence of Greece was proclaimed in the theatre. In 1881 Greek archaeologists, assisted by the French School in Athens, began to work on the site.

THE THEATRE★★★ *1 hour*

Set apart from the sanctuary *(southwest)* is the theatre, the most outstanding in the ancient world owing to the beauty of its setting, its magnificent lines and harmonious proportions. It was built in 4C by the Argive architect, Polykleitos the Younger and is set into the north slope of Mount Kynortion (now Harani) facing the valley sacred to Asklepios. In 1954 it was restored to make modern productions of the ancient repertory as well as musical recitals at which Dimitri Mitropoulos (1896-1960) and Maria Callas have performed.

The **theatre,** which can accommodate 14 000 spectators, forms a section of a circle slightly larger than a
semi-circle. It consists of 55 rows of
seats divided by a promenade *(diázoma)* into an upper and a lower
section. The seats of honour, reserved
for the magistrates and the priests,
were situated in the first row of the
upper section and in the back and
first row of the lower section; the
spectators in the rest of the lower
section probably had cushions to sit
on. The performance could be heard
and seen perfectly from every seat in
the theatre as can be demonstrated
today by whispering or rustling a
piece of paper in the centre of the
orchestra; the sound carries without
distortion to the top back corner of
the huge spread of terraces some
22.50m – 74ft from the ground.

There were two entrances at
ground level on either side of the
orchestra and steps up between the
rows of seats in both sections; the

Epidauros. – The Theatre

upper section was also served by two
ramps on either side of the seats.

The circular **orchestra**, where the chorus performed, is 20.28m – 2yds in diameter and marked at the centre by the base of the altar to Dionysos. Between the edge of the orchestra and the first row of seats there is a channel to take the rain water.

On the north side of the orchestra are the foundations of the stage and the proscenium incorporating a sort of arch which supported the scenery.

It is worth climbing the steps between the rows of seats to appreciate the contours and proportions of the theatre which are regulated by the "golden mean" (c8:13), particularly in the ratio between the lower and upper sections of seats.

The view from the top is very fine, particularly in the early evening when the sacred valley of Asklepios lies peacefully in the shelter of the surrounding hills.

ADDITIONAL SIGHTS

Leave the theatre, passing the museum *(p 110)* to reach the **gymnasium;** the central part of it was converted into an odeon by the Romans. Descend the ramp, which led up to the main entrance to the gymnasium, passing the remains of the **palestra** *(right)* on the way to the sanctuary.

Sanctuary of Asklepios★ (Hieron). – The main monuments are to be found here surrounded by a wall within which the sacred serpents were confined.

Temple of Asklepios. – An outline of rectangular foundations marks the site of the small Doric temple with a raised peristyle which was designed by the architect Theodotos (4C BC) who also assisted in the construction of the Mausoleum of Halikarnassos. The temple contained a statue in gold and ivory of Asklepios seated on a throne, a baton in his right hand and his left resting of the head of a serpent. South of the temple are the remains of the altar where the sacrifices were made.

Rotunda (Thólos). – More foundations *(west)* belong to the famous rotunda *(thólos – p 18)* which was built in 4C BC by the architect of the theatre, Polykleitos the Younger, as a mausoleum for the hero Asklepios.

The building consisted of two concentric colonnades – the outer one of tufa in the Doric order and the inner of marble in the Corinthian order. At the centre was a maze; its purpose has been the subject of many hypotheses: Asklepios' tomb, a pen for the sacred serpents, a ritual labyrinth like those in medieval cathedrals, a symbolic representation of a molehill since the god's name, Asklepios, is similar to the Greek word for a mole.

The rotunda was sumptuously decorated: different coloured marbles, paintings of Love and Inebriety and finely sculpted motifs.

Abaton. – To the north of the rotunda and the temple are the foundations of a portico which dates from the same period but was enlarged by the Romans. It was the dormitory where the sick slept in the hope that the god would appear to them in a dream.

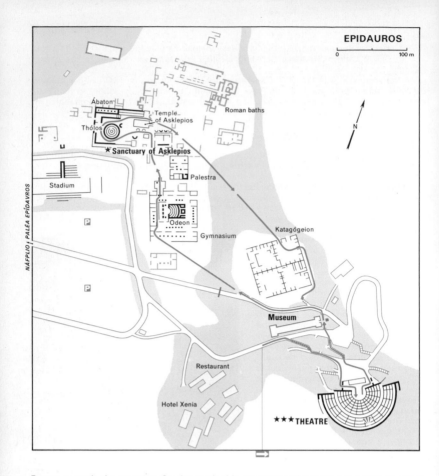

EPIDAUROS

0   100 m

Ábaton

Temple
of Asklepios

Roman baths

Thólos

★ Sanctuary of Asklepios

N

Stadium

Palestra

NÁFPLIO / PALÉA EPÍDAVROS

P

Odeon

Gymnasium

Katagógeion

P

Museum

Restaurant

Hotel Xenia

★★★THEATRE

Return towards the museum. On the north side are traces of a huge hotel *(katagogeion)* comprising 160 rooms arranged round four courtyards.

Museum. – *Open same times as the site; 11am to 7pm Tuesdays.* Although the chief sculptural finds on the site have been taken to the museum in Athens, the Epidauros museum contains several items of interest including some unusual stele bearing inscriptions (the accounts for the construction of the rotunda, descriptions of miraculous cures) and a collection of Roman medical instruments. There is a partial reconstruction of the rotunda using authentic elements: finely carved capitals and ceiling coffers.

Stadium. – It was built in 5C BC in a hollow in the ground. The starting and finishing lines are extant, 181.30m – 594ft apart. Stone seats were provided for the important people only.

EXCURSION

Paleá Epídavros. – Pop 1 344. *9km – 5 1/2 miles northeast.* Small fishing village and resort with several fish tavernas at the end of a picturesque valley planted with olive and citrus fruit trees.

EUBOIA (EUBOEA)★ _____ *Évia*

Central Greece – Pop 185 653 – Michelin map 𝟿𝟾𝟶 folds 18, 19, 30 and 31

Euboia runs parallel to the east coast of Attica and Boeotia to which it is linked by the bridge at Chalkis (Halkída) which is the capital. It is the second largest (3 580km² – 1 351sq miles) Greek island after Crete, being 150km – 93miles long and 10 to 50km – 6 to 31 miles wide.

It is well populated and fertile (beehives) with a varied landscape: cultivated plains and basins, verdant valleys, mountains partially clothed in forests of pine, chestnut and plane trees with the waters of the Aegean in the background.

For many years Euboia was called **Euripos** (Eurípos – the name of the narrows between it and the mainland) which developed into Negroponte *(p 79)*, the old Italian name.

Access. – *By car via the ferries (see Michelin map 𝟿𝟾𝟶) or via the bridge in Chalkis, by coach from Odós Liossíon in Athens or by train to Chalkis.*

Accommodation. – *There are many seaside resorts or holiday villages particularly on the southwest coast facing the mainland: (from south to north) Káristos, Marmári, Néa Stíra, Amárinthos, Ágios Minás, Erétria, Malakónda and Gregolímano.*

Touring. – *Follow the road which runs the length of the island from Káristos (south) to Loutrá Edipsoú (north) making two detours to Kími and Mount Dírfis; this itinerary takes about two days stopping over at Chalkis. Tourists with less time to spare are advised to visit the southern half between Káristos and Chalkis which includes a particularly spectacular stretch from Káristos to Stíra.*

TOWNS, SIGHTS AND RUINS *(travelling from south to north)*

Káristos. – Pop 4 081. This is a summer resort with a port used by fishing boats and ferries *(from Rafína)* surrounded by olive groves and vineyards. **Mount Óhi** (1 398m – 4 587ft) which rises behind the town was already being quarried in antiquity for its green cipolin marble. Under the Venetians the town was one of the three great baronies of Euboia.

On the top of Mount Folí stand the ruins of a huge castle with a double bailey which was built in 13C by Ravano delle Carceri and called **Castel Rosso** (Red Castle) owing to the colour of the stone. When the Emperor Baldwin II de Courtenay fled from Constantinople, he took refuge here in 1261 with **Otho de Cicon,** son of Sibylle de la Roche; in return for this hospitality Baldwin gave Otho a chased silver coffer containing St George's arm; two years later Otho himself offered this reliquary to the Abbey of Citeaux in Burgundy.

Eagles' Road★★★. – For about 30km – 18 1/2 miles between Káristos and Stíra the road runs along a ledge 700 to 800m – 2 300 to 2 600ft above sea level on the southwest coast of Euboia. Birds of prey hover over the bare and empty hillsides which offer splendid views down over Marmári, across the bay to the Petalíi Islands and into the cove at Pórto Láfia, a resort which is reached by a steep winding road.

The road is little used except by shepherds and spinners and the local buses.

Stíra. – Pop 473. The village on the slopes of Mount Kliossi is known for its marble quarries; to the east stood the mighty Frankish castle of Lármena. Ferries to Attica leave from Néa Stíra *(gravel beach; hotels)* down on the coast.

Dístos (Ruins). – *Access from the Káristos-Chalkis road by an earth track.* Isolated on flat open ground by a little lake lie the ruins of ancient Dystos which the Venetians converted into a fortress. The 5C BC walls are of polygonal construction with strengthened square towers.

Kími. – Pop 2 711. This little town, which is also known locally as Koúmi, is the main centre of a fertile region which produces olives, fruit, grapes and honey **(baklavá).** It has developed from the ancient town of Kyme whose inhabitants founded Cumae near Naples in Italy. The town stands on a beautiful site on a rocky plateau about 260m – 850ft above the Aegean Sea looking out towards the island of Skyros.

The ferry to Skyros leaves from the little port of Paralía Kímis *(sandy beach)* down on the coast *(4km – 21/2miles; bus).*

Erétria. – Pop 2 501. *Ferry Skála Oropoú on the mainland; sandy beaches.* Erétria was for many years the rival of Chalkis for possession of the rich Lelantine (Lefkandí) Plain. More recently it has also been known as **Néa Psará** since refugees from the island of Psará settled there in 1821 but the name Erétria is now re-established.

There are several traces of the ancient city which was extensive and prosperous; the main ones lie to the north: a fairly well preserved theatre (3C BC) at the foot of the acropolis with the foundations of a shrine to Dionysos nearby.

In the centre of the modern town are the ruins of a Temple to Apollo where the fine Archaic sculptures now in the Chalkis Museum were found.

Chalkis *(Halkída).* – *Description on page 79.*

Mount Dírfis. – From Néa Artáki there is a good road which passes through a region devoted to cereal and chicken farming and then climbs the lower slopes of Mount Dírfis.

Stení is a cool and shady mountain resort: its chalets are built on either side of a mountain torrent. There are many walks in the forests of chestnut and conifer trees which cover the slopes of Mount Dírfis (1 743m – 5 718ft); very varied flora.

Prokópi. – Pop 1 319. South of Mandoúdi, deep in the picturesque **Klissoúra Valley** lies Prokópi, formerly known as Achmet Aga. The banks of the stream which runs through the valley are covered by luxuriant vegetation: planes, poplars, walnuts and oleanders. In the Middle Ages the valley was commanded by a famous fortress on an almost inaccessible peak. More recently the area has been the estate of the Noel-Baker family, who have been careful but not uncontroversial landlords.

Oreí. – This is an ancient barony where the Venetians built a castle using materials from ancient structures. From the port there are fine views across the Oreí Channel to Mount Óthris on the mainland and the entrance to the Vólos Gulf *(north).*

Loutrá Edipsoú★. – Pop 2 198. *Ferries to Arkítsa on the mainland.* Its pleasant position by the sea made this important spa very fashionable in antiquity. Sulla, Augustus and Hadrian came to take the waters, which contain sulphur and are used to treat rheumatism and gynaecological complaints.

Beyond the neo-Classical pump room on the east side of the town are the hot springs with their sulphurous vapour; some of the water tumbles into the sea by a little beach in a smoking cascade.

Two attractive excursions can be made by car along the coast from Loutrá Edipsoú. One follows a new and spectacular corniche road southeast to **Ília,** a fishing village *(9km – 5 1/2 miles),* to Roviés *(29km – 18 miles)* and thence to **Límni** *(13km – 8 miles),* a fishing village well known to artists. From Límni a road rejoins the northern road. The other excursion, which is less picturesque, follows the bay westwards to Giáltra *(25km – 15 miles Rtn).*

ROME

A Michelin Green Guide

29 walks in the Eternal City :
  the most famous sites,
  30 centuries of history
  the art treasures in the museums.

GERÁKI Castle★★
Pírgos Gerakíou

Peloponnese – Lakonía – Michelin map 980 fold 41.

The ruins of Geráki Castle lie on an outlying spur of Mount Parnon, on the northern edge of the Lakonian Plain, about 4km – 2 1/2 miles from the little medieval town of Geráki (pop 1 638 – *tavernas*) with its many old houses and Byzantine churches which are decorated with 15C and 16C murals.

Tour *(about 3/4 hour).* – From Geráki take the road to *Ágios Dimítrios passing the cemetery* (attractive Byzantine **church of Agía Paraskeví**); *after 500m – 547yds turn left to the castle (signpost). Guided tour by the keeper (gratuity).*

Early in 13C William de Champlitte divided the Peloponnese, which he had just conquered, into 12 baronies and gave Lakonía, which contains Geráki, to Guy de Nivelet, a knight from the Franche Comté. His successor, John de Nivelet, built the present fortress in 1254 in imitation of the castle being built by William de Villehardouin in Mystra. The Franks did not hold Geráki for long; it passed to the Byzantines at the end of 13C.

Geráki. – Mount Taÿgetos in the background

The castle is shaped like an irregular quadrilateral formed by ramparts reinforced by strong towers; huge cisterns enabled it to withstand long sieges.

The tour includes several Gothic and Byzantine chapels, set on the slope, which are decorated with painted murals. **St George's Church** (13C), within the castle wall, has a nave and side aisles and is also decorated with paintings; a great Gothic tomb in a recess *(left)* bears the heraldic emblems of the Franks.

The parapet walk offers extensive **views**★★ of Mount Parnon (N), the Eurotas Valley running south to the sea and Mount Taÿgetos (W).

GÍTHIO

Peloponnese – Lakonía – Pop 4 054 – Michelin map 980 fold 41– Local map p 131

Gíthio boasts an attractive **site**, just west of the mouth of the River Eurotas (Evrótas), overlooking the graceful curves of the Lakonian Gulf and the outline of the island of Kythera which can been seen to the south on a clear day.

Access by boat, once or twice a week, from Piraeus and Kastéli (in Crete).

Gíthio is both a quiet seaside resort *(a few hotels)* and a port exporting the produce of Lakonía: olives, oil, rice, cotton, citrus fruits. In antiquity it played a role as the arsenal of Sparta. When Paris carried off Helen, the unfaithful wife of Menelaos, king of Sparta, they are said to have spent their first night together on the island of Kranai (now Marathónissi) before embarking for Kythera and thence for Troy and provoking the Trojan War which Homer described in the Iliad.

The harbour area consists of picturesque narrow streets below the ruins of a medieval castle; the street parallel to the quayside is lined by attractive Turkish houses with balconies. There is a small but well-preserved ancient theatre northwest of the town. On the island of Marathónissi there is one of the typical towers of Máni *(p 131).*

GLA Fortress

Central Greece – Boeotia – Michelin map 980 north of fold 30

Access. – *In Kástro take the road to Lárimna for about 500m – 550yds; then turn right into a stony track which circles the fortress. The entrance is on the northeast side.*

The fortress of Glá, which was originally surrounded by the dull waters of Lake Copaïs (Kopaïda) *(p 162),* is composed of a rocky plateau enclosed by a perimeter wall which was built in 14C-13C BC following the contours of the rock; it is 3km – 2miles long and over 5m – 16ft thick; there were four gates, the main one facing south.

Enter by the northeast gate which is flanked by square towers and turn right into a path which climbs up to the highest point on the island, 66m – 217ft above the level of the marshy plain. Late in the 19C the French School of Archaeology in Athens uncovered the remains of a Mycenaean type palace with two *megarons (p 17);* the stronghold has a panoramic **view** over the Copaïc Basin.

Join us in our never ending task of keeping up to date.

Send us your comments and suggestions, please.

Michelin Tyre Public Limited Company
Tourism Department
Davy House – Lyon Road – HARROW – Middlesex HA1 2DQ

HERAKLES' Road★★

Central Greece – Fthiótida – Michelin map 980 south of fold 17

This is a superb mountain road running from Brálos to Iráklia *(21km – 13miles, about 1 hour)* over the Fournatáki Pass (alt 590m – 1 935ft) between Mount Íti and Mount Kalídromo; before the motorway was built along the coast it was the main road between Central Greece and Thessaly.

Death of a hero. – When Herakles fell in love with Iole, his jealous wife, Deïaneira, sent him a tunic impregnated with what she thought was a love philtre but was in fact a poison given her by the centaur Nessos whom Herakles had mortally wounded for coveting his wife. As soon as the cloth touched his skin, Herakles was in agony as if his body was on fire. When he could bear the torment no longer, he built himself a pyre on Mount Íti and his companion Philoctetes set it alight. A shaft of lightning struck the earth and Herakles was carried into the next world.

The road. – It winds steeply through an impressive landscape with extensive views of Mount Kalídromo (1 375m – 4 511ft) (E), Mount Íti (2 152m – 7 060ft) (W) and Parnassos (2 457m – 8 061ft) (S).

The road descends into the Lamía basin near Iráklia revealing the unusual sight of the railway line from Athens to Thessalonika traversing the steep east face of Mount Íti through a series of tunnels linked by viaducts which span the river valleys.

HYDRA★★   *Ídra*

Saronic Gulf – Pop 2 732 – Michelin map 980 south of fold 30

Access by boat: from Piraeus in 3 1/2 hours by the regular service (stopping at Aigina, Méthana and Póros) and in 2 1/2 hours by the Express service; from Zéa (Piraeus) by hydrofoil in 2 hours; from Ermióni by the regular service in 1/2 hour. No cars allowed on the island.

An arm of the sea forming a strait (Kólpos Ídras) separates Hydra from the Argolid peninsula. The island consists of an impressive ridge of barren rock (55km² – 21sq miles) 18km – 11 miles long and rising to 590m – 1 936ft. The town of Hydra, which lies mid way along the coast facing the mainland, is invisible from the sea until one's ship arrives opposite the narrow gap in the sheer cliffs which leads into the natural harbour.

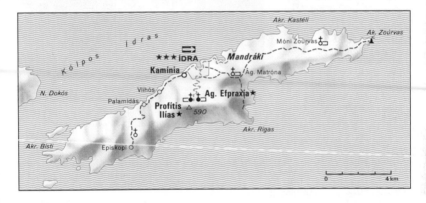

Water supply. – It seems that Hydra was once greener and more abundantly supplied with water than it is now. Pine woods covered the mountain and the lower slopes were terraced and cultivated. Huge underground cisterns, many of which are still in existence, collected the rain water which was then channelled to the gardens. The cisterns also made good hiding places for gold and other goods.

Gradually the surface water grew rarer, the pine forests were over exploited for ship building and the cultivated terraces were abandoned. Since 1960 water has been imported from the mainland by tanker.

A thriving maritime power. – In 15C Hydra began a quasi-autonomous existence; the inhabitants came to terms with the Turks and were protected against attack from abroad by the island's inhospitable coastline and their sailors' vigilance.

The first Hydriot ship was launched in 1657 but it was not until the middle of the following century that the ship yards began to produce in quantity; the ships which ranged from 100 to 400 tonnes traded throughout the Mediterranean and even across to America; the island made its fortune.

During the wars of the French Revolution and the Napoleonic Empire the Hydriots turned pirate when it suited them. Their two-masted, square-rigged brigs and swift and elegant polaccas slipped through the English blockade, sometimes with the aid of their canon, in order to bring wheat from the Peloponnese to Marseille where there was a large and prosperous Greek colony.

Cool and calculating and with a highly developed political sense, these ship owners constituted one of the forces in the War of Independence, not only supplying funds but also planning naval operations. In 1821 the Greek fleet was equipped by four Hydriot families: Koundouriótis, Tombázis, Voúlgaris and Miaóulis; it included the famous "fire ships" of **Andréas Miaóulis** (1769-1835), old vessels packed with explosive which were launched into the wind against the Turkish fleet and exploded on contact.

After independence part of the Hydriot fleet went back to sponge fishing in which it still engages in summer in the Aegean Sea.

HYDRA TOWN★★★ (ÍDRA)

The site★★★. – Defended by a few canon for a hundred years and more, the little port of Hydra, which is packed with yachts in the season, is hidden in a rounded inlet, bordered by old houses which fan out up the dry and rocky hillside towards the monastery.

There is usually a lively crowd strolling on the large smooth paving stones of the waterfront past the modest sailors' houses which have mostly been converted into cafés, tavernas, restaurants and pastry cooks' (speciality: almond cakes – *amigdalotá*) or into craft shops selling carpets and rush mats, jewellery and enamels, pots and ceramics; set back behind the houses on the quay is the 17C belltower belonging to the church of the monastery of the Virgin (Panagía).

The heat and bustle of the waterfront is counterbalanced by the cool peacefulness of the upper town where the ship owners had their elegant houses. The narrow but scrupulously clean streets slope steeply uphill; there are occasional glimpses down into the harbour; from time to time a file of donkeys or mules clatters by.

Ship owners' houses★. – Most of them were built early in 19C, often in imitation of Venetian palaces (loggias, internal courtyards) and have retained their state rooms decorated with carved wood mouldings and furnished in the style of the period. Many of these noble residences belonging to the leading citizens of the day have remained in the family; it is worth mentioning three which are on the west side of the harbour: the Voúlgaris house, the Tombázis house which is now a School of Fine Arts and the Koundouriótis house which has a remarkable courtyard.

Some of them can sometimes be visited; ask at the house.

(Photograph L. Y. Loirat/Explorer)

Hydra. – The port and town

EXCURSIONS

Prophet Elijah's★ (Profítis Ilías) and St Euphrasia's★ (Agía Efpraxía) Monasteries. – *1 3/4 hours on foot Rtn by Odós Miaoúli and the valley.* These two convents, one for men, the other for women, were built near a pine wood 500m – 1 640ft up; fine **views** of Hydra, the coast and the other Saronic islands.

Kamínia. – *3/4 hour on foot Rtn following the harbour quay round to the west.* There is a small fort still sporting its old 19C canon; attractive views of the harbour and the roadstead. Down among the rocks bathing platforms have been constructed.

The coast path continues to **Kamínia**, a quiet fishing hamlet with a shingle beach and several tavernas.

Mandráki. – *1 1/2 hours on foot Rtn or by the boat which shuttles to and fro in summer.*

Follow the quayside round to the east past the Merchant Navy Captains' School (**A**), which occupies an old ship owner's house. The road continues to Mandráki Bay *(hotel, beach)* formerly protected by two forts; this was the site of the 19C shipyards and the major part of the Hydriot fleet, which at its height numbered some 125 vessels and 10 000 sailors, used to anchor in the bay.

IOÁNINA★

Epiros – Pop 44 829 – Alt 520m – 1 706ft – Michelin map 980 fold 15

Ioánina, also known as Janena or Yannina, is the capital of Epiros, an administrative and commercial centre, the seat of a university and a tourist excursion centre. It is a modern town except for the old district near the lake which has an Islamic air owing to a bazaar and several mosques and minarets which date from the Turkish occupation.

Ali Pasha's city stands on the edge of an immense lake in a broad green valley, rich in pastureland and fields of tobacco, vines and cereals, against a backdrop of majestic mountains rising to 2 000m – 6 561ft. A good view of the **site★★** can be obtained by climbing up to the Tourist Pavilion (Touristikó Períptero) (**Z**) built in the regional style on a rise to the west of the town.

Local craftsmanship produces embroidery and silverwork, there are shops in Odós Avéroff (**YZ**). Gastronomic specialities include eels, frogs, trout and crayfish from the lake, cheese from Dodona and a sparkling white wine from the region of Zítsa.

HISTORICAL NOTES

Norman possession in 11C, capital of the despotate of Epiros early in 13C, dependence of the Serbian kingdom from 1345 to 1431, Ioánina then became Turkish until 1913 and had its hour of glory under the rule of Ali Pasha.

"The Lion of Ioánina". – Ali Pasha, who was born in 1744 in Tepelene in Albania, was made pasha of Ioánina by the Sultan in 1788. For more than thirty years, during which he expelled Napoleon's troops and the Souliots *(pp 108 and 120)*, he exercised almost sovereign power over his territory which was known in western Europe as Albania and extended from the Ionian Sea to Arta on the Ambracian Gulf in the south, to the Pindus range of mountains *(east)* and to Valona or even Durazzo in the north.

In his day Ioánina was like a capital ciy and developed into an important centre for Greek culture. Consuls were appointed by the major European nations and the British and French repersentatives vied with one another to exert influence over the pasha. Ali, however, cultivated both sides and also made sure of the support of the Greek partisans in the mountains, the Klephts *(p 24)* to assist him in his effort to become independent of the Sultan.

The Porte became alarmed at the growing power of Ali and in 1820 it sent an army of 50 000 men who besieged the citadel of Ioánina for 15 months. In the hope of negotiations Ali was lured to the island in the lake where he was surprised and killed by the Turks on 22 February 1822. His head was exposed in Ioánina.

Louis Dupré, who had the rare good fortune to capture a likeness of Ali Pasha, painted him *(p 24)* smoking his hookah in a boat floating among the reeds by the lakeside. He has captured the fierce and depraved expression of this cunning tyrant who had a harem of 500 women and was surrounded by a guard of assassins. In 1797 while Ali was allied to the French his daughter married General Roze but when the truce was broken Ali captured his son-in-law and sent him to Constantinople where the unfortunate man soon died. Acting on information from his daughter-in-law Ali also caused his son's favourite mistress, Euphrosine (Frosini), together with fifteen other women to be drowned in the lake for being unfaithful to their husbands.

Byron visits Ali Pasha. – On his first visit to Greece in 1809 Byron and his companion Hobhouse arrived in Ioánina in September and Ali, who was cultivating the support of the British against the French then in possession of the Ionian Islands, sent for them to Tepelene where he was staying. Byron described the scene: "I was dressed in a full suit of staff uniform with a very magnificent sabre. The Vizier (Ali) received me in a large room paved with marble; a fountain was playing in the centre; the apartment was surrounded by scarlet ottomans. He received me standing, a wonderful compliment from a Mussulman, and made me sit down on his right hand...".

Other Englishmen who visited Ioánina at the time included Col. William Leake, who was sent on a mission to Ali to make a military survey of the country, Henry Holland, Queen Victoria's physician, whom Ali consulted about his health, and C. R. Cockerell *(pp 35, 62 and 74)* who was "struck with the easy familiarity and perfect good humour of his (Ali's) manners"; he and his party were entertained to a dinner consisting of eighty six dishes, all of which had to be tasted at least.

SIGHTS *2 1/2 hours*

The Lake★★ (Límni Ioanínon). – A shady walk beneath the walls of the citadel along the edge of Lake Ioánina, also known as Lake Pamvótis, provides a pleasant view across the waters to the island where storks can be seen on the wing.

The lake is contained in a depression lined with alluvium. It collects the waters flowing down from Mount Mitsikéli *(north)* and its level varies according to the seasons and the outflow of the **swallow holes** *(katavóthres)* worn through the soft limestone round the shore. It is marshy in the northern part but in the south it reaches 12m – 40ft in depth; it is liable to sudden storms.

The Island★★ (Nissí Ioanínon) (Y). – *Access by boat about every half hour (crossing: 1/4 hour); landing stage Mavíli Square.*

This charming little wooded island *(restaurants, tavernas)* is surrounded by reed beds cut through by backwaters in which the residents moor their boats. It has a pretty lakeside village and five monasteries decorated with interesting frescoes. *Apply to the keeper who lives on the island; unaccompanied tour.*

The 16C **Monastery of Panteleimon,** secluded among enormous plane trees *(turn left at the end of the street coming from the landing stage)* is the best known: here can be seen the house with its wooden balcony (now a museum) where Ali Pasha was killed by the Turks. Beyond is the Monastery of St John the Baptist (Ágios Ioánnis Pródromos) with its 16C church and a cave which contained an ancient hermitage.

The **Monastery of the Philanthropiní** or Nikólaos Spanos *(turn right at the end of the street coming from the landing stage)* was built on a hill in 13C, but altered in 16C. The church is decorated with remarkable 17C **frescoes★**: in the narthex, the Annunciation, portraits of the founders of the monastery kneeling before St Nicholas, effigies of the ancient philosphers; in the sanctuary, the Life of Christ on the walls, the Communion of Saints in the apse.

The **Monastery of Stratigopoúlos** or Nikólaos Dílios dates from 11C; the church decorated with beautiful 16C **frescoes★** showing the Last Judgement and the Life of the Virgin (Narthex) and the Life of Christ with the Betrayal by Judas (sanctuary).

Fortress (Froúrio) (Y). – The huge fortress dominating the lake is surrounded by a wall which was built during the despotate of Epiros (13C) and restored by Ali Pasha.

It was inhabited by the Turks and then from 17C by Jews but is now almost deserted; it has retained an Islamic appearance provided by the narrow streets, the overhanging roofs of the houses and the former mosques; Ali pasha had his palace here on the top of the rock.

IOÁNINA ★

Aslan Aga Mosque ★ (Aslán Dzamí). – *Restoration work in progress.* The mosque was founded in 1619 on the site of an orthodox monastery; its slim pointed minaret still stands.

The building, which is composed of a vestibule, containing a recess for the worshippers' shoes, and a prayer chamber, has been converted into a little **Museum of Popular Art** *(open 8.30am to 1.15pm and 5.30 to 7.45pm (9.30am to 12.50pm Sundays); closed Mondays)*: handsome Epirot costumes and arms.

From the terrace there are very fine **views** ★ ★ of the lake and the surrounding mountains.

Below the mosque stands the former Turkish Library (A) roofed with several little domes; further west is the Old Synagogue (B), a reminder that in 19C there were nearly 6 000 Jews in Ioánina.

Inner Citadel (D). – It contains the tomb of Ali Pasha, a mosque and the former palace of "the Lion of Ioánina" which has recently been restored.

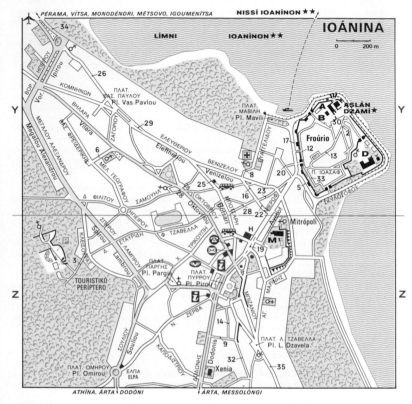

Archaeological Museum (Z M1). – *Open 8.45am to 3pm (9.30am to 2.30pm Sundays); closed Tuesdays; 100 Dr.*

It contains well-presented collections of objects found in the Ephyra Nekromanteion *(p 107)* (votive figurines in terracotta) and at Dodona *(p 117)* (bronze votive offerings); Hellenistic sarcophagi, Byzantine capitals, icons.

EXCURSIONS

Pérama Cave ★ ★ ★. – *6km – 3 3/4 miles to the north. Guided tours (about 1 hour) from 8am to 8pm; 60 Dr.*

The cave was discovered by chance during the Second World War when people were looking for shelter from aerial bombardment. It extends for about 1km – 1/2 mile and covers an area of 14 800m² – 5 714sq miles; the walls continuously stream with water.

Most of the caverns are very high and artistically lit to show off the splendid limestone concretions which occur in many hues (red, orange and even green) in the form of stalagmites and stalactites including excentrics, curtains, low walls and pools. The bones and teeth of cave bears have been found in the cave.

The exit, as opposed to the entrance, is the natural opening into the cave: superb **views** ★ ★ over Ioánina.

For those with time to spare it is worth continuing east along the road to Métsovo for several miles: extensive **views** ★ ★ from the overhanging road down over the valley, the lake and the town of Ioánina in its attractive mountain setting.

The Zagória country ★★. –
79km – 49miles Rtn – about 2 1/2 hours – plus 1 hour walking or sightseeing.

Take the road north which continues past the airport up a broad valley cut off to the east by the barrier of Mount Mitsikéli which rises to 1 810m – 5 938ft. After 19km – 12 miles turn right into a narrow tarred road which climbs towards Vítsa, overhanging the valley and producing beautiful views. This is the approach to the **Zagória country**, the "land beyond the mountains", which follows the renowned trout stream, the River Voidomátis, as it flows north into Albania. It is a region of forests (conifers, oaks, chestnuts) and pasture; the traditional habitat has not been disturbed; there are many houses of beautiful grey stone, with projecting upper storeys and wooden balconies, roofed with stone, churches with painted interiors and old "Turkish bridges". In these wild mountains, where bears and wolves still roam, Greek troops defied the advancing Italian forces when they invaded from Albania in November 1940.

10km – 6 1/4 miles after turning off the main road, there is a narrow tarred road to the right leading to a very unusual bridge (Géfira) with three arches downstream from **Kípi** which is the administrative centre of the Zagória country.

Vítsa ★. – Pop 140. The town is built on a picturesque site; most of the houses are in the traditional style.

Monodéndri ★. – Together with Kípi this is the main regional centre; many mountain style houses built of stone with shingle roofs.

Take the narrow road on the far side of the village which leads to the Monastery of Agía Paraskeví and the Víkos Gorge.

Víkos Gorge ★★★ (Farángi [or Harádra] Víkou). – The grey stone buildings of the Monastery of Agía Paraskeví cling to the rocks directly above a precipitous drop into the bottom of the gorge 1 000m – 3 281ft below, which the River Voidomátis has created.

Guided tours in the season only, 1 hour on foot Rtn; unadvisable for older people and those who suffer from vertigo. A path starting from the monastery winds down the face of the cliff past some terraces once cultivated by the monks and some caves which provided shelter for klephts *(p 24)* and hermits; it reaches a platform overlooking the confluence of the Voidomátis and a neighbouring mountain stream; the atmosphere is oppressive and wild.

The gorge continues downstream towards Kónitsa.

There is another magnificent view of the gorge from the hamlet of Osía which can be reached by a narrow road from Monodéndri.

Dodona ★★ (**Dodóni**). – *21 km – 13 miles south.*

Leave Ioánina by the road to Árta, turning right after 8km – 5 miles. A good tarred road climbs a mountain chain (magnificent views ★★ back over the Ioánina basin) to reach the ancient site of Dodona (alt 630m – 2 067ft) in a high fertile valley; to the southwest Mount Tómaros rises to 1 974m – 6 476ft.

Ancient Dodona grew out of a sanctuary dedicated to Zeus where a famous oracle flourished from the second millenium BC until 4C BC. This oracle made known its pronouncements through the whispering of the breeze in the leaves of a sacred oak tree. The message was interpreted by the priests, known as *Helloi* or *Selloi*, who were accustomed to sleep on the ground the better to be in tune with the god's manifestations. Later, however, the oracle was interpreted by priestesses.

Dodona was destroyed by barbarians in 6C AD but has been excavated by Greek archaeologists from 1873 to the present day.

Ruins. – *Open 9am to sunset; 100 Dr. Drama festival in summer. Tourism Pavilion.* Dodona was dominated by an acropolis, part of the walls still exist. The first ruins to be seen after the entrance are the remains of the stadium (late 3C BC) indicated by traces of the terraces of seats.

The **theatre** ★ ★ on the left is one of the largest (13m – 427ft broad by 22m – 72ft high) and one of the best preserved of ancient Greece. It was built in the Hellenistic period in the reign of Philip V of Macedon (late 3C BC) and was transformed into an arena under the Romans for gladiatorial and animal combats. At this time the arena was separated from the public by a wall which is still in place and by a channel for the evacuation of water. The outer wall of the structure is composed of massive blocks of grey stone; there is a fine view of the theatre from the top of the terraces of seats.

Beyond the theatre are the foundations of an assembly hall *(bouleuterion)* and a little temple to Aphrodite. Next come the remains of the **sanctuary to Zeus Naios** which included the precinct of the oracle of Zeus enclosing the sacred oak, the area devoted to the cult of Zeus, Dione (a primitive earth goddess) and Herakles (Hercules).

Finally, traces of a basilica with a nave and two aisles dating from 6C AD are a reminder that in the Byzantine period Dodona was the seat of a bishop.

KALAMÁTA

Peloponnese – Messinía – Pop 41 911 – Michelin map 980 folds 40 and 41

Kalamáta is not only the capital of the fertile region of Messenia (Messinía) *(p 9)* but also an agricultural market and an administrative and commercial centre. The town, which was rebuilt on a grid plan in 19C, stretches from the castle, at the foot of which part of the old town still survives, to the port, which is huge but not much used; it opens into a broad roadstead. A holiday resort is developing to the east along the coast.

Local specialities: fresh and preserved olives, figs, bananas, honey and sesame cakes, *rakí*.

Calamate, a Frankish city. – The Franks worked their way down the west coast of the Peloponnese from Patras and settled in Calamate and the Messenian delta, known to them as Val de Calamy, in 1206; they remained for over 200 years. William de Champlitte gave the fief of Calamate to Geoffrey I de Villehardouin who succeeded him in 1210 as Prince of Morea and built a castle. The de Villehardouin used to spend the winter in Kalamáta, enjoying the gentle climate free from the cold north wind; the surrounding country with its plains and rivers, its hills and meadows, was also to their taste.

William de Villehardouin was particularly attached to the castle where he was born in 1218 and where he died in 1278. Fluent in both Greek and French and keen on tournaments and courtly literature, he held court in a sumptuous manner together with his Greek wife Anna Comnena who was said to be as beautiful as Helen of Troy. In 1248 he assembled in Kalamáta the 400 French knights of Morea who were to join the Seventh Crusade led by Louis IX.

When William died without a male heir his position passed to his nephew, Guy II de la Roche, Duke of Athens. In 14C the town was in the hands of the Angevins of Naples and their Florentine allies and was not captured by the Byzantine despots of Mystra until 1425. Thereafter, except for two Venetian interludes from 1463-1479 and 1685-1718, it was under Turkish occupation.

SIGHTS

Castle (Kástro). – The castle built by the de Villehardouin stands on a rocky eminence overlooking the coastal plain on the site of the ancient acropolis; it incorporated an earlier church and houses. All that remain are traces of the 13C keep and the circuit walls which were repaired by the Venetians.

From the terrace *(Tourist Pavilion)* there is a view of Kalamáta and the Gulf of Messenia.

Bazaar. – Lively and teeming, the shops of the bazaar are grouped around a morning vegetable market in the old town between the museum and the double church of the Holy Apostles (chancel originally a 10C Byzantine chapel).

Museum. – *Open mornings.* Two handsome old houses near the bazaar now house the museum's collections: ancient statue of Hermes, Roman mosaics (Dionysos); souvenirs of the War of Independence: helmet belonging to the Maniot hero Mavromichalis (1765-1848).

EXCURSIONS

Messenian Gulf Road ★ ★ ★. – *Description page 135.*

Korone Riviera. – *52km – 32 miles – about 1 1/2 hours. Take the Pílos road which runs west across the Pámissos delta, after 22km – 14 miles turn left to Petalídi.*

Petalídi. – Pop 1 113. In 1828 the French expeditionary force to Morea disembarked in Petalídi under the command of General Maison to expel the Turks from the Peloponnese.

The road skirts the Messenian Gulf *(beaches, hotel, camping sites)* passing through undulating country where olives, oranges, figs, grapes, tomatoes and early vegetables are grown.

Kastélia. – This place is named after two castles built by the Franks in 13C.

Korone. – *Description page 122.*

Androússa. – Pop 726. *6km – 10 miles northwest via Messíni and Amfithéa. Androússa* is set among fig and olive trees on a slope overlooking the fertile Pámissos Valley. During the Frankish occupation it was known as Druyes, after the Burgundian fortress of that name which belonged to the de Courtenay family *(p 23)*, and became the see of a bishop. The "captains" of Druyes ruled from a castle of which the arched walls and a few towers still dominate Messenia.

Messene ★ ★. – *Description page 134.*

KALAMBÁKA

Thessaly – Tríkala – Pop 5 692 – Michelin map 980 fold 16 – Local map p 137

Kalambáka is a commercial and tourist centre, the usual starting point for a tour of the Metéora *(p 135).*

Cathedral (Mitrópoli). – The present 14C church, which stands on the heights to the north of the town *(signpost),* has taken the place of several earlier buildings; it incorporates much ancient or paleo-Christian (5C-6C) material which has been re-used.

It is built on the basilical plan with a nave and two aisles terminating in rounded apses and contains several original paleo-Christian features: the marble pulpit *(ambon),* the baldaquin and, at the back of the central apse, the steps on which the priests stood. The Cretan-style 16C frescoes are unfortunately somewhat blackened.

KALÁVRITA

Peloponnese – Achaia – Pop 1 802 – Michelin map 980 east of fold 28

Kalávrita (beautiful springs) is a pleasant cool summer resort *(hotels)* at 750m – 2 461ft above sea level ringed by mountain peaks rising to over 2 000m – 6 562ft and linked to the coast of Achaia by a famous narrow gauge rack railway *(p 197)* and a spectacular panoramic road.

From 1205 to 1230 the town was an important Frankish seigneury which was first held by Otho de Tournai and then belonged to the La Trémouille family, barons of Chalandritsa, early in 14C.

On 13 December 1943 the Nazis destroyed the town, which was a centre for the Resistance, and massacred 1 436 male inhabitants over 15 years of age *(memorial).*

EXCURSIONS

Monastery of Méga Spíleo★ and the Vouraïkós Gorge★★. – *11km – 6 3/4 miles northeast by the Trápeza road or the railway to Diakoftó. See page 197.*

Monastery of Agía Lávra. – *7km – 4 1/2 miles southwest. Open 8am to 1pm and 5pm to sunset; informal dress inadmissible.* Despite its remote position in the mountains where it was founded in 961, the monastery has earned its place in history. On 25 March 1821 **Germanós**, Archbishop of Patras, raised the standard of revolt against the Turks in the 17C conventual church which one can see before entering the present-day monastery.

Outside there is a terrace shaded by an enormous plane tree beneath which Germanós used to stand when he addressed the crowd. The monastery buildings *(guest house),* which were burnt by the Turks in 1821 and again by the Nazis in 1943, now house an interesting **museum**: manuscripts, icons, gold and silver ware, souvenirs of the War of Independence (the famous standard).

Above the monastery there is a path leading off the road *(signpost "Paleón Monastírion"; 1/2 hour on foot Rtn)* to the original **hermitage** where the monks lived until 1689: at the foot of the rock there is a chapel decorated with barely visible murals.

A hillock near the monastery bears the modern **Independence Monument.**

KARÍTENA

Peloponnese – Arkadía – Pop 229 – Michelin map 980 south of fold 28

The road running northwest from Megalopolis to Andrítsena is carried over the River Alpheios by a modern bridge which overshadows its 15C predecessor. From the bridge there is a spectacular view of the **site★★** of Karítena, a picturesque medieval town built into the curve of a hillside below a powerful Frankish castle commanding the mouth of the Alpheios Gorge.

Drive up to the square at the top of the town. Just below are the Church of Our Lady (Panagía) with a square stone belfry (17C) in the western style and St Nicholas', a small post-Byzantine church marked by a clump of cypress trees.

Castle★. – The first-class defensive site boasts a feudal castle, the stronghold of the barony of Karítena, which was created by the Franks in 1209 for the de Bruyères family; it was one of the strongest in the Frankish principality of Morea and consisted of 22 fiefs. The lord of Karítena, who was one of the "peers" of Morea, had the power to administer justice.

The castle was built in 1254 for Hugues de Bruyères and then passed to his son, **Geoffrey de Bruyères,** the famous "Sire de Caritène", a model of chivalry, whose exploits were told in the "Chronicle of the Morea". Karítena castle was sold in 1320 to the Byzantine Emperor Andronikos II Palaiologos; during the War of Independence Kolokotrónis defied Ibrahim Pasha from the security of its stout walls.

The triangular precinct, reinforced by towers, has only one entrance. Only the ruins of the residence of the lord of the castle remain against the south wall but several cisterns, some vaulted, some underground, have been preserved *(danger of falling).* From the top (alt 583m – 1 913ft) there are extensive **views★★** of the Alpheios Gorge (W), the Megalopolis basin (E) and Mount Lykaion (Líkeo) (S).

Alpheios Gorge★ (Alfiós). – *Follow the road to Andrítsena for about 15km – 9 1/4 miles.*
There are views back towards Karítena and down into the gorge created by the River Alpheios between the Megalopolis basin and Elis (Ilía). This succession of narrow passes, which was known in the Middle Ages as the Escorta, was guarded by the castles at Karítena, St Helena, Cumba...

Women in trousers and men and women wearing shorts or with bare shoulders are not allowed into churches and monasteries.

KARPENÍSSI

Central Greece – Evritania – Pop 5 100 – Michelin map 980 south of fold 16

Karpeníssi is a winter sports resort majestically situated in a high "alpine" valley (alt 960m – 3 150ft) south of the Timfristós range (alt 2 315m – 7 595ft). It is a very good centre for walks and excursions into the Evritanian pine forests.

It was near Karpeníssi that **Márkos Bótzaris** (1790-1823) was killed; he was a hero of the War of Independence who fought at Missolonghi (p 139) where he is buried.

Proussós Monastery. – *30km – 18 1/2 miles southwest by a good earth road. Open 9am to 1 pm and 5pm to sunset.* The monastery, which is isolated in the mountains, houses an icon of the Virgin said to have been painted by St Luke. The walls of the church are decorated with beautiful Byzantine and post-Byzantine mosaics.

KASSOPE★   *Kassópi*

Epiros – Michelin map 980 south of fold 15

A turning *(signpost "Ancient Kassopi")* on the inland road from Préveza to Igoumenítsa climbs the lower slopes of Mount Zálongo and offers glimpses of the colossal sculpted effigies of the "Souliot Women" *(see below)*.

After about 6km – 3 3/4 miles on a bend a path to the left leads to the ruins. Open 8.45am to 3pm (9.30 am to 2.30pm Sundays); 100 Dr.

Kassope, which was founded in 4C BC and later destroyed by the Romans, stood on the slopes of Mount Zálongo on a terrace which offers extensive views★ south over Préveza to Leukas and east over the Ambracian Gulf south of Árta.

Excavations have uncovered the agora and the remains of a portico, an odeon and a square structure built round a courtyard with a peristyle which may have been the *prytaneion* where the city magistrates met. Further off is the site of a theatre.

Zálongo Monastery. – *4km – 2 1/2 miles north.* In 1803 the Souliots (pp 108 and 115) who were fleeing from the troops of Ali Pasha took refuge in the monastery. To escape a worse fate sixty women climbed on to the bluff above the convent, where they performed their national dance (p 14), and then threw themselves together with their children over the precipice.

The line of impressive cement figures recalling their sacrifice was sculpted by Zongolopoulos and set up in 1954. Their desperate courage was also celebrated in a painting by Theophilos (p 127) and in verse by Byron in "Don Juan" and by Mrs. Felicia Hemans in "The Suliote Mother".

KASTORIÁ★

Macedonia – Kastoriá – Pop 17 133 – Michelin map 980 fold 4

Deep in the mountains, on the neck of a peninsula projecting into the picturesque waters of Lake Orestiáda, lies Kastoriá (alt 690m – 2 264ft), which legend says was founded by Orestes.

The charm of the old houses with their jutting balconies and the numerous little Byzantine churches has not been overwhelmed by the modern buildings. The inhabitants make their living by fishing and fur trading and the main street, Odós Mitropóleos, is lined by furriers' establishments.

For 500 years Kastoriá has prided itself on being involved in the furriery business, a trade which has traditionally been associated with the Jews. Exemption from import tax on the pelts, a concession granted during the Turkish occupation, and especial skill in making up rejected skins enables the workshops to produce coats and jackets and wraps.

Churches. – Once Kastoriá boasted 72 churches; now about fifty survive, some of which date from 10C. They are built of brick and stone on the basilical plan with barrel vaulting and remarkable frescoes by itinerant artists. The most interesting group is to be found in the eastern part of town:

St Stephen's★ (Ágios Stéfanos) is an 11C church decorated with Archaic frescoes of the same date showing hieratic figures: the beautiful carved wooden iconostasis is 13C-14C.

Ágii Anárgiri Valaám (10C-11C) contains 12C-13C frescoes (touching Entombment, figures of saints in the narthex).

St Nicholas' (Ágios Nikólaos) is an 11C church with 11C frescoes painted in warm tones.

Near the school *(gimnássio)* is a very attractive church dedicated to the Virgin (**Panagía Koubelídiki★**) which is decorated both outside and inside with 13C to 16C frescoes.

Lake Orestiáda★ (**Límni Kastoriás**). – Until quite recently the shores of the lake were marshy and infested with malaria. They were also inhabited by colonies of beavers whose skins were used by the furriers; the beaver *(castor in Latin)* may have given the town its name of Kastoriá.

On the promontory east of the town (via Leofóros Stratigoú Athanassíou) stands **Moní Mavrótissa★** *(2 hours on foot Rtn)*, a monastery with a double church which is decorated inside and out with 11C and 12C frescoes; very attractive view over the lake.

12km – 7 1/2 miles north of Kastoriá, on the road to Flórina, a **panoramic view★★** opens up of the lake set in the encircling mountains.

EXCURSION

Siátista. – Pop 5 701. *58km – 36 miles southeast.* From 16C to 18C Siátista was well known as a market for wine and leather before changing over to furs; it contains interesting examples of 18C Macedonian houses.

KAVÁLA ★

Macedonia – Kavála – Pop 56 375 – Michelin map 980 fold 7

Kavála, which was under Turkish domination from 1380 to 1913, still has an oriental air. It is the centre of the Macedonian tobacco industry, a bustling, lively town built on the shores of a broad and shining bay. The old district is huddled on a rocky promontory crowned by a citadel while the modern town extends westwards along the harbour. In the evenings it is agreeable to stroll along the quayside while the caïques put out to sea to go fishing by lamplight.

Twixt east and west. – Kavála, which was originally a colony founded by Thássos (p 186) and then became the port of Philippi (p 170) under the name of Neapolis, was a port of call throughout the Classical period; St Paul passed through with Silas on his way from Asia Minor to Philippi.

In the Middle Ages the town changed its name again to Christopolis; in 1306 bands of Catalans from Gallipoli landed in the port and then went on to defeat the Franks at the Battle of Cephisos (p 162) and to take possession of the Duchy of Athens. In 16C the French traveller **Pierre Belon** reported that the town housed many Jews and was called Bucephalos, after Alexander the Great's horse; this is probably the origin of its present name Kavála.

Kavála was the birthplace of the famous **Mehmet Ali** (1769-1849), viceroy of Egypt and reviver of its fortunes; as the father of Ibrahim Pasha (p 21) Mehmet Ali founded the dynasty which ruled in Egypt up to the time of King Farouk.

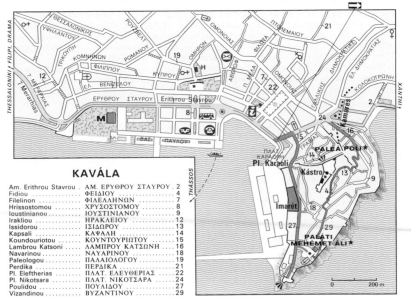

KAVÁLA

Old Town ★ (Paleá Póli). – Within the ramparts lies the picturesque old town; its narrow streets and steps wind between the Turkish houses with tiny courtyards and flowering balconies.

Starting from **Platía Karaolí**, a charming shady square lined by restaurants with outdoor terraces (fish specialities), walk up the narrow street, Odós Poulídou, which passes the Imarét (right).

Imarét. – This is a huge and unusual collection of buildings, designed in the Moslem style with many little domes, which is unfortunately derelict. The Imarét was founded by Mehmet Ali as a sort of alms house, run by Islamic monks (dervishes) for 300 poor men.

Higher up the hill the street opens into a small square where an equestrian statue of Mehmet Ali stands in front of his birthplace.

House of Mehmet Ali ★ (Paláti Mehémet Áli). – The keeper usually shows visitors round from 10am to 12 noon and 5 to 7pm; gratuity. This 18C house was the birthplace of Mehmet Ali, the son of a rich tobacco merchant of Albanian origin.

There is a magnificent view from the thick-set garden which surrounds the house; the wooden partitions and the lay-out are typical of a Turkish dwelling: stable and kitchen on the ground floor; on the first floor the householder's apartments and the harem which is fitted with moucharabies, wooden lattices which enable one to see out without being seen.

Walk out to the belvedere on the very tip of the promontory: extensive **view ★ ★** of the harbour, the town and the bay as far as Thássos Island; immediately below berths for shipping have been hewn out of the rock.

Walk through the old Turkish quarter, Odós Vizandinóu and Odós Fidíou, past a mosque and up to the Kástro.

Kástro. – The citadel stands on the site of an ancient acropolis and is surrounded by Byzantine ramparts, reinforced with towers; **views ★** of Kavála. The 16C aqueduct supplied the Old Town with water. Within the ramparts there is a cistern and prisons.

Walk down to the aqueduct by Odós Katsoni.

Aqueduct (Kamáres). – The aqueduct which spans the depression between the modern town and the old town was built in 16C by Suleiman the Magnificent to supply the Kástro with water from local springs.

Archaeological Museum (M). – *Open 8.45am to 3pm (9.30am to 2.30pm Sundays); 150 Dr.*

The collections are well presented in a modern building.

Room 1. Devoted to the excavations at Neapolis. Note the colossal Ionic capitals which came from the sanctuary of Parthenos (6C-5C BC) which has been excavated near the Imarét.

Room 2. The items displayed here come from the necropolis at Amphipolis *(p 34)*: carved stele, glass and gold Hellenistic jewellery.

KORONE   *Koróni*

Peloponnese – Messinía – Pop 1 376 – Michelin map 980 fold 40

The white houses of Korone with their pink tiled roofs are scattered over the slope of a promontory which protects a charming little port. A castle surmounts the high point at the end of the promontory while a long beach skirts the southern shore.

Korone, called Coron by the Franks, was conceded to the Venetians in 1206 and they used it for nearly three centuries as a port of call and trading port on the route to the Dardanelles; together with Methone *(on the west coast)* it was known as one of the "eyes of Venice" surveying the Mediterranean. It was taken by the Turks and then recaptured by the Venetians after a siege in 1685.

Citadel. – *Access by a steep street and steps; follow the sign "Hotel Panorama".*

The entrance to the very extensive citadel is an imposing Gothic gate built by the Venetians. The original circuit wall, which was reinforced with square towers, was strengthened in 15C and 16C by the Venetians and the Turks with bastions designed for the use of artillery. Views of Korone and the Messenian Gulf.

The citadel encloses a few scattered houses set in gardens, former storehouses, a Byzantine monastery and the remains of a basilica; part of the apse has been converted into a chapel.

KREMASTÁ, Lake★★   *Límni Kremastón*

Central Greece – Evritanía – Michelin map 980 south of fold 16

This is an artificial lake, the largest in Greece, which was created in the 1960s by the construction of a hydro-electric dam at the confluence of two rivers, the Ahelóos and the Tavropós; two villages are submerged beneath its glaucous waters, which spread on all sides like tentacles between the steep hillsides. *Tavernas.*

There are spectacular views of the reservoir from the Karpeníssi to Agrínio road which overlooks the lake from a great height except where it drops down to cross an arm of water by an elegant concrete bridge. The road to Karpeníssi is very beautiful although the surface is uneven in places.

Churches and monasteries are often closed between 1 and 5pm.

KYLLENE   *Kilíni*

Peloponnese – Elis – Pop 595 – Michelin map 980 fold 27

A seaside resort (Olympic Beach) and a small harbour sheltered by the **Kyllene headland** make up the modern town of Kyllene which has replaced the older town of Clarence, famous in the Middle Ages and now reduced to a few stones. *(Ferries to the Island of Zakynthos [Zante]).*

Proud Clarence. – Clarence was founded in 13C by the Crusaders on the shores of a sheltered bay and for two centuries was the major port of Morea under the de Villehardouin, the Angevins of Naples and the Venetians who called it Glarentza or Chiarenza.

Late in 13C and in 14C Clarence was one of the privileged possessions of the Angevin princes of Naples who would from time to time hold court there on a sumptuous scale. In those days, there was a great deal of traffic with their territories in Italy through the ports of Naples, Amalfi, Taranto, Bari and Manfredonia; the latter being one of the main crusader ports.

Being a port of call where Genoese ships and Venetian galleys *(p 82)* frequently put in, Clarence grew rich and populous, crowded with merchants, sailors, monks, knights, artists etc. The great European banks opened branches there including the Acciaiuoli who held first place. **Nicolo Acciaiuoli,** who was the chief adviser of Catherine de Valois and the princes of Taranto and came from a Florentine family which was in the service of the Angevins of Naples, became Prince of Cephallonia and Lord of Corinth; he was the patron of Boccacio who set one of the stories in his "Decameron" in Clarence.

In 13C the city had also obtained the privilege of issuing money and minted gold and silver coins of good quality which were highly valued on the money markets.

Through the marriage of Constantine Palaiologos, future despot of Mystra *(p 147),* in 1428, Clarence reverted to Byzantine control before falling into oblivion. The name survived in Great Britain into 20C: the title of Duke of Clarence was brought to the British throne by Phillipa, a great-niece of William de Villehardouin, who married Edward III of England.

City Ruins. – *10 minutes on foot from the modern town along the northwest waterfront.*

A few traces of the citadel are all that remain of Clarence: one can make out the footings of the curtain wall, a keep which was blown up by the Germans during the Second World War, and a huge church similar to the cathedral at Andravída *(p 123).*

EXCURSIONS

Vlacherna Monastery (Moní Vlahernón). – *On leaving Kilíni, turn right in the hamlet of Káto Panagía into a narrow road (signpost).* After 2km – 1 1/4 miles the road enters a verdant but deserted valley containing the monastery which takes its name from a famous church in Constantinople dedicated to the Virgin. The monastery was built in 12C in the Byzantine era but was altered under the the de Villehardouin when it was most probably served by a community of Cistercians *(to visit apply to the Orthodox nuns; open 9am to 1pm and 5 to 7pm).*

Although the brick walls of the abbey church suggest Byzantine influence, the surmounting corbelled cornice is in the western style and the external porch is Burgundian. In the interior too, certain architectural and decorative elements suggest French Gothic: nave and side aisles separated by columns, pointed arches over certain openings and early ogival arches in the narthex decorated with a lamb and a dove.

Kyllene Peninsula★. – From 13C to 15C the region between Kyllene and Andravída was the main base of the Frankish rulers of Morea *(p 23)* and was open to western influence. There are many monuments and other reminders of their occupation both on the promontory with the famous Clermont Castle (Chlemoutsi) and on the banks of the River Peneios which flows through the fertile plain of Elis; under the Turks the land deteriorated into its original state of marshland but in the last hundred years it has again been reclaimed.

Andravída. – Pop 3 335. The modern city is an unremarkable market town but in the Middle Ages, known as Andréville under the patronage of St Andrew, Andravída was the capital of Achaia, the seat of a Roman Catholic bishop and the principal residence of the de Villehardouin, a family from Champagne in France, who ruled Morea for almost the whole of 13C. They founded a famous "school of chivalry" and often called their barons together in an assembly.

The Templars had a church in Andréville, St James', where Geoffrey I, Geoffrey II (1218-1240) and William I de Villehardouin were buried. It also contained the tomb of Agnes of Achaia, who died in 1286; her tombstone has been found with an epitaph in French but the church has disappeared as has the monastery of St Nicholas of Carmel (13C).

Only part of the former church (13C) of the Dominicans remains *(on the outskirts of the town on the west side of the Patras road):* a large square chancel with early ogival vaulting and square chevet flanked by two chapels; traces of the nave and aisles are visible.

Chlemoutsi Castle★★. – *Description page 81.*

Gastoúni. – *South of Andravída.* Known as Gastogne in the Middle Ages, Gastoúni was another residence belonging to the Princes of Morea. There remains an 11C Byzantine church which was altered in 13C (Gothic north door); the interior contains some Byzantine paintings *(partially damaged)* and some naive icons *(bear right in the square where the road divides on the south side of the town).*

KYPARISSIA _____ *Kiparissía*

Peloponnese – Messinía – Pop 4 013 – Michelin map 980 south of fold 28

Kyparissia, the town of cypresses, is set just back from the coastline; in the Middle Ages it was called **Arkadia** after the people who were driven there from the neighbouring region to the east by the Slav invasions and was the personal fief of William de Villehardouin. After being destroyed in 1825 by Ibrahim Pasha *(p 21)* it is now a modern city, dominated by the ruins of a Frankish castle which had been built where an ancient and then a Byzantine acropolis had once stood. From the top there is a fine **view★** across the Ionian Sea to Zakynthos (NW)

Due west lie the **Strofádes Islands,** in antiquity the home of the Harpies (Snatchers), also called the Furies *(p 51)*; they were tempestuous divinities represented as birds with women's faces. They are also to be found among the symbols of medieval Christianity.

Ágrili. – *10km – 6 miles southwest.* Between the road and the sea rises the strange sight of a "medieval castle" and a house shaped like a horse which was designed by A. Fournarakis for a Greek who had made a fortune in America *(open to visitors).*

Peristéria Tombs. – *8km – 5 miles northeast; take the Pírgos road for 5km – 3 miles; turn right (signpost).* Among the green hills looking down into the narrow valley of the Peristéria, Professor Marinatos has excavated some royal tombs dating from the Mycenaean period *(work in progress).*

KYTHERA _____ *Kíthira*

Ionian Islands – Pop 3 354 – Michelin map 980 folds 41 and 42

Kythera, which was known to the Venetians as Cerigo, lies just off **Cape Malea** (Ákri Maléas), the southwest tip of the Peloponnese which creates a dangerous passage for sailors.

An artist's impression of Aphrodite's island would resemble the Garden of Eden; in reality the landscape is rather arid, recalling the Cyclades more than the Ionian Islands although it is to the latter group that Kythera has been joined throughout their history of occupation by the Turks, the Venetians (18C), the French (Revolution and Empire), and the British until 1864.

Access. – *There is a ferry service four times a week between Neápoli on the mainland, northwest of Cape Malea, and Agía Pelagía on the northeast coast of the island, which has replaced the former harbour of St Nicholas at Avlémonas further south; hydrofoil service twice a week from Zéa (Piraeus). There is also an air link with Athens, daily during the season. There is a modern hotel in Kapsáli and rooms to let. Honey is a speciality.*

Aphrodite's Isle. – Aphrodite, who is supposed to have sprung from the foam, was blown by the Zephyrs to Kythera which other legends cite as her birthplace. Then **Paris,** who had judged her to be more beautiful than Hera and Athena, built the first sanctuary to Aphrodite here on his way from the island of Kranai *(p 112)* to Troy. In fact the cult of the goddess of love seems to have been imported from Asia by the Phoenicians who came to these shores to collect the murex, a shell-fish which yields a purple dye.

Whatever the origins of the cult, several temples to Aphrodite were built but almost nothing remains. The largest contained a statue of the goddess made of myrtle which the Romans carried off to Rome.

Since then Kythera has enjoyed a reputation as a refuge for lovers who came to place themselves under the protection of Aphrodite's star. Francesco Colonna, the Venetian, took it as his subject in the "Dream of Poliphile" and Watteau painted it in an idyllic manner in his "Embarkation for the Island of Kythera".

To the south, in the waters off the island of **Antikythera,** in 1900 a sponge diver discovered an ancient wreck loaded with marbles and bronzes including the famous Ephebe of Antikythera (4C BC) which may be a likeness of Paris *(Athens Museum)*.

More recent excavations by the British School of Archaeology at Athens have explored various Minoan sites producing much valuable information.

SIGHTS

Kythera ★ (Kíthira). – Pop 268. The capital of the island occupies a very beautiful **site ★ ★** overlooking a magnificent roadstead and next to a rocky peak crowned by a Venetian citadel with a panoramic view; in October 1797 the citadel was heroically defended by 68 French soldiers under Captain Michel against the Russian fleet commanded by Admiral Ouchakov.

To the southeast lies the little port of Kapsáli and two magnificent bays separated by a promontory.

Milopótamos. – Here lie the ruins of a Byzantine and Venetian town with the lion of St Mark over the fortified gateway. The **cave of St Sophia** (Agía Sofía) has recently been restored *(1 1/2 hours on foot Rtn);* chambers which were used as chapels (traces of flooring and frescoes), passages with concretions and underground lakes.

LANGÁDIA

Peloponnese – Arkadía – Pop 821 – Michelin map 980 centre of fold 28

Langádia's picturesque and peaceful situation (alt 1 200m – 3 937ft) on a steeply sloping **site ★** beneath huge plane trees with a panoramic view of the surrounding mountains, makes it a pleasant summer resort on the road between Tripoli and Olympia.

On market days and local holidays the peasants come into town dressed in their traditional costumes: kilted skirts *(foustanélla)* for the men and shawls and embroidered aprons for the women.

LÁRISSA

Thessaly – Lárissa – Pop 102 048 – Michelin map 980 fold 17

Lárissa is a modern-looking town, the capital of Thessaly and an important junction on the south bank of the River Peneios; storks and bicycles are numerous. From 1389 to 1881 the town was occupied by the Turks who maintained a strong garrison. Now it is a market for agricultural produce and a food processing centre (sugar and dairy products).

Archaeological Museum. – *Open 8.45am to 3pm (9.30am to 2.30pm Sundays); closed Tuesdays; 100 Dr.* The museum is housed in an old mosque in the town centre at no. 2 in 31 August Street (Odós 31 Avgoustou); large collection of Greek, Roman and Byzantine funerary stele.

Venizelos Street (Odós Venizélou). – This is the main street in the old part of town. The low houses with their awnings and the open air street stalls are a lingering reminder of the Turkish occupation.

Venizelos Street runs down to the bridge which spans the River Peneios flowing between its steep green banks below the ancient acropolis: ancient traces, medieval castle *(restored)*.

LEFKÁDIA-NÁOUSSA ★ ★

Macedonia – Imathía – Michelin map 980 folds 4 and 5

The region of **Náoussa,** which is well known for its fruit (peaches, apricots, apples, strawberries etc.) and wine, is also famous for three unusual Macedonian *hypogea* (3C-2C BC), huge temple-like underground tombs situated out in the country near the little village of Lefkádia on the Véria to Édessa road.

Great Tomb. – *Signpost "Great Macedonian Tomb". Guided tours by the keeper (gratuity) every day from 8.45am to 3pm except Monday mornings and Friday afternoons.*

The tomb, which was excavated in 1954, is built of conchitic limestone. A flight of steps leads down to the two-storey façade; the lower section is Doric, the upper Ionic. It was decorated with paintings; those remaining show a warrior (probably Death), the god Hermes (leader of souls to the Underworld), Aiakos and Rhadamanthys (Judges of Hades) and battle scenes.

The interior comprises a vestibule and a chamber which still contains a sarcophagus.

Second Tomb. – *150m – 492ft beyond the Great Tomb, on the left of the path; guided tour by the keeper of the Great Tomb.*
Majestic steps descend to the superb columned façade of this *hypogeum* which is very well preserved both in its architecture and in its paintings.

Lysón Kalliklés Tomb. – *Closed temporarily: an iron ladder descends inside from the top of the vault.* This tomb is most unusual; it is in fact a burial vault for three families furnished with 22 funerary recesses inscribed with the names of the dead; ornamental paintings in an excellent state of preservation.

LEMNOS — *Límnos*

Aegean Islands – Pop 15 721 – Michelin map 980 fold 20

Bare plains in the east rise to rugged hills in the west. Lemnos is volcanic in origin; for this reason the Ancients thought it was the home of Hephaistos. During the Trojan War Philoctetes, who was companion to Heracles and inherited his arms, was abandoned on Lemnos because he had a gangrenous wound which smelt abominably.
During the Middle Ages Lemnos was occupied by the Venetians and then by the Genoese. It rose to prominence again in the First World War when the Allies used the vast Bay of Moúdros as a naval base before the landings at Gallipoli.

Access and accommodation. – *By ferry from Thessalonika, twice a week, about 6 hours, and from Kavála; by air from Athens, every day, 3/4 hour.* There is one resort, Mírina, with a spacious beach. Specialities: wine, fish, lobster, game in season.

Mírina. – Pop 3 744. The capital town and main harbour, which enjoyed a great reputation in antiquity, is pleasantly situated in a bay and dominated by a Venetian fortress. It is worth visiting the old houses with their wooden balconies and the museum which contains the considerable amount of material which has been excavated on the island.

Hephaistia (Ifestía). – This was an important city in the Classical and paleo-Christian eras. Italian archaeologists have excavated the remains of a theatre, houses, tombs and Byzantine basilicas.
On the opposite side of the bay at **Hlói** are "Philoctetes' Cave" and the ruins of a shrine to the Kabeiroi *(p 176)*, mysterious gods descended from Hephaistos.

LERNA — *Lérni*

Peloponnese – Argolis – Michelin map 980 fold 29 – south of Argos

On the northeast shore of the Argolic Gulf (Argolikós Kólpos) near the modern village of **Míli** lies the site of ancient Lerna. The narrow tract of land between the road and the seashore contains the Hydra Springs and the Lerna Marshes, which are now much reduced in size but still inhabited by huge eels; both evoke souvenirs of ancient legends.
This was the scene for one of the Labours of Hercules. He had to kill the many-headed **Hydra**, a water snake that lived in the marsh; when one of its heads was cut off, others grew in its place. The legend may symbolize an unsuccessful struggle to drain the marsh.
The ancient Greeks thought that the Lerna marshes were bottomless and an entrance to the Underworld.

Prehistoric remains. – *On leaving Míli going south bear left after a church into a path which leads to the excavations (200m – 220yds). Open 8.45am to 3pm (9.30am to 2.30pm Sundays); 100 Dr.*
The "House of the Tiles", which is protected by a roof, takes its name from the great quantities of tiles which were found among the foundations. The internal arrangement of this ancient palace, which dates from about 2200 BC, is perfectly visible. It is the only great building from the early bronze age to come down to us in such good condition; in fact it was destroyed by fire in 2100 BC and then covered by a protective layer of earth to form a tumulus. Articles excavated here are displayed in the Árgos Museum *(p 38)*.

Kástro. – *Take the path on the west side of the road on the edge of the village of Míli; fairly steep climb (3/4 hour on foot Rtn).*
The Frankish fortress of Lerna (13C-15C), which crowns a lesser peak of Mount Póntinos, consisted of three wards and commanded the southern approach to Argolis. The ruins provide a fine **view**★ of the plain of Árgos and the Gulf of Nauplion; on the south side stood the "Princess Tower" named after a member of the Enghien family who owned the region in the Middle Ages.

LESBOS★ — *Lésvos*

Aegean Islands – Pop 88 603 – Michelin map 980 fold 21

The Turks called Lesbos "the garden of the empire" because of its fertility; it is still sought after for its hilly wooded landscape, its huge sea inlets, the beauty of its traditional villages and its uncrowded beaches. Although there are few traces of earlier inhabitation, the Byzantines and Genoese have left some imposing fortresses and in the streets of the capital and the smaller towns there lingers a trace of the Middle East, only a few leagues away on the coast of Anatolia.
Lesbos, which is also known as **Mytilene**, the name of its capital, has a numerous population; its size (1 630 km² – 629sq miles) makes it the third largest island in Greece after Crete and Euboia. Market gardens, fruit trees and cereals thrive on the fertile soil which also supports over 11 million olive trees, the island's most important crop. A few soap factories, several distilleries producing the best *oúzo* in Greece, the hot springs in the spas and a flourishing tourist sector also contribute to the island's economy.

In keeping with the ancient tradition, Lesbos has a lively cultural scene composed of several literary, dramatic, musical and artistic societies. Several of Lesbos' citizens have achieved national recognition in the field of literature: Stratis Myrivilis, Ilias Venezis and the poet **Odysseas Elytis**, who was awarded a Nobel prize for literature in 1979.

Historical notes. – In antiquity the island was a thriving cultural centre, particularly in 7C and 6C BC when it nurtured the "Tyrant" Pittacos, one of the Seven Sages of Greece, Terpander, the musician and the poet Alcaeus; the famous woman poet **Sappho** *(p 128)* was a native of Lesbos. Theophrastos, philosopher and botanist, was born in Eressós in 372 BC and it was Lesbos that Longus (2C BC) chose as the setting for his pastoral romance "Daphnis and Chloe".

Following the division of the Roman empire Lesbos came under the control of Byzantium. In 1354 the island was given as a dowry by the Emperor John Palaiologos to his son-in-law Francesco Gattelusi from Genoa and it was administered by the Gattelusi until the Turkish conquest in 1462. Lesbos remained under Turkish occupation until 1912 and became part of the new Greek kingdom two years later. The disastrous campaign in Asia Minor *(p 21)* in 1922 led to the influx of thousands of refugees from Anatolia and the island lost for ever its rich continental possessions.

Access and accommodation. – *By air two flights daily from Athens and one from Thessalonika. By ferry daily (except Sundays) from Piraeus, stopping at Chios (about 12 hours) and once a week from Thessalonika.*

Lesbos has about twenty hotels in the categories A to C, mostly in Mytilene, Thermí and Míthimna; there are also many guest houses and rooms to let in the seaside villages and in Agiássos.

The road network is well maintained with many good secondary roads. Cars and motor scooters for hire in Mytilene and also Míthimna. Excursions by coach are organised by local firms. Banks in the main towns.

Festivals. – Religious festivals are celebrated on Lesbos with great enthusiasm and sometimes include very ancient elements. The feast of St Michael the Archangel, patron saint of the island, is celebrated on the third weekend after Easter at **Mandamádos** *(34km – 21 miles northwest of Mytilene)*. On Saturday afternoon a bull and several goats and sheep, decorated with flowers, are sacrificed beneath a great plane tree in the courtyard of the monastery. The spectators dip their handkerchieves in the blood and mark their foreheads to protect themselves from illness. A service including the baptism of children is held in the church in the presence of the Archbishop; the worshippers, who come from all parts of the island, throng to kiss a very old terracotta icon of the Archangel Michael. On the following day, after more ceremonies, the meat is distributed.

A similar celebration takes place in the last week in May near the town of **Agía Paraskeví** in the centre of the island. The procession on the Saturday, where horses and mules decorated with plumes parade to the sound of music, attracts the greater crowd. The bull is sacrificed on Saturday evening and on Sunday, after the church service and the distribution of the meat, there is horse racing. The sacrifice of the bull, which the Church only tolerates, is a remnant of the ancient cult of Mithras.

The Assumption of the Virgin on 15 August is celebrated with great show particularly in **Pétra** and **Agiássos**. All these festivals are accompanied by a secular fair with stalls selling craftwork, agricultural products and other goods.

TOWNS AND SIGHTS *(in alphabetical order – mileages from Mytilene)*

Agiássos. – Pop 3 294. *25km – 15 1/2 miles west*. The wooded lower slopes of the highest peak on the island (Mount Olympos, 968m – 3 235ft) frame this charming unspoilt town. A stroll up and down its shady paved streets reveals attractive cafés, fountains, sometimes a *sandoúri* (sort of cithar) player or an old woman wearing the old-fashioned full-skirted ankle-length culottes. A museum of religious and popular art is attached to the church.

Limónos Monastery. – *43km – 27 miles west*. Just beyond Kaloní on the Sígri road stand the impressive buildings of Lesbos' chief monastery. The 40 monks, whose social and educational work extends throughout the island, maintain two museums of religious and popular art.

Míthimna ★ (Molyvos). – Pop 1 250. *64km – 40 miles northwest*. Picturesque little town favoured by artists; beach and fishing port. The handsome houses, painted in pastel shades, climb the steep slope towards an impressive Byzantine-Genoese castle which offers views of the town and the coast. 3km – 2 miles east of Míthimna, beyond the beach at Eftaloú, a radio-active spring (46.8 °C – 124 °F) is captured in a covered bath before warming the sea water off the shingle beach.

Mytilene ★ (Mitilíni). – Pop 24 115. *Small beach below the castle*. The island capital is on the east coast facing Anatolia where in the past the citizens had trading interests. The castle, which stands on a promontory projecting seawards beyond the town and thus providing two harbours, one to the north and one to the south, was rebuilt in 14C by Francesco Gattelusi; some of the older construction work dates from 6C. Above the castle gates are the arms of the Palaiologos emperors of Byzantium (a two-headed eagle), the horseshoe of the Gattelusi and Arabic inscriptions.

Behind the slightly unexpected bulk of the neo-Classical church of Ágios Thérapon is the **Byzantine Museum** which houses some precious icons (13C-17C). An attractive villa on the road to the castle houses the Archaeological Museum: ceramics, Greek sculptures and some beautiful fragments of Roman mosaics from the "House of Menander" *(open 8.45am to 3pm [9.30am to 2.30pm Sundays]; closed Tuesdays; 100 Dr.)*

The district on the isthmus between the two harbours, which was the centre of town during the Turkish occupation, has retained some fine houses, the remains of a mosque and the cathedral which contains a very fine post-Byzantine iconostasis. The **"House of Lesbos"** (lesviakó spíti) contains a small museum of popular art and tradition *(tel: 28 550)*.

Northwest on a pine-clad slope are the remains of a Hellenistic theatre which was restored by the Romans; Pompey was so impressed by it that he had a replica built in Rome. Most of the terraces have disappeared – they were taken for building projects in the Middle Ages, in particular for the construction of the Gattelusi castle – but the size of the theatre (it seated 15 000 spectators) indicates the cultural importance of Lesbos in antiquity. From the upper terraces there is a fine view of the old town, the castle and the Turkish coast.

Pétra. – Pop 953. *60km – 37 miles west.* This quiet village beside its long stretch of sand was immortalised in a painting by Theophilos. The **rock**, which gives the village its name, is crowned by the Church of the Virgin (Panagía Glikofiloússa) which contains some remarkable icons; fine view of the surrounding countryside. At the centre of the village stands the **Vareldzidena house** with its graceful wooden balconies; the salon on the first floor is decorated with delicate paintings of the towns and fleet of the Ottoman Empire *(open except during the siesta)*. St Nicholas' Church (**Ágios Nikólaos**) contains 15C frescoes.

Plomári. – Pop 3 503. *42km – 26 miles southwest.* The second largest town in the island hides its steep streets of old houses in a hollow in the cliff face which is scarcely visible from a distance. The modern seafront provides cafés and restaurants as well as a tiny beach at the west end. East of the town extends a shingle beach, Ágios Issídoros, which is very popular. Plomári is famous throughout Greece for the high quality of its *oúzo.*

Sígri. – Pop 399. *95km – 59 miles west.* This fishing village (crayfish a speciality) nestles in a little bay, protected by a ruined Turkish fort and protected from the open sea by an island, Nissiópi. Several little beaches in the vicinity. Between Sígri and Eressós there is a **"petrified forest"** *(apolithoména déndra)* composed of fossilised trees which were buried under a layer of volcanic ash millions of years ago and then slowly revealed to view by erosion. The trees which are still upright reach up to 10m – 33ft in height and the trunks measure about 8m – 26ft round the bole. The forest spreads over a vast area but the most accessible trees are to be found on the south side of the Ándissa to Sígri road about 7km – 4 miles from Ándissa.

Skála Eressoú. – Pop 102. *90km – 56 miles west.* Skála Eressoú, which is the port for the larger village of Eressós, attracts many holiday-makers to its long sandy beach backed by tavernas and guest houses. **Ancient Eressós**, which was built on the slopes of a hill to the east of the village, is thought to be the birthplace of **Sappho**; as well as the remains of a few walls, there are two paleo-Christian basilicas decorated with mosaics and the ruins of a Genoese and a Turkish tower.

Thermí. – Pop 1 024. *11km – 7 miles north.* Loutropóli Thermís is a popular spa; its hot waters were known in antiquity for their curative properties. In the vicinity stand some traditional residential tower houses.

South of Thermí and west of the village of Mória are traces of an impressive **Roman aqueduct**. There are traces of another near the village of Lámbou Míli on the road to Kaloní.

Variá★. – Pop 661. *4km – 2 1/2 miles south of Mytilene.* Stratis Eleftheriadis-Teriade, famous critic and art dealer in Paris and native of Mytilene, built two museums on his property *(open 9am to 1pm and 5 to 7pm; closed Mondays).*

The **Theophilos Museum** presents 86 works by the famous naive painter Theophilos (1873-1934) who was born in Variá; the paintings are gaily coloured representations of popular scenes or incidents in Greek history. Other works by this artist are displayed in Makrinítsa, a village on Mount Pélion east of Vólos, and in the National Gallery in Athens.

On the same site under the olive trees stands the **Teriade Museum** which contains a rich library belonging to the art dealer and engravings and lithographs coloured by Chagall, Picasso, Fernand Léger, Matisse and Giacometti. There are also paintings by Jannis Tsarouchis and other works by Theophilos.

Vaterá. – *52km – 32 miles. South of Polihnítos.* This is the most beautiful beach on the island *(8km – 5 miles long).* A few hotels, guest houses and tavernas. There are traces of a paleo-Christian basilica on the Fokás headland and also east of the village.

(Photograph L. Y. Loirat/Explorer)

Amphorae

Ionian Islands – Pop 21 293 – Michelin map 980 south of fold 15

Leukas (Levkas), which was known by the Latins as **Santa Maura**, is almost linked to the mainland by a narrow strip of land forming a lagoon.

It is a mountainous island – the Eláti peak rises to 1 158m – 3 799ft – with several fertile valleys where wheat, olives and citrus fruits are cultivated; the vineyards produce an excellent red wine called Santa Maura.

After coming under Franco-Venetian domination during the Middle Ages, the island was occupied by the Turks from 1467 to 1684 when it was reconquered by the Venetians who held it until 1797.

Leukas has preserved a fair number of its old houses with balconies and projecting wooden superstructures; some of the women still wear traditional costume consisting of a green or brown skirt and a black shawl. The Leukas International Festival from 15 to 30 August presents traditional dances both local and foreign, plays and concerts.

Leukas was the birthplace of two great poets: Valaorítis (1824-1874) and Sikelianos (1884-1951) who restored the "Delphic Games".

Pratical information. – *Access by regular ferries across the canal which separates Leukas from the mainland. There are a few hotels in Lefkáda, Nídri and Vassilikí; camping at Vlihó, Póros and Vassilikí; restaurants and tavernas serving fish. Long sandy beaches along the narrow strip of land, also at Ágios Nikítas, southwest of Lefkáda. Embroidery and lacemaking are local crafts.*

Santa Maura Fort. – The fort was begun in 14C by the Orsini, lords of the Ionian Islands, passed to Gautier de Brienne, the Duke of Athens, in 1331 and then to the Tocchi, courtiers from the Angevin kingdom of Naples. Its present appearance, however, with its low curtain walls which are less easily attacked by canon and its massive bastions, owes most to the Venetians and the Turks. It was originally surrounded by the waters of the lagoon and reached by two bridges.

Inside the curtain wall are traces of the town of Santa Maura which was the capital of the island until 1684 and contained the famous collegiate church of Santa Maura, which the Turks converted into a mosque. The parade ground is still visible; from the ramparts there is an attractive view of Lefkáda and the lagoon.

Leukas Town (Lefkáda). – Pop 6 415. Leukas, the island capital, is a peaceful port on the lagoon with a Venetian atmosphere owing to the network of paved streets lined by low houses. Venetian influence is also responsible for the many little churches built by the great local families, with Classical façades, single naves and painted ceilings; Ágios Minás, at the end of the main street, has a very fine ceiling painted by Nicholas Doxarás in the middle of 18C.

Behind the cathedral in the main street is the tomb of the poet Valaorítis (1824-1874). Faneroméni monastery *(3km – 2 miles southwest)* provides **views★** of Leukas and the lagoon.

Lagoon. – It is only 1 to 2m – 4 to 6ft deep and therefore suitable for fish farming or the extraction of salt. The fishing includes eels and grey mullet whose eggs are used in the preparation of botargo *(avgotáraho)*, a relish of salt fish roe.

It is possible to drive round the north branch of the lagoon: huge beaches, windmills, view of Leukas which seems to float on the water.

Tour of the Island★★. – *88km – 55 miles – about 4 hours – plus 2 hours sightseeing; visitors pressed for time should turn back at Nídri.*

The road from Leukas first skirts the west side of the lagoon, with a view across the water of Fort St George, which was built by the Venetians in the late 17C; then it follows the east coast of the island which faces Etolía. On reaching Nídri turn left to visit the harbour.

Nídri Bay★★★. – The bay is sheltered by a screen of little islands covered with cypress and olive trees; an enchanting prospect is created by the natural contours of the site, the balmy air and the limpid light.

From the resort of Nídri (pop 592) there are boat trips round the bay *(1 to 1 1/2 hours)* which include:

– Madourí Island where Valaorítis' Italian villa nestles in an idyllic setting; after the union with Greece he retired here to write, having served in the Islands' Parliament under the British Protectorate;

– **Skorpiós Island,** owned by the shipping magnate, **Aristotle Onassis,** who was married on the island to Jacqueline Kennedy in 1968 and was buried there in 1976; the neighbouring island is a hunting reserve;

– Agía Kiriakí peninsula which contains the house and tomb of Dörpfeld (1853-1940), a German archaeologist and follower of Schliemann, who tried to identify Leukas as Odysseus' Ithaca;

– Meganíssi Island (pop 1 346) which has many inlets.

The road beyond Nídri looks down on **Vlihó Bay** which is joined to Nídri Bay by a narrow passage.

Póros. – Pop 274. Picturesque inlet below the village *(beach, taverna)*.

Vassilikí. – Pop 371. Charming fishing village on the edge of a fertile plain *(beach)*.

There are boat trips from Vassilikí *(3 hours Rtn; in season)* to the famous **Leukas Leap,** a high cliff 72m – 236ft above sea level *(lighthouse)* from which the poetess **Sappho** (6C BC – *p 120)* who had been deceived in love by the handsome Phaon, is supposed to have jumped to her death.

The headland (Ákri Doukáto) bears faint traces of a temple to Apollo whose priests used to jump off the cliff landing without harm owing to nets spread on the surface of the water to break their fall and to wearing something like wings.

The return journey up the west side of the island offers a direct view of Mount Eláti. In Komilió there is a junction with the rough road which leads to the Leukas Leap.

LEVÍDI

Peloponnese – Arkadía – Pop 1 442 – Michelin map 980 centre of fold 29

Small mountain resort (alt 860m – 2 822ft) overlooking the plain where the Arcadian town of Orchomenos stood in antiquity.

Church of the Dormition of the Virgin★ (Kimísseos Theotókou). – *Take the road to Orchomenos and Kandíla; after 2km – 1 1/4 miles turn right (signpost) into the track leading to the church. The keeper will show visitors round.*

A solitary enclosure planted with walnut trees and watered by springs surrounds this beautiful post-Byzantine church (17C). The interior is painted with murals which are interesting both for their picturesque detail and their pleasant colouring: scene from the Old Testament, Christ's Passion, the Dormition of the Virgin; effigies of oriental saints.

LIVADIÁ★

Central Greece – Boeotia – Pop 16 864 – Michelin map 980 north of fold 29

Livadiá, the capital of Boeotia, spreads out in a fan shape at the mouth of the gloomy Erkínas (Hercyna) Gorge which was thought in antiquity to be the entrance to the Underworld. It changed hands many times during the Middle Ages but under the Turkish occupation it became the second most important city in Greece after Thessalonika.

It is a lively town, an important junction in the road network and an industrial centre; the textile mills treat the cotton grown in the Copaïc Basin *(p 162)*. The upper town is graced by white houses with jutting wooden balconies dating from 18C and 19C, little shops shaded by broad Turkish awnings and tavernas where mini-kebabs *(souvláki)* and cherry conserve, the local specialities, are served.

SIGHTS *2 1/2 hours*

Park the car in the square in the centre of the modern lower town and take one of the streets which lead to the upper town. They follow the valley of the River Erkínas as far as a square which gives access to the Turkish bridge, the old houses and the fulling mills beside the stream.

Erkínas Gorge★★. – Walk upstream leaving the great square tower to the right. An old hump-backed stone bridge spans the river. On the east bank the **spring of Mnemosyne** (Remembrance) flows into a pool where niches for votive offerings have been carved out of the cliff face. A passage not far away leads to what is thought to be the **spring of Lethe** (Oblivion); its waters bestow forgetfulness of the past. Beneath the shade of the maple trees a hotel with a restaurant and a swimming pool has been built.

Continue up the gorge, deep into the rocky mountain where a few oleanders brighten the gloom. Only the cries of falcons break the silence of the canyon. There are fine views of the fortress and the Jerusalem hermitage.

Return to the square tower, which is at one end of the fortress' outer wall, and turn left into a path which follows the line of the wall past a beautiful Byzantine church with an apse and a dome.

Fortress★ (Kástro). – The fortress which stands on the top of Mount Elijah (Ágios Ilías) (alt 402m – 1319ft) controls the approaches to Thessaly. The position was first fortified in 13C by the Franks, who held Thebes, but the present fortress dates from 14C when the Catalans ruled the land. They had in their possession a remarkable relic, the head of St George, which eventually turned up in Venice.

The former outer bailey of the castle precedes the main gate which leads to the keep. Near it stands a chapel built on the site of a temple to Zeus. From the ramparts there are spectacular **views★★** of the Erkínas Gorge, the Jerusalem hermitage, the town and the mountains.

At the highest point there is a cave in which the oracle of an infernal divinity, Trophonios, was thought to operate: the oracle was consulted by **Pausanias,** who travelled in Greece in 2C AD and described the ritual and trials required at that time.

LOUTRÁKI★

Korinthía – Pop 6 823 – Michelin map 980 folds 29 and 30

Loutráki, which combines the old fashioned charm of a traditional spa with the more modern attractions of a seaside resort, is tucked into the crook of the Bay of Corinth at the foot of the Mount Geránia chain which rises to 1 351m – 4 432ft. Luxury hotels, a palm tree walk and a luxuriant public garden with oleanders, pine and eucalyptus trees bordering a little harbour all add to the visitor's pleasure.

Loutráki is the largest spa in Greece; its warm water which is radio-active is used in the treatment of renal infections and rheumatism. Loutráki water, which is alkaline and contains traces of magnesia, is sold in bottles throughout Greece.

EXCURSION

Heraion Headland★★★ (Akrotírio Iréo). – *46km – 29 miles Rtn – about 2 hours – plus 1 hour visiting*

At first a corniche road runs north from Loutráki offering admirable views *(left)* down on to the coast and the Bay of Corinth; then by a taverna (view north towards the headland crowned by a lighthouse) it bears right inland. On the outskirts of Perahóra (alt 350m – 1 148ft) turn left into a narrow road marked "Limni Heraion" which passes through olive groves and then skirts **Lake Vouliagméni** *(hotels, tavernas, camping)* which is linked by a channel to the sea. At the junction marked by a chapel bear right into an earth road which skirts the few traces of ancient Perachora which are scattered in an olive grove (ancient cistern on the left of the road) before reaching a car park.

LOUTRÁKI★

The **Heraion** (a sanctuary dedicated to Hera) is to be found on the rocky slopes of the headland which separates the Bay of Corinth from the Gulf. Its remote and wild **site★** is hidden in the bottom of a narrow valley which slopes down to the transparent waters of a sheltered cove below an acropolis.

From the car park walk down into the heart of the valley. Near a house are the ruins of a Hellenistic cistern; it is oblong in shape with a row of internal pillars. Higher up are the foundations of a temple to Hera Limenia (6C BC).

Excavations on the edge of the harbour have uncovered the foundations of an angled portico and a temple to Hera Akraia (6C BC).

The path from the car park to the lighthouse *(1/2 hour on foot Rtn)* provides a splendid **panorama★★★**, particularly at sunset, of the ancient site, the coast and mountains of the Peloponnese (SW), the Gulf of Corinth stretching northwest, the Halcyonic Gulf (Kólpos Alkionídon) on the north side of the headland and on the skyline to the north the Parnassos massif towering over Delphi.

The site, a rich deposit of Archaic Corinthian pottery, was excavated between 1930 and 1933 under Humfry Payne, Director of the British School at Athens, whose wife Dilys Powell mentions the dig in her book "An Affair of the Heart".

MÁNI★★

Peloponnese – Lakonía – Michelin map 980 fold 41

The southern spur of Mount Taÿgetos, which rises to 1 214m – 3 970ft, extends south between the Messenian and Lakonian Gulfs to form a promontory which ends in Cape Matapan (Akrí Ténaro), the southernmost point of continental Greece. This is the Máni peninsula, a wild and sparsely inhabited region, as remote and timeless as it was in feudal days. The barren windswept landscape and the grey villages with their abandoned towers create an unusual and even oppressive impression.

Northern or Messenian Máni is described on p 135.

A proud and courageous people. – The Maniots, who are thought to be descended from the ancient Spartans, originally came from the north of Lakonia from which they were expelled in 7C by invading Slavs. In the following centuries they managed to maintain a de facto autonomy from the succession of occupying forces – the Franks in 13C, the Byzantines, the Venetians and particularly the Turks against whom they rose in revolt in 1769 and 1821; **P. Mavromichális** (1765-1848) was one of the leaders in the War of Independence *(p 24)*.

Exclusive and bellicose, the Maniots lived in tribal villages under the rule of the local chiefs, sometimes confronting one another in vendettas; these disputes which could go on for generations explain their distinctive villages where the houses and even the fields were fortified. Writing of them in 17C Sir George Wheler described them as "famous as pirates by sea and pestilent robbers by land".

The Maniots also had a spirit of adventure. Some settled in Corsica in 17C, under the protection of the Republic of Genoa, forming communities in Paomia and later in Cargese. Others took up piracy, particularly in the Cyclades.

Few in number, the Maniots still live in their steep villages dotted with olive trees on the mountain slopes preserving the cult of honour and hospitality. The women still wear the long black dress and veil of the mourners in antiquity and perpetuate their tradition of singing funeral dirges *(mirológia)*.

The Towers. – There are about 800 towers, isolated or grouped in villages; the oldest go back to 15C; their height increased with the power of the family that built them. They were constructed of irregularly shaped blocks of stone, about 15m to 25m – 50ft to 80ft high and square in shape; they comprised three or four rooms, one above the other, linked by ladders and trap doors. Windows were small and few in number and the top floor was crenellated so that the tower looked like a castle keep.

The greatest concentration of towers is to be found in Kíta and Váthia in the south.

The churches. – Máni was probably converted in 9C and 10C and many of the churches and chapels date from 11C and 12C. They are small buildings in the traditional Byzantine style of a Greek cross plan surmounted by a dome; the walls are a mixture of stone with bands of brick. Some have gable-end belfries, a feature which may have been introduced by the Franks. Fragments of ancient or paleo-Christian marble have often been incorporated in the structure. The walls of the interior are decorated with charming 12-13C and 14C frescoes which are naive in treatment but very lively and illustrate the usual Byzantine themes; Frankish influence can sometimes be traced in the representation of knights and horses.

Unfortunately many of these churches are difficult to reach being isolated in the countryside; the keys are often kept at a neighbouring house. Here and there in the fields stands a lonely tombstone.

TOUR STARTING FROM GÍTHIO

160km – 100 miles, about 6 hours, plus 1 1/2 hours walking or visiting. The sites of interesting Byzantine churches are underlined in red on the map (p 131).

This tour can be completed in a day but for a leisurely pace, stopping to look at a few churches, it is better to take two days spending the night at Geroliménas.

Leave Gíthio by the road to Areópoli going south. The road climbs into the mountains through a gorge *(11km – 7 miles from Gíthio)* which was guarded by Passavant Castle at its northern end.

Passavant Castle (Passavás). – Briefly the merlons and crenellations *(restored)* of Passavant Castle appear on a bluff on the east side of the road. Its name recalls the medieval motto of the Neuilly family – passe-avant. It was built by Jean de Neuilly, lord of the barony who held the military title of "Marshal of Morea".

│ ★★

…aroúda. – Pop 31. The church
…11C-12C) is decorated with
…ome interesting and well
…reserved frescoes.

…nue along the Geroliménas

…ardenítsa. – Pop 86. 1km
…1 1/2 mile west of the road
(…signpost) lies St Saviour's
…church (Ágios Sotírios)
…which dates from 11C and
…2C. It has a porch and an
…nteresting apse with a sculp-
…ed decoration in Kufic
…cript; within are 13-14C
…rescoes revealing Frankish
…nfluences (knights, horses).

…ómia. – Pop 39. This village
…s scattered on the west side
…f the road with unusual
…iews★★ of the towers of
…íta.

…v and to the left of the road
…g to the village stands the
…Taxiarchs' Church *(key at
…ext house)* which is decora-
…ith a fine series of frescoes
…14C) illustrating the Life of

(Photograph GNTO)

Máni. – A village.

…íta. – Pop 123. The village is set in an olive grove to the east of the road. Despite
…e great number of towers it seems to be abandoned. In the hamlet of Tourlotí,
…t Sergius' Church (Ágios Sérgios) is well proportioned.

…outh of Kipoúla overlooking the Messenian Gulf rises a rocky bluff on which the
…amous castle of the Great Maina (Kástro tis Oriás) was built in 1248 by William de
…illehardouin; it was surrendered to the Byzantines in 1263.

Kíta the road runs down towards Geroliménas.

…eroliménas★. – Pop 76. This is a simple resort and fishing village, tucked into a rocky
…let in remote and wild surroundings.

…the road to Álika and bear right into a mediocre road leading to Váthia which rises
…lly on its rocky site on the horizon.

…áthia★★. – Pop 38. Forsaken by almost all its inhabitants, Váthia is the most
…npressive of the tower communities which are characteristic of the Máni. Stony paths
…ind between the silent towers and the empty houses mount to the top of the hill:
…ew★★ of Cape Matapan (Akrí Ténaro).

…Váthia the road continues south to **Pórto Kágio** (Quail Port) situated on the neck of
…cipitous peninsula which is favoured by game and ends in **Cape Matapan** (Akrí Ténaro)
…crowned by a temple to Poseidon; on 28 March 1941 a naval engagement took
…off Cape Matapan between the British and the Italians; the latter lost three cruisers.

…n to Álika and bear right into the road to Lágia over the ridge of the Máni. Beyond
…(towers) it descends down rock-strewn slopes past old marble quarries offering
…ificent and precipitous views★★ of the Maniot coast. Beyond Ágios Kiprianós it skirts
…ast coast of the Máni which is less inhospitable and indented than the western
…ard. The corniche road provides spectacular views of the coastline with its lonely
…and of the occasional villages and feudal ruins on the mountain slopes.

…kála. – Pop 206. An attractive sheltered inlet with a church at the water's edge.

…omohóri. – Pop 151. Typical village of tall towers dotted with cypress trees.

…° a mile beyond Flomohóri, turn right to Kótronas.

…tronas. – Pop 255. Small seaside resort set on the edge of a bay; fishing port.

…ɲ to Areópoli for the road to Gíthio.

MEGALOPOLIS   *Megalópoli*

…eloponnese – Arkadía – Pop 4 735 – Michelin map **980** folds 28 and 29

…egalopolis lies in the upper Alpheios Valley; it is known for its thermal power station,
…is fuelled by lignite from the neighbouring mines, and for an ancient ruined city.

…of Megalopolis. – *1km – 1/2 mile north on the Karítena road on the left (signpost);
…8.45am to 3pm (9.30am to 2.30pm Sundays).*

…ie ancient city of Megalopolis was built between 371 and 368 BC by Epaminondas
…t Sparta could be kept under surveillance and contained. As the headquarters of
…rcadian League" it played an important role in the Hellenistic and Roman periods.
…the native city of **Philopoimen** (253-183 BC), the "last of the Greeks", who sought
…ntain Greek unity in the face of Roman expansion, and of **Polybios** (204-122 BC),
…storian, who described the Roman conquest of Greece in his Histories. Ancient
…opolis was sacked several times and disappeared with the barbarian invasions.

…on. – The huge size of this assembly hall, which was designed to hold the "Ten
…and", the representatives of the Arcadian people, can be judged from the
…ations of the rectangular precinct and the many bases of columns within it. The

Continue along the Areópoli road which crosses the mountain chain; the western
is guarded by **Kelefá Castle,** a huge Turkish fortress (16C-17C) which appears on
side of the road.

At the road junction bear left to Areópoli.

    Areópoli★. – This is a large village (pop 611 – *tavernas*) in the typical Maniot
tradesmen's workshops (bakery), tower houses and churches. The Taxiarch
(18C), at the centre of the village, is unusual owing to the decoration so
the apse (signs of the Zodiac) and the side doors (escutcheons, angels a
saints); St John's Church, in a neighbouring street, is decorated with naiv
(18C).

At the junction with the road to Kótronas (left), bear right down to the Diróa

    Dirós Caves★★ (Spílea Diroú). – *Description p 106.*

Return to the Geroliménas road which runs along a sort of limestone terr;
between the mountain and the sea, dotted with villages of tower houses, such
and olives groves or Barbary fig trees. Below the road *(west)* lies Haroúda.

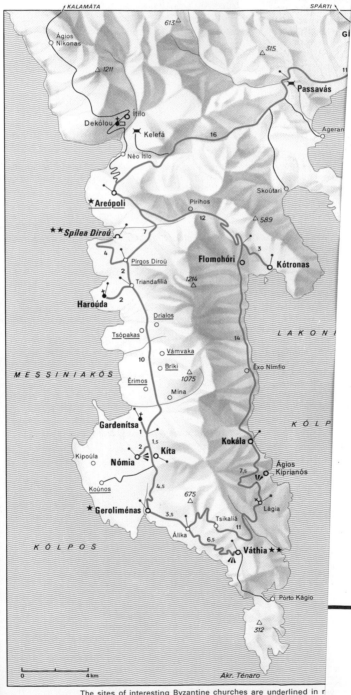

The sites of interesting Byzantine churches are underlined in r

hall was named after its founder; it measured 66m by 53m – 217ft by 174ft and the 67 pillars were placed so that almost all those present could see the speaker who stood in the centre of the side next to the theatre.

Theatre. – A fringe of shrubs makes a rustic crown for the theatre which is the largest in Greece (145m – 476ft in diameter) and could accommodate about 20 000 spectators on the 59 rows of seats; the acoustics were excellent. The lower rows, reserved for officials and members of the religious orders *(inscriptions)* are well preserved.

MÉGA SPÍLEO Monastery★

Peloponnese – Achaia – Alt 924m – 3 031ft – Michelin map 980 fold 29

Access either by car by the new road between Trápeza on the coast and Kalávrita (SW) or on foot or a donkey (summer only) (3/4 hour) by the path from Zahloroú in the Vouraïkós Gorge (p 197); taverna.

The monastery of Méga Spíleo (great cave), which attracts many pilgrims, appears at the foot of a bare rockface on a wild **site**★★ deep in the magnificent landscape of the Vouraïkós Valley.

It was founded in 8C by two hermits, Simeon and Theodore, following the discovery of a miraculous image of the Virgin which was found by Euphrosyne, a shepherdess, in a cleft in the rocks.

The monastery reached its apogee in the Middle Ages under the Palaeologi, the despots of Mystra *(p 147)* who sometimes used to stay there. The conventual buildings which were burnt down in 1934, have been rebuilt in a style which does not meet with unanimous approval. In 1981 there were 12 monks in residence.

Guided tour by a monk, offering; open 8am to 1pm and 5pm to sunset.

The rock church (17C) occupies the great cave from which the monastery takes its name. There is a beautiful door of embossed copper (early 19C); at the base is the Prophet Jesse beneath two scenes of the legend of the icon and effigies of archangels and the Virgin and Child. A recess harbours the miraculous image of the Virgin which was found by Euphrosyne and is attributed to St Luke.

The oratory consecrated to the founding saints is next to the cave where Euphrosyne is supposed to have discovered the miraculous Virgin. The "Treasury" is full of reliquaries, icons and Byzantine manuscripts, some of which date from 9C.

The guests' refectory and the household rooms (bakery, cellar etc.) may also be visited.

MELOS   *Mílos*

Cyclades – Pop 3 771 – Michelin map 980 fold 43

Austere and sombre and relatively untouched by tourism, Melos, like Santoríni, is an ancient volcano; the crater, now filled by sea water, provides a deep and safe haven which was used as a naval base by French squadrons during the Crimean War and again by the Allies in the First World War.

Riddled with mines and quarries, Melos grew rich in antiquity through the exploitation of obsidian, a hard vitreous volcanic stone which was made into axe or knife blades; later sulphur, alum and baryta were extracted. Nowadays Melos produces some good volcanic wines.

Practical information. – *Boat service daily from Piraeus; air service daily in the season from Athens. Small hotels at Skála Adamandás.*

The tribulations of the Venus de Milo. – During his voyage in the Levant in 1817 the Comte de Forbin, future director of the Museums of France, had noticed that Melos was rich in antiquities but had not been able to stay long enough to investigate.

Three years later two ships put in at Melos and two officers, Vautier and the future admiral **Dumont d'Urville** were struck by the beauty of the pieces of a marble statue which a local farmer had dug up in his field at the foot of the ancient acropolis.

They both alerted Louis Brest, the French consular agent on Melos, who sent a favourable report to Pierre David, the French consul in Smyrna, who told the **Marquis de Rivière,** the French ambassador to the Sublime Porte. The latter, who had already spoken to Vautier and Dumont d'Urville when they arrived in Constantinople, decided, in the absence of funds, to acquire the statue at his own expense and sent his secretary, the **Vicomte de Marcellus,** to Melos.

The young diplomat arrived on the island on 23 May 1820 only to be informed that the statue had been loaded on to an Albanian boat bound for Turkey where it was to be offered to the Dragoman, **Prince Nikolaki Morusi,** the Governor of the Cyclades. Marcellus laid claim to the statue saying that Brest had acquired it first and the island chiefs gave way, although Matterer, the captain of the ship, stated in his evidence that it was carried off against the wishes of the Greeks who were beaten back by the Frenchmen. In his own account of events Marcellus explains that the statue suffered no damage once it came into his care so the arms must have been lost during the earlier moves.

Marcellus had the five pieces of the statue sewn into canvas bags, he recompensed the island chiefs, paid the farmer and set sail for Piraeus where he showed the statue to the archaeologist Fauvel *(p 46)* before heading for Smyrna and Constantinople where he handed his treasure over to the Marquis de Rivière who presented it to Louis XVIII. The Venus de Milo, or more correctly the Melos Aphrodite, a masterpiece of 2C BC Hellenistic art, was put on display in the Louvre.

Aphrodite, however, had her revenge. On the orders of Prince Morusi the farmer was beaten and the island chiefs were whipped and fined 7 000 piastres; the Marquis de Rivière was never reimbursed for his expenses (30 000FF in those days); Brest had to wait six years for the post of vice-Consul which he coveted. In the end Prince Morusi and Dumont d'Urville died violent deaths; the former was executed on the order of the Captain Pasha and the latter was killed in a railway accident at Versailles in 1842.

133

MELOS

SIGHTS

Melos (Pláka). – Pop 735. The capital, which has a small museum, is dominated by the ruins of a Frankish castle incorporating a 13C chapel; panorama over the archipelago. Louis Brest *(see above)* is buried in the Roman Catholic church.

The ancient **acropolis**, where British archaeologists excavated a handsome *kouros,* now in the Athens Museum, extended down the hill towards the hamlet Klíma in the valley near where the Venus was discovered; traces of the precinct, Roman theatre *(restored)*, Paleo-Christian catacombs dating from 3C AD *(closed for restoration work)*.

Phylakope (Filakopí). – Excavations in the northeast of the island have uncovered traces of three superimpsed cities dating from different eras: the bronze age, the Minoan period (*c*1600 BC) and the Mycenaean (1200 BC). Their stone houses are the first indications of urbanism in the Cyclades and those built in the first period (old Cycladic) were decorated with frescoes which are now in the National Archaeological Museum.

EXCURSION

Kímolos Island. – Pop 787. *Take the ferry from Piraeus which stops at Kímolos twice a week or a boat from Voúdia on Melos. Rooms in private houses.*

This little island, which rises to 358m – 1 175ft, was called **Argentiera** (Silver Island) by western travellers owing to the colour of the soil from which cimolite, a sort of fuller's earth, was extracted; tales of ancient silver mines appear to be baseless.

In 17C it was used as a base by French pirates who scoured the archipelago and were brought to heel by Louis XIV. Then it became the residence of the French king's Pilot in the Levant; he was a consular agent with diplomatic immunity who was responsible for supplying His Majesty's French ships with pilots. For more than a century a family of French origin called Brest held the post; one of them, Louis Brest became famous, first for repulsing with the help of a few partisans two attacks by pirates from the Máni in 1815 and later for being involved in the negotiations for the purchase of the Venus de Milo *(p 133)*.

There is a 17C church in the village of Kímolos and ruined fortifications perched on the heights at Paleókastro with picturesque views of the islands.

MESSENE★★ _____ *Ithómi*

Peloponnese – Messinía – Michelin map ❾❽❽ south of fold 28

The ruins of ancient Messene lie against a majestic backdrop of mountains dominated by Mount Ithómi; at the centre stands the modern village of **Mavromáti** (pop 525).

Messene, the capital of Messenia, was for a long time a rebellious subject of Sparta which eventually destroyed the town; it was rebuilt by Epaminondas *(p 187)* who defeated the Spartans at Leuktra (371 BC) and in an effort to contain them constructed a defensive cordon consisting of Messene, Megalopolis, Mantineia and Árgos.

TOUR *about 3 hours*

A road runs across the site past the principal points of interest.

Circuit Wall★★. – The circuit wall, which dates from 4C BC and was well known in antiquity, had four gates, was over 9km – 5 1/2 miles long and turned the town into a sort of fortress. It was reinforced at regular intervals by towers and reached up to 2.50m – 8ft thick in some places; although only 4-5m – 13-16ft high it was protected by the escarpment below.

The best preserved section is on the north side of the site around the **Arkadia Gate** and forms a perfect system of defence. In fact the gateway consists of two sets of gates separated by an unusual round courtyard enclosed by strong walls constructed without mortar of stone blocks with projecting faces; the niches contained statues of the divinities who protected the city. The inner gate comprises an enormous monolithic lintel; the outer gate is flanked by two projecting square towers from which it could be protected by volleys of arrows and javelins.

Follow the ancient road (wheel ruts) out beyond the gate for a view of the ramparts; several tombs have been found in this area: handsome sarcophagus near to the Arkadia Gate.

Asklepieion★. – *Open 8.45am to 3pm (9.30am to 2.30pm Sundays).* A path leading off the road northwest of Mavromáti descends to a sanctuary dedicated to Asklepios (Aesculapius) which was formerly thought to be an agora *(signpost: Ithómi, Archaeological site; about 1/2 hour on foot Rtn)*.

Recent excavations have uncovered the foundations of a temple to Asklepios from the Hellenistic period together with a sacrificial altar. The temple stood in the centre of a courtyard surrounded by porticoes; the bases of the colonnades have been revealed; in the corners are traces of semicircular benches *(exedrae)*. As at Epidauros, next to the sanctuary there is a theatre which was also used as a meeting place for ritual ceremonies.

Lakonia Gate. – From Mavromáti drive up to the Lakonia Gate which provides a fine view of Mount Éva where there used to be a sanctuary to Dionysos; below lies the new Voulkáno Convent.

Mount Ithómi. – Alt 798m – 2 618ft. From the Lakonia Gate a steep path *(1 1/2 hours on foot Rtn)* climbs up past the remains of a temple to Artemis to the ancient **citadel of Ithome** (Ithómi).

At the summit is the old **Voulkáno Convent,** which was founded in 8C on the site of a temple to Zeus and abandoned in 1950. Under the Franks it housed a Templar commandery which later passed to the knights of St John of Jerusalem. Magnificent **views★★** of Messene, the region of Messenia and the southern Peloponnese.

MESSENIAN GULF Road★★★

Peloponnese – Messinía – Michelin map 980 folds 40 and 41

The magnificent road from Areópoli to Kalamáta, which often climbs high into the western foothills of the Taÿgetos chain, provides frequent views of the indented eastern shoreline of the Messenian Gulf where the empty waves sparkle into the distance.

The road passes through a varied landscape: fairly austere in the south on the edge of the Máni *(p 130)* where the ravines and slopes are partially covered by scrub and untended olive groves; more hospitable further north where cultivated basins alternate with terraced hillsides dotted with dark rows of cypress trees and clumps of pine trees.

The villages are very charming; their houses cluster on the hillsides round the main square with its fountain and giant plane tree in the shade of which a café is often to be found; there are many Byzantine and post-Byzantine churches.

All along the coast there are deserted little inlets perfect for bathing.
The coast from Areópoli round to Gíthio is described on pp 130-132.

FROM AREÓPOLI TO KALAMÁTA
80km – 50 miles – about 2 hours plus 2 hours for visiting

From Areópoli take the road north to Kalamáta; view of Kelefá Castle and Ítilo.

Ítilo. – *Map p 122.* The ancient capital of the Máni, now a wine-producing centre, stands on a hill facing the Turkish castle of Kelefá (16C and 17C) inland and a sheltered bay on the coast (Néo Ítilo) where Napoleon's fleet anchored in 1798 en route for Egypt. In 17C it was the port of embarkation for those Maniots who settled in Corsica *(p 130)*. On the slope below the road lies the **Dekólou Monastery** (18C); the church is decorated with frescoes and wood carvings (iconostasis, baldaquin).

At Langáda with its towers there are superb views down into the gulf.

Thalamés. – Pop 106. 13C church of St Sophia.

In an enclosure on the east side of the road between Thalamés and Nomitsí stands the **church of the Transfiguration** (Metamórfossis) which dates from 11C; unusual capitals carved with Byzantine motifs (peacocks, cockerels...); traces of frescoes.

Nomitsí. – Pop 109. Beside the road through the village stands the chapel of Sts Cosmas and Damian (Anárgiri); it takes the rare form of a cruciform plan within a square; it has a rooftop belfry and the interior is decorated with frescoes.

1km – 1/2 mile beyond Nomitsí the isolated chapel of St Demetrios appears on the left.

St Demetrios' Chapel ★ (Ágios Dimítrios). – This little chapel (13C) stands among the olives and cypresses on the terraced hillside facing Korone across the Messenian Gulf. Beyond a clump of pine trees, about 100m – 110yds further on, the whole of the Messenian Gulf is revealed in a magnificent **view★★★**.

The road continues on its steep and winding course to Kardamíli.

Kardamíli ★ – Pop 277: Kardamíli is a simple holiday resort and fishing port protected by a fortified islet offshore; its old houses cluster on the banks of a mountain stream. The best known church is St Spiridon's (13C): low relief carvings and fine pointed belfry with four storeys of arcading.

The land behind Kardamíli, now planted with olive trees, was once guarded by Beaufort Castle which was built by the Franks on a withdrawn site.

North of the town the road climbs offering superb **views★★** back over the Kardamíli basin and the coast and then descends into the Kámbos basin guarded by the medieval remains of Zarnáta Castle.

Koskarás Defile★. – The river has created a gorge which is spanned by a bold modern bridge. Park the car and climb down a short way to admire the design and the site. On emerging from the mountains the road enters the Kalamáta basin and skirts the shore until it reaches the town.

METÉORA★★★

Thessaly – Tríkala – Michelin map 980 fold 16

North of Kalambáka *(p 119)* in the northwest corner of the Thessalian plain a group of fantastic elephant-grey rocks rises up out of the trees in the flat Peneios valley. Perched on the top of these huge and precipitous columns of rock are the famous cenobitic monasteries known as the Metéora which means "in the air".

An unusual natural phenomenon. – These towers of rock stand on the border between the Píndos massif and the Thessalian plain at the lower end of the gorges carved by the waters of the Peneios and its tributaries in the limestone of the Píndos range. The flow of surface water has created the valley leaving the pillars of sandstone and tertiary conglomerate standing up to 300m – 984ft high above the surrounding plain. There are some sixty of these columns of rock, a favourite haunt of vultures.

Between heaven and earth. – It was in 11C that the first hermits sought refuge in the caves of the Metéora where the solitude and broad horizons favoured the mystic way of life. When the Serbs invaded Thessaly in 14C and brigands roamed the land, the hermits began to group together in monasteries. The first was founded by **St Athanasius** from Mount Athos, who established the Great Meteoron with nine monks on an almost inaccessible site. Others followed his example despite the considerable difficulties involved in transporting the building material to the top of the rocks by manpower or by hoist.

During the 15C and 16C the number of monasteries grew to 24 and the buildings were decorated with frescoes and icons by the great artists of the day such as **Theophanes,** a monk from Crete, who also worked on Mount Athos, and his followers. Unfortunately rivalry between the communities and a decrease in the number of vocations led to a decline; today only four monasteries are inhabited by monks or nuns: St Nicholas, the Great Meteoron, Varlaám and St Stephen's.

135

MÉTÉORA★★★

Originally the only access was by means of very long ladders which could be drawn up when not in use or in a basket or net suspended on ropes from a winch which was mounted in a tower above the void; according to travellers in the past the ropes were not replaced until they broke. Steps have now been cut in the rock face and there is a fine modern road serving the main monasteries.

TOUR *17km – 10 1/2 miles – about 1/2 hour – plus 3 hours visiting*

A tour based on Kalambáka will include the monasteries and magnificent views of the Píndos mountains and the Peneios valley; those with limited time are advised to visit the Great Meteoron and the Varlaám monasteries. *Formal dress required (p 30).*

Leave Kalambáka going west; soon after passing through Kastráki, leave the car and take the path on the left.

The Chapel of the Virgin on the "Column" of Doúpiani was part of the Doúpiani hermitage to which, until 14C, the scattered hermits were attached.

The road continues to the foot of St Nicholas' Monastery.

St Nicholas' Monastery★ (Ágios Nikólaos). – *Open 9am to 1pm and 3 to 6pm; 50 Dr.*
Although the monastery dates from 14C the church was built in 16C and was decorated at that time by Theophanes the Cretan with remarkable frescoes (the Last Judgment, the Dormition of St Ephraim) which were restored in 1960.

The road skirts the foot of the rock on which stands the Roussánou Monastery *(closed – see below)* and reaches a T junction. Bear left past the Varlaám Monastery *(see below)* to reach the Great Meteoron.

Great Meteoron Monastery★★ (Megálo Metéoro). – *Pop 6. Open 9am to 1pm and 3 to 6pm; closed Tuesdays; 50 Dr. Access by steps cut in the rock emerging near the tower with its winch and basket.*
The Great Meteoron is built on a broad platform of rock *(platís líthos)* (alt 534m – 1 752ft). It was founded as the Monastery of the Transfiguration (Metamórphosis) in 1356 by St Athanasius and enriched with relics and works of art by his successor St Ioasaph (John Uros), a member of the ruling family in Serbia.

Church. – The apse and the chancel date from 14C and are decorated with mid 15C frescoes; the rest of the building was rebuilt in mid 16C and consists of a huge narthex and an unusual transept built on the square cross plan with lateral apses roofed by domes, in accordance with an architectural style inherited from Mount Athos. The walls are decorated with contemporary frescoes, in an austere style, depicting the founders, St Athanasius and St Ioasaph *(west wall of the crossing)*; St Ioasaph's tomb is in the narthex. The bishop's throne, which is inlaid with mother of pearl, is a 17C work.

The **Refectory** (mid 16C), which lies to the north, next to the kitchen, is an imposing hall, divided into two aisles and roofed with domes. It now houses the Treasury: manuscripts, icons including some dating from 14C, liturgical ornaments, reliquaries and a carved cross of St Daniel.

From the southeast of the monastery there is an impressive **view** over the other pillars of rock, particularly the one bearing the Varlaám Monastery.

Retrace the last section of the road and bear right to the Varlaám Monastery.

Varlaám Monastery★★. – Pop. 8 *Open 8am to 12.30pm and 3 to 6.30pm.* A footbridge and a stairway lead up to the monastery which is perched above a ravine up which visitors and provisions used to be hoisted by the machinery in the winch tower (16C).

The monastery was founded in 1518 by two brothers, who belonged to a rich family called Aparas from Ioánina, on the site of a 14C cenobitic hermitage established by Barlaam.

(Photograph J. Bottin)

The Metéora.

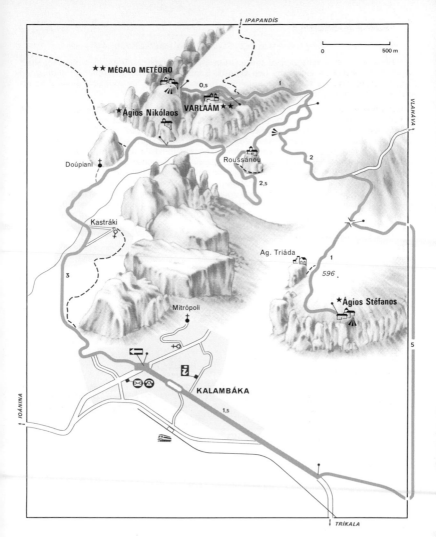

Church. – All Saints' (Ágii Pándes) Church, which incorporates the original 14C chapel dedicated to the Three Hierarchs, was completed in 1544 and is decorated with a remarkable collection of **frescoes**★★, restored in 1970.

The frescoes in the narthex, which date from 1566, recall the Last Judgment and the Life of John the Baptist; the walls are covered with figures of ascetics and there are portraits of the Aparas brothers near their tomb.

The frescoes in the church proper show western influence in the realistic poses and colours; they are the work of Frango Catellano of Thebes (1548): Christ in the dome, the Dormition of the Virgin and the Crucifixion on the west wall and effigies of St John of Damascus and St Cosmas Melodus on either side of the entrance.

The 17C frescoes in the Chapel of the Three Hierarchs are well preserved and include two masterly scenes: the Dormition of St John Chrysostom and the Dormition of St Ephraim the Syrian.

Also worthy of attention is the carved and gilded iconostasis (16C icon of the Virgin and Child) and the furnishings which are inlaid with mother of pearl.

Conventual buildings. – The refectory which houses the Treasury (including an icon of the Virgin by E. Tzanés), the infirmary, the store rooms (enormous barrel holding 12 000l – 2 640 gals), the wine press and the tower with its winch.

Return downhill to the road junction across the river; either bear right to Kastráki or, if there is time, bear left into the road which follows the slope of the hill: spectacular **view**★★ of the little **Roussánou Monastery** *(closed)*, rebuilt in 16C on a bizarrely shaped rock.

Further on at the second T junction the road on the right leads past the 15C and 17C buildings of **Holy Trinity Monastery** (Agía Triáda – pop 1) *(closed)*, crowning an enormous pillar of rock to St Stephen's Monastery.

St Stephen's Monastery★ (Ágios Stéfanos). – Pop 21. *Open 8am to 12 noon and 3 to 6pm; closed Mondays.* The convent is reached by a bridge spanning the chasm which separates the rock pillar from the mountain mass. It was founded in the late 15C on the site of a 12C hermitage and is now occupied by nuns. There are two churches: the older one was built in 15C on the basilical plan and is decorated with frescoes similar to those in the Church of the Transfiguration; the more recent is late 18C and contains a reliquary in which the head of St Charalambos is venerated.

There is a rich museum housing fine 16C and 17C icons by E. Tzanés, 17C illuminated manuscripts and 16C embroidery.

Splendid **views**★★ of the Peneios valley and Thessaly.

Return to the T junction and bear right downhill to Kalambáka.

Methone, the watchtower of the eastern Mediterranean, stands on a pleasant site★ overlooking a bay protected by two islands, Sapiéndza and Shíza, which provide good inshore fishing grounds. A beach adjoining the quiet fishing harbour with several hotels and tavernas makes it a pleasant place to stay.

A desirable possession. – A chance wind in 1204 blew Geoffrey de Villehardouin *(p 118)* into Methone harbour as he was returning from the Holy Land but he left soon after to join William de Champlitte in the conquest of the Peloponnese.

When the conquest was complete Methone was assigned to the Venetians who called it **Modon** and held it for nearly three centuries, except for a Genoese interlude from 1354 to 1403 when the Venetian fleet took its revenge and defeated the Genoese naval force under the French Marshal Boucicaut. Methone became a bishopric and earned its living by producing silk and supplying the Venetian galleys that put in on their way to Syria.

In 1500 however the Turkish army under Bayazid II captured the town after a month of bombardment. The Venetians returned in 1686 until 1715 when Methone once again fell to the Turks who held it until 19C. In 1824 Miaoúlis *(p 113)* attacked the Ottoman fleet with fire ships and burned 25 Turkish vessels.

Finally in 1828 General Maison recaptured Methone from Ibrahim Pasha and used the troops of the French expeditionary force to rebuild parts of the town.

Citadel★★. – *Open 8am to 7pm (6pm Sundays); 100 Dr; about 1 hour.*

The citadel was begun in 13C on the site of an earlier fortress in a very strong position on a promontory surrounded by the sea on three sides. Further building took place in 15C, 16C and 18C. Most of the construction is the work of the Venetians as is shown by the lions of St Mark and the carved escutcheons which adorn the building. During

Methone. – Boúrdzi Tower

the Venetian occupation a whole town was squeezed round the cathedral within the fortifications but when Chateaubriand visited Methone in 1806 on his way to the Holy Land the Turks were camping in tents and makeshift buildings.

Beyond the counterscarp a bridge built by General Maison spans the moat which was covered by cross-fire from the **Bembo bastion** (15C) *(right)* and the **Loredan bastion** (1714) *(left)* which was well provided with artillery.

An outer gate (early 18C) opens into a passage against the northern rampart (13C); a vaulted approach precedes the main gate, the **Land Gate** (13C) which has Gothic arches and gives access to the open space once occupied by the medieval town: on the right stands a wall of the keep rebuilt by the Turks in 16C; opposite is a monolithic granite column erected by the Venetians in 1494 and originally crowned by the lion of St Mark.

Follow the eastern rampart *(clockwise)*; on the left lies the port, on the right the confused remains of a Turkish bath, some cisterns, a powder magazine and the old Latin cathedral.

The **Sea Gate** on the south side of the citadel, which was rebuilt by the Turks using Venetian material (stone bearing a lion carving and the Foscolo arms), gives access to the picturesque **Boúrdzi Tower★**, which was rebuilt by the Turks in 16C on an island of rock and linked to the citadel by a bridge; climb to the platform for a splendid view★★ of the citadel, the harbour and the islands.

The western rampart with its five towers, which probably dates from 13C, leads back to the keep; most of its fortifications date from 15C but it was modernised in 18C (firing steps for artillery). On the landward side of the moat, at the very end of the counterscarp, there is another defensive construction called a redoubt.

Métsovo is admirably situated in a mountain comb just below the highest road pass in Greece (alt 1 705m – 5 594ft) which marks the border between Epiros *(west)* and Thessaly *(east)*. A few bears and wolves survive in the surrounding ancient forests of beech and pine trees. The little town is not only a summer resort offering the benefits of bracing mountain air but also a winter sports centre with skiing on the slopes of Mount Karakóli *(ski lift)*. Métsovo is famous for its trout, its spirits and its cheese as well as for its embroidered cloth and wood carvings.

Past reflections. – Métsovo, which is inhabited mainly by Vlachs *(p 13)*, was already prosperous under the Turkish occupation when the town enjoyed a relative autonomy. Many important families, Greek or Vlach, lived there, occasionally receiving the Klephts *(p 24)* who were being pursued by the occupying force. Certain of the families, such as the **Avéroff** and the **Tosítsa,** who had made their fortunes growing cotton in Egypt, bequeathed large sums to their native city as well as to Athens and the Greek state, thus contributing to the development of modern Greece.

Métsovo has moreover retained a character of its own. In the steep streets, paved with stones set on edge, there are mountain ponies loaded with wood, mules carrying packs and sheep herded by shepherds with crooks. The beautiful corbelled houses are roofed with stone.

Many of the inhabitants still wear the local dress: the men in dark blue, with baggy trousers or pleated skirt *(fustanélla)* and clogs adorned with pompons *(tsaroúhias);* the women in skirt, blouse and embroidered apron, a dark scarf on the head. On Sundays there is often traditional dancing in the square.

SIGHTS *2 hours*

Church of Agía Paraskeví. – At the centre of Métsovo there is a vast open space shaded by huge plane trees; nearby is the Church of Agía Paraskeví which contains a rich 18C **iconostasis★** carved with flamboyant motifs.

Follow the main street and turn left into a narrow street which climbs up to the museum *(signpost)* at the heart of the old district.

Museum★. – *Guided tours 8am to 1pm and 3 to 6pm; closed Thursdays; 50 Dr.*

The museum, which is devoted to local Epirot art, is housed in the Tosítsa family residence; Michael Tosítsa (1781-1858) founded the Polytechnic in Athens.

The interior has been richly adorned with carved woodwork (particularly the ceilings); the rooms are furnished with carpets and embroidered textiles and decorated with gold ornaments, beaten copperwork and icons. The huge reception room is particularly impressive with its divans and its monumental samovar.

Return to the main square and take the path on the right of the Bank of Greece *(signpost)* which leads down the slope into the Árahtos valley to St Nicholas' Monastery *(3/4 hour on foot Rtn).*

Monastery of St Nicholas★ (**Ágios Nikólaos**). – *Open 8am to 1pm and 5pm to sunset.*

This little convent has been pleasantly restored. A display of icons has been arranged in the narthex. The walls of the 14C church are painted with 16C-17C frescoes and the iconostasis is profusely decorated with gold and carving.

The conventual buildings contain the monks' cells, the room belonging to the Superior *(igoúmenos)* and the secret school where the children were taught during the Turkish occupation.

MISSOLONGHI _____ *Messolóngi*

Central Greece – Akarnanía – Pop 10 164 – Michelin map ⑨⑧⓪ north of fold 28

Missolonghi is famous for the death of Lord Byron and for a heroic siege. It lies on the edge of a lagoon, surrounded by salt marshes and fish ponds. Here one can taste botargo *(avgotáraho),* a relish made of salt fish roe from the tunny or the grey mullet.

10km – 6 1/2 miles to the east stood the ancient city of Calydon; the king had failed to sacrifice to Artemis who therefore sent a monstrous boar to ravage the whole region. The hunting and killing of the beast by **Meleager** and his companion Atalanta was a favourite scene with artists.

Missolonghi and the War of Independence. – The first Turkish attack was launched in 1822; the following year Missolonghi was again threatened. It was defended by **Márkos Bótzaris** *(p 108),* a Souliot.

Lord Byron enters the fray. – In January 1824 the great Philhellene poet Lord Byron arrived from Leukas accompanied by a doctor and nine servants. His wardrobe contained six military uniforms in various colours decorated with gold and silver braid, together with sashes, epaulettes, waistcoats and cocked hats, two gilded helmets and ten swords. More importantly he also brought funds raised by the London Greek Committee. His chief task was to unite and rally the various Greek factions. For relaxation he would paddle across the lagoon and go hunting on horseback over the flat country.

Byron's Death. – Riding home one day he was caught in a rainstorm and the chill April wind brought on a fever. His doctors resorted to bleeding but on 19 April 1824 he died. The Greeks proclaimed 21 days of mourning. His embalmed body was placed in a tin-lined case with 180 gallons of spirit in a large barrel and embarked for Zakynthos to a 37 gun salute. His remains arrived in London on the brig Florida but such was his reputation he was refused burial in Westminster Abbey. It was not until 1969 that a plaque was dedicated to him in Poets' Corner.

Fall of Missolonghi. – The final siege began in April 1825 when Reshid Pasha (known to the Greeks as Kiutahi) arrived at the head of 15 000 men; the besieged behind their feeble defences numbered only 5 000 but they fought furiously and made many sorties so that a year later they were still holding out when Ibrahim Pasha arrived with 10 000 Egyptian reinforcements.

The Greeks had run out of food and decided to make a mass sortie *(éxodos)* during the night of 22 to 23 April 1826. 9 000 set out including many women and children but they were decimated by the Turks who had been alerted by a traitor and only 1 800 reached Amphissa about 50 miles to the east. Chrístos Kapsális and the last defenders blew up the powder store burying themselves and their attackers under the ruins.

The impact of this historic gesture was magnified by the writings of Chateaubriand and Hugo and the paintings of Delacroix (Greece on the Ruins of Missolonghi), Ary Scheffer and David d'Angers.

Heroes' Garden. – Within the ramparts, which were restored by King Otho, and near the Sortie Gate is a pleasant garden planted with palm trees, oleanders and cypresses beneath which lie the tombs and commemorative monuments of the heroes of the War of Independence.

There is a tumulus to the nameless dead, a **statue of Byron** on the spot where his heart is buried and, on a platform *(right)*, the **tomb of Bótzaris** surmounted by a Child of Greece *(kóri tis Elládos)* reading the hero's name on a stone: the graceful white marble figure was sculpted in 1827 by David d'Angers.

Museum. – *In the Town Hall (Dimarhío) in the main square. Open daily 8am to 2pm (9.30am to 1pm Saturdays, Sundays, holidays).*

Souvenirs of the siege of Missolonghi and of the War of Independence are displayed on the staircase and first floor of the Town Hall. A room *(right at top of stairs)* contains souvenirs of Byron.

Downstairs a series of pictures shows local fishermen on the lagoon in their shallow square-sailed boats spearing fish with a multi-pronged implement.

EXCURSIONS

Tourlída. – Pop 7. *6km – 3 3/4 miles south; fish restaurants; beach.* The road south beside the lagoon gives a fine view of the stagnant waters gleaming in the pearly light; this is the haunt of many sea birds attracted by the rich fishing grounds (grey mullet, eels). The fishermen's huts are built on piles beside the fish hatcheries which are reached in huge flat-bottomed boats.

Etolikó. – Pop 4 368. *11km – 6 3/4 miles northwest.* Take the coast road which runs past the marshes and a salt refinery.

This picturesque little city on the lagoon reminds one of Venice. It was built in the Middle Ages on an islet commanding the entrance to an inlet and linked to the mainland by two symmetrical dykes. Miniature churches and the low houses of the fishermen and craftsmen line the network of narrow streets.

To the west at the mouth of the River Ahelóos the alluvion deposited by the river has created a fertile plain growing rice and water melons, the habitat of storks (many nests at Neohóri).

MONEMVASSÍA★★

Peloponnese – Lakonía – Pop 52 – Michelin map 980 folds 41 and 42

Visitors to Monemvassía experience the feeling that they have reached the world's end. This silent partially ruined medieval fortified town is half hidden in a slight depression on the southern face of a steep rock which stands just offshore creating a particularly spectacular **site**★★★.

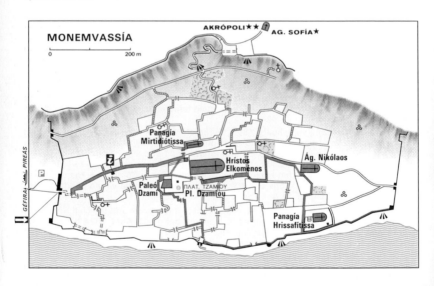

MONEMVASSÍA

AKRÓPOLI★★ AG. SOFÍA★

0   200 m

Panagía Mirtidiótissa

Hrístos Elkoménos

Ág. Nikólaos

Paleó Dzamí   ΠΛΑΤ. ΤΖΑΜΙΟΥ Pl. Dzamíou

Panagía Hrissafítissa

GÉFIRA — PIREAS

HISTORICAL NOTES

"The only entrance". – The rock, which is 300m – 984ft high, is linked to the mainland by a narrow causeway and a bridge and takes its name from the Greek words *"móni emvassía"* meaning "only entrance".

Monemvassía was fortified by the Byzantines against the Slav invasions but in 1248 after a three year blockade it fell into the hands of William de Villehardouin. The Franks repaired the castle but in 1263 William was obliged to return it to Michael VIII Palaiologos as part of his ransom *(p 147)*.

Under the Despotate of Morea *(p 147)* the Byzantines maintained an active trading port at Monemvassía which was on the route to Constantinople. In 1460 the town passed into the hands of the Pope for four years before becoming a Venetian possession. In 1540 it was captured by the Turks who held it until 1821 except for a brief period between 1690 and 1715 when it was retaken by the Venetians. During its time as a Venetian possession, when it was known as Malvasia or Napoli di Malvasia, Monemvassía was an important trading port and port of call in the Levant. The town was protected by a fortified bridge, 163m – 535ft long, carried on 13 arches which could be breached in time of danger, by a castle on the top of the rock and by a circuit wall which descended from the top of the hill, swung round along the seafront and up the hill again thus enclosing the town on three sides. In those days the population numbered 30 000 and was served by about 40 churches.

Throughout the Middle Ages and on into 19C Monemvassía exported Malmsey wine (known in French as Malvoisie as was the town too), a sweet white wine, produced mostly in the Aegean islands as well as locally, which was very popular in England. When the Duke of Clarence *(p 122)* was condemned to death by his brother Edward IV in 1477, he elected to be drowned in a butt of Malmsey wine.

In 1909 the Greek poet Yannis Ritsos was born in Monemvassía.

TOUR *about 4 hours*

It is possible to reach Monemvassía by road *(bus from Sparta)* but it is more spectacular to arrive by sea *(boats from Piraeus 3 times a week taking 9 hours; hydrofoil from Zéa [Piraeus] every day in the season taking 4 hours)*. Hotels and restaurants in Géfira (pop 547) on the mainland; one taverna, rooms and flats to let in Monemvassía. Food shops and bank (certain days only) in Géfira; extensive beach on the mainland shore. 1/2 hour on foot from Géfira to Monemvassía; taxis.

Monemvassia. – The main street

Old Town★★. – First there is the causeway – the "only entrance" – and the West Gate into the town which is a vaulted chicane; both it and the walls date from the Despotate but were repaired by the Venetians. Walk up the main street between the ancient houses to the main square.

Mosque Square (Platía Dzamíou). – This charming square extends southwards into a terrace graced by an 18C canon and the observation hole of an underground cistern. On the east side stands the **Church of Christ in Chains** (Christós Elkomenós), a former cathedral which was founded in 12C by the Byzantines and rebuilt late in 17C by the Venetians; note the detached belltower, as in Italy, and the symbolic peacocks carved in low relief on a piece of Byzantine sculpture which has been re-used in the façade.

Opposite stands the little church of St Paul, which dates from the late 10C and was converted into a mosque (Paleó Dzamí) by the Turks; it is to become a museum.

Southern Rampart. – From the main square walk down to the ramparts along the seafront and follow them eastwards. There are extensive views of the sea and the Peloponnese coast south towards Cape Malea; a postern gate gives access to the rocks where it is possible to swim.

Panagía Hrissafítissa. – The façade of this 16C church looks very Venetian with its framed doorway surmounted by an oculus; the open space in front was used as a parade ground. Near the ramparts stands a tiny chapel built over the "sacred spring"; it contains an icon from Chrysapha (Hrísafa) near Sparta.

It is worth pursuing the sentry walk to the corner bastion; return and descend to ground level to visit **St Nicholas'** (Ágios Nikólaos) which has a 16C Venetian doorway.

Return to the main square past several Venetian houses: door and window mouldings, flamboyant recesses and broad mouthed chimneys.

Panagía Mirtidiótissa. – This little church, which is up a steep rise, seems to belong to the Frankish period (13C); the façade frames a doorway surmounted by an oculus in the Venetian style. It was once a commandery belonging to the Templars and then to the Knights of St John of Jerusalem, as is shown by the sculpted escutcheon bearing the distinctive cross anchored of Pierre d'Aubusson *(p 223)*.

Citadel★★ (Akrópoli). – Originally it covered a wide area, amounting almost to a town on its own; the fortifications are for the most part Venetian (16C).

Visitors who cannot climb all the way up to the Citadel are advised to go half way up, if possible, for a very fine **view★★** of the lower town.

A vaulted passage in the fortified entrance emerges into an open space; take the path leading north up the hill to the church of St Sophia.

St Sophia★ (Agía Sofía). – St Sophia, the principal church of the citadel, is a large Byzantine church built on the edge of the cliff with a vertiginous **view★★★** of the sea below.

The building *(recently restored)* probably dates from 11C (capitals, low reliefs); it may have been occupied by Cistercians for a while during the Frankish occupation and was refurbished during the Despotate of Morea (14C-15C).

The church is built to a homogenous quandrangular plan with a narthex and an impressive dome supported on squinches. There are some unusual early Byzantine capitals in shallow relief, Byzantine marble carvings over the doors in the narthex and traces of murals.

There is a rough path leading to the highest point on the rock overlooking the isthmus and the mountains to the west; at its eastern end the rock is shaped like the prow of a ship pointing out to sea.

Return to the main gate and follow the sentry walk westwards to reach the highest point along the circuit wall: **splendid views★★** of the old town and the coast.

MYCENAE★★★

Peloponnese – Argolis – Michelin map 980 fold 29

Mycenae, city of the Atreids accursed of the gods, was the key to the opulent Argolid plain and occupied a wild and oppressive site★★★ on a rocky hill surrounded by a ring of barren mountains. The proud ruins of this city fortress, which dates from the second millenium BC, recall its Homeric epithet "rich in gold" and its warrior-kings, who pillaged and plundered and produced the Mycenaean civilisation _(see p 17)_.

LEGEND AND HISTORY

According to tradition Mycenae was founded by Perseus, son of Zeus and Danaë, who raised the city walls with the help of the Cyclops, giant builders who had but one eye in the middle of their forehead.

The tragedy of the Atreids. – After the Perseids came the Atreids whose complicated history with its trail of vengeance and death has been told by Homer in the Iliad and by Aeschylus, Sophocles and Euripides in their plays. The most well known of this accursed family are:

– **Atreus,** son of Pelops _(p 158)_, who killed the sons of his brother Thyestes and served them to him during a banquet.

– **Menelaos,** son of Atreus and king of Sparta, whose wife **Helen** was seduced by Paris, son of Priam, king of Troy, thus provoking the Trojan War.

– **Agamemnon,** Menelaos' brother, king of Mycenae and husband of **Clytemnestra,** Helen's sister; he was the leader of the Achaians in the expedition against Troy, the king of kings who ordered the sacrifice of his daughter Iphigenia at Aulis _(p 79)_ to obtain a favourable wind.

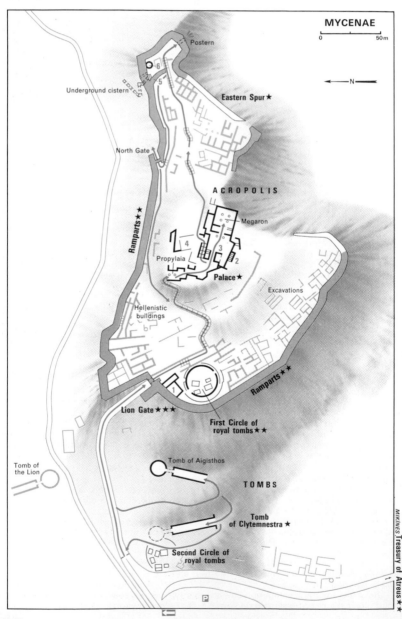

MIKÍNES Treasury of Atreus ★★

- **Aigisthos,** younger son of Thyestes who killed his uncle Atreus to avenge his father's death and became Clytemnestra's lover; she asked him to get rid of Agamemnon and his captive **Cassandra,** Priam's daughter, on their return from Troy.
- **Orestes,** son of Agamemnon and Clytemnestra, who is persuaded by his sister **Electra** to kill Clytemnestra and her lover Aigisthos; he is pursued by the Furies *(p 123)* but acquitted on the Areopagos in Athens by a jury presided over by Athena and then purified by Apollo on the *omphalos* in Delphi before ascending the throne of Mycenae; he gave his sister Electra in marriage to his faithful friend **Pylades.**

For many years these people were thought to be legendary figures. As a result of Schliemann's discoveries, historians and archaeologists now think that they really existed but that their actions have been transposed by the poets, above all by **Homer.** What is certain however is that from 16C to 12C BC when the Achaian city was destroyed by Dorian invaders, Mycenae was the richest and most powerful state in the Mediterranean world and had close relations with Crete and even Egypt.

Excavations. – By the time of Pausanias (2C BC) Mycenae was already reduced to a few overgrown ruins. Early in 19C however the Lion Gate and the so-called Tomb of Agamemnon was known to travellers, although the heraldic aspect of the lions led to certain false assumptions: a French scientific expedition to the Morea in 1828 thought they were looking at a Frankish castle.

Then came **Heinrich Schliemann** (1822-1890). He was a German businessman who made a fortune in the grocery trade and was obsessed with the Homeric heroes. Having retired from business at the age of 45, this brilliant amateur discovered the site of Troy on the coast of Asia Minor in 1874 while searching for King Priam's treasure.

Two years later he began to dig on the site of Mycenae in the hope of finding the tomb of Agamemnon and his retainers who were massacred by Aigisthos' assassins during a banquet. Guided by a sentence in Pausanias which said that Agamemnon had been buried within the city walls, Schliemann very soon discovered, just inside the Lion Gate, beneath a mound, the first circle of royal tombs containing 19 corpses which he thought were those of Agamemnon, Cassandra and their companions. The men wore golden face masks and golden breast plates; the women wore golden fillets, necklaces and bracelets. In 25 days a whole collection of jewellery, vases and precious items was recorded which is now the glory of the Mycenean room in the Athens Museum. These discoveries made a great stir.

Schliemann was followed at the end of the century by two Greek scholars, Stamatákes and Tsoúntas. Extensive excavations were undertaken this century by the British School in Athens in 1920 and again in the 1950s. Restoration work was begun by the Greek Archaeological School in 1951 when they also discovered the second circle of royal tombs near the tomb of Clytemnestra. Excavations are still in progress on the site within the western wall. *A museum is being built near the Tomb of the Lion to display the objects excavated on the site which are now in the National Archaeological Museum in Athens.*

TOUR *about 3 hours*

Access. – *The road running through the modern village of Mikínes (pop 440) is lined with tavernas and inns:* one of them, at the sign of Fair Helen (Belle Hélène) and King Menelaos, was mentioned by the Greek poet Seféris in some verses which have become famous.

Continue uphill to a car park (left); a short walk leads to the entrance to the archaeological site.

Open. – *8am to 5pm; 200 Dr. An electric torch is useful for visiting the tombs and the cistern. The site is slippery and fully exposed to the sun.*

ACROPOLIS

The hill on which the Acropolis was built is 278m – 912ft high and defended to the north and south by two deep ravines. The Acropolis is triangular in shape and surrounded by ramparts on all sides 900m – 2 953ft long. It housed the king, the royal family, the nobles and the palace guard. The town lay at the foot of the fortified acropolis. A few houses have been discovered below the acropolis on the left of the road.

Ramparts★★ and the Lion Gate★★★. – The "Cyclopean" fortifications date mostly from 14C-13C BC; they are built of undressed stone and vary in thickness from 3m to 8m – 10ft to 26ft.

The Lion Gate, which was the main entrance to the Acropolis, takes its name from the two wild animals sculpted on the huge monolithic pediment which measures 3.90m – 12 1/2ft at the base, 3.30m – 10 3/4ft in height and 0.70m – 2 1/4ft in width. The animals, probably lionesses, have lost their heads which were most likely inlaid and facing the front; the animals are standing on either side of a central column their front paws resting on a double altar which also supports the pillar and an entablature. This scene, which is Asiatic in inspiration, confronts the visitor from above the gateway, a symbol of Mycenaean power.

The gateway proper is flanked by two protective walls, the one on the right terminating in a tower. The entrance is 3.10m – 10ft high and 2.95m – 9 1/2ft wide; the huge size of the constituent monolithic blocks is quite astonishing; the lintel itself measures 4.50m – nearly 15ft in length, 0.80m – over 2 1/2ft in height and 1.98m – 6 1/2ft in depth and weighs over 20 tonnes. The wooden doors were reinforced by a bar which slotted into holes which are visible in the uprights.

Just over the threshold lay the porter's lodge *(left)* and the remains of a grain store (1) *(right)* where several carbonised grains of cereal were found in the bottom of some great jars.

First Circle of Royal Tombs★★. – On the right within the Lion Gate is the famous cemetery where Schliemann thought Agamemnon and his suite were buried but it is in fact much older (16C BC). Its circular outline is clearly marked by a double row of stones which formed a sort of palisade round the cemetery. It contained six shaft graves marked by stele decorated with low relief hunting scenes. The graves contained the bodies of 8 men, 9 women and 2 children accompanied by precious burial furnishings which are now displayed in the Athens Museum; the total weight of the golden articles reached 14kg – over 30lbs.

From the First Circle of Tombs take the paved "royal way" which leads from the Lion Gate up to one of the entrances to the royal palace past an area covered by houses and depositories *(southwest)* which is still being excavated.

Palace ★. – It dates from 15C BC and consists of three blocks of buildings extending as far as the eastern spur of the site. The main western block contains the **megaron** *(p 17)* which is fairly well preserved and the main stairs (2) comprising 18 steps.

The *propylaia* opened into the great courtyard (3) which was open to the sky. Beyond was the *megaron* which as can be seen from the ground plan was divided into a portico, a vestibule and the *megaron* itself, a royal chamber with a round hearth in the centre surrounded by four pillars (the bases are extant) supporting the roof; the floor was paved with slabs of gypsum and the walls were faced with stucco painted with decorative motifs in the Cretan style; the throne probably stood on the right.

The upper terrace of the palace has been altered by the later construction of a temple to Athena (4); only a few traces remain but there is a beautiful **view** of the site.

Visitors can either return to the Lion Gate or continue to the eastern spur of the site.

Eastern Spur ★. – The remains of a later set of fortifications (5), dating from 12C BC can be seen at this end of the fortress as well as an open cistern (6) from the Hellenistic period.

On the right a postern opens to the southeast revealing an interesting view of the ramparts from the outside. On the left is the entrance to an underground stair; its 99 steps bend round beneath the walls to a secret **cistern** 18m – 59ft below; it was supplied with water from the Perseia spring which flowed in terracotta conduits.

Follow the inside of the north rampart to the **North Gate** (2.30m – 7 1/2ft high; 1.50m – 5ft wide); the external approach is protected by a jutting section of wall from which the defenders of the citadel commanded the vulnerable side of their attackers, the right side of the body which is not protected by a shield. It is worth walking out through the gate for a few yards to get an overall view of the ramparts. Return into the citadel and take the path between the palace and the jumbled ruins of some Hellenistic buildings to regain the Lion Gate.

TOMBS

About 50m – 55yds from the Lion Gate turn left down to the entrance to **Aigisthos' Tomb** (15C BC); the vault has fallen in.
Pass on to "Clytemnestra's Tomb".

"Clytemnestra's Tomb" ★. – 14C BC. A communal royal tomb beneath a dome, more recent than the shaft graves. The path to the entrance is 35m – 38yds long and 5m – 5 1/2yds wide and leads to a door 5.48m – 18ft high surmounted by a lintel made of enormous blocks of stone; the bases of the framing columns are still visible on either side.

The huge round funeral chamber (diameter 13.50m – 44ft) is roofed with a dome *(recently reconstructed)* which reaches to 12.96m – 42 1/2ft above the floor. The lintel over the door is curved to follow the curve of the dome and extends on either side in a stone stringcourse.

Second Circle of Royal Tombs. – 17C BC. The lefthand side of Clytemnestra's Tomb impinges on this second circle of tombs which was excavated in 1951 and is older than the circle discovered by Schliemann. Unfortunately the stone surround composed of huge blocks of limestone is in poor condition.

The circle enclosed 24 graves, of which 14 were communal shaft graves, containing important archaeological material which is now in the Athens Museum: a remarkable rock crystal vase in the form of a duck.

Return to the car park and drive down the road to the entrance to the Treasury of Atreus (right).

Treasury of Atreus or "Tomb of Agamemnon" ★★. – 13C BC. This is the largest and the most beautiful of the nine communal beehive tombs which have been discovered to the west and southwest of the Acropolis of Mycenae. It was partially hewn out of the hillside and originally masked under a covering of earth; it is approached by a path 36m – 39yds long and 6m – over 20ft wide.

The door, which is 5.40m – nearly 18ft high and tapers towards the top, is framed by pilasters formerly preceded by two green marble half columns standing on bases which are still in position. The lintel is composed of two colossal blocks of stone: the one facing the interior is shaped to follow the curve of the dome and weighed about 120 tonnes. Resting on the lintel is a "relieving triangle" masked by a sculpted rectangular panel.

The round **funerary chamber** which is 13.39m – 44ft high and 14.60m – 48ft in diameter gives an impression of majestic strength. The skilful rows of stonework, each overlapping slightly towards the centre and cut away to form the conical vault, were ornamented with bronze rosettes and geometric motifs held in place with nails. A passage *(right)*, 2.50m – over 8ft high, with another relieving triangle over the entrance, leads into a smaller rectangular chamber hollowed out of the rock; some think it was the funeral chamber of the head of the family; others that it was the treasury itself.

GREEN TOURIST GUIDES
Picturesque scenery, buildings
Attractive routes
Touring programmes
Plans of towns and buildings.

MYKONOS★★   *Míkonos*

Cyclades – Pop 5 530 – Michelin map 𝟵𝟴𝟬 fold 32

The granite island of Mykonos is one of the most typical of the Cyclades. It is arid with wild wind-swept coasts; the outline of its cubic houses is clear cut; its windmills and chapels stand out against the brilliant transparent light.

Despite its reputation as a fashionable resort where people of all sorts congregate, Mykonos has nonetheless retained its peculiar timeless beauty. The island is moreover the starting point for an excursion to Delos *(p 95)*.

Access. – *By boat: every morning from Piraeus taking 5 or 6 hours; supplementary services in the afternoon in the season; daily (except Mondays) from Rafína, via Ándros and Tenos; the ships anchor at the entrance to the harbour.*

By air: from Athens twice a day during the season taking about 3/4 hour. Cars not allowed.

Hotels and restaurants. – In summer it is difficult to find room in the hotels but it is possible to lodge in a private house. In the town there are many tavernas (fish a speciality), cafés and tea rooms (*amigdalotá* made of almond paste). Lively night life: discotheques.

Beaches. – The most popular beaches (fine sand) are Platís Gialós (camping) and Ágios Stéfanos which can be reached by bus. On the south coast there are many sheltered inlets which are accessible by taxi or caique; some of them, such as Paradise and Super Paradise, are reserved for naturists. There is an excursion from Kalafáti beach (water skiing) to **Dragoníssi** : marine caves where a few seals live.

A cradle for sailors... and a haven for pirates. – In 13C to 14C Mykonos was a dependency of the Duchy of Náxos and ruled by the **Ghizi** of Venice; it remained in Venetian hands until 18C. They introduced Roman Catholicism and built the warehouses where the merchants of Venice and Marseille came for supplies.

Under the Turkish occupation, which was not strictly imposed, the difficulty of landing on the island because of the prevailing winds made it an ideal refuge for pirates, both Berber and Christian, who beached their dhows in the secluded inlets.

During the War of Independence the local sailors distinguished themselves in Tombazis' fleet. The island prided itself on its heroine, **Mando Mavrogenous,** who was young and rich, and at her own expense equipped two ships with which she repulsed about a hundred Algerian Berbers who suffered 17 dead and 60 wounded. In 1823 she composed the famous "Letter to the Women of Paris" extolling the struggle for Greek freedom. She died at a great age in poverty in Páros.

MYKONOS TOWN★★ (Pop 4 469)

The white buildings of Mykonos are linked by a network of narrow streets, originally intended to cut off the wind... and to frustrate pirates! Nowadays it is pleasant to wander about, always discovering new perspectives: arched or vaulted alleys, little squares shaded by an almond tree, or a pepper tree or a carob tree, pathways winding between high white walls topped by hibiscus and bougainvillea. There are said to be over 300 chapels on the island, built as votive offerings by the sailors, their domes painted in lively colours. The cuboid houses, their sharp lines softened by layers of whitewash, are charming with their flower bedecked balconies, their outside stairs, their shuttered and arched ground floors where there is sometimes the click-clack of a loom, their courtyards shaded by a vine or a fig tree. Here and there are craftsmen at work, old women talking, donkeys trotting past, street stalls and tavernas.

The harbour★★ (Limáni). – Caiques and old tubs bump against one another as the water laps against the curved marble quays. The lively waterfront is lined by the arcades of the 18C town hall, a lonely little chapel (**A**) dedicated to St Nicholas, patron saint of navigators, café terraces and craft shops as far as Mando Mavrogeneous Square where a monument (**B**) has been erected to the local heroine. From time to time the famous pelicans waddle into view.

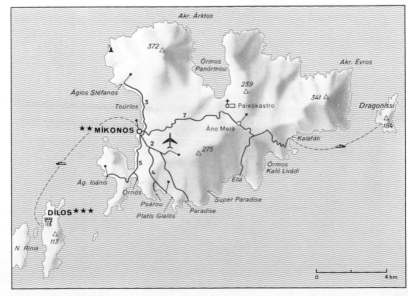

View of Mykonos★★. – A steep street, Odós Leondíou Bóni, leads up to the 16C **Boni windmill** (Mílos Bóni) which provides a splendid view of the town and the harbour, of the islands of Delos and Reneia (Rínia) (SW) and also of Syros (W) and Tenos (NW). At the end of a fine day the sunset seen from here is particularly splendid.

Old town★★. – *About 2 1/2 hours on foot.*

Start from Mando Mavrogeneous Square and walk to the Church of Agía Kiriakí (**D**) which contains the most beautiful icons on Mykonos.

Continue south along **Odós Androníkou,** a very busy street with many craft workshops; turn right into Odós Enopíon Dinámeon to visit a handsome 19C house (**N**), richly decorated and furnished.

Next comes a charming little square, surrounded by arcades and named after three wells (**Tría Pigádia**) (**E**); the legend says that unmarried girls should drink from each of the wells so as to find a husband.

Turn right to visit the cathedral (**F**) and the Roman Catholic church (**G**) which bears the Ghizi coat of arms above the door. The famous pelican Petros, which died in November 1985, used to parade in front of the Alexander Restaurant in the square.

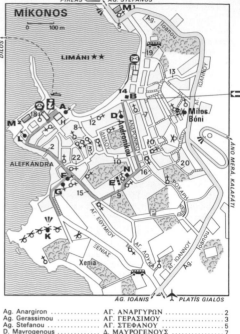

Ag. Anargiron	ΑΓ. ΑΝΑΡΓΥΡΩΝ	2
Ag. Gerassimou	ΑΓ. ΓΕΡΑΣΙΜΟΥ	3
Ag. Stefanou	ΑΓ. ΣΤΕΦΑΝΟΥ	5
D. Mavrogenous	Δ. ΜΑΥΡΟΓΕΝΟΥΣ	7
Drakopoulou	ΔΡΑΚΟΠΟΥΛΟΥ	8
Enoplon Dinameon	ΕΝΟΠΛΩΝ ΔΥΝΑΜΕΩΝ	9
Kalogera	ΚΑΛΟΓΕΡΑ	10
Kambani	ΚΑΜΠΑΝΗ	12
Leondiou Boni	ΛΕΟΝΤΙΟΥ ΜΠΟΝΗ	13
Mandos Mavrogenous	ΜΑΝΤΩΣ ΜΑΥΡΟΓΕΝΟΥΣ	14
Mitropoleos	ΜΗΤΡΟΠΟΛΕΩΣ	15
Panahrandou	ΠΑΝΑΧΡΑΝΤΟΥ	16
Paraportianis	ΠΑΡΑΠΟΡΤΙΑΝΗΣ	18
Polikandrioti	ΠΟΛΥΚΑΝΔΡΙΩΤΗ	19
Skardana	ΣΚΑΡΔΑΝΑ	20
Zani Pitaraki	ΖΑΝΝΗ ΠΙΤΑΡΑΚΗ	22

Turn left to reach the promontory on which the no less famous **windmills** (**K**) stand in a row; one of them is still in working order and when the wind blows miniature triangular white sails on the arms open up to catch the breeze; they look very decorative. The interior of the mill and its mechanism is open to view. Fine view of the town.

Return down the hill past the churches and turn left along the edge of the bay which is lined by a row of houses with balconies and loggias projecting over the water; this is **Alefkándra,** also known as **Little Venice.** The **Paraportianí Church** (**L**), composed of four independent chapels, curiously interlocked in a geometric pattern, stands on the site of the former castle. Picturesque old alleys lead back to the town hall and the harbour.

Archaeological Museum (M1). – *Open 8.45am to 3pm (9.30am to 2.30pm Sundays and holidays); closed Tuesdays; 100 Dr.*

Items excavated on the island of Reneia: vases and funerary objects transferred from Delos to Reneia by the Athenians in 426 BC during the purification of Delos *(p 96).* Unusual amphora (7C BC) found on Mykonos decorated with scenes from the Trojan War.

From the cliff above the museum there are remarkable **views★★** of Mykonos harbour and of the islands of Delos and Reneia.

Museum of popular art (M2). – *Open 4.30 to 8.30pm.* Traditional domestic interior.

Mykonos. – Little Venice

Peloponnese – Lakonía – Michelin map 980 north of fold 41

The ruins of Mystra occupy an exceptional **site**★★★ on a steep spur of Mount Taÿgetos overlooking Sparta and the Eurotas (Evrótas) valley. The Byzantine churches and monasteries, the ruined palaces and houses testify to the former splendour of the ancient capital of the despotate of Morea.

HISTORICAL NOTES

Franco-Byzantine conflicts. – The origins of Mystra seem to go back to the early 13C but the famous fortress was not built until 1249 when William de Villehardouin *(p 118)*, from Champagne in France, Prince of Morea and Duke of Achaia, began to construct "a superb castle, an impregnable stronghold" in the words of the "Chronicle of Morea" so as to control the region of Lakonía. The site was well chosen: a high bluff (621m – 2037ft) commanding the Eurotas Valley and protecting it from invasion by the Slav peoples living in the Taÿgetos mountains.

The Franks did not however hold Mystra for long. In 1259 **William de Villehardouin** was captured in Macedonia at Pelagoniá by the soldiers of Michael VIII Palaiologos, the emperor of Byzantium, then reigning in Nicaea, who was to recapture Constantinople from the Franks two years later. William was held prisoner for three years and only regained his freedom by ceding three fortresses to Michael: Monemvassía, the Great Maina and Mystra.

Once free the Prince of Morea defeated the Byzantines near to Leondári and then moved south again into Lakonía but he was never able to recapture the fortress of Mystra below which a town was beginning to develop.

"The Florence of the Orient" – At first Mystra was the seat of the Byzantine Governor of the province but in 14C and 15C under the dynasties of the Kantakouzenos and Palaiologos emperors it became the capital of the **despotate of Morea** which covered almost the whole of the Peloponnese and was reserved for the younger sons or brothers of the Emperor. In this way the despots who ruled in Mystra included Manuel Kantakouzenos (1348-1380), Theodore II Palaiologos (1407-1443) and **Constantine Palaiologos** (1443-1449); the latter, who was crowned emperor at Mystra, died in 1453 while defending Constantinople against the Turks.

The despots made Mystra a centre of Hellenic politics and culture. As well as building themselves a palace they arranged for the construction of many churches which combined the architectural formula of a cruciform plan beneath five domes with western features: detached belfries, apsidal chevets, extended naves, ogival arches and arcaded porches in the Cistercian style. The very skilful decoration usually took the form of frescoes instead of marbles and mosaics; the painting shows a striving for reality, movement and picturesque detail, attractive colouring and an expressive beauty which contrasts with the hieratism of former works.

The intellectual life of Mystra was even more brilliant under the auspices of the cultivated emperors such as John VI Kantakouzenos and particularly Manuel II Palaiologos who had spent two years in Paris.

Neo-Platonic philosophy which promotes the good and the beautiful was propounded by **Chrysolorás**, "the sage of Byzantium" who had also taught in Florence in 1397 where he influenced the teacher Guarino da Verona and the architect Brunelleschi.

In this sphere however the leading light was the humanist **Gemistos Plethon,** the Renaissance Plato, who headed a school preaching the renewal of moral values, social reform and a religion in which Christian dogma is reinforced with the ancient myths and the theories professed by Plato.

Plethon went to Florence in 1438 with the Emperor John VIII to attend the Council which was to prepare for the union of the Roman Catholic and Orthodox Churches; he so inspired his audience that Cosimo de' Medici decided to found an Academy of Platonism. Plethon died in Mystra in 1442 but his remains were removed in 1464 by Sigismond Malatesta, the "tyrant of Rimini" a mercenary leading an expeditionary force sent by Pope Pius II to try to drive the Turks from the Peloponnese.

Among the pupils of this great thinker one must mention **Bessarion** (1402-1472), a Greek who was trained in Mystra, spoke at the Council of Florence and was involved in the founding of the Academy of Platonism; as a Roman cardinal he preached a crusade against the Turks, failed to be elected pope and bequeathed his library to the Marciana Library in Venice.

Another Greek, **Constantine Láscaris,** a grammarian and philologist, went to Italy when the Byzantine empire fell and taught in Florence, Mantua and Milan, where in 1476 he published "Erotemata" (questions), the first book printed entirely in Greek; he lived in Rome among Bessarion's followers and died in 1501 in Messinia (Sicily) where he held a chair and taught Pietro Bembo.

The Turkish Yoke. – When Mystra was surrendered to the infidels in 1460 by Demetrios Palaiologos, the Emperor Constantine's brother, its churches were converted into mosques and the Despots' palace became the residence of the Pasha.

The town however continued to thrive on the silk industry and in 17C the inhabitants numbered 40 000.

From 1687 to 1715 Mystra was occupied by the Venetians; it was put to fire and the sword by the Russians under Count Orloff in 1770 and again by bands of Albanians ten years later; when **Chateaubriand** visited Mystra in 1806 the population had diminished to 8 000.

During the War of Independence the town was yet again pillaged and burned by the Egyptian troops of Ibrahim Pasha and afterwards it was abandoned in favour of the new town of Sparta which was founded in 1834.

The site was preserved from complete destruction by the work of the French School of Archaeology between 1896 and 1910 and was then studied by Gabriel Millet. More recently the Greeks have undertaken the restoration of monuments and frescoes.

MYSTRA★★★

TOUR *about 4 hours (3 hours excluding the castle)*

Prolific olive groves and plane trees line the road from Sparta which presents a very fine **view★★** of Mystra, standing out like a white patch on the dark bulk of Mount Taÿgetos. Beyond Néa Mistrás, a pleasant flower – bedecked village *(hotels and restaurants, tavernas)*, rise the ruins of old Mystra *(restaurant Xénia)* widely scattered over the hillside.

The ancient city consisted of three distinct sections contained within their respective precincts: the castle built by the de Villehardouin (Kástro), the Upper Town for the aristocracy and the Lower Town where the citizens lived among the many churches. There are two entrances: one to the Lower Town through the main gate and one to the Upper Town which can be reached by taking the new road which skirts the site.

Open 8.45am to 3pm (9.30am – 2.30pm Sundays and holidays); 200 Dr. As the tour is tiring, particularly in the heat of high summer, it is best to start as early as possible.

Coach trips from Sparta.

☐ LOWER TOWN★★

The 14C defensive wall enclosed the Metropolitan Church (Cathedral), several churches and monasteries, elegant houses and craftsmen's workshops.

Enter through the little **fort** which marks the site of the old town gate and turn right towards the Metropolitan which one passes (view of the apse and belfry) in order to reach the main door.

Metropolitan★★ (St Demetrios' Cathedral). – The Orthodox cathedral, which stands below street level, was founded in 1291 and altered in 15C.

First within the precinct there is a court with steps descending to the parvis of the cathedral; on the right there is a fountain decorated with the Byzantine eagle. The paving continues round the northeast side of the church into an 18C arcaded court overlooking the Eurotas Valley; the Roman sarcophagus decorated with a carving of a Bacchanalian revel was used as a basin for the Mármara Fountain *(p 151)*.

Church. – The structure was built late in 13C as a basilica with a central nave beneath a pitched roof and two vaulted side aisles of the same length. In 15C however Bishop Matthew reconstructed the upper part of the church on a cruciform plan with domes: in the nave the join between the 13C and 15C work is clearly visible and even accentuated by a sculpted frieze below which are traces of earlier paintings which have been mutilated.

The arcades in the nave rest on Byzantine capitals; the columns bear engraved inscriptions listing the privileges bestowed on the cathedral by the emperors. Part of the original marble paving with coloured inlay work has been preserved; set in the floor in front of the iconostasis is a stone bearing the crowned Byzantine eagle showing the place where Constantine Palaiologos is supposed to have been consecrated emperor of Byzantium in 1449. There are a few low relief sculptures (9C-11C) taken from the ruins of ancient Sparta; in the south aisle an unusual bishop's throne dating from 17C.

The 13C-14C **frescoes★** come from several sources; the painting on the apse vault evokes the theme of the Preparation (Hetoimasia): it shows an empty throne surmounted by the Byzantine cross symbolizing the expectation of the second coming of Christ for the Last Judgment: the angels grouped on either side of the throne wear ecstatic expressions on their faces.

A Last Judgment in the narthex assembles several scenes: prominent are two admirable angels opening the records of Good and Evil. The north aisle is decorated with episodes in the martyrdom of St Demetrios. A majestic representation of the Virgin and Child fills the central apse.

Museum. – The collection which was founded by Gabriel Millet is displayed in the old bishops' palace. Among the Byzantine sculptures are an Eagle seizing its prey (11C) and a Christ in Majesty (15C). There is an inscription bearing the monogram of Isabeau de Lusignan, wife of Manuel Kantakouzenos and a member of the French family which had ruled in Cyprus.

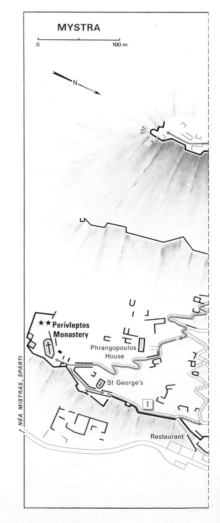

MYSTRA

0   100 m

N

U

★★ Perívleptos
Monastery

Phrangopoulos
House

St George's

☐ 1

Restaurant

NÉA MISTRÁS, SPARTI

Further west along the street stands the mortuary chapel of the Evangelístria (14C-15C); its well proportioned cruciform distyle structure stands in a little cemetery not far from the Brontocheion Monastery.

Brontocheion (Vrontohión) Monastery ★★. – Within its walls are two great churches: St Theodore's and the Odigítria.

St Theodore's Church ★. – The church was built on the cruciform plan late in 13C; it has been heavily restored but the apse was originally faced with ceramic tiles. The dome which rests on a sixteen sided tall drum is the most imposing feature both without and within where it is supported on eight pillars. The angles of the cruciform plan contain four funerary chapels, two of which *(east)* open into the arms of the transept, while the other two *(west)* open into the narthex which was added later.

Church of the Virgin Hodegetria ★★ (Odigítria). – The church was dedicated to the Virgin, who shows the way, and is also known as the Afendikó (belonging to the Master) because it was built in 14C by Pachomios, an important ecclesiastic in the Orthodox Church. Its architecture is a combination of the basilical plan with a nave and side aisles on the ground floor and the cruciform plan topped by domes in the upper storey, according to a design found only in Mystra.

The approach provides a spectacular view of the apse with triple windows, blind arches and the different roof levels. The bases and drums of columns suggest that the façade and sides of the church once boasted doorways like the Pandánassa *(p 150)*. Both the church and the belfry have been restored.

The interior is decorated with remarkable **murals ★★** (14C) by several different artists. The narthex is decorated with the Miracles performed by Jesus (Healing of the Blind Man, the Samaritan at the Well, the Marriage of Cana): the flowing lines of the composition, the harmony of the colours and the introspective expressions suggest the hand of a great artist, the equal of Duccio and Giotto.

The funerary chapel *(restoration in progress)* at the far end of the narthex *(left)* contains the tombs of Pachomios, shown offering his church to the Virgin, and Theodore I Palaiologos, shown both as despot and as the monk he became at the end of his life; among the other paintings is a very well preserved Procession of Martyrs in red raiment.

The walls of a second chapel at the other end of the narthex are covered with inscriptions copied from "chrysobulls", the imperial decrees granting goods and privileges to the monastery; the vault is painted with four angelic caryatids supporting the mandorla of Christ.

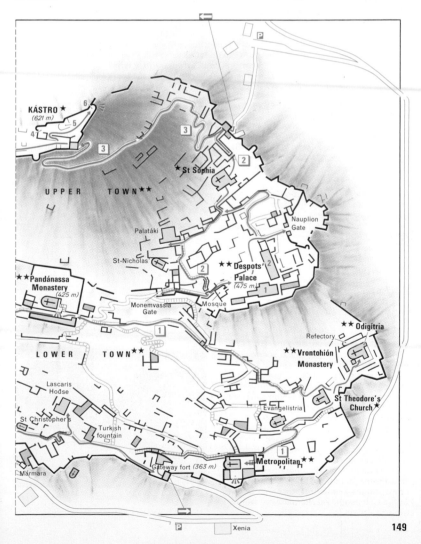

Walk up the nave between the marble columns – the first on the right is capped by an elegant capital – to appreciate the luminous central space formed by the huge dome resting on pendentives, the polygonal drum, the corner domes and the *gynecea* (galleries for women) over the narthex and side aisles.

The paintings on the ground floor, which were originally framed in coloured marble, are mostly effigies of saints; in the central apse are the saintly hieratic prelates: St Gregory of Nyssa, St Sylvester, St Basil, St John Chrysostom, St Gregory of Nazianzus etc. The brilantly coloured paintings in the galleries evoke the Resurrection and the Flight into Egypt; saints are portrayed on the walls *(access through the Chrysobulls Chapel)*. There are other paintings in the funerary chapels of the south aisle: the Dormition of the Virgin in the second chapel.

Leave the monestary precinct by the path leading uphill towards the Pandánassa Monastery. Visitors who wish to visit the whole site in one go should at this point turn up through the Monemvassía Gate to visit the north side of the Upper Town and the Castle before descending via the south side of the Upper Town to complete the tour of the Lower Town.

Pandánassa Monastery★★. – The monastery was founded by John Phrangopoulos, the chief minister of the Despotate, and dedicated to the Pandánassa (Queen of the Universe) in September 1428. It is now inhabited by a few nuns engaged in very fine embroidery work.

The main entrance leads into a narrow courtyard; on the left are the conventual cells; straight ahead are steps ascending to the church.

Church. – This beautiful building is a combination of two plans: a three-aisled basilica surmounted by a five-domed cruciform design. The belltower and the lower part of the apses, where western Gothic influence is marked, date from 14C, whereas the rest of the building is early 15C.

The main façade, which was originally embellished with a portico, is flanked by a superb Gothic belfry which shows French influence in the trefoil oculi, the Cistercian style arches framing the triple arcades and the small corner towers.

Flanking the belfry on its other side is the elegant east portico roofed with four shallow domes; it is a charming place to pause and enjoy the magnificent **view★★** of the Eurotas Valley. The southern façade is composed of three apses decorated with Gothic arches and a string of garlands, like an inverted arcade.

The first part of the interior of the church is the narthex which contains the tomb of Manuel Katzikis who died in 1445 and is shown in effigy on the wall. The church itself is decorated with **paintings★** from various periods. The best, which are lively and picturesque, date from 15C: on the upper section of the central apse a majestic Virgin Platytera and an Ascension; in the left transept Christ's entry into Jerusalem (notice the small figures pulling off their cloaks); in the galleries scenes from the Life of Christ (unusual representation of Lazarus rising from the dead wrapped in a winding sheet).

Beyond the Pandánassa Church the path descends past the **house of Phrangopoulos** (15C) with its balcony decorated with machicolations, to the Perívleptos Monastery.

Perívleptos Monastery★★. – This tiny monastery dates from the Frankish period (13C) but was altered in 14C when the murals were executed.

The entrance to the precinct is an attractive arched gateway; over the arch is a low relief showing a row of fleur de lys surmounted by the lions of Flanders flanking a circle containing the word *"perívleptos"* (which means "attracting attention from every side") in the form of a cross; this heraldic devise and motto indicate the founder of the monastery, who was one of the first two Latin emperors of Constantinople, Baldwin of Flanders or his brother Henry.

Church. – *Open 10am to 5pm.* From the gateway there is a picturesque view of the church with its two external funerary chapels beyond which rises a 13C tower; the ground floor of this tower has been converted into a refectory. One is struck by the typically French look of the 13C chevet which is Romanesque with its three canted apses and the fleur de lys carved between two rose windows.

A door to the right of the chevet leads into the interior which is decorated with an exceptional series of 14C **murals★★★** illustrating the New Testament and the Life of the Virgin. The harmonious composition, the expressive drawing and the variegated colouring of these scenes are as attractive as the movement of the figures and the picturesque detail:
– above the entrance door an admirable Dormition of the Virgin in which Christ is holding his mother's soul represented in the shape of a baby;
– in the central apse the Virgin in Majesty below and the Ascension above;
– in the right apse Christ sleeping, Peter's denial, Calvary;
– in the dome Christ Pantocrator surrounded by the Virgin and the Apostles; the empty throne symbolizes the expectation of the Last Judgment *(Hetoimasia)*; below are the Prophets;

(Photograph G.M. Guillou/Explorer)

Mystra. – Perívleptos Monastery

– on the arches framing the square base of the dome the Life of Christ including two very beautiful compositions representing the Nativity and the Baptism of Jesus.

The church is linked to the old monolithic **hermitage** which consists of a single chamber converted into a chapel and to St Catherine's Chapel, an early sanctuary surmounted by a belfry on the clifftop.

On leaving the Perívleptos Monastery take the path which passes **St George's,** a baronial funerary chapel, and the entrance *(right)* to the **Mármara,** which takes its name from a marble fountain, and St Christopher's *(left)*, another funerary chapel.

Láscaris House. – This is a fine example of a 14C patrician house which is thought to have belonged to the famous family which was related to the emperors of Byzantium and gave birth to the humanists, Constantine and John Láscaris. The vaulted chamber on the ground floor was probably the stables; a balcony decorated with machicolations looks out over the Eurotas Plain.

The building on the left was added later.

Return to the main entrance and drive up the hill to the Upper Town.

② UPPER TOWN ★★

The Upper Town which gives access to the Castle (Kástro) is enclosed within 13C ramparts; there were two entrances: the Monemvassía Gate (E) and the Nauplion Gate (W). Near the modern entrance from the upper car park stands Agía Sofía.

St Sophia★ (Agía Sofía). – This was the palace church, founded in 14C by the Despot Manuel Kantakouzenos, where the ceremonies of the Despotate were conducted and where Theodora Tocchi and Cleophas Malatesta, the Italian wives of Constantine and Theodore Palaiologos, were buried.

The church is distinguished by its tall narrow proportions and by its spacious narthex which is roofed by a dome. It is flanked on two sides by porticoes and funerary chapels.

Western influence is evident in the three-sided apses and in the detached belltower which echoes the Champagne style of architecture with its triple windows set within a round-headed arch; traces of an internal spiral staircase suggest that the tower was used as a minaret during the Turkish occupation.

In the interior beneath the dome there are fragments of the original multi-coloured marble floor. The most interesting murals are to be found in the apse (Christ in Majesty) and in the chapel to the right (fine narrative scene of the Nativity of the Virgin).

Follow the winding path downhill through the ruins to the Small Palace.

Small Palace (Palatáki). – This is a huge house incorporating a corner keep with a balcony. For defensive reasons only the upper floors had windows; the vaulted ground floor was lit by loopholes.

After passing St Nicholas' Church (17C), the path reaches the **Monemvassía Gate.** Turn back uphill past the ruins of a mosque into the open square in front of the Despots' Palace where the market was held during the Turkish occupation.

Despots' Palace★★. – It consists of two wings, set nearly at a right angle to one another; the northeast wing dates from 13C-14C, the northwest from 15C.

Northeast wing (1). – The building at the east end dates from 13C and was probably built either by the Franks or by the first Byzantine governors. Its structure and the pointed window arches suggest western Gothic influence; under the Despots it was probably used as a guardroom. Next in the range come two smaller buildings, the more northerly contained the kitchens serving the earlier building.

The last building in this range is a great structure with several storeys which dates from the second half of 14C. It was designed as the residence of Manuel Kantakouzenos with six rooms on each floor and a chapel. The north façade sports an elegant porch supporting a balcony decorated with machicolations overlooking the Lakonian plain.

Northwest wing (2). – This wing consists of an imposing three storey building constructed by the Palaiologi early in 15C.

The lowest floor which is partially underground is faced on the courtyard side by a row of round-headed arches supporting a terrace which provided access to the eight separate vaulted chambers on the middle floor. The top floor consisted of an immense hall, for receptions and entertainment, 36m – 118ft long by 10.50m – 34 1/2ft high. This chamber was lit by eight Gothic windows with stucco mouldings beneath eight round oculi and was heated by eight huge chimneys. The throne stood in the centre of the east wall in a shallow alcove.

Turn right at the south end of the wing down to the **Nauplion Gate** (13C) for a fine external view of the ramparts before returning to the modern entrance.

③ CASTLE★ (KÁSTRO)

A steep and winding path (steps) leads up to the Castle (Kástro) (3/4 hour on foot Rtn).

The plan of the original castle with its circuit walls and towers goes back to 13C and its founder de Villehardouin but the structure was much altered by the Byzantines, the Venetians and the Turks. William II de Villehardouin and his wife Anna Comnena held court there in grand style surrounded by knights from Champagne, Burgundy and Flanders.

The fortress consists of two baileys. The entrance to the first is guarded by a vaulted gateway flanked by a stout square tower; the southeast corner of the bailey is marked by an underground cistern and a huge round tower (3) which gives impressive **views★★** of the ravine facing Mount Taÿgetos.

The inner bailey *(northwest)* contained the baronial apartments (4) *(left on entering)*, another cistern and the castle chapel (5) of which only traces remain. The ruined tower (6) on the highest point provides spectacular **views★★** down into the many gullies in the wild slopes of Mount Taÿgetos where the ancient Spartans hurled their mal-formed babies; in the other direction lie the ruins of Mystra, modern Sparta and the Eurotas plain.

151

Central Greece – Akarnanía – Pop 9 012 – Michelin map 🔢🔢🔢 north of fold 28

This charming little city at the northwest end of the Gulf of Corinth was fortified by the Venetians in 15C. Under its medieval name of Lepanto it recalls the famous naval battle which took place in 1571 off Missolonghi. *Pleasant beach.*

The Battle of Lepanto (7 October 1571). – The battle, the last and greatest in which oar-propelled vessels were engaged, took place in the Bay of Patras to the leeward of Oxiá Island where the Christian fleet which had sailed from Cephallonia met the Turkish fleet from Lepanto.

The fleet of the Holy League was made up of contingents from the Papal States, Spain, Genoa, Naples, Malta and Venice under the command of **Don John of Austria** (1547-1578), the bastard son of Charles V and then 23 years old. The Turkish fleet of Sultan Selim was commanded by Ali Pasha and consisted of 200 galleys armed, as were the Christian ships, with from 5 to 7 cannon firing forward; some of the galleys came from Egypt and Algiers. In both fleets the majority of the sailors and galley slaves were Greek.

The 12 Venetian galleys, which formed the advance guard of the Christian fleet, were led by Don John holding a crucifix aloft. They were huge ships, with a castle at either end, fitted with about 15 cannon firing laterally; they carried 750 men of whom half manned the oars. They wrought havoc among the Turkish fleet most of which was destroyed. It was a severe blow to Turkish sea power.

The battle, in which Cervantes, the author of Don Quixote, lost the use of his left hand, was the subject of many paintings by celebrated artists; Titian, Tintoretto, Veronese...; it also inspired some verses: "The Lepanto", written by James I and printed in Edinburgh in 1591 and "Lepanto" a stirring ballad by G. K. Chesterton (1911).

Harbour. – The entrance to the oval basin is protected by two towers fortified with crenellations and merlons. From the parapet walk there are views of the town and the citadel half hidden in greenery and of the Peloponnese across the Gulf of Corinth.

Citadel. – *Access from the west of the town by a narrow tarred road which climbs up through the pine trees.*

The Venetian fortress, which is well preserved, dates from the Middle Ages; its walls extend downhill to link it with the harbour; other walls built laterally divide the town into compartments, each one forming a keep.

From the top there are views★ of the town and the straits; to the east lies an alluvial plain created by the material deposited by the River Mórnos.

Peloponnese – Argolis – Pop 10 611 – Michelin map 🔢🔢🔢 fold 29

Nauplion occupies a particularly delightful situation★★★ on a rocky peninsula projecting into the calm waters of the Argolic Gulf. It is a charming old town dominated by the citadel Acronauplia and the powerful Venetian fort of Palamedes. Nauplion is a pleasant place to stay and an excellent centre for excursions into the Argolid. Mediterranean cruise liners often drop anchor in the sheltered roadstead and harbour.

HISTORICAL NOTES

Palamedes the inventor. – Palamedes, whose father was Nauplios, the legendary founder of Nauplion and Poseidon's grandson, was looked upon as the king of the inventors by the ancient Greeks who attributed to him the invention of the Greek alphabet, lighthouses, money, number, weights and measures and military tactics. They also considered him to be as great a doctor – he recommended eating at regular intervals – as he was a distinguished astronomer.

Palamedes is said to have been at the siege of Troy and to have invented the games of dice and draughts to distract the besiegers in their long wait. He was killed by Odysseus and Diomedes who were jealous of his ingenious abilities.

The Lion of St Mark. – Nauplion passed from the Byzantines to the Franks in 1247; at first it was a fief belonging to **Otho de la Roche** and the Duke of Athens before passing to the Enghien family and descending through the female line via Marie d'Enghien to her Venetian husband, Pietro Cornaro, who transferred his rights over Nauplion to Venice.

From 1388 to 1540 Nauplion was held by the Venetians who fortified the city and Boúrtzi Island. They held out against the Turks until 1540 when Turkish forces occupied the region and made Nauplion capital of Morea. The new rulers neglected the defences but in 17C the town, together with Chios, was one of the main centres of trade with the West, exporting silk, morocco leather goods, wool, wax and cheeses.

In 1686 however Nauplion was recaptured by Venetian troops under **Francesco Morosini** *(pp 43 and 206)*. For thirty years under Morosini and his successors Nauplion was involved in great activity: new fortifications particularly at the **Palamedes Fort** by French engineers, Lasalle and Levasseur, new churches (St George's and St Nicholas'), new administrative and commercial buildings (warehouses), urban development and the influx of more people from elsewhere. As the capital of Morea and the chief town of Romania, which comprised Nauplion, Argos, Corinth and Tripoli, Nauplion then became known as **Napoli di Romania.**

This period of prosperity came to an end in 1715 with the return of the Turks whose army of 100 000 men recaptured Nauplion after a siege which cost them 8 000 lives. Pillage, massacre and deportations followed.

Nauplion capital of Greece. – When the War of Independence began in 1821, the Greek fleet, including the illustrious **Bouboulína** *(p 181)* in command of a corvette, had been blockading the harbour since the previous year. Three times the city repulsed the attackers but on 30 November 1822 **Staïkópoulos** with 350 men captured the Palamedes Fort and Nauplion was liberated from the Turks.

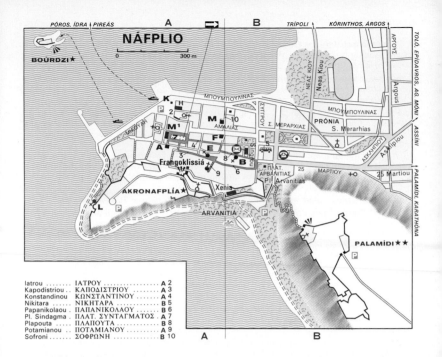

The city then became the centre of the struggle against the Turks. In 1827 English, French and Russian naval forces assembled offshore before attacking the Ottoman fleet at the Battle of Navarino. On 7 January 1828 **Kapodistrias,** the first Governor of Greece, installed his government in Nauplion and the city officially became the capital of Greece in the following year. The new administration, the foreign legations, the groups of Philhellenes *(p 24),* the troops and passing naval squadrons caused much excitement.

Unfortunately however bitter dissension developed among the Greeks and on 27 September 1831 Kapodistrias was assassinated on the steps of St Spiridon's Church by his political opponents. The Great Powers, England, France and Russia, turned to the son of King Ludwig I of Bavaria, **Otho of Bavaria,** who was 17 years old; his accession to the throne was ratified in 1832 by a National Assembly held in **Prónia,** the new suburb designed and commissioned by Kapodistrias.

Otho arrived in Nauplion on 18th January 1933 with his Council of Regents, 3 500 Bavarian soldiers and an embryonic court. During his stay **Kolokotrónis,** one of the chiefs of the Resistance, was condemned to death for disobedience to the established authority but the fierce soldier was reprieved and imprisoned only briefly in the Palamedes Fort.

Finally in autumn 1834 the capital of the new kingdom was transferred to Athens.

Otho's reign was marked by the construction of neo-Classical buildings with projecting balconies; the sober lines of the architecture give the city its aristocratic character. A colossal lion carved out of the rockface in Prónia commemorates the sacrifice of the Bavarian soldiers who fell in the Greek cause. There are other monuments and inscriptions recalling the heroic days of newly-won independence.

PRINCIPAL SIGHTS *1 day*

Palamedes Fort★★ **(Palamídi) (B).** – *Access by Leofóros 25 Martíou and the road leading to the east entrance or by 857 steps starting from Platía Arvaniliás.*

Open 10am to 4.30pm (3pm Sundays, holidays); 100 Dr; buffet-bar in summer.

The fortress was built on top of a hill, 216m – 709ft above sea level. It dates from the second Venetian occupation (1686-1715) and is a powerful complex of eight bastions linked by defilades, vaults, corridors and secret passages. It is well protected by watch towers and embrasures for guns and canon. Each bastion was designed to be self-sufficient and able to survive on its own if the neighbouring bastions were captured by the enemy.

The parapet walk provides magnificent **views** of Nauplion, the bay, the Argolid plain and the coastline of the Peloponnese.

One of the bastions, near the southeast gate, contains a splendid cistern; St. Andrew's bastion enclosed a courtyard overlooked by the quarters of the Governor of the Fort and by St Andrew's Chapel which is near the cell in which Kolokotrónis was detained.

Old Town★★. – *Itinerary shown on the plan starting from Platía Síndagma.*

Constitution Square (Platía Síndagma) (**A 7**). – This is the centre of Nauplion and the political forum during the struggle for independence, now named after the Constitution (Síndagma). From the square one can look up to Palamedes Fort on its hill.

At the west end of the square stands a naval warehouse built in 1713 by the Venetians and now converted into a museum (**M1**) while the cinema opposite was once a mosque.

In the southwest corner of the square, set back behind the Bank of Greece, is a flight of steps leading to another former mosque which is known by the Naupliots as the **Parliament** (**A A**) because it held the first meeting of the Greek National Assembly in 1822. It was also used for the session of the court which condemned Kolokotrónis, the "old man of Morea", to death in 1834.

From the centre of the east side of the square take Odós Kontandínou, a busy shopping street; turn right and left into Odós Plapoúta.

St George's Cathedral (Ágios Geórgios) (**B B**). – The church was built in 16C in a mixture of styles: Byzantine domes and Venetian arcades and campanile; the interior contains the throne of King Otho.

Turn right into Leofóros Singroú and return to the old town by Odós Papanikoláou, a narrow street crossed by several steep lanes leading up to the Acronauplia. One of these lanes on the left (Odós Potamianou) leads to the Frankish Church.

Frankish Church (Frangoklissiá) (**A**). – A flight of steps and an attractive 13C porch lead up to the church which was formerly the conventual chapel of a monastery built during the Frankish occupation. It was later converted into a mosque and then reverted to a Roman Catholic church dedicated to the Transfiguration.

Inside flanking the entrance stands a **Memorial to the Philhellenes,** who fell in the Greek War of Independence; it was erected on the initiative of a French Philhellene, Colonel Touret. Byron, Hastings and Church are among those named. Behind the high altar is the muslim prayer recess *(mihrab).*

Return down Odós Potamianou to St Spiridon's Church near a Turkish fountain.

St Spiridon's Church (Ágios Spiridónas) (**A E**). – This tiny Orthodox church was built in 1702 by the Venetians. Here on the threshold two members of the Mavromichalis family from the Máni assassinated Kapodistrias; a picture of the event hangs inside the church.

Continue along Odós Kapodistríou past another Turkish fountain and return to Constitution Square.

Seafront★★. – *About 2 hours on foot.* Starting from Platía Nikitará *(northwest corner),* take Leofóros Amalías; no 29 (**A F**) is the house where the first school for Greek officers was founded in 1829.

Turn right into Odós Sofróni which passes the Folklore Museum before reaching the waterfront (Aktí Bouboulínas).

The harbour. – It extends on both sides of Platía Iatroú, a square containing the Town Hall, St Nicholas' Church for sailors (early 18C) and the French **Philhellene Monument (A K)**, a marble pyramid erected in 1903 "in recognition of Marshal Maison, General Fabvier, Admiral de Rigny and French soldiers and sailors...". Views of the fortified Isle of Boúrdzi *(see below).*

The western waterfront (Aktí Miaoúli) which is lined by fish tavernas continues into a path which skirts the ramparts and the headland providing very fine views of the bay. Just short of the southern tip of the promontory a path *(left)* leads up to the **Chapel of the Little Virgin** (Panagítsa) (**A L**) clinging precariously to the rocky slope; during the Turkish occupation it contained one of the "secret schools".

*Continue along the coastal path to **Arvanitía,** Nauplion's beach.*

ADDITIONAL SIGHTS

Citadel of Acronauplia★ (Akronafplía) (**A**). – *Access on foot by one of the steep lanes leading off Odós Potamianou; by car by the road from Arvanitiá which skirts the Venetian bastion where the Hotel Xenia stands.*

First a Greek (traces of polygonal construction) and then a Frankish fortress were built on Acronauplia (alt 86m – 282ft). The final and major structure, which until recently housed a hospital, barracks and prisons, was built by the Venetians; it consists of several wards with the lion of St Mark over the gates.

From the walls there is a fine view down over the city, the harbour and the bay and up to the Palamedes Fort.

Isle of Boúrdzi★ (**A**). – *Closed temporarily for restoration work.*

During the last century the public executioner of Nauplion lived on the island. It was first fortified in 1471 by the Venetians to protect the harbour entrance and was reinforced early in 18C; the chief defence is a strong polygonal tower topped by a gun platform.

View of the city and its two citadels – Acronauplia and the Palamedes Fort.

Folklore Museum★ (**A M**). – *Open 9am to 1pm and 5 to 7pm; 9am to 2pm October to April; closed Tuesdays.*

The well-presented display includes not only a remarkable collection of costumes from the Peloponnese but also documents concerned with life in past centuries.

Archaeological Museum (**A M1**). – *Open 8.45am to 3pm (9.30am to 2.30pm Sundays; closed Tuesdays; 100 Dr.*

An old Venetian warehouse, built in 1713 and later used as a barracks, now houses several collections; the most interesting are of rare neolithic pottery and Archaic art found during excavations in the Argolid: bronze cuirasses, vases decorated in an oriental style, a fresco known as "the lady of Mycenae" and some astonishing idols found at Mycenae.

EXCURSIONS

Karathóna Bay and Beach★★. – *3km – 2miles south. Access by car by the road marked Palamídi from which a secondary road branches off to the bay. Plans for a seaside resort.*

A gently curving bay protected by an island encloses a huge sandy beach backed by a wood of eucalyptus trees. From the neighbouring heights, views of Palamedes Fort and the Acronauplia.

Tolon★ (Toló). – *12km – 7 1/2 miles southeast. Leave Náplio by the Epídavros road; after 1.5km – 1 mile turn right into a narrow road marked "Agía Moní".*

Agía Moní. – The monastery was founded in 1144 near the Kánathos Spring *(on the right below the convent)* which in mythology was supposed to return Hera to a state of virginity once a year. There is a guided tour by the monks *(offering)* of the 12C Byzantine church.

Return to the Epídavros road and continue for 2km – 1 1/4 miles. Turn right into the road to Toló and before reaching the coast turn left into the road to Drépano which passes a chapel near the Assíni acropolis.

Asine (Assíni). – The acropolis of the ancient city, which was mentioned by Homer in the Iliad, was excavated from 1922 to 1930 by Swedish archaeologists among whom was the future king of Sweden, Gustave VI: remains of ramparts which are part Mycenaean and Archaic (polygonal construction) and part Hellenistic. Huge beehive tombs have yielded many Mycenaean objects. From the top very fine **views**★★ of Tolon and the citrus orchards in the coastal plain.

Turn round and drive to Toló.

Tolon★ (Toló). – *Hydrofoil daily (except Sunday) from Zéa (Piraeus) in 4 hours.* Tolon is a fishing port and a pleasant seaside resort sheltered by the Asine promontory at the end of a long sandy beach with the islands of Rómvi and Platía offshore.

NÁXOS★

Cyclades – Pop 14 037 – Michelin map 980 folds 32 and 44

Náxos is the largest of the Cyclades and less oriental looking than its neighbours, particularly Páros, from which it is separated by a narrow channel only 5km – 3 miles wide. It is also the most attractive island with a varied landscape: rich coastal plains, verdant valleys and hills and the highest point in the archipelago, Mount Zeus (Náxos Días) which rises to 1 001m – 3 284ft.

Its resources lie in the plantations of citrus fruits, olives and figs, in the fields of cereals and vegetables and in the vineyards which produce excellent white and rosé wines; its specialities are honey and a citron liqueur *(kítro)*. The island is also very proud of its singers and dancers whose performances are appreciated throughout the whole of Greece.

Practical Information. – *Daily ferry from Piraeus between about 6.30 and 8am. Modest supply of hotels; many beaches including Ágios Geórgios in Náxos itself, Agía Ána and Pirgála. Buses and taxis; cars for hire.*

Ariadne and Dionysos in Náxos. – **Ariadne,** the daughter of Pasiphae and king Minos of Crete, fell madly in love with **Theseus,** helped him to overcome the Minotaur and then fled with him to escape Minos' anger. Theseus put in at Náxos on his way back to Athens but alas he left Ariadne asleep on the beach and when she woke all she could see of her faithless lover were the sails of his boat on the horizon.

Another boat arrived bearing the young **Dionysos** who was captivated by Ariadne's beauty; he married her and carried her off to Olympos.

Another version of the legend says that Ariadne died giving birth to Theseus' child.

The Dukedom of the Archipelago. – From 1207, when **Marco Sanudi** captured Náxos during the Fourth Crusade, until the island was taken by the Turkish pirate Barbarossa in 1566, Náxos was the seat of an important duchy administered by the Venetians. It was held by a succession of Venetian families – Sanudi, delle Carceri, Crispi – who resisted the pirate attacks by building towers or fortified houses *(pírgi)*, introduced Roman Catholicism, which is still the faith of the old families on the island, and rebuilt the capital giving it the appearance which it has more or less retained to this day.

NÁXOS TOWN★ (HÓRA)

The present town (Pop 3 735) is built on the site of the ancient city which was particularly flourishing during the Archaic era (7C to 6C BC); for a time the Naxiots administered the sanctuary on Delos.

Nowadays it is a picturesque little port set on a slope below the Venetian citadel. Under the arcades of the main square **(Platía)** are old cafés and tavernas where the Naxiots meet facing the pleasant view of the old harbour and the chapel of the Virgin (Panagía Mirtidiótissa) on its island. One can stroll beneath the balconies and vaults of the neighbouring streets; in Odós Ágiou Nikoumédou there are craft workshops and the house of an 18C saint, Nicomedes; sometimes one meets old men in local costume.

Strongili Portal. – It stands on Palace Island (Palátia), a circular *(strongilí)* islet north of the harbour, which is linked to the shore by a causeway where windmills once stood; the church of **St Anthony the Hermit** was built in 15C by the Knights of St John of Jerusalem.

The marble portal was the entrance to an Ionic temple to Apollo which was probably begun during the reign of the tyrant Lygdamis (6C BC) but never completed; the people called it "Ariadne's Palace". Fine views of the harbour and the town. *Small beach.*

Citadel (Kástro). – *From the main square (Platía) take Odós Apólonos uphill.* One can still see the line of the ramparts, built in 13C, to ward off pirate attacks.

The main gate is flanked by a huge tower; under the pointed arch, marked on the stone surround *(right)* as a standard measure for the local merchants is the Venetian metre. Within the gate is a quiet district where the streets are lined by houses built round internal courtyards with coats of arms carved above the door. These are the properties of the old Roman Catholic and aristocratic families, descended from the lords of Náxos.

Bear round to the right to reach the convent of the French Ursulines who run a school which was founded in 1672.

Beyond stands the old **ducal palace** which from 1627 housed the French College which was under the protection of the French king (escutcheon bearing the fleur de lys surrounded by the collar of the Order of the Holy Spirit) and accepted pupils from the Roman Catholic and Orthodox churches. Now the palace houses a museum *(closed temporarily for alterations)* displaying a fine collection of idols and Cycladic ceramics as well as a Hellenistic mosaic.

Nearby stands the **cathedral,** built in 13C by Marco Sanudi. The interior, consisting of a nave and two aisles, contains a superb Byzantine icon on the high altar: one side shows the Virgin and Child in the presence of the benefactor, a bishop; the other shows John the Baptist; there is also a painting (17C) of the Virgin of the Rosary surrounded by members of the Sommaripa family, and Venetian funeral plaques.

155

EXCURSIONS

Potamiá Valley ★ ★; Apólonas ★; Hrissóstomos. – *Round trip of 77km – 48 miles.*
The road crosses the rich coastal plain with its irrigation channels and screens of trees (market gardens, vineyards). Beyond Galanádo, Belónia tower comes into view *(right).*

Tower and church of Belónia. – The tower *(pírgos)* is a fine example of the fortified houses built by the Venetians as refuges against pirate attacks and used as country retreats in more peaceful times. It belonged to the Roman Catholic bishops of Náxos.

Beside it stands St John's (13C), a curious double church, Roman Catholic on the left and Orthodox on the right; the façade is decorated with the lion of St Mark and the interior has typically Gothic capitals with crockets.

The road continues towards Halkí with views of the orchards, vineyards and olive groves which cover the smiling green slopes of the **Potamiá Valley ★ ★**; among the trees beside the road stands the **church of Ágios Mámas** which was the seat of a bishop in the Byzantine era *(access by a track to the left 8km – 5 miles from Náxos);* further off are the ruins of **Apáno Kástro,** a 13C Venetian fortress. Halkí lies in the **Tragéa Valley,** surrounded by dense olive groves and dotted with Byzantine chapels and churches.

Halkí. – Pop 351. It is a prosperous little town with an interesting Byzantine parish church *(in the main street)* (9C-12C) decorated with frescoes and dedicated to the Virgin (Panagía Protothronís) and a very well preserved tower house, Pírgos Frangopoúlou.

Akádimi. – A path to the right, opposite a new church, leads *(1/4 hour of foot Rtn)* to a Byzantine church, the Holy Apostles (Ágii Apóstoli), half hidden among the olive trees and decorated with 13C frescoes.

Beyond Filóti there are spectacular views of the Tragéa Valley and the mountains.

Apíranthos. – Pop 882. Apíranthos is a centre for hand woven cloth; the narrow streets are picturesque; they contain a handsome fortified house and a small museum of Cycladic idols *(apply to the hairdresser's opposite).*

5km – 3 miles further on there are extensive views on either side of the road of both sides of the central ridge of the island, including the Kóronos region, which is rich in vineyards, orchards and olive groves, and marble or emery quarries.

Apólonas ★. – Pop 136. This charming village with a harbour and a beach nestles in a peaceful inlet. On the edge of the houses above the coast road to Náxos is an old marble quarry; abandoned on the edge lies a **kouros** *(p 19)* which was roughed out in 7C BC.

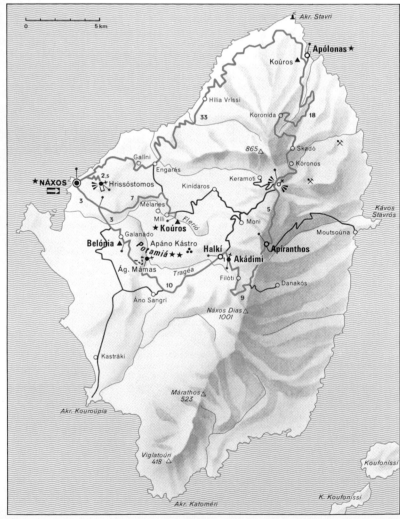

The return journey to Náxos follows the northwest coast by a sometimes rather poor road (several towers); 3km – 2 miles from Náxos a steep and narrow road leads up to the **Monastery of St John Chrysostom** (Hrissóstomos) which is painted a dazzling white; **view★** of the town of Náxos and the island of Páros across the strait.

Flerió Kouros★. – *12km – 7 1/2 miles east of Náxos. Take the road to Belónia. After 3km – 2 miles turn left and then left again 1km – 1/2 mile later to join the road to Míli. Beyond Míli follow the road to* **Mélanes Valley** *and then the track which descends to the stream. Leave the car and continue on foot.*

The Flerió *kouros*, incomplete and abandoned like the one at Apólonas, is also smaller and more recent (6C BC); it lies in a pleasant shady garden embowered in flowers.

NEMÉA★

Peloponnese – Korinthía – Michelin map 980 fold 29

Access. – *Half way between Corinth and Argos turn north into a side road leading to the ruins (Ancient Neméa) marked by a lone cypress tree (right) before Iráklio.*

Neméa is best known for Herakles' (Hercules') first "labour"; in a nearby cave Herakles surprised and strangled the fierce Nemean lion and dressed himself in its skin. The legend may have some basis in fact since there were lions in the region in the Mycenaean period as is shown by representations of lion hunts on items found at Mycenae.

In the Archaic and Classical periods the Nemean Games, which were celebrated by Pindar in his odes, were one of the four great games held in the Greek world. According to traditions they were founded by Herakles whose victory was honoured in conjunction with the glory of Nemean Zeus.

Nowadays the reputation of modern Neméa rests on its red wine, which is strong and sweet and known locally as "the blood of Herakles".

Ruins★. – *Open 8.45am to 3pm (9.30am to 2.30pm Sundays); 100 Dr.* The ruins lie in a valley bordered by Mount Kilíni (W) and the mountains of Argolis and Arcadias (S).

The largest remains belonged to a huge peripteral **temple** (6 by 12 columns) built in the Doric style in 4C BC and dedicated to Zeus. The *naós (p 18)*, which in 18C was shaded by a wild pear tree mentioned by all the travellers, is unusual in having Corinthian columns and a crypt. Three columns belonging to the temple are still standing and round the edge are the displaced drums of other columns. The centre of the façade is marked by a ramp; in front stood an immense sacrificial altar, narrow and elongated. Formerly a grove of sacred cypress trees ringed the sanctuary which was surrounded by buildings including nine houses *(oikoi)* on the south side built by the various states as lodgings for their representatives during the Games. There was a swimming pool as well as a "hotel" (20m by 80m – 66ft by 262ft) beside the main road running through the sanctuary.

South of the temple are traces of a palestra *(p 20)* and a gymnasium which was converted by the Byzantines into a church with a semi-circular apse; 500m – 550 yds to the southeast lie the ruins of a stadium and a theatre.

Museum★★. – *Open 8.45am to 3pm (9.30am to 2.30pm Sundays); closed Tuesdays; 100 Dr.*

In the entrance hall: documents about the excavations conducted between 1880 and 1912: engravings, drawings and photographs of the site in 19C; travellers' descriptions.

In the main gallery: rich collection of local coins (6C-3C BC), model of the sanctuary and stadium in 4C BC. A series of photographs records the excavations and locates where the objects were found. Exhibition of drawings and photographs of the ceramics depicting the athletic competitions. Mycenaean works found near Neméa.

NESTOR'S Palace★   *Anáktora Néstoros*

Peloponnese – Messinía – Michelin map 980 north of fold 40

Open 8.45am to 3pm (9.30am to 2.30pm Sundays): 100 Dr.
On a hill deep in the country north of Pylos on the road to Kyparissia lie the foundations of the Palace of Nestor *(covered)*. Despite his age, King Nestor commanded a large fleet of ships at the siege of Troy; Homer praised him for his wisdom. Here in his palace Nestor received **Telemachos,** when he came to ask for news of his father Odysseus.

The site of Nestor's palace was first explored in 1939 and then excavated from 1952 onwards by Carl Blegen *(p 63)*. The buildings, which were burnt in about 1200 BC by the Dorians, date from the Mycenaean era and were decorated with frescoes. They contained a large number of clay tablets bearing inscriptions which have contributed to our understanding of the Mycenaean language which is related to early Greek. Near the palace many tombs have been found including several beehive tombs.

The ruins reveal that the palace was similar to those in Crete or the Argolid (Mycenae, Tiryns) with two storeys (traces of stairs). The entrance *(propylon)* is flanked by two archive rooms where about 1 000 clay tablets were found. On the far side of the courtyard stood the **megaron,** the royal residence consisting of a vestibule and a large hall decorated with frescoes; at the centre was a round hearth, the throne was to the right.

The buildings on the east side of the court contain the queen's apartments which include a presence chamber with a central hearth next to a bathroom containing a **bath,** the only one known to have survived from this period. Around the outside of the palace are the servants quarters and storerooms containing numerous jars for oil or wine.

About 100m – 110yds east of the palace there is a restored beehive tomb *(access from the road to Hóra)*.

Hóra. – Pop 3 086. *4km – 2 1/2 miles northeast*. This town among the vineyards contains an interesting **archaeological museum** *(open 8.45am to 3pm; 9.30 am to 2.30pm Sundays; closed Tuesdays; 100 Dr)* which displays the objects excavated in the palace and the region: golden cups and jewellery from the Mycenaean period, finely wrought; fragments of frescoes and mosaics; mouldings of inscribed tablets.

The ruins of Olympia in the idyllic Alpheios Valley testify to the grandeur of the ancient sanctuary which through the Olympic Games was a symbol of Greek unity.

The site ★★. – Below the wooded slopes of **Mount Krónion** (alt 125m – 410ft – north) the sanctuary of Zeus shelters in a grove of trees between the Alpheios and its tributary the Kládeos. Upstream the valley of the Alpheios narrows between the foothills of the mountains of Arcadia; downstream it widens out towards the Elian plain in a fertile basin surrounded by gently rolling hills. Vines, rice, cotton, cereals, olives, Aleppo pines and cypresses form a lush setting which contrasts strikingly with the brooding grandeur of the other panhellenic sanctuary, Delphi.

Practical information. – *Access from Athens by railway (6 hours) or by coach. The modern town (Olimbía – pop 1 063) has many hotels, guest houses, restaurants and tavernas. Camping grounds are open all the year round. The ruins and the museum can be visited in half a day but it is pleasanter to take a whole day.*

LEGEND AND HISTORY

In the beginning a sacred grove... – The first primitive cult centre at Olympia seems to have been a sacred grove, the Áltis, which was succeeded by a sanctuary on Mount Krónion, dedicated to **Kronos**, son of Ouranos (the Sky) and Ge or Gaia (the Earth). Kronos, the god of Time, was supplanted by his son, Zeus, and pilgrimages began to flow.

This early period is illuminated by legends; the best known is about Pelops, the first prince of the Peloponnese. **Oinomaos,** the ruler of the region, had been warned by an oracle that his son-in-law would depose him. He therefore declared that any pretender to the hand of his daughter Hippodameia should compete in a chariot race and the loser would be put to death... Oinomaos owned an unbeatable team of horses!

Hippodameia seemed destined to remain unwed when Pelops, an Achaian chief, managed to bribe the driver of the royal chariot; he lost a wheel... and the race. Pelops then killed Oinomaos, married Hippodameia and became the ruler of the Peloponnese.

The Olympic Games. – According to the legend, after diverting the waters of the Alpheios to cleanse the stables of Augeas, king of Elis, **Herakles** (Hercules), son of Zeus, built a sacred precinct in the Áltis round the shrines of Pelops, Zeus and Hera. He also inaugurated competitions in athletics and gymnastics in honour of the conqueror of Oinomaos.

In fact, the institution of the Olympic Games seems to date from 8C BC when Iphitos, king of Pisa, and Lycurgus, the Spartan law giver, decided to organise a sporting competition among the Greek peoples. These games took place regularly every four years and while they were in progress a "sacred truce" was observed at Olympia lasting one month. The games reached the height of their popularity in 5C BC when even the more distant colonies took part.

The festivities, which included cult ceremonies and a great fair, took place in summer. The athletic contests themselves lasted for only five days but the competitors had to spend a long period at Olympia in advance training under the eye of the judges. From 150 000 to 200 000 peole are thought to have been attracted to the festival.

The competitors took part in the following events: in the stadium, running, boxing, wrestling, the pancration which was a combination of wrestling and boxing, and the pentathlon comprising running, jumping, wrestling, throwing the discus and the javelin; on the race course, horse racing and chariot racing in which the owner of the team rode in the chariot with the charioteer.

The victor in each event was crowned with a wreath of olive, cut with a golden scythe from the sacred olive tree, and attended a banquet; these heroes where celebrated by poets such as Pindar and immortalised in statues by sculptors. Their native cities often showed their pride by erecting a votive monument or a "treasury" to receive offerings in honour of the gods.

The most famous laureate was **Milo of Croton** in Magna Graecia (6C BC), six times victor in the wrestling, who could outrun race horses.

Grandeur and decline. – The Olympian Festival thrived for several centuries and Philip of Macedon even altered the Áltis precinct to make room for a monument bearing his name, the Philippeion.

In the Roman era **Nero** supplemented the athletic contests with music and poetry competitions so that he himself could take part... he received seven prizes! In 2C AD Hadrian and Herod Atticus carried out repairs, as they had done in other Greek sanctuaries, to houses, baths, aqueducts and nymphaea.

But the heart had gone out of the ceremonies; people no longer attended the games as a religious festival and then Theodosius prohibited the pagan cults; the Games were held for the last time in 393 AD. The statue of Zeus was sent to Constantinople where it was destroyed in a fire in 475 AD. Dilapidation and destruction assisted by earthquakes, rock falls from Mount Krónion and the Alpheios floods reduced the site to ruins; eventually it was covered in a 3 to 4m – 9ft to 13ft thick layer of mud.

Rediscovery and Excavation. – Although the location of the sanctuary was first raised in 1723 by Dom Montfaucon, a Parisian Benedictine, in a letter to Cardinal Querini, Archbishop of Corfu, the actual site was discovered in 1766 by Richard Chandler, an Englishman, who spent several years travelling in Greece at the expense of the Dilettanti and published an account of all he saw. In 1768 **Winckelmann**, the German antiquary, asked the Turks for permission to make investigations but he was assassinated soon afterwards.

The first excavations were conducted by the scholars accompanying the Morean Expedition *(p 24)* who explored the temple of Zeus in 1829 under the direction of the architect, **Abel Blouet:** three metopes and some mosaics were removed to the Louvre.

Nevertheless the credit for carrying out a systematic investigation of the sanctuary goes to German archaeologists, at the instigation of the historian **Ernest Curtius;** from 1875 to 1881 they spent six years excavating the sanctuary and many works of art.

THE RUINS ★★

Open 8.45am to 3pm (9.30am to 2.30pm Sundays); 200 Dr; about 2 hours; follow the route shown on the plan.

Secondary Structures

First on the right through the entrance are traces of the gymnasium and then the palestra *(p 20)*.

Gymnasium. – It was built in the Hellenistic era (3C BC) and surrounded by covered porticoes but most of them were swept away by the flood waters of the Kládeos; only the foundations of the eastern and southern porticoes remain.

Palestra ★. – The double colonnade of the porticoes, some of which has recently been re-erected, make it possible to envisage the Hellenistic palestra, a sports arena some 66m – 216ft square. The athletes, particularly the wrestlers, trained in the courtyard and bathed or anointed themselves with oil in the surrounding rooms.

South of the palestra lie the rather confused remains of a Roman villa and a Byzantine church which was constructed in the ruins of Pheidias' studio.

Pheidias' Studio. – The excavations of 1955 – 58 revealed the rectangular plan of the studio which was specially built for the sculptor Pheidias to work on his statue of Zeus. A cup bearing Pheidias' name was found among the ruins.

Leonidaion. – The ground plan of this huge hostelry is reasonably clear. It was built in 4C BC by a certain Leonidas from Náxos. It consists of four ranges of rooms set round an atrium with a circular pool in the centre.

Follow the Roman processional way which skirts the south side of the sacred precinct enclosing the sanctuary. The string of pedestals on the right once supported votive monuments. Next come the traces of a **bouleuterion** *(p 20)* which dated from 6C BC and consisted of two long chambers with an apse where the members of the council which administered the sanctuary used to hold their meetings.

Enter the sanctuary.

Sanctuary (Áltis)

The boundary of the sacred precinct was originally traced by Herakles, or so the legend says. In the Classical period the sanctuary covered an area about 200m – 656ft square and was slightly enlarged by the Romans. Over the centuries a collection of temples, altars and votive monuments accumulated.

On the right within the entrance stands a triangular pedestal which supported a Victory *(in the museum)*, an admirable statue by the sculptor Paionios.

Great Temple of Zeus ★★. – A ramp leads up to the terrace supporting the temple of Zeus which was built in 5C BC of local shell-limestone, covered with a layer of stucco. The chaotic heap of stones, the enormous drums and capitals of the columns thrown down by an earthquake in 6C AD create a dramatic effect.

The temple was built in the Doric order and had a peristyle with six columns at either end and 13 down the sides. Its dimensions (64.12m by 27.66m – 210ft by 91ft approximately) make it almost as large as the Parthenon. The pediments were decorated with sculptures *(in the museum)* illustrating the chariot race between Oinomaos and Pelops as well as the battle of the Lapiths and Centaurs; the friezes at the entrance to the *prónaos* and the *opisthódomos (p 18)* were composed of 12 sculpted metopes *(in the museum)* showing scenes from the Twelve Labours of Hercules *(p 194)*. The floor was paved with stone and mosaics, added later, some of which are still visible.

The *naós*, which consisted of a nave and two aisles, contained the famous statue of Olympian Zeus, one of the "Seven Wonders of the World". It was a huge chryselephantine figure, about 13.50m – 44ft high, representing the King of the gods in majesty, seated on a throne of ebony and ivory, holding a sceptre surmounted by an eagle in his left hand and a Victory, also chryselephantine, in his right; his head was crowned with an olive wreath.

The majestic effigy almost reached the ceiling of the *naós* and wooden galleries were built over the side aisles to enable people to see the figure more easily.

This masterpiece has almost entirely disappeared except for a few base reliefs from the throne illustrating the murder of Niobe's children; these sculptures, which were in Rome in 17C when Van Dyck copied them, are now in the Hermitage Museum in Leningrad.

Pausanias said that when Pheidias had finished his statue he asked Zeus if he was pleased with it and a flash of lightning was followed by thunder.

A few scattered stones north of the temple mark the site of the **Pelopion,** a place of worship dedicated to Pelops; nearby were the sacred olive tree and the great altar of Zeus.

Bear left towards a spinney which hides the remains of the Philippeion.

Philippeion. – One can make out the ground plan of this circular votive monument, which was built in 4C BC in the Ionic order. It was begun by Philip of Macedon and completed by Alexander the Great.

Temple of Hera ★ (Heraion). – A few columns have been re-erected among the remains of the imposing foundations of the temple of Hera.

The temple which was built in about 600 BC in the Archaic Doric order, was long and narrow; it measured 50m by 18.75m – 164ft by 62ft and had 6 columns at either end and 16 down the sides. These columns, originally of wood, were soon replaced by others of tufa, short and stout, to support the typical Archaic capitals shaped like round cushions. The footings of the *naós* were of tufa, the walls of brick.

Within stood an effigy of Hera, of which the colossal head has been found, and one of Zeus, as well as many other statues which included the famous Hermes by Praxiteles.

Exedra of Herod Atticus★. – This unusual Roman monument is recognizable from its semi-circular shape. It was built in 160 AD by the wealthy Athenian, Herod Atticus, as a conduit head supplying drinking water. It was composed of two basins, the lower of which was flanked by two round fountains which are still discernable. The exedra formed a sort of nymphaeum with niches containing effigies of the Emperor Hadrian and the imperial family and also of Herod Atticus and his family.

Terrace of the Treasuries. – Steps lead up to the terrace which bore some dozen treasuries, of which the foundations remain, and an altar consecrated to Herakles. These treasuries were built by the cities of Greek colonies (Mégara in Attica, Gela and Selinus in Sicily, Cyrene in Africa, Byzantium etc) in the form of small Doric temples in which offerings were made to the gods.

At the foot of the terrace is a row of pedestals on which stood the bronze statues of Zeus erected out of the proceeds of the fines which were imposed on those who broke the code of the Olympic Games.

Stadium★

In 3C BC a passage was built beneath the terraces to link the Sanctuary to the stadium. Originally covered with vaulting, of which a small section remains, it opened on to the floor of the stadium where the athletic competitions took place.

The starting and finishing lines are still visible; the distance between them

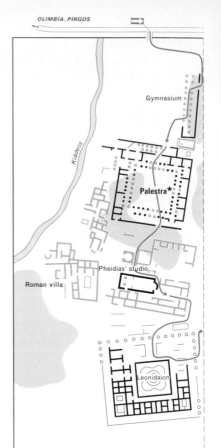

was a *stadion*, about 194 yards. The finishing line *(nearest the passage)* was marked by a cippus, a small low column acting as a goal or a marker round which the runners ran if the race consisted of more than one length of the stadium; the starting line was marked by several cippi – the runners took their marks between them.

The spectators, men only, were ranged on immovable wooden stands mounted on the bank surrounding the stadium. It was enlarged several times until it could accommodate 20 000 people. In the middle of the south side there was a paved marble enclosure where the judges sat.

Parallel with the south side of the stadium was the **race course,** 609m by 320m – 667yds by 350yds; it was destroyed in the Alpheios floods.

Return to the entrance through oleanders and pine trees.

MUSEUM★★

Open 8.45am to 3pm (9.30am to 2.30pm Sundays and holidays; closed Tuesdays; 250 Dr.

Around the central hall devoted to the pediments and metopes of the temple of Zeus is a series of rooms containing objects found during the excavations arranged in chronological order. In the entrance hall there is a model of the sanctuary. Opposite is the central hall; on the left is the first of the chronological rooms.

Central Hall. – The sculptures of the two **pediments★★** from the temple of Zeus have been more or less reconstructed with pieces found on the site. The originals were carved in Parian marble between 470 and 456 BC in a striking and monumental style.

East Pediment. – Zeus *(centre)* is presiding over the preparations for the chariot race between Oinomaos *(left)* and Pelops *(right);* at each end is an allegorical reclining figure representing the River Alpheios *(left)* and the River Kládeos *(right).*

West Pediment. – At the centre stands a statue of Apollo (3m – nearly 10ft high); on either side are the Centaurs, human from head to waist with equine bodies, attending the wedding of Peirithoös, king of the Lapiths, where they drank too much and tried to carry off the women and the young men *(ephebes)* of the Lapiths. Note the plastic qualities of the figures of Apollo and Deidamia, wife of Peirithoös *(right of Apollo).*

The hall also displays the **metopes★** from the temple frieze illustrating the Labours of Hercules *(p 194);* the treatment is sober and vigorous.

First Room. – Mycenaean and Geometric era. A showcase *(back left)* contains an unusual Mycenaean **helmet★**made of boar's tusks and a rare bronze horse (9C-8C BC).

Second Room. – Archaic era. There is a colossal **head of Hera★** *(back right)* made of tufa, very Archaic treatment, originally painted, which was excavated in the temple of the goddess; a huge terracotta acroterion richly decorated with multi-coloured stylised motifs; an elegant bronze winged figure – a siren *(centre left);* fine collection of helmets.

Third Room. – Archaic era. Reconstruction of the pediment of the Treasury of Mégara.

Fourth Room. – Archaic and Classical era. There is a remarkable terracotta group *(left),* an acroterion from a treasury, showing **Zeus abducting Ganymede**★★ *(c* 470 BC); Ganymede was a handsome youth who was abducted by Zeus while guarding his flocks and taken to Mount Olympos where he became the cup-bearer of the gods (note the cock in his left hand and the figures of Pegasus painted on the hem of Zeus' robe).

The **Victory**★ *(alcove)* has been shown by the sculptor, Paionios, at the moment of landing on earth; this figure was erected near the temple of Zeus by the Messenians and the Naupaktians to celebrate their victory over the Spartans.

There is also the helmet consecrated to Zeus by Miltiades before the Battle of Marathon, an ear and horn of a bull in bronze dedicated to Zeus in gratitude for an Olympic victory and a little bronze horse (460 BC).

Hermes Room. – The famous statue of **Hermes by Praxiteles**★★★, a 4C BC masterpiece of Classical art in highly polished Parian marble, was found in the temple of Hera, near to a pedestal bearing an inscription relating to the sculptor Praxiteles to whom the Hermes was also attributed by the historian Pausanias; certain scholars however assert that it is a Hellenistic or even Roman copy.

Hermes, the messenger of the gods, is carrying the infant Dionysos, son of Zeus and Semele, to entrust him to the care of the nymphs out of reach of Hera's jealousy. The perfection of the modelling and the harmony of the proportions are remarkable. Traces of colour on the lips and the hair show that the statue was originally painted.

Seventh and Eighth Rooms. – Among the works from the Roman period are an Antinoüs (Hadrian's favourite) and a marble bull dedicated to Zeus by Regilla, Herod Atticus' wife.

Many accessories used by athletes in the Games.

ADDITIONAL SIGHTS

Pierre de Coubertin Monument. – East of the ruins on the north side of the Trípoli road a ring of cypress trees marks the site of the mausoleum built in 1938 to contain the heart of **Baron Pierre de Coubertin** (1863-1937) who founded the modern Olympic Games. The modern cycle was started in 1896 in Athens with the assistance of the Greek millionaire **George Avéroff** (1818-1899) and the games have been held every four years ever since except in time of war.

Beside the monument stands the altar with the Olympic flame bearing the five Olympic circles, symbols of the union of the five continents of the world. At the opening of each Olympiad the sacred flame is carried from Olympia in Greece to the place where the Games are to be held.

Museum of the Olympic Games. – *Open 8am to 3.45pm in summer (9am to 4.45pm Sundays); 9 am to 5pm in winter.*

The museum was opened in 1978 in the modern town just off the main street; it contains many documents about the Games, particularly those held in Athens in 1896 and 1906.

EXCURSION

Skiloundía. – Pop 383. *20km – 12 1/2 miles south by the road to Kréstena and a minor road turning east.*

East of the modern town of Kréstena lie the ruins *(arhéa)* of the ancient city of Skillous consisting mainly of the foundations of a Doric temple to Athena built in 5C BC of shell limestone. Below the temple several ancient tombs have been excavated; one is composed of a huge terracotta vessel, like a *pithos (p 20)* laid on its side with enlarged mouth.

OLYMPOS, Mount★   *Óros Ólimbos*

Macedonia – Thessaly – Michelin map 980 north of fold 17

Olympos is a huge and complex massif composed of crystalline schist. It is the highest mountain range in Greece consisting of nine peaks exceeding 2 600m – 8 530ft. It is divided into Lower Olympos in the south where the wooded slopes are easy to climb and Upper Olympos, a succession of precipices cleft by deep ravines. Despite various earlier attempts the first successful ascent was made only in 1913 by two Swiss climbers, Baud-Bovy and Boissonas, accompanied by the Greek guide, Kokalos.

To the ancient Greeks Olympos was a mysterious mountain, usually wreathed in clouds, situated on the northern boundary of their world, far from the great cities; they thought it was the home of **Zeus** and the other gods which the Giants vainly tried to rival by piling Pelion upon Óssa; these are two lesser peaks to the southeast (1 551m – 4 760ft and 1 978m – 6 490ft respectively). In antiquity there were lions in the forests on Lower Olympos.

The main town on Olympos is **Litóhoro** *(hotels, tavernas),* the principal base for walking and climbing in the mountains *(apply in Litóhoro or to the Hellenic Alpine Club, 7 Odós Karagéorgi Servías, Athens).* The four major peaks, exceeding 2 800m – 9 186ft, form a rocky cirque: **Mítikas** or Pantheon reaches 2 917m – 9 580ft and Zeus' Throne or Crown (Stepháni) reaches 2 909m – 9 547ft.

ORCHOMENOS   *Orhomenós*

Central Greece – Boeotia – Pop 5 369 – Michelin map 980 fold 29

Orchomenos, which had been the capital of the Minyans in the prehistoric era and was rich and powerful in the Mycenaean period, was the rival of Thebes in antiquity.

It is now a small country town on the edge of what was formerly a huge marsh known as **Lake Copaïs** (Kopaïda). There are traces of drainage channels dug by the Minyans. In later centuries the flooding seems to have worsened owing to earthquakes blocking the natural outlets. Modern drainage work was begun at the end of 19C by Scots engineers; a network of canals was created to channel the water south towards the River Kifíssos which flows into Lake Ilíki and Lake Paralímni. Over a period of years nearly 200km² – 77sq miles of land was reclaimed. Until it was expropriated by the Greek Government in 1952, the estate was administered by the British Lake Copais Company. The land is used for animal husbandry and the cultivation of cotton, rice and cereals.

Battle of Kephisos (Kifíssos). – Near to Orchomenos, where the River Kifíssos flowed into Lake Copaïs there took place on 13 March 1311 a bloody battle which put an end to the Frankish domination of the Duchies of Thebes and Athens.

The foot soldiers of the Catalan Company *(p 121)* were drawn up on the right bank of the river and separated from the Frankish cavalry by a stretch of level ground, green but marshy. The 700 cavalry from Burgundy, Champagne and Flanders under the command of **Gautier de Brienne,** the Duke of Athens, did not notice that the ground was not firm. As they charged forward their heavy war horses sank into the quagmire. The riders were powerless to move and the light Catalan infantry had no trouble cutting them down. Only two knights escaped.

SIGHTS *3/4 hour*

The ruins of ancient Orchomenos and the Church of the Dormition of the Virgin face one another at the entrance to the modern town on the Kástro road.

Ancient ruins. – *Open 8.45am to 3pm (9.30am to 2.30pm Sundays); apply to the keeper.*
On the left of the theatre is the path *(drómos)* leading into the **Treasury of Minyas ★** (a legendary ancestor of the Minyans); this is a huge Mycenaean *thólos* tomb similar to the Treasury of Atreus at Mycenae; the roof has fallen in but the huge blue marble lintel is still in place over the door and the inner funerary chamber, linked to the main tomb by a corridor, has retained part of its original ceiling which is handsomely decorated.

The acropolis *(1 hour on foot Rtn)* gives a fine **panorama ★** over Orchomenos and the Copaïc region.

Church of the Dormition of the Virgin ★ (Kimísseos Theotókou). – *Opening times as for the ancient ruins.* The Byzantine church, which dates from 9C, belonged to a monastery built on the site of a temple dedicated to the Graces *(charites),* who were goddesses of Nature.

In 13C the monastery passed to the Cistercians who altered the church and the conventual buildings, leaving their distinctive architectural mark: the open narthex in front of the church like the one at Citeaux Abbey, the porch and the triple windows; the double arched arcading along one side of the old cloisters is also typical of the Cistercian style.

Inside the church is an unusual Byzantine paved floor. There are inscriptions in Greek letters and many Byzantine stones sculpted with symbolic motifs (winged dragons, doves, lions, deer, trees of life etc).

The upper part of the transept walls and the dome have recently been restored.

ÓSSIOS LOUKÁS Monastery★★

Central Greece – Boeotia – Alt 490m – 1 608ft – Michelin map 980 fold 29

Deep in the bauxite-bearing mountains on the borders of Boeotia and Phocis stands the Monastery of Holy Luke (Óssios Loukás). Its **position**★★ is peaceful and imposing on the edge of a rounded valley beneath the green slopes (olives) of Mount Helicon (Oros Elikónas).

The monastery was founded by a hermit, **Luke the Styriot,** who died in 953 and whose tomb became the object of pilgrimages. Like the abbeys at Daphne and Orchomenos, the convent was occupied in 13C and 14C under the Burgundian Dukes of Athens and Thebes by Cistercians who preferred an isolated site which they placed under the protection of the Virgin. The monastery was damaged by earthquakes in 16C and 17C and restored between 1960 and 1970; there are seven orthodox monks in residence. Despite its isolation in the mountains the major church is decorated with marvellous **mosaics**★★ and is a masterpiece of Byzantine art.

Practical information. – *Access by the Livadiá to Delphi road. Buses from Livadiá. Xenia Hotel-restaurant. Car park. Open 8am to 7pm (6pm Sundays); 100 Dr.*

TOUR
about 1 1/2 hours

The monastery precinct is shaped like an irregular pentagon at the centre of which stand two churches, one for the pilgrims and one for the community. The peripheral buildings comprise the monks' cells *(north and west sides)* and a refectory *(south side)* which was rebuilt after being damaged in a bombardment in 1943.

Pass through the main entrance into the precinct to arrive in front of the pilgrims' church (Katholikon); set back on the left is the conventual church (Theotókos).

Holy Luke's Church (Katholikon)★★. – The huge and typical pilgrimage church was built in 11C over the tomb of Luke the hermit.

Before examining the mosaics in detail it is advisable to walk round the church so as to understand its architecture and décor.

ÓSSIOS LOUKÁS MONASTERY

0   20m

← N →

Monks' courtyard

Theotókos ★

3
4 2

Crypt

Refectory

Cells

1

KATHOLIKON ★★

Courtyard

Cells

Tower

From the outside the building is typically Greek with its stonework resting on a course of bricks and the windows grouped together beneath semi-circular relieving arches. The church, which is preceded by a narthex, is built on the Greek-cross plan beneath a central dome supported on pendentives and with an apse jutting from its rectangular mass, as in Agía Sophía in Constantinople. The galleries were reserved for women.

The interior décor is mostly 11C; only the murals, which replaced damaged or lost mosaics, are later (16C-17C). The visitor will marvel at the multicoloured marbles which face the walls and pillars, the jasper and porphyry in the floor, the delicate sculptures which decorate the iconostasis and the extraordinary mosaics on the ceiling.

To examine the interior decoration start at the main door. The mosaics are set against a gold background, a typical example of the 11C hieratic style, sober and expressive, which was executed by artists from Thessalonika and Constantinople.

Narthex (1). – Fine mosaics:
– on the pediment above the nave door, a majestic effigy of Christ preaching;
– on the pediments of the arches on either side of the central doors, the Crucifixion and the Resurrection, a scene combined with the Descent into Hell *(right)* and effigies of Helen and Constantine, who initiated the devotion to the Holy Cross;
– on the central vault, the Virgin, the Archangels Gabriel and Michael and St John the Baptist;
– in the pediments above the arches on the west side, curious figures of oriental saints;
– in the lateral recesses, the Washing of the Disciples Feet *(north)* and Doubting Thomas *(south).*

(Photograph GNTO)

Óssios Loukás. – Mosaic

ÓSSIOS LOUKÁS Monastery★★

Dome (2). – The original mosaics were replaced by frescoes in 16C and 17C. In the centre figures Christ Pantocrator surrounded by the Virgin, St John the Baptist and the Archangels Michael, Gabriel, Raphael and Uriel; between the windows are the sixteen prophets. The pendentives are faced with charming mosaics evoking the Nativity, the Presentation in the Temple and the Baptism of Christ.

Iconostasis. – It is made of white marble and formerly hung with four great icons (1571), the work of the famous Cretan artist, Damaskinós, who taught El Greco *(stolen a few years ago)*.

Chancel and Apse (3). – The mosaic in the small dome above the altar symbolises Pentecost; in the apse is the Mother of God (Meter Theou). The two mosaics facing one another in the little apse *(right)* are among the most admired of all: Daniel in the lions' den and Shadrach, Meshach and Abed-nego in the fiery furnace.

North transept (4). – Fine mosaic of Luke the Hermit.

Crypt. – *Access from south side outside the church.* The crypt which contains the tomb of Holy Luke dates from 10C. The murals are 11C: note the Last Supper *(right of iconstasis)*.

Church of the Virgin★ (Theotókos). – A doorway beneath a double arch leads into the monastic "enclosure" and the open court in front of the church.

This church is very different from its neighbour; some people think it is contemporary with Luke the Hermit, 10C; others think it is 11C.

In fact, even if Luke's oratory did stand on this spot, it seems that the present church was built or rebuilt in 13C for the Cistercians according to the visible evidence: external porch with rib vaulting linking the church with the monastic buildings, nave and two aisles terminating in apses with flat external chevets, shape of the arches and the simplicity of the decoration.

The proportions of the narthex are admirable: the vault is supported on two columns with Corinthian capitals and the high dome rests on four granite columns with handsome carved capitals.

On leaving go round the south side of both churches into the monks' courtyard to compare the east ends: the Byzantine pilgrims' church is massive and crowned by a powerful round dome; the conventual church soars up to an elegant octagonal lantern. The east side of the precinct consists of another range of conventual buildings.

PÁRGA★★

Epiros – Pop 1 693 – Michelin map 980 west of fold 15.

Forests of pine trees and groves of olives and citrus fruits (citrons and particularly lemons) growing on the slopes on the Epirot coast make a green surround to Párga. It is a charming resort on a particularly attractive **site★★**; its white flower-hung houses cluster on the neck of a promontory flanked by two bays which are screened from the open sea by rocky islets and a huge gently curving sandy beach.

Párga provides a sheltered anchorage for coastal traders and for pleasure boats *(trips to the isle of Paxí organised in season)*. From 15C to 1797 Párga belonged to the Venetians who called it "Le Gominezze", the anchorage. Much against the will of the inhabitants, it was sold by the British to Ali Pasha *(p 115)* in 1817 and did not return to the Greeks until 1913.

Párga Bay

Venetian Fortress. – The fortress (now in ruins) was built late in 16C and later modified. It stood on a rocky peninsula now overgrown by trees – citrus, pines and cypresses – through which there are changing **views★★** of Párga, the bays and the islands: Panagía Island is marked by two chapels and a little fort built by the French in 1808. The Souliots *(p 108)* often found a refuge in the fortress during their struggle against Ali Pasha.

Michelin map 980 shows the picturesque routes, the interesting sites and monuments, viewpoints, rivers, forests etc.

PÁROS★

Cyclades – Pop 7 881 – Michelin map 𝟿𝟾𝟶 fold 32

Famous throughout antiquity for its white marble, the island of Páros at the centre of the Cyclades has a distinct character with its white houses, its domed churches and its windmills, the most typical of which are to be found at Parikía and Léfkes.

Practical information. – *Access by 3 or 4 ferries daily from Piraeus in 6 to 8 hours according to the number of stops. Most hotel accommodation in Páros (Parikía) and Náoussa. Several beaches the most popular being in Páros (Parikía) itself, at Kríos in Páros Bay and at Písso Livádi on the east coast. Buses, taxis; bicycles and motor scooters for hire.*

GEOGRAPHICAL AND HISTORICAL NOTES

The island has two excellent natural harbours on the west and north coasts; the terrain is hilly (rising to 771m – 2 530ft in Mount Profítis Ilías) and more or less barren, although the patches of colour, many appearing in the folds of the ground, are fields of barley, vineyards, orchards and groves of olives and figs which provide the islanders with a reasonable living. The island is well known for its white and rosé wines and its citron liqueur as well as for its sardines and shellfish.

In antiquity Páros grew prosperous owing to its fine grained white marble, called "lychnite" which was in great demand by architects (Solomon's Temple in Jerusalem) and by sculptors (Venus de Milo, Hermes by Praxiteles).

From 13C until it was captured by the Turks in 1537 Páros was a dependency of the Duchy of Náxos and under Venetian occupation. At the beginning of 17C William Petty, the Earl of Arundel's Chaplain, discovered the famous "Parian Chronicle" in the fortress; this was a chronological account of ancient Greek history, engraved in 3C BC on the stone which gave the assumed date of Homer's birth. In 17C the Capucines founded a monastery on the site of the present Roman Catholic church.

PÁROS TOWN★ (PARIKÍA)

Páros (Pop 2 716), the capital of the island, has developed on the site of the ancient city. The dazzling white of the buildings is accentuated by the vivid colours of the clusters of oleanders, bougainvilleas and hibiscus *(photo p 229)*. It is pleasant to stroll in the maze of narrow winding streets which are crowded with shops, chapels, blue domed churches (beautiful iconostases) and fountains, some of which date from 18C.

Kástro. – On the promontory on the site of the ancient acropolis stand the ruins of a 13C Venetian fortress; its walls incorporate some ancient fragments (marble columns, pieces of architrave). Some of these come from a temple; its foundations can be seen near the little church of St Constantine within the precinct. Beautiful view of Páros Bay.

Church of Our Lady of the "Hundred Doors"★ (Panagía Ekatondapilianí). – *At the far end of a square on the east side of the harbour. Open 9am to 1pm and 5 to 7pm.* The name may also be a corruption of Katapoliani meaning below the town. The first church was an important Byzantine sanctuary founded by St Helen, Constantine's mother; the present building dates from 6C only and may have been largely reconstructed in 10C. Under the Venetians it was the Roman Catholic cathedral, probably shared with the Orthodox.

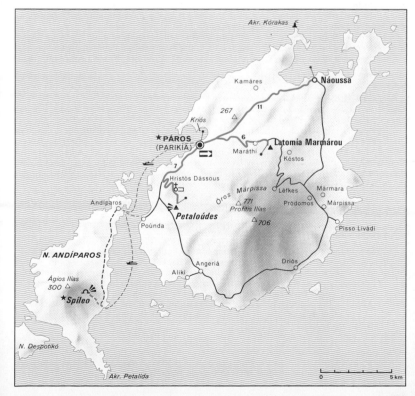

An unusual narthex, with rib vaulting and apses at either end, leads into the church itself which is a combination of a basilical building with a nave and two aisles and the Greek cross plan. Inside are galleries *(gynaecea)* for the women, a rare foundation shaft *(right transept)*, a Byzantine tabernacle on the high altar and the bishop's throne *(apse)*.

St Nicholas' Chapel *(left of the chancel)* which dates from 6C is supported on ancient columns; the iconostasis is 17C. The baptistry *(right of the church)* dates from 6C and was designed for baptisms by total immersion.

Museum. – *Beyond and to the right of the Church of the Hundred Doors. Open 8.45am to 3pm (9.30am to 2.30pm Sundays); closed Tuesdays; 100 Dr.* On display is a fragment of the Parian Chronicle; the main piece is in the Ashmolean Museum in Oxford. Effigy of Victory (Skópas school).

Grotto of the Nymphs. – *Below Hotel Xenia and the windmill hill.* Originally dedicated to a nymph cult, the grotto was Christianised by the building of a chapel.

EXCURSIONS

Butterfly Valley (Petaloúdes) (Psihopiána). – *7km – 4 1/4 miles south; follow the coast road; then turn left into a road leading to the monastery of Christ in the Forest (Hristós Dássous) and the valley of the butterflies (petaloúdes); 100 Dr.*

In spring and summer the fruit trees growing on the valley slopes are inhabited by swarms of butterflies (tap on the tree trunks to make the butterflies take wing). Attractive view of Andíparos; remains of a 16C Venetian castle.

Náoussa. – Pop 1 229. *10km – 6 1/2 miles northeast.* Náoussa is a fishing village with picturesque alleys situated deep in a wide rugged bay where the Russian fleet spent the winter in 1770 *(several small beaches in inlets which can be reached by boat);* down by the harbour a tower belonging to a castle built by the Dukes of Náxos.

Marble Quarries (Latomía Marmárou). – *6km – 3 3/4 miles east on the slopes of Mount Márpissa. Take the road towards the attractive village of Léfkes. Beyond Maráthi turn right into a track which leads up the valley to the famous quarries. The approach is marked by abandoned buildings.*

(Photograph Desmarteau/Explorer)

Páros. – Náoussa Harbour

Leave the car near the chapel and walk 100m – 110yds; pass through the low wall on the left and follow the path to the quarries.

There are three quarries *(latomía)* side by side with steeply sloping galleries, which are sometimes slippery, and penetrate deep into the mountain since the finest and whitest marble lies very deep. There is an ancient low-relief sculpture at one of the entrances.

Andíparos Island. – Pop 635. *Access daily in the season from Parikía by caique which goes to the beaches and the cave returning about 3pm. There is also a launch which crosses the channel from Poúnda.*

Cave ★ (Spíleo). – *Open 9am to 2pm; from the shore 1 hour of foot Rtn, donkeys in the season; bus from the village to the coast near the cave.*

The cave of Andíparos is about 165m – 541ft up on the slopes of Mount Ágios Ilías. The cave is well presented and consists of a vast chamber about 90m – 295ft deep (400 steps) with many concretions. At Christmas in 1673 the French Ambassador in Constantinople, M. de Nointel *(p 49)* arranged for midnight mass to be celebrated by the light of flaming torches; many people attended from the neighbouring island *(inscription).* In 19C the cave was visited by Byron and other romantic travellers.

PATRAS — *Pátra*

Peloponnese – Achaia – Pop 141 529 – Michelin map 980 fold 28

Patras, the modern capital of the Peloponnese and Achaia, is the third largest town in Greece and the major port on the west coast. Backed by a fertile hinterland of fruit orchards and vineyards (large wine-producing firms), it is also a commercial and industrial centre (textiles, tyres) and a university town. In 1821 it was burnt by the Turks and rebuilt on a geometric plan. Its arcaded streets and shady squares and harbour mole, where people gather in the evening, provide a pleasant stroll. The town carnival *(see table p 14)* is one of the most spectacular in Greece and the local cuisine is delicious: excellent gilt-head fish *(tsipoúres).*

It was here that Byron first set foot on Greek soil in 1809.

A religious city. – According to tradition Patras was converted to Christianity in the reign of Nero by St Andrew, the Apostle, who was crucified on an X-shaped cross, henceforward known as the St Andrew's cross. His tomb soon attracted many pilgrims and quarrels arose over his relics; in 4C some were removed to Constantinople while others were

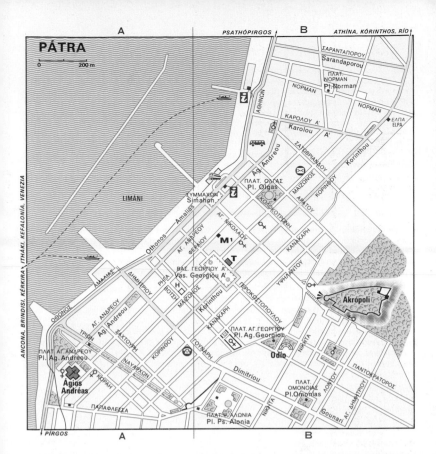

carried off by St Regulus (or Rule), the Bishop of Patras, who was shipwrecked off the coast of Fife and founded St Andrews in Scotland. The head however remained in Patras where in 805 a miraculous apparition of the Apostle put to flight the bands of Slavs who were attacking the city.

The religious role of Patras grew even greater with the Frankish occupation in 1205 when the city became the seat of a powerful barony first held by William Aleman from Provence; the Latin archbishop held jurisdiction over the whole of the Peloponnese and even became a baron in 1360. For their part the Dukes of Burgundy adopted St Andrew as their patron in war; the cross of Burgundy is a St Andrew's cross.

In 1408 Patras passed into the hands of the Venetians and Archbishop Pandolfo Malatesta presided over the completion of his cathedral in 1426. From 1429 to 1460 the city was ruled by the Despots of Mystra, the Palaiologi, and when Patras was captured by the Turks Thomas Palaiologos removed St Andrew's head to Rome where it was kept in St Peter's Basilica until 1964 when it was returned to Patras.

Having returned to the Orthodox fold, the see of Patras rose to fame in 1821 when Metropolitan **Germanós** gave the signal at the Monastery of Agía Lávra *(p 119)* for the revolt against the Turks; the latter took their revenge by setting fire to Patras which was rebuilt a few years later under the government of Kapodistrias.

SIGHTS

Fortress (Akrópoli) (B). – Early in 9C, on the site of the ancient acropolis, the Byzantines built a fortress, including two churches, which was subsequently enlarged and remodelled by the Franks (south and east curtain walls), the Venetians and the Turks. On the highest point rises the medieval **castle** defended by towers and a square keep still protected by a close set defensive wall.

The lower ward is also reinforced by towers and a round 17C bastion which offers a beautiful **view**★ of Patras and the Gulf of Patras as far as Cephallonia and Zakynthos as well as inland over the Achaian plain.

St Andrew's New Church (Ágios Andréas) (A). – This neo-Byzantine style church was completed in 1979 to receive the great pilgrimage which occurs on 30 November, St Andrew's Day.

The great icons of St Andrew and of the Virgin, the "Source of Life", are to be found at the end of the nave; there is also an impressive carved wooden chandelier. St Andrew's relics are displayed at the end of the side aisle: chased gold casket containing the saint's head, which was venerated in St Peter's Rome from 1462 until 1964 when it was returned to Patras by Pope Paul VI; reliquary of St Andrew's cross, held since 13C in the crypt of St Victor's in Marseille and sent back to Patras in 1980.

Odeon (Odío) (B). – The Roman odeon (2C AD) was restored in 1960.

Museum of popular art (B M1). – *Open 9.30am to 3pm; closed Tuesdays.*
Interesting collection of 18C popular dress; icons, arms, etc.

Municipal theatre (B T). – This elegant neo-Classical building with a loggia stands on the north side of a pleasant square; it was built in 1872 to designs by the architect Ziller.

EXCURSION

Río. – *7km – 4 1/4 miles northeast; camping, ferry to Andírio, many beaches nearby.*
The **Castle of Morea** on the headland, which is matched by the Castle of Roúmeli on the northern shore, commands the narrow passage *(2km – 1 1/4miles)* known as the Little Dardanelles which separates the Gulf of Patras from the Gulf of Corinth.

An earlier fortress built in 1499 by Sultan Bayazid II was destroyed by the Knights of Malta; the present 18C castle was built by the Venetians and strengthened by the Turks. In 1828 it was taken by the French expeditionary force after a siege of three weeks.

The castle (now a prison) is triangular in plan and surrounded by a moat; it has vast casemates and a bastion *(north)*; fine view over the straits.

PELION, Mount★★   *Pílio*

Thessaly – Magnissía – Michelin map 980 folds 17 and 18

Mount Pelion forms a well wooded and well watered promontory protecting Vólos Bay (Pagassitikós Kólpos) from the Aegean Sea. In high summer it is a haven of cool peacefulness where many people from Vólos and Athens choose to spend their holidays. Good roads and comfortable hotels add to the pleasure of visiting this charming region with its hill villages, its inviting bays and beautiful views; in winter there is good skiing.

Natural features. – The mountain range is formed of schist and is marked by sheer cliffs, and deep ravines. It culminates in **Mount Pelion** (Óros Pílio) at 1 551m – 5 089ft, extends north towards Mount Óssa (alt 1 978m – 6 488ft) and also south, curving west to form the Magnissía peninsula.

The relatively humid climate encourages a luxuriant growth of Mediterranean plants on the lower slopes and mountain types at altitude. Thus the olive groves (the famous Vólos olive), fruit orchards (apples, cherries, peaches...), walnut, hazel and pine trees give way higher up to forests of beeches, oaks and chestnut with ferns and mosses growing underfoot.

Houses. – The village centre is marked by a huge open space **(platía)** shaded by enormous plane trees. Owing to the abundant water sources, the houses are scattered; many are built in the traditional style with jutting upper storeys, supported on wooden corbels, and slate roofs with overhanging eaves. The local churches do not conform to the usual Orthodox style; they are rectangular, wide and low, with little apses, external galleries and detached belltowers.

Mythology. – The sense of mystery engendered by the mountain's impenetrable forests has given rise to many legends.

Pelion. – Traditional house

It was said by the ancients that during the battle **(Gigantomachia)** between the gods and the giants, the latter tried to challenge Olympos by piling Pelion on Óssa.

Mount Pelion was also the remote home of **Cheiron**, the wisest of the centaurs, who played an important part in the Greek fables. Having encouraged the marriage of Peleus and Thetis a nereid, he educated their son Achilles *(p 183)*, one of the heroes of the Trojan War. He was also responsible for the education of Asklepios, to whom he explained the use of herbs, and of Jason who used timber from Pelion for the boat in which he sailed with the 50 argonauts to Colchis (Black Sea) to find the Golden Fleece.

Tour starting from Vólos

162km – 100 miles – about 1 day

Leave Vólos (p 197) by Odós Venizélou in the direction of Portariá (east).

Anakassiá. – Pop 834. In the village, which lies to the left of the road, is the **Theophilos Museum** *(open until sunset; leave the car in the car park next to the church and walk to Odós Moussíou Theóphilou).* The museum is installed in the "House of Kondós", a beautiful building decorated with frescoes by the great primitive painter, Theóphilos (1873-1934), a native of Lesbos who spent part of his life in Vólos. The first floor contains scenes recalling the War of Independence.

The road continues to climb towards Portariá with a view over Vólos Bay; it passes close to **Episkopí**, a hill clothed in pines and cypresses and crowned with an old church which until 1881 was the seat of the bishop of Dimitriádi.

Portariá★. – Alt 650m – 2 133ft; pop 769. A pleasant resort in summer, cool and fresh, with a view up to Makrinítsa and down over Vólos Bay; beautiful village square with superb plane trees *(cafés, restaurants)* and characteristic houses.

From Portariá take the road (panoramic view) to Makrinítsa (3km – 2 miles).

Makrinítsa★★. – Alt 700m – 2 297ft; pop 546. *Leave the car in the square at the entrance to the village.* Makrinítsa occupies a magnificent **site★★** on a verdant slope facing Vólos Bay; it is pleasant to stroll through the steep and narrow streets among the splendid old houses; some of them are quite large and have been well preserved and restored.

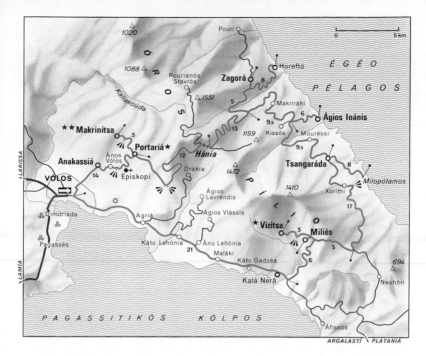

The main **square**★★ *(platía)* is especially attractive with its fountain, its plane trees and its tiny church (18C) which has external galleries decorated with low relief sculptures and beautiful icons within. Higher up is the former conventual Church of the Virgin (Panagía) (18C): Roman and Byzantine inscriptions on the walls.

Return to Portariá and continue to climb. Marvellous **views**★★★ across Vólos Bay to Mount Óthris, northwards into Thessaly and south to Euboia.

Hánia Pass (Agrioléfkes). – Alt 1 200m – 3 937ft. Winter sports resort *(hotel-restaurants; ski lift)*, set in beech and chestnut woods; there is a road from here to the summit of Mount Pelion.

The road descends towards the Aegean through beech and chestnut woods before reaching the level of the orchards. *13km – 8 miles from the pass bear left to Zagorá.*

Zagorá. – Pop 2 675. This was an important centre of Greek culture under the Turks when the Pelion region enjoyed a certain autonomy. Zagorá is a little town of houses set in orchards and gardens watered by many fountains. It was also a centre for hand-woven cloth which was exported by caïque from the port at Horeftó. The main **square** is at the top of the town near St George's Church (Ágios Geórgios) which contains a huge 18C **iconostasis**★, carved and gilded.
From Zagorá a side road plunges downhill to **Horeftó** (pop 64), a fishing village with a long beach of fine sand.

Return towards Hánia Pass; take the narrow but picturesque road to Tsangaráda.

Ágios Ioánis. – Pop 143. Very white beach at the foot of green hills.

Tsangaráda. – Alt 499m – 1 637ft; pop 605. Peaceful resort where the houses are dispersed among the trees; the village (pop 41) boasts one of the oldest and largest plane trees (15m – 49ft circumference) in Greece. Nearby is **Milopótamos** which has two beaches flanked by rocks.
Just beyond Xoríhti there is a splendid **view**★★ high above the coast (Milopótamos lies immediately below) and over the Aegean Sea to Skíathos and Skópelos.

At the next junction where the road continues south to Argalastí and **Plataniá** *(36km – 22 miles – pop 165 – beautiful sheltered beach)* bear right uphill to Vizítsa.

Vizítsa★. – Pop 169. Many typical old houses, some in poor condition.

Return downhill; fine **views**★★ of the peninsula and Vólos Bay.

Miliés. – Pop 745. This is a pleasant resort, which was a centre for Greek culture under the Turks and possesses a history library containing some rare volumes.

The road back to Vólos follows the line once taken by the famous Pelion railway along the shore of the bay; there are several beaches, the most popular being **Kalá Nerá** (pop 550): seafront promenade lined with eucalyptus trees, large beach of fine sand.

PELLA   *Péla*

Macedonia – Péla – Michelin map 980 fold 5 – northwest of Thessalonika

The ancient city of Pella was situated in the heart of the fertile Macedonian plain on the road from Édessa to Thessalonika. Under Philip II and Alexander the Great it was the capital of Macedon and it has not yet revealed all its secrets.

Pella, a royal city. – Late in 5C BC King Archelaos abandoned Aigai, identified with Édessa or, as recent excavations suggest, Vergína *(p 196)*, and moved to Pella where he built a splendid palace, probably in Old Pella (Paleá Péla). The palace was decorated with paintings by the famous Zeuxis (464-398 BC); here Archelaos maintained a sophisticated court, welcoming artists and men of letters, including **Euripides**, who died at Pella in 406 BC and whose play "The Bacchantes" was first performed in the town theatre.

Both **Philip II of Macedon** and **Alexander the Great** were born in Pella in 382 and 356 BC respectively. Alexander, who was the son of Philip and Princess Olympia, was educated in literature as well as the military arts; one of his tutors was Aristotle, a native of Chalcidice. Pella grew to be the largest town in Macedon and was linked to the sea by a canal 22km – 14 miles long but it was laid waste by the Roman Consul, Aemilius Paulus in 168 BC and never recovered.

Pella was mentioned or described by the Greek writers Herodotos, Thucydides and Xenophon and by the Roman historian Livy but it is the excavations begun in 1957 by Greek archaeologists that have revealed its vast extent and its grid plan which was recommended by the architect Hippodamos of Miletus *(p 64)*. Remarkable Hellenistic mosaic pavements (4C-3C BC) have also been excavated; they are made of red, white and black pebbles set in frames of lead or baked clay.

Ruins. – *Open 8.45am (9.30am Sundays) to 3pm; 100 Dr.*
The excavations on the north side of the road have uncovered the foundations of what must have been administrative buildings because no domestic objects have been found.

To the right lay a huge complex of buildings erected round a courtyard and an Ionic peristyle; some of the columns have been re-erected. Certain rooms were paved with mosaics: some geometric *(in situ),* others figurative *(in the museum).*

To the left are the foundations of other buildings; the most distant are decorated with fine mosaic pavements illustrating the Abduction of Helen and of Deïanira, the battle of the Amazons and a deer hunt signed by Gnosis.

3km – 2 miles away, on the Pella acropolis, near to the village of ancient Pella, recent excavations have discovered more ruins including a royal residence which could be Cassandra's palace. *Excavations in progress.*

Museum. – *Closed Tuesdays; 100 Dr.* Here are displayed the finds from the excavations including some superb **mosaic pavements**★ (4C-3C BC): the most beautiful show Dionysos seated on a panther (the god's favourite animal) and a lion hunt in which Krateros a comrade in arms *(p 103)* is supposed to have saved the life of Alexander the Great.

Among the other Hellenistic figures are a marble dog from a tomb, a head of Alexander, a small bronze statue of Poseidon and some attractive terracotta pieces.

PHILIPPI★★ _____ *Fílipi*

Macedonia – Kavála – Michelin map 𝟿𝟾𝟶 fold 7 (centre)

The road from Kavála to Dráma runs through the Macedonian plain where tobacco, wheat and corn grow on the well-drained land; it bisects the site of the ancient city of Philippi which was named after Philip II of Macedon; the ruins now visible are, however, more evocative of the Romans and the early Christians than of the Macedonians.

Roman and Christian Philippi. – After the assassination of Julius Caesar in 44 BC, his murderers, Brutus and Cassius, fled east with their forces and occupied the country east of the Adriatic.

Caesar's nephew Octavian and Antony marched against the Republican partisans and met them west of Philippi in October 42 BC. After various inconclusive engagements Antony and Octavian gained the advantage; Cassius first and then Brutus committed suicide. The victors then shared power until the Battle of Actium *(p 173).*

Later veterans of the victorious army were settled in Philippi which was granted the status of a Roman colony which meant that the inhabitants had the same rights as the Romans in Italy. The city quickly grew prosperous owing to its position on the Via Egnatia *(p 189),* its proximity to the gold mines of Mount Pangaion and the fertility of the surrounding countryside.

In 49 AD **St Paul** arrived from Neapolis and preached for the first time in Philippi; he was denounced and imprisoned for a period together with his companion Silas. Christianity spread rapidly as Paul was able to see when he returned to Philippi six years later. St Paul's Epistle to the Philippians was probably sent from Rome in 64 AD.

THE RUINS★★

Open 8am to 3pm (10am to 5pm Sundays); 150 Dr. Tourist Pavilion (café-restaurant) and large car park. Drama festival in summer.

East Section. – *Not open to the public but visible from the road.*
Coming from Kavála one enters Philippi by the **Neapolis Gate,** part of the Byzantine walls which still exist in places and were reinforced with towers and redoubts. The section running north climbs up to the Greek acropolis where three towers were built in the Middle Ages.

The area between the walls and the forum is still being excavated. The French School in Athens has discovered traces of a large **paleo-Christian basilica** which, an exception from usual, was built on an octagonal plan similar to St Vitale in Ravenna, a baptistry and a bishop's palace both of which were reached by a gateway on the Via Egnatia.

South Section★★. – *Access by steps from the modern road.*
The **Via Egnatia,** which is the first level below the modern road, formed the main street *(decumanus maximus)* of Roman Philippi; on the left of the steps are the ruts worn by the wagons which plied the road.

Forum★. – At the centre is a large marble-paved court measuring some 100m – 328ft by 50m – 164ft. Most of the forum was built in the reign of the Emperor Marcus Aurelius (161-180 AD). The plan is clearly recognizable: down the north side runs the Via Egnatia; the other three sides were bordered by steps and porticoes leading to the main municipal buildings which can be identified by their foundations.

Parallel with the Via Egnatia were fountains, a rostrum for speeches and commemorative monuments.

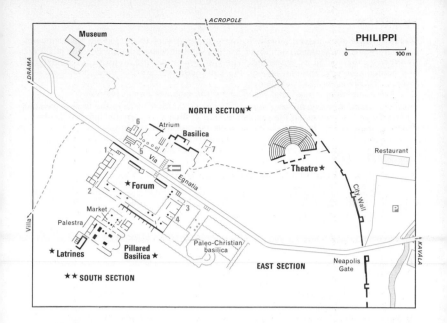

0   100 m

Museum

ACROPOLE

DRAMA

NORTH SECTION ★

6   Atrium   Basilica   7

Restaurant

1   5   Via

Theatre ★

City Wall

★ Forum

Egnatia

P

2

Villa

Market   3

4

Palestra

Paleo-Christian basilica

★ Latrines   Pillared Basilica ★

EAST SECTION

Neapolis Gate

KAVALA

★★ SOUTH SECTION

The west side is bordered by traces of a temple (1) and administrative buildings; in the southwest corner stands an unusual **upturned marble table** (2): the different sized cavities in it are thought to have been used for measuring; further on at the foot of the second column of the south portico there are holes in the ground for the game of marbles.

The east side was bordered by another temple (3) incorporating the fluted columns and a library (4).

Market. – On the far side of the street which runs parallel with the south side of the forum lay the market composed of shops and a hall supported on columns, some of which have been re-erected. Between them on the paving stones are the marks of various games. The southern section of the market was levelled in 6C for the construction of the Pillared Basilica.

Pillared Basilica ★. – Also known as the Direkler, which means pillars in Turkish, the basilica was begun in 6C but, so it seems, never finished because it proved impossible to construct a dome to cover such a large building. The huge pillars still in place, which are composed of ancient drums, and their Byzantine capitals, which are delicately carved with acanthus leaves, point to the ambitious nature of the building which had a narthex, a nave and

(Photograph GNTO)

Philippi. – The ruins

aisles and a rounded apse. On the north side, towards the forum, are traces of a baptistry and a chapel which housed the bishop's throne.

Roman Palestra. – There are a few traces of the palestra *(p 20)* (2C AD) beyond the narthex of the basilica.

Latrines ★. – Contemporary with the palestra and situated below the southwest corner is a huge Public Latrine, almost perfectly preserved. Most of the original marble seats and water ducts are still extant, as are the entrance steps.

Villa or Schola. – Further south in the fields *(1/4 hour on foot Rtn)* are traces of a building (3C AD) consisting of numerous rooms arranged round a peristyle courtyard; it was probably an elegant villa or a sort of farmers' guild.

North Section ★. – From the entrance climb up to the terrace which provides an extensive view southwest to Mount Pangaion.

Basilica with atrium. – It was built in 6C but was probably destroyed by an earthquake soon afterwards. From east to west it consisted of an apse, a nave and two aisles, a narthex and an atrium as in St Demetrios' in Thessalonika. There are still traces of the steps which descended into the "confessio" which housed the relics beneath the high altar.

Below the basilica, at road level, is the **Roman crypt** (5) which by 5C had come to be considered as the prison where St Paul and Silas were detained.

Higher up rear the massive blocks of the foundations of a Hellenistic temple (6); the Byzantines converted them into a cistern.

The path to the theatre passes at the foot of some little **rock sanctuaries** (7), recesses hollowed out of the rock.

Theatre ★. – The shell-shaped hollow in the lower slopes of the Acropolis hill contained a great theatre which dated back to 4C BC but was refurbished by the Romans in 2C AD and then remodelled in 3C when the stage was converted into an arena for gladiatorial and animal combats. The carvings on the entrance pillar are 3C; they show Mars and Victory, the divinities of circus games.

The theatre was modernised in 1959 for the summer drama festival.

Museum. – *Open from 9am to 5pm; closed Tuesdays; 100 Dr.* It contains the finds excavated by French archaeologists on the prehistoric site of **Dikili Tash**, near Philippi, the acroteria from the west temple in the forum and capitals from the Pillared Basilica.

PÍRGOS

Peloponnese – Elis – Pop 21 958 – Michelin map 980 fold 28

Pírgos is an agricultural market town and the capital of verdant **Elis** (Ilía); it is situated on the southern edge of the coastal plain of Elis. This alluvial land is now irrigated and very productive: vines, grain, fruit and vegetables (canneries). The neo-Classical 19C market hall is to be converted into a museum.

EXCURSIONS

Katákolo. – Pop 717. *13km – 8 miles west of Pírgos.* Seaside resort and port, linked to Pírgos by the railway. In the past the shipping was mostly involved in the export of currants; today the well protected harbour is used by a few merchant ships and by the cruise liners which call in to visit Olympia.

The peninsula to the south, which is called **Pondikó** (mouse) because of its shape, bears traces of the medieval castle of **Beauvoir,** which was built on Greek foundations; here in 1219 Geoffrey II de Villehardouin was made Prince of Achaia by his brother-in-law Robert de Courtenay, the Frankish emperor of Byzantium.

Fine views of the coast and the Ionian Sea.

Skafidiá Monastery. – *13km – 8 miles northwest of Pírgos.* A community of Orthodox nuns now inhabits this fortified monastery which dates from the Frankish period; it is pleasantly situated on a hill facing the Ionian Sea and Zakynthos Island.

PLATAIA   *Plateés*

Central Greece – Boeotia – Michelin map 980 north of fold 30

Only a few traces remain of the ancient city of Plataia, whose hoplites fought bravely at the battle of Marathon *(p 71);* they lie on a sloping terrace in a majestic situation at the foot of the north face of Mount Kithairon (Kitherónas). There is a fine **view** of the red earth of the fertile Boeotian plain.

Northeast of the site on the level ground by the River Assopós the battle of Plataia took place in 479 BC when the Greeks beat the Persians whose general, Mardonios, was killed. This victory, coming in the year after the battle of Salamis *(p 73),* forced the troops of Xerxes to leave Greece and so terminated the Persian Wars.

On the right of the road from Erithrés, just outside the modern town, are the ancient ruins, in particular traces of the 5C-4C BC circular walls reinforced by towers which were open on the inside.

PLATAMÓNAS Castle★

Macedonia – Pieriá – Michelin map 980 north of fold 17

On a hill which rises to 200m – 656ft between the sea and Mount Olympos stands the Frankish castle of Platamónas; it occupies a commanding position at the seaward end of the Vale of Tempe *(p 185)* guarding the road north to Thessalonika.

It was begun in 1204 by the Crusaders under Boniface de Montferrat, Prince of Thessalonika and constituted the fief of the Lombard baron, Orlando Pischia under the name of Chytra. In mid 13C it passed to the Byzantines and eventually to the Turks.
Open daily until sunset. Access by a footpath from the Thessalonika road in Néa Pandeleimónas.

The fortress is an interesting example of medieval military architecture. It consisted of three baileys. The walls of the outer rampart which was reinforced with towers varied in height from 7 to 9m – 23 to 30ft and were from 1.20 to 2m – 4ft to 6½ft thick. A very narrow entry leads to a double Gothic door beneath a rounded arch which was once part of a smaller castle. Beside the keep and some officers' quarters, the fortress contained five churches; the Turks destroyed all but one which they converted into a mosque.

Two more walls defended the approach to the **keep;** the entrance was 3.50m – 11½ft from the ground and could be reached only by ladders; note the rounded window arches, one of which is divided by a small central column.

PLATIÁNA

Peloponnese – Elis – Michelin map 980 south of fold 28

This village (pop 490) is known for the remains of the ancient city of **Typaneai** which occupy a hilltop to the south; the 3C BC walls are well preserved; there are traces of a theatre and cisterns.

Our Lady of Issóva. – *8km – 5 miles northeast.* At a junction between Platiána and Kalithéa (Záha) a road leads north through Tripití before descending to the ruins of the monastery of Issóva, now known as Palátia, which occupy a picturesque site near some springs.

The monastery was built by the Franks early in 13C and later restored after being burnt by the Byzantines in 1264. The roof of the huge Gothic abbey church (41m – 134ft long) has fallen in but the thick walls still stand pierced by windows with pointed arches heavily splayed. It is flanked by St Nicholas', another abandoned church which was probably intended for those of the Orthodox faith.

From the monastery there are beautiful distant views of the Alpheios Valley.

PÓROS★★

Saronic Gulf – Pop 3 929 – Michelin map 𝟿𝟾𝟶 fold 30

Access. – *From Piraeus by the regular boat service in 2 1/2 hours (stopping at Aigina and Méthana) and by the express boat service in 2 hours; from Zéa (Piraeus) by hydrofoil in 1 1/4 hours; from Galatás (Argolis) by launch or car ferry in 1/4 hour.*

Póros lies just off the east coast of the Argolid peninsula across a narrow strait which opens out at its western end into **Neorion Bay** (Órmos Neoríou) enclosed by splendid wooded hills. A canal divides the island into two parts: the major part, called **Kalavría,** is a limestone ridge rising to 390m – 1279ft; the minor is a volcanic islet called **Sfería** where Póros Town, the main port, is reflected in the calm waters of the strait opposite Galatás on the Argive shore. Its homely character and its verdant countryside (pine, olive and lemon groves) make it an agreeable place to stay or from which to make excursions to the Argolid peninsula: the lemon groves

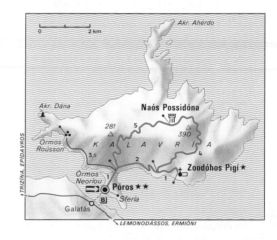

at Lemonodássos *(p 38)* and the ruins at Troizen, Epidauros, Tiryns and Mycenae.

Póros Town★★. – Pop 3 605. The white cuboid houses with jasmin trailing over the trellises and courtyards, mount the slopes of the promontory towards a blue painted belltower; from the top there is a **view★★** of the town, the roadstead and the hills of Troizen.

A stroll along the quay opens up a picturesque view of Galatás, the strait and the roadstead where in 1831 Miaoúlis' fire ships *(p 113)* set fire to the frigate Hellas which Kapodistrias wanted to lend to the Russian fleet to punish his rivals from Hydra.

In the typical fishermen's district *(east)* the cafés and tavernas serving fish dishes are decorated with naive paintings. The old arsenal *(west)* now houses a naval school.

The coast road *(turn left after crossing the canal)* runs westwards to Russian Bay (Órmos Roússon), a 19C Russian naval station (traces of storehouses) on a lonely site.

Temple of Poseidon (Naós Possidóna); **Monastery of the Source of Life★** (Zoodóhos Pigí). – *Round trip of 15km – 9 1/4 miles.*
The road climbs up to the ruins of a sanctuary to Poseidon (6C BC); only the outline on the ground remains but it is on a superb site near to a little pine forest overlooking the island and the Saronic Gulf.

From the temple follow the road downhill to the Monastery of the Virgin, the Source of Life (Zoodóhos Pigí), a white building set in a valley refreshed by many springs; the cloister with its noble cypress trees is open to the public *(from early morning to 1pm and 5pm to sunset);* fine view of the Argolid coast extending southwest to Cape Spathí.

Below the monastery there is a charming little beach *(tavernas).*

(Photograph Lorne/Explorer)

Póros. – Shop sign

PRÉVEZA

Epiros – Pop 12 662 – Michelin map 𝟿𝟾𝟶 fold 15

Préveza, which was founded in 3C BC by Pyrrhus *(p 38),* king of Epiros, guards the entrance to the Ambracian Gulf (Ambrakikós Kólpos) opposite Cape Akteion (Áktio) where the famous naval engagement, **the battle of Actium,** took place in 31 BC: Octavian, the future Emperor Augustus, routed the fleet of his rival, Antony who was accompanied by Cleopatra, queen of Egypt, and fled to Alexandria.

The town is now a port and seaside resort complemented by the facilities available at **Préveza Beach** *(21km – 13 miles north);* beach, camping sites, fish tavernas, all in the shade of the pine trees to the west of the town.

EXCURSIONS

Ruins of Nikopolis ★ (Nikópoli). – *7km – 5 miles north on the Ioánina road which crosses the site; tavernas.* Nikopolis was an important Roman and Byzantine city founded in 30 BC by Octavian Augustus after his victory at Actium. Tradition says that St Paul visited the city in 64 AD and it developed into an active centre of Christianity where the future pope St Eleutherius (2C) was born. The city was destroyed by the Bulgarians in 11C.

In 1798 the French and Souliot *(p 108)* troops who were occupying Préveza were annihilated by the forces of Ali Pasha *(p 115)* who took 1 200 prisoners and sent them on foot over the Balkans to Constantinople.

The city. – *Apply to the keeper of the museum, on the left coming from Préveza.* It consists of a badly ruined external wall dating from the time of Augustus and a huge internal Byzantine wall (6C) reinforced with towers. The main features are the museum (lion, Roman portraits), the remains of Doumetios' basilica (5C, mosaics) and Augustus' Odeon *(restored)* which from the top gives a good view of the ruined site.

The impressive traces of the **basilica of Alkyson** *(on the right of the road going towards the theatre)* were built in 6C by a bishop of that name; it comprises an atrium, a narthex a nave and four aisles; moulded doorframe and mosaics.

The theatre. – It is built against a hillside *(beware of snakes)* and dates from the time of Augustus although it must have been altered at a later date as is shown by the brickwork. The stage is well preserved and the rows of seats are clearly traceable. Around the upper rim are the holes which held the posts to support the sun awning.

On a hill to the north of the theatre, beyond the village of Smirtoúla, are the remains of a monument commemorating the victory of Actium, which was erected by Augustus on the very site where his tent had stood during the battle.

Vónitsa. – Pop 3 627. *17km – 10 1/2 miles southeast by the ferry and the gulf coast road.* From Cape Akteion on which a temple once stood where two *kouroi (p 19)* were excavated *(now in the Louvre in Paris)* the road reaches Vónitsa *(tavernas).* This little old town was once defended by a 17C Venetian **fortress** *(access on foot from the east side);* glimpses of the coast and the Ambracian Gulf.

PTOION, Sanctuary of _____ *Ptóo*

Central Greece – Boeotia – Michelin map 980 north of fold 30

Traces of a sanctuary to Ptoan Apollo lie on a wild and isolated mountain **site** ★.

Access. – *On the outskirts of the village of Akréfnio leave the tarred road and follow the signpost Naós Apóllonos for 5km – 3 miles to Kókino. At the next crossroads turn left into a steep, rough road with spectacular views down on to Lake Helice (Ilíki). About 3km – 2 miles from Kókino park the car by a chapel in a group of trees (right).*

Sanctuary Ruins (6C-3C BC). – The ruins *(unfenced)* extend over three superimposed terraces (alt 370m – 1 214ft) and were excavated by the French School of Archaeology at the end of the last century when several fine *kouroi (p 19)* dating from 6C-5C BC were found; they are now in the museum in Thebes and in the National Museum in Athens.

Lower terrace *(level with the chapel).* – Great compartmented cistern and fountain collecting water for use in a building where the purification rites took place.

Middle terrace. – Foundations of long parallel colonnades *(stoas).*

Upper terrace. – Tufa foundations of a Doric temple to Apollo; behind the temple, near to the pool of the sacred spring, is a cave; it was the site of the oracle of Apollo, which rivalled the one at Delphi.

PYLOS★★ _____ *Pílos*

Peloponnese – Messinía – Pop 2 107 – Michelin map 980 fold 40

Pylos, not to be confused with Homer's "sandy Pylos" *(p 157)* and better known as **Navarino**, a name which is probably derived from the Avars who lived in the area from 6C-9C, lies on the southern shore of a majestic **bay**★★ which is bounded on the seaward side by the rocky ridge of the island of Sphakteria (Sfaktiría). It is endowed with a good harbour and an excellent anchorage, 3km by 5km – 2 by 3 miles, with a depth of water varying from 20m – 66ft in the north to 60m – 197ft in the south.

The town, which boasts a superb beach, was built in 1829 by the French Expedition to Morea *(p 24)* and is a good base for making excursions into the southern Peloponnese. The focal point of Pylos near the port is Three Admirals Square (Platía Trion Návarhon) which is shaded by trees and bordered by arcades *(small archaeological museum; cafés, tavernas):* at the centre stands a monument to the three admirals commanding the victorious fleet at the Battle of Navarino.

A desirable possession. – The strategic importance of Navarino Bay was recognised both in antiquity and the Middle Ages but in those days the town and the harbour were at the northern end of the bay at the foot of the promontory which was crowned first by an acropolis and then by a medieval castle called Port de Junch or Joncs (Port of Rushes) owing to the marshy nature of the coastline; it is now called Old Castle (Paleó Kástro).

During the succeeding centuries the Venetians and the Turks fought for possession of this excellent anchorage; the Turks built a fortress to guard the southern approach; it is now called New Castle (Néo Kástro). It was captured in 1685 by the Venetian troops of Morosini.

Battle of Navarino: "an untoward event" – This was how the Duke of Wellington described the naval engagement which took place on 20 October 1827 between the allied fleet, made up of English, French and Russians, and the Turkish fleet which was at anchor in the bay.

The presence of the allied fleet was intended to intimidate Ibrahim Pasha, whose army, based at Navarino, was ravaging the Peloponnese, and to force the Porte to agree an armistice with the Greeks. The allied force, which was commanded by Admirals Codrington, de Rigny and de Heydden, consisted of 26 ships (11 English, 7 French and 8 Russian) with a total of 1 270 cannon. When they appeared at the southern entrance to the bay, a few shots fired by the nervous Turks started the action. The Turkish and Egyptian ships, which numbered 82, were caught in a trap without room for manœuvre and were annihilated despite their superior fire power (2 400 cannon) and the support of the artillery on the Néo Kástro; 6 000 Turks died against 174 Allies.

The Battle of Navarino created a great stir; it forced the Sultan to negotiate and paved the way for Greek independence.

SIGHTS

Néo Kástro ★. – *Access from the Methóni road; open 8am to 7pm.*
This citadel which dominates the town and the anchorage was built by the Turks in 16C on the site of an earlier structure but it was much altered in 1829 by the French who added the great cannon emplacements to the walls and the pentagonal keep with five bastions which was later converted into a prison.

The former mosque *(centre)* has been converted into a church. From the southwest redoubt there are remarkable **views** ★ over the bay and the island of Sphakteria; off its southern point lies an islet which bears a monument to the French who fell at Navarino and during the Expedition to Morea (1828-1830). A memorial to the British sailors who died at Navarino stands on a low rock called Chelonaki (little tortoise) in the harbour.

An underwater archaeological centre is in the course of construction.

Navarino Bay ★. – *In the season boats operate from Pylos to Sphakteria and Paleó Kastro.*

Paleó Kástro ★. – On a spur of rock near the northern approach rise the crenellated walls and towers of the **Castle of Port de Junch** which was built in 1278 by Nicolas II de St Omer, the Bailiff of Morea, on the foundations of an ancient acropolis. The castle consists of a circuit wall and a keep and commands the lagoon and the ancient port of Pylos *(bathing)*. At the foot of the cliff there is a cave with stalactites, named after King Nestor, which is linked to the castle by a second entrance higher up.

Sphakteria (Sfaktiría). – This uninhabited island is about 5km – 3 miles long and rises to 152m – about 500ft. It is the site of several monuments raised to commemorate those who died at the Battle of Navarino (particularly the Russians) and in the cause of Greek independence (the remains of Paul-Marie Bonaparte: *p 182*).

On the summit there are traces of an ancient fortress where 420 Spartans made a heroic stand against the Athenians during the Peloponnesian War (425 BC).

Nestor's Palace ★. – *14km – 9 miles north on the road to Hóra. Description p 157.*

SÁMOS ★

Aegean Islands – Pop 40 519 – Michelin map 980 fold 34

A narrow strait only 2km – 1 1/4 miles wide separates Sámos from the Turkish coast almost opposite Ephesus (Efes). The island is well known for its sweet red Muscat wine. The terrain is green and hilly culminating in Mount Kerketéas (alt 1 433m – 4 700ft).

Access by ferry from Piraeus, Mondays (in summer), Tuesdays, Wednesdays, Fridays, Saturdays and Sundays in about 12 hours; by air from Athens, 2 or 3 flights daily, in about 1 hour. A few hotels in Vathí, Kokári, Karlovássi, Pithagório; many beaches.

A glorious dictatorship. – Sámos, which was first known as Parthenadia in honour of Athena Parthenos, the virgin goddess, is also the birthplace of the goddess Hera.

In the Archaic period the island flourished; the people cultivated wheat, grapes and figs, produced ceramics and metals and traded widely. It reached its apogee in the middle of 6C BC under the rule of the enlightened tyrant **Polycrates.**

He commanded a fleet of 100 ships with which he made profitable raids throughout the Aegean. He accomplished several feats of engineering: a long mole to protect the port of Sámos which he rebuilt, shipyards for construction and repair, and an underground aqueduct in a tunnel, designed by the great architect Eupalinos of Mégara, which was one of the wonders of the ancient world. On the cultural side, he welcomed men of letters at his court, such as Anacreon, the lyric poet, he rebuilt the temple of Hera and fostered a school of sculpture which was characterized by its delicate work and produced the Hera of Sámos, an Archaic votive statue which stood in the Haraion and is now in the Louvre.

Alas, Polycrates, whose good luck was proverbial, fell into a trap set by the Persians and was crucified in 522 BC. Sámos became a Persian possession; it retained its prosperity but no longer played a political role. In antiquity Sámos produced or fostered several famous men: the mathematician Pythagoras (6C BC), the sculptor Pythagoras (5C BC), the philosopher Epicurus (4C BC) and the astronomer Aristarchos (c270 BC), who anticipated Copernicus in the discovery that the earth revolves around the sun.

In 1475 Sámos was captured by the Turks while under Genoese control.

SIGHTS

Sámos (Vathí). – Pop 5 575. The island capital with its pretty pastel coloured houses is divided into the lower town round the harbour and the upper town, Áno Vathí, which spreads up the hillside behind the port. The **museum** *(open 8.45am to 3pm; closed Tuesdays; 100 Dr)*, which is in the lower town behind the Xenia Hotel, displays an interesting collection of Archaic sculptures: ivories of Perseus and Medusa, the largest known *kouros (p 19)* (5m – 16 1/2ft high), which comes from the Heraion.

6km – 3 3/4 miles east of the town towards Kamára is the Monastery of Zoodóhos Pigí: extensive **views** ★ of the Sámos Strait and the Turkish coast.

Ancient Sámos ★. – The ruins extend over a large area.

Pithagório. – Pop 1 360. This is a popular port *(tavernas)* for fishing and pleasure boats; the foundations of the jetty are the ancient mole built by Polycrates. Above the town is the **Castle of Logothetes** which was built in 19C on the site of the ancient acropolis; the precinct contains traces of Roman and paleo-Christian building.

City. – On the hillside near Pithagório are traces of the 6C BC walls which were reinforced by towers. Turn off the Vathí road to reach the ruins of a theatre and then the famous underground **aqueduct** (Evpalínio), which is 1km – 1 094yds long and 2.50m – about 8ft in diameter and took some 15 years to complete; this masterpiece of 6C BC engineering was explored in 1853 by Victor Guerin; it provided the city with fresh water and was also used as a secret means of evacuation *(open [partially] 8am to 2pm, except Sundays)*.

Panagía Spilianí. – On the ancient site stands a picturesque hermitage with a chapel hiding the entrance to a mysterious cave.

Heraion ★ (Iréo). – *Open 8.45am to 3pm; 100 Dr.*
Facing the sea are the meagre ruins of the celebrated shrine of Samian Hera. The single column and the foundations show the position of the enormous temple of Hera which was rebuilt by Polycrates in 6C BC. The stylobate measured 55m by 112m – 180ft by 367ft and the temple incorporated at least 135 columns over 18m – 59ft high. Numerous votive offerings were made by pilgrims, particularly mariners; among them is a stone ship presented by the explorer Kolaios who sailed through the Straits of Gibraltar.
Distributed round the building are the remains of altars, smaller temples, baths and houses which mostly date from the Hellenistic and Roman periods; one can trace the route of the Sacred Way which was lined with votive monuments.

SAMOTHRACE _____ *Samothráki*

Thrace – Pop 2 871 – Michelin map 980 fold 8

The island measures 20km by 12km – 12 1/2 by 7 1/2 miles; from the low coastline the land rises to Mount Fengári (alt 1 611m – 5 285ft). It is a wild island, rarely visited owing to poor communications and a lack of safe harbours.
Access by ferry from Alexandroúpoli or Kavála, three times a week, about 3 hours.

Ruins of the Sanctuary of the Great Gods ★. – The sanctuary, which stands on the slopes of a ravine above Paleópoli, was dedicated to two mysterious subterranean divinities, the Kabeiroi, highly venerated by the Ancients who underwent initiation ceremonies in the sanctuary. The first excavations were undertaken in 1863 by Champoiseau, French consul in Adrianople (now Edirne), who discovered the famous **Victory of Samothrace** *(p 221)*, a masterpiece of Hellenistic art (3C BC), which is now in the Louvre in Paris.
The Anaktoron (1C BC), the Hall of Princes, was built of polygonal masonry and used for initiation ceremonies. The **Arsinoeion**, the largest rotunda in Greece, being over 20m – 65ft in diameter, was built in about 285 BC by Arsinoë, wife of king Lysimachos of Thrace. A rectangular precinct *(témenos) (p 16)* of which the foundations date from 4C BC contained an allegorical statue of Desire by the great sculptor Skópas. The **Hieron** *(p 16)*, an important 4C BC building with a Doric doorway *(columns re-erected)* and an apse was used for sacrifices.
Near the theatre, of which little remains, was the Victory fountain set in a rocky niche and decorated with the famous winged Victory, which was probably a votive monument as in Líndos; the hand was not recovered until 1950.
The Ptolemaion was erected by the king of Egypt, Ptolemy Philadelphos (280-264 BC) as a monumental gateway to the sanctuary.

Museum. – Models recall the former appearance of the main buildings in the Sanctuary of the Great Gods. The sculptures include a headless statue of Victory from the Hieron and a bust (5C BC) of **Tiresias,** the seer who was transformed into a woman for seven years and then made blind by Athena whom he had seen bathing.

SANTORÍNI ★★★ (THERA) _____ *Thíra*

Cyclades – Pop 7 328 – Michelin map 980 fold 44

The island of **Santoríni ★★★** (Thera), the southernmost of the larger Cyclades, is one of the most spectacular in the Mediterranean; it presents the awesome sight of a volcanic crater partially submerged by the sea. It is particularly impressive to approach by boat and enter the vast roadstead (10km – 6 1/2 miles in diameter) which is almost landlocked and encircles the still active cone. The blue of the water contrasts with the dark cliff face which is crowned by piles of white cubes, the houses of Ía *(north)* and Thíra, the capital.
Access by boat (some carry cars) from Piraeus daily in the season in about 12 hours, landing at Thira Steps (donkeys; cable car) or Athiniós (bus and taxis) or sometimes at Ía (donkeys); by air from Athens daily in the season. Many hotels particularly in Thíra and Kamári; guest houses and rooms to let; cave dwellings in Ía. Black volcanic beaches at Kamári and Eríssa (small hotels, camping). Buses and taxis; mini land rovers for hire.
The island's specialities are full-bodied wines, dessert grapes, broad beans, tomatoes and fish. Water is scarce; it is collected in cisterns or brought in by boat.

A Succession of disasters. – Santoríni has suffered many earthquakes and volcanic eruptions which have altered its configuration.

Tertiary Era. – At this period Santoríni was part of the Aegean continent which was composed of limestone sediment, marble and metamorphic schist. At the end of the Tertiary Era the continent sank and was covered by the sea with the exception of a few islands. Mount Profítis Ilías and the Méssa Vounó headland date from this period.

Quaternary Era. – A succession of underwater eruptions and subsequent outflows of lava made the island circular so that it was called Strongyli (round).

2000-1500 BC. – A civilised way of life developed on the island similar to that on Crete under the Minoans *(p 201)*. In *c*1500 BC the gases which had been building up under the lava exploded and created a huge central crater *(caldera)* which was filled by sea water rushing in through a breach in the southwest sector. A hail of ashes and slag fell on the remaining land burying entire cities (Akrotíri) while a gigantic tidal wave rolled south towards Crete.

236 BC. – While the island was being used as a naval base by the Egyptians (Ptolemaic dynasty) another earthquake in 236 created a second breach between Théra and Thirassía. In 197 an islet surfaced in the centre of the crater; it was later called Paléa Kaméni.

Christian Era. – This period was marked by the appearance (1573-1711) in the flooded crater of several volcanic cones, some of which fused together in 1867, 1925 and 1928 to form Néa Kaméni. The last quake in 1956 destroyed 2 000 houses and caused 50 deaths.

The Quest for Atlantis. – The first excavations on Santoríni were undertaken by Ferdinand Fouque, a geologist, who had been present at the eruption in 1867 and then proceeded to make probes on Thirassía and in the Akrotíri combe. He discovered traces of buildings and pottery and in 1869 he published an article in the Revue des Deux-Mondes showing that at the time of the great eruption in 1500 BC an advanced civilisation was flourishing on Thera.

A hundred years later the Greek archaeologist, **Professor Marinatos,** renewed investigations in the Akrotíri combe in the hope of proving a theory he had formed before the Second World War. He had been working in Crete when he noticed volcanic deposits on land which was far removed from any volcano. He had then made the connection with the eruption in 1500 BC and put forward the idea that Minoan Crete and Santoríni had belonged to the same land mass, Atlantis, where an advanced and highly civilised people had been engulfed suddenly by fire and water as Plato had described.

Marinato's discovery of frescoes at Akrotíri similar to those found at Knossos *(p 210)* on Crete wàs proof that before 1500 BC the same type of civilisation flourished on Santoríni as on Crete; this did not however prove the existence of Atlantis.

Kalliste, Thera, Santoríni. – After the great eruption several generations of Phoenicians occupied the island which was known as Kalliste (most beautiful). In about 9C BC a party of Spartans arrived under the leadership of Theras, in whose honour Kalliste was named Thera. The island remained a colony or ally of Sparta and little is known about its history until the Hellenistic period when the Egyptian Ptolemies were attracted by its strategic position in the centre of the Aegean *(p 179)*. Christianity took root in Thera very early; St Irene of Thessalonika, the island's future patron, died there in 304. Following the capture of Constantinople by the Crusaders in 1204, the island passed into the hands of the Venetians for the next four hundred years and they made it a dependency of the Duchy of Naxos and then of Crete. They called it Santoríni after a shrine dedicated to St Irene. The population often suffered from the rivalry between the grand Latin families and the Turko-Venetian conflict. In this respect the period of Turkish occupation (1579-1821) was the most peaceful and prosperous. After gaining independence in the modern Greek state, the island officially resumed its ancient name of Thera (Thíra) but the majority of Greeks continue to call it Santoríni.

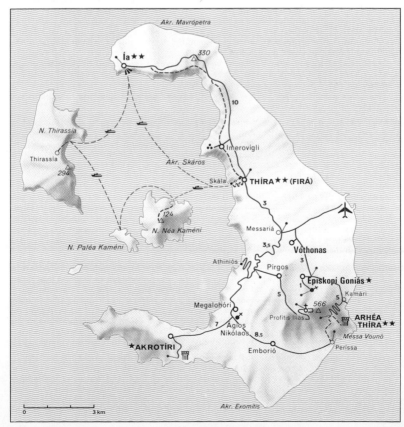

SANTORÍNI★★★

THERA TOWN★★ (THÍRA or FIRÁ; Pop 1 573)

Seen from sea level in the crater, where the water is so deep (400m – 1 312ft and over) that it is impossible to drop anchor, the island capital seems to perch precariously 300m – 984ft on the top of the precipitous cliff. The cliff face itself is of interest owing to the many layers of volcanic debris laid down after each eruption: bands of black lava, rust-coloured slag, purple grey ash, puzzolana which is sought after for making cement and at the top a light-coloured layer of pumice stone which is quarried for export.

From the landing stage (Skála) a stepped path *(587 steps)* zig-zags up the cliff face offering spectacular views★★ down into the water-filled crater; an army of mules carrying tourists wends its way up or down to the accompaniment of cries and bustle *(300 Dr per person)*. There is also the cable car *(300 Dr)*.

The town, a maze of picturesque narrow streets, seems to be suspended above the sea like a balcony; from the terrace in front of the Orthodox Cathedral there are splendid views★★★, particularly at sunset and after dark, of the sea, the volcanic islands (Kaménes), the crater and Thirassía Island. On the eastern side of the town a layer of lava, covered by stocky vineyards slopes down to the Mediterranean and the island of Anáfi.

New district. – This district on the north side of the town was rebuilt after the earthquake in 1956; the curved roofs are specifically designed to resist earth tremors. This is where the Roman Catholics congregate; they have been numerous on Santoríni (nearly half the population) since the Venetian occupation from 1204 to 1537. Next to the cathedral, dedicated to St John the Baptist, in the Dominican convent there is a carpet weaving workshop *(open to visitors; shop)*. The schools belonging to the Sisters of St Vincent-de-Paul and the Lazarists closed down after the catastrophe in 1956. On the corner between the Cathedral and the Convent stands the handsome Ghizi house containing a collection of furniture, engravings and ceramics *(closed at present)*.

Museum. – *Open 8.45am to 3pm; 9.30am to 2pm Sundays and holidays; closed Tuesdays; 100 Dr.*

It houses the sculptures and ceramics from the Mycenaean to the Roman period which have been found on the island, particularly at Ancient Thera. The museum also displays material from the excavations at Akrotíri. Another museum, devoted to prehistoric archaeology is due to open near the Orthodox cathedral.

EXCURSIONS

Boat trip in the crater★★★. – *Leaving from Firá and Ía; in Firá apply to one of the tourist agencies in the main square (bus terminal). Allow 15 to 20 minutes to descend on foot to the waterfront. Take appropriate shoes for walking to the crater and a swimming costume; the trip takes from 2 to 5 hours according to the programme.*

The view of the towering cliffs of the caldera from the deck of a small boat is most impressive; the trip includes a close look at several other volcanic features. The boat stops first at **Néa Kaméni**; a tiring but not difficult walk *(1/2 hour)* over the old cinders leads to the centre of the volcano which emits whisps of sulpherous smoke: panoramic view of the outline of the original Round Island. For those who do not dally over the walk possibility of a refreshing dip from the black pumice rocks.

The boat stops next at the entrance to an inlet in **Paleá Kaméni**; during the swim to the shore the water grows warmer and is coloured red by the soft volcanic mud of the inlet; bubbles of gas erupt on the surface of the sea.

At lunchtime *(Greek time: 2.45pm)* the boat arrives at the island of **Thirassía** *(taverna on the beach)*. At the top of the cliff *(donkeys)* there is a quiet little village of white and blue houses and a view of the caldera *(tavernas)*.

The boat returns to Firá via the Skála of Ía *(see below)* skirting the forbidding and precipitous cliffs of the caldera.

Ía★★. – *10km – 6 miles. Access from Firá by bus or on foot (3 hours) by the cliff-top path* (very fine views of the caldera).

The new church at **Imerovígli** contains a very beautiful iconostasis in carved wood, the only piece rescued from the old building which was destroyed in the earthquake in 1956. Below the village *(west)* on **Cape Skáros** traces of old walls, almost indistinguishable from the rock, indicate the site of the Venetian capital; the path is not easy.

Further north the corniche road runs near the edge of the cliffs and provides a good view east over the carefully tended land descending in broad terraces down to the sea.

Ía★★ (pop 360), which was the first town on the island before the earthquake in 1956, is slowly restoring its damaged buildings on the slopes of the crater. Life here is more peaceful and traditional than in its rival Firá. There is a splendid view★★★ from the northwestern end of the village of the crescent shape of the island, the caldera and the volcanoes at its centre.

Vóthonas; Episkopí Goniás★. – *7km – 4 1/2 miles south by the Kamári road.* A narrow road *(right)*, half sunken in the ground, leads to the unusual village of **Vóthonas** (pop 309), which is partially hidden in a fold in the layer of pozzolana. All that can be seen above the surrounding countryside are palm tree fronds, a few domes and the graceful belltower of the church. *Return to the Kamári road.* Near Méssa Goniá (pop 191) a track *(right)* runs south of the village to the church at **Episkopí Goniás★** (also Panagía Episkopís), one of the most beautiful on the island. It was founded by the Byzantine emperor, Alexis Comnenos late in 11C and the frescoes date from about 1100; re-use of ancient columns.

"Fortified" villages. – *8 to 15km – 5 to 9 miles south of Firá.* **Pírgos** (pop 420), the highest village on the island, is composed of concentric streets, the last ring of houses forming a rampart; there are several handsome neo-Classical houses and traces of a Venetian castle. 4km – 2 1/2 miles southeast of Pírgos stands the Prophet Elijah Monastery (Profítis Ilías) which was founded in 1711 *(no longer open to the public)*; above it rises the peak of the same name, the highest point on the island (556m – 1 824ft; *prohibited military area)*.

Just beyond the village of **Megalohóri** (attractive belfry astride a street), about 500m – 550yds short of the turning to Períssa, stands St Nicholas' Chapel, an unusual little building in white marble dedicated to **Ágios Nikólaos Marmarítis;** it is an ancient funerary temple (3C BC), perfectly preserved and dedicated to the goddess Basileia.

Just outside **Emborío** (pop 1 039) lie the remains of a Venetian fortress which enclosed some ancient houses and the 15C Church of the Virgin.

All these villages have several churches with domes or belltowers.

RUINS OF ANCIENT THERA★★ (ARHÉA THÍRA)

Access from Kamári by a concrete road winding steeply uphill; leave the car at the saddle and take the path leading up to the ruins. There is also a footpath up from Períssa (1 1/2 hours of steep climbing).

Ancient Thera was founded in 9C on a magnificent site★★ high above the Aegean Sea. It was a considerable city in antiquity with 5 000 inhabitants and 700 cisterns and reached the height of its importance under the Egyptian Ptolemies (300-150 BC) who established a naval base in the port at Kamári (then called Oia). Ancient Thera declined under the Romans and was abandoned in 13C.

The first section of the ruins is Byzantine (fortifications and chapels).

Témenos of Artemidoros. – A Ptolemaic admiral was responsible for this sacred enclosure which has retained its altar of Concord and some inscriptions engraved in the rock walls. There are unusual sculptures representing Artemidoros, the lion of Apollo, the eagle of Zeus and the dolphin of Poseidon.

Agora. – It was divided into two parts; the first was overlooked by a temple to Dionysos at the top of a flight of steps and the second by the Royal Portico, a Roman structure of which the bases of the central colonnade can be seen. Behind the agora was a residential district.

Beyond the agora is the theatre *(left)* which dates from the Ptolemaic period but was repaired by the Romans; the sacred way leads to the temple of Apollo.

Temple of Apollo. – It consisted of a *naós* and a *prónaos (p 18)* of which the foundations remain and was preceded by a court *(right)* flanked by two chambers. Beyond lie the terrace and the gymnasium of the Ephebes.

Terrace and gymnasium of the Ephebes. – On the terrace, which dates from 6C BC, the Ephebes, young men doing their military service, engaged in naked exercises and dances, **gymnopaidia;** graffiti in their honour have been written on the rock walls.

Below the terrace at the tip of the headland are traces of the gymnasium (2C BC) where the Ephebes lived overlooking a courtyard; in the north corner of the court was a shrine dedicated to Herakles and Hermes who were venerated by the Ephebes. The baths, of which the foundations are visible, were built by the Romans.

On the way back, take the street by the theatre which climbs to the left towards the **Sanctuary of the Egyptian gods,** Isis, Serapis and Anubis which is cut out of the rock.

EXCAVATIONS AT AKROTÍRI★

Access by bus from Firá. Open 8am to 1pm and 3 to 6pm; closed Mondays; 150 Dr. Keep to the official path.

The excavations, which are roofed over, are gradually revealing a Minoan city dating from 1000 BC which was buried when the volcano at the centre of the island erupted in 1500 BC. Many discoveries have been made including the famous frescoes which are now in the National Archaeological Museum in Athens.

After the eruption Akrotíri was protected and preserved by a thick layer of impervious pumice stone. Part of the city has been excavated revealing the streets and paved squares, the two-storey houses of which the stairs, doors and windows have been partially restored. The huge jars *(pithoi)* in which stores were kept have been left where they were found.

The city must have been evacuated by its inhabitants before the catastrophe because no bodies have been found.

SIKYON   *Sikióna*

Peloponnese – Korinthía – Michelin map 𝟿𝟪𝟢 centre of fold 29

From Kiáto *(10km – 6 1/4 miles by car Rtn)* take the small road marked "Ancient Sikyon" which climbs through vineyards, groves of citrus fruits, olives and almond trees, crosses the motorway, passes through the modern village of Sikióna (Vassilikó pop 872) and reaches the ancient site.

The ruins of Sikyon on their hilltop overlooking the fertile coastal plain and the Gulf of Corinth recall an earlier ancient city which flourished in the Archaic period, particularly under the tyrant Kleisthenes who built a *thólos* and a monopteral monument at Delphi early in 6C which were replaced in 5C by a Treasury. The city of Sikyon then stood in the plain but it was rased to the ground in 30 BC by Demetrius Poliorketes, a king from Asia Minor, and rebuilt on the plateau: it became famous for its school of painting on wax which produced among others Pamphilos, the master of Apelles. According to Pausanias, this latter city was destroyed by an earthquake.

Ruins. – *Museum and site open 8.45am to 3pm.* There are remains from both the Hellenistic and the Roman periods. Beyond the museum, which stands on the site of the old Roman baths, is a large theatre (3C BC) *(restored)* on the right built against the flank of the former acropolis. Below to the left are the foundations of a huge gymnasium (72m by 69m – 236ft by 226ft) on two levels bordered by porticoes and linked by a central staircase between two fountains which are clearly identifiable. The ground also shows traces of a temple, presumably dedicated to Apollo, and a senate house *(bouleuterion).*

Although modern Sparta is built on the fertile banks of the Eurotas (Evrótas) at the foot of the snow-capped slopes of Mount Taÿgetos on the site of ancient Sparta (Lakedaimon), it has nothing in common with the austere and bellicose city of antiquity which triumphed over Athens at the end of the Peloponnesian War. The modern town was developed in the reign of King Otho after 1834; it is a provincial administrative centre, the capital of Lakonía, its straight streets lined with orange trees intersecting at right angles; it is also on the tourist route for those visiting the ruins at Mystra.

HISTORICAL NOTES

An aristocratic and military state. – In the Mycenaean period Sparta was part of the kingdom of Menelaos, Helen's husband. Remains from this period have been found near to Sparta, not only at the Menelaion itself (Geráki road) but also at **Amyklai** (Amíkles – 7km – 4 1/4 miles south) where there was a sanctuary to Apollo containing the tomb of Hyacinthos who was loved by Apollo. There are also the beehive tombs at **Vapheio** (Vafió) on a hill near Amíkles which have yielded the famous golden horn-shaped vessels (rhytons) in the Athens Museum.

The period when Sparta was most influential however was from 9C to 4C BC, first in the Peloponnese, which was conquered except for Árgos, and then throughout Greece.

The Greeks respected the skill of the Spartan soldiers even if they did not approve of the oligarchic constitution which had been drawn up, according to tradition, in about 900 BC by the famous lawgiver **Lycurgus.** At the head of the state were two kings, who were the military leaders, assisted by a council of 28 elders and five "ephors" who had executive power.

The population was divided into three classes: the Spartiates, the warrior class, between 5 000 and 10 000 in number, who were also land owners and holders of government posts; the Perioikoi, who were traders and artisans or farmers, free-men who paid tax; the Helots, serfs without legal status but very numerous.

Spartan way of life. – The Spartiates were forbidden to work; instead they spent almost all their time in barracks, training in combat and practising an athletic war dance known as the Pyrrhic. They ate communally, living mainly on herbs and wild roots; their famous black broth, pork stewed in the animal's blood, was a banquet to them.

At 7 the boys were drafted into youth troops inured to physical exercise. They slept on the ground and were sometimes obliged to practise stealing without being caught; a well-known anecdote tells how a youth who had stolen a fox cub and hidden it beneath his tunic, preferred to let it maul him rather than reveal his booty. On reaching adulthood at the age of 20 the young Spartiates faced a series of initiation tests, the _krypteia;_ they were flogged, sometimes to death, and abandoned without resources in the countryside; they proved themselves by killing any Helots who tarried out of doors after dark.

The girls also were given to strenuous exercise and shocked the other Greeks by their plunging necklines. The married women were not expected to be faithful to their husbands; their lovers were chosen with a view to procreation. It was the married women who presented the newly graduated hoplites with their traditional shield and plumed helmet.

The Spartiates were austere and laconic soldiers but they gave up their lives without hesitation, as did **Leonidas** and his companions at Thermopylae _(p 188)_ in 480 BC. Their numbers diminished continually and eventually they were beaten by Epaminondas in 371 BC at Leuktra near to Thebes _(p 187)._ From then on the city declined and was supplanted by Mystra; gradually ancient Sparta was abandoned until it turned into a desert of stones.

The Spartans are generally thought to have scorned the arts but in 6C and 5C they had talented bronzesmiths who produced the statuettes which are now displayed in the museums of Sparta and Athens and also in the British Museum.

SIGHTS _1 hour_

Archaeological Museum (M). – _Open 8.45am to 3pm (9.30am to 2.30pm Sundays), closed Tuesdays; 100 Dr. Start in the room on the right of the entrance._

The museum, which is surrounded by a pleasant garden, displays the finds from local excavations, particularly Sparta and Amyklai (Amíkles): Archaic low relief sculpture (6C BC), one of which represents Helen and Menelaos; a votive statue of the Dioscuri, Helen's brothers (5C BC); effigy of a hoplite, in marble, thought to be Leonidas (5C BC); head of Apollo or Dionysos (4C BC) discovered in 1978; Archaic bronze statuettes; terracotta masks from the sanctuary of Artemis Orthia; Roman mosaics...

Ancient ruins. – Most of them date from the Hellenistic or Roman periods.

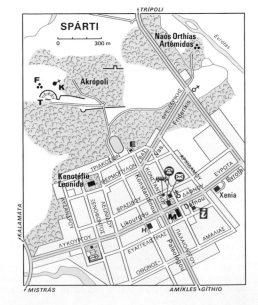

"Leonidas' Tomb" (Kenotáfio Leonída). – This is in fact the base of a small Hellenistic temple; Leonidas' tomb was to be found on the Acropolis.

A modern statue (**E**) of the hero has been erected nearby at the northern end of the main street, Odós Konstandínou.

Akropolis (Akrópoli). – The remains of the Acropolis buildings are half hidden in an olive grove on high ground north of the modern town (signpost: Ancient Sparta). Go through the Byzantine wall and bear left to reach the theatre (**T**) which dates from 1C BC. Above it are the foundations of a temple to Athena (**F**).

At the very top, agreeably situated among fragrant pine and eucalyptus trees next to a spring stands an old Byzantine monastery, Óssios Nikónas (10C AD) (**K**).

Sanctuary of Artemis Orthia (Naós Orthías Artémidos). – The oleanders and rushes on the banks of the River Eurotas – a favourate theme with earlier writers – now screen the ruins of a temple (7C-6C) and an amphitheatre which were excavated by British archaeologists.

It was here that the ritual endurance tests of young Spartiates took place: flogging and athletic dances with masks which were offered to Artemis.

SPETSAE★★   *Spétses*

Saronic Gulf – Pop 3 729 – Michelin map 980 south of fold 30

Access from Piraeus by the regular boat service in 3 1/2 hours or by the express service in 2 3/4 hours; from Zéa (Piraeus) by hydrofoil in 2 1/2 hours; from Kósta by launch in 1/2 hour; from Portohéli by the express service or by hydrofoil in 1/2 hour.

Official permission required for the use of cars; bicycles and motor scooters for hire.

Spetsae is popular with the Athenians who often own houses on the island.

In antiquity it was known as Pityoussa, the island of pine forests; their cool shade and the fragrant resin-scented air in summer, together with the peaceful atmosphere, are still attracting visitors to the island.

Culinary specialities are the almond cakes *(amigdalotá)* and the fish prepared in the Spetsiot manner (baked in the oven in white wine).

Like its rival Hydra, Spetsae grew rich through piracy in the Mediterranean during 18C and 19C. The island contributed nobly to the struggle against the Turks with the vessels built in its shipyards.

Bouboulína, a Greek heroine (1771-1825). – Lascarína Pinótzis was born in prison in Constantinople, the daughter of a Hydriot captain who was condemned to death by the Turks.

Her mother fled to Spetsae, where in 1788 Lascarína married Giannoutzás, a Spetsiot captain, whom she accompanied on several sea voyages but who died in 1798 when his ship was sunk by Barbery pirates. She married a second time, Boúboulis, another sailor, but he too was killed by pirates.

Her husbands' deaths made Bouboulína a rich woman; she owned shipyards and a fleet of brigs and schooners which she supplemented in 1821 with a powerful corvette, the Agamemnon, which flew her personal colours.

Sailing at the head of her squadron, dressed in the striped Spetsiot costume and wearing a huge wimple, Admiral Bouboulína took part in the naval engagements in 1821 and 1824, participating

Spetsae. – Street paving

in acts of piracy and in particular making a significant contribution to the blockade of Nauplion.

On returning to Spetsae she became involved in violent family quarrels caused by her son's seduction of a daughter of the Koutsís family. She died, a victim of the vendetta, from a gunshot wound in the head in her house in Kounoupítsa on 22 May 1825.

SPETSAE TOWN★★ (SPÉTSES) – Pop 3 655

Spetsae is a spacious town, consisting of two districts round the harbour, Dápia and Paleó Limáni, as well as the upper town, Kastéli. It is pleasant to stroll past the ship owners' and sailors' houses set in their gardens. Very often the threshold is decorated with a mosaic of pebbles depicting ships, animals or marine motifs.

Dápia and Paleó Limáni. – The modern port (Dápia) consists of an inlet enclosed between two jetties where caiques and motor boats are moored. The waterfront is lined by a string of administrative buildings, the harbour master's house and several tavernas. Beyond the town hall, in **Kounoupítsa**, the courtyard (unusual mosaics) of Bouboulína's house can be seen *(on request)*. In the other direction towards Kokinariá, stands the **Méxis house**, which was built late in 18C by Hadziyannis Mexis, a wealthy ship owner, and is now occupied by a museum devoted to the lives of great 19C Spetsiots.

Further along the coast near the lighthouse (SE) lies the old port, Paleó Limáni. Its many creeks are filled with shipyards, caulking stations and moorings for the yachts and caiques which have replaced the 19C brigs.

In 1821 the first flag of independent Greece was flown from the belltower of **St Nicholas' Monastery** (Ágios Nikólaos). When **Paul-Marie,** the son of Lucien Bonaparte, was killed in 1827 by a pistol exploding on board the frigate Hellas just offshore, his body was brought to the monastery, preserved in a barrel of oil and kept in a cell for five years before being taken to Sphacteria *(p 175).*

South of Paleó Limáni, beyond the headland, extends the rocky shore round **Agía Marína** *(tavernas).*

Kastéli. – The upper town above Dápia looking across to the Argolid peninsula was fortified by the Venetians in 16C; there are three churches, of which the largest, Holy Trinity (Agía Triáda), contains a beautiful carved wood iconostasis.

Zogeriá Bay★★ (Órmos Zogeriás). *– Take the coast road northwest (5 hours on foot Rtn); 2 hours by bicycle Rtn).* The road runs past what was once a distinguished boys' school (1927-83), founded

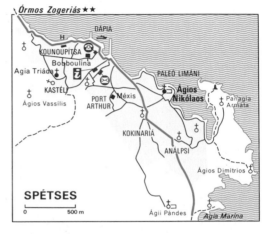

by a Spetsiot tobacco baron, Sotírios Anárgyros, on the lines of an English public school. Two of the English masters who taught there have written novels using their experience: John Fowles' "The Magus" and Kenneth Matthews' "Aleko".

The road continues, cut into the hillside, through forests of Aleppo pines, round the heads of several creeks until it reaches the huge bay at Zogeriá, a beautiful site facing north up the Bay of Nauplion *(tavernas in summer).*

Just off the southeast coast of Spetsae lies **Spetsopoúla,** an islet belonging to the shipping magnate, Niarchos, who has turned it into a game reserve and a harbour for his yachts, including the Creole, the largest three-master in the world.

SPORADES★★   *Vóries Sporádes*

Magnissía – Michelin map **980** folds 18 and 19

The Northern Sporades extend in a chain northwest of Euboia; there are four main islands – Skíathos, Skópelos, Alónissos and Skyros *(with a regular boat service)* – accompanied by numerous smaller islands *(sporádes* means dispersed). The countryside is hilly and wooded, with picturesque villages of white houses cascading down the slopes to the sea, and secluded creeks with beaches ideal for bathing or under-water fishing.

The population follows its traditional way of life: raising sheep and goats, tending vines, olive groves and orchards, fishing with nets or by lamplight, boat building *(caïques)* in Skíathos and Skópelos. Local crafts still thrive: furniture, ceramics, hand-woven cloth... Fish and seafood (lobsters, giant prawns) occur frequently in the local dishes.

May and June are the pleasantest months but the islands are popular throughout the summer when they enjoy constant sunshine tempered by the north wind *(meltémi).*

Skíathos★★. – Pop 4 129. *Access by ferry in 2 hours from Vólos in Thessaly or in 2 1/4 hours from Ágios Konstandínos in Boeotia, in 5 hours from Kími on Euboia; by air from Athens in 3/4 hour.*

Skíathos Island, which has become very fashionable, is a southern extension of the Pelion range; it is covered with pine and olive trees and rises to 438m – 1 437ft. The jagged coastline creates numerous sandy creeks and a splendid lagoon bordered by pine trees. **Koukounariés Beach★★**, a stretch of fine sand over 1km – 1/2 mile long, backed by pine trees *(access from Skíathos-Town by bus or caïque).*

Skíathos Town★. – Pop 3 838. Skíathos is the capital of the island and a cosmopolitan resort in summer. It was rebuilt in 1830 on two hills overlooking a broad and sheltered roadstead; its two harbours, one for fishing boats and one for pleasure craft, are protected by an islet (Boúrdzi) which was fortified in the Middle Ages. The shady waterfront is crowded by cafés and fish tavernas. In town one can visit the house of the novelist Aléxandros Papadiamántis (1851-1911) who often wrote about Skíathos in his work.

In summer there are boat trips round the island; in passing one can admire the Blue Grotto, **Laláría** beach with its "pierced rock" and the Kástro. *Daily excursions to Skópelos and Alónissos.*

Kástro★. – *On the north coast; access by boat (1 1/2 hours) or on foot (4 hours Rtn) from Skíathos Town.*

The track passes two monasteries – Evangelístria (beautiful iconostasis of carved wood in the church) and Ágios Harálambos – before reaching the ruins of the medieval fortress (Kástro). It was the capital of the island until about 1825 and stood on a promontory, accessible only by a drawbridge. It contained 300 houses and 22 churches, two of which are well preserved: Christchurch contains a 17C carved wooden iconostasis.

Skópelos★. – *Access by ferry from Kími on Euboia, Vólos in Thessaly or Ágios Konstandínos in Boeotia; hotels in Skópelos Town, rooms in private houses.*

Skópelos is the most densely populated (pop 4 451) of the Sporádes and also the most fertile. It grows vines, olives, almonds and above all plums which make excellent prunes when dried in the oven.

Like Skíathos, Skópelos is well supplied with creeks and charming sandy beaches but it also has a traditional side and the women sometimes still wear the local dress – a skirt embroidered with flowers and a velvet bodice. Traces of the Minoans have been found, in particular the tomb of King Staphylos who may have introduced the grape *(staphíli)* to the island. Skópelos boasts some 350 churches and chapels together with about ten 17C and 18C monasteries; white buildings against the green landscape.

Skópelos Town★. – Pop 2 668. It is a pleasure to stroll along the quayside by the harbour under the shade of the plane trees and through the narrow streets of the town; among the houses with their stone shingled roofs are many small churches or chapels.

The medieval **castle** (Kástro) contained many houses and several religious buildings including St Athanasius' Chapel which was built in 9C on the foundations of an ancient temple. From the top of the ruins there is a fine view of Skópelos and the archipelago.

Alónissos. – *Access by ferry from Vólos and Agios Konstandínos three times a week; from Kími once a week. Bungalow hotel.*

The island is quite large but has few inhabitants (pop 1 554); it has a wild landscape of woods and mountains. Fishing, shepherding and agriculture are practised. Sea caves.

Skyros★. – *Access: by ferry from Kími on Euboia (2 hours) and from Vólos in Thessaly (11 1/2 hours) landing at Linariá; by air from Athens daily (except Wednesdays) (50 minutes). Beaches on the east coast at Gírísmata, Mólos, Magaziá (Skyros Town), Meálos and Ahíli; on the west coast at Theotókos, Ágios Pétros, Agalipa, Atsítsa, Ágios Fokás, Péfkos, Linariá and Kalamítsa; on the south coast in Trís Boúkes Bay (shingle) and at Glyfáda on Sarakíniko Island.*

Skyros Island (pop 2 575) is the largest of the Sporades and consists of two mountainous islets linked by an isthmus. It has a rougher, more primitive character than its neighbours. The southern half, called **Vounó** (mountain), is barren and steep and mainly covered with holm-oak scrub although well supplied with springs in the north; it is known not only for its semi-wild herds of sheep and goats but also for its small **horses**, similar to Shetland ponies, which may date from Classical times. The northern half of the island, called **Meroi**, is fertile and cultivated and well wooded with pine forests. The island has a strong tradition of excellent craftsmanship: carved and painted furniture, hand-woven and embroidered cloth, carpets, basketwork and ceramics.

The traditional baggy blue trousers, thick black or white gaiters and distinctive Skyrian sandals *(trohadia)*, modelled on ancient sandals, are still worn by some of the older men.

Fresh fish, crustaceans and honey are plentiful. The creeks and caves along the coast invite one to explore. In summer there are excursions by road and boat.

Skyros Town★. – Pop 2 217. The main town, Skyros also called Hóra, has two hotels and a large sandy beach at Magaziá. Its tiny white cuboid houses more typical of the Cyclades *(p 92)* are crowded on the inland face of a steep rock crag, spilling over into the valley and climbing up to the castle on the summit. It is a pleasure to stroll through the network of narrow alleyways and steps *(no cars)* which pass under arches and open into courtyards. Traditionally the living room with its carved wooden furniture and its curved chimneybreast *(alóni)* bearing three rows of hooks and shelves is adorned with copper articles and porcelain plates.

Kástro. – The Venetian fortress was built on the old acropolis where **Achilles** *(p 168)* is supposed to have been brought up, dressed like a girl, among the daughters of King Lykomedes, so as to escape the dismal destiny which overtook him at the siege of Troy. Just below it the famous monastery of St George nestles on a ledge of rock above the town; the church dates from 10C. There is an unusual **view★★** over Skyros Town where the stepped roofs of the houses form a chequerboard.

Phaltaïts Folklore Museum. *Open daily 10am to 1pm and 5 to 8pm (4 to 5pm in winter). Donation.*

An old Skyrian mansion on the northeast edge of the town houses a fascinating collection of Skyrian handicrafts, both traditional and modern: jewellery, embroidery, textiles, local costumes, wood carvings, furniture, ceramics and bronze and copper household articles. Reconstruction of a local interior. Books about Skyros.

Archaeological Museum. – *Open daily 8.45am to 3pm (9.30am to 2.30pm Sundays and holidays); closed Tuesdays.*

This museum, which was recently completed next to the Phaltaïts Museum, houses articles and sculptures excavated on the island (6C BC to 3C AD).

Rupert Brook Memorial and Grave. – On a bastion on the northeast edge of the town *(by the museums)* stands a statue to immortal poetry in memory of Rupert Brook.

The poet's grave lies in a grove of olive trees in a valley on the southern shore of the island in Trís Boúkes Bay *(1 hour by road from Skyros or by boat from Linariá)*. When Rupert Brook died of septicaemia on a French hospital ship in April 1915 on the eve of sailing for the Dardanelles, his last wish was to be buried on the island of Skyros.

STYMPHALIA Lake★   *Stimfalía*

Peloponnese – Korinthía – Michelin map 980 centre of fold 29

Access. – *37km – 23 miles southwest of Kiáto.* A good road, marked Stimfalía, crosses the groves of citrus fruit trees in the coastal plain and then climbs the eastern foothills of Mount Kilíni overlooking the Gulf of Corinth: a smiling landscape of pine woods and vines cultivated as bushes to produce the dried grapes known as "currants". The road then descends into the huge and barren depression at the bottom of which lies Lake Stymphalia *(tavernas).*

The Lake★. – Below the acropolis of the city of Stymphalia extends an immense reed-covered marsh surrounded by a ring of dark peaks rising to 2 000m – 6 560ft; its depth and surface area vary according to the season. A touch of anguish seems to emanate from the bleak and inhospitable landscape.

A profound silence hangs over this vast tract of land which is inhabited only by rare herds of cows or flocks of sheep grazing in the custody of a herdsman swathed in a thick cloak and carrying a crook; Stymphalia is on the borders of Arcadia.

The Stymphalian Birds. – The gloomy waters of Lake Stymphalia inspired fear in the ancient Greeks; according to the legend the lake was haunted by nauseating birds with huge wings which seized on passers-by, suffocating them in their grasp and killing them with their beaks before eating them. **Herakles** (Hercules) rid the region of them as the fifth of his Twelve Labours *(p 194)* by killing them with his arrows and then offering them to Athena.

Old Abbey of Zaraká. – On the east side of the road from Kiáto are the ruins of a Cistercian monastery built in 13C. The church was Gothic: the pillars in the nave were formed of engaged columns and the chancel was square according to the usual Cistercian practice. The cloisters were on the south side. A single tower marks the entrance to the precinct.

Kastaniá. – *20km – 12 1/2 miles Rtn from the west end of the lake.* Pop 138. From the lake a road winds past rocky outcrops and coniferous forests to an old mountain village; its houses are traditional with balconies and pantile roofs. It is a quiet place to spend a few days *(hotel Xenia)* on the slopes of **Mount Kilíni** (also Zíria) (2 376m – 7 790ft) which in antiquity was supposed to be the haunt of white blackbirds.

SYROS★   *Síros*

Cyclades – Pop 19 669 – Michelin map 980 fold 32

Syros enjoys a privileged position at the centre of the archipelago; its main town Ermoúpoli is the capital of the Cyclades. The island, which is steep and barren on the eastern seaboard, is green and cultivated on the opposite slope. The vast roadstead at Ermoúpoli provides a safe and deep anchorage; in the late 19C it was the first port in Greece and is still the hub of seaborne traffic between the islands.

Access from Piraeus by several ferrys daily in 4 to 5 hours.

The Pope's Island. – In 13C the Venetian and Genoese who occupied the island sought a refuge from pirates and founded Ano Syra (Áno Síros) on the southern peak where they implanted Roman Catholicism. This version of Christianity prevailed even after 1537 when the Turks captured the island because under the "Capitulations" agreed between François I and the Sultan the religious institutions established by the Latins were placed under the protection of France.

The Capucines were the first to arrive in 1633, followed by the Jesuits, the Ursulines and the Lazarists of St Vincent de Paul. The religious "Houses" dispensed justice and organised schools and hospitals. In 1717 the botanist Tournefort wrote that Syros, then called **Syra,** was the most Catholic island in the archipelago with 6 000 Roman Catholic as against 12 Orthodox families. Nowadays Syros is still a Roman Catholic see.

Birth of a refugee town. – Syra had always been a focal point on the shipping routes between Athens, Constantinople, Alexandria and the other ports of the Levant and in the aftermath of Greek independence the island's importance grew.

Starting in 1821 thousands of Greeks, who were driven out of Chios and other Aegean islands by the Turks, found refuge on the then uninhabited shores of Syra Bay.

Gradually a new town developed; it was placed under the patronage of Hermes, the god of Commerce, and called Hermoupoli (Ermoúpoli). Totally Greek, it grew rapidly and by 1828 it already had 14 000 inhabitants. At one time there was even a possibility of it becoming the capital of the newly established Greek kingdom.

In fact, Ermoúpoli flourished until the end of the century. Maritime trade, ship yards, textile workshops, tanneries, the production of wrought iron and ships' prows all enriched the cosmopolitan inhabitants. The town acquired the appearance which it has to a large extent retained: foreign architects such as Chabeau (French) and Ziller (German) contributed to the construction of public buildings, elegant houses with wrought iron balconies and the handsome villas in Vapória where the ship owners, bankers and rich merchants lived. The establishment of schools, printing presses, newspapers and even a literary circle sustained a high level of intellectual activity. A flourishing social life was expressed in the Carnival, theatre or opera, concerts and balls.

The opening of the Corinth Canal in 1893 dealt Ermoúpoli a serious blow and it was supplanted by Piraeus. There was renewed activity in the port during the Second World War when Goulandris, a shipping magnate, built the Neorion floating dock.

SIGHTS *1 1/2 hours*

From the entrance to the bay there is an arresting view of the **setting★★** of the town with its white houses spread up and down the steep slopes and divided into distinct districts: on the waterfront, Ermoúpoli, built in 19C, the administrative and commercial centre; above, on two hills divided by a valley, Áno Síra *(left),* the old Roman Catholic town dating from 13C and Vrondádo *(right),* where the Orthodox live, which was built in 19C as an offshoot of Ermoúpoli.

Ermoúpoli – Pop 13 876. The "new" town was built in the neo-Classical style.

The quays. – The waterfront, with its cafés, shipping lines, tavernas and confectioners selling the Turkish Delight *(loukoúmi)* for which the island is famous, has a fine view of the port and the anchorage protected by Donkey Island (Gaidouníssi).

Platía Miaoúlis. – The huge square with its marble paving, its palm trees and pavement cafés is the setting for the evening stroll *(perípato* or *vólta)*, which is so common in Mediterranean countries, and also for concerts given in the bandstand.

The neo-Classical architectural style is well in evidence in the arcades along the south side, in the majestic building designed by Ziller (1878) which is both the Town Hall and the Law Courts, and also in the Library. The attractive marble theatre, a small-scale replica of the Scala in Milan, in the adjoining square was designed by Chabeau in 1862.

Administrative district. – Apollo Street (Odós Apóllonos) is the axis of the administrative and commercial district, which looks rather forsaken but nevertheless presents a group of solid 19C buildings : regional administrative offices *(Nomarhía),* Chamber of Commerce, banks and fine mansions with balconies.

The road up to St Nicholas' Church (blue dome) passes through Vapória, a residential district with elegant villas overlooking a little bay.

Áno Síros. – Pop 1 275. *Access by taxi or on foot by Odós Omírou and steps (3/4 hour Rtn).* The road passes near the French school (St George's) which takes 160 pupils and the French hospital run by the Sisters of Charity *(right).*

Áno Síros, the old Roman Catholic town, is criss-crossed by steep and winding streets lined by chapels (Our Lady of Carmel) and convents (Jesuits). Side by side in a square at the top of the hill are the bishop's palace and St George's Cathedral, built in the Venetian style. From the terrace there is a **view★** down the valley between Áno Síros and Vrondádo to Ermoúpoli and the harbour.

TEMPE, Vale of★ — *Témbi*

Thessaly – Lárissa – Michelin map 980 north of fold 17

On the northern border of Thessaly the valley of the River **Peneios** narrows into a dark and mysterious but verdant gorge, once known as the "Wolf's Mouth" (Likóstomo). The ravine, which is 5km – 3 miles long, was caused by a seismic fracture between Olympos and Óssa; it formed a channel into which the Peneios directed its course so draining the Lárissa lake to the sea.

The laurels of Apollo. – In antiquity this region was sacred to Apollo, son of Zeus and Leto. After killing the python at Delphi *(p 100)* he came to wash in the waters of the Peneios. There he fell in love with the nymph Daphne who was changed into a laurel tree *(dáphni)* to escape from Apollo's advances. Disappointed, Apollo gathered a sprig of the laurel and planted it at Delphi near the Kastalian spring. Every eighth year, as a token of remembrance, pilgrims went to Tempe from Delphi to gather a symbolic laurel branch.

The Vale of Tempe was much praised in antiquity for its cool freshness compared with the torrid summer climate of the Macedonian and Thessalian plains. It enchanted the Emperor Hadrian who had it re-created by landscape architects in the grounds of his villa at Tivoli near Rome.

SIGHTS *1/2 hour*

It is advisable to visit the Vale of Tempe, with its clumps of plane trees, oleanders and rhododendrons, by travelling upstream from east to west as most of the lay-bys are on the north *(right)* side of the road.

Daphne's (or Apollo's) **Spring.** – Shady site, cool and restful.

Agía Paraskeví. – This important place of pilgrimage dedicated to the Virgin is on the north bank of the River Peneios at the foot of an impressive cliff of rock. From the footbridge over the river there is a beautiful **view★** of the Vale and the plane trees spreading their graceful arms over the water. On a rocky pinnacle are the remains of a medieval castle, one of the six fortresses which guarded the pass.

Aphrodite's Spring. – It is down by the river beneath the sheltering plane trees.

TENOS — *Tínos*

Cyclades – Pop 7 731 – Michelin map 980 fold 32

In the Greek world Tenos is famous for pilgrimages on 25 March and 15 August to the miraculous icon of the Annunciation of the Virgin. It is a mountainous island; its terraced slopes, on which barley and vines are grown, are often swept by the north wind *(meltémi).*

The island is also well known for its Venetian style **pigeon lofts** which number upwards of a thousand; these are white towers decorated with delicate geometric patterns, often done in open-work (fine collection at **Kámbos**). Scarcely less numerous are the **churches** and **chapels**, some of which contain treasures of popular art inspired by Byzantine or Venetian tradition.

Tenos was a fief of the Venetian Ghisi family in 13C and, like Mykonos, it was the last of the Cyclades to fall to the Turks in 1718; for this reason the Roman Catholic faith is professed by nearly 50% of the population, grouped in the centre of the island round the bishop's residence at Xinára and the girls' school at Loutrá.

Access by daily ferry from Piraeus and Rafína; many hotels and rooms to let in town; hotel at Klónia (2.5km – 1 1/2 miles). Local buses or organised excursions.

Tenos Town. – Pop 3 879. Set in a broad bay, the white capital of the island is both a port and a pleasant little town, its narrow streets bustling with traders and craftsmen.

Church of Panagía Evangelístria. – A broad steeply sloping street, which some pilgrims climb on their knees, leads up to the imposing white marble church which dominates the town. The church was built in 1823 following the discovery in 1822 by Sister Pelagia of a miraculous icon, the object of the pilgrimages which attract the sick and the faithful.

A great court enclosed by porticoes surrounds the church which is approached by a ceremonial flight of steps. On the left of the entrance in the nave is the holy icon, encrusted in jewels and hung about with countless votive offerings: hearts, legs, silver lamps, boats etc.

On the left below the church are the "caves" where the icon was discovered; a neighbouring building contains a little museum of religious art (icons).

Archaeological Museum. – *Open 8.45am to 3pm (9.30am to 2.30pm Sundays); closed Tuesdays; 100 Dr.* In 1969 a building was constructed beside the approach road to the church in the style of the island pigeon lofts; among other exhibits it houses a colossal provisions vase *(pithos)* dating from 7C BC and found at Exómvourgo, as well as objects from the excavation of the sanctuary of Poseidon and Amphitrite.

Exómvourgo. – *9km – 5 1/2 miles plus 1 hour on foot Rtn; from the Stení-Falatádos crossroads drive to the monastery and park the car nearby; continue on foot by a fairly difficult path.*

On the hilltop (alt 553m – 1 814ft) stands Exómvourgo, a Venetian citadel built on the site of an ancient acropolis; below extended the town, also fortified, which the Venetians named Sant' Elena.

From the top **panorama over the island and the northern Cyclades.**

The Villages. – There are about 50 villages on Tenos; they were built inland from the coast, with narrow winding streets and vaulted passages, as much for protection against the wind as against the pirates of earlier centuries. The most interesting include **Istérnia** with its two churches and **Pánormos** (or Pírgos), the home of famous painters and sculptors, with a beautiful beach down by the sea. The unusual **Kehrovouníou Convent,** in the northeast of the island, is a village in miniature, housing about sixty nuns.

THÁSSOS★★

Macedonia – Kavála – Pop 13 111 – Michelin map 980 fold 7

Thássos, famous in antiquity for its gold and marble, lies just off the coast of Eastern Macedonia. Its wooded mountain scenery, its creeks and bathing beaches as well as its excellent hotels make it a delightful island resort for holidays.

Access by ferry from Kavála to Órmos Prínou and Thássos-Liménas (three sailings per day; 1 1/2 hour crossing) and from Keramotí to Thássos-Liménas (six sailings per day; 1/2 hour crossing). Main beaches at Makríamos, Alikí, Potamiá and Limenária Bay. Local specialities: fresh fish, honey and retsína. Classical drama festival in summer.

From yellow gold to black gold. – The island, which covers about 440m² – 170sq miles and rises in Mount Ipsári or Psári to about 1 127m – 3 698ft, is composed of marble and grey-green gneiss. Ample rainfall in autumn and winter sustains the luxuriant vegetation which clothes the landscape. There are several sorts of pine tree: sea pines, Aleppo pines and Corsican pines; also Cypresses, olives, oaks, chestnuts, walnut and even poplars...

In antiquity, particularly from 7C to 5C BC Thássos was of considerable economic importance owing to its exports of oil and wine, of white marble and of gold and silver; the metal was used to mint money throughout the Mediterranean. In those days the inhabitants ruled part of the Macedonian coast including Kavála and Thessalonika.

Then the island entered on a period of relative quiet until the arrival of the Romans who reactivitated the production of wine and marble. In 15C Thássos was occupied for a period by the Genoese who set up a trading post under the Gatteluzzi, the lords of Lesbos and Samothrace. Finally the Turks took over and Thássos became the personal fief of Mehmet Ali *(p 121)* and his family from 1813 to 1902.

Interest in Thássos was renewed in 1971 when oil was discovered off-shore.

THÁSSOS TOWN★ (pop 2 300)

The modern town, which is also known as **Liménas** (Port), extends westwards in a lively string of café terraces and tavernas set about with trees. The considerable traces of the ancient Greek civilisation, which the French School in Athens has been excavating since 1910, are spread over a vast area enclosed within a marble wall which dates from 5C BC; a few of the gates are still decorated with low relief carvings.

Eastern ramparts and the acropolis★ – *2 hours on foot Rtn.* Starting behind the long Turkish building with balconies overlooking the caïque harbour, the path runs along inside the ramparts and then climbs up above the ancient port; the outline of the old jetties can be traced beneath the water. A little way offshore lies the islet of Thassopoúla.

After passing the modest shipyards and the remains of a 5C paleo-Christian basilica set on a promontory, the path climbs up by the wall which is superbly constructed in places with polygonal blocks. Half way along is the **theatre;** it was built in the Hellenistic period but remodelled by the Romans as an arena for wild beast fights.

Continue uphill to the acropolis.

Acropolis★. – There were three peaks in a line separated by two narrow saddles.

On the first peak stood a sanctuary to Pythian Apollo which was converted into a fortress by the Genoese who reused the old material on the original foundations.

The second peak, which forms a terrace, boasted a temple to Athena; the 5C foundations are still visible.

At the base of the third is a small rock sanctuary dedicated to Pan; from the peak there are beautiful **views**★★ of Thássos Island and the Aegean Sea as far as Samothrace.

Agora★ – *Open 8.45am to 3pm; entrance near the museum.*

The agora, which has recently been excavated, was not far from the harbour and surrounded by porticoes and studded with monuments of all sorts; it was linked to the neighbouring shrines by the Ambassaders *(Theories)* Passage which was decorated with low relief sculptures (sent to the Louvre in Paris in 1864).

An anti-clockwise tour round the agora takes in three porticoes: on the right of the entrance traces of the southwest portico, which dates from the Roman period and was supported by 33 Doric columns (remains of a monumental altar in south corner); then traces of the southeast portico, of the same period, of which three columns have been re-erected (at the far end the base of a monument to Glaukos set up in 7C BC); finally traces of the "oblique" portico and of a 5C paleo-Christian basilica.

Within the open space the archaeologists have excavated the remains of a *thólos (p 18)*, an altar dedicated to the deified Theagenes, a Thassian who had been victorious in the Olympic Games, and some round stone benches *(exedrae)*.

Museum. – *Open 8.45am to 3pm (9.30 to 2.30pm Sundays); closed Tuesdays; 100 Dr.*

It displays the items found during the excavations and some interesting sculptures. Room 1 (central hall): colossal *kouros (p 19)* carrying a ram (6C BC) from the acropolis and a very realistic head of Silenus (5C BC); Room 2: two 6C BC works found in the temple of Artemis, a mirror handle in bronze and an extraordinary ivory lion's head; the other rooms: an effigy of Dionysos (3C BC) from the Hellenistic period, two heads by the School of Skópas (4C BC, a base relief from a Roman altar to Cybele showing griffins devouring a doe and Roman portraits from the empire (Julius Caesar, Claudius, Hadrian).

TOUR OF THE ISLAND★★ *79km – 49 miles, about 3 hours*

There is a good road which follows the wooded coastline not far from the shore. It passes inlets and beaches or crosses tiny coastal basins, cuts into the cliff face.

Leaving Thássos-Liménas in a southeasterly direction the road first climbs to **Panagía** (pop 899), the ancient capital of the island; the houses have balconies and schist roofs.

Alikí★ *(tavernas)* on the south coast is built on an attractive site on the neck of a peninsula consisting entirely of marble quarries which seem to have been abandoned only yesterday. There was an ancient city here as is proved by the remains of a double sanctuary; the edge of the hill bears traces of two paleo-Christian basilicas.

Limenária (pop 1 448) is a fishing village and a lively summer resort.

Along the west coast the road passes many fishing villages *(skála)*. If there is time make a detour to **Mariés** *(29km – 18 miles Rtn)*, a pretty village in the traditional style.

THEBES   *Thíva*

Central Greece – Boeotia – Pop 18 712 – Michelin map 980 fold 30

Thebes, capital of the rich and fertile Boeotia, which was one of the most famous cities in ancient Greece, is now only a commercial centre, a busy but undistinguished town. It was rebuilt in the last century, after an earthquake, to a regular plan on the hill where the acropolis of Cadmea once stood.

MYTHOLOGY AND HISTORY

According to legend, Thebes was founded by Cadmos, a Phoenician, who was guided to the spot by a cow marked with a magic sign. Then **Amphion**, son of Zeus and Antiope, built the city walls, moving the enormous stones into place with the sound of his lyre. Finally Cadmos, who had married Harmonia, had a daughter Semele who became the mistress of Zeus and mother of Dionysos.

Ill-fated Oedipus! – The most famous Theban, however, is Oedipus, son of Laios, king of Thebes, and Jocasta. When Laios was told by an oracle that Oedipus would kill his father and marry his mother he had him exposed on Mount Kithairon (Kiterónas) to die of cold and hunger but some shepherds rescued the boy who was brought up by the King of Corinth in ignorance of his true parentage.

On reaching manhood Oedipus left Corinth; near Thebes he quarrelled with a man and killed him; it was Laios. At that time the Theban countryside was being terrorised by the **Sphinx**, a winged monster with a lion's body and a woman's bust, which devoured those passing by who were unable to answer the riddles it posed. Jocasta's brother, **Creon**, offered the throne of Thebes and Jocasta's hand to anyone who would rid the country of the Sphinx. Oedipus accepted the challenge and was asked "What is it that walks on four legs in the morning, on two at noon, on three in the evening?" "Man" answered Oedipus. He was right. In vexation the Spinx threw herself into an abyss. Oedipus became king of Thebes and married his mother, thus fulfilling the oracle's prediction.

Later, however, when Oedipus discovered the truth, he put out his eyes and Jocasta hanged herself. Oedipus left Thebes accompanied by his daughter Antigone to lead a wandering life until his death at Colona (Kolonós) near Athens.

Proud Antigone! – After Oedipus' death, Antigone returned to Thebes to be with her sister Ismene and her brothers Eteocles and Polyneices. These two quarrelled, entered into fratricidal combat and died. Their uncle Creon, the traitor, took his opportunity and seized power, forbidding Antigone to bury Polyneices who had allied himself with the seven champions of Argos, an incident recalled by Aeschylus in his play "Seven against Thebes". Oedipus' daughter defied man-made laws to follow her conscience and buried her brother before suffering her own punishment which was to be buried alive. Sophocles took this sad story as the theme of his tragedy "Antigone".

Lucky Pindar! – Thebes' moment of glory came in 4C BC when she headed the Boeotian Confederacy and defeated Sparta at Leuktra in 371 near Plataia, initiating a period of Theban hegemony over Greece which lasted ten years. Two men **Epaminondas** and

Pelopidas, took the credit for reorganising the Theban army which centred on a core of crack troops the famous "Sacred Band" composed of 300 young nobles who swore to fight together until death.

After the death of Epaminondas at the battle of Mantineia in the Peloponnese in 362 BC Thebes, Athens' long-time rival, declined and in 336 the city was destroyed by Alexander except for the house of Pindar the poet (518-438 BC).

Magnificent Nicholas! – Thebes regained a certain importance as a commercial centre in the Byzantine period when the silk industry flourished. It also resumed its political importance in 1205 when the Crusaders occupied the region. Boeotia and Attica fell to Otho de la Roche, from Burgundy, who settled in Thebes. When he died without issue, his nephew, Guy I, inherited Athens and Attica while his niece, Bonne, received Boeotia as her dowry when she married Otho of St-Omer whose descendants took the title of the Duke of Thebes. It was **Nicholas of St Omer** (1258-1294) who built the castle of Cadmea and decorated it lavishly. It was captured however in 1311 and dismantled by the Catalans who defeated the Franks at the battle of Kephisos *(p 162).*

ARCHAEOLOGICAL MUSEUM★

Open 8.45am to 3pm (Sundays 9.30am to 2.30pm); closed Tuesdays; 100 Dr.
The museum stands near a 13C **Frankish tower,** once part of the castle built by the St Omer family, at the northern entrance to Thebes. It contains Boeotian antiquities: in the room on the right of the entrance, Archaic sculptures including *(centre)* a superb 6C BC **kouros★★** *(p 19)* from the French excavations at Ptoion *(p 174)* ; in the third room funerary steles in black stone (5C BC) showing representations of warriors; in the fourth room a series of sarcophagi from the Mycenaean period (13C BC) painted with funerary scenes showing keeners, ritual ceremonies etc.

THERMOPYLAE★   *Thermopíles*

Central Greece – Fthiótida – Michelin map 980 south of fold 17

The pass of Thermopylae is famous for its heroic defence by Leonidas and his Spartans. Hemmed in in antiquity between Mount Kalídromo (S) and an arm of the sea, the Maliac Gulf, the pass was the main route from Thessaly into Southern Greece. In those days the pass was much narrower than it is now; the modern motorway follows the ancient shoreline. Subsequently the estuary of the River Sperhiós silted up forming a coastal plain which now produces olives and cotton.

An unequal struggle. – In 480 BC, ten years after the battle of Marathon *(p 71),* another "Great Army" of Persians led by **Xerxes,** Darius' son, crossed the Hellespont (the Dardanelles) and invaded Greece. Thus began the Second Persian War which Herodotos described in his History.

When the myriads of Persian soldiers (according to modern historians they numbered about 30 000) arrived at Thermopylae they found the Greeks, only 8 000, entrenched behind the Phocian wall. "Surrender your arms" cried Xerxes to Leonidas. "Come and take them" replied the Spartan commander.

The Persians attacked but for two days suffered heavy losses. Then a traitor showed them a way over the mountains so that they could turn the Greek defence and, despite the Phocian troops, take the Greeks in the rear.

When Leonidas saw what was planned, he made the bulk of the army withdraw and prepared to defend his position with 300 Spartans and 700 Thespians. He was forced to retreat to a knoll (Kolonós) under a hail of arrows to which he responded with "So much the better, we will fight in the shade" The Spartans were killed to the last man; Leonidas' body was beheaded and then crucified on the orders of Xerxes who had lost his two brothers in the engagement.

Fortunately for the Greeks the subsequant engagements at Salamis *(p 73)* and Plataia *(p 172)* resulted in victory and the Persians were driven out of Greece.

Leonidas' Monument. – *On the north side of the road.* The monument was unveiled in 1955 by King Paul of Greece. It is constructed of white marble and decorated with low relief sculptures of the battle; it is crowned by a bronze statue of the Spartan leader, bearing arms and wearing his helmet.

On the other side of the road is the knoll, **Kolonós,** where the Spartans took their final stand; a mausoleum has been constructed bearing an inscription –
"Go, tell the Spartans, thou who passest by,
That here obedient to their laws we lie".

Thermopylae. – Leonidas' Monument

Hot springs (Loutrá). – *500m – 547yds beyond the monument, on the south side of the road near a petrol station.* Known in antiquity as the "Baths of Herakles" these sulphurous waters which emerge at the foot of the mountain have given their name to the locality; Thermopylae literally means "hot gates".

Thessalonika (Salonica), the second largest town and port in Greece, is also the capital of Macedonia and the seat of the Ministry of Northern Greece. It is a modern looking town spreading up the hillside with a thriving intellectual (University: Panepistímio), commercial and industrial life (pop 406 413; 725 785 including the suburbs).

The city is flanked on the west by an industrial zone of factories, by a residential district on the east and on the heights to the north by an oriental quarter; the centre on the waterfront is marked by **Platía Aristotélous**, a square open to the sea. Thessalonika's position at the head of a deep bay, its tree-lined streets, smart shops and Byzantine churches make it attractive to visitors but they should avoid the summer heat and the rigours of winter when the head of the bay sometimes freezes over.

HISTORICAL NOTES

Thessalonika, an imperial city. – Thessalonika was founded in 315 BC by Kassander, a Macedonian general *(diádochos)* who named the city after his wife Thessalonika, sister of Alexander the Great. Under Roman rule it developed into an important port and staging post on the **Via Egnatia**, which linked Dyracchium (Durazzo in Albania) with Asia Minor and was the main highway for Roman penetration of the Levant. In 148 BC it became the capital of the Roman province of Macedonia and was an important cultural centre which was visited by Cicero when he went into exile in 58 BC. **St Paul** visited Thessalonika twice during his journeys in 50 and 56 AD and preached in the Synagogue despite the hostility of certain Jews; he also founded the church to which he addressed several Epistles.

Early in 4C Thessalonika became the main residence of the Emperor Galerius under whose edict Christians were persecuted; in 306 a Roman officer of Greek origin, St Demetrios was martyred. The **Emperor Theodosius the Great** (379-395) gave official standing to the Christian religion which he had embraced during a serious illness. His conversion did not however prevent him from ordering the massacre of 7 000 Thessalonians in the circus in reprisal for the murder of one of his generals; later he repented and submitted to the penitence imposed by St Ambrose, Bishop of Milan.

Under the return to order following the Barbarian invasions in the reign of the Emperor of Byzantium, **Justinian** (527-565), Thessalonika became the second city of the Eastern Empire after Byzantium and many churches were built. St Cyril, the philosopher, future apostle of the Slavs and probable inventor of the Cyrillic alphabet, was born there in 827.

From anarchy to prosperity. – After a period of uncertainty caused by dissension among the Byzantines, Thessalonika was caught up in the capture of Constantinople by the Fourth Crusade and from 1204 to 1224 was an archbishopric and capital of a Latin kingdom of which the first king was Boniface de Montferrat.

Thessalonika was returned to Byzantium and fell prey to anarchy until it was captured by Sultan Mourad II in 1430. There followed a period of prosperity which was further enhanced by the arrival in 1492 of 20 000 Jews who had fled from Spain; they were skilled in working with wool, silk and precious stones. They formed a community of craftsmen and merchants who traded throughout Europe. They spoke Ladino a form of Castilian written in Hebrew script, wore caftans and greatcoats trimmed with fur and by 17C numbered about 30 000, nearly half the population.

The modern period. – Under the Turks Thessalonika was allowed a certain autonomy and its economy developed in the late 19C; in 1888 it was linked by railway to Central Europe and from 1897 to 1903 a new port was constructed by a French company. It was the cradle of the Young Turks who deposed Sultan Abdul Hamid in 1909 and of **Kemal Ataturk** (1881-1938) who was the first President of the Turkish republic.

In 1912 Thessalonika was returned to Greece. During the First World War from 1915-1918 it was the headquarters of the allied armies in the East and of the Greek government of National Defence under Venizélos *(p 204)*. In September 1918 Greek troops joined the allies in clearing Macedonia of the enemy and advancing into Serbia and Bulgaria; those who fell in the campaign are buried in the allied military cemetery at Diavatá (north of Thessalonika).

When a large part of the city was destroyed by fire in 1917, leaving 80 000 people without shelter, it was rebuilt in concrete according to plans drawn up by the French architect Hébrard who designed the beautiful central perspective. In 1941 Thessalonika was occupied by the Germans who deported some 50 000 Jews. The city suffered another disaster in 1978 when an earthquake damaged most of the monuments and caused serious harm to the churches.

Industry and commerce. – Thessalonika stands at the crossroads of the land and sea routes linking western Europe with the Levant; it has long been a trading centre which now organises an International Fair (Diethní Ékthessi, **BZ**) each September. Local industry which is grouped to the west of the city has traditionally concentrated on textiles, tobacco, food (sugar, oil...) to which other activities have recently been added: an oil refinery, fertiliser factories, a steel works, a cement works etc. The traffic in the port, fifty per cent of which is hydrocarbons, is constantly increasing.

Life in Thessalonika. – Parking places are scarce; there is however a car park in the centre, Platía Eleftherías, and other places near the International Fair ground. The smart shops are concentrated in two streets: Odós Mitropóleos and Odós Tsimiskí.

The local cuisine is more heavily spiced than southern Greek food and shows more Turkish influence. The chief specialities are fish and "doner kebab" which is slices of meat layered on an upright spit revolving in front of a fire; it is carved vertically in thin slivers as it cooks. Chocolate sweets and pastries are also very popular and delicious. The main restaurants are to be found down near the seafront, while the tavernas are grouped round the central market. In the evening people gather on the terraces of the large cafés in the main square, Platía Aristotélous.

The beach, **Agía Triáda (BZ)**, is on the southern shore of the bay; at the weekends there is a ferry plying to and fro.

PRINCIPAL SIGHTS *3 1/2 hours on foot*

Start from the main square, **Platía Aristotélous★**, a broad paved area lined with large hotels and cafés, which terminates the central axis of the city overlooking the sea.

Turn left *(south)* along the **seafront★★** (Odós Vassiléos Konstandínou) past restaurants and luxury boutiques: extensive views of the harbour and the bay.

White Tower★ (Lefkós Pírgos – BZ). – *Open 9am to 7pm (8am to 6pm Sundays); closed temporarily for repair work.* The tower was originally incorporated in the ramparts which surrounded the city; it stood in the southeast corner and was the main defensive element in the section fronting the sea which was pulled down in 1866. The tower was rebuilt by the Turks in 15C and used during the following century as a prison for Janissaries *(p 24)*, the Sultan's personal guards, who sometimes betrayed their master. Thus, when the janissaries revolted in 1826 against Mahmoud II, he had them confined to the tower and massacred. The building became known as the Bloody Tower, an unwelcome title which the Turks decided to suppress by painting the walls with whitewash and renaming it the White Tower.

The tower is 35m – 115ft high and built of stones interspersed with bricks. From the top there is a view of the city and the harbour.

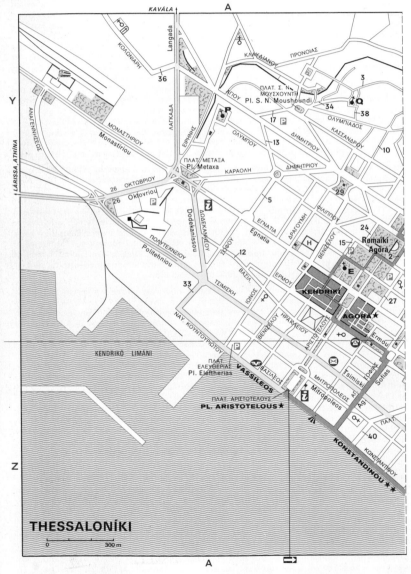

THESSALONÍKI

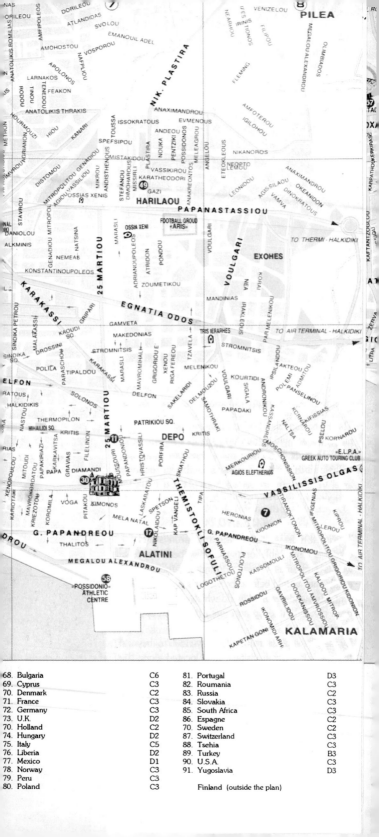

Beyond the White Tower on the seafront stands an equestrian statue of Alexander the Great (BZ B); behind it extends a park which is bordered down the east side by Odós Desperai and the Archaeological Museum.

Archaeological Museum★★★ (Arheologikó Moussío – BZ). – *Open 8am to 7pm (6pm Sundays); closed Tuesdays; 200 Dr.*

The building houses ceramics and other objects excavated from sites in Macedonia and Thrace but the most interesting exhibits are the Treasures of ancient Macedon, recently discovered in various tombs in Northern Greece.

Treasures of ancient Macedon★★★ – This stunning collection of precious objects, which is housed in a specially built wing of the museum, consists mainly of offerings in bronze, silver or gold found in tombs dating from 4C BC and the Hellenistic period, including the famous "royal tomb" at Vergína *(p 196)*.

Treasury of Síndos. – Here are the objects excavated from 121 tombs (dating from 6C – 5C BC) in the cemetery at Síndos, west of Thessalonika. The men's tombs yielded weapons, helmets of the so-called Illyrian type covered in gold leaf together with gold face masks. Several types of chariots and carts made of welded iron and small three-legged tables were also found. The women's graves produced gold jewellery (brooches, pendentives and pins) showing filigree work and milling.

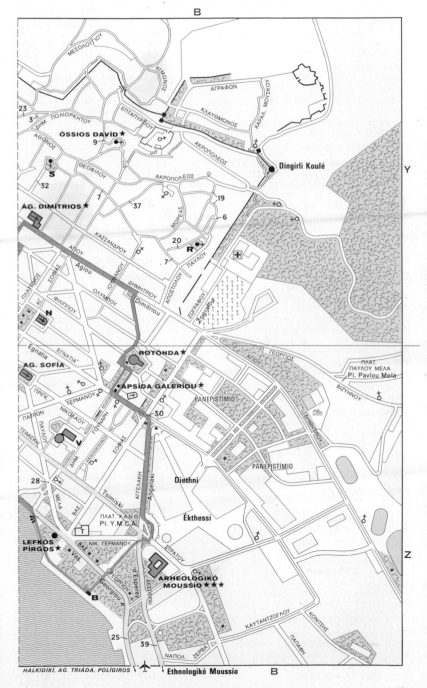

Vergína Treasure. – A reconstruction of the royal tomb made by Professor Andrónikos of the University of Thessalonika is illustrated by a model and slides; the tomb, which is thought to be that of Philip II of Madecon (4C BC), consisted of a chamber and an antechamber which produced some remarkable objects.

(With the permission of Prof. Andronikos)

Thessalonika. – "Larnax" from Vergína

A golden coffer (larnax) weighing over 8kg – 171bs is decorated with a twelve-pointed star, the emblem of the Macedonian kings; it contained the bones of the dead and was found in a sarcophagus in the antechamber to the tomb.

A quiver covered in gold leaf embossed with scenes from the sack of Troy vies in exquisite craftsmanship with vases in silver and polychrome ceramic.

Another huge golden coffer (illustration), larger and heavier (10kg – 221bs), is decorated with a sixteen point star; it probably contained the bones of Philip II, whose exquisite golden crown of oak leaves is also on display.

There are some very expressive and minutely carved portraits in ivory, probably of the royal family of Macedon: Philip II with a beard, his wife Olympia and their son Alexander.

Dervéni Treasure. – This is the material found in some 4C BC tombs at Dervéni (north of Thessalonika): golden jewellery (earrings), vases in silver or bronze and a huge cup in bronze gilt with appliquéd figures on the neck and reliefs illustrating the life of Dionysos.

Sculptures. – These are arranged in chronological order in the hall and five other galleries (proceed clockwise): a kouros and a kore (p 19) without their heads, funerary reliefs, Roman copies of Muses from the Odeon, Roman portraits including one in bronze of the Emperor Alexander Severus (3C). In the hall stands a 4C marble arch from Galerius' palace.

Proceed north (Odós Angeláki) past the International Fair ground and bear left.

Arch of Galerius ★ (Apsída Galeríou – BZ). – The arch was part of a monument erected in 4C AD at the main crossroads of the Roman city in honour of the Emperor Galerius. The brick pillars were faced with stone decorated with low reliefs celebrating Galerius' victories over the armies of Persia, Mesopotamia and Armenia.

The south pillar is the best preserved. On the outer face starting at the base: war scenes with elephants and a lion; a sacrifice showing Galerius (right) and his father-in-law Diocletian (left) ; Galerius' triumph; Galerius addressing his soldiers. On the inside face, at the base: Mesopotamia and Armenia, represented by two women making their submission; above: Galerius in combat.

Proceed north up to St George's Church, formerly Galerius' Mausoleum.

St George's Church ★ (Rotónda – BZ). – *Closed for restoration.*

The building was erected in 4C AD as a circular mausoleum for the Emperor Galerius, who was not however buried within since he died far away in Sofia. In the following century, under Constantine and Theodosius the Great, the mausoleum was converted into a church by the addition of an apse to the east; the main entrance then faced south down the street lined by porticoes which led to the Arch of Galerius and the imperial palace.

Converted into a mosque under the Turks (minaret), the building now houses a lapidary museum. The interior was decorated with mosaics on a gold ground of which a few survive, particularly at the base of the dome where eight saintly martyrs can be seen in prayer against a background of architectural compositions.

Continue north and then bear left into Odós Ágiou Dimítriou to reach the church of the same name.

St Demetrios' Church ★ (Ágios Dimítrios – BY). – *Open 7am to 9pm.* This impressive building marks the site of the martyrdom and tomb of St Demetrios, patron saint of Thessalonika. After the fire in 1917 the church was totally restored to reproduce the 7C basilica which was preceded by an atrium; some of the old material (marbles, columns, mosaics) were re-used. To the left are traces of Roman baths.

The interior, which is surprisingly large, has a nave and four aisles lit by three rows of windows. Carved capitals crown the superb ancient columns in green, white and red marble which have been re-used; their different lengths have been accommodated by mounting them on bases of the appropriate height.

The pillars on either side of the entrance to the apse are decorated with small 7C **mosaics ★★** of very fine design and colouring: (right pillar) Demetrios and a deacon bearing the Gospel, Demetrios between the two founders of the church, then St Sergius; (left pillar) Demetrios between two children, then the Virgin and St Theodore, a later composition.

The relics of St Demetrios, which were recovered from Italy in 1978, are venerated before the iconostasis. A stairway descends from the apse (right) into a crypt (small lapidary museum; *open 8.45am to 3pm, closed Tuesdays*) where, according to tradition, the miraculous oil which flowed from the saint's tomb beneath the high altar was collected.

At the back of the church near the nave (right) there is a 15C Florentine sarcophagus. The external chapel is thought to mark the site of St Demetrios' original tomb.

Return down the central axis of the city to the seafront.

Forum (Romaïkí Agorá – AY). – Recent excavations have uncovered traces of the Roman forum which date for the most part from 1C AD: base of a double portico which framed the forum and also the terraces of an odeon (small theatre).

Further down on the right stands the church of Our Lady of the Coppersmiths surrounded by a garden.

Church of Our Lady of the Coppersmiths (Panagía Halkéon – AY E). – This little brick church was built in 11C as the parish church of the coppersmiths and other smiths who plied their trade in the surrounding streets; it is a typical Byzantine church built on the Greek cross plan with a central dome and a façade flanked by two towers over the narthex.

The road then passes through the centre of the picturesque **Central Market** ★ (Kendrikí Agorá – AY). Bear left to the Church of the Holy Wisdom in Odós Ermoú.

Church of the Holy Wisdom ★ (Agía Sophía – BZ). – The church, which probably dates from 8C AD, is remarkable for its huge dimensions and its unusual design; the standard basilical plan of a nave and two aisles with galleries is combined with the Greek cross plan beneath a dome.

The interior displays some very unusual **capitals** ★ with acanthus leaf decorations which were probably taken from a 5C building. The **mosaics** (9C-10C) in the dome depict the Ascension of Christ.

Odós Agías Sophías leads back to the seafront and Platía Aristotélous.

ADDITIONAL SIGHTS
Churches are usually closed between 12.30 and 5pm.

Ramparts ★ (ABY). – The principal section of the ramparts encloses the Upper Town and the ancient acropolis where the network of streets and the terraced houses suggest an eastern bazaar. The ramparts were built late in 4C on Hellenistic foundations and were altered in 14C by the Byzantines and again in 15C by the Turks who employed Venetian engineers.

Starting near the cemetery in Odós Zográphou, proceed north outside the walls; at one point there is a section built of massive pieces of stone which dates from the Hellenistic period. Higher up stands the great **Chain Tower** (Dingirlí Koulé – BY) dating from 15C. Before reaching it pass within the walls so as to gain entrance to the acropolis. From this side the ramparts, which have been recently restored, make a fine sight linking the two towers named after Manuel Palaiologos and Andronikos II (14C). *Return by the same route.*

Holy David's Church ★ (BY). – The church which dates from 5C contains a well preserved **mosaic** ★ of the same date representing the Vision of Ezekiel.

Twelve Apostles' Church (Dódeka Apóstoli – AY P). – This is an attractive 14C church built on the Greek cross plan with three apses in the sanctuary, a design typical of the Palaiologos "Renaissance" The external brickwork is ingeniously arranged to form decorative geometric motifs; the internal columns supporting the dome have Corinthian capitals; the mosaics and frescoes are 14C.

St Catherine's Church (Agía Ekateríni – AY Q). – This small but perfectly proportioned brick church dates from 13C, as do the frescoes and mosaics inside.

St Nicholas' Church (Ágios Nikólaos Orfanós – BY R). – *Open 9.45am to 3pm; closed Tuesdays; 100 Dr.* 14C church and frescoes.

Prophet Elijah's Church (Profítis Ilías – BY S). – 14C building with three apses in the elegant sanctuary; superb monolith columns in the transept.

Church of the Virgin (Panagía Ahiropíitos – BY N). – It dates from 5C but has been heavily restored; monolithic columns with Byzantine capitals; traces of mosaics.

Galerius' Palace (Anáktora Galeríou – BZ V). – An open space, Platía Navarínou, reveals the plan of the brick built imperial Roman palace which was arranged round a rectangular courtyard with porticoes.

Macedonian Ethnological Museum (Ethnologikó Moussío). – *68 Odós Vasilissis Olgas – BZ via Odós Vas. Geórgiou (south of the plan). Open 9.30am to 2pm; closed Thursdays.* This 19C mansion houses rich collections devoted to the popular art and traditions of Northern Greece: architecture, costume, crafts; reconstruction of the lifestyle of the nomadic Sarakatsani *(footnote p 63)* and of Macedonian high society early this century.

TIRYNS★★   *Tírintha*

Peloponnese – Argolis – Michelin map 980 fold 29

Set on a bluff in the centre of a plain, the fortress of Tiryns is a Cyclopean structure dating from 13C BC, a well preserved masterpiece of ancient military architecture.

On every side extend the huge citrus plantations of the Argolid plain; in the neighbouring town stand the buildings of the first national school of agriculture which was founded under Kapodistrias' government (1828-1831).

The misfortunes of Amphitryon. – According to legend, Tiryns was founded before Mycenae by a certain Proitos aided by Cyclopes from Asia Minor. Like Mycenae it came under Perseus' rule; then it was governed by the son of Perseus and Andromeda, Alkaios, who was succeeded by Amphitryon.

Amphitryon, king of Tiryns, had married his cousin **Alkmene,** who was as virtuous as she was beautiful, but before consummating the union he was bound by an oath to avenge the deaths of Alkmene's brothers, who had been killed in a quarrel with the Teleboans.

As a result Amphitryon went into exile in Thebes and Zeus, who was captivated by Alkmene's beauty, took advantage of Amphitryon's absence to introduce himself to Alkmene disguised as her husband.

Following her union with first a god and then a mortal Alkmene gave birth to two sons; the one, lacking in ability, was called Iphikles and took after Amphitryon while the other, brave and strong, was called **Herakles** (Hercules) and took after Zeus. As a demigod, although only 18 months old, Herakles was able to strangle the serpents sent to kill him by Hera, the jealous wife of Zeus.

Later in a fit of madness he killed his children and the Pythia at Delphi ordered him to enter the service of Eurystheus, king of Argos, who set him the **Twelve Labours** to accomplish: to strangle the Nemean lion, to execute the many-headed hydra of Lerna, to run down the hind of Ceryneia, to capture the Erymanthian boar, to cleanse the Augean stables, to destroy the Stymphalian birds, to tame the Cretan bull, to capture the man-eating horses of king Diomedes, to obtain the girdle of the Amazon queen, to carry off the cattle of Geryon a three-headed monster, to fetch the golden apples from the Garden of the Hesperides and finally to bring back Cerberus from Hades.

In the Achaian period (13C BC) Tiryns was subject to Mycenae and under Agamemnon took part in the Trojan war. During the Dorian invasion (12C BC) it was an independent kingdom with about 15 000 inhabitants; it was frequently in conflict with its neighbour Árgos. In 468 BC the Argives captured the city and laid it waste; its role was finished.

ACROPOLIS★★

Open 8.45am to 3pm (9.30am to 2.30pm Sundays); 100 Dr; about 1 hour.

"Wall-girt Tiryns" as Homer described it, stands on a long and narrow rocky limestone bluff only 20m – 66ft above the surrounding plain but the sea came in closer in antiquity so that its isolated position and the strength of its walls made it almost impregnable.

The ruins now visible date, for the most part, from the late 13C BC. They cover an area measuring 300m – 328yds by between 45m and 100m – 49yds and 109yds and comprise the palace on the upper level and on the lower an elliptical precinct enclosing buildings for military, religious and economic use and to house the service quarters.

Fine **views** of Árgos and the Argolid, Mycenae, Nauplion and the bay.

The site has been excavated by the German School of Archaeology and the acropolis has provided some frescoes *(in the Athens Museum)*, ceramics and terracottas *(in the Nauplion Museum)*.

Ramparts★★. – 7m to 10m – 23ft to 33ft wide and about 1 500m – 1 640yds long, the walls reach 7.50m – 25ft high in places. They were compared by Pausa-

TIRYNS

nias to the Pyramids and their Cyclopean structure using roughly shaped stones, up to 3.50m by 1.50m – 11ft by 5ft in size, is very impressive.

The ramp, which was broad enough for a chariot, leads up to the main entrance to the acropolis; an attacker advancing up the ramp would have been exposed on his righthand side (unprotected by his shield) to projectiles hurled by the defenders; the gateway, which was closed by wooden doors, was reinforced by two flanking towers.

On passing through the gateway, turn left into the passage (1) enclosed between the outer wall and the wall of the palace which is 11m – 36ft high at this point; it was a real death-trap; if the attackers managed to force the gate they could easily be annihilated at this point by projectiles hurled from every side.

Palace★. – The door to the palace is marked by a stone threshold, 4m – 13ft long by 1.45m – 4 3/4ft wide, containing holes for hinges, and by one of the jams containing the socket for the wooden bar which held the doors shut.

Within is the forecourt with a flight of steps *(left)* leading down to the east casemates.

East Casemates★★ – A narrow gallery, 30m – 98ft long, with a vaulted roof, was built in the thickness of the ramparts; it had six chambers or casemates leading off it which were used by the garrison as stores or barrack rooms. The heavy blocks of stone and the gloom which reigns in these military quarters create an oppressive and timeless atmosphere.

Great Propylaia. – The monumental main entrance, of which traces remain, was the forerunner of the Great Propylaia on the acropolis in Athens which was designed to the same plan: an inner and an outer porch covering a central passage. The Great Propylaia leads into the great court of the palace from which a staircase descends through a right angle to the **south casemates,** similar to those in the eastern ramparts.

Smaller Propylaia (2). – This entrance links the great court to the inner or Megaron Court.

Inner Court. – Its dimensions are 20m by 15m – 66ft by 49ft and it was originally covered with white cement; it was enclosed on three sides by porticoes of which traces remain; at the far end rose the façade of the *megaron (p 17)*. On the right within the entrance stood the royal altar (3).

Megaron. – As at Mycenae the *megaron* had a porch, a vestibule, a central hearth surrounded by wooden pillars on stone bases; the king's throne stood on the right. The walls were faced with stucco and decorated with paintings in the Cretan style. In 7C or 6C the *megaron* was replaced by a temple to Hera; some of the foundations are visible. The royal apartments were on two floors on the north and east sides of the *megaron*.

Walk out through the rear court of the palace to reach the western ramparts.

Steps and western ramparts★★ – A flight of 80 steps winds down inside the crescent-shaped wall to a postern gate; it is one of the most unusual features of the defences. If an attacking force had succeeded in breaching the postern gate and reaching the steps, it would have been assailed on all sides by the defenders and even if some of the attackers had managed to win through they would have fallen into a sort of trap at the top of the steps. There was moreover an additional bastion protecting the heart of the acropolis.

It is worth descending the steps and going out through the postern gate to admire the western ramparts and then continuing to another postern gate further north which opens into the lower ward of the acropolis. From there it is about as far again to see the drinking water cisterns which were situated outside the ramparts but reached from within by underground passages, only recently discovered.

Return eventually to the main entrance to the site.

TRÍKALA

Thessaly – Tríkala – Pop 40 857 – Michelin map 980 fold 16

Tríkala is an important agricultural market at the heart of the fertile province of Thessaly. In antiquity it was well known for its sanctuary to Asklepios, which was the oldest in Greece. For a time under the Turkish occupation it became the capital of the province.

Old town. – Containing the main churches and a picturesque bazaar, it spreads over the lower slopes of Mount Ardáni below a Byzantine castle.

Old Mosque. – South of the town on the road to Kardítsa stands a 16C mosque with an imposing dome; it is being restored to house a museum.

EXCURSION

Pórta Defile★ (Stená Pórtas). – *2km – 1 3/4 miles southwest. Take the road to Píli; beyond the village climb for about 1km – 1/2 mile up the south bank of the Portaïkós which rises in the Píndos range.*

Bridge★ – The bridge, which was built in 16C by the monk Bessarion, is narrow and high and spans the river in one impressive arch beneath the peaceful shade of the plane trees at the entrance to the pass.

Return to Píli, cross the stream and climb up the north bank. Soon a church appears below in a rural setting to which a group of cypress trees adds a solemn touch.

Sanctuary of the Virgin of the Gateway★ (Pórta Panagía). – *Open mornings or key available from a nearby house, Mr. Souflias.* In this charming rural setting there are two distinct buildings.

The eastern church is built in the Latin style of architecture to judge by the dressed stone, the obvious transept, the outline of certain openings, the nave buttressed by side aisles and the remarkable chevet with an apse and smaller canted apses. In the interior the entrance to the chancel is framed by mosaics of Christ and the Virgin and Child which show a flexibility and freedom of composition not found in Byzantine hieratism.

The western church is Orthodox, designed according to the Greek cross plan beneath a dome; it was probably rebuilt in 15C but the façade and the stone walls seem to date from 13C and to be the work of a western mason. The 15C fresco in the interior of the dome follows the Byzantine tradition with a severe Christ accompanied by a solemn legion of saints.

The remote site, the western architectural influences and the date of construction, when John I and John II Doukas, who owed allegiance to Guy II de la Roche *(p 43)*, were masters of Thessaly, all suggest that this double church, like the one at Óssios Loukás *(p 163)*, belonged to a Cistercian Abbey.

TRÍPOLI

Peloponnese – Arkadía – Pop 21 311 – Michelin map 980 fold 29

Trípoli is the capital of Arcadia (Arkadía) and the central point in the road network of the Peloponnese. The town is built in the centre of a high flat plain (alt 663m – 2 175ft in the limestone massif formed by erosion and surrounded by mountains of up to 2 000m – 6 560ft. The relatively high altitude means that even in summer the climate is cool and fresh; Trípoli is therefore a pleasant centre for tourists who can make excursions into the quiet and attractive countryside of the Arcadian basin which was evoked by Virgil and Poussin (the Shepherds of Arcadia).

In 18C under the name of Tripolizza, the town was the residence of the Pasha of Morea and very Turkish-looking according to Chateaubriand. It was destroyed in 1824 by Ibrahim Pasha but rebuilt: the central square is bordered by the metal awnings typical in the mountains whereas Areos Square is open and planted with gardens; the Bazaar lies to the south on the Kalamáta road.

EXCURSIONS

Tegéa. – *10km – 6 1/4 miles southeast. Follow the Sparta road for 8km – 5 miles; in Kerassítsa turn left (signpost "Ancient Tegéa").*

Lying in the fertile plain, Tegéa was the most important city in Arcadia in antiquity; it came under Spartan domination in 6C BC and was finally destroyed by barbarians in 5C AD. It was resurrected under the name of Nikli by the Byzantines and in 13C it was the seat of the important Frankish barony of **Niclès** and of a latin bishopric; a few miles to the south during the Frankish occupation were held the great verbena fairs which have left their mark in the name of the village Vérvena.

Paleá Episkopí. – A shady park enclosed the modern church which incorporates some material from the 5C paleo-Christian basilica of Nikli; elements from antiquity and from the Middle Ages.

Temple of Athena. – Between 1889 and 1910 the French School of Archaeology in Athens excavated the foundations of the famous **Temple of Athena Alea** (4C BC) which housed the Archaic ivory statue of the goddess and the remains of the Calydonian boar *(p 139)*. The building was designed and decorated by statues and sculptures by the great Parian sculptor, Skopas; several fragments have been found; the most beautiful, representing the Calydonian hunt (Calydonian boar, head of Atalanta) are displayed in the Athens Museum, others in the little local museum *(closed Tuesdays; 10 Dr)*.

Mantineia (Mandínia). – *11km – 7 miles north on the Olympia road; after 9km – 5 1/2 miles turn right.*

In antiquity Mantineia was a fortified city, rivalling Tegéa for control of the plain which was irrigated then and covered with crops and oak woods although it is barren today. Beneath its walls in 362 BC fell Epaminondas *(p 187)*, the famous Theban general, who was pursuing the Spartan army of Agesilaos.

The excavations *(right of the road)* conducted by the French School of Archaeology have uncovered traces of the walls, 4km – 2 1/2 miles long and reinforced with towers, as well as the foundations of several buildings including a theatre, an agora and several temples.

On the opposite side of the road stands a **church** ★ which is dedicated to the Virgin, the Muses and Beethoven. This extraordinary building was erected between 1970 and 1978 by an American architect of Greek origin who used every possible material (marble, ashlar stone, brick, wood) aiming at a synthesis of several styles (Egyptian, Greek Byzantine) and incorporating every imaginable sort of decoration (sculpture, frescoes, stained glass, mosaics, enamels, gold and silver work); the effect of this combination is a joy to those who appreciate surrealism.

VÉRIA

Macedonia – Imathía – Pop 37 087 – Michelin map 980 fold 5

Véria is well sited on a spur of Mount Vérmio overlooking the Macedonian plain; it is an important fruit market (peaches, apples etc.) and has the appearance of a modern town. Among the concrete buildings, however, hidden in courtyards and blind alleys, are a few Turkish houses and Byzantine churches.

In 54 AD St Paul came from Thessalonika to preach to the Jewish community.

The ramparts have been converted into a walk: extensive **views** over the plain.

Christchurch ★ **(Ágios Hristós).** – *Guided tour by the keeper.* At the centre of the town near the main crossroads stands a Byzantine church built of brick and recently restored. It is decorated with a remarkable collection of early 14C frescoes signed by Kaliergis: the Virgin and angels in the apse, scenes from the Life of Christ, Orthodox saints etc.

Archaeological Museum. – *Open 8.45am to 3pm (9.30am to 2.30pm Sundays); closed Tuesdays; 100 Dr.* The museum contains objects from various periods: prehistoric, Archaic, Hellenistic and Roman.

EXCURSION

Vergína and Palatítsa ★ – *15km – 9 1/2 miles southwest of Véria on the road to Melíki; after 12km – 7 1/2 miles turn right to the modern village of Vergína; at the end of the village turn left by the sign "to the Royal Tombs".*

Royal tombs. – *Excavations in progress; not open at present.* Two huge tumulus tombs, dating from 4C BC, have been under excavation by Professor Andrónikos since 1977. One is decorated with beautiful frescoes. The other, which consists of a vestibule and an inner chamber, has yielded a magnificent collection of funerary objects *(displayed in the Thessalonika museum, p 191)* which indicate that it was the tomb of Philip II of Macedon *(p 169)*. Vergína is therefore probably the site of ancient **Aigai**, which was the capital of Macedon before being superseded by Pella, and the royal burial ground.

(With the permission of Prof. Andronikos)

Vergína. – Section of the great tomb

A third tomb of the same type has been discovered nearby.

Lastly in 1982 the archeologists discovered the site of the theatre where Philip II was assassinated.

Follow the sign "to the Macedonian Tomb and to the Palace".

Macedonian Tomb ★ (Romeou's Tomb). – *On the left of the road; guided tour by the keeper of Palatítsa (gratuity).* This is a 3C *hypogeum* with an Ionic façade and marble doors *(temporarily removed).* The funeral chamber still contains the marble throne which shows traces of its original painted decoration.

The road reaches a platform whence a footpath climbs up to the Palatítsa.

Palatítsa ★ – *Open 8.45am to 3pm (9.30am to 2.30pm Sundays); closed Tuesdays; 100 Dr.*

Traces of this little palace *(palatítsa),* which dates from the Hellenistic period, were discovered in 1861 by a French archaeologist, Heuzey. An old oak tree is now growing at the centre of the terrace where the palace once stood. The buildings were altered in the Middle Ages and in 15C were the residence of a Byzantine princess called Vergína; the palace was later destroyed by the Turks.

The plan of the ancient palace can still be traced on the ground. The rooms were arranged round a Doric peristyle courtyard; several had mosaic floors; one has been restored to reveal a pleasant décor combining geometric, floral and figurative motifs.

Extensive views of the site of the ancient city and over the plain to the sea (E).

VITÍNA

Peloponnese – Arkadía – Pop 857 – Michelin map 980 folds 28 and 29

This little old town northwest of Tripoli makes a popular summer resort (alt 1 050m – 3 444ft) with its clean air and its walks in the pine forests of the neighbouring mountains where the god Pan was born. Vitína has preserved the features of a typical mountain town: fine stone houses with broad arched doorways and balconies, some of which are covered. It is a pleasure to wander through the narrow streets and up and down the picturesque steps which offer glimpses of the surrounding countryside.

Local craftsmen engage in wood turning and wood sculpture.

VÓLOS

Thessaly – Magnissía – Pop 71 378 – Michelin map 980 fold 17 – Local map p 169

Vólos stands at the head of its vast bay (Pagassitokós Kólpos) which is almost completely cut off from the Aegean Sea by the arm of the Magnissiá peninsula. It is the latest in a long line of settlements; an earlier one was ancient Iolkos, the port from which Jason *(p 168)* and the Argonauts set sail in search of the Golden Fleece.

Vólos is subject to frequent earthquakes, the most recent of which occurred in 1955, so that the town today looks very modern and its straight streets, laid out on the grid pattern, are lined by special "anti-quake" houses three or four storeys high. There is a pleasant promenade along the seafront bordered by hotels, cafés and restaurants. Vólos olives are famous.

Vólos is a good starting place for excursions into Mount Pelion *(p 168).*

Economic activity. – Vólos is the third port in Greece after Piraeus and Thessalonika. It exports the local regional products – cereals, cotton, tobacco, olives, oil, wine and fruit – and also heavy industrial manufactures – machinery and other metal products – which are transported by ship to the Middle East, particularly Syria. Vólos is also the home port for the ships serving the Northern Sporades *(p 182).*

About 8km – 5 miles from the city centre there is an industrial zone with 44 factories: cement works, tanneries, textiles, cigarettes, oil etc.

Archaeological Museum ★. – *Open 8.45am to 3pm (9.30am to 2.30pm Sundays); closed Tuesdays; 100 Dr.*

It displays an astonishing series of about 300 marble funerary stele which date from the Hellenistic period. Many of them are painted or carved with scenes from the life of the dead person. Most of them were taken from the necropolis at Dimitriáda in 50 AD to reinforce the city walls, which is where they were found.

Some tombs have been reconstructed to illustrate the funerary rites and customs practised in prehistory and antiquity. There are also collections of neolithic objects from the sites at Sésklo (4 000 BC), Dimíni etc, and Mycenaean vases excavated at Iolkós.

VOURAÏKÓS Gorge★★

Peloponnese – Achaia – Michelin map 980 folds 28 and 29

From the heights of Mount Aroánia, which rises to 2 340m – 7 677ft, the River Vouraïkós flows down into the Corinthian Gulf some 50km – 30 miles, to the north. Along its course it has worn a deep channel through the soft limestone rock creating a fantastic gorge, dark and narrow, through which runs a picturesque narrow-gauge railway.

Rack railway from Diakoftó to Zahloroú ★★ – *12km – 7 1/2 miles, about 1 hour. Departures from Diakoftó 8.10, 10.16am, 12 noon, 3.10 and 7.06pm.*

The narrow gauge Decauville railway, which was built late in the last century from Diakoftó on the coast to Kalávrita, is a particularly bold feat of engineering. It runs for 22km – nearly 14 miles along a vertiginous route – through tunnels, along overhangs, across bridges and viaducts and on a rack in certain sections where the incline is steeper than 7 %. Since 1962 Diesel engines have replaced the ancient steam locomotives which dated back to 1900 and had a top speed of 35km – 22 miles per hour.

VOURAÏKÓS Gorge★★

On leaving **Diakoftó** (pop 1 724) station the train crosses the foothills of Aroánia, passing through vineyards and orchards (famous for cherries), before entering the gorge between high sheer cliffs which are riddled with caves. The railway line crosses from one side to the other high above the racing torrent; the grey-green water gleams far below swirling round the blocks of stone. Here and there the austerity of the bare rock is relieved by patches of colour in the shape of oleanders and oak and plane trees growing in clumps.

Zahloroú (pop 84) lies on a natural terrace overlooking a narrow basin. The charming little station is half hidden in the trees between the rockface and the stream *(tavernas, small hotel)*. From there it is 3/4 hour on foot or by donkey (in summer only) up a winding path (fine views towards Kalávrita) to the Monastery of Méga Spíleo *(p 133)*, which can also be reached by road.

The train continues to the terminus at Kalávrita *(p 119)*.

ZAKYNTHOS★ _____ *Zákinthos*

Ionian Islands – Pop 30 014 – Michelin map ⑨⑧⓪ fold 27

Access by ferry from Kilíni in 1 1/2 hours, several times a day in summer; by air and coach from Athens daily. Boat from Argostóli (Cephallonia).

Despite being shaken by earthquakes Zakynthos is still the "Flower of the Levant" *(Fior di Levante)* praised by the Venetians for its gentle climate, its luxuriant flora, its fertile soil and the charm of its inhabitants.

The island, which is 403km² – 156sq miles in extent, rises in the west in a chain of limestone peaks reaching 756m – 2 480ft and levels out to the east in a fertile plain producing olives, citrus fruits and good white wines (Delizia, Verdea). The tar deposits in the south near Kerí were used in antiquity for caulking ships.

Beaches of fine sand, particularly at **Laganás** *(hotels, tavernas)* and Argássi.

Cultural centre. – From 1489 to 1797 Zakynthos belonged to Venice which maintained an oligarchy of nobles inscribed in a Golden Book; this was a period of intense activity.

When Crete fell to the Turks in 1669 many artists moved to Zakynthos and contributed to the Ionian School of painting which combines the Byzantine tradition and the Ventian Renaissance. Local architecture was also marked by the Venetian influence: arches and arcading and bell towers separate from their churches...

In the late 18C and early 19C Zakynthos became a breeding ground for poets, whose work was a blend of the Hellenic and Italian cultures: **Ugo Fóscolo** (1778-1827), a master of romantic Italian literature, who campaigned for the independence of Italy and died in England; **Dionysos Solomós** (1798-1857), educated in Cremona, who became the poet of Greek independence and was the author of the Greek National Anthem – "The Hymn to Liberty" – translated into English by Rudyard Kipling; **Andréas Kálvos** (1792-1867), who travelled to Zurich and London with Fóscolo and also supported the Greek struggle for independence in his poetry; he too died in England.

Nowadays, the poets have been succeded by popular singers who perform the famous local barcarolles *(minóres)*.

ZAKYNTHOS TOWN★

Zakynthos Town is the capital (pop 9 764) and the main port of the island. The churches, palaces and squares with their fountains and surrounding arcades, which were built during the Venetian occupation, have made the town one of the most picturesque in the Adriatic after Dubrovnik. Although much of the town was destroyed in an earthquake in 1953, it has been rebuilt in the Venetian style. Soft nougat *(mandoláto)* is a speciality.

Kástro★. – *Admission: 100 Dr.* The old Venetian citadel, set on a hill, 100m – 361ft up, survived the earthquake and provides an extended **view★★** of the town, the bay and the coast of the mainland from Missolonghi (NE) to Pylos (Navarino) (SE).

Art Museum.★ – *Platía Solomoú. Open 8.45am to 3pm; closed Tuesdays; 100 Dr.*
Many items recall old Zakynthos: model of the theatre, paintings and engravings, furniture. There is a rich collection of icons from 16C to 19C by Damaskinós, Tzanés etc. and religious paintings by the 17C and 18C Ionian School: massive iconostasis from the church of the Pantocrator, frescoes and murals from the churches of St George in Zakynthos, St Andrew in Volímes etc.

Church of Our Lady of the Angels★ (Kiría ton Angélon). – *Behind the Hotel Xenia; key at no 34 Odós Louká Karnér.* Elegant Venetian Renaissance façade and 17C iconostasis.

Solomos Museum. – *Platía Ágiou Márkou. Open 9am to 2pm and 6 to 8pm*
Tombs of Solomós and Kálvos on the ground floor; icons and souvenirs of famous citizens (portrait of Fóscolo) on the first floor.

EXCURSION

Alikés Corniche★; Volímes. – *86km – 53 miles Rtn, about 2 hours plus 1 hour sightseeing.*

After skirting the citadel, the road runs northwest through a rural area (vineyards and country houses surrounded by gardens) before reaching **Alikés,** a sheltered seaside resort with a fine sandy beach facing Cephallonia across the sea. The road passes some salt marshes before climbing the Alikés corniche; from the top there is a **panorama★★** of the plain of Zakynthos to the south, of the Kyllene peninsula including Chlemoutsi on the mainland, of the Gulf of Patras (NE) and of Cephallonia (N).

Before reaching Volímes, one can make a detour to the left to visit the **Convent of Anafonítria,** occupied by an order of nuns, where St Denys, the patron saint of the island, died in 1622; medieval tower.

Volímes (pop 484) is an old mountain village producing carpets in the local style. To the north lies the picturesque **"Blue Grotto"** accessible only by boat.

CRETE

Crete is different from the other islands in the Greek archipelago. Despite the increase in tourists, particularly noticeable on the north coast, the wild grandeur of the landscape has not been spoiled and the inhabitants have retained their traditional qualities of pride, honesty and hospitality. "The island of the gods" as Homer described it, was the cradle of the Minoan civilisation which flourished in the eastern Mediterranean two thousand years before Christ.

In the countryside Cretan men sometimes still wear their traditional dress: tall boots, baggy breeches and a fringed turban (mandíli). On feast days they dance to the music of three-stringed lyres.

Access. – By air: Olympic Airways operates several flights daily from Athens to Herakleion (Iráklio) and Chania (Haniá) (3⁄4hour flight); in summer there are also flights from Crete to Rhodes, Santoríni, Páros, Mykonos and Thessalonika. By sea: ferries from Piraeus to Herakleion or Chania overnight; there are also regular sailings between the Dodecanese and the Cyclades and the ports of Crete; twice a week there is a ferry from Piraeus to Kastéli (W of Chania) which takes 1 1/2 days and calls at various places on the east coast of the Peloponnese: Pláka (Leonídio), Monemvassía, Gíthio and Kythera.

Accommodation. – In winter it is mild on the coast but cold and snowy inland; the spring, however, although it can be chilly, brings a profusion of flowers (anemones, oleanders, orchids). The summer is very hot but from time to time refreshing winds *(meltémi)* blow down from the north. Autumn is marked by a more agreeable temperature and fewer tourists.

From the simplest to the most luxurious, the hotels can be divided into two main types: ordinary urban hotels and holiday hotels, designed specifically for tourists and usually sited on the north coast.

The restaurants and tavernas, which are plain but not expensive, offer several tasty dishes such as lamb with artichokes *(arnáki me angináres)* and, near the sea, excellent fish: swordfish *(ksífi),* red mullet *(barboúni),* mullet *(kéfalos),* crayfish *(karavída).* Cretan cheeses *(féta, graviéra, manoúri)* are well known; so also is yoghurt with honey. The local wines are full bodied with a good nose and bottled under various names: Minos, Lato, Angelo, Gortys etc. but the most typical are sold in carafes in the country inns. Those who are partial to liqueurs will want to try *rakí* (very different from Turkish raki) and *tsikoudía,* a strong and fruity marc.

Touring. – The great east-west road from Sitía to Kastéli via Ágios Nikólaos, Herakleion, Rethymnon and Chania forms the axis of touring in Crete. Several roads branch off it leading to the south coast over the mountains.

If one has only a few days (4 or 5) available, Herakleion makes a good base from which to make excursions to the archaeological sites (Knossós, Phaistos, Mália etc.) or natural features (Lassíthi Plateau) as well as other places on the north coast.

If one has more time (a fortnight) available, one can first visit Herakleion and its neighbourhood and then take the axis road east and west making detours inland and to the south coast.

GEOGRAPHY

Crete is the largest island in the Greek archipelago and the fifth largest in the Mediterranean. It is 8 305km² – 3 200sq miles in extent with a population of 502 165. From east to west it measures about 260km – 162 miles and is between 12 and 50km – 7 1/2 and 31 miles wide. It lies on the same latitude as Rabat in Morroco.

Physical features. – Crete is composed of a ridge of limestone mountains which have been heavily eroded to form numerous inland basins, gorges, chasms and caves (over 3 000). There are three major peaks which are capped with snow from November to June: Lefká Óri (White Mountains) (2 453m – 8 048ft), Ida (Ídi) (2 456m – 8 058ft) and Díkti (2 148m – 7 047ft). The Herakleion plain *(north)* and the Messará plain *(south)* are at either end of the central depression which forms the fertile heart of Crete where the earliest Mediterranean civilisations were nurtured. The northern coast, which is mostly flat, is punctuated with gulfs and bays and inlets whereas the tall, semi-barren cliffs of the southern coast plunge sheer into the sea less than 300km – 186 miles from Libya.

Agriculture. – Agriculture flourishes in the coastal plains, the inland basins and on the lower slopes in the valleys. Both wheat and rice are grown; irrigation enables orchards of citrus fruits to thrive beside the olives which are grown for the extraction of their oil. Vineyards tend to be concentrated in the broad valley south of Herakleion. Early vegetables, tomatoes, cucumbers, artichokes etc. are grown under glass while bananas have been introduced in the Messará plain and round Ierápetra. Both fruit and vegetables are exported to Piraeus and the rest of Europe.

Sheep and goats are reared in the mountains.

30 km

0

Akr. Síderos

Vái
Itanós
Paleókastro
Toploú
20
Káto Zákros
Sítia
30
Móhlos
Sfáka
Plátanos
19
Akti Mirambélou
Ag. Nikólaos
20
Gourniá
14
Ierápetra
Hers. Spinalónga
Spinalónga
28
Elounda
Sísma
15
Lató
Kritsá
Panagía Kerá
Dikti 2148
53
A. Viános
Mírtos
Árvi
Neápoli
Kardiótissa
Psihró
Lassíthi
Diktéo Ándro
40
Límáni Hersoníssou
Máliá
Potamiés
43
Pigí
Kastéli
Ágios Pandeleímonas
Varvári
18
Knossós
17
Paleókastro
IRÁKLIO
Ag. Pelagía
Ag. Stavrós
Akr. Stavrós
Fódele
48
Tílissos
Arhánes
Vathípetro
Giouhtas
54
Górtis
Messará
Pírgos
Kalí Liménes
Anógia
Axós
Vrondíssi
Zarós
Míres
Festós
Kamáres
Valsamónero
Ag. Triáda
Mátala
Akr. Lithíno
Idi 2456
Idéo Ándro
Ormos Messarás
Ag. Galíni
Melidóni
Bali
Arkádi
Ag. Triáda Mesará
47
Réthimno
N. Día
N. Hríssi
N. Gávdos
Koufoníssi
Frangokástelo
Omalós
Xilóskalo
Samariá
Ag. Rouméli
Sfakiá
Lefká Óri 2453
40
32
Vríses
Áptera
Ormos Soúdas
Mouzourás
Hers. Akrotíri
Gouvernéto
Ag. Triáda
Táfos Venizélou
20
Haniá
Soúda
Farángi Samariás
36
Akr. Spáda
Rodopós
Goniá
41
Kastéli
Kíssamos
Polirínia
Plátanos
1071
Paleohóra
Falássarna
N. Gramvoússa
Akr. Voúxa
Akr. Kriós

Minoan Crete. – From about 2500 BC to 1000 BC Crete was the centre of a brilliant civilisation supposed to be of mythical origin. According to both Homer and Hesiod, Zeus was born in Crete where the nymph Europa, whom he had abducted, bore him a son **Minos**, who became a wise and powerful king. He started a dynasty which presided over the Minoan civilisation; archaeologists have identified four broad periods.

Pre-Palace Period (2500-200 BC) is marked by domed circular tombs which have yielded grave goods: jewellery, seals, "Cycladic" statuettes, pottery.

Old Palace Period (2000-1700 BC) covers the first palaces which were built round a central courtyard bordered by the public reception and cult rooms and the private royal apartments. Traces of such palaces have been found in Knossós, Phaistos and Mália, which according to legend were the princely seats of Zeus' sons, Minos, Rhadamanthos and Sarpedon; mountain-top sanctuaries have also been discovered. The pottery, known as Kamáres ware, since the first examples were found in 1900 in Kamáres Cave on Mount Ida, is decorated with exuberant polychrome patterns. The island was the centre of a maritime empire, trading with Egypt and the Middle East and exporting olives, grain, vegetables and wine. In about 1700 BC an earthquake brought devastation.

New Palace Period (1700-c1500 BC) is so called because new palaces were built on the sites of the earlier ones at Knossós, Phaistos, Mália and also on a fourth site at Zákros. The new palaces were larger and more richly decorated; the royal apartments in particular consisted of several floors, lit by light wells, serviced by a network of stairs and corridors and supplied with piped water. The walls are covered with low-relief sculptures or clean-lined paintings usually depicting obscure cult scenes featuring the double headed axe or symbolic bull's horns, ritual bull-leaping events, processions and animal and, in exceptional circumstances, human sacrifices *(p 208)*. There are also representations of graceful priestesses presented in profile with a single eye facing straight ahead. The script current during this period, known as **Linear B**, was deciphered in 1953.

The Minoan civilisation extended beyond Crete into the Mediterranean basin and several traces of it have been found particularly in Thera (Santoríni – *p 176*) but in about 1500 BC a second earthquake, probably connected with the volcanic eruption on Thera, seems to have produced a tidal wave which destroyed the new palaces.

Post-Palace Period (1500-1100 BC) is marked by the Achaian invasion, which introduced the customs of the Mycenaeans (burial of warriors with their arms, palaces with a *megaron* *(p 17)*, and then by gradual fusion with mainland Greece.

Rome and Byzantium. – In 67 BC the Romans took possession of Crete which together with Cyrenaica formed a Roman province with its capital at Gortyn where many traces of brick buildings, temples, sculptures and mosaics from this period have been found. In 59 AD St Paul landed on the south coast at Kalí Liménes; his disciple Titus was later sent to convert the island to Christianity.

From 395 to 1204, except for a brief Arab intervention between 824 and 961, Crete came under the sway of Byzantium, as the many churches demonstrate.

Under the claw of the Venetian lion. – Following the Fourth Crusade in 1204 Crete was assigned to the Venetians who retained it for four hundred years despite local revolts. They divided the island into four districts, Chania, Rethymnon, Sitia and Candia (Herakleion) which was the residence of the Duke of Candia, a magistrate appointed by the Grand Council in Venice for two years. The Venetians built many fortresses on Crete and made it their main base, controlling the sea routes used by their merchant galleys trading with the Levant. Civil servants, ship owners and merchants from Venice settled in the Cretan towns; churches, loggias, houses and fountains in the Venetian style can still be seen today. Colonists settled in the more fertile valleys.

Finally Dominicans and Franciscans arrived preaching oecumenism: several churches (St Catherine's in Herakleion, Kritsá, Valsamónero, Toploú etc.) have two naves side by side, one for the Orthodox and one for the Latin rite.

"Cretan Renaissance" – The fall of Constantinople to the Turks in 1453 brought Crete an influx of artists and men of letters.

Churches and monasteries were enriched with frescoes and icons by painters of the famous **"Cretan School"** in which the traditional Byzantine formality was softened by Italian influence evident in the representation of volume and the arrangement of the figures: in Nativity scenes the Virgin is shown sitting or kneeling but not lying down. This school, which in 16C migrated to Metéora and Mount Áthos, reached its apogee with Damaskinos *(p 208)* and particularly Domenico Theotokópoulos, known as El Greco (1541-1614) *(p 209)*, a painter of icons, who emigrated first to Venice, then to Rome and finally to Spain. Later in 17C other artists such as Tzanes settled in the Ionian Islands.

The most famous work of literature was the great poem "Erotokritos"by Vinkentios Kornáros; it was based on a French work about the trials of two lovers which reached a happy ending but contained many Greek and Cretan elements.

Crete under the Turks. – The Turkish occupation of Crete, which followed the capture of Herakleion *(p 205)* in 1669, was very harsh; some Cretans had to convert to Islam while others took refuge in the mountains. Revolts erupted, particularly in 1770 under the leadership of the Sfakiot, Dasklogiánnis *(p 217)*; there were several more in 19C.

Finally in 1878 Crete acquired a certain measure of autonomy under the aegis of the Great Powers and the regency of Prince George of Greece. It was thanks to the great liberal Cretan politican, Eleutherios Venizélos (1864-1936) *(p 204)*, that Crete was finally attached to Greece in 1913.

The Battle of Crete (1941). – After occupying mainland Greece the Germans turned their attention to Crete. In May 1941 they carried out an audacious airborne operation with 500 transport aircraft and 80 gliders carrying parachutists and infantrymen. On 21 May 3 000 parachutists captured Máleme aerodrome to the west of Chania which served the Germans as a base for their penetration along the north coast of the island.

The British, Australian and New Zealand troops under General Freyberg were obliged to retreat over the White Mountains to embark at Sfakiá. It took the Germans only ten days to capture the whole island but it cost them 6 000 of their best men.

ÁGIOS NIKÓLAOS★★

Lassíthi – Pop 8 130 – Michelin map 980 fold 39

Regular ferries to Sitía, Rhodes and Santoríni.

Ágios Nikólaos (St Nicholas) is a smart and lively resort, its white houses cover the slopes above the sparkling waters of Mirambélo Bay. It is pleasant to take an evening stroll along the quays of the lake and the fishing harbour where cafés, tavernas and restaurants spill out on to the pavement in typical Mediterranean style. The beaches and moderns hotels lie along the coast to the north. Ágios Nikólaos makes a good centre from which to explore the eastern end of the island.

Local speciality: *soumáda,* a refreshing almond drink.

Lake Voulisméni★ – Steep slopes honeycombed with caves encircle this pretty little lake. Its waters reflect the boats, cafés and shops which line the quays under the shade of tamarisk trees. Formerly it was known as "Artemis' Pool" and believed to be bottomless but in fact it is 64m – 210ft deep; the channel to the sea was dug in 1870.

Archaeological Museum. – *Open 8.45am to 3pm; closed Sundays; 100 Dr.*

The museum, which is on the road to Iráklio, contains finds from local excavations, particularly articles from the Minoan or Archaic Greek periods (Lató terracottas).

EXCURSIONS

Spinalónga Peninsula★ (Hersónissos Spinalónga). – *43km – 27 miles, about 1 hour.* Leave Ágios Nikólaos by Odós Koundoúrou which turns into a very beautiful corniche road providing frequent **views★★** over Mirambélo Bay. Once over a little pass the road runs down to the modern village of **Shísma** (Eloúnda – Pop 1 109) which is known for its luxurious hotels. In the village turn right *(sign Oloús)* into a track suitable for vehicles which runs through onetime salt pans created by the Venetians. By two windmills the road crosses a bridge over a canal which was dug through the neck of the peninsula in 1898 by French sailors from the allied occupation forces; on the right rise the remains of ancient Oloús.

Oloús. – Owing to earthquakes most of the ruins lie under the sea but an enclosure on the left beyond the bar contains traces of a paleo-Christian basilica with a fragment of 6C or 7C mosaic floor decorated with geometric motifs and fish.

Spinalónga Island. – *Access by boat from Eloúnda.* Off the northern end of the peninsula lies a rocky islet on which the Venetians built a fortress in 16C. They held it until 1715 when it passed to the Turks. Between 1904 and 1958 the island was a leper colony.

Return to Ágios Nikólaos via **Neápoli** (W of Eloúnda), once the home of **Pétros Filargés** (1340-1410), a Franciscan monk who became archbishop of Milan in 1402 and Pope Alexander V in 1409.

Kritsá★ and Lató★. – *Description pages 211-212.*

ANÓGIA

Réthimno – Pop 2 449 – Alt 740m – 2 428ft – Michelin map 980 fold 38

The majestic site of this mountain town *(24 miles west of Iráklio)* lies at the foot of **Mount Ida** (Ídi), also known as Mount Psilorítis; its summit (alt 2 456m – 8 058 ft) is snow-capped almost all the year. Anógia *(tavernas)* was rebuilt after being destroyed by the Germans in 1944 and is now a centre for local crafts (weaving, embroidery).

EXCURSIONS

Idaian Cave (Idéo Ándro). – *22km – 14 miles south plus 1/2 hour on foot Rtn. Open from spring to autumn (except when excavations are in progress); apply to the keeper, Mr. Xylouris in Anógia.*

Just before Anógia coming from Iráklio a narrow road branches off *(left)* leading to the Nída Plateau (alt 1 370m – 4 495ft) and the Idaian Cave (alt 1 540m – 5 052ft).

The sacred cave of Ida high on the mountain may have been the birthplace of Zeus *(p 212).* It was first excavated at the end of 19C by Italian archaeologists who discovered objects dating from 9C BC including several decorated bronze shields which are now displayed in the museum in Herakleion.

Recent excavations by Greek archaeologists have produced countless objects tracing the history of the cave from the neolithic period to 5C BC: objects made of gold, silver, pottery and rock crystal as well as small ivory pieces fashioned with skill (probably imported from Syria). The cave attracted pilgrims from all over the Greek world.

Axós. – Pop 228. *6km – 4 miles west.* At the entrance to the village *(left)* stands **St Irene's Church,** a beautiful and typically Byzantine building except for the Gothic doorway in the façade. The frescoes in the interior date from the first half of 14C.

ÁPTERA

Haniá – Michelin map 980 east of fold 37

Branching off the main east-west highway is a minor road which leads up to a plateau above Soúda Bay. The ruins belong to a town which flourished from 5C BC to the Byzantine period when it became a bishopric. Within the precinct are the remains of temples, a Roman theatre and an impressive underground **Roman cistern** with three bays.

From the fort at the far end of the promontory there is a very fine **view★★** of the mountain *(south)* and of **Soúda Bay★** *(north),* a huge natural harbour 8km – 5 miles long by 2km – 1 1/4 miles wide; the entrance is protected by two fortified islets which were held by the Venetians until 1715. The largest ships can anchor in Soúda Bay so that it serves both as the commercial port of Chania *(ferries to Piraeus)* and as a strategic naval base.

ARKÁDI Monastery★

Réthimno – Michelin map 𝟿𝟾𝟶 centre of fold 38

Arkádi Monastery *(car park; Tourist Pavilion)* is one of the most impressive places in Crete as much for its site on the edge of a plateau overlooking a wild gorge as for a gloriously tragic incident in the struggle against the Turks. In 1866 some 1 000 Cretans, including many women and children, took refuge in the monastery and, after holding out in a desperate combat for two days against 12 000 Turkish soldiers, decided to blow themselves up with the powder magazine rather than yield; Gabriel, the superior of the monastery and the soul of the resistance, perished together with 829 other people.

A few monks still live in the monastery *(open 8.30am to 1pm and 3 to 5pm)*. It was founded in 11C and its bare walls and austere exterior make it look like a fortress. A shady walk leads to the door and a vaulted passage gives access to the large courtyard in front of the church.

The church façade is striking; it is built of golden stone and dated 1587. The Corinthian columns, the arcading and the Italian-style oculi give it a Renaissance look while the curves and counter-curves of the pediments add a touch of the Baroque.

The convent buildings date from 17C but have been altered since. The cellars, the kitchen, the huge refectory, the powder magazine and a small museum (souvenirs of Gabriel) are open to the public.

CHANIA★ *Haniá*

Haniá – Pop 47 338 – Michelin map 𝟿𝟾𝟶 fold 37

Chania, which is served by the port at Soúda *(ferries to Piraeus)* and the airport at Akrotíri, lies in a fertile coastal basin which produces citrus fruits and potatoes. The capital of Crete until 1971, it is now a hard-working modern town, which suffered greatly in the German bombardment in 1941. Nevertheless a picturesque old district has survived round the Venetian port (Enetikó Limáni). *Beaches to the west of the town.*

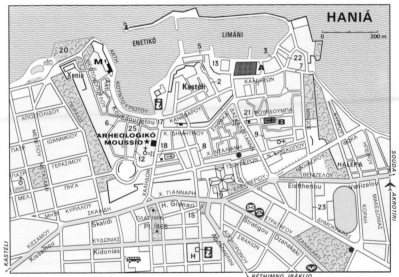

Ag. Markou	ΑΓ. ΜΑΡΚΟΥ	2	Pl. Mahis tis Kritis	ΠΛΑΤ. ΜΑΧΗΣ ΤΗΣ ΚΡΗΤΗΣ 15
Akti Enosseos	ΑΚΤΗ ΕΝΩΣΕΩΣ	3	Pl. El. Venizelou	ΠΛΑΤ. ΕΛ. ΒΕΝΙΖΕΛΟΥ 17
Akti Tombazi	ΑΚΤΗ ΤΟΜΠΑΖΗ	5	Pl. Patr. Athinagora	ΠΛΑΤ. ΠΑΤΡ. ΑΘΗΝΑΓΟΡΑ 18
Douka	ΔΟΥΚΑ	6	Pl. S. Venizelou	ΠΛΑΤ. Σ. ΒΕΝΙΖΕΛΟΥ 19
Epimenidou	ΕΠΙΜΕΝΙΔΟΥ	7	Pl. Talo	ΠΛΑΤ. ΤΑΛΩ 20
Gavaladon	ΓΑΒΑΛΑΔΩΝ	8	Pl. 1821	ΠΛΑΤ. 1821 21
Kalistou	ΚΑΛΙΣΤΟΥ	9	Radamanthios	ΡΑΔΑΜΑΝΘΥΟΣ 22
Kondilaki	ΚΟΝΔΥΛΑΚΗ	12	Trikoupi	ΤΡΙΚΟΥΠΗ 23
Pl. Katehaki	ΠΛΑΤ. ΚΑΤΕΧΑΚΗ	13	Zambeliou	ΖΑΜΠΕΛΙΟΥ 25

Old town★. – The old town which follows the curve of the harbour, is used only by caiques and coasting vessels; it was built from 13C onwards by the Venetians who enclosed it within a wall which was rebuilt in 16C according to the plans of the great engineer Sammicheli *(p 208);* a few segments of the wall are still standing.

Kastéli district. *East.* – This is the old district round the citadel which contained the Latin cathedral, the Venetian Governor's palace, the administrative buildings (Customs, Archives), the houses of the leading citizens and the Arsenal (**A**), of which a few curious vaulted structures have survived, where the galleys were repaired. On the quayside the former Janissaries' *(p 24)* mosque (late 17C) now houses the Tourist Office.

Merchants' District★. *West.* – Walk along the quay (Aktí Koundouriótou) which is very busy and thronged with tavernas offering fish and seafood dishes (sea urchins).

The beautiful old house *(north end)* is now a **naval museum (M1)** *(open 10am to 2pm; also 5 to 7pm Tuesdays, Thursdays and Saturdays; closed Mondays; 50 Dr);* the exhibits are well presented: historic documents and detailed model ships.

The charming little streets behind the museum contain old Venetian houses with balconies and stone doorways sometimes ornamented with sculpted coats of arms.

From time to time there is a view of the harbour between the houses.

Archaeological Museum★ (Arheologikó Moussío). – *Open 8.45am to 3pm (9.30am to 2.30pm Sundays); closed Tuesdays; 100 Dr*. The museum is housed in an old church which was built in 14C in the Venetian Gothic style as the conventual church of a Franciscan convent and dedicated to St Francis; it has a nave and two aisles with ogival vaulting. The Turks converted it into a mosque.

The exhibits include painted sarcophagi and ceramics from the Minoan and post-Minoan periods and Roman mosaics.

The stone exhibits are displayed in the garden beneath the palm trees and other exotic plants round a fine hexagonal Turkish fountain.

St Nicholas' Church (Ágios Nikólaos) (B). – It was built as a Dominican chapel, converted into a mosque with a minaret and became an Orthodox church in 1918; the neighbouring streets are quite picturesque.

EXCURSION

Akrotíri Peninsula (Hersónissos Akrotíri). – *40km – 25 miles by car Rtn*. The peninsula which divides Soúda Bay from Chania Bay is made of limestone and riddled with caves.

Leave Haniá via Halépa which is a residential district to the east; after 6km – 4 miles turn left towards Venizelos' Tomb.

Venizelos' Tomb★ (Táfos Venizélou). – The tomb stands on the top of a hill named after the Prophet Elijah (Profítis Ilías) *(restaurants)*, where the Greek flag was raised by the Cretan rebels in 1897 and shot down by the navies of the Great Powers.

A great stone marks the grave of the Cretan statesman **Elefthérios Venizélos** (Chania 1864 – Paris 1936); he was a lawyer and leader of the Greek liberal party who campaigned for Crete to be united with Greece and for Greece to enter the First World War on the side of the Allies; his son Sophoclés Venizélos (1894-1964) is buried beside him. There is an extensive **view★★** over Chania and its bay and south to the White Mountains (Lefká Óri).

Follow the signs to the Airport and at the end of the runway turn left into the road to Mouzourás and then almost immediately left again to Agía Triáda.

Holy Trinity Monastery (Agía Triáda). – *Restoration in progress*. It was founded early in 17C by Tzangaroli, a Venetian; the church and the belltower are in the Italian Classical style. In 1980 there was only one monk left.

Gouvernéto Monastery. – A walk *(about 1 hour on foot Rtn)*, starting from Agía Triáda leads to the monastery of St John of Gouvernéto which was rebuilt and fortified in 1548 by the Venetians. The cave of St John the Hermit is nearby.

GONIÁ Monastery

Haniá – Michelin map 980 fold 37 – between Haniá and Kastéli.

The monastery of Our Lady Gonia (Moní Kirías Goniás), which is also called the Hodegetria (Moní Odigítrias), was founded by the Venetians in 1618; since its position on the coast was of military importance it also served as a fortress and was frequently damaged and restored.

The church and the adjacent chapels *(open 8.30am to 1pm and 3 to 5pm)* contain an interesting collection of **icons★** several of which date from 16 and 17C: the very moving Crucifixion of Christ.

From the terrace behind the church there is a very fine **view★** of Chania Bay.

GORTYN★   *Górtis*

Iráklio – Michelin map 980 fold 38

The impressive ruins straggling beneath the olive trees on either side of the road from Phaistos (Festós) evoke the past glory of Gortyn, capital of a Roman province and seat of the first Christian bishop of Crete.

Proud Gortyn. – The city began to develop in 7C BC forming an acropolis on a hill on the west bank of the little river Lethe and it soon supplanted Phaistos as the capital of the Messará Plain. In about 500 BC a sort of civil and criminal code was drawn up regulating social relationships: the famous **Twelve Tables of Gortyn**.

Although Hannibal took refuge in Gortyn in 189 BC after being defeated by the Romans, the city nevertheless fell to the Romans in 67 BC and they made it the capital of a province comprising Crete and parts of North Africa known as Cyrenaica. As the seat of the provincial Governor the city went in for a spate of building in 2C, particularly under Trajan, using stone from the huge quarries in the neighbouring mountains; many administrative and religious buildings were erected at this time.

Christianity took root in Gortyn in 1C AD with the arrival of **Titus** who was sent by St Paul to convert the Cretans and became their patron saint. In 260 AD during the persecution ordered by the Emperor Decius the Christian community produced its first martyrs, the Holy Ten (Ágii Déka), who are remembered in the name of a local village (pop 766 – *museum*). In 4C AD, following the recognition of Christianity by the Emperor Constantine, Gortyn became a bishopric with jurisdiction over all the churches in Crete; richly decorated sanctuaries began to proliferate.

Gortyn was still prosperous during the Byzantine period but fell into decay after the Arab invasion in 9C.

When the Italian monk Buondelmonti visited the city in 15C it was in ruins but he was nontheless impressed by its size and compared it with Florence.

Excavations were first conducted in 1884 by the Italian School in Athens and continued in 1970.

MAIN SIGHTS *1/2 hour*

Park in the car park on the right of the road coming from Iráklio. Open 8 am to 7pm (6pm Sundays); 100 Dr.

St Titus' Basilica ★ (Ágios Títos). – This important building, which is thought to date from 7C, was erected on the site of Titus' martyrdom. The basilical plan of a nave and two aisles has been combined with the cruciform plan; the arms of the transept have apsidal ends. The chevet formed of three parallel apses is still standing; a few fragments of the carved decoration are on display in the Historical Museum in Herakleion.

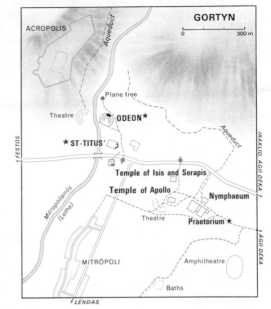

On the north side of the basilica was an agora; the city had two.

Odeon ★. – The little theatre, which has been restored, consists of semi-circular terraces supported by vaulting and was built early in 2C AD under Trajan on the site of and with materials taken from an earlier rotunda *(thólos – p 18)*. Here and there lie damaged statues.

At the rear of the Odeon under the vaulting of the outer corridor are several blocks of stone taken by the Romans from the earlier building and bearing the text of the Twelve Tables of Gortyn. The Dorian letters which number 17 000 were inscribed in about 480 BC and the lines are written alternately from left to right and right to left; the text deals with individual liberty, property, inheritance, adultery, violence, etc.

Nearby stood an evergreen plane tree in memory, so legend would have it, of the love of Zeus and Europa which gave birth to Minos, Sarpedon and Rhadamanthos.

OTHER SIGHTS

Return towards Iráklio and then take the path on the right level with the sign for Gortyn.

Temple of Isis and Serapis. – The remains of a cella and a purification basin mark the site of this 2C temple which was dedicated to two Egyptian gods whose worship was widespread in the Roman world: Isis was the symbol of the universal feminine and Serapis was seen by the Romans as a manifestation of Jupiter. On the architrave is inscribed the dedication made by Flavia Phyrila and her sons.

Temple of Pythian Apollo. – Traces of a great sanctuary which dates from the Archaic period (inscriptions) but was rebuilt later; the *prónaos (p 18)* is Hellenistic, the columns of the cella and the altar are Roman.

Residency ★ (Praetorium). – Recent excavations have uncovered the impressive ruins of the praetorium, a huge building which was both the Governor's residence and the seat of the provincial administration; first built of brick in 2C under Trajan, it was reconstructed in 4C following an earthquake. It is possible to identify a vast chamber (basilica), the baths and the courtyard of a temple surrounded by a portico; the drums of the columns rest beside the bases. Several damaged statues have been recovered.

Nymphaeum. – Opposite the praetorium is a nymphaeum which was built in 2C as a grotto dedicated to the nymphs and converted into a fountain in the Byzantine era; it was supplied with water by an aqueduct.

HERAKLEION★   *Iráklio*

Iráklio – Pop 101 634 – Michelin map 980 fold 39

Now the capital city and principal port of Crete, the commercial and administrative centre of the island, the medieval city of **Candia** has developed enormously since the Second World War. Nonetheless it is still surrounded by its 16-17C ramparts and is not unattractive owing to its lively atmosphere and the contrast between port and town, broad avenues and narrow streets, modern buildings and traditional houses. It is a good base for excursions into the centre of the island.

The favourite meeting places for both tourists and locals are Liberty Square (Platía Eleftherías) and Venizelos Square (Platía El. Venizélou) with their pavement cafés, book shops and newspaper kiosks, and Daidalos Street (Odós Dedálou) with its souvenir shops, local crafts (jewellery and icons), restaurants and tavernas.

It is also worth eating in the fish tavernas down by the harbour particularly in the evening; sometimes there is music performed on the Cretan "lyre".

HISTORICAL NOTES

According to legend, Herakleion takes its name from Herakles (Hercules) who landed on Crete to accomplish one of his Twelve Labours *(p 194)*: to master the Cretan bull which was ravaging the kingdom of Minos at the instigation of Poseidon.

When Crete fell in 827 to the Arabs, they set up a fortified camp on the site of Herakleion surrounded by a ditch – El Khandak – from which the Venetians, who arrived in 13C, derived the name Candia which applied not only to the city but to the island itself. Under the Venetians the city became a commercial and military centre, the key to the rest of Crete; they erected many churches, public and private buildings and an arsenal.

The Cretans however hated the Venetians who oppressed them with heavy taxes.

The Great Siege (1648-1669). – In 1648 the Turks landed on Crete, most of which they occupied, and laid siege to Candia. During the following twenty years they made 69 assaults on the city while the besieged carried out 89 sorties. The pressure increased in 1667 when the Grand Vizier assembled 80 000 men and the largest canon in Europe.

As the Venetians held out under their commander **Francesco Morosini** (1619-1694), who twenty years later delivered Athens from the Turks *(p 43)*, Christendom grew concerned. Finally Louis XIV sent a naval force led by the **Duc de Beaufort**; the ships carried 6 000 soldiers under the command of Marshal de Navailles. Beaufort was killed during a sortie which failed and, after losing 1 000 men, the expeditionary force withdrew.

Morosini now had only 4 000 defenders and the city was under heavy bombardment; on 5 September 1669 he surrendered. About 30 000 Christians and 110 000 Muslims had died during the siege, which marked the end of Venetian sway in the eastern Mediterranean.

Under the Turkish occupation Candia gradually lost its importance to Chania which became the capital of Crete until 1971.

MAIN SIGHTS *3 hours*

Archaeological Museum ★★★ (Arheologikó Moussío). – *Open 8am to 7pm (6pm Sundays); in winter 8am to 5pm; closed Mondays; 150 Dr.*

In the shade of the garden stands a stele raised in memory of the Duc de Beaufort and his 1 000 French soldiers who fell during the siege of Candia. The museum is devoted to the Minoan civilisation discovered at the end of the last century; it is preferable to visit the museum after seeing the archaeological sites of Knossós, Phaistos, Mália and Zákros.

The exhibits are arranged in chronological order and are mainly the product of the excavations complemented by reconstructions (models or watercolours) of the main palaces. The most interesting rooms are Room IV and Room VII.

Room I: Neolithic and Pre-Palace Periods (5 000 – 2 000 BC). Among the funerary articles Vassilikí vases with a red decoration on a light ground *(case 6)*, alabaster and soapstone vessels, golden jewellery from Móhlos Island (west of Sitía) *(cases 7 and 17)*, seals used as signets or as lucky charms *(cases 11 and 18)*.

Rooms II and III: Old Palace Period (2 000 – 1 700 BC). Little remains of the palaces and mountain shrines of this period but excavations have produced votive offerings and a remarkable series of **Kamáres ware:** vases, amphorae, jugs with spouts, cups and goblets elegantly decorated with spirals and flowers.

In the centre of Room III in case 41 is the **Phaistos Disk;** the hieroglyphs inscribed in a spiral on the clay (not yet deciphered) are suggestive of the labyrinth of the Minotaur. Case 43 contains an astonishing bowl in Kamáres ware decorated with white flowers in relief which was found at Phaistos.

Room IV: New Palace Period (1700 – c1500 BC) Masterpieces of Minoan civilisation. On the left on entering *(case 50)* are the famous **snake goddesses,** faience statuettes of barebreasted priestesses (symbols of fecundity) found in the central shrine at Knossós. Next *(case 51)* is a soapstone vase in the shape of a bull's head used for religious libations: the eye is rock crystal and the muzzle outlined with mother of pearl. Two other cases *(56 and 57)* display an extraordinary ivory **acrobat** involved in the ritual bull leaping and a set of pieces made of incrusted ivory. At the far end of the room is an alabaster ritual vessel (rhyton) shaped like a lion's head *(case 59)*.

Room V: New Palace Period. Everyday articles of porphyry (lamps, weights) and alabaster (amphorae). Clay tablets with inscriptions in Linear A and B scripts.

Room VI: New Palace Period. Funerary objects. The group of sacred dancers in terracotta comes from a *thólos* tomb at Kamilári, southwest of Phaistos *(case 71, right)*, a libation jug *(case 80)*, gold jewellery *(cases 87 and 88, centre)*.

Room VII: New Palace Period (1700-c1500 BC). This room is one of the richest in the museum. On entering one's attention is claimed by the huge bronze double-headed axes. The first three cases display three black soapstone vessels used for ritual libations and found at Agía Triáda:

– the **Harvester Vase** *(case 94)* decorated with a procession of peasants and musicians in low relief;

– the **Chieftain Cup** *(case 95)* showing several people of whom one, a Chief or Prince, has long wavy hair and is wearing jewellery;

– the **Boxer Vase** *(case 96)*, a conical rhyton decorated with athletics and ritual bull-leaping scenes.

Note the curious copper ingots weighing 30kg – 66lbs *(cases 97 et 99)* and the jewellery: famous **golden pendant** composed of two foraging bees which was found at Mália *(case 101, centre of the room)*.

Rooms VIII and IX: New Palace Period. In the first room note the objects discovered since 1962 in the palace at Zákros: ritual vases including a rock crystal rhyton *(case 109)* with pearl handles which was reconstructed by the museum workshop from a multitude of fragments.

The main exhibit in the second room is an amphora decorated with an octopus *(centre case)*.

Room X: Post-Palace Period (c1500-1100 BC). The art of this period is characterized by large female figures with headdresses of birds, horns and poppies *(case 133, at the back)*.

Rooms XI and XII: Sub-Minoan and Geometric Period (1100-650 BC). Interpenetration of the Minoan, Greek and Oriental styles. At the back of the first room *(case 148)* are female idols and a curious chariot drawn by bulls; in the second room are cinerary urns with lids and bronze objects found in a cave on Mount Ida *(case 169)*.

Room XIII: Minoan sarcophagi from the Post-Palace Period (c1500-1100 BC) often look like baths or chests. There is a wooden model of the Palace of Knossós as it may have been in about 1400 BC.

Rooms XIV, XV and XVI (first floor): A Gallery and two rooms are devoted to Minoan frescoes from the New Palace Period, which show similarities with frescoes from the Palace of Mari (Sumerian civilisation). They have been reconstructed from fragments – some parts are in relief – and show the high quality of mural painting in the palaces of this period.

One of the chief exhibits in the museum, the **Agía Triáda sarcophagus,** is to be found in the centre of Room XIV: the painted decoration has a funerary theme – sacrifice of a bull, priestesses pouring libations, people bearing offerings going to meet death. On the walls are the **Prince of the Lilies,** crowned with lilies and peacock feathers, a bull's head in relief and an acrobat in a bull-leaping scene – all from Knossós.

Room XV contains the famous **"Parisienne",** found at Knossós and so named by Sir Arthur Evans because of the malicious charm of her expression; the small-scale but well preserved figure represents a priestess. Room XVI next door contains other well known frescoes: the Monkey collecting saffron, a dancer and "an officer of the black guard".

Some minor rooms on the first floor are temporarily closed.

Old port★ (Paleó Limáni). – The old Venetian port is now devoted to fishing boats. Parts of the **Venetian Arsenal (A)** are to be found at the far end of the harbour: stores, docks and in particular the hangar where the galleys were brought out of the water for caulking and repair.

The entrance to the harbour is commanded by the Koúles, the **Venetian fortress** *(open 8.45am to 3pm; 9.30am to 2.30pm Sundays; 100 Dr)* still bearing the lion of St Mark; it was built in 16C and has been recently restored. It has massive walls pierced with embrasures for canon, a cistern, a powder magazine and casemates communicating with stores for canon balls. Fine views of the port and town.

Odós 1866. – In the morning the street is the scene of a lively **market★** full of smells and colour selling local products: yoghurt and honey, herbs including dittany which is drunk as an infusion, ornamental bread rings, raisins, figs, citrus fruits, cheeses, fish and meat...

At the end of the street are two contrasting fountains: the Bembo fountain, erected by the Venetians in 1588, and a Turkish fountain converted into a street stall.

El. Venizélos Square. – This is a pleasant paved area reserved for pedestrians only; the basin of the 17C **Morosini Fountain (B)** is decorated with nereids, tritons and dolphins... (the upper basin, supported on lions, may come from an earlier 14C fountain).

Leading out of the southeast corner of the square is a street reserved for pedestrians, Odós Dedálou, where the tavernas and boutiques invite one to take a stroll.

St Mark's Church (Ágios Márkos) **(D)**. – Italianate in style with an external portico and a nave and two aisles supported on tall columns, it was the cathedral of Candia during the Venetian occupation; the Turks converted it into a mosque.

The building (14C, restored) is now used for exhibitions, conferences, concerts; the walls are decorated with copies of Byzantine frescoes.

Venetian Loggia (E). – The reconstruction has been carried out in the style of the 17C original which was inspired by the Venetian architect, Palladio. It was here that the money changers set up their stalls and the merchants met to discuss business.

OTHER SIGHTS

St Catherine's Church (Agía Ekateríni) **(F)**. – In 16C and 17C this church was attached to the convent of St Catherine of Sinai which organised a school; its pupils may have included El Greco *(p 209)* one of whose early works was a landscape of Mount Sinai.

It is a shared church with two centres of worship. The one on the left, dedicated to the Holy Ten (Ágii Déka) *(p 204)*, dates from 13C; it has heavy ogival vaulting; the elegant Venetian façade with pilasters, tympanum and oculus is later, probably 15C. The other dates from 16C; the façade and the barrel-vaulted nave lit by oculi reveal the influence of Italian architecture.

The interior *(open 9am to 1pm; also 4 to 6pm Tuesdays, Thursdays and Fridays; 150 Dr)* contains six remarkable **icons** ★★ by **Damaskinós** who worked in Venice and the Ionian Islands from 1574 to 1582 before returning to Crete. These works, which were formerly at the Vrondissí monastery *(p 218)* combine the traditional Byzantine formality of composition and picturesque realism with the Italian feeling for form. Compare the unusual scene of the Council of Nicaea condemning Arianism, in the Byzantine style, with the Last Supper and the Adoration of the Magi which owe much to Tintoretto.

Venetian Walls (Enetiká Tíhi) (16-17C). – The town walls are 5km – 3 miles long and reinforced by seven large bastions with lateral projections called "orillions"; they were the work of **Michele Sammicheli** (1484-1559), an architect who had designed the fortifications of Padua and Verona and came to Crete in 1538. The road running along under the walls leads to the **Martinengo Bastion** (Promahónas Martinéngo) on the top of which is the tomb **(G)** of the great Cretan writer Kazantzákis (1883-1957); the inscription reads: I hope for nothing, I fear nothing, I am free.

History Museum (Istorikó Moussío) **(M1)**. – *Open 9am to 1pm and 3 to 5.30pm; closed Sundays; 150 Dr.*

Its collections, which illustrate Cretan history from the Byzantine period down to the present day, include: sculptures from St Titus' Basilica at Agía Triáda; pieces from the loggia, fountains and Venetian houses in Candia; Venetian and Turkish tomb stones; Byzantine icons; embroidery, jewellery and traditional Cretan fabrics; documents on the Battle of Crete (1941).

Note the reconstructions of Kazantzákis' study and a 19C Cretan interior.

St Titus' Church (Ágios Títos) **(K)**. – The church was built by the Venetians in 16C; the Turks transformed it into a mosque; it is now the Metropolitan (cathedral) church.

In the narthex *(left)* is a reliquary containing St Titus' head which was returned by the Venetians in 1966.

EXCURSIONS

Knossós ★★★. – *5km – 3 miles south. Description p 210.*

Kazantzakis Museum. – *15km – 9 1/2 miles SE of Iráklio at Varvári Pediádos (Mirtiá). Open 9am to 1pm; also 4 to 8pm Sundays, Mondays, Wednesdays and Saturdays; closed Thursdays; November to February, 9am to 2pm Sundays only; 150 Dr.*

This little museum is devoted to the life of the Greek novelist Kazantzakis: manuscripts of his books which have been published in 53 countries and translated into 41 languages, theatrical costumes used in presentations of his plays, photographs and some of his personal possessions.

Mount Gioúhtas ★; **Vathípetro.** – *21km – 13 miles south. – Take the road to Knossós and 5km – 3 miles beyond the site turn right to Arhánes;* the road runs through a region of vineyards in which many traces of Minoan buildings have been discovered: palaces, graveyards (at Foúrni in particular), "villas"; temples where human sacrifices were occasionally made to avert an imminent or insuperable danger.

On the far side of Arhánes, 3km – 2 miles beyond Hotel Dias, bear right into an unsurfaced road which leads to the top of Mount Gioúhtas *(signpost)*.

Mount Gioúhtas ★. – In this mountain (alt 811m – 2 661ft), which has yielded a number of votive offerings from a Minoan shrine, the god Zeus is supposed to be entombed. The mountain's silhouette can indeed be said to resemble the profile of a man asleep which popular belief claims to be Zeus himself.

From the pilgrimage church at the top on the edge of a steep cliff there is a vast **panorama** ★★ over Herakleion and the sea (N), Mount Díkti (E) and Mount Ida (W).

Return to the road to Pírgos; after 1km – 1/2 mile turn right (signpost) into a track which leads to the ruins of Vathípetro.

Vathípetro Villa. – Excavations on this pleasant site have uncovered a large-scale agricultural enterprise from the Minoan period: central courtyard, stores, potter's workshop, shrine; it has even been possible to identify an oil press and a wine press.

Tylissos (Tílissos). – *14km – 8 3/4 miles southwest; coming from Iráklio bear left on entering the village.*

On the top of the hill are traces of three Minoan villas from the New Palace Period *(open 8.45am to 3pm; 9.30am to 2.30pm Sundays; 100 Dr).*

Near the entrance walk round the remains of Villa B *(right)* and then walk anti-clockwise round the whole of the ruins to reach the entrance to Villa C of which the northeast corner is marked by a circular cistern. Further on the right is the vestibule next to the porter's lodge: next are several rooms, some of which as still partially paved, passages and stairs.

Beyond are the remains of Villa A; its entrance was divided by two pillars: to the right were the stores, to the left a paved corridor leading to a little court or light well *(p 211)* surrounded by various rooms. The enormous bronze cauldrons in the Herakleion Museum were found in this villa.

Fódele★; **Balí**★. – *48km – 30 miles west. Leave Iráklio by the Chania Gate and take the new road to Réthimno.* At the end of the bay the road passes Paleókastro, a Venetian fortress, leaves the fishing village of **Agía Pelagía** (pop 215 – *good beaches*) on the right and then reaches the Fódele Valley.

Fódele Valley★. – This recess in the mountainside is thought to be the birthplace of the painter Domenico Theotokópoulos, known as **El Greco** (1541-1614) *(pp 208 and 218).* Its slopes are covered with olive and carob trees; the well irrigated valley bottom is carpeted with orange and lemon groves.

1km – 1/2 mile before reaching the village, take the path on the right *(1/2 hour on foot Rtn; signpost "House of Theotokópoulos")* which fords the river, skirts a charming Byzantine church (frescoes inside) and ends in front of El Greco's father's house; it stands in a pleasant spot facing the austere grandeur of the barren mountain tops.

Return to the coast road and continue to the righthand turning down to Balí (poor road).

Balí★. – Pop 141. The village *(tavernas)* in a little creek offers good fishing and walking along the spectacular and rugged rocky coast which conceals a few small isolated beaches.

IERÁPETRA

Lassíthi – Pop 8 575 – Michelin map 980 fold 39

There is a certain oriental feeling about Ierápetra which is the most southern town in Europe and enjoys a mild winter climate. It is a market for the agricultural products of the coastal plain: wine, oil, fruit, early vegetables and particularly tomatoes which are grown under glass throughout the year. It is also a popular resort with a long sandy beach bordered by a promenade lined with tamarisk trees and tavernas.

The port, which is devoted to fishing and coastal traffic, is not unattractive; the entrance is commanded by a 13C **fortress** with square bastions.

The old town still bears traces of the Turkish occupation: a fountain and a minaret.

EXCURSION

Áno Viános★. – Pop 1 101. *53km – 33 miles west.* The road passes through heavily eroded country before reaching the verdant Mírtos Valley (oranges, bananas, vines). Beyond Péfkos a track bears left down to **Árvi** *(beach, inns),* a fishing village surrounded by banana plantations and overlooked by a monastery of unusual construction.

Áno Viános★ stands on a spectacular site in a mountain cirque overlooking a great sweep of olive trees.

KASTÉLI or KÍSSAMOS

Haniá – Pop 2 749 – Michelin map 980 fold 37

Known in antiquity as Kíssamos, Kastéli is now an excursion centre and a market town (good quality wine, olives, early vegetables, citrus fruit). Its position in the centre of Kíssamos Bay (Kólpos Kissámou) is well sheltered by the Rodopós promontory *(east)* and by the Gramvoússa promontory *(west);* northwest lies **Gramvoússa Islet,** which was fortified by the Venetians and held by them until the end of 17C; it then became a pirates' retreat until 19C. *Ferries to Kythera, the Peloponnese and Piraeus.*

EXCURSIONS

Falássarna. – *17km – 10 1/2 miles west. Take the road west to Plátanos.* In the village turn right into an unsurfaced road which leads down to the sea; fine views down over the rich coastal plain: olive groves, tomatoes under glass.

7km – 4 1/4 miles beyond Plátanos, past a café-bar, the road reaches the ancient ruins of Falássarna, scattered over a lonely site on the neck of a rocky peninsula on which an acropolis once stood; the position of the harbour is still visible although it is now dry since volcanic movements have raised the level of the coastline by about 8m – 26ft.

Polirinía. – Pop 127 – *6km – 3 3/4 miles south.* Picturesque village on a bluff of rock which provides a fine view of Kíssamos Bay; traces of an ancient city founded in 8C BC.

KASTÉLI

Iráklio – Pop 1 271 – Michelin map 980 centre of fold 39

Kastéli *(tavernas)* is a large village; on Saturdays a lively market is held.

3km – 2 miles north on the road to Limáni Hersoníssou, just before Pigí, an unsurfaced road bears right *(sign)* to **St Pantaleon's Church** (Ágios Pandeleímonas), which is hidden by trees on a cool and shady site *(café-taverna);* it is an interesting church, built on the basilical plan with a nave and two aisles, terminating in apses; it was probably rebuilt during the Venetian period using fragments of earlier buildings (ancient capitals, Byzantine sculptures); the sanctuary is decorated with 14C frescoes and beautiful icons.

KNOSSÓS ★★★

Iráklio – Michelin map 980 fold 39 – 5km – 3 miles south of Iráklio

The maze of corridors, passages, rooms and stairways, which make up the Palace of Knossós, is one of the major sights of Crete. The palace, which was excavated and partially reconstructed by the British archaeologist, Sir Arthur Evans, was the first of the Minoan palaces to be discovered and proved to be the largest.

MYTHOLOGY BASED ON HISTORY

King Minos. – Knossós, "the chief city of King Minos, whom great Zeus took into his confidence every nine years" (Homer), developed out of a very complicated building, the **Labyrinth** – "The Palace of the Axe" – since the double-headed axe was the main ritual symbol of the Minoan religion. The palace is supposed to have been designed by the cunning **Daidalos**, at Minos' request, to confine the **Minotaur**, a monster with a man's body and a bull's head.

Minos used to feed his enemies to the Minotaur and every nine years the Athenians, whom he had conquered, had to deliver a human sacrifice of seven youths and seven maidens. It was as part of the tribute that **Theseus** arrived from Athens and seduced Ariadne, King Minos' daughter; she gave him the thread obtained from Daidalos which Theseus unwound as he penetrated the Labyrinth and was thus able to fine his way out after killing the Minotaur and escape from the palace with Ariadne (p 155).

To punish Daidalos for revealing the secret of the Labyrinth Minos had him imprisoned within the palace but Daidalos constructed some wings using birds' feathers and wax and escaped from the palace with his son Ikaros.

Alas for Ikaros, he flew too close to the sun which melted the wax and the unfortunate young man fell into the sea near to the present island of Ikaría (west of Sámos in the Aegean) while his father succeeded in reaching Cumae in Italy.

Excavation of the palace. – The existence of Knossós had been suggested by Schliemann interpreting the Homeric epic as if it were history, as he had done for Troy and Mycenae. In 1878 a Cretan, Minos Kalokairinos, who had been the first to identify the site, had undertaken some excavations but it was the great British archaeologist, **Sir Arthur Evans** (1851-1941) who began to dig in earnest in 1900 and who gained the credit for discovering the palace and making it live again.

The site of Knossós on a hill was already inhabited in the neolithic period; in about 2000 BC a palace was built which was destroyed in 1700 BC. It was replaced by a new palace at the centre of a town with about 50 000 inhabitants; it is traces of this palace which can be seen today.

In c1500 BC an earthquake and a tidal wave, provoked, it seems, by the eruption of the volcano on Santoríni, laid waste the new palace which was however also sacked and occupied for a short period by the Mycenaeans. It was finally destroyed by fire between 1375 and 1250 BC. Nonetheless a settlement survived in the neighbourhood and in 4C BC Knossós was still of some importance in politics. Eventually at the end of 3C BC it was supplanted by Gortyn (p 204).

THE PALACE

Open 8am to 7pm (6pm Sundays); about 2 hours; 200 Dr.

Beyond the entrance gate, pass through a copse into the West Court, a paved area which was probably an agora. On the left are three pits for the disposal of discarded sacred objects and the base of an altar (1) in front of the entrance; behind it are the foundations of the palace about 1m – 3ft high. There were no fortifications and the buildings comprised about 1 300 rooms.

On the right is the West Entrance supported by a single central column of which the base remains. This entrance gave access to the **Corridor of the procession** (2); the walls were decorated with frescoes showing a procession of people bearing offerings (Herakleion Museum).

Upper Floor. – Next turn left to reach the grand entrance (3) *(propylaia)*, a pillared porch at the foot of the grand staircase to the upper floor; a section, including a copy of a fresco (bearers of offerings) has been reconstructed.

The upper floor comprised a certain number of pillared rooms, some of which have been restored and decorated with copies of frescoes. They may have been used as reception rooms: the famous "Parisienne" (p 207) may have formed part of the decoration.

To the west of this suite of rooms runs a long corridor serving a series of narrow storerooms piled high with provision jars *(pithoi)* some of which are still in place.

To the east another staircase leads down into the central courtyard.

Central Courtyard. – The courtyard is 60m – 197ft long by 29m – 95ft wide and surrounded by the main buildings: shrines, royal apartments etc. It (or the theatre) was probably the site of the perilous acrobatic ritual bull-leaping.

Sanctuary ★★. – Down the west side of the courtyard lie the rooms devoted to religious use on either side of the staircase.

On the right a vestibule (4), in the centre of which Evans placed a prophyry basin, leads into the "Throne Room" (5) which contains a bench and the alabaster throne on which the High Priestess of the Labyrinth may have sat; the Griffin Frescoes are reconstructions. Opposite the throne, steps beneath arches descend to a lustral basin.

On the left another vestibule (6) leads into the two "pillar crypts" (7) *(opposite)* where the ritual ceremonies took place (double axe heads carved on the pillars) and into the Treasury (8) *(right)* beneath which ritual objects were found, in particular the famous "snake goddesses" (Herakleion Museum); the sacred serpents may have been kept here.

Prince of the Lilies Fresco. – On the south side of the courtyard, in the passage which forms the end of the Corridor of the Procession, is a copy of the fresco of the Prince of the Lilies; the original is displayed in the Herakleion Museum.

Royal Apartments ★ ★ ★. – On the east side of the courtyard are the royal apartments, occupying four floors of rooms, two above the level of the courtyard and two below, built into the slope of the hill above the river with a view over the countryside. Here, as in other parts of the palace, there are light wells to provide the circulation of air and the partial lighting of the rooms.

A flight of steps (9) adjoining a light well leads to the royal apartments which are linked by a network of passages and corridors.

The first room is the Hall of the Double Axes (10) which may have been the Guard Room and is separated by a screen from the King's Room (11) which contained a wooden throne.

Queen's Chamber (12). – The room is lit by a light well and decorated with a copy of the Dolphin Fresco; adjoining is a tiny bathroom (13) with a bath made of clay. This material was also used to make the piping which carried the palace's supply of fresh water under pressure.

From the royal apartments a covered portico, which served as a promenade (points of view) leads to the outbuildings on the north side of the palace.

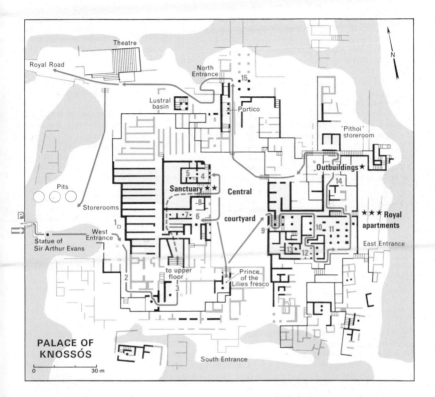

PALACE OF KNOSSÓS

Outbuildings ★. – There were workshops for craftsmen, stone polishers, potters (14) (remains of kilns), tailors, gold and silver smiths, and storerooms.

The **store containing the "pithoi"** *(p 20)* is astonishing; these huge terracotta jars (partially reconstructed) were used to store wine, oil, grain, honey etc.; this store dates from the first palace.

Return to the central courtyard and bear right down a passage which was suitable for vehicles.

This lane is lined by a portico decorated with animal sculptures, including a bull, and leads to what Evans called the Customs House (15); its square pillars are thought to have supported a banqueting hall on the floor above. On the left is the north entrance to the palace; outside it *(left)* is a lustral basin.

The **"Royal Road",** about 4m – 4yds wide and paved, probably led to Katsámbas and Amnisós, the harbours to the east of Herakleion which served Knossós.

On the right of the road stands a set of terraces in a good state of repair which are thought to belong to a sort of theatre, mentioned by Homer as the setting for ritual dances. *From there return to the west entrance.*

KRITSÁ ★

Lassíthi – Pop 1 910 – Michelin map 🅹🅸🅾 east of fold 39

Kritsá is a picturesque little town; its streets, arches and steps cling to the mountain slope among almond orchards overlooking Mirambélo Bay. Beneath the broad roofs and balconies craftsmen offer their wares for sale: woollen cloth, carpets, jewellery, leather boots. This was the location chosen for the film of "Christ Recrucified" based on the novel by Kazantzakis. In the summer season traditional folklore festivals (enactment of a Cretan wedding) are held.

EXCURSIONS

Lató Ruins★. – *3km – 2 miles northeast. Leave Kritsá by the road to Ágios Nikólaos and then turn left by the cemetery into an unsurfaced road leading to Lató.*

This isolated and awesome site★★ has been excavated since 1967 by archaeologists from the French School in Athens who have found traces of an ancient town scattered over the slopes of a sort of suspended amphitheatre.

Lató was founded in 8C BC on a saddle between two crags, each crowned by an acropolis; the position of the agora is indicated by the rectangular open space at the centre of the site; there are traces of a small shrine and a cistern at its centre.

The steps on the left of the agora, which were probably used for public assemblies or games, led up to a **Prytaneion** (3C BC) where the magistrates met in a small court surrounded by a peristyle. From the northern acropolis, reached via the ruins of houses, there is an extensive view down to Ágios Nikólaos.

From the other side a path leads to a polygonal wall retaining a terrace on which stands a little **temple of Apollo** (4C–3C) together with an altar for sacrifices. Beyond the terrace a series of steps indicates the site of a theatre.

Panagía Kerá Church★. – *1km – 1/2 miles from Kritsá on the Ágios Nikólaos road. Open 8.45am to 3pm (9.30am to 2.30pm Sundays); 100 Dr.*

A clump of cypress trees *(left)* conceals a charming white church, dedicated to the Virgin (Panagía). It was built in 13C, at the beginning of the Venetian occupation, on a small scale but well proportioned; it has a nave and two aisles terminating in apses. The church contains a remarkable series of 14C and 15C **frescoes**★★, both sophisticated and naive, in vivid colours.

The frescoes in the right aisle depict the Life of St Anne, her husband Joachim and the Virgin Mary: note the Birth of Christ being announced to the Shepherds and the Journey to Bethlehem.

On the left wall of the nave are Herod's Banquet and the Last Supper; on the right Paradise with the Virgin and the Patriarchs, Abraham, Isaac, Jacob, receiving the souls of the blessed and also the Massacre of the Innocents.

The frescoes in the north aisle, which date from 15C, are dedicated to St Anthony: the most curious *(right)* shows another interpretation of Paradise, with Peter leading Eve to the gates of the Celestial City, while the Virgin is represented with the Patriarchs bearing the souls of the elect; various saints *(left)* accompany the benefactors of the church.

LASSÍTHI Plateau★★

Lassíthi – Michelin map 980 fold 39

800m – 2 625ft up in the Díkti mountains, which rise to 2 148m – 7 047ft in the south, lies the Lassíthi Plateau, an enormous hanging basin in which rich alluvial soil has collected. The plateau is divided up into fertile fields, formerly irrigated by thousands of windmills which are gradually disappearing.

Places to stay in Dzermiádo, Ágios Geórgios and Psihró.

TOUR *about 1/2 day*

Approach to the plateau by the north slope★★. – The road from Limáni Hersoníssou winds its way up the slope through hairpin bends offering spectacular views down into the Avdoú Valley which is deep and narrow but the valley floor is carpeted with orchards and orange groves. At the entrance to **Potamiés** (pop 494) there stands a tiny church *(left)* built in the Venetian Gothic style; the doorway has a pointed arch; the interior is decorated with 14C frescoes. More 14C frescoes in a good state of preservation are to be found in the little monastery of **Kardiotíssa** *(signpost)* just before the village of Kerá.

On the way up to the plateau there is a row of old corn mills, one of which is still working *(open to the public in the season).*

The Plateau★★. – The unexpected expanse of the Lassíthi Plateau, 12km by 6km – 7 1/2 miles by 3 1/2 miles, hemmed in by mountains, is an attractive sight, particularly in summer if the irrigation windmills are turning. Wind power is gradually being replaced by motors which are more efficient and easier to use.

The whole plateau is involved in agriculture (cereals, potatoes, fruit) and has retained its traditional methods of working: threshing floors, draught donkeys and mules, blacksmiths and wheelwrights, etc).

After skirting the plateau the road reaches **Psihró** (pop 248): on the far side of the village an unsurfaced road *(sign: Diktéo Ándro)* leads to a Tourist Pavilion near a car park.

Diktean Cave★ (Diktéo Ándro). – *Open 8.45am to 3pm (9.30am to 2.30pm Sundays); 100 Dr. From the car park walk or ride up on a mule (1/4 hour) to the cave mouth; then walk down a steep and sometimes slippery slope by candle light; wear suitable shoes and warm clothing; the tour lasts about 1/2 hour.*

The deep and mysterious Diktean cave, like the Idaian Cave *(p 202)*, is supposed to have sheltered Rhea, the mother of Zeus, who was fleeing from her husband Kronos who had the annoying habit of devouring her children; thus Zeus, the master of the gods, was born in a cave, suckled by the goat Amalthea and fed by the bee Melissa.

The Diktean cave was a shrine from the Minoan period to the Archaic period and it has yielded many cult objects: altars, bronze statuettes, votive offerings, miniature double axes etc. The path descends past enormous rocks for about 60m – 197ft to a little lake. The lower section of the cave contains a variety of stalagmites and stalactites.

Michelin Main Road Maps
Greece 980, Great Britain/Ireland 986, Germany 987, Italy 988,
France 989, Spain/Portugal 990, Yugoslavia 991.

212

LIMÁNI HERSONÍSSOU

Iráklio – Pop 2 183 – Michelin map 980 fold 39

Limáni Hersoníssou is strung out round a little bay, a sizable seaside resort and a fishing village with many tavernas serving fish. In antiquity it was a port for Lyttos and the ancient city, which extended further west than the present one, retained its importance in the Roman period (fountain decorated with fish mosaics on the quay) and on into the beginning of the Christian era.

Paleo-Christian Basilica. – On the rocky peninsula which shelters the bay to the north on a fine site overlooking the port are the foundations of a Christian basilica (6C). The ground plan can be deduced from the remains of the floor, partially decorated with wavy mosaics.

Beyond and below the church at the end of the promontory are Roman fish tanks cut into the rock at sea level.

MÁLIA ★★

Iráklio – Michelin map 980 fold 39

3km – 2 miles east of the modern village of Mália *(hotels and restaurants)* a narrow road to the left *(north)* penetrates the ruins of the huge Minoan city which covers a rocky platform facing the sea.

The site was discovered by Joseph Hatzidakis and since 1921 has been excavated by the French School of Archaeology. The excavations at Mália are of particular interest since the site ceased to be inhabited at the end of second millennium BC and is not therefore cluttered with traces of later construction. The majority of the many finds made there are in the Heraklion Museum.

The palace★★. – *Open 8.45am to 3pm; Sundays 9.30am to 2.30pm; about 1 hour.*

This Minoan palace, which was destroyed in *c*1500 BC, was smaller and less luxurious than Knossós *(p 210)* but similar in lay out, being built round an outer and central courtyard.

PALACE OF MÁLIA

Outer courtyard. – This court is a paved area crossed by a roadway and bordered on the east side by the foundations of the western façade of the palace. This range of buildings contained *(from right to left)* eight huge grain silos, a series of storerooms reached by a broad internal corridor, and the royal apartments.

Walk up the east side of the court towards the sea *(north)* as far as the Minoan paved road which leads to the north entrance to the palace past an enormous terracotta vessel *(pithos)* (1) *(p 20)*, 1.75m – nearly 6ft high, which could hold over 1000 litres – 220 gallons of oil or wine.

North entrance. – First there is a vestibule (2) and then a portico supported on pillars of which the bases remain. On the lefthand near a row of storerooms was another *pithos* (3). To the right lay the North Court which gave access to the royal apartments. *A corridor leads to the central courtyard.*

Central courtyard. – The north and east sides are bordered by porticoes and the western range of buildings was used, as at Knossós, for religious and official activities. At the centre of the courtyard is a shallow pit for sacrifices.

The sanctuary was in the northwest corner. The royal lodge or throne room (4), which overlooked the court, is marked by a terrace in front of which lies a Byzantine cannon ball (5). Next are the steps of a staircase (6) which led to the upper floor, and then a cult room (7) with two square pillars engraved with the symbolic double axe.

Beyond the four monumental steps (8) in the southwest corner near the South Entrance to the palace is a circular stone table **(kérnos)** (9) which has a central hollow and many others round the circumference, where, it is thought, the faithful placed their offerings (according to another interpretation it is a gaming table).

The buildings on the eastern side of the courtyard comprise the royal Treasury next to the East Entrance to the palace, followed by a range of storerooms *(not open)* which still contain drains in the floor and marble benches against the walls, on which stood jars of oil and wine. The rooms next in the range have been identified by the archaeologists as the kitchens.

The north side of the court is taken up with a hall (10) with two rows of rectangular pillars, which may have been a banqueting hall; it is flanked by a vestibule (11) *(left)*.

213

MÁLIA★★

The town. – *Excavations in progress in the "mu" area, Old Palace Period.* On leaving the palace, follow the Minoan paved roadway which passes the agora *(right)* and leads to the **Hypostyle Crypt** which was excavated after the Second World War and is protected by a roof. The steps at the end gave access to meeting rooms, still partially furnished with benches, which were probably part of the Prytaneion, where the city magistrates met. It is flanked by storerooms.

Other buildings used for religious purposes and houses, where the ground floor and basement have often survived *(not at present accessible),* have been discovered on the outskirts of the town.

The Krysólakos ("gold pit") necropolis on the north side near the sea was certainly a royal graveyard; it contained the famous "bee pendant" now in the Herakleion museum.

MELIDÓNI Cave★

Réthimno – Michelin map 980 fold 38 – between Iráklio and Réthimno

A good metalled road *(2km – 1mile)* leads from the village of Melidóni *(sign: Spileon)* to this huge deep cave where a tragedy occurred in 1824. After an uprising against the Turks some 400 people, mainly women and children, took refuge in the cave; the Turks partially blocked the mouth with boulders and then made a fire in the restricted entrance; the people inside were asphyxiated.

From the mouth of the cave there is a fine view towards Mount Ida.

MIRAMBÉLO Coast★★   *Aktí Mirambélou*

Lassíthi – Michelin map 980 fold 39

From Ágios Nikólaos eastwards to Móhlos *(47km – 30 miles)* the road follows a well-chosen route along the magnificent rocky coast of Mirambélo Bay, first at sea level and then, after the Ierápetra turning, slightly higher up. This road leads to or passes by many attractive inlets, some of them suitable for bathing, and offers repeated views down over the gentle curve of the shining bay dotted with headlands and islands and up to the mountains inland. The land is planted with tomatoes, beans and olive trees.

SIGHTS

Gourniá★. – *Open 8.45am to 3pm (9.30am to 2.30pm Sundays); no charge.* On a hill above Mirambélo Bay lie the ruins of a Minoan city which dates from 1500-1450 BC and has been almost entirely excavated by American archaeologists. The town plan is clearly visible owing to the low walls marking out the streets, lanes, squares, buildings and modest houses of the craftsmen and tradesmen.

Enter the site by the path on the east side, not far from the main road, and follow the path on the right which climbs round the ruins emerging in a paved street which bears left towards the agora and is lined with houses separated by lanes and steps; the third house on the right is particularly well preserved: it has a shop and rooms on the ground floor and the beginning of the stairs leading to the floor above.

Overlooking the agora stands the palace which is reached by a flight of steps.

It is possible to return to the entrance by another street running through the lower part of the city.

Plátanos viewpoint★★. – From a terrace by the roadside near a café-bar there are splendid views down on to Psíra Island and across Mirambélo Bay to Spinalónga peninsula.

Móhlos★. – Pop 101. *Tavernas.* In Sfáka turn left into a road which descends for 7km – 4 1/4 miles to a little quay hidden in an inlet opposite a tiny island where a mass of Minoan material was found which is now in the Herakleion Museum.

PHAISTOS★★   *Festós*

Iráklio – Michelin map 980 fold 38

On a outlying spur of Mount Ida – a magnificent **site★★** with an endless view of the Messará plain – stand the ruins of the Minoan palace of Phaistos which was founded by Rhadamanthos. Excavations carried out by the Italian School of Athens have identified two superimposed buildings; one dates from 2000-1650 BC and the other, which is similar in plan to the palace at Knossós, is more recent, dating from 1650-1400 BC.

Open 8am to 7pm (6pm Sundays); 1 hour; 150 Dr. Tourist Pavilion.

Start in the North Court (traces of Hellenistic and Roman structures) (1); then go down the steps (2) which lead to the base of the Propylaia and the theatre.

Theatre. – It is composed, like the one at Knossós, of straight terraces, in this case eight, facing the West Court, an open space for dancing and ritual games outside the palace. There was a little shrine (3) in the northeast corner.

Great Propylaia. – An imposing flight of steps leads up to the Propylaia, a monumental entrance consisting of a pillared hall (4). Beyond and to the left is a huge peristyle (5) surrounded by the royal apartments, to the east of which lies a range of domestic buildings where the famous "Phaistos Disk" *(p 207)* was discovered.

Royal Apartments. – On the north side lies the "King's Megaron" consisting of a reception room (6) and a lustral bath (7) for ritual purification, which is down several steps; on the south side is the "Queen's Megaron" (8): one of the rooms has retained its original alabaster paving. A small court (9) and a corridor (10) lead into the central court.

Central Court. – The vast open rectangle was flanked on the east and west sides by pillared porticoes while the north side contained the entrance to the royal apartments. As at Knossós it was probably used for displays of bull-leaping. There is a well (11) in the southwest corner.

Behind the west portico are traces of a crypt with two pillars (12) and a room surrounded with benches (13), both part of a **sanctuary**. Further along is a pillared hall (14), faced with alabaster, leading into a corridor lined with storerooms.

Storerooms. – The rows of storerooms down both sides of the corridor contained supplies of cereals, oil and wine in enormous terracotta jars *(pithoi)*; in the last storeroom on the right (15) there was a device for collecting the oil which flowed from the receptacles.

Bear right to return to the entrance. Southwest of the West Court lie the ruins of the first palace *(not open at present)* which has yielded many examples of Kamáres ware.

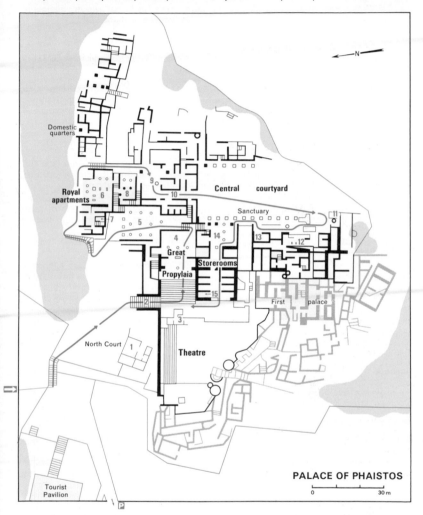

PALACE OF PHAISTOS

0   30 m

EXCURSIONS

Agía Triáda ★. – *3km – 2 miles west along a road (turn right at the junction after rejoining the road from Iráklio) which ends in a cul-de-sac. Car park, Cretan flutes for sale; open 10am to 4pm; 100 Dr.*

The ruins here, as at Phaistos, occupy a fine site (its ancient name is unknown) overlooking the Messará Plain and Bay. The ruins were excavated by the Italians. To the left is a small palace; to the right and below lies a village. The local graveyard produced the famous painted sarcophagus, now in the Herakleion Museum.

The palace. – It may have been the residence of a dignitary or a relative of the princes of Phaistos. Pass the grand staircase *(left)* leading up to the Altar Court and follow the paved ramp, which leads down towards the sea, past the north front of the palace; the redans are typical of Minoan architecture. This range of buildings, which was at least two storeys high (traces of stairs), comprised a central block containing the reception rooms, storerooms and the royal *megaron* with its alabaster cladding still in place. The west wing was built round small courts or light wells as living accommodation; some of the rooms have retained some of their original fittings: slate floors, benches, alabaster plaques, channels for draining off water.

Further on stands St George's Church, a small 14C building decorated with delicate Byzantine sculptures which have been re-employed.

Mycenean Village. – It was built later (1375-1100 BC) on the north side of the palace. The east side of the *agora* was bordered by a portico with shops.

PHAISTOS★★

Mátala★. – Pop 337 – *15km – 9 1/4 miles southwest.*

Mátala *(hotels, tavernas)* is a little fishing village with a broad sandy beach and plenty of fresh fish. It lies in a peaceful bay almost cut off from the sea by the rocky islet blocking the entrance. According to the myth, it was here that Zeus swam ashore in the shape of a bull bearing Europa on his back *(pp 201 and 205)*.

Mátala is however better known for its **caves**★ which are to be found in the parallel strata of tufa on the north side of the beach. They may originally have been used as tombs but have also served as places of worship and troglodite dwellings: benches, beds and recesses hollowed out of the stone.

Agía Galíni★. – Pop 271. *18km – 11 miles northwest.* This is a charming and very popular resort, with a picturesque harbour and many tavernas serving fish. There are boat trips to the sea caves along the coast.

Kalí Liménes. – Pop 75. *25km – 15 1/2 miles south.* This peaceful bay was not disfigured by oil storage tanks when St Paul put in on his last voyage to Rome.

RETHYMNON★   *Réthimno*

Réthimno – Pop 17 736 – Michelin map 980 fold 38

The traditional character of a Cretan town, a blend of Venetian and Turkish influences, is best preserved in Rethymnon. It is pleasant to stroll past the fish tavernas which throng the quays, through the old and narrow streets to the fortress. Crafts such as weaving and embroidery are of high quality and the Wine Festival in July attracts a big crowd.

SIGHTS

Old Town★. – From the main square, near the Public Garden, pass through a late 16C Venetian gate in the walls; on the right is a minaret. Turn left into Odós Konstandinopóleos, a busy shopping street lined by Turkish houses with louvres and balconies.

Former Nerandze Mosque. – A slim **minaret**★ set back from the street *(left)* marks the position of a domed mosque *(open 9am to 1pm and 5 to 7pm)* which has replaced a 17C Venetian convent; from the top of the minaret there is a view of the town and the surrounding country.

Further down the street are two Venetian monuments: the Loggia *(right)* and the Arimondi Fountain *(left)*.

Loggia. – It was built early in 17C as an Exchange before being converted into a mosque by the Turks; it has massive pillars and rustic stonework. It now houses the **archaeological museum** *(open 8.45am to 3pm; closed Tuesdays; 100 Dr)* which displays sculpture, bronzes, jewellery from the Minoan, Greek and Roman periods and a remarkable collection of money.

Arimondi Fountain. – Three Corinthian columns mark this monumental fountain (1629).

Odós Thessaloníkis★. – This street near the Arimondi Fountain contains several 16C-17C Venetian houses built of stone with elegant stone doorways decorated with coats of arms next to 18C-19C Turkish houses with balconies and wooden projections.

Harbour. – During the Venetian occupation Malmsey wine *(p 141)* was exported from here; now the harbour is used by fishing boats and coasters. The old vaulted houses on the quayside have been converted into cafés and tavernas which open at the back into a parallel street, Odós Arkadíou.

Venetian Fortress (Fortétza or **Froúrio).** – *Open 9am to 4pm; 50 Dr.*

It was built on the promontory between 1574 and 1582. The south face is reinforced with curious bastions which have an orillion (rounded projection) on one side and a redan on the other. The fortress was captured by the Turks in 1645.

The main entrance is on the east side in the angle made by the bastion. It is protected by an outwork called a barbican. Over the gateway is the Lion of St Mark. On entering follow the ramparts round to the left (views of the town and the harbour).

At the centre of the fortress stand a rectangular building which was once a prison and a domed building which was built as the Latin cathedral of St Mary of the Angels and converted into a mosque by the Turks. Elsewhere are ruined houses, stores, barracks, cisterns, powder magazines and a Byzantine chapel.

SAMARIÁ Gorge★★★   *Farángi Samariás*

Haniá – Michelin map 980 fold 37

In the heart of the White Mountains (Lefká Óri) the surface water has worn away a huge ravine which runs for 18km – 11 1/4 miles from the Omalós Plateau down to the Libyan sea; this is the wild and sometimes awesome Samariá Gorge.

Practical information. – It is possible to walk down the gorge between May and October only. It takes 5 to 6 hours of sometimes hard walking owing to the steep descent at the beginning and to the summer sun but the path is clearly marked; it is important to be well shod. *Tourist Pavilion at the top end of the gorge; places to stay in Agía Rouméli, on the coast.*

The simplest way of visiting the gorge is to join an organised all-day excursion starting from Chania, Herakleion or various other centres, by putting down your name in your hotel or a tourist agency or the EOT. A coach takes the walkers to the top of the gorge. They are picked up at the other end in Agía Rouméli by boat which delivers them about 1 1/2 hours later in Sfakiá where the coach is waiting.

Those who do not want to walk the gorge from end to end may go as far as the viewing platform and then turn back *(1/2 hour on foot Rtn)*.

Tour. – The road up to the gorge passes over the **Omalós Plateau** (alt 1 050m – 3 445ft), a barren and austere depression surrounded by mountains; it is uninhabited and covered in snow in winter but cultivated nonetheless with cereals and potatoes and used for sheep rearing. After passing through Omalós *(tavernas)* the road ends in **Xilóskalo** on the edge of the gorge *(car park)*.

First a flight of wooden steps *(xilóskalo)* and then a twisting path descends among pine and plane trees down a steep slope to a viewing platform. There is an impressive **view**★★ of the ravine between sheer rock walls which rise to over 2 000m – 6 561ft and are the refuge of the last of the local wild goats *(agrími)*.

The path goes on down through the woods descending rapidly to the bottom of the gorge. In a little clearing stands St Nicholas' Chapel.

Half way down the gorge there is a handful of houses, **Samariá**, now deserted; the name of the hamlet derives from Osía María, Holy Mary, to whom the local church was dedicated. Beyond the village is the narrowest section of the gorge where the distance between the vertical walls, which rise to 300m – 984ft, is not more than 2 or 3m – 7 to 10ft.

Eventually the stream bed, which is flanked by oleanders, widens out and reaches **Agía Rouméli** (pop 100), known in antiquity as Tarrhia, on the edge of the Libyan Sea. From here the boats make the trip to Sfakiá at the foot of towering rocky cliffs.

SFAKIÁ★★

Haniá – Pop 334 – Michelin map 980 fold 37

From **Vrísses** *(tavernas; famous for yogurt and honey)*, a pleasant well-shaded village by a stream just off the main east-west highway, there is a good road which covers the 40km – 25 miles to Sfakía (or **Hóra Sfakión**) across the White Mountains (Lefká Óri). As the road descends 1 000m – 3 281ft towards the south shore there are dramatic, even vertiginous, **views**★★★ of the wild and scantily inhabited coast and the Libyan Sea.

Sfakiá was once a considerable town with 3 000 to 4 000 inhabitants, trading with Africa. Although it is now only a small place it is still the capital of the Sfakiots, a belligerent and unyielding people, with fair hair and blue eyes, who tended sheep in the mountains and were at the root of most of the uprisings against the Venetians and Turks; in 1770 a Sfakiot called **Daskaloyánnis** (Teacher John) led a revolution against the Turks but he was defeated and flayed alive in Herakleion.

Nowadays it is a quiet resort *(Hotel Xenia, guest houses, tavernas)* beneath the ruins of a 16C Venetian fort with a picturesque little harbour and a boat service to **Agía Rouméli** (pop 100) at the bottom of the Samariá Gorge *(p 216)*. In 1941 British troops were evacuated from Sfakiá *(p 201)*; 7 000 soldiers were taken off the island despite the Stuka bombardment.

EXCURSION

Frangokástelo★. – *15km – 9 1/4 miles east by the coast road and an unsurfaced track; taverna.*

The massive outline of the "Frankish castle" is visible from afar; it was built in 1371 by the Venetians as a defence against pirates, Turks and insurgent Sfakiots.

It is rectangular in plan with crenellated walls and a square tower at each corner, one of which was reinforced to form the keep. Over the sea gate the lion of St Mark looks down on the remains of a deserted harbour next to a fine sandy beach. The ruined fort surveys the empty sea as if it were at the end of the world.

SITÍA

Lassíthi – Pop 6 659 – Michelin map 980 fold 40

Sitía is a pleasant resort on the bay of the same name, defended by the ruins of a former Venetian fortress; nevertheless the white and ochre cuboid houses give it a slightly African appearance. It is pleasant to stroll under the shade of the enormous tamarisk trees where the cafés and tavernas set out their chairs and tables. A museum of local traditions has been opened recently. The archaeological museum *(open 8.45am to 3pm; closed Sundays)* displays the finds from local excavations.

Sitía is supposed to be the birthplace of Myson, one of the Seven Sages of Greece and even today the citizens of Sitía enjoy a reputation for composure and integrity. The town earns its living by exporting sultanas.

EXCURSIONS

Toploú Monastery (Moní Toploú). – *20km – 12 1/2 miles northeast; follow the Palékastro road for 14km – 8 3/4 miles and then bear left up to the plateau. Open from sunrise to 1pm and 5pm to sunset.*

The monastery emerges from a fold in the bare hillside; its thick walls and rare windows make it look like a fortress. It was founded in 14C by the Venetians as Our Lady of the Cape but has been refurbished many times, particularly in 15C and 17C after being damaged in the uprisings against the Turks; during the Second World War it was a centre of resistance against the Germans. The monastery is the owner of nearly the whole of Cape Síderos but there is only one monk in residence.

A handsome Gothic door opens into the entrance court which leads into an inner court surrounded by arcades and the stairs up to the cells. The church is built in the Venetian style with pointed vaulting. It contains a very rich **icon**★★ by an 18C Creto-Venetian master, Ioánnis Kornáros (Cornaro); it is a masterpiece portraying several biblical scenes in naive and realistic detail.

Váï Palm Grove ★. – *28km – 17 1/2 miles northeast.* The road continues through a barren landscape to Váï, which appears unexpectedly looking strangely like an oasis. A palm grove *(restaurants, camping)* consisting of about 5 000 palm trees fringes a fine sandy beach.

Return to the crossroads and turn right to Itanós, 2km – 1 1/4miles away.

Itanós. – In a lonely setting on the northeast tip of Crete, where the land forms a promontory indented by wild creeks, lie traces of an ancient town which was inhabited up to the Byzantine period: sites of two acropoli, Hellenistic foundations of a terrace and remains of a large basilica.

VRONDISSÍ Monastery

Iráklio – Michelin map 980 fold 38

3.5km – 2 1/4 miles northwest of Zarós bear right into a track which rapidly reaches Vrondissí Monastery situated on a terrace on the south face of Mount Ida with a magnificent view. Beneath the ancient plane trees that shade the entrance stands a beautiful **Renaissance fountain** (15C), built in marble by the Venetians; it bears the effigies of Adam and Eve.

As is often the case in Crete, the church is shared, with one aisle for the Latin rite and one for the Orthodox.

EXCURSION

Valsamónero Monastery ★. – *7km – 4 1/2 miles west. Take the road to Kamáres and on leaving Vorízia bear left into an indifferent track which leads to Valsamónero (signpost).*

The church of Ágios Fanoúrios, which belongs to Valsamónero Monastery *(open 7.30am to 2pm or key in Vorízia),* is in the Italian style of architecture. It also has two parallel aisles preceded by a narthex. The older aisle (14C) on the left contains some remarkable **frescoes** ★ (also 14C) depicting scenes from the Life of the Virgin and the saints, in particular John the Baptist; other frescoes (15C) decorate the righthand aisle and the narthex.

According to tradition, **El Greco** *(pp 208 and 209)* stayed in this monastery *(now deserted)* to study not only the frescoes but also the famous icons by Damaskinos which are now displayed in St Catherine's Church in Herakleion.

ZÁKROS★★   *Káto Zákros*

Lassíthi – Michelin map 980 fold 40

A remote but very beautiful **site** ★★, deep in a little bay *(beach, tavernas)* on the east coast of Crete, has been excavated by Greek archaeologists who have uncovered the remains of the palace of Zákros, the fourth great Minoan palace after Knossós, Phaistos and Mália. The path to the palace winds down the side of a deep ravine, the Valley of Death, which was used in antiquity as a necropolis: there are spectacular views down into the bay.

Palace ★. – *Open 9am (10am Sundays) to 5pm. Entrance from the northeast.* The buildings, which were destroyed in about 1500 BC by the earthquakes accompanying the eruption of the Santoríni volcano, were arranged, as in the other Minoan palaces, around a central court. On the north side was a large kitchen, the only one of its kind that has been identified with certainty; the reception rooms and place of worship lay to the west; opposite on the east were the royal apartments belonging to the sovereign and his consort and including a round basin which may have been used as a cistern; to the south stood the workshops and storerooms with an adjoining well.

The town extended south towards the sea: in those days Zákros was an important place trading with Egypt and the Orient.

RHODES
AND THE DODECANESE

The Dodecanese is a group of twelve islands, as the name suggests (*dódeka* in Greek means twelve), and a few smaller islets. These are Rhodes and Kós, the main islands, Pátmos, Léros, Kálimnos, Níssiros, Tílos, Syme, Hálki, Astypálea, Kárpathos and Kássos. To these is added Kastelórizo (Megísti), an island off the south coast of Turkey.

These mountainous and picturesque islands, also known as the **Southern Sporades,** played an important role in antiquity and during the Middle Ages when faced with the Turkish threat. Occupied by the Italians in 1912 they joined the Greek state in 1948.

RHODES★★★   *Ródos*

Dodecanese – Pop 87 833 – Michelin map 𝟵𝟴𝟬 fold 47

Close to the southwest tip of Asia Minor lies Rhodes, the island of roses. Its flower gardens and gentle climate, its beautiful buildings, its excellent beaches and tourist facilities make it attractive to visitors. Lovers of art and history will delight in evoking its glorious past, rich in souvenirs of antiquity and the Middle Ages.

Access by air from Athens: 4 or 5 flights daily in about 1 hour; in summer: 1 flight daily from Crete, 3 flights per week from Santoríni, 1 flight daily from Mykonos, 4 flights per week from Páros, 2 flights per week from Thessalonika; by ferry from Piraeus: 1 or 2 boats daily in the season in about 15 hours according to the number of stops.

Accommodation. – There are over 130 hotels, almost all modern, with a total of 30 000 beds, grouped mainly in Rhodes Town and along the northwest coast between the capital and the airport close to extensive but fairly exposed beaches. The east coast, which is more sheltered, has several good places to stay between the capital and Kalithéa.

International cuisine except in a few tavernas where fish is served; good local wines, in particular "Chevaliers de Rhodes", "Líndos" and "Embonas".

Transport. – A week is time enough in which to visit the island; there are no hotels in the south but as the road round the island is now surfaced almost all the way, it is possible to make a succession of trips starting from Rhodes Town by bus *(bus station in Mandráki near the New Market)* or by taxi *(booked for the whole day)* or by hire car. Daily boat service from Rhodes to Líndos in the season *(departure 9am, return 7pm)*.

RHODES ★★★

GEOGRAPHICAL AND HISTORICAL NOTES

The island is long, 77km – 48 miles, and narrow, 37km – 23 miles, with a low straight coastline broken only in the centre. The terrain is mountainous, rising to 1 215m – 3 986ft in **Mount Atáviros,** and composed of limestone and schist which supports a flora of conifers together with semi-tropical shrubs, red hibiscus, mauve bougainvilleas and white scented jasmin, since the average temperature in winter is 13° C – 56°F. The coastal plains are devoted to the cultivation of vines, barley, figs and citrus fruits.

The island of Helios. – According to the Greek myths, Rhodes in the guise of the nymph Rhodia was given to **Helios** the sun-god, and his descendants founded the three main towns: Ialyssos (near Filérimos), Líndos and Kámiros.

In 7C BC these three cities were already trading throughout the Middle East as far as Egypt and founding colonies in the neighbouring islands, on the coast of Asia Minor and even in Italy (Naples, Gela); the people were already engaged in the production of gold jewellery and of ceramics decorated with oriental motifs of plants and animals in stylised form. In 6C BC the cities were wisely governed by the "tyrants" who achieved a high degree of prosperity. In 408 BC the three cities jointly founded the city of Rhodes which was not slow to supplant them.

During 3C and 2C BC, despite disputes with the Macedonians and the Romans, the island became the main maritime power in the eastern Mediterranean owing to its fleet and its wealth. The arts flourished, particularly a school of sculpture which became famous and exported its work far afield: e.g. the Colossos of Rhodes, by Chares of Lindos (265 BC), the Aphrodite of Rhodes, the Victory of Samothrace, a masterpiece attributed to Pythekritos, and the Laocoon in the Vatican.

From the Cross of St John to the Cross of Savoy. – The arrival in 1306 of Foulques de Villaret and his Knights of St John of Jerusalem *(p 222)* brought a period of unrest which lasted until 1522. The island was the advance bastion of Christianity against the Turks and the Knights engaged in extensive building works: walls, the town and port of Rhodes, fortresses at Filérimos, Líndos, Arhángelos and Monólithos, forts to repel pirate attacks, monasteries and churches. The Provençal Gothic style was used; thus in Rhodes Town the Palace of the Grand Master recalls the Papal Palace in Avignon, St John's Church is similar to the Church of Notre Dame-des-Doms in Avignon and the gates in the ramparts are like those in Villeneuve-lès-Avignon.

The Turks left few traces apart from some mosques and fountains but it was during their occupation that the famous "Rhodes faience", with its brilliant enamels, was commercialised; this consists of plates and flagons decorated with stylised oriental motifs which some historians think have been produced in Líndos since the time of the Knights of St John while others maintain that they come from Nicaea (Isnik) in Asia Minor.

When the citizens of Rhodes rose against the Turks in 1912, the Italians intervened and annexed the island, where they encouraged tourism, improved the roads, constructed public buildings and hotels and restored, sometimes insensitively, the ancient monuments.

Eventually on 7 March 1948 Rhodes became part of the Greek state.

The distances to the places below are measured from Rhodes Town.

ASKLIPIÍO (Pop 363 – *east coast; 65km – 40 miles*)

Interesting village owing to its site, its old houses and its fortress. The Church of the Dormition of the Virgin, which dates from the Byzantine period (1060), is decorated with a fine collection of frescoes.

ÉMBONAS (Pop 1 148 – *west coast; 62km – 39 miles*)

Émbonas, which is surrounded by famous vineyards, has kept its old-fashioned ways and women can still be seen spinning or wearing leather boots to protect them from snakes while working in the fields. In some houses the walls are hung with "Rhodes faience" plates and dishes.

In Émbonas it is possible to arrange to climb **Mount Atáviros** (alt 1 215m – 3 986ft) with a guide *(6 hours on foot Rtn)*; from the top where a sanctuary to Zeus once stood there is a fine view.

FERAKLÓS CASTLE (*east coast; 37km – 23 miles*)

Drive through the hamlet of Heráki (pop 54; *taverna*) and leave the car at the foot of the hill; fairly stiff climb *(3/4 hour on foot Rtn)*. Only a few ruined walls now remain of what was one of the largest castles ever built by the Knights of St John but there is a very fine view★★ of the bays on either side of the promontory; to the south the fortress at Líndos is silhouetted on the skyline.

KALITHÉA SPA★ (*east coast; 15km – 9 miles*)

The waters, which were known to the ancients and recommended by Hippocrates, are effective in the treatment of ailments of the liver and the gall bladder. In 1929 the Italians built a little spa with white pavilions in the oriental style pleasantly set among the pine and palm trees but it is no longer in use.

Charming sandy beach in a rocky inlet.

KÁMIROS★ (*west coast, 33km – 20 1/2 miles*)

In antiquity, Kámiros was one of the three great cities of Rhodes, which occupied a beautiful site on a hill set back from the seashore at the heart of a fertile region covered with fig and olive groves. It was founded so says the legend, by Althaimenes, Minos' grandson, destroyed by an earthquake in 2C BC and rediscovered in 1859; it has been excavated by French (1863-64) and Italian archaeologists.

Ruins. – *Open 8.45am to 3pm (2.30pm on Sundays); 100 Dr.*

Excavations have brought to light traces of Hellenistic and Roman buildings which occur in the following sequence up the hillside;

– a 3C BC sanctuary consisting of a Doric temple, approached by a flight of steps; the bases of the columns remain and one column which has been re-erected; lower down there is a semi-circular seat *(exedra)*, and an area for sacrificial altars;

– an area of Hellenistic houses, several with peristyles (columns re-erected);

– an agora lined by a long 3C AD portico *(stoa)* built over a 5C-6C BC cistern which was reached by two flights of steps and supplied the houses below it with water;

– a temple dedicated to Athena Kamíria dating from 5C BC.

Near to Kámiros Skála, 13km – 8 miles SW, on a spur facing the sea are traces of **Kámiros Castle★** (Kastélo) *(access by a poor road: 1.2km – 3/4 mile plus 1/4 hour of foot)* contemporary with the Knights Hospitaller; the arms of two Grand Masters – Aimeri d'Amboise and Fabrizio del Carretto – are sculpted on the outside; within is a chapel.

LÍNDOS★★ (Pop 661 – *east coast; 50km – 31 miles*)

The blue sea, the white houses of the old town and the forbidding walls of the medieval fortress crowning a rise combine to make Líndos a spectacular **site★★★** where three civilisations – ancient, Byzantine and medieval Greek – have left their mark; there is a fine view of the Grand Port facing north at the foot of the hill.

Líndos is a simple resort *(guest houses, rooms in private houses)* with an attractive beach in one of the sheltered bays which lie on either side of the isthmus containing the Grand Port and St Paul's Port. Specialities: hand-woven cloth, ceramics.

The coast nearby was used in the film "The Guns of Navarone".

Leave the car in the upper car park on the right on arriving.

A maritime and religious stronghold. – With its two natural harbours and its easily-defended hill, Líndos has been inhabited since the prehistoric era and by 10C BC a temple to Athena had been built on the hilltop. It was in 7C BC that colonists set out from Líndos and founded Gela in Sicily and Parthenope (now Naples) in Italy.

In 6C BC **Cleobulos,** one of the many benevolent dictators in Greece, ruled Líndos. He was one of the Seven Sages of Greece and was reputed to express himself in enigmas.

The cult of the gods was succeeded by Christianity. Tradition has it that St Paul landed in St Paul's Port at the end of his third missionary journey. After the Byzantines and the Genoese came the Knights Hopitaller who turned Líndos into an imposing fortress, defended by 12 Knights and a Greek garrison. When the Grand Master, **Foulques de Villaret,** was deposed in 1317 for misconduct, he took refuge in Líndos; later he was obliged to go to Avignon and defend himself before John XXII, a native of Cahors in France.

Acropolis and fortress★★. – *Access by a path and steps (1 hour on foot or by donkey Rtn); open 8am to 7pm in summer (6pm Sundays); 150 Dr.*

The hilltop, which is 116m – 381ft above sea level, bears extensive traces of ancient and medieval monuments.

At the foot of the escarpment inside the first gate there is an *exedra (p 20)* hollowed out of the rock on the left and a ship's prow which bore a statue of Agesandros, the priest of Poseidon. This statue was the work of the Rhodian sculptor, Pythekritos; the Victory of Samothrace *(p 176)*, which occupied a similar position, is also attributed to him.

Fortress. – The present building was begun under Grand Master Fulvian (1421-1437) and completed under Pierre d'Aubusson (1476-1503). A long flight of steps, skirting the Governor's palace on the left, leads up to the entrance tower crowned by a bartisan. A vaulted passage emerges on the right of the old Gothic Governor's palace near to St John's Chapel consisting of three apses, a nave and two aisles marked off by the bases of pillars.

Take a second vaulted passage under the Governor's palace on the left which emerges below the acropolis.

(Photograph J. Bottin)

Líndos

Acropolis. – Early this century the site was excavated by Danish archaeologists and then restored by Italians. About twenty columns mark the position of the great Doric portico *(stoa)* which was preceded by a great staircase leading up to the sanctuary entrance *(propylaia)*.

The very ancient **sanctuary to Athena Lindia,** which Pindar mentioned in one of his Odes, was specially venerated in antiquity because of the miracles which took place there; the temple, which housed a statue of the goddess in gold and ivory, was built above a cave inhabited by a seer of which the entrance was in the cliff face below. The traces which remain date from the 4C BC and consist of the foundations, some Doric columns and the walls of the *naós (p 18)* which have been re-erected and the bases of votive statues, one of which was presented by Alexander the Great.

From the hilltop there are splendid **views★★★** of the headland and the coast; on the north side are the Great Port and Líndos beach; to the south the inlet named after St Paul who was supposed to have landed there.

Town★. – It is pleasant to stroll through the narrow streets of the town past the white terraced houses; the most beautiful, built for the rich ship owners or sea captains, have pointed arches and are decorated with roses, plants and birds in the Gothic style. Some of the internal courtyards are adorned with Rhodian ceramics.

The **Church of the Virgin** (Panagía) in the town centre, which is dated 1489-1490 and bears the arms of Pierre d'Aubusson, is in fact older; the Knights restored it and added the western narthex; the interior is decorated with 18C frescoes.

View of Líndos★. – *2km – 1 1/4 miles by car Rtn.* From the upper car park drive up a narrow unsurfaced road to a rocky peak which offers an unusual view down into St Paul's Bay on the right while straight ahead is the fortress dominating the ancient theatre, its terraced seating hewn out of the rock.

MONÓLITHOS CASTLE★★ *(west coast; 70km – 44 miles)*

Access by a narrow turning north of Monólithos village; signpost "Froúrion".
The Knights of Rhodes built Monólithos castle on a spectacular **site★★** at the top of a rocky escarpment some 200m – 656ft above the wild and jagged coastline. A path leads up to the fortress which contains two cisterns and a chapel; the **view** extends across the sea to Hálki Island.

PETALOÚDES (Butterfly Valley)★ *(west coast; 24km – 15 miles)*

Entrance signposted. Open 8am to sunset; 1 hour on foot Rtn; 30 Dr; restaurants.
From June to September this shady rockstrewn valley is filled with myriads of orange and black butterflies attracted by the scent emanating from the leaves of a sort of maple tree. A path climbs up the valley and is carried on wooden bridges over the narrow stream which tumbles downhill in cascades and waterfalls. It is necessary to make a noise or throw stones to provoke the butterflies to rise from the rocks and bushes where they are resting and swirl into the air in colourful clouds.

PROFÍTIS ILÍAS (Mount Elijah) Alt 798m – 2 618ft *(west coast; 49km – 30 1/2 miles)*

The mountain, named after the Prophet Elijah, rises from wooded hills where herds of deer roam. A small summer resort *(chalets-hotels)* has been built among the pines and cedars and cypresses on the upper slopes providing a peaceful cool retreat in hot and sultry weather. Beautiful views of the neighbouring peaks and along the west coast.

RHODES TOWN★★ (RÓDOS) Pop 40 392

This is a resort of international repute, as popular in winter as it is in summer; particularly with the Scandinavians and the Germans. The former city of the Knights of St John of Jerusalem is situated at the northeastern end of the island, facing the Turkish coast across its double harbour. There are a few ancient remains but more important is the superb medieval "City" restored by Italian architects early this century and a lively modern town, bright with flowers and tourist attractions: beaches, hotels, touring agencies, night-clubs and countless boutiques.

Specialities: jewellery, silverware, ceramics and furs.

Entertainments: Son et Lumière every evening in the gardens near the Palace; traditional dances every evening in summer in the Old Town *(signpost);* Wine Festival in Rodíni Park during the summer season.

Knights of Rhodes. – Founded in 11C to protect pilgrims in the Holy Land, the order of the Hospitallers of St John of Jerusalem, was both a religious and a military body maintaining a church and a hospital in Jerusalem as well as a mighty stronghold at Acre.

After the capture of Acre by the Turks in 1291, the Knights of St John had to leave the Holy Land; they moved first to Cyprus then to Rhodes, a Genoese possession, which became their main base in their struggle against the Turks in the eastern Mediterranean.

The knights were divided into seven nations known as "tongues" – France, Provence, Auvergne, Aragon, Castille, Italy and England – each "tongue" having its own "inn" to live in and being governed by a bailiff. The whole order, in which the French were the majority, was ruled by the Grand Master; French and Latin were the official languages. The knights took vows of poverty and chastity and were assisted by squires.

When the Knights Templar were suppressed in 1312 and their possessions and duties passed to the Hospitallers, the latter built a fleet which took part in the papal crusades. In 1331 in particular the Hospitallers signed a treaty with the French, the Italians and the Byzantine emperor against the Turks; then at the end of 14C they joined in the naval campaign conducted by Marshal Boucicaut *(p 138)*.

In 1444 and again in 1480 Rhodes was besieged by the Turks but without success. In 1482 the Grand Master, **Pierre d'Aubusson** received Prince Djem with great ceremony. Djem was the son of Mahomet II and unhappy rival of his brother Bayazid; he was sent to Bourganeuf, the grand priory in France of the Auvergne "tongue", but later removed to Italy where he died in 1495.

Unfortunately a third siege in 1522 proved fatal to the Knights. For a good six months 650 knights and about 1 000 auxiliaries held out against an army of 100 000 Turks led by Suleiman the Magnificent but, despite the efforts of Pope Hadrian VI to come to their aid, the Knights were obliged to surrender, betrayed by a defector. On 1 January 1523, the Grand Master, **Villiers de l'Isle-Adam** (1464-1534) and the 180 knights who had survived left Rhodes for Malta, where they eventually arrived after many peregrinations in 1530.

(Photograph Bibliothèque Nationale, Paris)

Rhodes. – The siege of 1480

THE CITY ★★★

Tour 2 1/2 hours; plan p 224; it is also worth visiting at night.

Fortress ★★ (Collachium – CZ). – The knights and their attendants lived in this part of the city which was fortified on all four sides and called collachium; the internal wall, which no longer exists, ran parallel with Odós Sokrátous.

Enter the fortress by the Amboise Gate.

Amboise Gate (Píli Amboise – **CZ**). – An arched bridge over a moat approached the gate which bears the arms of the Order and those of the Grand Master, **Aimeri d'Amboise,** who had it built in 1512. A vaulted entrance in the thickness of the outer wall and a narrow passage lead into the lists and thence to St Anthony's Gate (**CZ A**) which opens into the Palace Square, the former outer court of the Palace; on the right once stood **St John's Chapel,** belonging to the Order, where the knights were buried and where the hand of John the Baptist, given to Pierre d'Aubusson by Sultan Bayazid, was kept for veneration.

St John's Lodge (CZ D), which has ogival vaulting and was reconstructed by the Italians, was both a meeting place and a grand entrance to the Palace.

Palace of the Grand Masters ★ (Paláti Magálon Magístron – **CZ).** – *Open 8am to 7pm (6pm Sundays); closed Tuesdays; 150 Dr.*

The Grand Masters' residence, which was built in 14C in the northwest corner of the ramparts, more nearly resembles a fortress than a palace. In fact it acted as a supplementary line of defence since it was protected by a moat, crenelated walls and towers, a keep and three underground floors of storerooms to hold victuals and munitions. It was converted into a prison by the Turks, severely damaged by the explosion of a munition store in 1856 and restored by the Italians.

The palace is built round a central court surrounded by arcades paved with marble. The staterooms *(first floor),* which are furnished in the Italian manner, contain a series of Hellenistic and Roman mosaics from neighbouring islands: note the Lion Hunt. The room containing a double row of columns was the chapter house of the Order.

Knights Street ★★ (Odós Ipotón – **CZ**). – This is a medieval cobbled street lined by the "Inns", 15C and 16C Gothic buildings in which the Knights lived according to their "tongue".

The Provençal Inn *(left)* is linked by an arch to the Spanish Inn. Further down on the same side are the Chaplain's House and the chapel of the French "tongue" (14C) with a recess containing a statue of the Virgin and Child.

Next comes the façade of the **French Inn** (**CZ E**), the largest and most beautiful of all the inns, where Prince Djem stayed in 1482; above the tierce-point doorway is an inscription to Aimeri d'Amboise, Grand Master from 1505 to 1512.

The **Italian Inn (CZ F)** further down on the left bears the arms of the Italian Fabrizio del Carretto who was Grand Master from 1513 to 1521.

Knights Street ends in Hospital Square which is flanked by St Mary's Church *(left),* the English Inn *(east side)* and the Hospital *(right).*

St Mary's Church (Panagía Kástrou – **DZ**). – The church was built in 12C on the Greek cross plan and transformed into a Latin cathedral in the Gothic style by the Knights who fortified the east end incorporating it into the ramparts. Subsequently the Turks turned it into a mosque. The plane tree *(right)* was used by the Turks as a gibbet for hanging people.

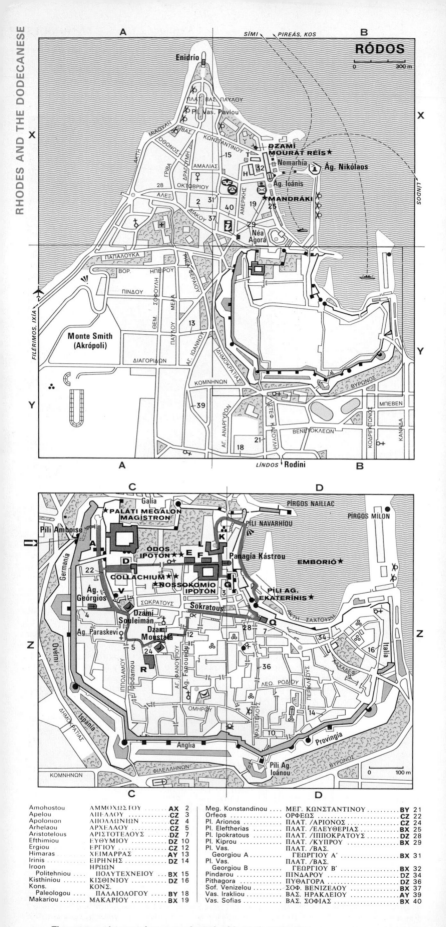

The maps and town plans are oriented with north at the top.

English Inn (DZ G). – It was built in 1483 and bears the coat of arms of England.

Knights' Hospital and Archaeological Museum★ (Nossokomío Ipotón – **CZ**). – *Open 8.45am to 3pm (9.30am to 2.30pm Sundays); closed Tuesdays; 150 Dr.*

This impressive building was begun in 1440 and completed under Pierre d'Aubusson, Grand Master from 1478 to 1505. Above the Gothic arch of the doorway rises the east end of the chapel bearing the arms of Jean de Lastic, Grand Master from 1437 to 1454, who bequeathed 10 000 florins to the building. Beyond the door a vaulted passageway leads into an inner court surrounded by a gallery supported on arcades; there were shops on the ground floor and rooms with fireplaces above.

The hospital proper, which was administered by a bailiff from the French "tongue", was reached by a staircase to the upper floor. The **Great Ward of the Sick** was divided in two and contained 32 communal beds which could accommodate about 100 sick men; the doors and ceiling are of cedar wood. Some of the knights' funerary plaques, formerly in St John's Church, are displayed here. Note the chapel entrance which is delicately carved with festoons and the alcoves where those with contagious diseases were isolated.

Next door is the former refectory communicating with the kitchens.

The museum contains some remarkable ancient sculpture: a 6C BC *kouros* from Kámiros; the funeral stele of Timarista to whom her daughter Krito is saying farewell (5C BC) found at Kámiros; Aphrodite "Thalassia", also called Venus Pudica (3C BC); head of the god Helios (2C BC); effigy of Dionysos with a beard, Hellenistic work (2C BC); the **Aphrodite of Rhodes,** 1C BC masterpiece in the form of a small statue of the goddess rising from the waves and smoothing her hair; two small statues of Asklepios and his daughter Hygieia; a bust of the Greek poet Menander (3C BC).

Leave Hospital Square by the northwest corner, passing in front of St Mary's Church to reach Platía Alexándrou, a small square containing the **Inn of the Auvergne (CZ K)** (14C); above the Gothic doorway is an inscription dating from 1513 which mentions **Guy de Blanchefort,** nephew of Pierre d'Aubusson who was assigned to Djem while he was in Rhodes and later in Bourganeuf, northeast of Limoges in France.

Pass under the arch into another square; the fountain at the centre has been created out of Byzantine baptismal fonts; on the right *(east side)* is the façade of the Inn of the Auvergne with an outside stair and loggia; on the left *(west side)* the former arsenal.

Arsenal (Arméria – **CZ L).** – The main building (14C) was used as the infirmary before the construction of the Great Hospital and is adorned with the allusive arms of Roger de Pinsot, Grand Master from 1355 to 1365. One wing contains the **Museum of Decorative Arts** *(open 9am to 1pm Mondays, Wednesdays, Fridays; 100 Dr);* furniture, costume and a beautiful collection of Rhodian ceramics.

Continue north to the ruins of a temple to Aphrodite and then turn right *(east)* through the Arsenal Gate (Píli Navarhíou – **DZ**) on to the harbour quay.

Harbour★ (Embório – **DZ**). – Now known as the Commercial Harbour, it has always been a safe anchorage. In the days of the Hospitallers the entrance was closed by an enormous chain strung between the square Naillac Tower (Pírgos Naillac), the base of which is extant, and the Mill Tower (Pírgos Mílon) named after a row of mills on the east jetty.

From the waterfront on the seaward side of the Arsenal Gate there is a fine perspective *(south)* of the ramparts with the minarets of the Turkish district in the background, and the Marine Gate in the centre.

Marine Gate★ or St Catherine's Gate (Píli Agías Ekaterínis – **DZ**). – This impressive gate with its four machicolated towers was placed under the protection of the Virgin and Child flanked by St Peter and John the Baptist who appear on a low-relief *(unfortunately damaged);* the Lily of France appears between the arms of the Order and those of Pierre d'Aubusson who caused the gate to be built in 1478.

Re-enter the town by the Marine Gate.

Town★ (CDZ). – Bear left through the gate into **Platía Ippokrátous** with its Turkish fountain; on the far side stands the Merchants' Loggia; behind it (SE) lay the Jewish district.

Merchants' Loggia (Q). – Early 16C building with an outside stairway; the ground floor was a meeting place while the upper floor was used as a courtroom for hearing trade disputes. The building was initiated by Pierre d'Aubusson and completed by Aimeri d'Amboise whose arms appear on the façade and on the lintel respectively.

Turn west along Odós Sokrátous which marks the northern limit of the Turkish district.

Turkish district★. – Busy and thriving, **Odós Sokrátous** was the main street of the Bazaar. Walk up as far as the former Aga mosque on the corner of Odós Fanouríou, one of the oldest and most picturesque streets in the Town and turn left into it. Then take the second turning on the right which leads to Platía Aríonos to see the 18C **Mustapha mosque** (Dzamí Moustafá) and the **Turkish Baths (R),** which have recently been restored, a luxurious establishment dating from the time of Suleiman the Magnificent (16C).

Take Odós Arheláou and Odós Ipodámou (NW) past the 15C Church of Agía Paraskeví *(left)* to reach the **Suleiman Mosque** (Dzamí Souleimán) *(open 8am to 8pm),* which was formerly the Church of the Holy Apostles and has an elegant Italian Renaissance doorway. Turn off into Odós Apolloníon to visit **St George's Church** (Ágios Geórgios – no 18), a picturesque little 15C building, designed on a circular plan and reinforced with huge flying buttresses.

Return along Odós Apolloníon and turn left into Odós Orféos passing beneath the **Clock Tower (V)** or belfry to return to St Anthony's Gate and Amboise Gate.

ADDITIONAL SIGHTS

West and South Ramparts★★ (CDZ). – *Guided tours at 2.45pm Mondays and Saturdays; starting in the courtyard of the Grand Masters' Palace; 2 hours; 150 Dr.*

The walls, which are 4km – 2 1/2 miles long, already existed when the Knights arrived but they rebuilt them almost entirely and continued to strengthen them, particularly under Pierre d'Aubusson, Aimeri d'Amboise and Villiers de l'Isle-Adam. The moat was over 20m – 66ft deep in places and the walls up to 5.30m – 17ft thick. Large platforms were built at the base of the towers to assist in firing the canon. The walls were divided into sections, called "boulevards", each "tongue" was responsible for the defence of a boulevard.

The rampart walk runs anti-clockwise from the Amboise Gate to St John's Gate (Píli Ágiou Ioánou or Kóskinou), giving a fine view of the bastions jutting into the flower-bedecked moat and of the forest of minarets in the Turkish town. It covers four boulevards assigned respectively to Germany (Germanía), the Auvergne (Ovérni), Spain (Ispanía) and England (Anglía); the next two boulevards running east to the shore were assigned to Provence (Provingía) and Italy (Italía).

Return clockwise skirting the external glacis to the Amboise Gate and beyond to the seventh boulevard, assigned to France (Galía), for a different view of the system of fortifications.

Mandráki★ (BX). – Mandráki, meaning a small enclosure, is the name given to a well-protected harbour. This little harbour in Rhodes, which was in use in antiquity, is now devoted to pleasure craft and excursion boats (Líndos and Syme).

On either side of the entrance the Italians erected a column supporting a bronze deer (a buck and a roe), the symbolic animals of Rhodes. According to tradition this was originally the site of the **Colossus of Rhodes**, a bronze statue of the sun-god Helios, 30m – 98ft high; it was numbered among the Seven Wonders of the ancient World and was thought to stand astride the harbour entrance; it was brought down in an earthquake in 226 BC and the pieces were later put up for sale.

The east mole, which has three windmills on it, ends in **St Nicholas' Tower** (Ágios Nikólaos), a strong outer defence work built in 1464 by Grand Master Zacosta; it was placed under the protection of St Nicholas of Bari, the patron saint of navigators, and commanded the sea approach to Rhodes. Views of the harbour and the town; *musical entertainment in the evenings.*

The northern part of the town west of Mandráki was built during the Italian period from 1912 to 1945. Liberty Square (Platía Eleftherías), a lively stretch of waterfront with pleasant gardens, is closed at the southern end by the unusual New Market (Néa Agorá), built round a central courtyard, and on the north by St John's Church (Ágios Ioánis) which was rebuilt in the Gothic style on the model of the original which stood by the Grand Masters' Palace *(p 223)*. Platía Vassilíou Georgíou B, the administrative centre, is bordered by monumental buildings in the oriental Gothic style: the regional administrative offices *(Nomarhía),* former seat of the Italian Governor, the Town Hall *(Dimarhío)* (H) and the theatre (T).

Further north, the charming **Murad Reis Mosque★** (Dzamí Mourát Réïs), which is named after one of Suleiman's admirals, stands in a grove of eucalyptus trees surrounded by the typical tomb stones of a muslim cemetery; the graves of the men are distinguished by a turban, those of the women by a sort of pineapple.

Aquarium (Enidrío) (AX). – *Open until 8pm; 50 Dr.* Mediterranean marine creatures – turtles, groupers, lampreys and octopi – are presented in a reconstruction of their natural habitat.

Rodini Park. – *2km – 1 1/4 miles southeast, on the right of the road to Líndos.* Attractive physic garden, green and fresh, supplemented by a small zoo. The "Wine Festival" is held here from July to September; free wine tasting.

Mount Smith (Akrópoli) (AY). – *4km – 2 1/2 miles or 1 1/2 hours on foot Rtn; no 5 bus from the New Market.*

Several elements of the ancient city, which was founded in 5C BC, still exist, more or less reconstructed by the Italians: the theatre (2C BC) – only the lower terrace is authentic, the stadium (2C BC) and the temple to Pythian Apollo indicated by three columns.

St Stephen's Mount is now called Mount Smith after Admiral Sir Sidney Smith of the British Navy who lived in Rhodes early in 19C; from the top there are superb **views★★** particularly at sunset of the shoreline, Syme Island and the Turkish coast.

EXCURSIONS

Mount Filérimos★ (alt 267m – 876ft). – *13km – 8 miles by car by the road to Ixiá turning left in Triánda, a modern village.*

The ancient city of Ialyssos stood on a very fine site overlooking the coastal plain. The city was probably founded by the Phoenicians and then occupied by the Dorians and the Achaians. In the Middle Ages the Genoese laid siege to the Byzantines and were besieged in their turn by the Knights of St John; during the siege of Rhodes in 1522 Suleiman set up his headquarters on the site.

Beneath the pines and cypresses on the acropolis *(open 8.45am to 3pm; 100 Dr)* are the foundations of a 4C BC temple and a paleo-Christian basilica incorporating an old baptistry. The Gothic monastery, which was built by the Knights and restored by the Italians, has a quadruple church: for the Roman Catholics and the Orthodox, the Knights and relics; a miraculous image of the Virgin was kept in the church.

There is a vast **panorama★★** of the northern end of the island to be seen from the top of the Knights' fortress on the edge of the headland. St George's Chapel *(on the right on returning to the exit),* partially underground, is decorated with 14C and 15C Gothic murals representing scenes from the New Testament and the Knights with their patron saints.

On the southern slope of the hill there stands a monumental ancient Doric fountain *(not accessible at present).*

Syme★ (Sími). – *Daily boat service in the season from Mandráki harbour, Rhodes, returning at about 6pm; two small hotels on Syme.*

The island is barren and the inhabitants earn their living by fishing or gathering sponges. The main town has quite an air with its attractive neo-Classical houses with tiled roofs and pediments. The boats put in on the southwest coast below the 18C Panormítis Monastery *(rooms to let).*

KÓS★★

Pop 20 890 – Michelin map 980 fold 46

Kós is the second most important island in the Dodecanese after Rhodes. It lies northwest of the latter, close to the coast of Asia Minor near Bodrum (Halikarnassos). It is a fertile island, blessed with smiling countryside and a mild climate and rich in reminders of Classical Greece and the Knights of St John who held Kos from 1315 to 1522.

The island is 45km – 28 miles long by 11km – 7 miles wide and rises to 846m – 2 776ft high. It is well supplied with rain and springs and produces cereals, vegetables, fruit such as water melons, citrus fruits and grapes; chicken farming is also common.

Kós was the birthplace of **Hippocrates,** the "Father of Medicine", in about 460 BC. He wrote several medical treatises which are the basis of the Hippocratic Oath, a sort of moral code which doctors swear to observe. Another famous native was **Apelles,** the artist who flourished in the reign of Alexander the Great (336-323 BC).

Access. – By boat or car ferry belonging to the Piraeus-Rhodes line, daily service taking between 12 and 17 hours according to the number of stops. By air, daily flights from Athens to Andimáhia in about 3/4 hour, from Rhodes to Andimáhia and Léros to Andimáhia. In the season there is a boat service between Kos and Bodrum (Halikarnassos) in Turkey.

Accommodation. – Kós Town, the capital, has a good choice of hotels, restaurants and fish tavernas. Specialities: local wine, fish and seafood.
  Municipal tourist office on the seafront (Aktí Koundourióti).
  Buses and taxis; car and bicycle hire. Many beaches.

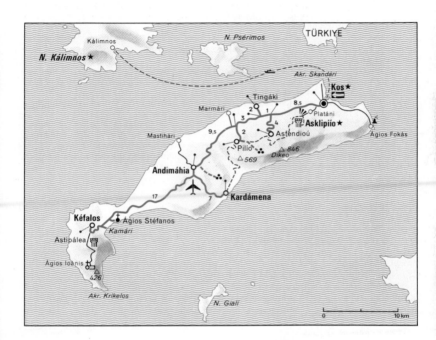

KÓS TOWN★ Pop 11 851

Kós, which is the capital and main resort of the island, has a significant Ottoman minority. Between the harbour, Mandráki, in the bay and the majestic castle of the Knights of St John on the hill are grouped the white arcaded houses, the terraced cafés, the palm lined walks and gardens of flowering red hibiscus which give the town its charm.

The centre of the town for tourists is **Plane Tree Square★** (Platía tou Platánou) which takes its name from the enormous plane tree (14m – 46ft in girth) beneath which Hippocrates, the famous doctor, is supposed to have taught his pupils (in fact the tree is only 500 years old). Next to the tree stands a covered Turkish fountain composed of ancient materials which have been re-employed, such as the sarcophagus converted into a basin.

The "loggia mosque" (1786), on the south side of the square, has a double portico and was probably used in the past as a merchants' exchange.

Knights' Castle★ (Kástro). – *Open 8.45am to 3pm (9.30am to 2.30pm Sundays); closed Tuesdays; 100 Dr.*

There are two concentric sets of walls with massive towers at the corners; the inner wall was built between 1450 and 1476 and the outer wall was added between 1495 and 1514 by Grand Masters Pierre d'Aubusson, Aimeri d'Amboise and Fabrizio del Carretto. The stone of which they are constructed includes pieces taken from ancient buildings, particularly the Asklepieion *(p 228):* note the Hellenistic frieze over the entrance door.

The outer wall, which was the work of Italian engineers, is reinforced at the critical points by bastions for artillery: the Carretto bastion, a round tower in the southwest corner on the left of the entrance, resembles its counterpart in Rhodes while the Aubusson tower, a polygonal structure in the northeast corner, commands the harbour entrance. The parapet walk gives a succession of picturesque views of the inner wall with its coats of arms of the Knights, the town, the harbour, the sea and Bodrum (Halikarnassos) Bay.

KÓS★★ – Kós Town★

Agora and harbour district. – In the days of the Knights of Rhodes, the medieval town adjoining the harbour was called **Lango;** it was surrounded by ramparts of which a few traces remain. The district was destroyed by an earthquake in 1933 and archaeologists have conducted a systematic excavation of part of the Hellenistic and Roman city: the pavement of an agora, the foundations and two columns of a temple to Aphrodite, eight Corinthian columns of a stoa and the footings of a paleo-Christian basilica.

St John's Church, a small 15C domed building, dates from the time of the Knights.

Archaeological Museum. – *Open 8.45am to 3pm (9.30am to 2.30pm Sundays); 100 Dr.* The museum, which is in Liberty Square (Platía Eleftherías), displays the product of excavations carried out on the island: an interesting collection of Hellenistic and Roman sculpture including a statue of Hippocrates, another of Hygieia the goddess of Health, a figure of Mercury seated, effigies of women wearing the *peplos* and portraits.

At the centre of the courtyard is a mosaic representing Hippocrates and Asklepios.

Greco-Roman district. – On either side of the road called Odós Gregoríou lie extensive excavations including traces of a temple of Dionysos, a colonnaded palestra, baths, houses decorated with mosaics and frescoes and a Roman road with its original paving. The Italian archaeologists carried out some reconstruction work: a court with peristyle surrounded by latrines *(forica),* a small theatre *(odeon)* and a Roman house decorated with mosaics.

Asklepieion★ (Asklipiío). – *4km – 2 1/2 miles south. Open 8am to 7pm (6pm Sundays); 100 Dr.* Four terraces cut into a hillside overlooking the Kos plain mark the site of this important sanctuary which was consecrated to Asklepios (Aesculapius), the healer and son of Apollo. It was built late in 4C BC to commemorate the skills of Hippocrates and, like Epidauros, it was both a place of worship and a treatment centre served by eminent priest-healers, the Asklepiades, who formed a famous medical school.

To the left of the lower terrace lie the ruins of the Roman baths. The ancient monumental entrance *(propylaia)* leads up to the second terrace which was lined with porticoes enclosing the curative sulphurous waters.

At the centre of the third terrace stands a monumental altar to Asklepios, flanked *(right)* by traces of an Ionic Hellenistic temple and *(left)* by a Roman temple; the former, which was originally decorated with paintings by Apelles, son of Praxiteles, (Aphrodite Anadyomene), contained the sanctuary treasury and the votive offerings of the pilgrims seeking cures. Note also the semi-circular public seat *(exedra).*

On the top terrace, on the same axis as the steps, stood the great temple of Asklepios; the black and white marble steps were part of a 2C BC Doric temple, six columns broad by eleven long. The sides and back of the terrace were bordered by porticoes.

There are magnificent **views★★** down over the sanctuary and the surrounding woods to the town of Kós and over the sea to the Turkish coast.

EXCURSIONS

Road to Kéfalos★. – *108km – 67 miles Rtn.* The road runs the length of the island with side roads leading to Tingáki, a charming little port *(fish tavernas)* on the north coast, and to Asfendioú and Pilío with its Hopitallers' castle *(2km – 1 1/4 miles on foot beyond the village)* in the hills to the south.

Andimáhia. – Pop 1 460. There is a path running south *(6km – 3 3/4 miles Rtn)* to the Hospitallers' fortress, which was built to a rectangular plan and contains the ruins of churches, houses and cisterns; over the entrance are the arms of the Order and of Aimeri d'Amboise.

Kardámena. – Pop 1 212. Attractive village on the south coast; sandy beach *(tavernas).*

Kéfalos. – Pop 1 976. South of Kéfalos lie the ruins of the Greek city of Astypalaia (Astipálea) and of St Stephen's (Ágios Stéfanos), a paleo-Christian basilica. There is a beautiful beach at Kamári east of Kéfalos.

Kálimnos★. – Pop 14 457. Boats sail daily at 8am from the seafront (Aktí Koundourióti) in Kós Town to this rocky island which is known as the sponge divers' island *(1 to 2 hour crossing; return to Kós at about 6pm).* Here one can find the peace and charm of an island which is not specially geared to the demands of tourism *(a few small hotels).*

PATMOS★★

Dodecanese – Pop 2 607 – Michelin map 980 folds 33 and 34

The most northerly of the Dodecanese is formed by the coalition of three volcanic islets, the largest of which boasts the main town, known as Hóra or Pátmos, situated below the fortified monastery of St John. The island earns its living from agriculture and fishing; it has retained its insular character and a certain mystical ambiance reflecting the memory of **St John the Divine,** the "disciple whom Jesus loved"; he was exiled under the emperor Domitian and from 95 to 97 AD he lived on Pátmos where he had his vision of the Apocalypse.

Access and accommodation. – By boat from Piraeus daily taking 8 to 10 hours according to the number of stops; from Rhodes daily in summer *(landing at Skála on the east coast).* Hotels at Skála and Grígos; numerous inlets and secluded beaches (shingle).

TOUR *about 3 hours*

From Skála there is a road suitable for cars *(6km – 3 3/4 miles by bus or taxi; 2 hours Rtn on foot or mule)* up to the cave of the Apocalypse *(left of the track)* and then on to St John's Monastery: fine views of the coast and the neighbouring islands.

Cave of the Apocalypse★. – Enclosed within a small monastery is the spot where St John received his divine revelation through terrifying dreams which his disciple Prochoros wrote down from his dictation.

St John's Monastery★★ (Ágios Ioánis Theológos). – *Open 8am to 12 noon and 3 to 6pm; 7am to 11am Sundays and holidays; 50 Dr.*

This monastery was founded in 1088 by St Christodoulos, who had received the island as a gift from the Byzantine emperor Alexis Comnenus. It was fortified in 15C by the Venetians to serve as a stronghold but remodelled in 17C. In 1461 it was placed under the personal protection of Pope Pius II Piccolomini and the Turks respected it. Externally the building looks like a fortress; its towers and grey walls contrast with the white houses of Hóra. Some twenty monks, compared with 150 formerly, live in the monastery; they observe a particularly solemn celebration of Easter, the Feast of the Assumption and the Feast of St John.

A fortified doorway leads into the interior which consists of a maze of courtyards, stairs and terraces which provide admirable **views**★★ of the island, the archipelago and the Turkish coast.

Church. – The outer court is a curious 17C structure braced with reinforcing arches against earthquakes. St Christodoulos' Chapel, containing the marble sarcophagus of the founder saint, abuts the narthex which is decorated with frescoes depicting the life of St John on Pátmos. The church itself is built on the Greek cross plan and the lower part dates back to 11C; the most striking frescoes (13C) are in the Lady Chapel *(right)*; they show Abraham and the three angels and the Virgin between the Archangels Michael and Gabriel. The frescoes in the refectory also date from 13C.

Treasury. – This is one of the richest treasuries in Greece after those on Mount Athos. The items are well presented: large collection of Byzantine icons (11C to 13C), embroidered vestments embellished with gold and silver thread (15C to 18C), religious plate in gold and silver adorned with diamonds and enamels (17C in particular), carved crosses, jewels and precious objects...

Library. – It contains 15 000 printed volumes and a priceless collection of over 1 000 manuscripts: fragments of the famous Codex Purpureus on purple vellum (early 6C), the Book of Job (8C), illuminated evangelistaries and cartularies (12C to 14C), the founding charter (chrysobull) of the monastery...

Hóra. – Pop 748. Interesting 16C, 17C and 18C houses, some of which belonged to the ship owners whose vessels competed in 19C with those of Hydra, Spetsae and Psará.

Páros. – Church at Parikía

Herakleion (Crete) .... *Towns, sights, ruins and tourist regions.*

Ikaros, témenos ...... *Mythological and historical people or specialist terms explained in the text.*

(Peloponnese) .... *Province or tourist region.*

(The spelling used in this index is either a phonetic transcription from demotic Greek (with stress accents) or reflects the Greek spelling; variants are common : e.g. Chalkis may also be written as Khalkis, Halkis, or Halkída.)